Lecture Notes in Computer Scie

T0238553

Commenced Publication in 1973
Founding and Former Series Editors:
Gerhard Goos, Juris Hartmanis, and Jan van Leeuwen

Val Tannen   Limsoon Wong
Leonid Libkin   Wenfei Fan
Wang-Chiew Tan   Michael Fourman (Eds.)

In Search of Elegance in the Theory and Practice of Computation

Essays Dedicated to Peter Buneman

 Springer

Volume Editors

Val Tannen
University of Pennsylvania, Department of Computer and Information Science
3330 Walnut Street, Philadelphia, PA 19104, USA
E-mail: val@cis.upenn.edu

Limsoon Wong
National University of Singapore, School of Computing
13 Computing Drive, Singapore 117417, Singapore
E-mail: wongls@comp.nus.edu.sg

Leonid Libkin
Wenfei Fan
Michael Fourman
The University of Edinburgh, School of Informatics
10 Crichton Street, Edinburgh EH8 9AB, UK
E-mail: {libkin; wenfei@inf.ed.ac.uk}, michael.fourman@ed.ac.uk

Wang-Chiew Tan
University of California, Department of Computer Science
1156 High Street, Santa Cruz, CA 95064, USA
E-mail: wctan@cs.ucsc.edu

ISSN 0302-9743   e-ISSN 1611-3349
ISBN 978-3-642-41659-0   e-ISBN 978-3-642-41660-6
DOI 10.1007/978-3-642-41660-6
Springer Heidelberg New York Dordrecht London

Library of Congress Control Number: : 2013951160

CR Subject Classification (1998): H.2, D.3, H.3, F.3, F.4.3

LNCS Sublibrary: SL 1 – Theoretical Computer Science and General Issues

Typesetting: Camera-ready by author, data conversion by Scientific Publishing Services, Chennai, India

Printed on acid-free paper

Springer is part of Springer Science+Business Media (www.springer.com)

Val Tannen   Limsoon Wong
Leonid Libkin Wenfei Fan
Wang-Chiew Tan   Michael Fourman (Eds.)

In Search of Elegance in the Theory and Practice of Computation

Essays Dedicated to Peter Buneman

 Springer

Volume Editors

Val Tannen
University of Pennsylvania, Department of Computer and Information Science
3330 Walnut Street, Philadelphia, PA 19104, USA
E-mail: val@cis.upenn.edu

Limsoon Wong
National University of Singapore, School of Computing
13 Computing Drive, Singapore 117417, Singapore
E-mail: wongls@comp.nus.edu.sg

Leonid Libkin
Wenfei Fan
Michael Fourman
The University of Edinburgh, School of Informatics
10 Crichton Street, Edinburgh EH8 9AB, UK
E-mail: {libkin; wenfei@inf.ed.ac.uk}, michael.fourman@ed.ac.uk

Wang-Chiew Tan
University of California, Department of Computer Science
1156 High Street, Santa Cruz, CA 95064, USA
E-mail: wctan@cs.ucsc.edu

ISSN 0302-9743   e-ISSN 1611-3349
ISBN 978-3-642-41659-0   e-ISBN 978-3-642-41660-6
DOI 10.1007/978-3-642-41660-6
Springer Heidelberg New York Dordrecht London

Library of Congress Control Number: : 2013951160

CR Subject Classification (1998): H.2, D.3, H.3, F.3, F.4.3

LNCS Sublibrary: SL 1 – Theoretical Computer Science and General Issues

Typesetting: Camera-ready by author, data conversion by Scientific Publishing Services, Chennai, India

Printed on acid-free paper

Springer is part of Springer Science+Business Media (www.springer.com)

Foreword

When we started this project we contacted a number of Peter Buneman's PhD students, postdocs, and colleagues, both in the academic departments that Peter belonged to, and in the larger scientific communities to which he contributed. We asked them if they would contribute a chapter to this Festschrift and we were deeply moved by the enthusiasm our query elicited. So here we are, a group of people for whom Peter was, and still is, a teacher, a mentor, a collaborator, or a colleague, sometimes several of these, with our scientific offerings. All of us, moreover, are fervent admirers of Peter Buneman the computer scientist and are proud to consider ourselves friends of Peter Buneman the wonderful man.

Let us mention briefly some of Peter's seminal scientific achievements. We cannot do justice in this preface to the depth and breadth of Peter's long, distinguished, and continuing career. By necessity, and perhaps selfishly, we shall choose a few items about which we might be better prepared to write.

A dominant theme in Peter Buneman's work is the quest to unite the fields of databases and programming languages. We expect that the majority of the readers of this Festschrift will come from these two communities. For these readers, it is interesting to note that Peter's early work was in two completely different areas: brain modeling (see his articles in *Nature*) and mathematical phylogeny. His work in the latter area underlies most modern techniques that evolutionary biologists use to reconstruct phylogenies.

Peter has made many seminal contributions to the field of databases. In his quest to bring richer data models and more flexible query constructs to database systems, he made comprehensive use of ideas from the field of programming languages, in the process making signal contributions to that field as well. He extended ideas from functional programming languages and from type theory to show how one can unify and enrich various querying paradigms for relational and post-relational data models such as complex values. This led to his study of the principles that underlie Web-like data, and he is a co-author of the first textbook on this subject. All this work, as well as his more recent investigations of the principles of modeling data provenance and of data archiving, is characterized by a most seductive mathematical elegance. For those of us who already had such a proclivity, it was encouraging and reassuring that a scientist of Peter's stature would lead us in this style!

In addition to his masterful work on the theory of computing, Peter Buneman always saw the computer scientist as a contributing citizen to the larger field of science. We already mentioned that he worked on mathematical models for neuroscience. He started working on phylogenies in order to help scholars who were studying the transmission of medieval manuscripts (but the biologists ended up benefitting most from his work). The work he did in the 1990's on monad-based query languages was very successfully used in the integration "on-the-fly" of non-relational genomics data sources (to the great surprise of some participants in the

Human Genome Project). It was again motivation from scientists and scholars as Web-users that led Peter to study the provenance of data that are continually copied and transformed. More generally, he became one of the founders of the field of *digital curation* including the creation at the University of Edinburgh of a center with this name. Recent years have seen Peter initiating and successfuly completing a project to bring broadband Internet to one of the more remote corners of the Scottish Highlands. With this he took one more step: from citizen of science to citizen of the society at large. Peter is now playing an active rôle in spreading high-speed Internet access to the less well-connected, lobbying government and providing advice and practical assistance to communities.

Many of the contributions to this Festschrift belong to the field of databases. Some belong to the field of programming languages and a few to other fields. When we contacted the potential contributors we offered them free choice of topic(s). We feel that the final result displays an exciting variety, just as Peter Buneman's career does! We also encouraged the contributors to choose their co-authors as they felt appropriate. The result is that the complete list of authors includes many more people and we are delighted that they agreed to help us celebrate Peter. We would be remiss, however, if we didn't provide an exact list of the principals (one or more for each paper), since this foreword is also written on their behalf.

August 2013

Val Tannen
Limsoon Wong
Leonid Libkin
Wenfei Fan
Wang-Chiew Tan
Michael Fourman

also on behalf of

Serge Abiteboul
Samson Abramsky
Hassan Aït-Kaci
James Cheney
Vassilis Christophides
Susan Davidson
Alin Deutsch
Irini Fundulaki
Floris Geerts
Georg Gottlob
Martin Grohe
Carmem Hara
Rick Hull
H.V. Jagadish
Anastasios Kementsietsidis
Sanjeev Khanna

Bertram Ludaescher
David Maier
Renée Miller
Tova Milo
Heiko Müller
Rishiyur Nikhil
Atsushi Ohori
Gordon Plotkin
Lucian Popa
Dan Suciu
Keishi Tajima
Jan Van den Bussche
Stijn Vansummeren
Victor Vianu
Stratis Viglas
Scott Weinstein

Table of Contents

Models for Data-Centric Workflows[*]

Serge Abiteboul[1] and Victor Vianu[2]

[1] INRIA Saclay
[2] UC San Diego and INRIA Saclay

Abstract. We present two models for data-centric workflows: the first based on business artifacts and the second on Active XML. We then compare the two models and argue that Active XML is strictly more expressive, based on a natural semantics and choice of observables. Finally, we mention several verification results for the two models.

1 Introduction

Workflows and database systems are two essential software components that often have difficulties interoperating. Data-centric workflow systems alleviate this problem by providing an integrated approach to data management and workflows. They allow the management of data evolution by tasks with complex sequencing constraints, as encountered for instance in scientific workflow systems, information manufacturing systems, e-government, e-business or healthcare global systems.

Data-centric workflows have evolved from process-centric formalisms, which traditionally focus on control flow while under-specifying the underlying data and its manipulations by the process tasks, often abstracting them away completely. In contrast, data-aware formalisms treat data as first-class citizens. A notable exponent of this class is the *business artifact model* pioneered in [17], deployed by IBM in commercial products and consulting services, and further studied in a line of follow-up works [4,6,9,10,5,15,13,14]. Business artifacts (or simply "artifacts") model key business-relevant entities that evolve in response to events in their life-cycle. See [11] for a brief survey on the topic.

Another effort at modeling data-centric workflows relies on Active XML (AXML). An AXML document consists of an XML document with embedded function calls, modeling tasks in the workflow. Each call generates a data-carrying task which in turn can spawn additional sub-tasks. The functions are specified using queries based on tree patterns [3,1]. See [2] for a discussion on how Active XML can serve as a workflow model.

Business artifacts and AXML provide two different paradigms for specifying data-centric workflows. A natural question concerns their relative expressive power. We describe a semantics introduced in [7] for comparing the expressiveness of workflow systems relative to a set of observables, and argue that Active XML is strictly more expressive than the variant of business artifacts presented here.

[*] This work has been partially funded by the European Research Council under the European Community's Seventh Framework Programme (FP7/2007-2013) / ERC grant Webdam, agreement 226513. http://webdam.inria.fr/

V. Tannen et al. (Eds.): Buneman Festschrift, LNCS 8000, pp. 1–12, 2013.

Several recent works have considered the problem of verifying business artifacts [8,7] and Active XML systems [3]. The verification problem consists of statically checking whether all runs satisfy desirable properties expressed in an extension of linear-time temporal logic (LTL). The presence of data results in a challenging infinite-state verification problem, due to the infinite data domain. Rather than relying on general-purpose software verification tools suffering from well-known limitations, the above works address this problem by identifying relevant classes of business artifacts and Active XML systems for which fully automatic verification is possible. We briefly summarize these results.

2   The Business Artifact Model

We describe a minimalistic variant of the business artifact model, adequate for conveying the flavor of the approach. The presentation is informal, relying mainly on a running example (the formal development is provided in [8,7]). The example models an e-commerce business process in which the customer chooses a product and a shipment method and applies various kinds of coupons to the order. After the order is filled, the system awaits for the customer to submit a payment. If the payment matches the amount owed, the system proceeds to shipping the product.

In the minimalistic model, an artifact is simply an evolving record of values. The values are referred to by variables (sometimes called *attributes*). In general, an artifact system consists of several artifacts, evolving under the action of *services*, specified by pre- and post-conditions. For simplicity, we use a single artifact with the following variables

```
status, prod_id, ship_type, coupon, amount_owed,
amount_paid, amount_refunded.
```

The status variable tracks the status of the order and can take values such as "edit_product", "received_payment", "shipping", "canceling", etc. Thus, status can be viewed as recording the current stage of the order processing. In conjunction with pre-and-post conditions of services, this allows simulating a classical form of sequencing based on finte-state automata. However, unlike classical process-centric approaches, the sequencing can also depend on properties of the *data*.

The artifact system is equipped with a database including the following tables, where underlined attributes denote keys. Recall that a key is an attribute that uniquely identifies each tuple in a relation.

```
PRODUCTS(id, price, availability, weight),
COUPONS(code, type, value, min_value, free_shiptype),
SHIPPING(type, cost, max_weight),
OFFERS(prod_id, discounted_price, active).
```

The database also satisfies the following foreign keys:

```
COUPONS[free_shiptype] ⊆ SHIPPING[type] and
OFFERS[prod_id] ⊆ PRODUCTS[id].
```

The starting configuration of every artifact system is constrained by an initialization condition, which here states that status initialized to "edit_prod", and all other variables to "undefined". By convention, we model undefined variables using the reserved constant λ.

The Services. Recall that artifacts evolve under the action of services. Each service is specified by a pre-condition π and a postcondition ψ, both existential first-order ($\exists$FO) sentences. The pre-condition refers to the current values of the artifact variables and the database. The post-condition ψ refers simultaneously to the current and *next* artifact values, as well as the database. In addition, both π and ψ may use arithmetic constraints on the variables, limited to linear inequalities over the rationals.

The following services model two of the business process tasks of the example. We use primed artifact variables x' to refer to the *next* value of variable x.

choose_product. The customer chooses a product.

$$\pi : \texttt{status} = \text{"edit\_prod"}$$
$$\psi : \exists p, a, w(\texttt{PRODUCTS}(\texttt{prod\_id}', p, a, w) \wedge a > 0)$$
$$\wedge \texttt{status}' = \text{"edit\_shiptype"}$$

choose_shiptype. The customer chooses a shipping option.

$$\pi : \texttt{status} = \text{"edit\_ship"}$$
$$\psi : \exists c, l, p, a, w(\texttt{SHIPPING}(\texttt{ship\_type}', c, l) \wedge$$
$$\texttt{PRODUCTS}(\texttt{prod\_id}, p, a, w) \wedge l > w) \wedge$$
$$\texttt{status}' = \text{"edit\_coupon"} \wedge \texttt{prod\_id}' = \texttt{prod\_id}$$

Notice that the pre-conditions of the services check the value of the status variable. For instance, according to **choose_product**, the customer can only input her product choice while the order is in "edit_prod" status.

Also notice that the post-conditions constrain the next values of the artifact variables (denoted by a prime). For instance, according to **choose_product**, once a product has been picked, the next value of the status variable is "edit_shiptype", which will at a subsequent step enable the **choose_shiptype** service (by satisfying its pre-condition). The interplay of pre- and post-conditions achieves a sequential filling of the order, starting from the choice of product and ending with the claim of a coupon. A post-condition may refer to both the current and next values of the artifact variables. For instance, consider the service **choose_shiptype**. The fact that only the shipment type is picked while the product remains unchanged, is modeled by preserving the product id: the next and current values of the corresponding artifact variable are set equal.

Pre- and post-conditions may query the database. For instance, consider the function **choose_product**. The post-condition ensures that the product id chosen by the customer is that of an available product (by checking that it appears in a PRODUCTS tuple, whose availability attribute is positive).

Semantics. The semantics of an artifact system consists of its *runs*. Given a database D, a run is an infinite sequence $\{\rho_i\}_{\geq 0}$ of artifact records such that ρ_0 and D satisfy the initial condition of the system, and for each $i \geq 0$ there is a service S of the system such that ρ_i and D satisfy the pre-condition of S and ρ_i, ρ_{i+1} and D satisfy its post-condition. For uniformity, blocking prefixes of runs are extended to infinite runs by repeating forever their last record.

We note that the full business artifact model is still in flux. In its current state (e.g., see [12]), the model allows artifact attributes containing collections, rather than just atomic atoms. It also provides richer forms of control, achieved by a *hierarchy* of services.

3   Active XML Workflows

We next describe the specification of workflows in Active XML. We use a model called *Guard Active XML* (GAXML for short) [3,7].

GAXML documents are abstractions of XML with embedded service calls. A GAXML document is a forest of unordered, unranked trees, whose internal nodes are labeled with tags from a finite alphabet and whose leaves are labeled with tags, data values, or function symbols. More precisely, a function symbol $!f$ indicates a node where function f can be called, and a function symbol $?f$ indicates that a call to f has been made but the answer has not yet been returned. For example, a GAXML document is shown in Figure 1.

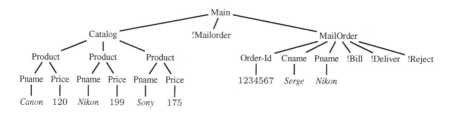

Fig. 1. A GAXML document

The GAXML document may be subject to constraints specified by a DTD, as well as Boolean combinations of tree patterns. For example, the negation of the pattern in Figure 3 (a) says that an Order ID uniquely determines the product and customer names. In patterns, double edges denote descendant and single edges the child relation.

A GAXML document evolves as a result of making function calls and receiving their results. A call can be made at any point, as long as a specified pre-condition, called a *call guard*, is satisfied. The argument of the call is specified by a query on the document, producing a forest. Both the call guard and input query may refer to the node at which the call is made (denoted *self*), so the location of the call in the document is important. The result of a function call consists of another GAXML document, so a forest, whose trees are added as siblings of the node x where the call was made. After the answer of a call at node x is returned, the call may be kept or the node x may be deleted. This is specified by the schema, for each function. If calls to $!f$ are kept, f is called *continuous*, otherwise it is *non-continuous*.

For example, consider the `MailOrder` function in Figure 1. Intuitively, its role is to fetch new mail orders from customers. For instance, one result of a call to the function `!MailOrder` may consist of the subtree with root `MailOrder` in Figure 1. Since new orders should be fetched indefinitely, the call `!MailOrder` is maintained after each result is returned, so `MailOrder` is specified to be continuous. On the other hand, consider the function `!Bill` occurring in a `MailOrder`. This is meant to be called only once, in order to carry out the billing task. Once the task is finished, the call can be removed. Therefore, `Bill` is specified as a non-continuous function.

Consider again the function `MailOrder`, whose role is to fetch new orders from external users or services. Since the function is processed externally, the semantics of its evaluation is not known. We call such a function *external*. Its specification consists only of its call guard and input query, and its answer is only constrained by signature information provided by the schema. In addition to external functions, there are functions processed internally by the GAXML system. These are called *internal*. For example, `Bill` is such a function. When a call to `Bill` is made at a node x labeled `!Bill`, the label of x turns to `?Bill` (to indicate that a call has been made whose answer is still pending) and the call is processed internally. Specifically, the call generates a new GAXML document (a *running call*) that evolves until it satisfies a condition called *return guard*. Intuitively, the return guard indicates that the task corresponding to the call has been completed and the result can be returned. The contents of the result is specified by a *return query*. For example, the answer to a call to `Bill` can be returned once payment has been received. The answer, specified by the return query, provides the product paid for and amount of payment (see Example 1).

Once the result of a call has been returned, the GAXML document of the completed running call is removed. In order for the result to be returned at the correct location (next to node x), a mapping called *eval* is maintained between nodes where calls have been made and GAXML document corresponding to the running call (e.g., see Figure 2). The system evolves by repeated function calls and answer returns, occurring one at a time non-deterministically. This may reach a *blocking instance* in which no function can be called and no result can be returned, or may continue forever, leading to an infinite run. For example, runs of the Mail Order system are always infinite since new mail orders can always be fetched. For uniformity, we make all runs infinite by repeating blocking instances forever.

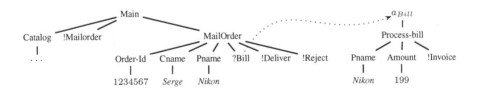

Fig. 2. An instance with an *eval* link

Note that call guards provide a very useful form of control. In particular, they are instrumental in enforcing desired ordering among tasks. For instance, in the Mail Order example, to enforce that delivery of a product can only occur after billing has been completed, it is sufficient for the call guard of !Deliver to check that neither !Bill nor ?Bill occur in the subtree corresponding to the order.

Example 1. The function Bill used in Figure 1 is specified as follows. It is internal and non-continuous. Its call guard is the pattern in Figure 3 (b), checking that the ordered product is available. The input query is the query in Figure 4. Assuming that Invoice is an external function eventually returning Payment (with product and amount paid), the return guard and return query of Bill are shown in Figure 5.

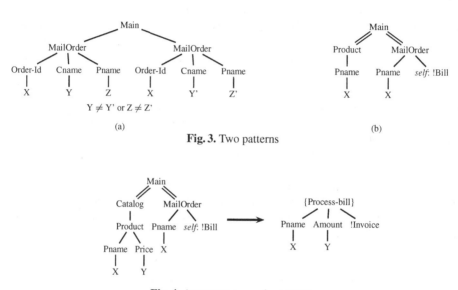

Fig. 3. Two patterns

Fig. 4. Argument query for !Bill

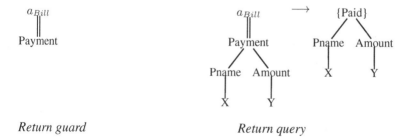

Return guard   *Return query*

Fig. 5. Return guard and query for !Bill

In GAXML, workflow control is provided by the guards associated with functions. There are many other possible ways to control sequencing of tasks. In [7], the following alternative workflow control mechanisms are also discussed:

Automata. The automata are non-deterministic finite-state transition systems, in which states have associated tree pattern formulas with free variables acting as parameters. A transition into a state can only occur if its associated formula is true. In addition, the automaton may constrain the values of the parameters in consecutive states.

Temporal Properties. These are expressed in a temporal logic with tree patterns and Past LTL operators. A temporal formula constrains the next instance based on the history of the run.

Subject to some minor technical assumptions, it is shown in [7] that the power of guards, automata, and temporal logic as workflow specification mechanisms is the same. More surprisingly, static constraints alone can largely simulate all three control mechanisms.

4   Comparing Business Artifacts and Active XML Workflows

We have discussed two models of data-centric workflows: business artifacts and Active XML. A natural question is whether their expressiveness can be measured and compared. The models are quite different in their representation of data and events, so a direct comparison is meaningless. In [1], a framework is developed for comparing workflow specification languages, by mapping different models to a common abstraction using the notion of *workflow view*. Depending on the specific needs, a workflow view might retain information about some abstract state of the system and its evolution, about some particular events and their sequencing, about the entire history of the system so far, or a combination of these and other aspects. Even if not made explicit, a view is often the starting point in the design of workflow specifications. This further motivates using views to bridge the gap between different specification languages.

To see how this might be done, consider a workflow W specified by tasks and pre/post conditions and another workflow W' specified as a state-transition system, both pertaining to the same application. One way to render the two workflows comparable is to define a view of W as a state-transition system compatible with W'. This can be done by defining states using queries on the current instance and state transitions induced by the tasks. To make the comparison meaningful, the view of W should retain in states the information relevant to the semantics of the application, restructured to make it compatible with the representation used in W'. More generally, views may be used to map given workflows models to an entirely different model appropriate for the comparison. In [1], the general notion of workflow view is defined and a form of bisimulation over views is introduced to capture the fact that one workflow simulates another. The bisimulation applies to the *tree of runs* of the systems to be compared.

Using the framework based on views, it is shown in [1] that Active XML is strictly more expressive than business artifacts (without arithmetic and data depedencies). Specifically, Active XML can simulate business artifacts, but the converse is false.

The first result uses views mapping XML to relations and functions to services, so that artifacts become views of Active XML systems. For the negative result we use views retaining just the trace of function and service calls from the Active XML and the artifact system. This is a powerful result, since it extends to *any* views exposing *more* information than the function/service traces.

5   Verification

The verification problem for business artifacts as well as Active XML workflows has been considered in several recent works [3,8,7]. The problem consists of checking, for a given workflow specification and temporal property, whether all runs of the workflow system satisfy the property. For instance, one may want to verify whether some static property (e.g., all ordered products are available) and some dynamic property (e.g. an order is never delivered before payment is received) always hold. The temporal properties are specified in extensions of LTL, linear-time temporal logic. The presence of an unbounded data domain yields a challenging infinite-state verification problem.

In order to specify temporal properties we use an extension of LTL. Recall that LTL is propositional logic augmented with temporal operators such as $\mathbf{G}$ (always), $\mathbf{F}$ (eventually), $\mathbf{X}$ (next) and $\mathbf{U}$ (until) (e.g., see [18]). For example, $\mathbf{G}p$ says that p holds at all times in the run, $\mathbf{F}p$ says that p will eventually hold, and $\mathbf{G}(p \rightarrow \mathbf{F}q)$ says that whenever p holds, q must hold sometime in the future. In order to take into account data, we consider extensions of LTL in which propositions are interpreted by statements on current snapshots of the system. The language used to express the statements is dependent on the particular data model. For business artifacts, the language is FO, yielding the extension LTL(FO). For Active XML, the language consists of tree patterns, yielding LTL(*Tree*). We consider each model in turn.

Verification for Business Artifacts. For business artifacts, propositions are interpreted as quantifier-free FO formulas using current and next artifact values, constants, and the database. For example, suppose we wish to specify the property that if a correct payment is submitted then at some time in the future either the product is shipped or the customer is refunded the correct amount. The property is of the form $\mathbf{G}(p \rightarrow \mathbf{F}q)$, where p says that a correct payment is submitted and q states that either the product is shipped or the customer is refunded the correct amount. Moreover, if the customer is refunded, the amount of the correct payment (given in p) should be the same as the amount of the refund (given in q). This requires using a global variable x in both p and q. More precisely, p is interpreted as the formula $\mathtt{amount\_paid} = x \wedge \mathtt{amount\_paid} = \mathtt{amount\_owed}$ and q as $\mathtt{status} = \text{"shipped"} \vee \mathtt{amount\_refunded} = x$. This yields the LTL(FO) property

$$\forall x \mathbf{G}((\mathtt{amount\_paid} = x \wedge \mathtt{amount\_paid} = \mathtt{amount\_owed})$$
$$\rightarrow \mathbf{F}(\mathtt{status} = \text{"shipped"} \vee \mathtt{amount\_refunded} = x))$$

Note that, as one would expect, the global variable x is universally quantified at the end.

For artifact systems and properties without arithmetic constraints or data dependencies it was shown that verification is decidable [8]. The complexity is PSPACE-complete for a fixed number of attributes, and EXPSPACE otherwise. This is the best one can expect, given that even very simple static analysis problems for finite-state systems are already PSPACE-complete.

It turns out that the verification algorithm can be extended to specifications and properties that use a *total order* on the data domain, which is useful in many cases. This however complicates the algorithm considerably, since the order imposes global constraints on runs. The verification algorithm was first extended in [8] for the case of a dense countable order with no end-points (such as the rationals). This was later generalized to an arbitrary total order by Segoufin and Torunczyk [16] using automata-theoretic techniques. In both cases, the worst-case complexity remains PSPACE.

Unfortunately, the above decidability result fails even in the presence of simple data dependencies or arithmetic. As shown in [8,7], verification becomes undecidable as soon as the database has at least one key dependency, *or* if the specification of the artifact system uses simple arithmetic constraints allowing to increment and decrement by one the value of some atributes. Therefore, a restriction is imposed in [7] to achieve decidability.

The restriction is designed to limit the data flow between occurrences of the same artifact attribute throughout runs of the system that satisfy the desired property. As a first cut, a possible restriction would prevent any data flow path between unequal occurrences of the same artifact attribute. Let us call this restriction *acyclicity*. While acyclicity would achieve the goal of rendering verification decidable, it is too strong for many practical situations. In the example of Section 2, a customer can choose a shipping type and coupon and repeatedly change her mind and start over. Such repeated performance of a task is useful in many scenarios, but would be prohibited by acyclicity of the data flow.

To this end, we define in [7] a more permissive restriction called *feedback freedom*. Intuitively, paths among different occurrences of the same attribute are permitted, but only as long as each value of the attribute is independent on its previous values. This is ensured by a syntactic condition that takes into account both the artifact system and the property to be verified. We omit here the rather technical details. It is shown in [7] that feedback freedom of an artifact system together with an LTL(FO) property can be checked in PSPACE by reduction to a test of emptiness of a two-way alternating finite-state automaton. Feedback freedom turns out to ensure decidability of verification in the presence of linear constraints, and also under a large class of data dependencies including keys and foreign keys.

Verification of Active XML Workflows. Properties of Active XML workflows are expressed in LTL(*Tree*), an extension of LTL in which propositions are interpreted by tree patterns. For example, suppose that we wish to verify the following property:

Every product for which a correct amount has been paid is eventually delivered.

To formulate the property, we use tree patterns with variables binding to data values (without going into details, let us denote such a language of tree patterns by *Tree*).

The above property can be expressed in the language LTL(*Tree*) as follows. We start out with the LTL formula $\mathbf{G}(p \rightarrow \mathbf{F}q)$. The proposition p is replaced by the tree pattern

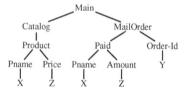

checking that the payment received for product X of order Y is in the right amount Z. The proposition q is replaced by the tree pattern

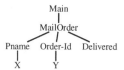

checking that product X of the same order Y is eventually delivered. Note that we wish X and Y to be the same in the tree patterns for p and q, so these are globally quantified; in contrast, Z is locally quantified. The resulting LTL(*Tree*) formula is shown in Figure 6.

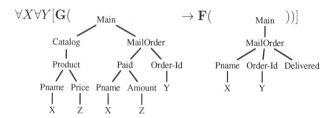

Fig. 6. An LTL(*Tree*) formula

It is shown in [3] that verification of LTL(*Tree*) properties of Active XML workflows is decidable in 2-EXPTIME, under a syntactic restriction ensuring that the workflow has only runs of bounded length.

6   Conclusion

Data-centric workflows are increasingly prevalent and there is a need for high-level models and languages for specifying and reasoning about them. In this note, we presented two such models: business artifacts (initiated at IBM Research), and Active XML (developed at INRIA). In both models, data is a first-class citizen, and it evolves as a result of events in its life cycle. However, there are significant differences in the two approaches. The data in business artifacts is relational, while in Active XML it is an extension of XML. Events in the life-cycle are modeled in business artifacts by services specified by pre-and-post conditions, while Active XML models events by function calls embedded in the data. To compare such distinct models, we proposed an approach based on workflow views that map different models to a common abstraction, and a notion of bisimulation on the trees of runs of the abstracted systems. Using this framework, we showed that Active XML is strictly more expressive than business artifacts (for the variants presented here). This is not suprising given that Active XML is a much richer model. A more detailed discussion of the ability of Active XML to capture the facets of an artifact model, as informally described in [17], is presented in [2], where it is argued that Active XML can in fact capture all aspects of the artifact approach. Moreover, the notions of subtask and of collection of artifacts are naturally built into the model, whereas the business artifact model as in [8,7] has to be extended in order to model them. Such extensions are indeed discussed in [12].

We finally reviewed some recent results on the automatic verification of workflows in both languages. These suggest that automatic verification may be feasible for a practically significant class of workflows and properties.

References

1. Abiteboul, S., Bourhis, P., Vianu, V.: Comparing workflow specification languages: A matter of views. In: ICDT (2011)
2. Abiteboul, S., Bourhis, P., Galland, A., Marinoiu, B.: The axml artifact model. In: TIME, Symposium on Temporal Representation and Reasoning, pp. 11–17 (2009)
3. Abiteboul, S., Segoufin, L., Vianu, V.: Static analysis of active XML systems. ACM Trans. Database Syst. 34(4) (2009)
4. Bhattacharya, K., Caswell, N.S., Kumaran, S., Nigam, A., Wu, F.Y.: Artifact-centered operational modeling: Lessons from customer engagements. IBM Systems Journal 46(4), 703–721 (2007)
5. Bhattacharya, K., Gerede, C.E., Hull, R., Liu, R., Su, J.: Towards formal analysis of artifact-centric business process models. In: Proc. Int. Conf. on Business Process Management (BPM), pp. 288–304 (2007)
6. Bhattacharya, K., et al.: A model-driven approach to industrializing discovery processes in pharmaceutical research. IBM Systems Journal 44(1), 145–162 (2005)
7. Damaggio, E., Deutsch, A., Vianu, V.: Artifact systems with data dependencies and arithmetic. In: ICDT (2011)
8. Deutsch, A., Hull, R., Patrizi, F., Vianu, V.: Automatic verification of data-centric business processes. In: ICDT, pp. 252–267 (2009)
9. Gerede, C.E., Bhattacharya, K., Su, J.: Static analysis of business artifact-centric operational models. In: IEEE International Conference on Service-Oriented Computing and Applications (2007)
10. Gerede, C.E., Su, J.: Specification and verification of artifact behaviors in business process models. In: Krämer, B.J., Lin, K.-J., Narasimhan, P. (eds.) ICSOC 2007. LNCS, vol. 4749, pp. 181–192. Springer, Heidelberg (2007), http://www.springerlink.com/content/c371144007878627
11. Hull, R.: Artifact-centric business process models: Brief survey of research results and challenges. In: OTM Conferences (2), pp. 1152–1163 (2008)
12. Hull, R., Damaggio, E., Fournier, F., Gupta, M., Heath, F.T., Hobson, S., Linehan, M.H., Maradugu, S., Nigam, A., Sukaviriya, P., Vaculín, R.: Introducing the guard-stage-milestone approach for specifying business entity lifecycles. In: Proc. of 7th Intl. Workshop on Web Services and Formal Methods, WS-FM (2010)

13. Kumaran, S., Liu, R., Wu, F.Y.: On the duality of information-centric and activity-centric models of business processes. In: Bellahsène, Z., Léonard, M. (eds.) CAiSE 2008. LNCS, vol. 5074, pp. 32–47. Springer, Heidelberg (2008)

14. Küster, J.M., Ryndina, K., Gall, H.C.: Generation of business process models for object life cycle compliance. In: Alonso, G., Dadam, P., Rosemann, M. (eds.) BPM 2007. LNCS, vol. 4714, pp. 165–181. Springer, Heidelberg (2007)

15. Liu, R., Bhattacharya, K., Wu, F.Y.: Modeling business contexture and behavior using business artifacts. In: Krogstie, J., Opdahl, A.L., Sindre, G. (eds.) CAiSE 2007 and WES 2007. LNCS, vol. 4495, pp. 324–339. Springer, Heidelberg (2007)

16. Segoufin, L., Torunczyk, S.: Automata based verification over linearly ordered data domains. In: Int'l. Symp. on Theoretical Aspects of Computer Science, STACS (2011)

17. Nigam, A., Caswell, N.S.: Business artifacts: An approach to operational specification. IBM Systems Journal 42(3), 428–445 (2003)

18. Pnueli, A.: The temporal logic of programs. In: FOCS, pp. 46–57 (1977)

Relational Databases and Bell's Theorem

Samson Abramsky

University of Oxford
samson.abramsky@cs.ox.ac.uk

Abstract. Our aim in this paper is to point out a surprising formal connection, between two topics which seem on face value to have nothing to do with each other: relational database theory, and the study of non-locality and contextuality in the foundations of quantum mechanics. We shall show that there is a remarkably direct correspondence between central results such as Bell's theorem in the foundations of quantum mechanics, and questions which arise naturally and have been well-studied in relational database theory.

1 Introduction

Our aim in this paper is to point out a surprising formal connection, between two topics which seem on face value to have nothing to do with each other:

- Relational database theory.
- The study of non-locality and contextuality in the foundations of quantum mechanics.

We shall show, using the unified treatment of the latter developed in [3], that there is a remarkably direct correspondence between central results such as Bell's theorem in the foundations of quantum mechanics, and questions which arise naturally and have been well-studied in relational database theory.

In particular, we shall see that the question of whether an "empirical model", of the kind which can be obtained by making observations of measurements performed on a physical system, admits a classical physical explanation in terms of a local hidden variable model, is mathematically equivalent to the question of whether a database instance admits a universal relation. The content of Bell's theorem and related results is that there are empirical models, predicted by quantum mechanics and confirmed by experiment, which do not admit such a universal relation. Moreover, while the original formulation of Bell's theorem involved probabilities, there are "probability-free" versions, notably Hardy's construction, which correspond directly to relational databases.

In fact, we shall show more broadly that there is a common mathematical language which can be used to described the key notions of both database theory, in the standard relational case and in a more general "algebraic" form covering e.g. a notion of probabilistic databases, and also of the theory of non-locality and contextuality, two of the key quantum phenomena. These features are central to

V. Tannen et al. (Eds.): Buneman Festschrift, LNCS 8000, pp. 13–35, 2013.
© Springer-Verlag Berlin Heidelberg 2013

current discussions of quantum foundations, and provide non-classical resources for quantum information processing.

The present paper is meant to be an introduction to these two topics, emphasizing their common content, presented in a manner which hopefully will be accessible to readers without prior knowledge of either.

How should this unexpected connection be interpreted? One idea is that the notion of contextuality is rather fundamental, and we can see some outlines of a common 'logic of contextuality' arising from this appearance of common structure in very different settings.

Ideally, some deeper connections can also be found, leading to interesting transfers of results and methods. A first step in this direction has already been taken, in joint work with Georg Gottlob and Phokion Kolaitis [4], in the closely related field of constraint satisfaction. An algorithmic question which arises naturally from the quantum side (see [2]) leads to a refined version of the constraint satisfaction paradigm, *robust constraint satisfaction*, and to interesting new complexity results.

2   Relational Databases

2.1   Review of Basic Notions

We shall begin by reviewing some basic notions of relational database theory.

We start with an example to show the concrete scenario which is to be formalized.

Example. Consider the following data table:

branch-name	account-no	customer-name	balance
Cambridge	10991-06284	Newton	£2,567.53
Hanover	10992-35671	Leibniz	€11,245.75
. . .	. . .	. . .	. . .

Let us anatomize this table. There are a set of *attributes*,

$$\{\text{branch-name}, \text{account-no}, \text{customer-name}, \text{balance}\}$$

which name the columns of the table. The entries in the table are 'tuples' which specify a value for each of the attributes. The table is a set of such tuples. A database will in general have a set of such tables, each with a given set of attributes. The *schema* of the database — a static, syntactic specification of the kind of information which can reside in the database — is given by specifying the set of attributes for each of the tables. The state of the database at a given time will be given by a set of tuples of the appropriate type for each of the tables in the schema.

We now proceed to formalize these notions.

We fix some set $\mathcal{A}$ which will serve as a universe of attributes. A database schema Σ over $\mathcal{A}$ is a finite family $\Sigma = \{A_1, \ldots, A_k\}$ of finite subsets of $\mathcal{A}$.

At this — surprisingly early! — point, we come to an interesting juncture. There are two standard approaches to formalising the notion of relation which can be found in the relational database literature. One — the 'unnamed perspective' [1] — is to formalize the notion of tuple as an ordered n-tuple in D^n for some set D of data values; a relation is then a subset of D^n. This is motivated by the desire to make the connection to the standard notion of relational structure in first-order logic as direct as possible. This choice creates a certain distance between the formal notion of relation, and the informal notion of table; in practice this is not a problem.

For our purposes, however, we wish to make a different choice — the 'named perspective' [1]: we shall formalize the notion of tuple, and hence of relation, in a fashion which directly reflects the informal notion. As we shall see, this will have both mathematical and conceptual advantages for our purposes. At the same time, there is no real problem in relating this formalism to the alternative one found in the literature. Note that the style of formalization we shall use is also commonly found in the older literature on relational databases, see e.g. [26].

We shall assume that for each $a \in \mathcal{A}$ there is a set D_a of possible data values for that attribute. Thus for example the possible values for **customer-name** should be character strings, perhaps with some lexical constraints; while for **balance** the values should be pairs (**currency**, **amount**), where **currency** comes from some fixed list (£, €, ...), and **amount** is a number. These correspond to *domain integrity constraints* in the usual database terminology.

Given $A \in \Sigma$, we define the set of A-tuples to be $\prod_{a \in A} D_a$. Thus an A-tuple is a function which assigns a data value in D_a to each $a \in A$.

In our example above, the first tuple in the table corresponds to the function

$$\{\textbf{branch-name} \mapsto \text{Cambridge}, \textbf{account-no} \mapsto 10991{-}06284,$$

$$\textbf{customer-name} \mapsto \text{Newton}, \textbf{balance} \mapsto £2,567.53\}$$

A relation of type A is a finite set of A-tuples. Given a schema Σ, an *instance* of the schema, representing a possible state of the database, is given by specifying a relation of type A for each $A \in \Sigma$.

Operations on Relations. We consider some of the fundamental operations on relations, which play a central rôle in relational databases. Firstly, relations of type A live in the powerset $\mathcal{P}(\prod_{a \in A} D_a)$, which is a boolean algebra; so boolean operations such as union, intersection, and set difference can be applied to them.

Note that the set of data values may in general be infinite, whereas the relations considered in database theory are finite. Thus one must use set difference rather than an 'absolute' notion of set complement.

Next, we consider the operation of projection. In the language of A-tuples, projection is *function restriction*. That is, given an A-relation R, and a subset $B \subseteq A$, we define:

$$R|_B := \{t|_B : t \in R\}.$$

Here, since $t \in \prod_{a \in A} D_a$, $t|_B$ just means restriction of the function t to B, which is a subset of its domain. This operation is then lifted pointwise to relations.

Now we consider the independent combination of relations, which is cartesian product in the standard formalism. The representation of tuples as functions leads to a 'logarithmic shift' in the representation[1], whereby this operation is represented by *disjoint union* of attribute sets.

Given an A-relation R and a B-relation S, we form the disjoint union $A \sqcup B$, and the $A \sqcup B$-relation

$$R \otimes S := \{t \in \prod_{a \in A \sqcup B} D_a \ : \ t|_A \in R \ \wedge \ t|_B \in S\}.$$

Of course, as concrete sets A and B may overlap. We can force them to be disjoint by 'tagging' them appropriately, e.g.

$$A \sqcup B := \{0\} \times A \ \cup \ \{1\} \times B.$$

The minor housekeeping details of such tagging can safely be ignored.[2] We shall henceforth do so without further comment.

This is only a subset of the operations available in standard relational algebra [26]. A more complete discussion could be given in the present setting, but this will suffice for our purposes.

2.2   The Functorial View

We shall now show how the relational database formalism, in the style we have developed it, has a direct expression in functorial terms. This immediately brings a great deal of mathematical structure into play, and will allow us to relate some important database notions to concepts of much more general standing.

We shall assume the rudiments of the language of categories, functors and natural transformations. All the background we shall need is covered in the charming (and succinct) text [25].

We shall consider the partial order **Att** of finite subsets of $\mathcal{A}$, ordered by inclusion, as a category.

We shall define a functor $\mathcal{T} : \mathbf{Att}^{\mathrm{op}} \longrightarrow \mathbf{Set}$ where $\mathcal{T}(A)$ is the set of A-tuples. Formally, we define

$$\mathcal{T}(A) := \prod_{a \in A} D_a,$$

and if $A \subseteq B$, we define the *restriction map* $\rho_A^B : \mathcal{T}(B) \longrightarrow \mathcal{T}(A)$ by

$$\rho_A^B : t \mapsto t|_A.$$

---

[1] Think of $2^a 2^b = 2^{a+b}$, and hence $\log(xy) = \log(x) + \log(y)$.

[2] The relevant result is the coherence theorem for monoidal categories [20].

It is easy to verify functoriality of $\mathcal{T}$, which means that, whenever $A \subseteq B \subseteq C$,

$$\rho_A^B \circ \rho_B^C = \rho_A^C,$$

and also that $\rho_A^A = \mathrm{id}_A$. Thus $\mathcal{T}$ is a *presheaf*, and restriction is exactly function restriction.

We also have the covariant powerset functor $\mathcal{P} : \mathbf{Set} \longrightarrow \mathbf{Set}$, which acts on functions by direct image: if $f : X \longrightarrow Y$, then

$$\mathcal{P}f : \mathcal{P}X \longrightarrow \mathcal{P}Y :: S \mapsto \{f(x) : x \in S\}.$$

We can compose $\mathcal{P}$ with $\mathcal{T}$ to obtain another presheaf

$$\mathcal{R} := \mathcal{P} \circ \mathcal{T} : \mathbf{Att}^{\mathrm{op}} \longrightarrow \mathbf{Set}.$$

This presheaf assigns the set of A-relations to each set of attributes A; while the restriction map

$$\rho_A^B : \mathcal{R}(B) \longrightarrow \mathcal{R}(A)$$

is exactly the operation of relation restriction, equivalent to the standard notion of projection in relation algebra, which we defined previously:

$$\rho_A^B : R \mapsto R|_A.$$

Natural Join. One of the most important operations in relational algebra is *natural join*. Given an A-relation R and a B-relation S, we define an $(A \cup B)$-relation $R \bowtie S$:

$$R \bowtie S := \{t \in \prod_{a \in A \cup B} D_a : t|_A \in R \wedge t|_B \in S\}.$$

We shall now show how this operation can be characterized in categorical terms.

Note firstly that since the powerset is naturally ordered by set inclusion, we can consider $\mathcal{R}$ as a functor

$$\mathcal{R} : \mathbf{Att}^{\mathrm{op}} \longrightarrow \mathbf{Pos}$$

where $\mathbf{Pos}$ is the category of posets and monotone maps. $\mathbf{Pos}$ is order-enriched; given monotone maps $f, g : P \to Q$, we can define the pointwise order:

$$f \leq g \ \equiv \ \forall x \in P.\, f(x) \leq g(x).$$

Now suppose we are given attribute sets A and B. We consider the following diagram arising from the universal property of product in $\mathbf{Set}$.

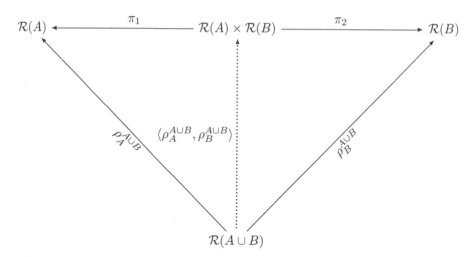

Proposition 1. *The natural join* $\bowtie: \mathcal{R}(A) \times \mathcal{R}(B) \to \mathcal{R}(A \cup B)$ *is uniquely characterized as the left adjoint of* $\langle \rho_A^{A \cup B}, \rho_B^{A \cup B} \rangle$; *that is, as the unique map satisfying*

$$\text{id}_{\mathcal{R}(A \cup B)} \leq \bowtie \circ \langle \rho_A^{A \cup B}, \rho_B^{A \cup B} \rangle, \qquad \langle \rho_A^{A \cup B}, \rho_B^{A \cup B} \rangle \circ \bowtie \leq \text{id}_{\mathcal{R}(A) \times \mathcal{R}(B)}.$$

The fact that in general a relation $R \in \mathcal{R}(A \cup B)$ satisfies only

$$R \subseteq R|_A \bowtie R|_B,$$

with strict inclusion possible, corresponds to the fact that natural join is in general a 'lossy' operation. Lossless joins correspond exactly to the case when equality holds.

2.3   The Sheaf-Theoretic View

We shall now show, building on the presheaf structure described in the previous sub-section, how a number of important database notions can be interpreted geometrically, in the language of sheaves and presheaves.

Schemas as Covers and Gluing Conditions. We shall interpret a schema $\Sigma = \{A_1, \ldots, A_k\}$ of finite subsets of $\mathcal{A}$ as a *cover*. That is, we think of the attribute sets A_i as 'open sets' expressing some local information in the sense of related clusters of attributes; these sets cover $A := \bigcup_{i=1}^{k} A_i$, the global set of attributes for the schema. Conversely, we think of the global set A as being decomposed into the local clusters A_i; which is exactly the standard point of view in databases.

The basic idea of sheaf theory is to analyze the passage from local to global behaviour in mathematical structures. A number of important notions in databases have exactly this character, and can be described naturally in sheaf-theoretic terms.

An instance $(R_1, \ldots, R_k)$ of a schema Σ is given by specifying a relation $R_i \in \mathcal{R}(A_i)$ for each $A_i \in \Sigma$. In sheaf-theoretic language, this is a family of local sections, defined over the open sets in the cover. A central issue in geometric terms is whether we can glue these local sections together into a global section defined over $A := \bigcup_{i=1}^{k} A_i$.

More precisely, we can ask:

Does there exist a relation $R \in \mathcal{R}(A)$ such that $R|_{A_i} = R_i$, $i = 1, \ldots, k$.

We say that the *gluing condition* is satisfied for the instance $(R_1, \ldots, R_k)$ if such a relation exists.

This has been studied as an algorithmic question in database theory, where it is referred to as the *join consistency property*; it is shown in [17] that it is NP-complete.

Note that a *necessary condition* for this to hold is that, for all $i, j = 1, \ldots, k$:

$$R_i|_{A_i \cap A_j} = R_j|_{A_i \cap A_j}. \tag{1}$$

Indeed, if such an R exists, then

$$R_i|_{A_i \cap A_j} = (R|_{A_i})|_{A_i \cap A_j} = R|_{A_i \cap A_j},$$

using the functoriality of restriction, and similarly for $R_j|_{A_i \cap A_j}$.

We shall say that a database instance $(R_1, \ldots, R_k)$ for which this condition (1) holds has consistent projections, and refer to the family of relations in the instance as a *compatible family*.

These notions can be generalized to apply to any presheaf. If the gluing condition can *always* be satisfied, for any cover and any family of compatible elements, and moreover there is a *unique* element which satisfies it, then the presheaf is a sheaf.

It is of course a well-known fact of life in databases, albeit expressed in a different language, that our relational presheaf $\mathcal{R}$ is *not* a sheaf.

In fact, we have the following:

Proposition 2. *An instance $(R_1, \ldots, R_k)$ satisfies the gluing condition if and only if there is a universal relation R for the instance.*

Here we take a universal relation for the instance by definition to be a relation defined on the whole set of attributes from which each of the relations in the instance can be recovered by projection. This notion, and various related ideas, played an important rôle in early developments in relational database theory; see e.g. [22,12,19,21,26].

Thus the standard notion of universal relation in databases corresponds exactly to the standard notion of solution to the gluing condition in sheaf theory, for the particular case of the relational presheaf $\mathcal{R}$.

It is also standard that a universal relation need not exist in general, and even if it exists, it need not be unique. There is a substantial literature devoted to the issue of finding conditions under which these properties do hold.

There is a simple connection between universal relations and lossless joins.

Proposition 3. Let $(R_1, \ldots, R_k)$ be an instance for the schema $\Sigma = \{A_1, \ldots, A_k\}$. Define $R := \bowtie_{i=1}^k R_i$. Then a universal relation for the instance exists if and only if $R|_{A_i} = R_i$, $i = 1, \ldots, k$, and in this case R is the largest relation in $\mathcal{R}(\bigcup_i A_i)$ satisfying the gluing condition.

Proof. We note that, if a relation S satisfies $S|_{A_i} = R_i$, $i = 1, \ldots, k$, then $S \subseteq \bowtie_{i=1}^k R_i$ by the adjoint property of the natural join. Moreover, since projection is monotone, in this case $R_i \subseteq S|_{A_i} \subseteq (\bowtie_{i=1}^k R_i)|_{A_i} \subseteq R_i$.   □

There are further categorical aspects of relational databases which it might prove interesting to pursue. In particular, one can define categories of schemas and of instances and their morphisms, and the construction of colimits in these categories may be applicable to issues of data integration. However, we shall not pursue these ideas here. Instead, we will turn to a natural generalization of relational databases which arises rather effortlessly from the formalism we have developed to this point.

3   Algebraic Databases

We begin by revisiting the definition of the relational presheaf $\mathcal{R}$ in terms of the covariant powerset functor $\mathcal{P}$. An alternative presentation of subsets is in terms of *characteristic functions*. That is, we have the familiar isomorphism $\mathcal{P}(X) \cong \mathbf{2}^X$, where $\mathbf{2} := \{0, 1\}$ is the 2-element boolean algebra.

We can also use this representation to define the functorial action of powerset. Given $s : X \to \mathbf{2}$ and $f : X \to Y$, we define $f^*(s) : Y \to \mathbf{2}$ by

$$f^*(s) : y \mapsto \bigvee_{f(x)=y} s(x). \tag{2}$$

It is easy to see that this is equivalent to

$$f^*(s)(y) = 1 \iff \exists x \in S.\, f(x) = y.$$

Here S is the subset of X whose characteristic function is s.

We can specialise this to the case of an inclusion function $\iota : A \hookrightarrow B$ which induces a map $\mathbf{2}^B \to \mathbf{2}^A$ by restriction:

$$s : B \to \mathbf{2} \quad \mapsto \quad (s|_A) : A \to \mathbf{2}.$$

What we obtain in this case is exactly the notion of *projection* of a relation, as defined in the previous section.

The advantage of this 'matrix' style of definition of the powerset is that it can immediately be generalized rather widely. There is a minor caveat. In the above definition, we used the fact that **2** is a *complete* boolean algebra, since there was no restriction on the cardinality of the preimages of f. In the database context, of course, all sets are typically finite.[3] We shall enforce a finiteness condition explicitly in our general definition.

We recall that a *commutative semiring* is a structure $(R, +, 0, \cdot, 1)$, where $(R, +, 0)$ and $(R, \cdot, 1)$ are commutative monoids, and moreover multiplication distributes over addition:

$$x \cdot (y + z) = x \cdot y + x \cdot z.$$

Many examples of commutative semirings arise naturally in Computer Science: we list a few of the most common.

- The reals
$$(\mathbb{R}, +, 0, \times, 1).$$

More generally, any commutative ring is a commutative semiring.
- The non-negative reals
$$(\mathbb{R}_{\geq 0}, +, 0, \times, 1).$$

- The booleans
$$\mathbf{2} = (\{0, 1\}, \vee, 0, \wedge, 1).$$

More generally, *idempotent* commutative semirings are exactly the distributive lattices.
- The min-plus semiring

$$(\mathbb{R}_{\geq 0} \cup \{\infty\}, \min, \infty, +, 0).$$

We also note the rôle played by *provenance semirings* in database theory [14,9,11].

We fix a semiring R. Given a set X, the *support* of a function $v : X \to R$ is the set of $x \in X$ such that $v(x) \neq 0$. We write $\mathsf{supp}(v)$ for the support of v. We shall write $\mathcal{V}_R(X)$ for the set of functions $v : X \to R$ of *finite* support. We shall write $\mathcal{D}_R(X)$ for the subset of $\mathcal{V}_R(X)$ of those functions $d : X \to R$ such that

$$\sum_{x \in X} d(x) = 1.$$

Note that the finite support condition ensures that this sum is well-defined.

We shall refer to elements of $\mathcal{V}_R(X)$ as R-valuations on X, and of $\mathcal{D}_R(X)$ as R-distributions.

We consider a few examples:

- If we take $R = \mathbf{2}$, then $\mathcal{V}_R(X)$ is the set of finite subsets of X, and $\mathcal{D}_R(X)$ is the set of finite non-empty subsets.

---

[3] The sets of data values D_a may be infinite, but only finitely many values will appear in a database instance.

– If we take $R = (\mathbb{R}_{\geq 0}, +, 0, \times, 1)$, then $\mathcal{D}_R(X)$ is the set of discrete (finite-support) probability distributions on X.

Algebraically, $\mathcal{V}_R(X)$ is the free R-semimodule over the set X [13].

These constructions extend to functors on **Set**. Given $f : X \to Y$, we define

$$\mathcal{V}_R(f) : \mathcal{V}_R(X) \to \mathcal{V}_R(Y) :: v \mapsto [y \mapsto \sum_{f(x)=y} v(x)].$$

This restricts to $\mathcal{D}_R$ in a well-defined fashion. Taking $R = \mathbf{2}$, we see that $\mathcal{V}_R(f)$ is exactly the direct image of f, defined as in (2).

We can now generalize databases from the standard relational case to 'relations valued in a semiring' by replacing $\mathcal{P}$ by $\mathcal{V}_R$ (or $\mathcal{D}_R$) in our definition of $\mathcal{R}$; that is, we take $\mathcal{R} := F \circ \mathcal{T}$, where F is $\mathcal{V}_R$ or $\mathcal{D}_R$ for some commutative semiring R. We recover the standard notion exactly when $R = \mathbf{2}$. In the case where $R = (\mathbb{R}_{\geq 0}, +, 0, \times, 1)$ and $F = \mathcal{D}_R$, we obtain a notion of probabilistic database, where each relation specifies a probability distribution over the set of tuples for its attribute-set.

Moreover, our descriptions of the key database operations all generalise to any semiring. If we apply the definition of the functorial action of $\mathcal{V}_R$ or $\mathcal{D}_R$ to the case of restriction maps induced by inclusions, we obtain the right notion of *generalised projection*, which can be applied to any algebraic database. We have already seen that we recover the standard notion of projection in the Boolean case. In the case where the semiring is the non-negative reals, so we are dealing with probability distributions, projection is exactly *marginalization*.

We also note an important connection between probabilistic and relational databases. We can always pass from a probabilistic to a relational instance by taking the *support* of the distribution. Algebraically, this corresponds to mapping all positive probabilities to 1; this is in fact the action of the unique semiring homomorphism from the non-negative reals to the booleans.

In general, many natural properties of databases will be *preserved* by this homomorphic mapping. This means that if we show that such a property is *not* satisfied by the support, we can conclude that it is not satisfied by the probabilistic instance. Thus we can leverage negative results at the relational level, and lift them to the probabilistic setting.

We shall see a significant example of a probabilistic database in the next section.

4   From Databases to Observational Scenarios

We shall now offer an alternative interpretation of the relational database formalism, with a very different motivation. This will expose a surprising connection between database theory, and on face value a completely different topic, namely Bell's theorem in the foundations of quantum mechanics [8].

Our starting point is the idealized situation depicted in the following diagram.

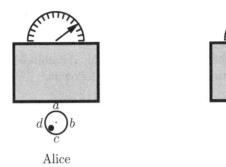

Alice   Bob

There are several agents or experimenters, who can each select one of several different measurements $a, b, c, d, \ldots$ to perform, and observe one of several different outcomes. These agents may or may not be spatially separated. When a system is prepared in a certain fashion and measurements are selected, some corresponding outcomes will be observed. These individual occurrences or 'runs' of the system are the basic events. Repeated runs allow relative frequencies to be tabulated, which can be summarized by a probability distribution on events for each selection of measurements. We shall call such a family of probability distributions, one for each choice of measurements, an *empirical model*.

As an example of such a model, consider the following table.

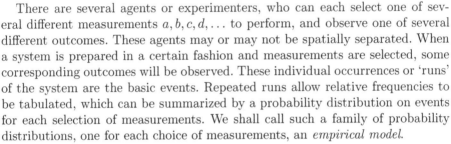

	$(0,0)$	$(1,0)$	$(0,1)$	$(1,1)$
$a\ b$	$1/2$	0	0	$1/2$
$a'\ b$	$3/8$	$1/8$	$1/8$	$3/8$
$a\ b'$	$3/8$	$1/8$	$1/8$	$3/8$
$a'\ b'$	$1/8$	$3/8$	$3/8$	$1/8$

The intended scenario here is that Alice can choose between measurement settings a and a', and Bob can choose b or b'. These will correspond to different quantities which can be measured.[4] We assume that these choices are made independently. Thus the *measurement contexts* are

$$\{a, b\}, \quad \{a', b\}, \quad \{a, b'\}, \quad \{a', b'\},$$

and these index the rows of the table. Each measurement has possible outcomes 0 or 1.

Note that, with a small change of perspective, we can see this in database terms. Take the global set of attributes $\mathcal{A} = \{a, a', b, b'\}$, and consider the schema

$$\Sigma := (\{a, b\}, \{a', b\}, \{a, b'\}, \{a', b'\}).$$

For each $a \in \mathcal{A}$, we take $D_a := \{0, 1\}$.

---

[4] For example, in the quantum case these settings may correspond to different directions along which to measure 'Spin Up' or 'Spin Down' [29].

For each $A \in \Sigma$, we have a 'table' in the algebraically generalized sense discussed in the previous section. That is, we have a distribution $d_A \in \mathcal{D}_R \circ \mathcal{T}(A)$, where $R = \mathbb{R}_{\geq 0}$ is the semiring of non-negative reals. Thus d_A is a probability distribution on $\mathcal{T}(A)$, the set of A-tuples.

To make a direct connection with standard relational databases, we can pass to the support of the above table, which yields the following:

	$(0,0)$	$(1,0)$	$(0,1)$	$(1,1)$
$a \; b$	1	0	0	1
$a' \, b$	1	1	1	1
$a \; b'$	1	1	1	1
$a' \, b'$	1	1	1	1

This corresponds to the instance of the schema Σ where for each $A = \{\alpha, \beta\} \in \Sigma \setminus \{\{a, b\}\}$, there is the 'full' table of all possible tuples:

α	β
0	0
0	1
1	0
1	1

while for $\{a, b\}$ we have the table with only two tuples:

a	b
0	0
1	1

Thus we have a formal passage between empirical models and relational databases. To go further, we must understand how empirical models such as these can be used to draw striking conclusions about the foundations of physics.

5 Empirical Models and Hidden Variables

Most of our discussion is independent of any particular physical theory. However, it is important to understand how quantum mechanics, as our most highly confirmed theory, gives rise to a class of empirical models of the kind we have been discussing.

To obtain such a model, we must provide the following ingredients:

- A quantum state.
- For each of the 'measurement settings', which correspond to attributes in database terms, a physical observable or measurable quantity. Each such observable will have a set of associated possible outcomes, which will correspond to the set of data values associated with that attribute.

The 'statistical algorithm' of quantum mechanics will then prescribe a probability for each measurement outcome when the given state is measured with that observable.

Although we shall not really need the details of this, we briefly recall some basic definitions. For further details, see e.g. [24,29].

A Crash Course in Qubits

Whereas a classical bit register has possible states 0 or 1, a qubit state is given by a *superposition* of these states. More precisely, a (pure) qubit state is given by a vector in the 2-dimensional complex vector space $\mathbb{C}^2$, *i.e.* a complex linear combination $\alpha_0|0\rangle + \alpha_1|1\rangle$, subject to the normalization constraint $|\alpha_0|^2 + |\alpha_1|^2 = 1$. Here $|0\rangle, |1\rangle$ is standard Dirac notation for the basis vectors $[1,0]^T$ and $[0,1]^T$.

Measurement of such a state (in the $|0\rangle$, $|1\rangle$ basis) is inherently probabilistic; we get $|i\rangle$ with probability $|\alpha_i|^2$.

There is a beautiful geometric picture of this complex 2-dimensional geometry in real three-dimensional space. This is the Bloch sphere representation:

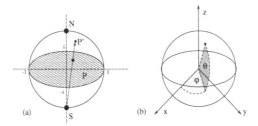

The pure qubit states correspond to points on the surface of the sphere. However, this one-qubit case does not yet provide non-classical resources for information processing. Things get interesting with n-qubit registers

$$\sum_i \alpha_i |i\rangle, \qquad i \in \{0,1\}^n.$$

It is at this point, in particular, that *entanglement phenomena* arise.

A typical example of an entangled state is the Bell state:

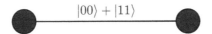

$$|00\rangle + |11\rangle$$

We can think of two particles, each with a qubit state, held by Alice and Bob. However, these two particles are entangled. If Alice measures her qubit, then if she gets the answer $|0\rangle$, the state will collapse to $|00\rangle$, and if Bob measures his qubit, he will get the answer $|0\rangle$ with certainty; similarly if the result of Alice's measurement is $|1\rangle$. This non-local effect creates new possibilities for quantum information processing.

Mathematically, compound systems are represented by the *tensor product*, $\mathcal{H}_1 \otimes \mathcal{H}_2$, with typical element

$$\sum_i \lambda_i \cdot \phi_i \otimes \psi_i.$$

Superposition encodes *correlation*.

Entanglement is the physical phenomenon underlying Einstein's 'spooky action at a distance'. Even if the particles are spatially separated, measuring one has an effect on the state of the other.

Bell's achievement was to turn this puzzling feature of quantum mechanics into a theorem: quantum mechanics is *essentially non-local*.

5.1 Bell's Theorem

We look again at the empirical model

	$(0,0)$	$(1,0)$	$(0,1)$	$(1,1)$
(a,b)	1/2	0	0	1/2
(a,b')	3/8	1/8	1/8	3/8
(a',b)	3/8	1/8	1/8	3/8
(a',b')	1/8	3/8	3/8	1/8

This can be realized in quantum mechanics, using a Bell state

$$\frac{|00\rangle + |11\rangle}{\sqrt{2}},$$

subjected to measurements in the XY-plane of the Bloch sphere, at relative angle $\pi/3$. Systems of this kind have been the subject of extensive experimental investigation, and the predictions of quantum mechanics can be taken to be very highly confirmed.

The question we shall ask, following Bell, is this: Can we explain these empirical findings by a theory which is *local* and *realistic* in the following sense.

- A theory is realistic if it ascribes definite values to all observables for every physical state, independently of the activities of any external observers.
- A theory is local if the outcomes of measurements on spatially separated subsystems depend only on common causal factors. In particular, for space-like separated measurements, the outcomes of the measurements should be independent of each other.

We allow for the fact that there may be salient features in the theory determining the outcomes of measurements of which we are not aware. These features are embodied in the notion of *hidden variable*. Thus we take measurement outcomes to be determined, *given some value of this hidden variable*. Moreover, we assume that this hidden variable acts in a local fashion with respect to spatially separated subsystems.

This gives a general notion of theory which behaves in a fashion broadly consistent with classical physical intuitions. The import of Bell's theorem is exactly that *no such theory can account for the empirical predictions of quantum mechanics*. Hence, given that these predictions are so well-confirmed, we must abandon the classical world-view which underpins the assumptions of local realism.

To give a precise statement of Bell's theorem, we must formalize the notion of local hidden variable theory. We shall give this in a streamlined form, which can be shown to be equivalent to more general definitions which have been considered (see e.g. Theorem 7.1 in [3]).

We shall explain this notion in relation to the Bell table given above. We have a total set of four measurement settings we are considering, two for Alice and two for Bob:
$$\{a, a', b, b'\}.$$
A simultaneous assignment of outcomes (0 or 1) to each of these is given by a function
$$s : \{a, a', b, b'\} \longrightarrow \{0, 1\}.$$
The fact that an (unknown) hidden variable may be affecting the outcome is captured by saying that we have a probability distribution d on the set of all such functions s. Such a probability distribution can be taken to be a canonical form for a hidden variable.

The requirement on this distribution d to be consistent with the empirical data is that, for each of the experimentally accessible combinations of measurement settings
$$\{a, b\}, \quad \{a', b\}, \quad \{a, b'\}, \quad \{a', b'\},$$
the restriction (or marginalization) of d to this set of measurements yields exactly the observed distribution on outcomes from the corresponding row of the table. For example, we must have $d|\{a, b\} = d_1$, where
$$d_1(0,0) = d_1(1,1) = 1/2, \quad d_1(0,1) = d_1(1,0) = 0.$$

A precise statement of a particular instance of Bell's theorem can now be given as follows:

Proposition 4. *There is no distribution d on the whole set of measurements which yields the observable distributions by restriction.*

Proof. Assume for a contradiction that such a distribution d exists. It will assign a number $X_i \in [0, 1]$ to each $s_i : \{a, a', b, b'\} \longrightarrow \{0, 1\}$. There are 16 such functions: we enumerate them by viewing them as binary strings, where the j'th bit indicates the assignment of an outcome to the j'th measurement, listed as a, a', b, b'.

The requirement that this distribution projects onto the distributions in the empirical model translates into 16 equations, one for each entry in the table. It suffices to consider 4 of these equations:
$$\begin{aligned}
X_1 + X_2 + X_3 + X_4 &= 1/2 \\
X_2 + X_4 + X_6 + X_8 &= 1/8 \\
X_3 + X_4 + X_{11} + X_{12} &= 1/8 \\
X_1 + X_5 + X_9 + X_{13} &= 1/8
\end{aligned}$$

Adding the last three equations yields
$$X_1 + X_2 + X_3 + 2X_4 + X_5 + X_6 + X_8 + X_9 + X_{11} + X_{12} + X_{13} = 3/8.$$

Since all these terms must be non-negative, the left-hand side of this equation must be greater than or equal to the left-hand side of the first equation, yielding the required contradiction. □

This argument seems very specific to the probabilistic nature of the empirical model. However, an important theme in the work on no-go theorems in quantum mechanics is to prove results of this kind in a probability-free fashion [15,16]. This will bring us directly into the arena of relational databases.

5.2 Hardy's Construction

Hardy's construction [16] yields a family of empirical models which can be realized in quantum mechanics in similar fashion to the Bell model. However, these families exhibit a stronger form of non-locality property, which does not depend on the probabilities, but only on the support.

We exhibit an example of a support table arising from Hardy's construction.

	$(0,0)$	$(1,0)$	$(0,1)$	$(1,1)$
(a,b)	1	1	1	1
(a',b)	0	1	1	1
(a,b')	0	1	1	1
(a',b')	1	1	1	0

This arises from a probability table by replacing all positive probabilites by 1.

Note that we can view this table as encoding a small relational database, as in our discussion in the previous section. There will be four relation tables in this database, one for each of the above rows. The table corresponding to the first row will have the full set of tuples over $\{0,1\}$. The tables for the second and third rows will have the form

α	β
0	1
1	0
1	1

while that for the fourth row will have the form

a'	b'
0	0
0	1
1	0

The property which shows the non-locality of this model is the exact relational analogue of the probabilistic version we considered in relation to the Bell model.

Proposition 5. *There is no A-relation R, where $A = \{a, a', b, b'\}$, which is consistent with the empirical observable supports; that is, for which $R|\{\alpha, \beta\}$ yields the relational table for all $\{\alpha, \beta\}$, $\alpha \in \{a, a'\}$, $\beta \in \{b, b'\}$.*

In database language, this says exactly that there is no 'universal relation' on the whole set of attributes which yields each of the 'observable relations' by projection.

Proof. We argue similarly to the case of the Bell model, except that we are now working over the Boolean semiring rather than the non-negative reals. The existence of a relation R thus reduces to a Boolean satisfiability problem. An equation $\sum_i X_i = 1$ simply asserts the disjunction of the boolean variables, while an equation $\sum_i X_i = 0$ asserts the conjunction of the negated variables. Again it suffices to consider four of the equations which can be read off the Hardy table:

$$X_1 \ \vee \ X_2 \ \vee \ X_3 \ \vee \ X_4$$
$$\neg X_1 \ \wedge \ \neg X_3 \ \wedge \ \neg X_5 \ \wedge \ \neg X_7$$
$$\neg X_1 \ \wedge \ \neg X_2 \ \wedge \ \neg X_9 \ \wedge \ \neg X_{10}$$
$$\neg X_4 \ \wedge \ \neg X_8 \ \wedge \ \neg X_{12} \ \wedge \ \neg X_{16}$$

Since every disjunct in the first formula appears as a negated conjunct in one of the other three formulas, there is no satisfying assignment. □

There is a precise sense in which the Hardy result is stronger than the Bell result. In fact, we have the following.

Proposition 6. *If an empirical model has a local hidden-variable model in the probabilistic sense, then its support table has a universal relation. Thus failure to have a universal relation implies failure to have a local hidden-variable model in the probabilistic sense.*

Proof. This follows simply from the fact that the map from the non-negative reals to the booleans which takes all non-zero elements to 1 is a semiring homomorphism. □

The converse to this result is false. For example, the support table arising from the Bell model *does* have a universal relation, as can easily be verified.

Note that the Hardy table, and indeed all such tables arising from quantum mechanics, satisfies the compatibility condition which we discussed in Section 2.3. In fact, compatibility corresponds precisely to the physical condition of *no-signalling*, and the fact that quantum models satisfy the condition is exactly the content of the No-Signalling theorem of quantum mechanics. See [3] Section 8 for an extended discussion of this point.

6   No-Go Theorems, Global Sections and Universal Relations

We shall now develop a more general perspective on the results we have discussed in the previous section.

Following the geometric language we introduced in Section 2.3, we see that the existence of a hidden-variable model is equivalently expressed as the existence of a *global section* which glues together the family of empirical accessible distributions or relations.

Thus non-locality and related no-go results can be understood in terms of *obstructions to the existence of global sections*, a central issue in the pervasive applications of sheaves in geometry, topology, analysis and number theory.

In terms of databases, such results can be understood as expressing obstructions to the existence of universal relations for given instances of the database.

We shall now discuss two further types of no-go results, which can be understood in terms of yet stronger forms of obstruction.

6.1 Strong Contextuality

If we consider the argument for the Hardy construction, it can be understood as saying that there is no relation over the global tuples which 'covers' all (and only) the observable tuples. But now suppose we consider a much weaker requirement: we simply ask for *one global tuple* which projects consistently into all the relations in the database instance.

Note that the Hardy model does meet this condition. The global assignment

$$\{a \mapsto 1,\ a' \mapsto 0,\ b \mapsto 1,\ b' \mapsto 0\}$$

does project consistently into the support table for this model. The Bell model similarly meets this condition.

If even this, much weaker requirement *cannot* be met, then we have a much stronger form of no-go theorem. We say that such a situation exhibits *strong contextuality*.

The question now arises: are there models coming from quantum mechanics which are strongly contextual in this sense?

We shall now show that the well-known GHZ models [15], of type $(n, 2, 2)$ for all $n > 2$, are strongly contextual. This will establish a strict hierarchy

$$\text{Bell} < \text{Hardy} < \text{GHZ}$$

of increasing strengths of obstructions to non-contextual behaviour for these salient models.

The GHZ model of type $(n, 2, 2)$ can be specified as follows. We label the two measurements at each part as $X^{(i)}$ and $Y^{(i)}$, and the outcomes as 0 and 1. For each context C, every s in the support of the model satisfies the following conditions:

- If the number of Y measurements in C is a multiple of 4, the number of 1's in the outcomes specified by s is even.
- If the number of Y measurements is $4k+2$, the number of 1's in the outcomes is odd.

A model with these properties can be realized in quantum mechanics, using the GHZ state

$$\frac{|0 \cdots 0\rangle + |1 \cdots 1\rangle}{\sqrt{2}}.$$

Proposition 7. *The GHZ models are strongly contextual, for all $n \geq 3$.*

Proof. We consider the case where $n = 4k$, $k \geq 1$. Assume for a contradiction that we have a global section $s \in S_e$ for the GHZ model e.

If we take Y measurements at every part, the number of 1 outcomes under the assignment is even. Replacing any two Y's by X's changes the residue class mod 4 of the number of Y's, and hence must result in the opposite parity for the number of 1 outcomes under the assignment. Thus for any $Y^{(i)}$, $Y^{(j)}$ assigned the *same* value, if we substitute X's in those positions they must receive *different* values under s. Similarly, for any $Y^{(i)}$, $Y^{(j)}$ assigned different values, the corresponding $X^{(i)}$, $X^{(j)}$ must receive the same value.

Suppose firstly that not all $Y^{(i)}$ are assigned the same value by s. Then for some i, j, k, $Y^{(i)}$ is assigned the same value as $Y^{(j)}$, and $Y^{(j)}$ is assigned a different value to $Y^{(k)}$. Thus $Y^{(i)}$ is also assigned a different value to $Y^{(k)}$. Then $X^{(i)}$ is assigned the same value as $X^{(k)}$, and $X^{(j)}$ is assigned the same value as $X^{(k)}$. By transitivity, $X^{(i)}$ is assigned the same value as $X^{(j)}$, yielding a contradiction.

The remaining cases are where all Y's receive the same value. Then any pair of X's must receive different values. But taking any 3 X's, this yields a contradiction, since there are only two values, so some pair must receive the same value.

The case when $n = 4k+2$, $k \geq 1$, is proved in the same fashion, interchanging the parities. When $n \geq 5$ is odd, we start with a context containing one X, and again proceed similarly.

The most familiar case, for $n = 3$, does not admit this argument, which relies on having at least 4 Y's in the initial configuration. However, for this case one can easily adapt the well-known argument of Mermin using 'instruction sets' [23] to prove strong contextuality. This uses a case analysis to show that there are 8 possible global sections satisfying the parity constraint on the 3 measurement combinations with 2 Y's and 1 X; and all of these violate the constraint for the XXX measurement. □

6.2   The Kochen-Specker Theorem

Kochen-Specker-type theorems [18] can be understood as *generic strong contextuality results*. In database terms, they say that, if the database schema has a certain combinatorial structure, then *every instance* satisfying some conditions is strongly contextual. This can be interpreted in the quantum context in such a way that the conditions will be satisfied by *every* quantum state, and hence we obtain a state-independent form of strong contextuality result.

The condition which is typically imposed on the instances, assuming that the possible data values for each attribute lie in $\{0,1\}$, is that *every tuple contains exactly one* 1. If we think in terms of satisfiability, this corresponds to a 'POSITIVE ONE-IN-k-SAT' condition.

To show that the Kochen-Specker result holds is exactly to show that there is no satisfying assignment for the corresponding set of clauses.

The simplest example of this situation is the 'triangle', *i.e.* the schema with elements

$$\{a,b\}, \{b,c\}, \{a,c\}.$$

However, this example cannot be realized in quantum mechanics [3].

An example which can be realized in quantum mechanics, where $\mathcal{A}$ has 18 elements, and there are 9 sets in the database schema, each with four elements, such that each element of $\mathcal{A}$ is in two of these, appears in the 18-vector proof of the Kochen-Specker Theorem in [10].

U_1	U_2	U_3	U_4	U_5	U_6	U_7	U_8	U_9
A	A	H	H	B	I	P	P	Q
B	E	I	K	E	K	Q	R	R
C	F	C	G	M	N	D	F	M
D	G	J	L	N	O	J	L	O

Here the schema is $\Sigma = \{U_1, \ldots, U_9\}$.

We shall give a simple combinatorial condition on the schema Σ which is implied by the existence of a global section s satisfying the 'POSITIVE ONE-IN-k-SAT' condition. Violation of this condition therefore suffices to prove that no such global section exists.

For each $a \in \mathcal{A}$, we define

$$\Sigma(a) := \{A \in \Sigma : a \in A\}.$$

Proposition 8. *If a global section satisfying the condition exists, then every common divisor of $\{|\Sigma(a)| : a \in \mathcal{A}\}$ must divide $|\Sigma|$.*

Proof. Suppose there is a global section $s : \mathcal{A} \to \{0,1\}$ satisfying the condition. Consider the set $X \subseteq \mathcal{A}$ of those a such that $s(a) = 1$. Exactly one element of X must occur in every $A \in \Sigma$. Hence there is a partition of Σ into the subsets $\Sigma(a)$ indexed by the elements of X. Thus

$$|\Sigma| = \sum_{a \in X} |\Sigma(a)|.$$

It follows that, if there is a common divisor of the numbers $|\Sigma(a)|$, it must divide $|\Sigma|$.   □

For example, if every $a \in \mathcal{A}$ appears in an even number of elements of Σ, while Σ has an odd number of elements, then there is no global section. This corresponds to the 'parity proofs' which are often used in verifying Kochen-Specker-type results [10,28]. For example, in the 18-attribute schema with 9 relations given above, each attribute appears in two relations in the schema; hence the argument applies.

For further discussion of these ideas, including connections with graph theory, see [3].

7   Further Directions

We mention some further directions for developing the connections between databases and the study of non-locality and contextuality in quantum mechanics.

- We may consider conditions on the database schema which guarantees that global sections can be found. The important notion of *acyclicity* in database theory [7] is relevant here. On the probabilistic side there is a result by Vorob'ev [27] (motivated by game theory), which gives necessary and sufficient combinatorial conditions on a schema for *any* assignment of probability distributions on the tuples for each relation in the schema to have a global section; that is, for a universal relation in the probabilistic sense to always exist for any probabilistic instance of the database. Rui Soares Barbosa (personal communication) has shown that the Vorob'ev condition is equivalent to acyclicity in the database sense. This provides another striking connection between database theory and the theory of quantum non-locality and contextuality.
- A logical approach to Bell inequalities in terms of logical consistency conditions is developed in [5]. It would be interesting to interpret and apply this notion of Bell inequalities in the database context.
- The tools of sheaf cohomology are used to characterize the obstructions to global sections in a large family of cases in [6]. In principle, these sophisticated tools can be applied to databases. There may be interesting connections with acyclicity in the database sense.

We can summarise the connections which we have exposed between database theory and quantum non-locality and contextually in the following table:

Relational databases	measurement scenarios
attribute	measurement
set of attributes defining a relation table	compatible set of measurements
database schema	measurement cover
tuple	local section (joint outcome)
relation/set of tuples	boolean distribution on joint outcomes
universal relation instance	global section/hidden variable model
acyclicity	Vorob'ev condition

Acknowledgements. Discussions with and detailed comments by Phokion Kolaitis are gratefully acknowledged. Leonid Libkin also gave valuable feedback. This paper was written while in attendance at the program on 'Semantics and Syntax: the legacy of Alan Turing' at the Isaac Newton Institute, Cambridge, April–May 2012.

References

1. Abiteboul, S., Hull, R., Vianu, V.: Foundations of Databases. Addison-Wesley, Reading (1995)
2. Abramsky, S.: Relational Hidden Variables and Non-Locality. Studia Logica 101(2), 411–452 (2013)
3. Abramsky, S., Brandenburger, A.: The sheaf-theoretic structure of non-locality and contextuality. New Journal of Physics 13(2011), 113036 (2011)
4. Abramsky, S., Gottlob, G., Kolaitis, P.: Robust constraint satisfaction and local hidden variables in quantum mechanics. In: Rossi, F. (ed.) Proceedings of the International Joint Conference in Artificial Intelligence (IJCAI) (2013)
5. Abramsky, S., Hardy, L.: Logical Bell Inequalities. Physical Review A 85, 062114 (2012)
6. Abramsky, S., Mansfield, S., Barbosa, R.S.: The cohomology of non-locality and contextuality. In: Proceedings of Quantum Physics and Logic 2011. EPTCS, vol. 95, pp. 1–15 (2012)
7. Beeri, C., Fagin, R., Maier, D., Yannakakis, M.: On the desirability of acyclic database schemes. Journal of the ACM (JACM) 30(3), 479–513 (1983)
8. Bell, J.S.: On the Einstein-Podolsky-Rosen paradox. Physics 1(3), 195–200 (1964)
9. Buneman, P., Tan, W.C.: Provenance in databases. In: Proceedings of the 2007 ACM SIGMOD International Conference on Management of Data, pp. 1171–1173. ACM (2007)
10. Cabello, A., Estebaranz, J.M., García-Alcaine, G.: Bell-Kochen-Specker theorem: A proof with 18 vectors. Physics Letters A 212(4), 183–187 (1996)
11. Cheney, J., Chiticariu, L., Tan, W.C.: Provenance in databases: Why, how, and where. Foundations and Trends in Databases 1(4), 379–474 (2009)
12. Fagin, R., Mendelzon, A.O., Ullman, J.D.: A simplified universal relation assumption and its properties. ACM Transactions on Database Systems (TODS) 7(3), 343–360 (1982)
13. Golan, J.S.: Semirings and their Applications. Springer (1999)
14. Green, T.J., Karvounarakis, G., Tannen, V.: Provenance semirings. In: Proceedings of the Twenty-Sixth ACM SIGMOD-SIGACT-SIGART Symposium on Principles of Database Systems, pp. 31–40. ACM (2007)
15. Greenberger, D.M., Horne, M.A., Zeilinger, A.: Going beyond Bell's theorem. In: Kafatos, M. (ed.) Bell's Theorem, Quantum Theory, and Conceptions of the Universe, pp. 69–72. Kluwer (1989)
16. Hardy, L.: Quantum mechanics, local realistic theories, and Lorentz-invariant realistic theories. Physical Review Letters 68(20), 2981–2984 (1992)
17. Honeyman, P., Ladner, R.E., Yannakakis, M.: Testing the universal instance assumption. Information Processing Letters 10(1), 14–19 (1980)
18. Kochen, S., Specker, E.P.: The problem of hidden variables in quantum mechanics. Journal of Mathematics and Mechanics 17(1), 59–87 (1967)
19. Korth, H.F., Kuper, G.M., Feigenbaum, J., Van Gelder, A., Ullman, J.D.: SYSTEM/U: A database system based on the universal relation assumption. ACM Transactions on Database Systems (TODS) 9(3), 331–347 (1984)
20. Mac Lane, S.: Categories for the working mathematician, vol. 5. Springer (1998)
21. Maier, D., Ullman, J.D.: Maximal objects and the semantics of universal relation databases. ACM Transactions on Database Systems (TODS) 8(1), 1–14 (1983)
22. Maier, D., Ullman, J.D., Vardi, M.Y.: On the foundations of the universal relation model. ACM Transactions on Database Systems (TODS) 9(2), 283–308 (1984)

23. Mermin, N.D.: Quantum mysteries revisited. Am. J. Phys. 58(8), 731–734 (1990)
24. Nielsen, M.Q.C., Chuang, I.: Quantum Computation and Quantum Information. Cambridge University Press (2000)
25. Pierce, B.C.: Basic category theory for computer scientists. The MIT Press (1991)
26. Ullman, J.D.: Principles of database systems. Prentice-Hall (1983)
27. Vorob'ev, N.N.: Consistent families of measures and their extensions. Theory of Probability and its Applications 7, 147 (1962)
28. Waegell, M., Aravind, P.K.: Parity proofs of the Kochen-Specker theorem based on the 24 rays of Peres. Arxiv preprint arXiv:1103.6058v1 (2011)
29. Yanofsky, N.S., Mannucci, M.A.: Quantum computing for computer scientists, vol. 20. Cambridge University Press, Cambridge (2008)

High-Level Rules for Integration and Analysis of Data: New Challenges

Bogdan Alexe[1], Douglas Burdick[1], Mauricio A. Hernández[1],
Georgia Koutrika[2], Rajasekar Krishnamurthy[1], Lucian Popa[1],
Ioana R. Stanoi[1], and Ryan Wisnesky[3]

[1] IBM Almaden Research Center
{balexe,drburdic,mahernan,rajase,lpopa,irs}@us.ibm.com
[2] HP Labs
koutrika@hp.com
[3] Harvard University
School of Engineering and Applied Sciences
ryan@cs.harvard.edu

1   Introduction and Motivation

Data integration remains a perenially difficult task. The need to access, integrate and make sense of large amounts of data has, in fact, accentuated in recent years. There are now many *publicly* available sources of data that can provide valuable information in various domains. Concrete examples of public data sources include: bibliographic repositories (DBLP, Cora, Citeseer), online movie databases (IMDB), knowledge bases (Wikipedia, DBpedia, Freebase), social media data (Facebook and Twitter, blogs). Additionally, a number of more specialized public data repositories are starting to play an increasingly important role. These repositories include, for example, the U.S. federal government data, congress and census data, as well as financial reports archived by the U.S. Securities and Exchange Commission (SEC).

However, in all of these cases, the data has become increasingly more heterogeneous and less structured. Even within one source (e.g., SEC or DBpedia), bits and pieces of data about the same real-world entity (such as a person, a company or a product) are often buried in text, html, XML, or other formats, and spread over many documents. In order to make sense of all this data at the aggregated level, it is necessary to build an entity or concept-centric view [10] of the domain, where clean and rich entities, together with their relationships, are aggregated from the myriad of unstructured or semi-structured pieces of data. It is these entities and relationships that will provide the real value to a human user or to the subsequent applications that need to consume information. In fact, many companies (so called data aggregators) have started to emerge in this space, aiming to create integrated value on top of the underlying raw data.

However, achieving the level of integration that is required in such practical scenarios is a challenge. There are many types of techniques that need to be put together in a complex data processing flow. These techniques include: *information extraction* [11] (to produce structured records from text or semi-structured

V. Tannen et al. (Eds.): Buneman Festschrift, LNCS 8000, pp. 36–55, 2013.
© Springer-Verlag Berlin Heidelberg 2013

data), *cleansing and normalization* (to be able to even compare string values of the same type, such as a dollar amount or a job title), *entity resolution* [13] (to link records that correspond to the same real-world entity or that are related via some other type of semantic relationship), *mapping* [14] (to bring the extracted and linked records to a uniform schematic representation), and *data fusion* [6] (to merge all the related facts into one integrated, clean object). In practice, these steps are often implemented in general purpose languages (e.g., Java, Perl), using ETL tools, or using general data manipulation languages (e.g., XSLT, Pig Latin). Often, the emphasis is on the low-level operations (sort, pipe, duplicate elimination, join, string matching, etc.) without a high-level view of the data integration steps. Most of the time, there is no explicit entity or object view, but rather tuples, arrays, key/value pairs.

In this paper, we advocate the need for a *high-level language or framework* to describe the main logical operations of data integration (e.g., entity extraction, entity resolution, mapping, fusion) and analysis (e.g., aggregation, view creation, temporal analysis). We emphasize the logical specification aspects rather than the physical implementation. In addition to ease of specification or programmability, such a framework would also enable better readability, better reuse and better customization of data integration and analysis (to other domains, other tasks, other views). The target users of such framework are developers that need to perform complex, industrial-strength data integration tasks.

We will illustrate the paper with an end-to-end scenario of integration that is focused on people and company entities. This scenario is drawn from our own experience, as part of the Midas project [3,7] at IBM, with integrating data from DBpedia and especially SEC, which we have used extensively as a source for integration in the financial domain. Similar challenges or technologies will apply to other scenarios of integration from public data sources. We will focus our discussion on the high-level rules and declarations that are needed to accomplish the various integration steps. For each of the important tasks, the rules are shown in a candidate syntax that takes inspiration from existing formalisms, languages and tools for information extraction, entity resolution and schema mapping. However, rather than fixing on a concrete language, the goal is to illustrate the features that need to be supported in such a language, as well as the challenges. Coming up with an actual integrated language that combines all these features together is a separate challenge in itself with many design choices.

This is mostly a vision paper, with the goal of raising the attention of interested researchers towards this area.

Note Some of the ideas and desiderata described in this article have subsequently led to the development at IBM of a high-level integration language called HIL [22].[1] This language includes declarative constructs for entity resolution and for mapping and fusion of data, and is now extensively used within IBM for large-scale integration over structured and unstructured data (e.g., social media, news articles, financial disclosures, enterprise data, etc.). The exact

---

[1] Thus, from a timeline point of view, this book chapter describes work that precedes the development of HIL.

language design choices and primitives of HIL, as well as its compilation and execution, are described in [22]. While HIL answers some of the research challenges outlined in this article, several important problems remain largely open, such as the need for tools or systems to support large-scale data exploration or to assist users with the actual development of a *good* set of data analysis rules.

1.1 Overview of the Paper

We start in Section 2 by describing some of the features of the data in DBpedia, as well as the challenges involved in data exploration, which is a phase that *precedes* the actual writing of the rules. We then illustrate some concrete rules for extracting facts from DBpedia. Here, the output of an extraction rule has a relatively simple structure (or schema), but the input is semi-structured and largely heterogeneous. Extraction from completely unstructured data (i.e., text) [11] is highly related in this context; however, in this paper, we focus our attention specifically on extraction from semi-structured data (e.g., RDF, or XML, or JSON). We also note that extraction from text, technically, is of a different nature and is discussed extensively elsewhere (e.g., [8]).

In addition to giving examples of extraction rules, we also include a discussion of the need for automatic or semi-automatic extraction of structured records that is based on data examples. Such technology, while non-trivial, would be particularly useful when the developer is in the exploration phase and does not know enough about the data and its peculiarities. Based on a few examples that are representative of the type of entities that the developer is interested to extract, the system must first be able to derive all the other entries that are "similar" to the given examples. More challenging, the system should come up with a set of extraction rules that would result in such entries. While existing work on query discovery based on data instances [18,27] or on schema mapping design based on examples [1,21] may provide a starting point here, new types of algorithms will have to be developed to account for highly heterogeneous data with "less" schema (such as DBpedia).

The next integration component that we address is entity resolution, in Section 3. Rather than looking at specific algorithms or implementations that match records based on various similarity measures on their fields, we take a higher-level approach where the goal is to provide the *specification* framework for entity resolution. We advocate a framework that is based on logical constraints that are similar, in spirit, to the dependencies used in data exchange [15]. However, different from data exchange where the dependencies are source-to-target, our entity resolution constraints are target-to-source: they define *declaratively* all the desired properties of the target (i.e., of the links) in terms of the sources. Furthermore, these constraints incorporate disjunction (of the alternative matching rules that may apply), rely on user-defined functions for computing similarity of values, and can include cardinality constraints (e.g., to express many-to-one type of links). We include a discussion to illustrate the differences between this framework and previous approaches such as the Dedupalog language [2].

One of the main research problems that we outline, as part of declarative entity resolution, is the compilation of the declarative constraints into an execution plan that produces a good instantiation of the links. An important related question is formulating the semantics of the declarative constraints, which then needs to be implemented by the execution plan. Finally, a major challenge for entity resolution, which goes beyond the design of the specification language, is the development of methods and tools to help users interactively resolve the inherent ambiguities in their specification. These tools can help users refine the declarative constraints, based on the actual data sets that need to be linked, to ultimately achieve a high quality specification for entity resolution.

We discuss mapping and transformation, as well as data fusion and aggregation aspects in Section 4. While there is work on schema mapping tools [14], data exchange semantics [15], and data fusion methods [6], our goal is to develop an expressive scripting language that allows developers to combine non-trivial mapping, fusion and aggregation tasks (e.g., that are often not possible within a schema mapping tool paradigm) with the declarative entity resolution and extraction operations discussed earlier. At the same time, we emphasize simplicity and ease of programming as important requirements for the language design.

We discuss several other related papers and systems in Section 5 and conclude the paper in Section 6, where we reiterate the need for a single, unified framework that incorporates all the aspects outlined in the previous sections.

2   Data Exploration and Extraction

The first step before the actual writing of extraction and integration rules is the *exploration* phase, where a human user needs to understand what is in the source data and what can be extracted. This step is usually expensive; any help that a system or tool can provide in assisting the human user can be valuable. Even if the user has an idea of what concepts need to be extracted, the form in which these concepts manifest in the actual data source can vary significantly. Hence, heterogeneity is a challenge.

We start with an example from DBpedia to illustrate the issues. We focus on financial companies (e.g., Bank of America, Citigroup); the goal here will be to extract structured records that are relevant for such financial companies and that are deemed useful towards building the final integrated view. First, we assume that the DBpedia data set is given as a set of JSON records, each corresponding to one entity. A record has a subject field (which is also the identifier of that entity), and then all the various properties recorded for that entity. This JSON representation can be easily obtained from the RDF version of Dbpedia, which records RDF triples of the form (subject, property, value).[2] The conversion from RDF to JSON is already a step towards a more unified view of the data, since it yields full objects rather triples. However, the format of these objects is wildly heterogeneous, even for the same "type" of entity, as we shall see shortly. A large

---

[2] See the Ontology Infobox Properties data set at
http://wiki.dbpedia.org/Downloads.

```
{                                                    {
  "assets": "US$ 2.264 trillion",                      "areaServed": "Worldwide",
  "foundation": "1904",                                "assets": "$ 1.119 trillion (2007)",
  "homepage": [ "http://www.bankofamerica.com",        "companyName": "Goldman_Sachs",
             "http://www.bofa.com" ],                  "companySlogan": "Our clients\' interests always come first",
  "industry": [ "Banking", "Financial services" ]      "companyType": "Public_company",
  "keyPeople": [                                        "foundation": "1869",
   "Bryan Moynihan",                                    "founder": ["Marcus_Goldman", "Samuel Sachs"],
   "(President and CEO)",                               "homepage": "http://www.gs.com/",
   "Charles Holliday",                                  "industry": "Finance_and_insurance",
   "(Chairman)"                                         "keyPeople": [
  ],                                                     "Lloyd_Blankfein",
  "location": [                                          "(Chairman & CEO)",
   "Charlotte,_North_Carolina",                          "Gary_Cohn",
   "United_States",                                      "(President & COO)",
   "North_Carolina"                                      "David Viniar",
  ],                                                     "(Executive VP & CFO)"
  "name": "Bank of America Corporation",                ],
  "numEmployees": "288000",                             "location": [ "United_States", "New_York_City" ],
  "slogan": "Bank of Opportunity",                      "marketCap": "$ 65.91 billion (2007)",
  "subject": "Bank_of_America",                         "numEmployees": "30,522 (2007)",
  "type": "Public_company",                             "products": [
  "wikiPageUsesTemplate": "Template:infobox_company"     "Financial_services",
},                                                       "Investment_bank"
                                                        ],
                                                        "revenue": "$ 87.968 billion (2007)",
                                                        "subject": "Goldman_Sachs",
                                                        "wikiPageUsesTemplate": "Template:infobox_company"
                                                      },
```

Fig. 1. Sample DBpedia records

part of the subsequent processing will be devoted to extracting the relevant parts of the objects of interest, bringing the extracted parts to a uniform format, and then linking and integrating them with data from other sources (e.g., SEC).

Figure 1 illustrates two sample input records, in JSON, corresponding to the DBpedia entries for Bank of America and Goldman Sachs. Even though both of these records represent entities of a similar type (i.e., financial institutions), there is significant variation in the structure of the records (i.e., the attributes that are present, their types), in the naming of the attributes, and in the values and format of the values that populate the attributes. For example, Goldman Sachs has attributes such as "founder" and "marketCap", while Bank of America does not include these attributes. Goldman Sachs has a "companyName" attribute, while the equivalent attribute for Bank of America is "name". The "homepage" attribute for Goldman Sachs is a single string, while the similar attribute for Bank of America is an array of strings. Finally, the values themselves are not always clean or cleanly organized. For example, Bank of America includes "Banking" and "Financial services" under the "industry" attribute; the corresponding information for Goldman Sachs is actually distributed over two attributes ("industry" and "products"). Furthermore, the entries under the "keyPeople" attribute, in both records, are a mixture of person names and positions (titles), without an explicit tagging of the data.

After exploring several more representative DBPedia entries for financial companies, the user may decide on a set of important *concepts* to be extracted from this collection of heterogeneous records. Each concept is based on a subset of

```
FinancialCompany =
    for (r in DBpedia)
    let industryTerms = extractIndustries (r.industry),
        compName = extractCompanyName (r)
    where contains (compName, "Bank|Insurance|Investment") or
            (some (i in industryTerms) satisfies
                contains (i, "bank|banking|insurance|finance|financial"))
    return {company_id: r.subject,
            name: compName,
            foundation: r.foundation,
            industry: industryTerms,
            revenue: cleanDollarAmount (r.revenue)
            }
```

Fig. 2. Extraction rule for financial companies

attributes and, hence, it is a piece of a schema. In our scenario, the user may be interested in the following three concepts.

FinancialCompany (company_id, name, foundation, industry, revenue, ...)
CompanyAddress (company_id, street1, street2, zipcode, city, state, country)
KeyPeople (person_name, titles, company_name, age, biography, ...)

Note that, in general, the schema for these concepts must be *open* (see the above ... notation) to account for possibly other attributes of interest that may be added later. The high-level integration language will have to be flexible and account for such open schema by either not requiring the user to explicitly having to define the schemas of the concepts, or by using advanced programming language features such as record polymorphism to represent extensible record types [24,25,28].

Finally, other concepts can be defined later from either the same source (DB-Pedia) or from other sources (e.g., SEC, as we will see later). All of these extracted concepts will then be processed together, in the subsequent integration flow, to generate clean target entities with richer structure.

We focus next on how to extract the data to populate such concepts from the underlying collection of heterogeneous records.

2.1 Extraction Rules: Examples

Figure 2 gives a first example of a rule that extracts data for financial companies from DBpedia. This rule populates into the FinancialCompany concept. There may be other rules to further populate into this same concept (and possibly add new attributes). Thus, the actual instance of a concept will be given by a union of extraction rules.

The rule uses an XQuery-like syntax (although other types of syntax could also be used) to express the search for DBPedia records that match the characteristics of a financial company and also to express the extraction of the relevant attributes. Note the complex predicate that is used in the where clause to recognize a financial company. This predicate includes multiple string matching conditions that are based on financial keywords. Note also the extensive presence of user-defined functions (UDFs) that are used for various purposes:

- to *clean* the data in the individual attributes. For example, cleanDollarAmount is a function that transforms various heterogeneous string values that represent dollar amounts into a standardized form. Concretely, strings such as "$ 87.968 billion (2007)" and "US$ 2.264 trillion" could be transformed into "$87.96 billion" and "$2.26 trillion", respectively.
- to *extract* certain expected strings from an input record or value (e.g., extractCompanyName from r and extractIndustries from r.industry).
- more generally, to account for the heterogeneity in the input data or structure. For example, extractIndustries must account for the fact that the input r.industry could be a string such as "Finance_and_insurance" or an array such as ["Banking", "Financial services"]. The function must uniformly generate an array of terms identifying the various relevant industries (i.e., ["finance", "insurance"] from the first input and ["banking", "financial services"] from the second input).

  As another example, extractCompanyName has to account for the fact that the company name can appear under various attributes in the input record r (e.g., sometime name, and sometime companyName). Furthermore, the value itself must be normalized (e.g., "Goldman_Sachs" must be transformed to "Goldman Sachs").

  Note that the extracted and normalized industry terms and company name are used both in the predicate in the where clause that identifies a financial company and in the output of the rule.

In Figure 3, we show another example of an extraction rule from DBPedia, to produce records for the key people that are associated with the financial companies. As before, the rule makes use of UDFs to restrict to financial companies. An additional UDF extractNameTitles is used to convert an array of strings into a set of structured records with explicit name and titles fields. For example, the array of uninterpreted strings that is the value of the keyPeople field in the "Goldman Sachs" record in Figure 1 is converted into a set of three records:

```
{ name: "Lloyd Blankfein", titles: ["Chairman", "CEO"] }
{ name: "Gary Cohn", titles: ["President", "CEO"] }
{ name: "David Viniar", titles: ["Executive VP", "CFO"] }
```

Note that the above UDF must employ a name recognizer as well as a title recognizer. Also, it must take into account the sequence in which the names and the titles appear in the input string. In particular, the function must detect that the titles of a person follow the actual person name, and also it must be able to handle the absence of title information (e.g., two consecutive names).

```
KeyPeople =
    for (r in Dbpedia)
    let industryTerms = extractIndustries (r.industry),
        compName = extractCompanyName (r),
        peopleTitles = extractNameTitles (r.keyPeople)
    for (p in peopleTitles)
    where  contains (compName, "Bank|Insurance|Investment") or
            (some (i in industryTerms) satisfies
                contains (i, "bank|banking|insurance|finance|financial"))
    return {person_name: p.name,
            titles: p.titles,
            company_name: compName,
            age: null,
            biography: null
            }
```

Fig. 3. Extraction rule for key people

2.2   Challenges in Data Extraction

In general, extraction rules can be fairly complex and the development time can
be extensive. On the one hand, they can be seen as a form of mapping rules that
require many UDFs. On the other hand, however, they differ from traditional
schema mappings in that the source schema, here, is very loose or non-existent.
This makes it harder to benefit from schema mapping tools [14], which assume
that the source schema and the target schema are both manageable and matched
within a user interface, which is then used to drive the generation of the mapping
rules. Generating a meaningful schema for DBpedia, even for a small portion of
it, would mean generating a large number of union or choice types to account for
the variation in the structure (even for the same type of entity). The ability to
load, use and manage such schema within a mapping tool is a research challenge
in itself.

A somewhat different research question is the following: *Can we generate or
learn extraction rules directly from the data and/or from examples?* The starting points for such generation would be: the input source data (e.g., DBpedia),
an existing library of UDFs (for normalization, cleansing, etc.), and a set of
representative examples of the intended output data. Existing work on query
discovery based on data instances [18,27] or on schema mapping design and refinement based on examples [1,21] may provide some foundations towards solving
this problem. However, most of the existing work on query or mapping discovery has been restricted to the case of fixed, strictly relational, schemas; it is not
clear to what extent their methods or ideas generalize to a highly heterogeneous
environment.

The Lixto [20] system, aimed at extracting data from heterogeneous web documents, takes a different approach where a visual tool can be used to specify
the various patterns that navigate a tree-like structure and select the relevant

subsets of nodes. Although it uses example documents as a starting point, this framework is closer in spirit to the paradigm of visual query builders. One downside of Lixto is that, in a highly heterogeneous environment (like DBpedia), a user may end up having to specify a large number of navigation and selection patterns to account for all the variations in the structure (or instance values) of the objects to be extracted. Being able to further automate the process and to reduce the amount of user interaction is left as an open question.

Coming back to data examples, a related and possibly simpler research question than that of generating the extraction rules is the following: Given the input source data, and a set of representative examples of the output data, *is there a procedure that directly extracts all output records that are similar to the given examples?* In other words, instead of generating rules to extract data, one could employ a procedure that performs the extraction starting from the given examples. In more concrete terms, a developer manually extracts records for, say, "Bank of America", "Goldman Sachs", "American Express" and "Visa", and then asks the procedure to extract all other "similar" such records from the input. Of course, defining what similar means is one of the challenges here.

3   Entity Resolution

To illustrate the problem of entity resolution, assume now that another extraction process uses SEC (rather than DBpedia) as a data source and extracts facts about key executives of public companies. The relation SecPerson, shown below, associates with each person a set of employment records that span, possibly, multiple companies over many years.

SecPerson (name, cik, employment: (company, position, date), ...)

Note that the relation is nested in that the employment attribute is itself a relation (i.e., a set of records with attributes for company, position and date). In general, the support for a nested data model is a pre-requisite for any system or language that aims at integrating richly structured entities from heterogeneous data sources.

Specific to SEC data, each person is associated with a unique key (cik) that is globally identifies a person across multiple SEC filings. In contrast, such key does not always exist for DBpedia. Hence, before we can merge the information about people extracted from the two data sources (SEC and DBpedia), we need to be able to link or relate corresponding records in the two data sources that refer to the same person. This problem is widely known as *entity resolution.* Let us assume that we add a record id field (rid) to each KeyPeople record. Then, in an abstract sense, the problem of entity resolution becomes one of creating links of the form (rid, cik). Note that we use cik on the right side, since we know that cik is a key that identifies a person entity in SecPerson. However, on the left side, we use the entire record id, since we do not have a key of a person there. Essentially, we need to link multiple records, in general, in KeyPeople to exactly one person entity in SecPerson, by exploiting information such as name and also

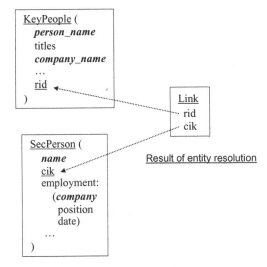

Fig. 4. Entity resolution diagram

other contextual information such as employment. Figure 4 depicts schematically the concrete entity resolution scenario that we are considering.

3.1 Declarative Constraints for Entity Resolution

We now illustrate the logic that is needed to express the above entity resolution problem. We advocate a declarative formalism where one specifies the properties or *constraints* that the outcome of entity resolution (i.e., the link table) must satisfy, without having to specify a concrete procedure or implementation for computing this outcome. It will be the role of the underlying system to materialize a good solution (i.e., a set of links) that satisfies the specified constraints in the best possible way.

For our entity resolution example, we show in Figure 5 a set of declarative constraints that can be used to specify the desired properties of the link table. We believe that such constraints (and their extensions) should form the basic ingredients of any language that attempts to specify entity resolution at a high-level.[3] We explain the constraints first and then discuss the issues involved in building a language and system that implements such specification.

First, we have provenance or identification constraints that specify the attributes or combinations of attributes that identify the source objects to be

---

[3] However, the syntax of the actual language does not have to have follow the logical notation we use here. Furthermore, some of these constraints may be implicit in the semantics of the language.

Link [rid] ⊆ KeyPeople [rid]
Link [cik] ⊆ SecPerson [cik]

Link : rid → cik

(m) <u>every</u> Link
   <u>satisfies</u>
     KeyPeople.person_name = SecPerson.name
  <u>or</u>
     (KeyPeople. person_name ~$_{name}$ SecPerson.name
     <u>and</u>
     KeyPeople.company_name <u>in</u> SecPerson.employment [company]
)

Fig. 5. Declarative constraints for entity resolution

linked. In this example, the two inclusion dependencies from Link to the sources specify that the projection of Link on rid must be a subset of the projection of KeyPeople on rid and, similarly, the projection of Link on cik must be a subset of the projection of SecPerson on cik. Thus, the intention behind Link is to be a subset of all the pairs of rid and cik values that appear in the two sources. In general, it is up to the user to define what constitutes the identifier of an object of interest for entity resolution. The framework we suggest is independent of what makes the identifier of an object. As a result, we can naturally capture most types of entity resolution described in the literature, from record linkage and deduplication [17,23] to reference reconciliation [12] and to more general, semantic type of linkage among entities (e.g., the relationship between companies and subsidiaries). To follow some of the terminology in the literature, in our example, the first type of object that participates in Link can be viewed as an entity reference (since it refers indirectly to an actual person, via person name and other non-identifying attributes), while the second type of object can be viewed as an entity (since it identifies a person in SEC).

The next constraint in the specification is a functional dependency (on the Link table) to specify that an rid from the first source must be linked to a unique cik in the second source. Note that, in this example, it is is ok to have multiple rid's linked to the same person cik. Thus, by using a functional dependency, we encode an N:1 type of entity resolution (where multiple objects of interest in one source must be linked to a single object in another source). For 1:1 type of entity resolution, we would write a functional dependency in the other direction as well. For an N:M type of entity resolution, we do not need to specify any functional dependencies.

The final constraint in this example, probably the most important, is used to declare a disjunction of all the valid reasons for why two objects can match. Essentially this constraint specifies that a link can exist only if at least one of several matching conditions holds. The matching conditions are formulated with respect to the source tuples that are related via the link. In the example, we can have a match because of exact equality of person names, or because of similarity of person names (via a user-defined similarity predicate) and, moreover, because the company_name in the KeyPeople record appears in the employer set in the SecPerson record. Note that the second matching condition relaxes the equality on person names, when compared to the first matching rule, but at the same adds a strenghtening condition that is based on employment information. Note that the employment-based condition, although a strengthening, may apply to less tuples (those that have a non-empty employment set in SecPerson). In practice, one will have to formulate multiple matching conditions, in order to improve the recall of entity resolution. Furthermore, each matching condition has to be strong enough to prevent the generation of accidental links.

Other types of constraints that appear in practice are structural type of constraints requiring properties such as transitivity of matching or variations of it. Such constraints are needed to specify clustering behavior or to specify the linking of two objects in two sources due to another object in a third source that links to them.

A slight extension to this basic framework of constraints allows us to express *collective entity resolution* [5], where the task is to create multiple, inter-related types of links (rather than to create a single type of link). For example, assume that we have the following two source relations:

    Paper (pid, title, venue, year, ...)
    Venue (venue, conferenceOrJournal, sponsor, ...)

In this context, we may want to specify links between papers *and* links between venues. Assume that the first type of link is represented as a binary relation PaperLink(pid1, pid2), while the second type of link is represented as a binary relation VenueLink(venue1, venue2). Then, the matching rules for one type of link may depend on the other type of link. For example, we can declare the matching conditions for VenueLink as follows:

    every VenueLink satisfies
        ... (some similarity condition on venue names) ...
    or
        ... (other condition) ...
    or
        exists (p1 in Paper, p2 in Paper)
            p1.venue = VenueLink.venue1 and p2.venue = VenueLink.venue2 and
            PaperLink (p1.pid, p2.pid)

In particular, the last condition says that a possible reason for a venue link is that there exist two papers that are linked via PaperLink and whose venues are the two venues related by the link.

Note that in the framework we suggest, we do not *force* the generation of links, but rather define them *implicitly* through a declaration of the possible matching rules. For example, satisfying the last matching condition in the above constraint does not mean that a VenueLink tuple will necessarily be created, since the existence of such tuple may be prevented due to other constraints. In fact, creating such link may be the wrong choice sometimes (e.g., a conference version and a journal version of a paper may be linked via PaperLink, but that does not mean that the conference and the journal represent the same venue). The disjunction allows us to enumerate, declaratively, all the possible reasons for why a link may exist without forcing the link generation. It is then the job of the underlying system to take into account all the constraints to reach a good set of links, as we discuss in the next section.

Other frameworks aimed at declarative entity resolution exist. Perhaps, the most comprehensive one is the Dedupalog [2] language which allows the use of constraints, expressed in a Datalog style of syntax, to drive the identification of duplicate entities. Several remarks are in order here. First, Dedupalog limits itself to links that are equivalence relations, thus focusing strictly on deduplication. In contrast, we require a more flexible framework for links that represent more general semantic relationships, going beyond the "same-as" type of relationship. Furthermore, Dedupalog rules are not entirely declarative. Generally speaking, rules in Dedupalog are a guideline for the implementation, and the intention of a rule is to populate links based on conditions on the sources or other links. Since forcing links may create inconsistencies in the result, Dedupalog compensates by allowing some rules to be soft: for such rules, links are "likely" to be generated. The system then figures out to what extent to satisfy these rules (e.g., by attempting to minimize the overall number of constraint violations). As a consequence, an important downside is that the result of Dedupalog evaluation does not satisfy, in a precise first-order logic sense, the Dedupalog rules that were given as a specification. Furthermore, it may not be easy for a user of the system to understand the properties of the final result.

In contrast, the matching constraints that we envision have a purely declarative flavor, where we specify all the desired properties on the target links, without worrying about how to actually generate the links. This achieves a better separation between specification and execution. Furthermore, we require all the declarative constraints to be satisfied, in a precise first-order logic sense, by any solution that implements the specification. Ultimately, we believe that such framework forms a better foundation for entity resolution that is transparent and high-quality while at the same time high-level.

3.2   From Declarative Constraints to Execution: Challenges

There are many foundational and architectural challenges that need to be solved, in order to achieve a functional framework for declarative entity resolution. The main research questions here will be to define precisely the language that captures all of the above types of constraints, to formulate its semantics, and to investigate the expressive power and computational aspects of the language. We outline some of the issues here, and leave further details, solutions or algorithms for future work.

One of the main problems for declarative entity resolution is the ability to execute or compile the declarative constraints that specify the desired properties of entity resolution into a more procedural plan that implements the specification. But what do we want this implementation to actually compute? Ultimately, we need one instance for Link that is a good solution, satisfying all the constraints. But there may be many such good solutions. This is similar, in some aspects, to data exchange semantics [15], where we can also have multiple solutions. For our example in Figure 5, we could have an instance (Solution 1) with one link satisfying the first disjunct in constraint (m), and another instance (Solution 2) that is exactly identical but replaces that one link with a new link satisfying both disjuncts in constraint (m). Intuitively, Solution 2 is a better solution, since it contains a stronger link (a link for which there is a stronger matching evidence).

While in the previous example, Solution 1 is dominated by Solution 2 and could be replaced by it, it is easy to come up with "good" instances for Link that are incomparable. For example, there could be multiple candidate links, satisfying the same disjuncts of constraint (m), each linking a KeyPeople record to a different cik. Since all of these links cannot co-exist together due to the functional dependency rid → cik, each of these links will be in a different good solution. The presence of incomparable "good" solutions is a more challenging situation than in data exchange, where universal solutions (i.e., the "good" solutions in data exchange) are all equivalent, and furthermore there is always a unique core universal solution. Thus, the entity resolution problem is inherently more ambiguous than the data exchange problem.

One of the more challenging aspects is therefore to design an *interactive* sytem for entity resolution that brings the human user in the loop in order to resolve ambiguity. Conceptually, the interactive system must take the initial specification (i.e., the constraints) and then enumerate through multiple good solutions for Link. In particular, the differences between these solutions must be pinpointed to the user, which can then decide how to further resolve these differences (for example, by adding stronger matching clauses to (m)). An essential part of the problem is being able to compactly represent and efficiently navigate through the space of all different solutions. This problem of efficient, interactive enumeration of a space of solutions, is similar in spirit to the problem addressed in [9] in the context of schema integration. There, multiple solutions for the schema integration problem are defined implicitly via a set of constraints (of a simpler nature than here), and the question is how to interactively explore and refine the space of solutions, in order to reach one final integrated schema. While similar in spirit, the problem of navigating through solutions for entity resolution is likely more challenging, especially due to the fact that the size of the data, in general, is much larger than the size of schemas.

4   Mapping and Fusion

We illustrate next how mapping and fusion operations can be used to put all the extracted facts together into rich entities, by also making use of the result of

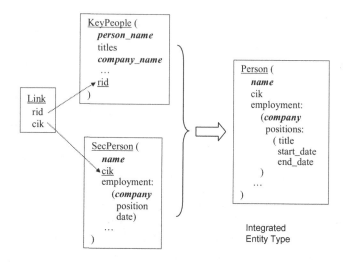

Fig. 6. From extracted facts and links to integrated entities

entity resolution. While there is extensive work on schema mapping tools [14], data exchange semantics [15], and data fusion methods [6], there is not much work towards developing an actual scripting language that allows developers to combine all the necessary ingredients (mapping, fusion, aggregation, entity resolution, schema definition), while still maintaining simplicity and ease of use. An important aspect behind such desired language is the ability to express non-trivial ways of fusion and aggregation of data that are often not possible in a typical schema mapping tool, but are essential for developing industrial-strength data integration flows.

4.1   An Example of Transformation

To illustrate the issues, consider the (simplified) scenario shown in Figure 6 where the goal is to take the extracted facts (i.e., KeyPeople and SecPerson) as well as all the links generated so far, and create unified entities that conform to a target Person type or schema. The desired target entity type contains, in general, a union of many of the attributes from the sources. However, the structure is generally richer than in the sources, with various nesting levels to better aggregate and organize information. Furthermore, it is often the case that a target attribute represents a non-trivial aggregation over a set of source values. In this example, the employment history of Person has a two-level nesting where, for each company, we want a listing of all known positions with the given company, together with the start/end dates (as best as they can be inferred from the sources.) Part of the task here is to construct the nested structure, where we list the unique companies for which a person works, the unique positions the person held, and also to compute the start/end dates from the input facts.

```
Person =
  for (s in SecPerson)
  return {name: s.name,
          cik: s.cik,
          employment: for (e in s.employment)
                      group by comp = normalizeCompanyName (e.company)
                      return { company: comp,
                               positions: for (g in Group)  // Group is the group of all (company, position, date)
                                                            // records having the same normalized company value
                                          group by pos = normalizeTitle (g.position)
                                          return { title : pos,
                                                   start_date: minDate (Group),
                                                             // Group is now the group of all (company, position, date)
                                                             // records having the same normalized company and position
                                                   end_date: maxDate (Group)
                                                 }
                             }
         }
}
```

Fig. 7. Transformation from SecPerson to Person

Computing the start/end date for a position is an example of *temporal aggregation*. These values that must be aggregated from all the input evidence (i.e., input dates) for a person working for a given company in a given position. Concretely, the fact that person X worked for a company C in some position P may be appear in multiple extracted records (possibly from many documents, each with a different date). This is especially true for SEC, which is a temporal archive that keeps track of past history, and where information must be periodically filed by the companies and their executives (even if nothing changed). Thus, in order to infer the start date for position P, we must look globally across all the sources and all the extracted records that mention person X as working for company C in position P and return the earliest known date.

Figure 7 shows an example of transformation that achieves the intended result for Person when considering the SecPerson in isolation (thus, ignoring KeyPeople and Link). The transformation is written in an pseudo-query language that abstracts features from query languages such as XQuery and Jaql [4]. The transformation consists of multiple levels of for statements that construct the structure of the target. To start with, the top-level part populates the name and the cik fields in Person. The rest of the transformation then makes essential use of the group by operation to put the target data into the desired form and also to perform aggregation. First, the employment records under SecPerson are grouped by the company name. Notably, the company name must be normalized to account for name variations for the same company. As a result of normalization and grouping, we obtain a set of unique company entries, each with an associated group containing all the records that share the same normalized company name. The group itself can then be further accessed by using the reserved word Group. A second level of grouping, this time by normalized position, produces the listing of unique positions. Finally, start_date can now be computed by taking the minDate function over the current group of records. A symmetric computation takes place for maxDate.

4.2   Mapping and Fusion: Making It Easier

Even though it achieves the intended result, given SecPerson alone, the transformation in Figure 7 is neither declarative nor easy to write. The programmer has to be quite familiar with the semantics of group by and has to understand the implicit collections over which aggregation needs to be performed. Furthermore, things become a lot more complex when additional data (e.g., KeyPeople from DBpedia, or other extracted records from other types of filings in SEC) need also to be fused into the Person entity. In such case, the above transformation has to be either rewritten to account for the new sources (and links), or its result must be integrated with the result of similar transformations from the other sources. However, the integration itself is low-level and complex, since the target components in Person, at various levels in the hierarchy, must be merged with the new data, and the values for start/end dates must be re-aggregated to account for the new data.

So, how do we make all this easier? The solution that has been tried in the past is to use graphical schema mapping tools [14] to help generate or re-generate the transformations. However, the process becomes clumsy when the transformations are complex and require a lot of aggregation and, ultimately, customization that is beyond the realm of the tool. Hence, we still need a language-level solution, but one that is more declarative and easier to use than writing raw transformations such as the one above.

The alternative that we are investigating is a rule language that allows for decorrelation of complex transformations via a mechanism that is similar to Skolem functions. As an example, the earlier transformation in Figure 7 can be rewritten as a simple rule where the value of employment is given by an explicit function call Employment(s.cik) that replaces the entire query block in the box. In other words, we would write:

```
Person = for (s in SecPerson)
            return {
                        name: s.name,
                        cik: s.cik,
                        employment: Employment (s.cik)
              }
```

Of course, explicit rules have to be written to define the value of the Employment function. The advantage is that the rule to populate the top-level part of Person does not need to know about how Employment is defined. The actual definition of Employment as a function parameterized by cik is delegated to separate rules that use possibly different data sources and that could rely themselves on other similar Skolem functions. Hence, we achieve a separation of concerns that can make the entire specification process more scalable and easier to evolve.

Another advantage of the decorrelation approach is that the Skolem functions themselves become first-class objects in the language, and can be used to express important parts of the integration logic that otherwise would be implicit. For example, the aggregation start_date: minDate(Group) can be rewritten as:

start_date: minDate (EmploymentProvenance (cik, comp, pos))

where EmploymentProvenance is now an explicit function that associates a triplet (cik, company, position) to the set of all source records that mention the fact that the person given by cik worked for company in the given position. As before, separate rules have to be written out to explicitly define EmploymentProvenance. But, again, the rule to aggregate and compute start_date need not know about how the provenance function is defined. Hence, we achieve the same separation of concerns.

Fleshing out the concrete details for this language, such as the type system, the allowed constructs, the efficient support for the functions that decorrelate the rules, as well as the integration with declarative entity resolution and extraction operations, falls outside the scope of this paper. Here, we outlined the issues as well as some of the motivation for why there is, still, a need for a good programmable language to address mapping and fusion in the context of the larger data integration.

5 Further Related Work

We have already discussed some of the relevant and recent work in the areas of entity resolution, schema mapping, data exchange and data fusion. We mention now a few other related research papers and systems. Ajax [19] is an early data cleaning framework. However, it was focused on matching and clustering and less on mapping and fusion. In particular, Ajax had no high-level constructs to support complex fusion and temporal aggregation, and had no notion of logical entities. On the other end of the spectrum, iFuice [26] combines mapping with fusion of data. However, iFuice includes no entity resolution (it assumes instead that the links are given), and fusion is focused narrowly on individual atomic attributes rather than applying on richer entity types.

More recently, the work on the interaction between matching dependencies and data repairs [16] combines record matching and data repairing for better data quality. As part of the high-level specification, matching dependencies (MDs) are used to identify or equate components of tuples in different data sets, while conditional functional dependencies (CFDs) are used to specify certain equalities of values within a given relation. In order to achieve a clean data set, cleaning rules implement the collection of MDs and CFDs by following certain pre-defined strategies (e.g., by using master data) to actually force the correction of the data. However, like in Dedupalog, matching dependencies only look at equivalence (same-as) type of linkage. Moreover, the notion of an entity (or entity link) is only implicit with matching dependencies. Furthermore, there is no notion of mapping or transformation from one entity type to another. In contrast, we are interested in a framework where entities have rich types and their properties (including the links) are first-class citizens. Additionally, we emphasize the programmability and customization aspect behind the cleansing, merging, transformation and aggregation of complex entities from the input data and the links.

6   Concluding Remarks

In summary, we outlined a vision of a high-level framework that covers multiple important steps in data integration. We exemplified rules and UDFs for extraction from semi-structured, heterogeneous data, which is complementary to text extraction. We outlined the need for and the challenges involved in learning or generating the extraction rules from examples. We illustrated the use of constraints as a foundation for declarative entity resolution, and outlined the challenges involved in defining the semantics and the compilation methodology for the declarative constraints. We further illustrated the types of rules for mapping and fusion that are needed to generate clean, unified entities.

It is important to emphasize that it is the combination of all these ingredients together (extraction, entity resolution, mapping, fusion) that gives enough expressive power to tackle complex, end-to-end data integration tasks. It is often the case that different types of rules must be interleaved together as part of the integration flow. Therefore, all the outlined components must be, ideally, part of a single framework that can be easily used by domain experts to specify and deploy sophisticated data integration flows for various scenarios. A further important factor that permeates all aspects of such framework is the need for tools that will assist users in various phases such as the data exploration or the development and refinement of the actual rules for entity resolution, for fusion, or for further analysis of the data.

References

1. Alexe, B., ten Cate, B., Kolaitis, P.G., Tan, W.C.: Designing and Refining Schema Mappings via Data Examples. In: SIGMOD, pp. 133–144 (2011)
2. Arasu, A., Ré, C., Suciu, D.: Large-Scale Deduplication with Constraints Using Dedupalog. In: ICDE, pp. 952–963 (2009)
3. Balakrishnan, S., Chu, V., Hernández, M.A., Ho, H., Krishnamurthy, R., Liu, S., Pieper, J., Pierce, J.S., Popa, L., Robson, C., Shi, L., Stanoi, I.R., Ting, E.L., Vaithyanathan, S., Yang, H.: Midas: Integrating Public Financial Data. In: SIGMOD, pp. 1187–1190 (2010)
4. Beyer, K., Ercegovac, V., Gemulla, R., Balmin, A., Eltabakh, M., Kanne, C.C., Ozcan, F., Shekita, E.: Jaql: A Scripting Language for Large Scale Semistructured Data Analysis. In: VLDB (2011)
5. Bhattacharya, I., Getoor, L.: Collective entity resolution in relational data. TKDD 1(1) (2007)
6. Bleiholder, J., Naumann, F.: Data Fusion. ACM Comput. Surv. 41(1) (2008)
7. Burdick, D., Hernández, M.A., Ho, H., Koutrika, G., Krishnamurthy, R., Popa, L., Stanoi, I.R., Vaithyanathan, S., Das, S.: Extracting, Linking and Integrating Data from Public Sources: A Financial Case Study. IEEE Data Eng. Bull. 34(3), 60–67 (2011)
8. Chiticariu, L., Krishnamurthy, R., Li, Y., Raghavan, S., Reiss, F., Vaithyanathan., S.: SystemT: An Algebraic Approach to Declarative Information Extraction. In: ACL, pp. 128–137 (2010)
9. Chiticariu, L., Kolaitis, P.G., Popa, L.: Interactive Generation of Integrated Schemas. In: SIGMOD Conference, pp. 833–846 (2008)

10. Dalvi, N.N., Kumar, R., Pang, B., Ramakrishnan, R., Tomkins, A., Bohannon, P., Keerthi, S., Merugu, S.: A Web of Concepts. In: PODS, pp. 1–12 (2009)
11. Doan, A., Naughton, J.F., Ramakrishnan, R., Baid, A., Chai, X., Chen, F., Chen, T., Chu, E., DeRose, P., Gao, B.J., Gokhale, C., Huang, J., Shen, W., Vuong, B.Q.: Information Extraction Challenges in Managing Unstructured Data. SIG-MOD Record 37(4), 14–20 (2008)
12. Dong, X., Halevy, A.Y., Madhavan, J.: Reference Reconciliation in Complex Information Spaces. In: SIGMOD Conference, pp. 85–96 (2005)
13. Elmagarmid, A.K., Ipeirotis, P.G., Verykios, V.S.: Duplicate Record Detection: A Survey. IEEE TKDE 19(1), 1–16 (2007)
14. Fagin, R., Haas, L.M., Hernández, M., Miller, R.J., Popa, L., Velegrakis, Y.: Clio: Schema Mapping Creation and Data Exchange. In: Borgida, A.T., Chaudhri, V.K., Giorgini, P., Yu, E.S. (eds.) Conceptual Modeling: Foundations and Applications. LNCS, vol. 5600, pp. 198–236. Springer, Heidelberg (2009)
15. Fagin, R., Kolaitis, P.G., Miller, R.J., Popa, L.: Data Exchange: Semantics and Query Answering. TCS 336(1), 89–124 (2005)
16. Fan, W., Li, J., Ma, S., Tang, N., Yu, W.: Interaction between Record Matching and Data Repairing. In: SIGMOD Conference, pp. 469–480 (2011)
17. Fellegi, I.P., Sunter, A.B.: A Theory for Record Linkage. J. Am. Statistical Assoc. 64(328), 1183–1210 (1969)
18. Fletcher, G.H.L., Gyssens, M., Paredaens, J., Gucht, D.V.: On the Expressive Power of the Relational Algebra on Finite Sets of Relation Pairs. IEEE TKDE 21(6), 939–942 (2009)
19. Galhardas, H., Florescu, D., Shasha, D., Simon, E., Saita, C.A.: Declarative Data Cleaning: Language, Model, and Algorithms. In: VLDB, pp. 371–380 (2001)
20. Gottlob, G., Koch, C., Baumgartner, R., Herzog, M., Flesca, S.: The Lixto Data Extraction Project - Back and Forth between Theory and Practice. In: PODS, pp. 1–12 (2004)
21. Gottlob, G., Senellart, P.: Schema Mapping Discovery from Data Instances. Journal of the Association for Computing Machinery (JACM) 57(2) (2010)
22. Hernández, M.A., Koutrika, G., Krishnamurthy, R., Popa, L., Wisnesky, R.: HIL: A High-Level Scripting Language for Entity Integration. In: EDBT, pp. 549–560 (2013)
23. Hernández, M.A., Stolfo, S.J.: The Merge/Purge Problem for Large Databases. In: SIGMOD Conference, pp. 127–138 (1995)
24. Ohori, A.: A Polymorphic Record Calculus and Its Compilation. ACM Trans. Program. Lang. Syst. 17(6), 844–895 (1995)
25. Ohori, A., Buneman, P.: Type Inference in a Database Programming Language. In: LISP and Functional Programming, pp. 174–183 (1988)
26. Rahm, E., Thor, A., Aumueller, D., Do, H.H., Golovin, N., Kirsten, T.: iFuice - Information Fusion utilizing Instance Correspondences and Peer Mappings. In: WebDB, pp. 7–12 (2005)
27. Sarma, A.D., Parameswaran, A.G., Garcia-Molina, H., Widom, J.: Synthesizing View Definitions from Data. In: ICDT, pp. 89–103 (2010)
28. Wand, M.: Complete Type Inference for Simple Objects. In: LICS, pp. 37–44 (1987)

A New Framework for Designing Schema Mappings

Bogdan Alexe[1] and Wang-Chiew Tan[2]

[1] IBM Research - Almaden, San Jose, CA
balexe@us.ibm.com
[2] University of California, Santa Cruz, CA
tan@cs.ucsc.edu

Abstract. One of the fundamental tasks in information integration is to specify the relationships, called *schema mappings*, between database schemas. Schema mappings specify how data structured under a source schema is to be transformed into data structured under a target schema. The design of schema mappings is usually a non-trivial and time-intensive process and the task of designing schema mappings is exacerbated by the fact that schemas that occur in real life tend to be large and heterogeneous. Traditional approaches for designing schema mappings are either manual or performed through a user interface from which a schema mapping is interpreted from correspondences between attributes of the source and target schemas. These correspondences are either specified by the user or automatically derived by applying schema matching on the two schemas.

In this paper, we examine an alternative approach that allows a user to follow the "divide-design-merge" paradigm for specifying a schema mapping. The user can choose to independently design schema mappings for smaller portions of the source and target schema. Afterwards, the user can interact with the system to refine and further design schema mappings through the use of data examples. Finally, in the merge phase, a global schema mapping is generated through the correlation of the individual schema mappings.

Keywords: Schema mappings, data examples, merge.

1 Introduction

The need to combine information that resides in heterogeneous, and typically independently created data sources often arises in enterprises. In today's information age, where vast amounts of (un)structured data is available on the Web, and where many data sources collected or curated by different organizations are made publicly available (e.g., [20, 34]), the demand for technology that can effectively combine disparate data sources goes well beyond enterprises. The process of combining different data sources into one is called *information integration*, which is a broad term that encompasses *data integration* and *data exchange*. The goal of *data integration* is to create a single virtual view of the underlying data sources and provide seamless and transparent access to these data sources through the virtual view. On the other hand, the goal of *data exchange* is to create a materialized view of the underlying data sources.

Systems such as Multibase [32] and EXPRESS [31] have pioneered the study of data integration and data exchange respectively and considerable research effort has been

V. Tannen et al. (Eds.): Buneman Festschrift, LNCS 8000, pp. 56–88, 2013.
© Springer-Verlag Berlin Heidelberg 2013

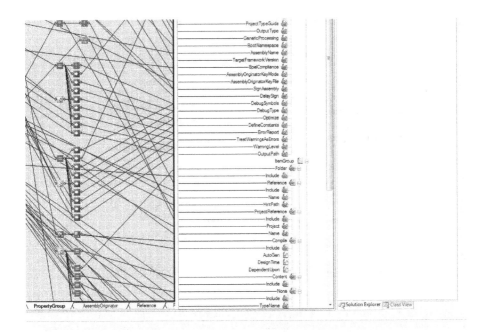

Fig. 1. Screenshot of a mapping design tool (from [12])

put into addressing information integration challenges since Multibase and EXPRESS. In practice, information integration is still a difficult and time-consuming process that incurs high costs in terms of money and human effort and recent reports provide strong evidence of this. For example, [12] stated that information integration is frequently "the biggest and most expensive challenge that information-technology shops face" and "information integration is thought to consume about 40% of their budget".

Even though data integration and data exchange differ in their goals, they share a common abstraction, called *schema mappings*, which describe the relationship between database schemas. In research prototypes such as Clio [16] and HePToX [15], the term *schema mappings* is used to refer to the high-level declarative specfication that specifies the semantics of translating data from the *source schema* to the *target schema*. However, commercial data transformation systems such as Altova Mapforce [25], Stylus Studio [33] and Microsoft BizTalk Mapper [13] often refer to schema mappings or *data mappings* as the executable script (e.g., XQuery or SQL) that can be used to translate data from the source schema to the target schema. Regardless of terminology, most of these tools work in two steps. First, a visual interface is used to solicit all known *attribute correspondences* between elements of the two schemas from the user. Such correspondences are usually depicted as arrows between the attributes of the source and target schemas. For illustration, Figure 1 presents a screenshot of a mapping design tool with a number of correspondences between attributes of a source schema on the left and a target schema on the right. Once the correspondences are established, systems such as Altova MapForce, Stylus Studio, and Microsoft Biztalk Mapper, interpret them directly

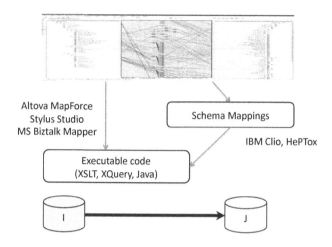

Fig. 2. Generic architecture of schema mapping design systems

into an executable script (e.g., XQuery or SQL query), which can be executed on an instance of the source schema to obtain an instance of the target schema. Other systems such as Clio or HePToX, interpret the correpondences into an internal representation (which we refer to as schema mappings in this article), and this representation can be compiled over different runtimes. Often, the user will need to refine the schema mapping (whether as an internal representation or an executable script) that is derived from such tools in order to achieve the desired transformation semantics.

The previously outlined two-step schema mapping design framework is illustrated in Figure 2. While this framework provides a method for end users to visually specify a schema mapping, it lacks support for reusability and for modularity in design; A schema mapping between two schemas must always be designed all-at-once. In particular, this methodology does not allow the design of a schema mapping to be divided up and designed modularly in different steps with intermediate schemas. Furthermore, the user must be familiar with the language of schema mappings in order to refine them. For the rest of this article, we will describe a new framework for designing schema mappings that will overcome some of the limitations of existing schema mapping design tools. Details of this framework can be found in the dissertation of Bogdan Alexe [8].

2 Our Divide-Design-Merge Framework

Our framework for designing schema mappings between two schemas follows three main steps: Divide, Design, and Merge, as outlined in Figure 3. This new framework overcomes some of the aforementioned limitations of the existing mapping design paradigm.

Since smaller mappings tend to be easier to create and understand, our framework allows a schema mapping between large source and target schemas to be divided up

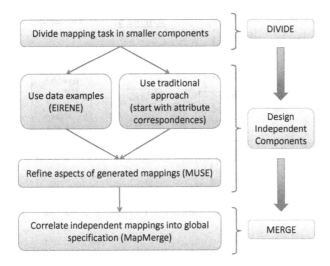

Fig. 3. Divide-Design-Merge Workflow

and designed through independent components. Furthermore, the design of each such schema mapping can be broken up into multiple smaller intermediate steps which involve intermediate schemas. Each of the schema mappings can either be designed with existing approaches (i.e., via attribute correspondences) or via our new approach (i.e., Eirene component system) that requires the user to specify *data examples*, which are pairs of source instance and expected target instance. After this, various components of a schema mapping can be refined through our Muse component system. Finally, in the merge phase, a global schema mapping is generated through the correlation of the individual mapping components (i.e., MapMerge component system). In this new framework, schema mappings that have been previously designed for some of the components can be saved, reused, and customized further at a later time.

We note that in the divide phase, the process of dividing or breaking up schema mappings into smaller "chunks" that are more amenable to design and understanding is entirely driven by the user. It will be interesting work to further design a component that will suggest strategies for such divisions.

2.1   An Example

As mentioned before, the user may choose to divide the design task into smaller components that can be designed independently. For instance, in Figure 4, the design of a schema mapping from schema S_1 to schema S_4 can be divided into a sequence of steps, involving the intermediate schemas S_2 and S_3. Existing schema mapping design tools would only allow designing a monolithic end-to-end schema mapping from S_1 to S_4. In our framework, the user can design smaller mappings independently and merge them together at the end. For instance, the user can start by designing the mapping, denoted by t_1, from *Group* in S_1 to *Dept* in S_2, then the mapping t_2 relating a join of *Works* and

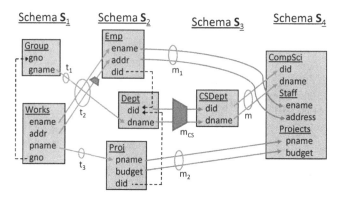

Fig. 4. Designing a schema mapping from the first schema S_1 to the last schema S_4

Group to *Emp* and *Dept*, and so on. For this toy example, it is conceivable that the user would successfully design a mapping directly from S_1 to S_4 (or even S_1 to S_2) with relatively little effort. However, in real-life scenarios, it is typically difficult to understand the entire schemas and to grasp the complexities of the desired global transformation all at once.

Eirene. The design of each component mapping can be driven by data examples. A data example is a pair of input and output instances. Intuitively, a data example specifies the expected output for a given input and represents a partial specification of the desired semantics. This is beneficial, since users may be familiar with their data and the use of data examples is akin to specifying test cases during program debugging to ensure that programs behave as intended.

The Eirene component of our system is a schema mapping design component that takes as input a set of data examples provided by the user. In turn, Eirene outputs a schema mapping that "fits" the set of data examples, if such schema mapping exists. Referring back to Figure 4, the design of t_2 can be achieved through Eirene by providing a data example that reflects the transformation semantics that the user expects from the mapping. In this case, the source instance of the data example may consist of a *Group* tuple and a *Works* tuple that agree on their *gno* attributes, while the target instance may consist of an *Emp* tuple and a *Dept* tuple that have the same *did* value. Furthermore, the tuples may be specified in such a way that the *gname* and *dname* values are the same across the *Group* and *Dept* tuple. In addition, the *ename* and *addr* of the *Works* tuple are identical, respectively, to the *ename* and *addr* of the *Emp* tuple in the target. This reflects that the desired transformation semantics is to migrate *gname, ename, addr* to the corresponding "locations" in the target. For this data example, the system will determine that a fitting schema mapping exists, and it will generate such mapping that will produce the desired target instance on the corresponding source instance of each data example.

Eirene can also be used to refine a schema mapping that already exists. To do this, Eirene will first generate a set of *canonical data examples* for the existing mapping. The user can then "tweak" the canonical data examples, and Eirene will generate a new mapping that fits, if possible. Alternatively, a schema mapping can also be designed using the traditional methodology via attribute correspondences, imported from previous design work, and augmented with new attribute correspondences and additional customizations.

Muse. The Muse component of our system assists the user with refining the existing schema mappings. The focus of Muse is to use data examples to help the user refine two important mapping features: *grouping semantics* and *disambiguation*. The basic idea behind Muse is to present the user with different data examples, where each data example represents a specific (grouping/disambiguation) semantics of the underlying specification. The choices made by the user will allow the Muse system to automatically refine the underlying specification.

Referring to Figure 4 again, Muse can assist the user with specifying how the nested *Staff* set of tuples should be grouped under the *CompSci* root of schema S_4. The semantics of grouping *Staff* is determined by its set identifier, which consists of a *Skolem function* parameterized by some of the attributes in schemas S_2 and S_3. By presenting differentiating examples that can be used to distinguish among alternative grouping semantics, Muse helps the user determine which attributes should be used to parameterize the nested set identifier of *Staff*.

In addition, Muse can also help the user understand the right interpretation of a visual specification. This part of Muse works with traditional schema mapping design systems, where the user specifies a set of attribute correspondences between a source and a target schema. (A *visual specification* consists of the source and target schema, and the attribute correspondences.) A visual specification is *ambiguous* if more than one schema mapping can be interpreted from the visual specification[1]. In case a visual specification is ambiguous, our Muse system will detect the ambiguity and present the user with a carefully constructed "data example" that essentially represents the transformation semantics of all alternative schema mappings. The target instance of the "data example" contains choices of data values on certain attributes of tuples. Each selection of a value from a choice by the user will prune away some schema mappings among the set of all possible schema mappings that can be interpreted from the visual specification. At the end, when all choices have been made, only one schema mapping will remain.

MapMerge. When all component schema mappings are designed, the *MapMerge* schema mapping operator [6] can be invoked to automatically generate a meaningful overall mapping between each pair of source and target schemas. MapMerge takes as input a set of schema mappings between the same source and target schema, and it returns a schema mapping that correlates the specifications given by the individual mapping components. As we shall show, this orchestration phase is necessary since simply considering the union of input mappings is inadequate in general; in the context of data exchange, simply taking the union of input schema mappings may result in the loss

---

[1] In systems such as Clio, a default schema mapping is generated when a visual specification is ambiguous. The user can choose among alternative mappings by manually inspecting the loss alternatives and picking one of the alternatives.

of certain data associations and also lead to a more "redundant" target instance. These deficiencies can be easily avoided if the relationships across input mappings are carefully considered in the context of source and target schemas. A schema mapping that results from a MapMerge of input mappings is experimentally shown to overcome these deficiencies when compared with a simple union of the input mappings [6].

Finally, the end-to-end mapping for flows of mappings, such as from the first schema S_1 to the last schema S_4 in Figure 4 can be obtained using a new algorithm that combines MapMerge with mapping composition [18] to correlate flows of schema mappings.

3   Background and Related Work

We define the basic concepts and terminology that will be used, as well as discuss prior approaches to schema mapping design.

Schemas and Instances. A *relational schema* R is a finite sequence $(P_1, \ldots, P_k)$ of relation symbols, each of a fixed arity. An *instance* K over R is a sequence $(P_1^K, \ldots, P_k^K)$, where each P_i^K is a relation of the same arity as P_i. We shall often write P_i to denote both the relation symbol and the relation P_i^K that interprets it. Here, we assume that all values occurring in relations belong to some fixed infinite set dom of values. A *fact* (or *tuple*) of an instance K over a schema R is an expression $P(a_1, \ldots, a_m)$ such that P is a relation symbol of R and $(a_1, \ldots, a_m) \in P^K$. We denote by $\mathrm{adom}(K)$ the *active domain* of an instance K, that is to say, the set of all values from dom occurring in facts of K. A relational schema can be associated with a set of key/foreign key constraints.

Referring back to Figure 4, schema S_1 consists of two relation symbols *Group* and *Works*. The key/foreign key constraint associated with S_1, denoted in the figure via the dashed line, requires that in each instance of S_1, for each *Works* tuple, there must exist a unique *Group* tuple such that they agree on the value of the *gno* attribute. An example of a possible valid instance of S_1 is shown below, where *John* works in group number 123 and the name of group 123 is *CS*.

$$\{\mathrm{Group}(123, \mathrm{CS}), \mathrm{Works}(\mathrm{John}, \mathrm{NY}, \mathrm{Web}, 123)\}$$

In Muse and MapMerge, we use an extension of the relational model that allows for the representation of nested data: the *nested relational* (NR) model [19, 28]. The NR model generalizes the relational model where tuples and relations are modeled as *records* and respectively, *sets* of records. In the NR model however, an element, such as a set of records, may be nested inside another element, such as a record, to form hierarchies. In the following we will use the terms record and tuple, as well as set and relation, interchangeably. To simplify our discussions, we assume that XML schemas are modeled using a single schema root of record type whose elements are all of set type. We also assume strict alternation of set and record types. As an example, consider schema S_4 in Figure 4. This is a nested schema, where each root *CompSci* record contains nested *Staff* and *Projects* sets.

In a nested relational schema, nested sets have associated identifiers called *SetIDs*, also referred to as *grouping functions*. They are *Skolem functions*. In an instance of a nested relational schema, the parameters of each Skolem function serving as a grouping function are instantiated with actual data values, hence providing unique set identifiers for each nested set in the instance. By convention, we use SKN to denote the SetID name of a nested set N in a schema. For example, the SetID name of the nested set *Projects* in the schema $\mathbf{S}_4$ mentioned above is SKProjects (or SKProjs, or simply SK when there is no ambiguity). We sometimes refer to a nested set N simply as SKN. We assume that every nested set in a schema has a different SetID name.

Schema Mappings. A *schema mapping* or *mapping* is a triple $(\mathbf{S}, \mathbf{T}, \Sigma)$ where $\mathbf{S}$ is a source schema, $\mathbf{T}$ is a target schema that is disjoint from $\mathbf{S}$, and Σ is a set of constraints. The largest class of constraints we consider is a subset of *second-order tuple generating dependencies (SO tgds)* [18]. One way to express this type of constraints is through the following logical formalism expressed in a query-like notation:

$$\textit{for } \mathbf{x} \textit{ in } \bar{S} \textit{ satisfying } B_1(\mathbf{x}) \textit{ exists } \mathbf{y} \textit{ in } \bar{T} \textit{ where } B_2(\mathbf{y}) \textit{ and } C(\mathbf{x}, \mathbf{y})$$

Here, the symbol $\bar{S}$ represents a vector of relation symbols (possibly repeated), while $\mathbf{x}$ represents the tuple variables that are bound, correspondingly, to these relations. A similar notation applies to the *exists* clause for the vector $\bar{T}$ of target relation symbols and $\mathbf{y}$ of tuple variables that are bound to these relations. The conditions $B_1(\mathbf{x})$ and $B_2(\mathbf{y})$ are conjunctions of equalities over the source and, respectively, target variables. Note that these conditions may equate variables with constants, allowing the definition of *user-defined filters*. The condition $C(\mathbf{x}, \mathbf{y})$ is a conjunction of equalities that equate target expressions (e.g., y.A) with either source expressions (e.g., x.B) or *Skolem terms* of the form $F[x_1, \ldots, x_i]$, where F is a function symbol and $x_1, \ldots, x_i$ are source variables or other Skolem terms. Skolem terms are used to relate target expressions across different SO tgds.

Both Muse and MapMerge components of our system use the language of schema mappings specified by SO tgds over nested relational source and target schemas, while the Eirene component focuses on SO tgds without Skolem terms over relational source and target schemas. A constraint of this type may also be called, simply, a *tuple-generating dependency* or *tgd* [17]. In some situations we will refer to a tgd by the equivalent term *GLAV (Global-Local-As-View) constraint*. GLAV constraints have been extensively studied in the context of data exchange and data integration [21, 22]. In cases where $\bar{S}$ and $\bar{T}$ refer to source and, respectively, target relation symbols, then the tgd is referred to as *source-to-target tgds* or *s-t tgds* in short. They are also used in such systems as Clio [16] and HePToX [15].

Two examples of SO tgds that relate schemas $\mathbf{S}_1$ and $\mathbf{S}_2$ in Figure 4 are given below:

(t_1):
for g *in* Group
exists d *in* Dept
where d.dname=g.gname

(t_2):
for w *in* Works, g *in* Group
satisfying w.gno = g.gno *and* w.addr="NY"
exists e *in* Emp
where e.ename=w.ename *and*
            e.addr=w.addr *and* e.did=$F[g]$

The constraint t_1 is a tgd that states that for every record g in the relation *Group*, there must be a record d in *Dept* where *dname* of d is the same as *gname* of g. Here,

g and d are record variables that range over records in *Group* and, respectively, *Dept*. The second assertion t_2 is an SO tgd that states that for every record g in *Group* and every record w in *Works*, where their *gnos* are identical and the *addr* value of the *Works* record is "NY", there must be a record e in *Emp* where the conditions in the <u>*where*</u> clause are satisfied. Note that "$e.did = F[g]$" states that the *did* value of e is dependent on g through the Skolem function F. Thus, $F[g]$ is a *Skolem term*.

Note that our SO tgds do not allow equalities between or with Skolem terms in the <u>*satisfying*</u> clause. While such equalities may be needed for more general purposes [18], they do not play a role for data exchange and can be eliminated, as observed in [36].

Solutions. Let $\mathcal{M} = (\mathbf{S}, \mathbf{T}, \Sigma)$ be a schema mapping. An instance I of $\mathbf{S}$ will be called a *source instance*, and an instance J of $\mathbf{T}$ will be called a target instance.

We say that J is a *solution of I w.r.t.* $\mathcal{M}$ if $(I, J) \models \Sigma$, i.e., if (I, J) satisfies every constraint in Σ. In general, there are many possible solutions for a source instance I under a schema mapping $\mathcal{M} = (\mathbf{S}, \mathbf{T}, \Sigma)$.

To illustrate, in line with the previous examples, suppose the source schema consists of the relation symbol *Group*, the target schema consists of the relation symbol *Dept*, and the schema mapping $\mathcal{M}$ is specified by the constraint t_1 given as an example above. Consider the source instance $I = \{\mathrm{Group}(123, \mathrm{CS}), \mathrm{Group}(456, \mathrm{EE})\}$ and the target instances

$$J_1 = \{\mathrm{Dept}(N1, \mathrm{CS}), \mathrm{Dept}(N2, \mathrm{EE})\}$$
$$J_2 = \{\mathrm{Dept}(N1, \mathrm{CS}), \mathrm{Dept}(456, \mathrm{EE})\}$$
$$J_3 = \{\mathrm{Dept}(N1, \mathrm{CS})\}.$$

Both J_1 and J_2 are solutions for I w.r.t. $\mathcal{M}$, but J_3 is not. Observe that the solutions J_1 and J_2 contain values (namely, $N1$ and $N2$) that do not occur in the active domain of the source instance I. Intuitively, these values can be thought of as labeled nulls.

As we shall describe later, a central concept in both Eirene and Muse is the concept of a *data example*. Given a source schema $\mathbf{S}$ and a target schema $\mathbf{T}$ respectively, a *data example* is a pair (I, J) such that I is an instance of $\mathbf{S}$ and J is an instance of $\mathbf{T}$.

Data Exchange, Homomorphisms, and Universal Solutions. *Data exchange* is the following problem: given a schema mapping $\mathcal{M} = (\mathbf{S}, \mathbf{T}, \Sigma)$ and a source instance I, construct a solution J for I such that $(I, J) \models \Sigma$. As we just saw, a source instance may have more than one solution with respect to a given GLAV schema mapping. We will be interested in *universal solutions*, which were identified in [17] as the preferred solutions for data exchange purposes. Universal solutions are defined in terms of *homomorphisms*, as follows.

Let I_1 and I_2 be two instances over the same relational schema $\mathbf{R}$. A *homomorphism* $h : I_1 \to I_2$ is a function from $\mathrm{adom}(I_1)$ to $\mathrm{adom}(I_2)$ such that for every fact $P(a_1, \ldots, a_m)$ of I_1, we have that $P(h(a_1), \ldots, h(a_m))$ is a fact of I_2. We write $I_1 \to I_2$ to denote the existence of a homomorphism $h : I_1 \to I_2$. In our previous example, we have that $J_1 \to J_2$ since the function $\{\mathrm{N1} \to \mathrm{N1}, \mathrm{CS} \to \mathrm{CS}, \mathrm{N2} \to 456, \mathrm{EE} \to \mathrm{EE}\}$ is a homomorphism from J_1 to J_2. We say that I_1 and I_2 are *homomorphically equivalent* if there is a homomorphism from I_1 to I_2 and a homomorphism from I_2 to I_1.

Let $\mathcal{M} = (\mathbf{S}, \mathbf{T}, \Sigma)$ be a schema mapping and let I be a source instance. A target instance J is a *universal solution* for I w.r.t. $\mathcal{M}$ if the following hold:

1. J is a solution for I w.r.t. $\mathcal{M}$.

2. For every solution J' of I w.r.t. $\mathcal{M}$, there is a homomorphism $h : J \rightarrow J'$ that is constant on $\operatorname{adom}(I) \cap \operatorname{adom}(J)$, that is to say, $h(a) = a$, for every value $a \in \operatorname{adom}(I) \cap \operatorname{adom}(J)$.

Intuitively, universal solutions are the "most general" solutions. Furthermore, in a precise sense, they represent the entire space of solutions (see [17]). For this reason, universal solutions have become the standard semantics for data exchange. Going back to our previous example, note that J_1 is a universal solution for I w.r.t the schema mapping $\mathcal{M}$ specified by the constraint t_1. In contrast, J_2 is not a universal solution for I w.r.t. $\mathcal{M}$, since there is no homomorphism from J_2 to J_1 that is constant on $\operatorname{adom}(I) \cap \operatorname{adom}(J_2)$.

Chase and Canonical Universal Solutions. For GLAV schema mappings $\mathcal{M}$ (and in fact for the wider class of SO tgds), a variant of the *chase procedure* can be used to compute, given a source instance I, a *canonical* universal solution for I w.r.t. $\mathcal{M}$ in time bounded by a polynomial in the size of I (see [17]).

Intuitively, the chase provides a way of populating the target instance J in a minimal way, by adding the tuples that are *required* by Σ. For every instantiation of the *for* clause of a dependency in Σ such that the *satisfying* clause is satisfied but the *exists* and *where* clauses are not, the chase adds corresponding tuples to the target relations. Fresh new values (also called *labeled nulls*) are used to give values for the target attributes for which the dependency does not provide a source expression. Additionally, Skolem terms are instantiated by nulls in a consistent way: a term $F[x_1, \ldots, x_i]$ is replaced by the same null every time $x_1, \ldots, x_i$ are instantiated with the same source tuples. Finally, to obtain a valid target instance, we must chase (if needed) with any target schema constraints. For our earlier example, the target instance J_1 is the result of chasing the source instance I with the constraint t_1. The tuple $\operatorname{Dept}(N_1, \operatorname{CS})$ appears in J_1 since it is asserted by the *exists* clause of t_1, when the *for* clause of t_1 is instantiated with the tuple $\operatorname{Group}(123, \operatorname{CS})$ from I. The *CS* value is propagated from the source *Group* tuple to the target *Dept* tuple because of the equality condition in the *where* clause of t_1. Furthermore, the fresh labeled null N_1 is introduced since t_1 does not provide a source expression for the *did* attribute of the target *Dept* tuple. The tuple $\operatorname{Dept}(N_2, \operatorname{EE})$ in J_1 is obtained in a similar fashion. Since J_1 is the result of chasing I with t_1, we have that J_1 is a *canonical universal solution* for I w.r.t. the schema mapping specified by the constraint t_1.

In practice, mapping systems such as Clio do not necessarily implement the chase with Σ, but generate queries to achieve a similar result [19, 28].

3.1 Prior Schema Mapping Design Systems

A *mapping system* is a graphical user interface that allows a user to visually specify a schema mapping (i.e., data transformation) that translates data from one schema into another. Mapping systems can be categorized as either *function-based* or *relationship-*

based [30]. In function-based mapping systems, schema mappings are specified operationally, as a workflow of operators, which is very similar to the way Extract-Transform-Load (ETL) processes are specified in ETL tools. These systems tend to be highly expressive since the user is allowed to define custom operators. At the same time, these systems are aimed at relatively advanced technical users, as users are required to specify and understand the workflow of operations that constitute the overall semantics of the data transformation at hand.

Relationship-Based Mapping Systems. In contrast, the only type of input required of users of *relationship-based* mapping systems is the specification of high-level relationships between elements (i.e., attributes or sets of attributes) of the source and target schemas. The design methodology of relationship-based mapping systems is shown in Figure 2. The user starts the mapping design process by providing, through a graphical interface, all known *attribute correspondences* (i.e., lines between elements) between elements of a source schema S (typically shown on the left of the graphical interface) and a target schema T (typically shown on the right of the graphical interface). An example of a graphical interface typical of a relationship-based mapping system was presented in Figure 1. Sometimes, a schema matching module [29] is used to suggest or derive attribute correspondences.

The source and target schemas, together with the attribute correspondences, form a *visual specification* of the schema mapping intended by the user. Since all that is required as input is the specification of attribute correspondences, this methodology is generally more accessible to non-technical users who may understand their data and the relationships between schema elements.

For commercial mapping systems (e.g., Altova Mapforce [25], Stylus Studio [33], and Microsoft BizTalk Mapper [13]), the visual specification is compiled directly into a runtime executable code (e.g., in XSLT or XQuery or SQL or Java) that implements the intended relationships that are captured by the visual specification. *Data exchange* can be achieved by applying the generated executable code on an instance I of the source schema S to derive an instance J of the target schema T.

On the other hand, research prototypes such as Clio [16], HePToX [15], and Spicy++ [26] first compile the visual specification into SO tgds or GLAV constraints. To illustrate, consider schemas S_1 and S_2 in Figure 4, and the visual specifications represented by the groups of arrows denoted by t_1 and t_2, respectively. From the visual specification, the declarative schema mappings (t_1) and (t_2) which are expressed as constraints described earlier are first generated. These schema mappings (t_1) and (t_2) can then be compiled into runtime executable code.

One advantage of using schema mappings to specify the relationship between two schemas as an intermediate form is that they are more amenable to the formal study of data exchange and data integration. Many properties of data integration and data exchange, and rigorous studies of operators for manipulating schema mappings have been investigated as a consequence of such logical formalisms [21].

Limitations of Existing Schema Mapping Design Methodologies. Existing schema mapping design systems do not provide the capability for automatically combining pre-existing schema mappings that are independently designed over different and possibly overlapping parts of a source and target schema. To derive the overall schema mapping between the two schemas, the pre-existing schema mappings are typically "integrated" manually or the overall schema mapping is re-designed from scratch.

The ability to automatically combine different schema mappings that are designed over the same source and target schema allows one to design a schema mapping between two schemas by focussing on smaller components of the schemas. Such a feature is especially useful when the schemas are large and far too complex for the entire mapping to be designed all-at-once. On a similar note, relationship-based mapping systems offer very little support for designing a schema mapping through designing a workflow of (smaller) schema mapping steps. In other words, the procedural methodology offered by function-based mapping systems is sometimes desirable when schemas are large and too complex to be designed in one step.

Finally, even though relationship-based mapping systems tend to be more user-friendly, they cannot be used to generate any arbitrary schema mapping. These systems derive a fixed set of possible schema mappings from a given visual specification, and the derived schema mappings may not correspond to what a user desires. It is typically the case that the user will have to manually tweak or create a schema mapping with the desired semantics.

For the rest of this article, we overview our new framework for designing schema mappings, which overcomes the limitations described earlier. Section 4 describes how data examples can be used to derive and refine a schema mapping interactively. Section 5 describes our MapMerge operator which correlates different schema mappings over the same source and target schema to produce an overall schema mapping which preserves "data associations". In the same section, we also describe how MapMerge together with the composition operator can be leveraged to allow one to design a schema mapping between a source and target schema by designing a workflow of small schema mapping steps. Details of these subsystems can be found in [1–3, 5, 10].

4   Interactive Mapping Design and Refinement via Data Examples

In our new framework, a schema mapping can be designed with existing approaches or interactively with our new approach through the Eirene component system. In Eirene, the user specifies data examples, which are pairs of source instance and expected target instance and the Eirene component system will provide a schema mapping that "fits" the given data examples, if possible. The user can continue to refine various components of a schema mapping through our Muse component system.

4.1   Eirene

The Eirene system supports the design of *GLAV (Global-and-Local-As-View)* schema mappings over a relational source and a relational target schema interactively via data examples. For the rest of this section, we shall use the term *schema mappings* to refer to GLAV schema mappings.

Recall that a *data example* is a pair (I, J) consisting of a source instance and a target instance that conform to a source and target relational schema. The Eirene workflow is

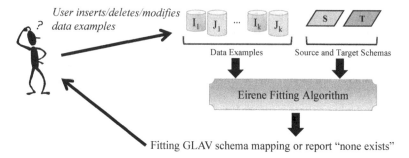

Fig. 5. Workflow for interactive design of schema mappings via data examples

depicted in Figure 5. The interaction between the user and Eirene begins with the user providing an initial finite set $\mathcal{E}$ of data examples, where each data example in $\mathcal{E}$ provides a partial specification of the semantics of the desired schema mapping. Furthermore, the user stipulates that, for each data example (I, J), the target instance J is a *universal solution for I* w.r.t. the desired schema mapping. Intuitively, the target instance J is a "most general" target instance that, together with I, satisfies the specifications of the desired schema mapping. Eirene responds by generating a schema mapping that *fits* the data examples in $\mathcal{E}$ or by reporting that no such schema mapping exists. Here, we say that a schema mapping $\mathcal{M}$ *fits a set $\mathcal{E}$* of data examples if for every data example $(I, J) \in \mathcal{E}$, the target instance J is a universal solution of the source instance I w.r.t. $\mathcal{M}$. The *refinement process* can continue where the user may modify the data examples in $\mathcal{E}$ to arrive at another finite set $\mathcal{E}'$ of data examples. Again, Eirene responds by testing whether or not there is a schema mapping that fits $\mathcal{E}'$. Eirene reports a fitting schema mapping if one exists. Otherwise, it reports that no fitting schema mappings exist. The process of modifying data examples and generating fitting schema mappings can be repeated until the user is satisfied.

Data examples were considered in [3, 7, 35] as a means to illustrate and help understand schema mappings. In [9], several different notions of "fitting" were explored, including the just defined notion of fitting in terms of universal examples. However, universal solutions, being the most general solutions, are natural as data examples because they contain just the information needed to represent the desired outcome of migrating data from source to target. In particular, they contain no extraneous or overspecified facts, unlike arbitrary solutions. In addition, note that the alternative notion of "fitting" with solutions in place of universal solutions gives rise to a trivial "fitting" problem since, in this case, the schema mapping with an empty set of constraints would "fit" every data example (I, J). In fact, it would be the "most general fitting schema mapping".

Logical Formalism for Schema Mappings. We will often express GLAV constraints using a logical formalism, which is syntactically different, but equivalent to the query-like notation described in Section 3. In this logical formalism, a constraint is a first-order sentence of the form

$$\forall \mathbf{x}(\varphi(\mathbf{x}) \rightarrow \exists \mathbf{y} \psi(\mathbf{x}, \mathbf{y}))$$

where $\varphi(\mathbf{x})$ is a conjunction of atoms over the source schema $\mathbf{S}$, each variable in $\mathbf{x}$ occurs in at least one atom in $\varphi(\mathbf{x})$, and $\psi(\mathbf{x}, \mathbf{y})$ is a conjunction of atoms over the

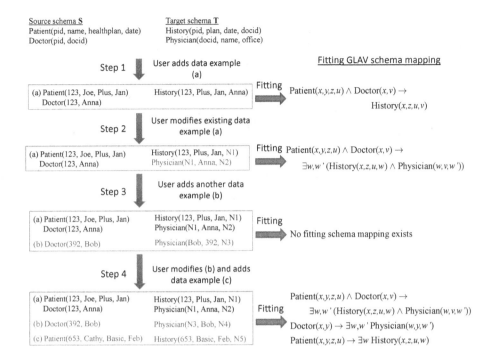

Fig. 6. An example of the workflow in Figure 5

target schema $\mathbf{T}$ with variables from $\mathbf{x}$ and $\mathbf{y}$. By an *atom* over a schema $\mathbf{R}$, we mean a formula $P(x_1, \ldots, x_m)$, where $P \in \mathbf{R}$ and $x_1, \ldots, x_m$ are variables, not necessarily distinct. For notational simplicity, we will often drop the universal quantifiers $\forall \mathbf{x}$ in the front of GLAV constraints. To draw an analogy to the query-like notation introduced in Section 3, the atoms in the $\varphi(\mathbf{x})$ conjunction correspond to the atoms in the *for* clause, while repeated appearances of a variable from $\mathbf{x}$ correspond to equalities specified in the *satisfying* clause. A similar analogy holds between the $\psi(\mathbf{x}, \mathbf{y})$ formula and the *exists* and *where* clauses.

An Example Run of Eirene. Suppose a user wishes to design a schema mapping between the source schema and target schema shown in the top-left corner of Figure 6. The source schema has two relations: Patient and Doctor, and the target schema has two relations: History and Physician.

Step 1. The user adds a single data example, shown in the first box, which essentially states that *Anna* is the doctor of *Joe*, whose health plan is *Plus*, and date-of-visit is *Jan*. In the target relation, there is a single fact that consolidates this information, omitting the patient name. Based on this single data example, Eirene will infer the schema mapping shown on the right of the box. This schema mapping states that whenever a Patient tuple and Doctor tuple agree on the *pid* value (i.e., a natural join between Patient and Doctor), create a target tuple with the *pid*, *healthplan*, *date*, and *docid* values from Patient and Doctor.

Step 2. The user may choose to refine the data example further, perhaps after a realization that there was a typographical error in the data example that is just entered. The modified data example is shown in the second box. For this data example, the source instance remains unchanged, but the user has now modified the target instance to consist of two tuples: a History tuple and a Physician tuple which are "connected" through the value *N1*. Observe that the values *N1* and *N2* in the target instance do not occur among the values of the source instance and they, intuitively, represent unknown and possibly different values. Based on this single data example, our system infers the desired schema mapping shown on the right. The new schema mapping asserts that information from the inner join of Patient and Doctor should be migrated to the target relations, with appropriate nulls to represent unknown and possibly different values.

Step 3. In the third box of Figure 6, the user adds a second data example (b). Eirene now reports that no schema mapping can fit the two data examples (a) and (b). This is because the pattern of data migration in data examples (a) and (b) are inconsistent. According to (b), every Doctor(pid,docid) fact in the source must have a corresponding Physician(docid,pid,office) fact in the target. Observe that the *pid* value is copied to the second column of the corresponding Physician fact. However, this is inconsistent with what (a) states: a Doctor(pid, docid) has a corresponding Physician(_,docid,_) fact in the target, and *docid* gets copied to the second column of the corresponding Physician fact instead.

Step 4. In the fourth box, the user modifies data example (b) and adds a third data example (c). Based on these data examples, Eirene reports the schema mapping shown to the right of the fourth box. Essentially, the schema mapping migrates information from the outer join of Doctor and Patient to the corresponding relations in the target.

Our algorithm that underlies Eirene is shown in Figure 7. It solves the *fitting generation problem* and relies on a *homomorphism extension test* that is a necessary and sufficient condition for the *fitting decision problem*.

Given a source schema **S**, a target schema **T**, and a finite set $\mathcal{E}$ of data examples that conform to the schemas, the *GLAV Fitting Decision Problem* asks to tell whether or not there is a GLAV schema mapping $\mathcal{M}$ that fits $\mathcal{E}$. The *GLAV Fitting Generation Problem* asks to construct a GLAV schema mapping $\mathcal{M}$ that fits $\mathcal{E}$, if such a schema mapping exists, or to report that "None exists", otherwise.

The GLAV Fitting Algorithm. As seen in Figure 7, our algorithm has two main steps. Given a finite set $\mathcal{E}$ of data examples, the first step of the algorithm uses the homomorphism extension test to check whether there exists a GLAV schema mapping that fits $\mathcal{E}$. If no such fitting GLAV schema mapping exists, then the algorithm simply reports that none exists. Otherwise, the second step of the algorithm proceeds to construct a GLAV schema mapping that fits the set $\mathcal{E}$.

Homomorphism Extension Test Let (I, J) and (I', J') be two data examples. We say that a homomorphism $h : I \rightarrow I'$ *extends to a homomorphism* $\widehat{h} : J \rightarrow J'$ if for all $a \in adom(I) \cap adom(J)$, we have that $\widehat{h}(a) = h(a)$. The homomorphism extension test checks the following: for every pair of data examples from the given set $\mathcal{E}$, test whether every homomorphism between the source instances of the two examples extends to a homomorphism between the corresponding target instances. If this homomorphism

---

Algorithm: GLAV Fitting

Input: *A source schema* **S**, *a target schema* **T**, *and a finite set* $\mathcal{E}$ *of data examples* $(I_1, J_1) \ldots (I_n, J_n)$ *over* **S**, **T**.

Output: *Either a fitting GLAV schema mapping or 'None exists'*

// Homomorphism Extension Test: Test for existence of a fitting GLAV schema mapping

for all $i, j \leq n$ **do**
       for all homomorphisms $h : I_i \rightarrow I_j$ **do**
              if not(h extends to a homomorphism $\widehat{h} : J_i \rightarrow J_j$) **then**
                    fail('None exists')

// Construct a fitting canonical GLAV schema mapping

$\Sigma := \emptyset$
for all $i \leq n$ **do**
       add to Σ the canonical GLAV constraint of (I_i, J_i)
return $(\mathbf{S}, \mathbf{T}, \Sigma)$

Fig. 7. The GLAV Fitting Generation Algorithm

extension test fails, the algorithm immediately reports that no GLAV schema mapping can fit the set $\mathcal{E}$ of data examples.

To illustrate the failure of the homomorphism extension test, we refer back to Figure 6 and the set of data examples resulting after Step 3 of the depicted workflow. The homomorphism $\{392 \rightarrow 123,\ \texttt{Bob} \rightarrow \texttt{Anna}\}$ from the source instance of data example (b) to the source instance of data example (a) cannot be extended to a homomorphism between the corresponding target instances. Any such homomorphism would necessarily map the value Bob to N1, as well as 392 to Anna. Consequently, in this case, the homomorphism extension test fails, and the algorithm terminates. If the homomorphism extension test succeeds, the fitting algorithm proceeds to construct the fitting schema mapping.

Constructing a Fitting Canonical GLAV Schema Mapping In this step, the algorithm proceeds to construct the *canonical GLAV schema mapping* of $\mathcal{E}$. The concept of a canonical GLAV schema mapping is similar to that of a *canonical conjunctive query*. If (I, J) is a data example, then the *canonical GLAV constraint of* (I, J) is the GLAV constraint $\forall \mathbf{x}(q_I(\mathbf{x}) \rightarrow \exists \mathbf{y} q_J(\mathbf{x}, \mathbf{y}))$, where $q_I(\mathbf{x})$ is the conjunction of all facts of I (with each value from the active domain of I replaced by a universally quantified variable from $\mathbf{x}$) and $q_J(\mathbf{x}, \mathbf{y})$ is the conjunction of all facts of J (with each value from $\mathrm{adom}(J) \setminus \mathrm{adom}(I)$ replaced by an existentially quantified variable from $\mathbf{y}$). The *canonical GLAV schema mapping of* $\mathcal{E}$ is the schema mapping $\mathcal{M} = (\mathbf{S}, \mathbf{T}, \Sigma)$, where Σ consists of the canonical GLAV constraints of each data example in $\mathcal{E}$. For example, the canonical GLAV schema mapping for the set of data examples resulting after Step 4 of the workflow in Figure 6 is specified by the three GLAV constraints depicted on the right of the box containing the data examples. Notice that this step takes time linear in the size of the given set $\mathcal{E}$ of data examples.

It is important to point out that the canonical GLAV schema mapping of a given set of data examples need *not* fit this set of examples. In fact, this is what makes the GLAV fitting generation problem interesting and nontrivial. Consider the set $\mathcal{E}$ consisting of the data examples

$$(\{S(a,b)\}, \{T(a)\}) \text{ and } (\{S(c,c)\}, \{U(c,d)\}).$$

The canonical GLAV schema mapping of $\mathcal{E}$ is specified by the GLAV constraints

$$\forall xy(S(x,y) \rightarrow T(x))$$
$$\forall x(S(x,x) \rightarrow \exists z U(x,z))$$

This schema mapping does not fit $\mathcal{E}$, as the second data example violates the first constraint. Note also that our homomorphism extension test in the first step of the algorithm would detect this: the homomorphism h that maps $S(a,b)$ to $S(c,c)$ does not extend to any target homomorphism from $T(a)$ to $U(c,d)$. Hence, in this case, our algorithm will terminate after the first step and report that "None exists".

Next, we report results that show the correctness of our algorithm, that our algorithm returns the "most general" fitting schema mapping, if a fitting schema mapping exists, that our algorithm is complete for GLAV schema mapping design, the complexity of our algorithm, and our implementation.

Correctness. The correctness of the GLAV fitting generation algorithm is given by the following result.

Theorem 1. *Let $\mathcal{E}$ be a finite set of data examples. The following are equivalent:*

1. *The canonical GLAV schema mapping of $\mathcal{E}$ fits $\mathcal{E}$.*
2. *There is a GLAV schema mapping that fits $\mathcal{E}$.*
3. *(Homomorphism Extension Test) For all $(I, J), (I', J') \in \mathcal{E}$, every homomorphism $h : I \rightarrow I'$ extends to a homomorphism $\widehat{h} : J \rightarrow J'$.*

Theorem 1 shows that the homomorphism extension test is a necessary and sufficient condition for determining whether GLAV schema mapping fitting $\mathcal{E}$ exists. Furthermore, this condition is also a necessary and sufficient condition for determining whether the canonical GLAV schema mapping of $\mathcal{E}$ fits $\mathcal{E}$.

Most General Fitting GLAV Schema Mapping. Given a finite set $\mathcal{E}$ of data examples, there may be many GLAV schema mappings that fit $\mathcal{E}$. If there is a GLAV schema mapping that fits $\mathcal{E}$, we showed that the canonical GLAV schema mapping is the most general GLAV schema mapping that fits $\mathcal{E}$.

Let $\mathcal{M} = (\mathbf{S}, \mathbf{T}, \Sigma)$ and $\mathcal{M}' = (\mathbf{S}, \mathbf{T}, \Sigma')$ be two schema mappings over the same source and target schemas. We say that $\mathcal{M}$ is *more general than* $\mathcal{M}'$ if Σ' logically implies Σ, i.e., if for every data example (I, J) such that (I, J) satisfies Σ', we have that (I, J) also satisfies Σ. For example, both $R(x,y) \rightarrow P(x,y)$ and $R(x,x) \rightarrow P(x,x)$ fit the data example $(\{R(a,a)\}, \{P(a,a)\})$ with the latter mapping being more general. In this case, the GLAV fitting algorithm will return the latter mapping $R(x,x) \rightarrow P(x,x)$.

This result, along with the correctness of the GLAV fitting algorithm, imply that if a fitting GLAV schema mapping exists for a given set $\mathcal{E}$ of data examples, then our GLAV fitting algorithm returns the most general GLAV schema mapping that fits $\mathcal{E}$. Note that this most general schema mapping is unique up to logical equivalence.

Completeness for Design. Our method of designing schema mappings via data examples is complete for schema-mapping design.

Theorem 2. For every GLAV schema mapping $\mathcal{M}$, there is a finite set of data examples $\mathcal{E}_{\mathcal{M}}$, such that, when given $\mathcal{E}_{\mathcal{M}}$ as input, the GLAV fitting algorithm returns a schema mapping that is logically equivalent to $\mathcal{M}$.

In other words, every GLAV schema mapping can be produced (up to logical equivalence) by our GLAV fitting algorithm with an appropriate set of data examples.

Complexity. The most general schema mapping produced by our GLAV fitting generation algorithm has size linear in the size of the input set of data examples. We showed that this linear bound on the size of the most general schema mapping cannot be improved in general. In contrast, the first step of the GLAV fitting algorithm can be exponential, since the number of homomorphisms between two database instances can be exponential. Hence, the GLAV fitting algorithm runs in exponential time in the worst case. We showed that the GLAV fitting decision problem is complete for the second level Π_2^p of the polynomial hierarchy, hence, in all likelihood, it is harder than NP-complete.

Implementation. We implemented our approach as a prototype in Java 6, with IBM DB2 Express-C v9.7 as the underlying database engine, running on a Dual Intel Xeon 3.4GHz Linux workstation with 4GB RAM. Eirene stores data examples in the IBM DB2 database system and implements the homomorphism extension test as a set of DB2 user-defined functions. Intuitively, each function is associated with a data example and it tries to find a witness to the failure of the homomorphism extension.

The high worst-case complexity of the GLAV fitting problem notwithstanding, the experimental results that we have obtained demonstrate the feasibility of interactively designing schema mappings using data examples. In particular, our experiments show that our system achieves very good performance in real-life scenarios. For more details, we refer the interested reader to the experimental evaluation presented in [1].

4.2 Muse

Muse allows a user to refine various aspects of an existing schema mapping specification, based on the choices made by users on a series of data examples that are presented by the system. The Muse workflow is shown in Figure 8. In contrast, the Eirene system derives schema mappings from data examples provided by the user.

The Muse system is largely inspired by the work of Yan *et al.* [35], which was the first to present data examples to users so that users' feedback can be used for refining schema mappings. Like [35], Muse uses data examples to differentiate between alternative mapping specifications and infer the desired mapping semantics based on a user's actions. However, we go significantly beyond the techniques and space of alternative mappings supported by [35].

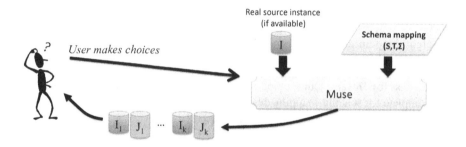

Fig. 8. Interactive refinement of various aspects of schema mappings via data examples

First, Muse is capable of helping a user derive the desired grouping semantics for a mapping specification through choices made on data examples. For instance, to infer whether a user wishes to group projects by a a company's name and location or only by a company's name, Muse will construct a sequence of choice questions with data examples. The selection of data examples made by the user allows Muse to infer the desired grouping semantics. The number of choice questions and the size of each data example are usually small. They correspond roughly to the number schema elements that could be used for grouping and each data example consists of at most two tuples per (nested) relation.

Second, as in [35], Muse helps a user choose among alternative interpretations of an ambiguous mapping. Intuitively, a schema mapping is *ambiguous* if it specifies, in more than one way, how an atomic target schema element (or attribute) is to be obtained. For example, the schema mapping that is generated from the visual specification could be ambiguous because the visual specification may assert (through attribute correspondences) that a project supervisor is a project manager and a project tech-lead at the same time. In other words, it is not clear whether to extract the manager's name or the tech-lead's name (or both) from the source database as the supervisor of a project in the target database and hence the ambiguity. When this happens, the user is asked to select among a small set of data choices to fill in the target instance of a data example that is constructed by Muse. The data example and choices are carefully chosen so that they reflect all possible interpretations of the ambiguous mapping. Furthermore, the user's actions on these choices translate into a unique interpretation. Apart from our ability to handle nested XML-like data, Muse is also different from [35] in that we show all possible interpretations of an ambiguous schema mapping in *one compact representation* (i.e., the data example together with data choices in the target instance of the data example). In contrast, all different target instances are shown to the user in [35]. The discussion of ambigious mappings will be omitted from this article. However, details can be found in [8].

Finally, unlike previous work which relies exclusively on an available source instance to illustrate mappings, Muse can construct its own synthetic data example whenever a meaningful data example cannot be drawn from the actual source instance or when the source instance is unavailable. It is important to note that for a given source instance, schema mappings that are logically inequivalent may produce the same target instance

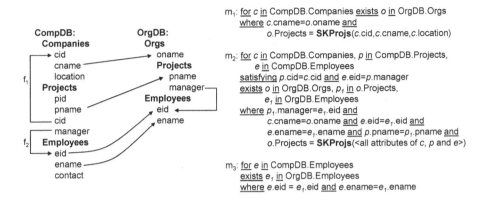

Fig. 9. A mapping scenario

on the given source instance. Muse is able to automatically detect such situations and construct a synthetic source instance that will illustrate differences in all design alternatives as needed. In fact, our experiments justify that this feature of Muse is necessary to help design mappings for some real mapping settings and instances.

Naturally, an advanced user can always choose to tweak or specify the desired schema mapping function directly without using Muse. Muse is useful for cases where such direct manipulation of code is not preferred.

Design of Grouping Functions. Grouping or combining related data together is an essential functionality of many integration systems. We now describe how the grouping design wizard Muse-G of Muse can be used to infer the desired grouping function through a sequence of choices made by the user on data examples.

The Muse-G wizard is always able to infer a grouping function that has the same grouping semantics as the actual grouping function that the user has in mind. As the data examples illustrate the different possibilities of grouping, Muse-G can also be very useful when the user only has a partial understanding of the desired grouping semantics.

In what follows, we overview the basic algorithm behind Muse-G when there are no functional dependencies (FDs) in the source schema. Details of this algorithm and extensions to handle keys (and FDs in general) in the source schema, as well as our experimental results can be found in [8].

Except for topmost-level sets, every nested set in the target schema of mapping generation tools (e.g., [14, 19, 28]) has a *default grouping function*, where the arguments consist of only atomic attributes. For example, there are no grouping functions for *Orgs* and *Employees* in the target schema of Figure 9. However, the default grouping function for *Projects* in m_2 according to [19] is

$$SKProjs(c.cid, c.cname, c.location, p.pid, p.pname, p.cid, p.manager, e.eid, e.ename, e.contact)$$

This means that *Projects* records are grouped according to the values of all attributes of the *Companies*, *Projects* and *Employees* source records. If SKProjs(*cname*) is the grouping function instead, then *Projects* records are grouped according to *cname* of

Companies records (i.e., *oname* of *Orgs* records). (We write SKProjs(*cname*) instead of SKProjs(*c.cname*) when there is no ambiguity.)

In tools such as Mapforce, Stylus Studio and [14, 19, 28] the arguments of the grouping function have to be explicitly modified or specified. This can be difficult when schemas are large and the number of possible arguments for a grouping function tends to be large as a consequence. Indeed, if there are n possible attributes to group by, then there are in fact 2^n choices of grouping functions. Furthermore, it may not be obvious to a user, what the n possible grouping attributes are (see [19, 28]).

Muse-G takes as input a schema mapping $(\mathbf{S}, \mathbf{T}, \Sigma)$. The user can choose to design any grouping function that occurs in Σ. We assume that there is a real source instance I from which Muse-G can draw real data examples whenever possible, and show how Muse-G constructs its own examples otherwise. To illustrate our algorithm, we use the schema mapping $(\mathbf{S}, \mathbf{T}, \{m_2\})$, where $\mathbf{S}$, $\mathbf{T}$ and m_2 are the source and target schemas and respectively, mapping, of Figure 9.

Step 1. The first step is to determine an order to the set of grouping functions that the user wishes to (re)design in a mapping in Σ by performing a breadth-first traversal of $\mathbf{T}$ starting from the root. This yields, for our example, the order *Orgs*, *Employees*, and *Projects*. Since *Orgs* and *Employees* are top-level sets without grouping functions, Muse-G will only prompt the design of grouping functions for *Projects* (i.e., SKProjs) in m_2.

Step 2. Next, we determine the set $poss(m_2, \text{SKProjs})$ of all possible arguments for SKProjs according to m_2. According to the schema of *OrgDB*, a *Projects* SetID is nested inside an *Orgs* tuple. According to the *for* clause of m_2, the existence of an *Orgs* tuple is dependent on the existence of a *Companies* tuple, an *Employees* tuple, and a *Projects* tuple which agrees with the *Companies* and *Employees* tuples on the values of *pid* and *manager*, respectively.

This means that $poss(m_2, \text{SKProjs})$ consists of the set of attributes in the *Companies*, *Projects* and *Employees* records, which is $\{cid, cname, location, pid, pname, pid, manager, eid, ename, contact\}$. Note that the sets $poss(m, \text{SK})$ are in fact identical for all nested sets SK occurring in m. In other mapping formalisms, however, they may be different (see [19] for details). However, to simplify our subsequent discussion, we will assume that $poss(m_2, \text{SKProjs}) = \{cid, cname, location\}$.

Step 3. Suppose the user has SKProjs(Z) in mind, where $Z \subseteq poss(m_2, \text{SKProjs})$. In what follows, we show how Muse-G proceeds to construct data examples to present choices to the user in order to infer the desired grouping function.

Construct Data Examples. To determine whether or not an attribute A from $poss(m_2, \text{SKProjs})$ is to be included in the grouping function of SKProjs, Muse-G carefully constructs a small source instance I_e such that two differentiating target instances are obtained: regardless of what the rest of the grouping attributes might be, one is the result of including the attribute A as part of SKProjs in m_2, and the other omits it.

Suppose the attribute under consideration is *cid*. An example source instance I_e with two tuples, as shown below, will be constructed:

$$I_e : \{Companies(c_1, n_1, l_1), Projects(p_1, pn_1, c_1, e_1), Employees(e_1, en_1, cn_1),$$
$$Companies(c_2, n_1, l_1), Projects(p_2, pn_2, c_2, e_2), Employees(e_2, en_2, cn_2)\}$$

Observe that each relation in I_e has two tuples. Furthermore, every attribute value of every tuple is distinct, except for *cname* and *location* values of *Companies* tuples. The reason for this is so that the target instances generated by m_2 with SKProjs(*cid*,y), where $\mathbf{y} \subseteq \{cname,location\}$, versus m_2 with SKProjs(y) will be non-isomorphic. Indeed, the former target instance will contain two distinct *Projects* sets, while the latter consists of only one *Projects* set.

To obtain a real source instance, Muse-G generates the following query that will be executed against the actual source instance, if available, to retrieve real tuples for the example instance I_e.

$$Q^{I_e} : Companies(c_1, n_1, l_1) \wedge Companies(c_2, n_1, l_1) \wedge$$
$$Projects(p_1, pn_1, c_1, e_1) \wedge Projects(p_2, pn_2, c_2, e_2) \wedge$$
$$Employees(e_1, en_1, cn_1) \wedge Employees(e_2, en_2, cn_2) \wedge c_1 \neq c_2$$

All variables of Q^{I_e} are universally-quantified. The two *Companies* tuples must disagree on *cid* (the probed attribute) and agree on *cname* and *location* as explained earlier.

If $Q^{I_e}(I)$ returns an empty result, Muse-G will present the user with the synthetic instance I_e, shown earlier. Alternatively, a "semi-real" I_e may also be constructed by putting together various real values drawn from I (e.g., use *cid*, *cname* and *location* values drawn from the corresponding columns of the *Companies* relation to create a *Companies* tuple in I_e, regardless of whether these values participate in a real *Companies* tuple). However, this may lead to combinations that are misleading to the user. On the other hand, if $Q^{I_e}(I)$ returns a non-empty result, Muse-G constructs a real example based on the returned values. A possible real example constructed in this way is shown in Figure 10(a), where each tuple in *Companies*, *Projects* and *Employees* exists in I.

Next, Muse-G obtains two differentiating target instances shown in Scenarios 1 and 2 in Figure 10(a), by chasing I_e with mappings d_1 and respectively, d_2. Here, d_1 and d_2 are identical to m_2 except they have SKProjs(*cid*) and respectively, SKProjs() as grouping functions for *Projects*. Now, Muse-G asks the user "which target instance looks correct"?

Note that the instance I_e has been carefully crafted so that the chase of I_e with d_1 is isomorphic to the chase of I_e with d_1', where d_1' is a mapping obtained from m_2 by replacing SKProjs with SKProjs($\{cid\} \cup Y$), where $Y \subseteq \{cname, location\}$. Since *cname* and *location* values are identical for the two *Comp* tuples in I_e, the mapping d_1 has the same effect as d_1' on I_e. Similarly, d_2 has the same effect as d_2' on I_e, where d_2' is obtained from d_2 by replacing SKProjs with SKProjs(Y). Hence, based on the user's choice of Scenario 1 or 2, Muse-G correctly determines whether *cid* is part of the user's desired grouping function. So with one question, we either eliminate all mappings using *cid* (not only SKProjs(*cid*), but SKProjs(*cid*, *cname*), SKProjs(*cid*, *location*), and SKProjs(*cid*, *cname*, *location*)), or we eliminate all mappings that do not use *cid* in the skolem function for *Projects*.

Continuing with our example, suppose the user has the grouping function SKProjs(*cname*) in mind. She would select Scenario 2 in Figure 10(a). We now repeat the process for the other attributes *cname* and *location*. Figure 10(b) shows the example source instance and the two scenarios obtained by considering the attribute *cname*. The two source *Companies* tuples must differ on the values of *cname* and agree on the values of *location*. Note that the *cid* values of the two *Companies* tuples are not required

Example source: Target instances:

Companies	Scenario 1:	Scenario 2:
11 IBM NY	**OrgDB**	**OrgDB**
12 IBM NY	**Orgs**	**Orgs**
Projects	IBM	IBM
P1 DB 11 e4	**Projects**:SK(11,**y**)	**Projects**:SK(**y**)
P2 Web 12 e5	DB e4	DB e4
Employees	IBM	Web e5
e4 Jon x234	**Projects**:SK(12,**y**)	**Employees**
e5 Anna x888	Web e5	e4 Jon
	Employees	e5 Anna
	e4 Jon	
(a)	e5 Anna	

Note:
y ⊆ {IBM,NY}

Example source: Target instances:

Companies	Scenario 1:	Scenario 2:
11 IBM NY	**OrgDB**	**OrgDB**
14 SBC NY	**Orgs**	**Orgs**
Projects	IBM	IBM
P1 DB 11 e4	**Projects**:SK(IBM,**y**)	**Projects**:SK(**y**)
P4 WiFi 14 e6	DB e4	DB e4
Employees	SBC	WiFi e6
e4 Jon x234	**Projects**:SK(SBC,**y**)	SBC
e6 Kat x331	WiFi e6	**Projects**:SK(**y**)
	Employees	DB e4
	e4 Jon	WiFi e6
(b)	e6 Kat	**Employees**
		e4 Jon
		e6 Kat

Note:
y ⊆ {NY}

Example source: Target instances:

Companies	Scenario 1:	Scenario 2:
11 IBM NY	**OrgDB**	**OrgDB**
13 IBM SF	**Orgs**	**Orgs**
Projects	IBM	IBM
P1 DB 11 e4	**Projects**:SK(IBM,NY)	**Projects**:SK(IBM)
P2 Web 13 e5	DB · e4	DB e4
Employees	IBM	Web e5
e4 Jon x234	**Projects**:SK(IBM,SF)	**Employees**
e5 Anna x888	Web e5	e4 Jon
	Employees	e5 Anna
	e4 Jon	
(c)	e5 Anna	

Fig. 10. Probing on (a) *cid*, (b) *cname*, and (c) *location* when the user has SKProjs(*cname*) in mind

to be identical, since *cid* is not an argument of SKProjs. The user will pick Scenario 1 in Figure 10(b), since she wants to group *Projects* by *cname*, and Muse-G infers that *cname* is an argument to SKProjs. Figure 10(c) shows the data examples that are presented to the user when the attribute *location* is under consideration. The user will pick Scenario 2. Since *cname* is part of the grouping, the *Companies* tuples must agree on the *cname* values, otherwise, Muse-G would not be able to infer whether *location* is part of the groping from the user's choice in Figure 10(c). At this point, Muse-G concludes and returns SKProjs(*cname*).

Recall that we have assumed above that $poss(m_2, \text{SKProjs})$ is $\{cid, cname, location\}$ for simplicity, when in fact it consists of all attributes of *Companies*, *Projects* and *Employees* records. In this case, Muse-G concludes only after subsequently probing all the attributes of *Projects* and *Employees* records (the user will choose Scenario 2 in each case). Note also that it is conceivable for Muse-G to generate homomorphically equivalent target instances (i.e., target instances with a homormophisms into each other) for Scenarios 1 and 2 (e.g., Figure 10(b)). However, it is always possible for the user to distinguish between such instances, as they are non-isomorphic.

Muse-G infers the desired grouping function by presenting the user a *small* number of choice questions, where each choice question consists of a *small* source instance with two target instances that correspond to the two possible choices in this question.

Small Number of Choices, Small Data Examples. For each nested set SK in a mapping m, there are 2^n different grouping functions where $n = |poss(m, \text{SK})|$. However, Muse-G determines the desired grouping function by asking the user only $|poss(m, \text{SK})|$ questions. In fact, if there is at most one key per nested set, then Muse-G performs a careful reordering of the questions posed to the user. The questions pertaining to the attributes in the key are asked first. In general, using this strategy, at most n questions are needed to infer the desired grouping function. If the user decides to include the key attributes in the grouping function, then the number of questions is equal to the number of key attributes. It is also important to note that all real source schemas that we have encountered in our experimental evaluation fall into this category.

Furthermore, for each choice, Muse-G constructs a small source example. The size of the source example is twice the number of "$x \in X$" clauses in *for* clauses of m. This typically means that there are at most two tuples in each nested set.

We refer the interested reader to [2] for a report on our experience with Muse on publicly available mapping scenarios.

5   Modular Design of Schema Mappings

5.1   Overview

As outlined in Section 2, in our Divide-Design-Merge methodology, the user can choose to design a schema mapping by focusing on designing smaller and easier to understand mappings, using data examples as much as possible. In the previous section, we have presented our techniques for designing and refining schema mappings via data examples. However, simply taking the independently designed schema mapping components and using them as the specification for the global schema mapping may not achieve the desired semantics. This may lead, as it will be explained later, to problems such as data redundancies and loss of data associations. Hence, the design workflow is not complete without a mechanism for correlating the set of independent schema mappings resulting after the previous phase into a meaningful global schema mapping (see Figure 3). This is the role of the MapMerge schema mapping operator, presented in this section. This operator allows for the modular construction of complex and larger schema mappings from multiple "smaller" schema mappings between the same source and target schemas into an arguably better overall schema mapping.

Since the mappings given as input to MapMerge can be as simple as individual attribute correspondences, MapMerge supersedes previous mapping generation algorithms such as the ones in Clio [16]. In addition, as we will show later, MapMerge can be used in conjunction with the schema mapping composition operator [18, 23, 27] to correlate flows of schema mappings in a meaningful way.

5.2 Motivating Example

To illustrate the ideas behind MapMerge, consider first a mapping scenario between the schemas S_1 and S_2 shown in the left part of Figure 4. The goal is data restructuring from two source relations, *Group* and *Works*, to three target relations, *Emp*, *Dept*, and *Proj*. In this example, *Group* (similar to *Dept*) represents groups of scientists sharing a common area (e.g., a database group, a CS group, etc.) The dotted arrows represent foreign key constraints in the schemas.

Independent Mappings. Assume the existence of the following (independent) schema mappings from S_1 to S_2. The first mapping is the constraint t_1 in Figure 11(a), and corresponds to the arrow t_1 in Figure 4. This constraint requires every tuple in *Group* to be mapped to a tuple in *Dept* such that the group name (*gname*) becomes department name (*dname*). The second mapping is more complex and corresponds to the group of arrows t_2 in Figure 4. This constraint involves a custom filter condition; every pair of joining tuples of *Works* and *Group* for which the *addr* value is "NY" must be mapped into two tuples of *Emp* and *Dept*, sharing the same *did* value, and with corresponding *ename*, *addr* and *dname* values. (Note that *did* is a target-specific field that must exist and plays the role of key / foreign key). Intuitively, t_2 illustrates a pre-existing mapping that a user may have spent time in the past to create, possibly using the techniques based on data examples from Section 4. Finally, the third constraint in Figure 11(a) corresponds to the arrow t_3 and maps *pname* from *Works* to *Proj*. This is an example of a correspondence that is introduced by a user after loading t_1 and the pre-existing mapping t_2 into the mapping tool.

The goal of the system is now to (re)generate a "good" overall schema mapping from S_1 to S_2 based on its input mappings. We note first that the input mappings, when considered in isolation, do not generate an ideal target instance.

Indeed, consider the source instance I in Figure 12. The target instance that is obtained by minimally enforcing the constraints $\{t_1, t_2, t_3\}$ is the instance J_1 also shown in the figure. The first *Dept* tuple is obtained by applying t_1 on the *Group* tuple $(123, CS)$. There, $D1$ represents some *did* value that must be associated with CS in this tuple. Similarly, the *Proj* tuple, with some unspecified value B for *budget* and a *did*

Input mappings from **S₁** to **S₂**:

(t_1) _for_ g _in_ Group _exists_ d _in_ Dept
    where d.dname = g.gname

(t_2) _for_ w _in_ Works, g _in_ Group
    satisfying w.gno = g.gno, w.addr = "NY"
    exists e _in_ Emp, d _in_ Dept
      where e.did = d.did,
      e.ename = w.ename, e.addr = w.addr,
      d.dname = g.gname

(t_3) _for_ w _in_ Works _exists_ p _in_ Proj
    where p.pname = w.pname

(a)

Output of MapMerge(**S₁**, **S₂**, {t_1, t_2, t_3}):

for g _in_ Group _exists_ d _in_ Dept
    where d.dname = g.gname, **d.did = F[g]**

for w _in_ Works, g _in_ Group
    satisfying w.gno = g.gno, w.addr = "NY"
    exists e _in_ Emp
      where e.ename = w.ename, e.addr = w.addr,
        e.did = F[g]

for w _in_ Works, g _in_ Group
    satisfying w.gno = g.gno, w.addr = "NY"
    exists p _in_ Proj
      where p.pname = w.pname, p.budget = H₁[w],
        p.did = F[g]

(b)

Fig. 11. (a) Schema mappings from **S₁** to **S₂** in the scenario of Figure 4. (b) Output of Map-Merge.

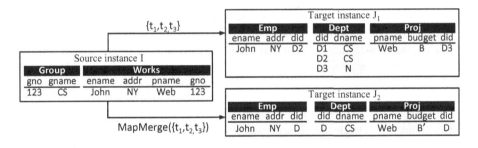

Fig. 12. An instance of **S₁** and two instances of **S₂**

value of $D3$ is obtained via t_3. The _Emp_ tuple together with the second _Dept_ tuple arc obtained based on t_2. As required by t_2, these tuples are linked via the same did value $D2$. Finally, to obtain a target instance that satisfies all the foreign key constraints, we must also have a third tuple in _Dept_ that includes $D3$ together with some unspecified department name N.

Since the three mapping constraints are not correlated, the three did values ($D1$, $D2$, $D3$) are distinct. (There is no requirement that they must be equal.) As a result, the target instance J_1 exhibits the typical problems that arise when uncorrelated mappings are used to transform data: (1) _duplication of data_ (e.g., multiple _Dept_ tuples for CS with different did values), and (2) _loss of associations_ where tuples are not linked correctly to each other (e.g., we have lost the association between project name Web and department name CS that existed in the source).

Correlated Mappings via MapMerge. Consider now the schema mappings that are shown in Figure 11(b) and that are the result of MapMerge applied on $\{t_1, t_2, t_3\}$. The notable difference from the input mappings is that all mappings consistently use the same expression, namely the Skolem term $F[g]$ where g denotes a *Group* tuple, to give values for the did field. The first mapping is the same as t_1 but makes explicit the fact that did is $F[g]$. This mapping creates a unique *Dept* tuple for each distinct *Group* tuple. The second mapping is (almost) like t_2 with the additional use of the same Skolem term $F[g]$. Moreover, it also drops the existence requirement for *Dept* (since this is now implied by the first mapping). Finally, the third mapping differs from t_3 by incorporating a join with *Group* before it can actually use the Skolem term $F[g]$. Furthermore, it inherits the filter on the $addr$ field, which applies to all such *Works* tuples according to t_2. As an additional artifact of MapMerge, it also includes a Skolem term $H_1[w]$ that assigns values to the $budget$ attribute, which was initially left unspecified. The target instance that is obtained by applying the result of MapMerge is the instance J_2 shown in Figure 12. The data associations that exist in the source are now correctly preserved in the target. For example, Web is linked to the CS tuple (via D) and also $John$ is linked to the CS tuple (via the same D). Furthermore, there is no duplication of *Dept* tuples.

Flows of Mappings. Taking the idea of mapping reuse and modularity one step further, an even more compelling use case for MapMerge in conjunction with mapping composition [18, 23, 27], is the *flow-of-mappings* scenario [4]. The key idea here is that to design a data transformation from the source to the target, one can decompose the process, in line with the Divide-Design-Merge approach, into several simpler stages, where each stage maps from or into some intermediate, possibly simpler schema. Moreover, the simpler mappings and schemas play the role of reusable components that can be applied to build other flows. Such abstraction is directly motivated by the development of real-life, large-scale ETL flows such as those typically developed with IBM Information Server (Datastage), Oracle Warehouse Builder and others.

To illustrate, suppose the goal is to transform data from the schema $\mathbf{S}_1$ to the nested schema $\mathbf{S}_4$ of Figure 4, where *Staff* and *Projects* information are grouped under *CompSci*. The mapping or ETL designer, following the divide-and-merge methodology, may find it easier to first construct the mapping between $\mathbf{S}_1$ and $\mathbf{S}_2$ (it may also be that this mapping may have been derived in a prior design). Furthermore, the schema $\mathbf{S}_2$ is a normalized representation of the data, where *Dept*, *Emp* and *Proj* correspond directly to the main concepts (or types of data) that are being manipulated. Based on this schema, the designer can then produce a mapping m_{CS} from *Dept* to a schema $\mathbf{S}_3$ containing a more specialized object *CSDept*, by applying some customized filter condition (e.g., based on the name of the department). The next step is to create the mapping m from *CSDept* to the target schema $\mathbf{S}_4$. Other independent mappings are similarly defined for *Emp* and *Proj* (see m_1 and m_2).

Once these individual mappings are established, the same problem of correlating the mappings arises. In particular, one has to correlate $m_{\mathrm{CS}} \circ m$, which is the result of applying mapping composition to m_{CS} and m, with the mappings m_1 for *Emp* and m_2 for *Proj*. This correlation will ensure that all employees and projects of computer science departments will be correctly mapped under their correct departments, in the target schema.

In this example, composition itself gives another source of mappings to be correlated by MapMerge. While similar with composition in that it is an operator on schema mappings, MapMerge is fundamentally different in that it correlates mappings that share the same source schema and the same target schema. In contrast, composition takes two sequential mappings where the target of the first mapping is the source of the second mapping. Nevertheless, the two operators are complementary and together they can play a fundamental role in building data flows. In Section 5.4 we will give an overview of an algorithm that can be used to correlate flows of mappings.

5.3 Correlating Mappings: Key Ideas

How do we achieve the systematic and, moreover, *correct* construction of correlated mappings? After all, we do not want arbitrary correlations between mappings, but rather only to the extent that the *natural* data associations in the source are preserved and no extra associations are introduced.

There are two key ideas behind MapMerge. The first idea is to exploit the structure and the constraints in the schemas in order to define what natural associations are (for the purpose of the algorithm). Two data elements are considered associated if they are in the same tuple or in two different tuples that are linked via constraints. This idea has been used before in Clio [28], and provides the first (conceptual) step towards Map-Merge. For our example, the input mapping t_3 in Figure 11(a) is equivalent, in the presence of the source and target constraints, to the following enriched mapping:

t_3': *for* w *in* Works, g *in* Group *satisfying* w.gno = g.gno
   exists p *in* Proj, d *in* Dept *where* p.pname = w.pname *and* p.did = d.did

Intuitively, if we have a w tuple in *Works*, we also have a joining tuple g in *Group*, since *gno* is a foreign key from *Works* to *Group*. Similarly, a tuple p in *Proj* implies the existence of a joining tuple in *Dept*, since *did* is a foreign key from *Proj* to *Dept*.

Formally, the above rewriting from t_3 to t_3' is captured by the well-known chase procedure [11, 24]. The chase is a convenient tool to group together, syntactically, elements of the schema that are associated. The chase by itself, however, does not change the semantics of the mapping. In particular, the above t_3' does not include any additional mapping behavior from *Group* to *Dept*.

The second key idea behind MapMerge is that of *reusing* or borrowing mapping behavior from a more general mapping to a more specific mapping. This is a heuristic that changes the semantics of the entire schema mapping and produces an arguably better one, with consolidated semantics.

To illustrate, consider the first mapping constraint in Figure 11(b). This constraint (obtained by skolemizing the input t_1) specifies a general mapping behavior from *Group* to *Dept*. In particular, it specifies how to create *dname* and *did* from the input record. On the other hand, the above t_3' can be seen as a more *specific* mapping from a *subset* of *Group* (i.e., those groups that have associated *Works* tuples) to a *subset* of *Dept* (i.e., those departments that have associated *Proj* tuples). At the same time, t_3' does not specify any concrete mapping for the *dname* and *did* fields of *Dept*. We can then borrow the mapping behavior that is already specified by the more general mapping. Thus, t_3' can be enriched to:

t_3'': *for* w *in* Works, g *in* Group *satisfying* w.gno = g.gno
    exists p *in* Proj, d *in* Dept
    where p.pname = w.pname *and* p.did = d.did *and*
        d.dname = g.gname *and* d.did = $F[g]$ *and* p.did = $F[g]$

where two of the last three equalities represent the "borrowed" behavior, while the last equality is obtained automatically by transitivity. The other borrowed behavior that we will add to t_3'' is the user-defined filter on *addr*. This filter already applies, according to t_2, to all tuples in *Works* that join with *Group* tuples, and are mapped to *Emp* and *Dept* tuples. The resulting constraint t_3''' has the following form:

t_3''': *for* w *in* Works, g *in* Group *satisfying* w.gno = g.gno $\boxed{and\ w.\text{addr} = \text{"NY"}}$
    exists p *in* Proj, d *in* Dept
    where p.pname = w.pname *and* p.did = d.did *and*
        d.dname = g.gname *and* d.did = $F[g]$ *and* p.did = $F[g]$

Finally, we can drop the existence of d in *Dept* with the two conditions for *dname* and *did*, since this is repeated behavior that is already captured by the more general mapping from *Group* to *Dept*. The resulting constraint is identical[2] to the third constraint in Figure 11(b), now correlated with the first one via $F[g]$. A similar explanation applies for the second constraint in Figure 11(b).

The MapMerge Algorithm. MapMerge takes as input a set $\{(\mathbf{S}, \mathbf{T}, \Sigma_1), ...,(\mathbf{S}, \mathbf{T}, \Sigma_n)\}$ of schema mappings over the same source and target schemas, which is equivalent to taking a single schema mapping $(\mathbf{S}, \mathbf{T}, \Sigma_1 \cup ... \cup \Sigma_n)$ as input. The algorithm is divided into four phases. The first phase decomposes each input mapping assertion into basic components that are, intuitively, easier to merge. In Phase 2, we apply the chase algorithm to compute associations (which we call *tableaux*), from the source and target schemas, as well as from the source and target assertions of the input mappings. The latter type of tableaux is necessary to support user defined joins that may not follow foreign key constraints. By pairing source and target tableaux, we obtain all the possible *skeletons* of mappings. The actual work of constructing correlated mappings takes place in Phase 3, where for each skeleton, we take the union of all the basic components generated in Phase 1 that "match" the skeleton. Phase 4 is a simplification phase that also flags conflicts that may arise and that need to be addressed by the user. These conflicts occur when multiple mappings that map to the same portion of the target schema contribute with different, irreconcilable behaviors. For a complete presentation of the MapMerge algorithm, we refer the interested reader to [5].

Evaluation. To evaluate the quality of the data generated based on MapMerge, we introduced a measure that captures the similarity between a source and target instance

---

[2] Modulo the absence of $H_1[w]$, which is introduced to ensure that no target attributes are left unassigned.

by measuring the amount of data associations that are preserved by the transformation from the source to the target instance. We used this similarity measure in our experiments, on a mix of real-life and synthetic mapping scenarios, to show that the mappings derived by MapMerge are better than the input mappings. Our experiemental results are presented in [5].

5.4 Correlating Flows of Schema Mappings with MapMerge and Composition

As discussed in the introduction, we can bring modular design of mappings beyond sets of parallel mappings between the same pair of schemas, towards assembling general flows of mappings. To generate meaningful end-to-end transformation specifications for such flows, we have to bring along into the picture the sequential mapping composition operator [18]. This operator can be used to obtain end-to-end mappings from chains of successive mappings. In contrast, MapMerge assembles sets of "parallel" mappings. These two operators can be leveraged in conjunction to correlate flows of mappings.

Recall the example of the flow of mappings in Figure 4. The individual mappings can be assembled into an end-to-end mapping from the schema S_1 to the schema S_4 through repeated applications of the MapMerge and composition operators. To exemplify, the specialized mapping for *Dept* records between S_2 and S_4 is a result of composing the m_{CS} and m mappings. Furthermore, the right correlations among the *Dept*, *Emp*, and *Proj* records that are migrated into S_4 can be achieved by applying MapMerge on m_1, m_2, and the result $m_{CS} \circ m$ of the previous composition.

Flow Correlation Algorithm. We provide here an overview of our flow correlation algorithm. The complete details of this algorithm can be found in [5]. A flow of mappings can be modeled as a multigraph whose nodes are the schemas and whose edges are the mappings between the schemas. Recall that a mapping consists of a pair of source and target schemas as well as a set of constraints specified by SO tgds. In this algorithm, a mapping between a source and a target schema is either part of the input, or a consequence of applying MapMerge or mapping composition. Our algorithm assumes that the graph of mappings is acyclic. In addition, for the purposes of this algorithm, we assume that the MapMerge operator does not lead to outstanding residual equality constraints. Integrating such constraints with the mapping composition operator is a problem we plan to investigate in future work.

The flow correlation algorithm, which is shown in Figure 13, proceeds through alternative phases of applying the MapMerge and mapping composition operators, and terminates when no further progress can be made. In a MapMerge phase, the multigraph modeling the flow is essentially transformed into a regular graph. For any pair of schemas S_i, S_j, the set of mappings $\mathcal{M}_{ij}$ going from S_i to S_j is replaced by the result of applying MapMerge on $\mathcal{M}_{ij}$. In a mapping composition phase, for any distinct schemas S_i, S_j, S_k in the flow such that M_1 is a mapping from S_i to S_j and M_2 is a mapping from S_j to S_k, the result $M = M_1 \circ M_2$ of composing M_1 and M_2 is added to the flow. We use here the mapping composition algorithm in [18], since it applies to schema mappings specified by SO tgds.

Our correlation algorithm keeps track, via the set $\mathcal{C}$, of the mappings being added to the flow in the composition phase. As a result, a mapping is not re-added to the flow

---

Algorithm CorrelateFlow($\mathcal{M}$)

Input: A set of schema mappings $\mathcal{M}$.
Output: The set of schema mappings $\mathcal{M}$ after correlation.

Let $\mathcal{S}$ be the set of schemas that are either source or target schemas for the mappings in $\mathcal{M}$.
Initialize $\mathcal{C} = \emptyset$
Repeat
      [Phase 1] MapMerge
            For every pair $(\mathbf{S}_i, \mathbf{S}_j)$ of distinct schemas in $\mathcal{S}$
                  Let $\mathcal{M}_{ij}$ be the set of mappings from $\mathbf{S}_i$ to $\mathbf{S}_j$ in $\mathcal{M}$.
                  Remove the mappings in $\mathcal{M}_{ij}$ from $\mathcal{M}$
                  Add MapMerge($\mathcal{M}_{ij}$) to $\mathcal{M}$
      [Phase 2] Composition
            Initialize $\mathcal{N} = \emptyset$
            For every triple $(\mathbf{S}_i, \mathbf{S}_j, \mathbf{S}_k)$ of distinct schemas in $\mathcal{S}$
                where there exist in $\mathcal{M}$ a mapping $\mathbf{M}_1$ from $\mathbf{S}_i$ to $\mathbf{S}_j$ and
                                      a mapping $\mathbf{M}_2$ from $\mathbf{S}_j$ to $\mathbf{S}_k$
                Let $\mathbf{M} = \mathbf{M}_1 \circ \mathbf{M}_2$
                If $\mathbf{M} \notin \mathcal{C}$ (this composition was not considered before), add $\mathbf{M}$ to $\mathcal{N}$
            Add the mappings in $\mathcal{N}$ to $\mathcal{M}$, and to $\mathcal{C}$
Until $\mathcal{N}$ is empty.
Return $\mathcal{M}$.

Fig. 13. The mapping flow correlation algorithm

if the result of composing the same mappings was computed and added to the flow previously in the execution of the algorithm. The algorithm terminates when no new mappings can be added to the flow in the composition phase, and returns the correlated flow of mappings $\mathcal{M}$. After executing this algorithm, the flow of mappings will contain at most one mapping between each pair of schemas (with each mapping typically being a set of correlated formulas).

6   Conclusion

This article presents a new framework for designing schema mappings between large schemas. This new framework allows a user to divide-and-conquer the design of large schema mappings by designing the schema mappings between smaller portions of the participating schemas. These smaller schema mappings can be designed independently of the rest through the specification of data examples or through the use of traditional schema mapping design tools. Such individually designed schema mappings can then be correlated and merged into one that better represents the associations in the source data, whenever possible.

Acknowledgements. This article presents an overview of work that has been investigated in the dissertation of Bogdan Alexe, whose academic genealogy can be traced back to Peter Buneman.

The authors are grateful to Balder ten Cate, Laura Chiticariu, Mauricio A. Hernández, Phokion G. Kolaitis, Renée J. Miller, and Lucian Popa for their collaboration on various aspects of this work. This work is supported by NSF Grant IIS-0905276 and a Google Faculty Award. Part of this work was done while Tan was at IBM Research - Almaden.

References

1. Alexe, B., ten Cate, B., Kolaitis, P.G., Tan, W.C.: Designing and Refining Schema Mappings via Data Examples. In: SIGMOD Conference (2011)
2. Alexe, B., Chiticariu, L., Miller, R.J., Pepper, D., Tan, W.C.: Muse: a System for Understanding and Designing Mappings. In: SIGMOD Conference, pp. 1281–1284 (2008)
3. Alexe, B., Chiticariu, L., Miller, R.J., Tan, W.C.: Muse: Mapping Understanding and deSign by Example. In: ICDE, pp. 10–19 (2008)
4. Alexe, B., et al.: Simplifying Information Integration: Object-Based Flow-of-Mappings Framework for Integration. In: Castellanos, M., Dayal, U., Sellis, T. (eds.) BIRTE 2008. LNBIP, vol. 27, pp. 108–121. Springer, Heidelberg (2009)
5. Alexe, B., Hernández, M.A., Popa, L., Tan, W.C.: MapMerge: Correlating Independent Schema Mappings. PVLDB 3(1), 81–92 (2010)
6. Alexe, B., Hernández, M.A., Popa, L., Tan, W.C.: MapMerge: Correlating Independent Schema Mappings. VLDB Journal 21(1), 1–21 (2012)
7. Alexe, B., Kolaitis, P.G., Tan, W.C.: Characterizing Schema Mappings via Data Examples. In: ACM PODS, pp. 261–272 (2010)
8. Alexe, B.: Interactive and Modular Design of Schema Mappings. Ph.D. thesis, University of California, Santa Cruz (2011)
9. Alexe, B., ten Cate, B., Kolaitis, P.G., Tan, W.C.: Characterizing schema mappings via data examples. ACM TODS 36(4) (2011)
10. Alexe, B., ten Cate, B., Kolaitis, P.G., Tan, W.C.: Eirene: Interactive design and refinement of schema mappings via data examples. PVLDB (Demonstration Track) (2011)
11. Beeri, C., Vardi, M.Y.: A Proof Procedure for Data Dependencies. JACM 31(4), 718–741 (1984)
12. Bernstein, P.A., Haas, L.M.: Information Integration in the Enterprise. Commun. ACM 51(9), 72–79 (2008)
13. Microsoft BizTalk Server, http://www.microsoft.com/biztalk
14. Bonifati, A., Chang, E.Q., Ho, T., Lakshmanan, L.V.S.: HepToX: Heterogeneous Peer to Peer XML Databases (2005),
    http://www.citebase.org/abstract?id=oai:arXiv.org:cs/0506002
15. Bonifati, A., Chang, E.Q., Ho, T., Lakshmanan, V.S., Pottinger, R.: HePToX: Marrying XML and Heterogeneity in Your P2P Databases. In: VLDB, pp. 1267–1270 (2005)
16. Fagin, R., Haas, L.M., Hernández, M., Miller, R.J., Popa, L., Velegrakis, Y.: Clio: Schema Mapping Creation and Data Exchange. In: Borgida, A.T., Chaudhri, V.K., Giorgini, P., Yu, E.S. (eds.) Conceptual Modeling: Foundations and Applications. LNCS, vol. 5600, pp. 198–236. Springer, Heidelberg (2009)
17. Fagin, R., Kolaitis, P.G., Miller, R.J., Popa, L.: Data Exchange: Semantics and Query Answering. TCS 336(1), 89–124 (2005)
18. Fagin, R., Kolaitis, P.G., Popa, L., Tan, W.C.: Composing Schema Mappings: Second-Order Dependencies to the Rescue. TODS 30(4), 994–1055 (2005)
19. Fuxman, A., Hernández, M.A., Ho, H., Miller, R.J., Papotti, P., Popa, L.: Nested Mappings: Schema Mapping Reloaded. In: VLDB, pp. 67–78 (2006)
20. International Nucleotide Sequence Database Collection, http://www.insdc.org

21. Kolaitis, P.G.: Schema Mappings, Data Exchange, and Metadata Management. In: PODS, pp. 61–75 (2005)
22. Lenzerini, M.: Data Integration: A Theoretical Perspective. In: PODS, pp. 233–246 (2002)
23. Madhavan, J., Halevy, A.Y.: Composing Mappings Among Data Sources. In: VLDB, pp. 572–583 (2003)
24. Maier, D., Mendelzon, A.O., Sagiv, Y.: Testing Implications of Data Dependencies. TODS 4(4), 455–469 (1979)
25. Altova MapForce, http://www.altova.com
26. Marnette, B., Mecca, G., Papotti, P., Raunich, S., Santoro, D.: ++spicy: an opensource tool for second-generation schema mapping and data exchange. PVLDB 4(12), 1438–1441 (2011)
27. Nash, A., Bernstein, P.A., Melnik, S.: Composition of Mappings Given by Embedded Dependencies. In: PODS, pp. 172–183 (2005)
28. Popa, L., Velegrakis, Y., Miller, R.J., Hernández, M.A., Fagin, R.: Translating Web Data. In: VLDB, pp. 598–609 (2002)
29. Rahm, E., Bernstein, P.A.: A Survey of Approaches to Automatic Schema Matching. VLDB Journal 10(4), 334–350 (2001)
30. Roth, M., Hernández, M.A., Coulthard, P., Yan, L., Popa, L., Ho, H.C.T., Salter, C.C.: XML Mapping Technology: Making Connections in an XML-centric World. IBM Sys. Journal 45(2), 389–410 (2006)
31. Shu, N.C., Housel, B.C., Taylor, R.W., Ghosh, S.P., Lum, V.Y.: EXPRESS: A Data EXtraction, Processing, and REStructuring System. ACM Trans. Database Syst. 2(2), 134–174 (1977)
32. Smith, J.M., Bernstein, P.A., Dayal, U., Goodman, N., Landers, T.A., Lin, K.W.T., Wong, E.: Multibase: Integrating Heterogeneous Distributed Database Systems. In: AFIPS National Computer Conference, pp. 487–499 (1981)
33. Stylus Studio, http://www.stylusstudio.com
34. U.S. Census Bureau, http://www.census.gov
35. Yan, L., Miller, R., Haas, L., Fagin, R.: Data-Driven Understanding and Refinement of Schema Mappings. In: SIGMOD, pp. 485–496 (2001)
36. Yu, C., Popa, L.: Semantic Adaptation of Schema Mappings when Schemas Evolve. In: VLDB, pp. 1006–1017 (2005)

User Trust and Judgments
in a Curated Database with Explicit Provenance

David W. Archer[1], Lois M.L. Delcambre[2], and David Maier[2]

[1] Galois Inc., Portland, OR 97204
[2] Portland State University, Portland, OR 97207-0751
dwa@galois.com, {lmd,maier}@cs.pdx.edu

Abstract. We focus on human-in-the-loop, information-integration settings where users gather and evaluate data from a broad variety of sources and where the levels of trust in sources and users change dynamically. In such settings, users must use their judgment as they collect and modify data. As an example, a battlefield information officer preparing a report to inform his or her superiors about the current state of affairs must gather and integrate data from many (including non-computerized) sources. By tracking multiple sources for individual values, the officer may eliminate a value from the current state whenever all of the sources where this value was found are no longer trusted. We define a conceptual model for a curated database with provenance for such settings, the Multi-granularity, Multi-provenance Model (*MMP*), which supports multiple insertions and multiple (copy-and-)paste operations for a single database element, captures the external source for all operations, and includes a Data Confidence Language that allows users to confirm or doubt values to record their atomic judgments about the data. In this paper, we briefly summarize the MMP model and show how it can be extended to support potentially complex operations including compound judgment operators (such as merging tuples to achieve entity resolution), while capturing a complete record of data provenance.

1   Introduction: Our Data-Curation Setting

Our work is motivated by our interest in a data curation setting – typically a human-in-the-loop setting – where a user is continually making judgments about the trustworthiness of data items. Green *et al.* point out that users often consider where data came from and how or by whom it has been modified in making such judgments [Green07]. As observed by Buneman *et al.*, [Buneman06] data curators are quite naturally performing information integration as they "use a wide variety of sources to select, organize, classify and annotate existing data into a database on some topic." Buneman and his colleagues also identified copy-and-paste as one of the key operations performed by data curators and noted that keeping track of the provenance due to user actions (in the form of data manipulations) is as important as keeping track of the resulting data. Their work was motivated, in part, by settings where the collective scientific community works together to evolve local copies of a single, shared database.

V. Tannen et al. (Eds.): Buneman Festschrift, LNCS 8000, pp. 89–111, 2013.

Our focus is on a somewhat different setting for curation where there are many competing and perhaps conflicting sources for (ordinary) data and where users may prepare different data products (from the same contributing data) to support different purposes. As an example, a battlefield information officer must collect and verify data for use by the local commander to decide on near-term actions. Alliances and allegiances can change, so a data source trusted yesterday might be in question today. In the same way, operations performed on data by a particular user during a particular time period may be in question. A user in this setting integrates data largely through manual, curatorial activities and each decision that he or she makes embodies his or her judgment.

The setting we envision has the following requirements:

- **track provenance of all operations that create or modify data** – The provenance record should include: the source of the information, the user (or automated process) who performed the operation, and the timestamp. The system must track queries (including materialized queries) and all data manipulation (DML) operations including copy-and-paste. We consider copy-and-paste as using an internal source (a value elsewhere in the same database) and insert as using an external source (some separate file or system). Since the schema may evolve over time, the provenance record should also track data definition (DDL) operations such as create or alter table statements.

- **record multiple internal and external sources for values** – Allowing users to indicate multiple sources for values is important in this setting. Consider a schema: Employee(Name, ID) with a relation instance containing one tuple <Bob, 8>. The source of this tuple could be recorded in the provenance record when it was originally inserted. User Betty could then find an additional external or internal source of information that confirms that Bob's ID is 8 and record this source as additional provenance for the tuple. In such a system, a single value in the database may have multiple histories based on DML operations alone.

- **provide full access to provenance and data** – Since users are aware of the actions performed on the data as well as the sources, they may find it useful to browse and query both data and provenance, including selecting data based on provenance. For example, user Candice might query Betty's database in order to search for data about Bob that was inserted from source S. Users may also wish to see the database as it existed at previous points in time.

- **allow users to record their confidence in data** – In this setting, users are often engaged in checking or corroborating data. Thus, it is useful to allow users to (simply) record their confidence (or lack thereof) in a value. For example, Candice might choose to record in the database that she has confidence in <Bob, 8>, perhaps because Bob told her that his ID is 8. Similarly, she might choose to record that she has reason to doubt some other data. Other users may consider these expressions of confidence and doubt when making their own judgments about the data.

We define trustworthiness of data to be a function of the user's trust in the sources from which the data came, the operations performed on it, the users who performed those operations, and the time periods when they were performed. Calculating a value of trustworthiness for an item of data thus requires that we: capture its provenance (as described above); allow the user to express levels of trust in the information sources, operations, and users represented in that provenance; and provide a method for computing a consistent mathematical valuation over that provenance and those levels of trust. These needs lead to one additional requirement:

- **determine user trust in external sources, users and timestamps with trustworthiness calculations** – By recording the level of trust in sources, (earlier) users who manipulated data, and in time periods, a user should be able to compute the current trustworthiness of data. Thus the system should support a systematic calculation of trustworthiness of data based on the provenance record much like the provenance polynomials developed by Green et al. [Green07b].

This paper presents the Multi-granularity, Multi-Provenance (*MMP*) Model [Archer11], a conceptual model designed to support this setting for data in a relational database. As a conceptual model, MMP is designed to make it easy for a user to browse and understand the complete record of the database as it evolved, with a complete record of its provenance. The state of the database at a point in time is called a *face*. MMP represents the complete record of user actions as a series of faces, ordered by timestamp, where each face is labeled with the identity of the user who performed the operation that created the face, the operation performed, and the timestamp at which the operation was applied. MMP includes a *Data Confidence Language (DCL)* that allows a user to confirm or doubt a given value; such operations are reflected in the provenance record (with the user and the date) but do not modify the value. Provenance is represented explicitly in MMP as links from components (i.e., relations, attributes, tuples, or values) in the current face to the components in the immediately preceding face from which the component was derived. MMP records provenance for query, data manipulation (DML), data definition (DDL), and data confidence (DCL) operations at various levels of granularity (i.e., table, attribute, tuple, and value) as appropriate for each operator in the model (multi-granularity) and explicitly allows for values to be inserted or (copy-and-)pasted multiple times, from different sources (multi-provenance). MMP represents external sources explicitly; provenance links are also used to connect each component (e.g., that was inserted) to the external source referent from which it was taken. MMP also includes a sub-language for use with traditional relational selection and projection operators that allows a user to select data based on its provenance [Archer10].

MMP builds on prior work in database provenance that records the provenance of tuples in a query answer, and prior work in curated databases that records the provenance of DML operations including the copy-and-paste operation. These previous works treat provenance as part of the data, affected by the same operations that affect data, and stored as additional schema elements (typically an additional attribute value for each tuple) along with data. Such an approach has several shortcomings with respect to how we expect provenance to be used. Because these models do not distinguish provenance from data, a user is left to manage and maintain provenance explicitly. For example, the user must take care not to delete or over-write provenance during each operation he or she performs. For the same reason, provenance must be queried using the query language for data, instead of allowing query language specifically for querying provenance. In these previous works it is possible to write a query that returns the provenance of selected data, but it is difficult to write a query that selects data based on its provenance. This difficulty arises because provenance is typically encoded in some sort of expression (e.g., polynomial) in an ordinary attribute; accessing data based on provenance would require parsing the provenance expressions. Because provenance in these models is treated as additional attribute values stored with data, deletion of the data leaves no place to retain its provenance, yet that provenance may be an important part of the provenance record of other data (previously derived from the deleted data) that is still present in the database. Because provenance in these models is stored as individual attribute values along with the data, these approaches limit data to having a single "history", preventing the system from representing, for example, multiple insertions of the same data from distinct sources. Because the relational model used in this prior work does not provide for recording provenance of all granularities of the data, it is not possible to represent some aspects of provenance. For example, this prior work does not support provenance for entire relations or entire attributes within relations. These models require complex computation and recursion over the database to convert "one-step" histories into a representation suitable for querying the full lineage of data. MMP addresses each of these shortcomings by providing a conceptual model where provenance has its own representation, semantics, and query language, and is managed independently of the data it describes. MMP also goes beyond these existing approaches by capturing additional information in the provenance record, including the external source (that was consulted), the user, and timestamp of each operation, by introducing data confidence operators, and by supporting multiple insert and paste operations for a value, a tuple, or a relation.

This paper contributes an overview of the MMP conceptual model and its formal definition and an explanation of how MMP operations can be easily combined in transactions to support complex operations including compound judgment operations. We illustrate this capability via an entity resolution operation (where two tuples are combined based on user judgment).

We describe the MMP model in Section 2 and provide an overview of its formal definition in Section 3. The formal definition allows us to demonstrate that MMP correctly supports polynomials [Green07b], extended to handle the additional features of external sources, DDL, DCL, and multiple insert and copy-and-paste operations. In Section 4, we describe how complex operations can be defined in MMP and we show how MMP supports trust-evaluation using polynomial expressions. Section 5 compares the work to related work in the field. Section 6 provides conclusions and a discussion of future work.

2   The Multi-granularity, Multi-Provenance Model (*MMP*)

The goal for MMP is to show the end-user a complete picture of both data and provenance in an understandable manner. MMP represents data and provenance orthogonally, with data accessible for users to create, modify, or delete but with provenance created as a by-product of the user operations and never modified. An MMP instance consists of a set of external sources (each represented as an un-interpreted token), a series of faces where each face is one instance of the database, and a set of provenance links from components in a face to components in the preceding face or to external sources.

Figure 1 shows two simple MMP instances with the current face shown in front with predecessor faces ordered. The left side of Figure 1 shows provenance links to an external source based on a tuple being inserted from that source (for example, based on user Betty inserting tuple <Bob, 8> into relation A from source X). The right side of Figure 1 shows provenance links introduced from the new face to the immediately preceding face when a relation is (copied and) pasted from another relation (for example, based on Betty copying the entirety of relation A from an existing relation B). In each case, the newly introduced face is labeled with the operation, user, and timestamp that led to the face. (The user is omitted in Figure 1 for brevity.) The left side of Figure 1 shows the provenance links for the tuple as well as *inherited* provenance links (described below and shown as dotted lines) for the attribute values in the tuple. The right side of Figure 1 shows provenance links at all four levels of granularity; relation A has a provenance link to relation B and additional provenance links (shown as dotted lines) are inherited as follows. Each attribute in relation A has a provenance link to the corresponding attribute in B; the tuple in A has a provenance link to the corresponding tuple in B; and each value in the tuple has a provenance link to its corresponding value. MMP defines provenance at the highest appropriate level of granularity for each supported operation and includes a set of inheritance rules that can compute the complete set of provenance links. As a result, MMP instances store the minimum explicit provenance links to represent complete provenance. For example, for the right hand side of Figure 1, an MMP instance need only store the single relation-level provenance link. For the left hand side of Figure 1, an MMP instance need only store the single tuple-level provenance link. The remaining links may be inferred from those links. In this paper, we focus on provenance links for tuples and values (assuming those links have been either induced directly by an MMP operation or deduced using the inheritance rules). Note that the database schema may change from one face to the next, based on DDL operations. The details of the inheritance rules for provenance and how DDL operations are supported in MMP can be found elsewhere [Archer11]. Once created, provenance links are permanent[1] and immutable.

In MMP, implicit, automatically derived provenance links, called *continuity links*, connect an unchanged component in one face to the identical component in the

---

[1] In an operational system, a user (with the appropriate privileges) should be able to delete the oldest faces and the associated provenance links that are deemed no longer useful.

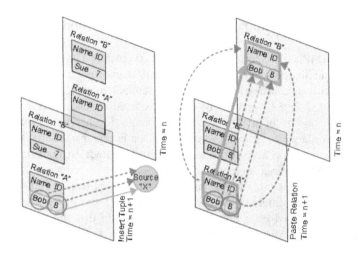

Fig. 1. Successive faces of two different *MMP* instances, with explicit and inherited links to an external source (left) for an insert operation and with explicit and inherited provenance links (right) for a (copy-and-)paste operation. Inherited links are shown as dotted lines.

Table 1. MMP operators (new operators shown in *bold*)

Note: *r* = relation, *t* = tuple, *a* = attribute, *v* = value, *s* = (external) source	
Note: for the paste operations: subscript *s* indicates source and subscript *t* indicates target	
Data Definition Operators (DDL)	**Data Manipulation Operators (DML)**
Create Relation(r)	*Insert Value(r, t, a, v, s)*
Create Source(name)	*Drop Value(r, t, a, s)*
Create Attribute(r, a)	*Insert Tuple(r, (a, v[, a, v, ...], s))*
Drop Relation(r)	*Drop Tuple(r, t, s)*
Drop Attribute(r, a)	*Paste Value(r$_t$, t$_t$, a$_t$, r$_s$, t$_s$, a$_s$)*
Data Confidence Operators (DCL)	*Paste Tuple(r$_t$, r$_s$, t$_s$)*
Confirm Value(r, t, a, v, s)	*Paste Relation(r$_t$, r$_s$)*
Doubt Value(r, t, a, v, s)	**Query Operators**
	select, project, join, union

immediately preceding face, called the *predecessor* of the component in the new face. Continuity links to predecessors are not shown in Figure 1 and are generally not shown to the user, though they are available when querying provenance.

The MMP operators are shown in Table 1, with new operators (beyond those found in a relational DBMS) shown in ***bold***. Each operator takes an MMP instance and creates a new MMP instance with at most one additional face, where the effect of the operator is reflected in the newly introduced face using the standard definition of relational database operators. MMP includes operators that create or drop attributes in a relational schema and operators that insert and drop values in a tuple, with the obvious semantics. The new Create Source DDL operator allows the user to introduce

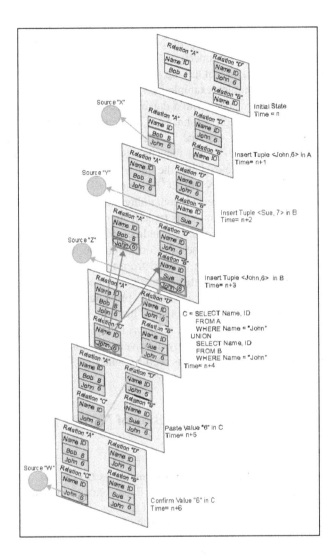

Fig. 2. MMP example showing three Inserts, one (materialized) query, a Paste, and a Confirm operation

a new external source reference (which is represented as an uninterpreted text string, in the current model). Create Source is the only operator that does not add a face to its input instance—it only augments the set of external sources. MMP includes new DML operators that allow a user to insert or drop individual values and that allow a user to paste a value, tuple, or relation. In MMP, a user can issue multiple insertions and pastes of data, with each represented as an additional source in the data's provenance, as long as the data inserted or pasted is identical to the existing data. A data component appears in all faces following the one in which it was created.

Every data item in a face has an associated *expired* flag that is initially set to *false*. When data is dropped (i.e., deleted) by an MMP operator, the expired flag is set to *true* in succeeding faces. MMP operators that correspond to standard relational operators[2] consider only the data that has the *expired* flag equal to *false*.

Figure 2 shows a more complex example using MMP, with seven successive faces. In this example, user Candice starts with a database containing relation A (with tuple <Bob, 8>), relation D (with tuple <John, 6>), and empty relation B. Candice first inserts <John, 6> into A from external source X. She then inserts <Sue, 7> into relation B from external source Y, and then inserts <John, 6> into relation B from external source Z. Next, Candice executes the query "C = SELECT Name, ID FROM A WHERE Name = "John" UNION SELECT Name, ID FROM B WHERE Name = "John". As a result, relation C is created, containing the single tuple <John, 6>. Next, Candice re-pastes the ID value "6" into this tuple from relation D, to indicate that D is another source of the same data. Finally, Candice indicates that she has additional confidence in "6" as John's ID because of information she found in external source "W". (The user and the timestamp are omitted from the labels in this example.) We see that insert operations and the confirm and doubt operations induce provenance links only to external sources. Queries induce provenance links at the relation, attribute, tuple, and value levels. For example, the value 6 in the query result has provenance links to the 6 from each of the relations involved in the query. A Confirm operation, the last one shown, induces only a provenance link to the external source used. (Continuity links to predecessors, as well as inherited links, are not shown in Figure 2.)

3   Overview of the Formal Definition of MMP

An MMP *instance M* consists of the following:

- **A finite sequence of relational databases instances $D = (d_1, d_2, ..., d_n)$**, where n is the current number of database instances. Each database instance in D is called a *face*. Each face d_i consists of a finite set of relations. Each *relation* consists of a finite set of tuples sharing a common schema consisting of a finite set of attributes. Each tuple includes at most one value from the domain of each attribute of the schema for the relation. The set of *components* C_i in a face d_i is the union of the relations, attributes, tuples, and values in d_i. Note that components are distinguished by the face in which they appear. For example, if a relation is present in face i (prior to an operation on the database) and is also present in face $i + 1$ (after that operation is applied), then an MMP instance would include two distinct components (one belonging to C_i and one belonging to C_{i+1}) to represent the relation appearing in the two faces. $C = \bigcup_{i=1}^{n} C_i$ is the set of components in D.

---

[2] MMP includes a predicate sublanguage for use in the relational algebra select and project operators; this sublanguage supports inspection of the expired flag. All other MMP operators work only with unexpired data.

- **A set of** *labels* $l_D = TS \times OpD \times U$. For a label $<ts, op, u>$ in l_D, $ts \in TS$ is a timestamp, $op \in OpD$ describes an operation from the MMP language as it was invoked, and $u \in U$ identifies a user of M.
- **A labeling function** λ_D**:** $D \rightarrow l_D$ that associates a label with each face $d \in D$, which indicates when the face was created, the operation involved, and the the user who applied the operation. We require that D is ordered by increasing timestamps of the labels of its faces.
- **A finite set** S **of** *external source referents* that represent external sources.
- **A finite set of** *provenance links* L, where each $l_p \in L$ is a hyper-edge from a component $c_{n+1} \in d_{n+1}$ to a non-empty set of components *in* d_n or an edge from a component $c_{n+1} \in d_{n+1}$ to an external source referent $s \in S$. A provenance link $l_p(c_{n+1}, B_n)$ indicates that the components in B_n, where $B_n \subseteq C_n$, collectively give rise to component c_{n+1} as a result of the operation that induced d_{n+1}. A provenance link $l_p(c_{n+1}, s)$ indicates that external source s gave rise to c_{n+1} as a result of an operation that induced d_{n+1}.
- **A finite set of** *continuity links,* each from a component in one face to the corresponding component in the immediately preceding face (if it exists), which is called the *predecessor*. The (partial) function *predecessor:* $C \rightarrow C$ delivers the predecessor of a component. Continuity links represent the implicit, trivial derivation of a component in d_{n+1} from its existence in d_n. All components in d_{n+1} not affected directly by the operation that created d_{n+1} have such a link.

Each MMP (non-query) operator and each composition of MMP query operators that constitute a single query takes an instance M with current database face d_n and produces a new instance M' with the following items added, as appropriate for the operator: zero or one additional face d_{n+1}, zero or more additional provenance links (from components in d_{n+1} to components in d_n or from components in d_{n+1} to external sources), a new labeling function λ_D (identical to the existing labeling function except that it is defined for one additional face, if the operator introduced a new face), a new set S with zero or one additional sources, and a new predecessor function (extending the existing predecessor function to the newly introduced components in d_{n+1} to define the new continuity links). An initial instance M consists of a single empty face, an empty set of sources (S), an empty set of provenance links (L), a labeling function defined only for the first face with a label $<time = 0$, null, null$>$ and an empty predecessor function.

3.1   Provenance Induced by MMP Operations

The provenance links that we introduce from components in one face to components in the immediately preceding face can be viewed as an explicit representation of the polynomials introduced by Green, *et al.* [Green07b], extended to handle the MMP operators, to represent provenance links from a component to an external source reference (when appropriate), and to support the labels associated with each operation. In MMP, we introduce one provenance link from a component c to a set B_n

of components to represent each distinct derivation for c. When the set B_n consists of more than one component, all of the components in B_n, collectively, are required for the derivation of c. The detailed description of the semantics of the MMP operations is defined elsewhere [Archer11]; we briefly describe how the MMP operators induce provenance here. Let M be an *MMP* instance with current face d_n. All of the operators (except Create Source) induce a new face d_{n+1} into M with the following modifications.

MMP DDL Operations:

Create Relation(r) adds a new empty relation named r to face d_{n+1}. *Create Attribute(r, a)* adds a new attribute to relation r in face d_{n+1}. The *Drop Relation* and *Drop Attribute* operations set the expired flag for the relevant component in d_{n+1} to *true*. None of these DDL operators induce provenance links. Note that *Create Source(name)* simply adds *name* to S and does not induce a new face and thus does not induce a label.

MMP DCL and DML Operations:

The *Confirm Value(r, t, a, v, s)* operation (and similarly *Doubt Value*) creates face d_{n+1} identical to face d_n and introduces a provenance link from the value v (for ·attribute a in tuple t in relation r) in face d_{n+1} to external source referent s.

The *Insert Value(r, t, a, v, s)* operation adds the new value v (for attribute a in tuple t in relation r), in face d_{n+1} and creates a provenance link from v to external source referent s, in the case when a value does not exist for attribute a in tuple t in relation r in face d_n. Similarly, *Insert Tuple(r, (a, v[, a, v, ...], s))* introduces a new tuple into face d_{n+1} for relation r with a provenance link to s if the tuple does not yet exist in face d_n. If the value or the tuple exists in d_n, then the existing value or the tuple must be identical to the inserted value or tuple. In this case, the effect of the *Insert Value* or *Insert Tuple* operator is to introduce a new face with the a provenance link from the value or tuple in the new face to the designated source referent s (effectively a re-insert operation).

Drop Value(r, t, a, s) and *Drop Tuple(r, t, s)* set the expired flag to true for the value or tuple, respectively, and introduce a provenance link from the value or tuple to source s.

The three paste operations, *Paste Value(r_t, t_t, a_t, r_s, t_s, a_s)*, *Paste Tuple(r_t, r_s, t_s)*, and *Paste Relation(r_t, r_s)*, where subscript t indicates the *target* and subscript s indicates the *source*, insert the source value (for relation r, tuple t, attribute a), tuple (for relation r, tuple t), or relation (for relation r)—in the case when it does not exist—and creates a provenance link from the target value, tuple, or relation to the source value, tuple, or relation. If the component exists in d_n, then it must be identical to the pasted component. In this case, the paste operation creates a provenance link, as described above, from the component in d_{n+1} to the component from which it was copied in d_n (effectively a re-paste operation).

MMP Queries:

All relations mentioned in a query must be in the current face, d_n, of an MMP instance M. A query in this form produces a new face d_{n+1} with the query result relation r_{new} (assuming that r_{new} is not yet in face d_{n+1}), using the normal semantics of these operators. Although the MMP model induces provenance for relations, attributes, tuples, and attribute values as described elsewhere [Archer11], we describe here only the provenance for tuples in the query answer. We define the provenance links introduced by query operators, recursively.

The cross product operator, $r_{new} = r_{n,1} \times \ldots \times r_{n,A}$, for input relations $r_{n,x}$, $1 \le x \le A$, on face d_n, induces one provenance link for each tuple t_{new} in the query result r_{new}. Each result tuple is linked by this provenance link to all of the tuples, one from each $r_{n,x}$, $1 \le x \le A$, that contributed to t_{new}. MMP introduces a single provenance link for each tuple t_{new} in the query result because all of the tuples from face d_n together are needed to derive t_{new}, for the cross product operator.

The select operator, $\sigma_{condition}(r_{n,i})$, for some input relation r_i on face d_n, induces one provenance link for each tuple t_{new} in the query answer that connects t_{new} to the identical tuple t_{old} in d_n. There is at most one such tuple.

The project operator, $r_{new} = \pi_{columnList}(r_{n,i})$, for some input relation r_i on face d_n, induces one provenance link for each tuple t_{new} in the query result that connects t_{new} to one of the tuples in r_i that resulted in t_{new}. The project operator introduces one provenance link for each tuple in face d_n from which t_{new} was derived because they each represent an independent derivation for t_{new}.

The union operator, $r_{new} = r_{n,1} \cup \ldots \cup r_{n,A}$, for input relations r_x, $1 \le x \le A$, on face d_n, induces multiple provenance links for each tuple t_{new} in the query result, one for each tuple in an input relation that is identical to t_{new}. MMP introduces multiple provenance links because any one of the identical tuples from an input relation can independently result in t_{new}.

To represent the provenance of complex queries in *MMP*, SPJU queries are first converted to the following form, with A terms in a multiway union:

$$\pi_1 \sigma_1 \left(r_{1,1} \times \ldots \times r_{1,q_1} \right) \cup \ldots \cup \pi_A \sigma_A \left(r_{A,1} \times \ldots \times r_{A,q_A} \right)$$

The attribute list for the project operators (π_i, $1 \le i \le A$) and the conditions for the select operators (σ_i, $1 \le i \le A$) are not shown in this expression. All input relations are on the current face and the result relation is created on the new face introduced by this query; we omit the subscript for face on the relations shown here, for simplicity. One can view the provenance induced by a query of this form as the provenance induced in four successive faces where the first face contains the results of the multiway cross-product operators, the second face contains the result of the select operators (each with the result from the appropriate cross-product operator as input), the third face contains the result of the project operators (each with the result from the appropriate select operator as input), and the fourth face contains the result of the multiway union. In MMP, without loss of generality, we compose the provenance links from these four faces; the resulting provenance links are induced from tuples in the final query answer in d_{n+1} to the appropriate tuples in d_n.

3.2   Provenance Polynomials in MMP

Green *et al.* [Green07b] show how to express several forms of database provenance using algebraic expressions from various underlying semi-rings. The resulting polynomial expressions can be stored as text strings in an annotation field that is added to the tuples to represent provenance. The explicit and implicit (inherited and continuity) provenance links in MMP, with provenance represented separately from relational data, capture the information present in the most expressive polynomials defined by Green et al. for use in Orchestra. In MMP, we extend the work of Green *et al.* in the following ways:

- We represent multi-generation (not just single-generation) provenance by composing polynomials.
- We include the operations performed, identity of users performing them, and time at which they were performed.
- We include provenance due to DDL and DML in addition to query operations.
- We allow for polynomials at all levels of granularity: relation, tuple, and attribute value.

Since MMP allows multiple insert and paste operations for a single tuple or value and since each such insert or paste operation can independently contribute the tuple or value in question, the polynomial expressions for MMP use the + operation to combine the provenance from such multiple insert and paste operations. Also, as in Green *et al.*'s approach, the + operation is used to combine the provenance links induced by the union and project query operators.

Consider an MMP instance M with components C and external source referents S. In the following discussion we refer to components in C and S and variables that represent those components in our polynomial expressions interchangeably. Let $V = C \cup S$. We define $Prov^{SN}$ to be a semi-ring $(V, +, \bullet, 0, 1)$, where + is algebraic addition and $\bullet$ is algebraic multiplication. The provenance of $c \in C$ is represented by a polynomial expression in $Prov^{SN}$ where + represents that any of its terms alone gives rise to c, and $\bullet$ represents that all of its terms together give rise to c. For example, if the provenance of c is $x_1 \bullet x_2 + x_3$, for $c \in C$ and $x_1, x_2,$ and $x_3 \in V$, then c is present in V because both x_1 and x_2 were present as inputs to an operation that had c as output, and is independently present because x_3 was present as an input to a (possibly distinct) operation that gave rise to c.

Let K be the set of constants, if any, introduced by queries that have previously run on M. Assume that we want to compute the provenance of a component c. Let C_{stop} be a set of components[3] of the same type as c in M specified by the user beyond which no provenance should be represented in the polynomial expression. Let B be the subset of C that appears in the face of the MMP instance immediately preceding the face in which c appears. Let $c' = predecessor(c)$, if it is defined. Note that any component has at most one predecessor consisting of the identical copy of the

---

[3] Typically, all of the components in C_{stop} are in the same face, but they need not be.

component c in the immediately preceding face (based on the continuity link between components unaffected by the operation that created the new face). Let c originate N provenance links, $l_1(c, B_1), \ldots, l_N(c, B_N)$, where link l_X, $1 \leq X \leq N$, has a terminal at each $b_{X,Y} \in B_X$, $1 \leq Y \leq |B_X|$. For a component c in face d_n of M, the provenance of c in $Prov^{SN}$ is defined recursively as

$$Prov^{SN}(c) =$$

$$\left[\begin{array}{l} c \quad \text{if } c \in \left(S \cup K \cup C_{stop} \right) \\[2mm] \sum_{X=1}^{N} \left(\prod_{Y=1}^{|BX|} Prov^{SN}(b_{X,Y}) + Prov^{SN}(c') \quad \text{if } c \in (S \cup K \cup C_{stop}) \right. \\ \qquad\qquad\qquad \text{and } c' = predecessor(c), if\ predecessor(c)\ is\ defined \\[2mm] \sum_{X=1}^{N} \left(\prod_{Y=1}^{|BX|} Prov^{SN}(b_{X,Y}) \right) \quad otherwise \end{array} \right.$$

Here, summation indicates the $+$ operation in $Prov^{SN}$, and product indicates the $\bullet$ operation in $Prov^{SN}$. Recursion stops when original sources, constants induced by queries, or stopping points specified by the user are encountered. By including the option for stopping points, we can represent as many generations of a component's provenance as the user wishes to see. If C_{stop} is the set of components in the face immediately preceding the one where c first appears, then $Prov^{SN}(c)$ is the single-generation provenance of c, comparable to most provenance representations from the literature. If C_{stop} is the empty set, then $Prov^{SN}(c)$ is the complete multi-generation provenance of c, which traces back every provenance path to a query constant or an external source.

As an example, consider the MMP instance in Figure 2. Assume that the attribute value 6 for the ID attribute value in tuple 1 of relation D on face n is a constant induced by a previous query. Let $S = \{W, X, Y, Z\}$ represent the external sources shown in Figure 2. Let c be the attribute value of 6 for the attribute ID in the first tuple of relation C at $time = n + 6$. Then

$$Prov^{SN}(c) = Prov^{SN}(n1) + W$$

where n1 = predecessor (c) (i.e., the value 6 in the first tuple of relation C in face n + 5), and W is the source for the Confirm value operation shown in the label for face n + 6. Expanding further, we see that

$$Prov^{SN}(c) = (Prov^{SN}(n2) + Prov^{SN}(n3)) + W$$

where n2 = predecessor(n1) (i.e., the value 6 in the first tuple of relation C in face n + 4) and n3 is the value 6 in first tuple of relation D based on the provenance link to face n + 4. Following another step of expansion, we see then that

$$Prov^{SN}(c) = (Prov^{SN}(n4) + Prov^{SN}(n5)) + Prov^{SN}(n6) + W$$

where n4 is the value 6 in the first tuple of relation A in face n + 3 and n5 is the value 6 in the first tuple of relation B in face n + 3 based on the provenance links for the query shown in the label for face n + 4. And n6 = $predecessor$(n3) (i.e., the value 6 in relation the first tuple in relation D in face n + 3). Continuing, we see that

$$Prov^{SN}(c) = Prov^{SN}(n7) + Z + Prov^{SN}(n8) + W$$

where n7 = $predecessor$(n4) (i.e., the value 6 in the second tuple of relation A in face n + 2), Z is the source of the Insert tuple operation shown in the label of face n + 3, and n8 = $predecessor$(n6) (i.e., the value 6 in the first tuple of relation D in face n + 2). Next, we see that

$$Prov^{SN}(c) = Prov^{SN}(n9) + Z + Prov^{SN}(n10) + W$$

where n9 = $predecessor$(n7) (i.e., the value 6 in relation A in face n + 1) and n10 = $predecessor$(n8) (i.e., the value 6 in the first tuple of relation B in face n + 1). Finally,

$$Prov^{SN}(c) = X + Z + n11 + W$$

where X is the source of the Insert tuple operation shown in the label of face n + 1 and n11 = $predecessor$(n10) (i.e., the value 6 in the first tuple in relation D in face n). As described above, n11 was introduced by an earlier query; thus n11 ∈ K.

The recursive expansion of $Prov^{SN}$ expressions terminates in polynomial time, because provenance graphs are acyclic, traversal follows the indicated direction of the directed edges in our graphs, (i.e., from d_{n+1} to d_n), and no provenance links originate from external source or query-constant nodes.

We extend the definition of $Prov^{SN}$ to include variables representing the label associated with the provenance link. To do so, we introduce the function $LabelToVars$, which maps the label on the relevant face to a product of representative variables:

$$Prov^{SN}(c) =$$

$$
\begin{bmatrix}
c & \text{if } c \in \left(S \cup K \cup C_{stop}\right) \\
\sum_{X=1}^{N}\left(\prod_{Y=1}^{|BX|} LabelToVars(\lambda_D(d_n))Prov^{SN}\left(b_{X,Y}\right) + Prov^{SN}(c') & \text{if} \\
c \in \left(S \cup K \cup C_{stop}\right) \text{ and} \\
c' = predecessor(c), \text{if } predecessor(c) \text{ is defined} \\
\sum_{X=1}^{N}\left(\prod_{Y=1}^{|BX|} LabelToVars(\lambda_D(d_n)) Prov^{SN}\left(b_{X,Y}\right)\right) & \text{otherwise}
\end{bmatrix}
$$

Face d_n in the above expressions is the face in D that contains the component $b_{X,Y}$. Simply stated, each step through an ancestor $b_{X,Y}$ of c induces a product of variables $LabelToVars(\lambda_D(d_n))$ where one variable represents the user, one represents the operation, and one represents the timestamp of the label applied at that step. As an example, for the face with the label <n+1, 'Insert tuple', 'Candice'>:

$$LabelToVars(<n+1, \text{'Insert tuple'}, \text{'Candice'}>) = \tau_{1\text{time}} \bullet \tau_{1\text{op}} \bullet \tau_{1\text{user}}$$

where $\tau_{1\text{time}}$ represents the timestamp n+1, $\tau_{1\text{op}}$ represents the operations 'Insert tuple', and $\tau_{1\text{user}}$ represents 'Candice'. Thus the value of $Prov^{SN}(c)$ from the example above is:

$$\tau_{1\text{time}} \bullet \tau_{1\text{op}} \bullet \tau_{1\text{user}} \bullet X +$$
$$\tau_{2\text{time}} \bullet \tau_{2\text{op}} \bullet \tau_{2\text{user}} \bullet Z +$$
$$\tau_{3\text{time}} \bullet \tau_{3\text{op}} \bullet \tau_{3\text{user}} \bullet n11 +$$
$$\tau_{4\text{time}} \bullet \tau_{4\text{op}} \bullet \tau_{4\text{user}} \bullet W$$

4   Exploiting Judgments in MMP

The DDL, DML, DCL and query language of MMP allow users to manipulate a curated database with provenance. We view each such action as embodying the judgment of a user or a (possibly automated) proxy of a user. Thus we view the MMP model as providing the capability to support and capture basic, atomic judgments of users. Here we describe how additional, compound judgment operations can be supported in MMP.

Defining a priori the allowable set of judgment operations assumes that we could anticipate the needs of a wide variety of users. Instead, we augment the MMP model with a means to implement such higher-level operations via sequences of primitive operations in a transaction or compound operation. We also show how MMP data and provenance can be used to make a trust assessment about components based on user valuations of trustworthiness for sources, users, operations, and timestamps that appear in the provenance. These two extensions are described in the subsections below followed by an example of a compound judgment operation for entity resolution.

4.1   Compound Operations (Transactions) in MMP

An MMP transaction consists of a sequence of MMP operations. The intermediate and final results of a transaction are thus represented by a sequence of consecutive faces in an MMP instance. To distinguish transactions in MMP, we add two components to the label associated with each face in an MMP: a transaction type and a transaction identifier. The transaction type is a string representing the name of the compound operation that was performed. For example, the transaction type might be "entity resolution". The transaction ID is a natural number (distinct from the timestamp) and is strictly monotonically increasing across transactions. Note that, for simplicity, we assume here that users issue transactions one at a time. All of the faces in a given transaction have the same transaction type, identifier, and user and, as a result, all of the faces for one transaction are consecutive in an MMP instance.

Recall from Section 3 that an MMP instance includes a labeling function λ_D: D $\rightarrow l_D$, which associates a label drawn from a set of labels $l_D = TS \times OpD \times U$ with each newly introduced face $d \in D$. We introduce transactions into MMP by extending l_D:

$$l_D = TS \times OpD \times U \times TT \times ID$$

where TT is a set of strings identifying recognized transaction types and ID is a natural number representing the transaction's unique identity. We correspondingly extend the *LabelToVars* function to accept our new definition of face labels as input and produce two additional variables in the product (one variable for transaction type and one for transaction ID).

4.2   Provenance Polynomial Evaluation in MMP

For a given component c in an MMP instance and a given set of stopping points, the provenance polynomial for the component, $Prov^{SN}(c)$, follows from the MMP instance, as described in Section 3.2. Each polynomial expression includes symbols that represent provenance *constituents*: external sources, users, timestamps, operations, transaction types, transaction IDs, and constants introduced by queries. If the set of stopping points is empty, then these symbols are the only ones that can appear in the polynomial expression. If the set of stopping points is non-empty, then the polynomial expression may also include symbols that represent individual components, just as the symbols in a polynomial expression as defined by Green *et al.* represent individual tuples.

There are many ways to evaluate trust using a polynomial. One way to do so is to replace each symbol in the polynomial by its current *trust value*. As a simple example, consider a trust value as either 0 or 1, indicating that a constituent is not trusted (0) or is trusted (1). Using the approach of Green *et al.* where trust values are 0 or 1 and + and • have the ordinary semantics of arithmetic, evaluating a polynomial results in a value that is 0 (if the component that corresponds to this polynomial expression cannot be derived from trusted components based on the current trust values) or a natural number t greater than 0 (if the component that corresponds to this polynomial expression can be derived in t distinct ways from trusted components). In general, all trust values must be known in order to compute the current state of the database. In practice, trust values need only be supplied for the symbols that appear in the polynomials for the components of interest.

Recall that in Section 3.2 we defined $V = C \cup S$ to be the variables in our provenance semi-ring $Prov^{SN}$. One simple way to define trust is as a function *trust:* V $\rightarrow \{0, 1\}$ that delivers the trust value for each symbol in V, assuming a simple binary trust model. The trust function could also use values in the range $[0, 1]$ to represent a finer granularity of trust. Given a component c in the latest face of M, a set of stopping points C_{stop}, and a *trust* function, we define the *ProvEval* operator as follows. *ProvEval(c, C_{stop}, trust)* is the value resulting from evaluation of $Prov^{SN}(c)$ using the function *trust*. The evaluation proceeds by normal substitution of values taken from *trust(c)* for each variable representing c. The resulting mathematical expression is then evaluated in the MMP provenance semi-ring to produce a numerical value, which is the valuation of $ProvEval(c, C_{stop}, trust)$.

As an example of provenance evaluation, recall that Candice was the user who applied all the operations in Figure 2 in our earlier example. Assume that Betty is interested in establishing the trustworthiness of Bob's ID value of 6, recorded in the first tuple of relation C in Figure 2. Let component d be a stopping point for provenance computation. Assume that each operation is in a distinct transaction, with no predefined transaction type. Then:

$$\tau_{1time} \bullet \tau_{1op} \bullet \tau_{1user} \bullet \tau_{1ttype} \bullet \tau_{1tid} =$$
$$LabelToVars(<n+1, \text{“Insert tuple”}, \text{“Candice”}, null, T1>)$$

$$\tau_{2time} \bullet \tau_{2op} \bullet \tau_{2user} \bullet \tau_{2ttype} \bullet \tau_{2tid} =$$
$$LabelToVars(<n+3, \text{“Insert tuple”}, \text{“Candice”}, null, T2>)$$

$$\tau_{3time} \bullet \tau_{3op} \bullet \tau_{3user} \bullet \tau_{3ttype} \bullet \tau_{3tid} =$$
$$LabelToVars(<n+4, \text{“Query”}, \text{“Candice”}, null, T3>)$$

$$\tau_{4time} \bullet \tau_{4op} \bullet \tau_{4user} \bullet \tau_{4ttype} \bullet \tau_{4tid} =$$
$$LabelToVars(<n+5, \text{“Paste value”}, \text{“Candice”}, null, T4>)$$

$$\tau_{5time} \bullet \tau_{5op} \bullet \tau_{5user} \bullet \tau_{5ttype} \bullet \tau_{5tid} =$$
$$LabelToVars(<n+6, \text{“Confirm value”}, \text{“Candice”}, null, T5>)$$

Let c be the component that is the value 6 in the first tuple of relation C on face n+6 in Figure 2. Then the provenance polynomial for c is:

$$Prov^{SN}(c) = \tau_{3time} \bullet \tau_{3op} \bullet \tau_{3user} \bullet \tau_{3ttype} \bullet \tau_{3tid}((\tau_{1time} \bullet \tau_{1op} \bullet \tau_{1user} \bullet \tau_{1ttype} \bullet \tau_{1tid} \bullet X) \bullet$$
$$(\tau_{2time} \bullet \tau_{2op} \bullet \tau_{2user} \bullet \tau_{2ttype} \bullet \tau_{2tid} \bullet Z)) + \tau_{4time} \bullet \tau_{4op} \bullet \tau_{4user} \bullet \tau_{4ttype} \bullet \tau_{4tid} \bullet n11$$
$$+ \tau_{5time} \bullet \tau_{5op} \bullet \tau_{5user} \bullet \tau_{5ttype} \bullet \tau_{5tid} \bullet W$$

Here we show three possible definitions for the trust function:

Element of $Prov^{SN}(c)$	Trust function A	Trust function B	Trust function for entity-resolution example
X	1	0	1
Z	1	1	0
n11	1	1	1
W	1	1	1
all τ variables	1	1	1

Using trust function A from the above table, $Prov^{SN}(c)$ evaluates to 3 indicating that there are three independent, trusted derivations that give rise to c. If, for example, we modify the trust function such that X maps to 0 to indicate that X is not trustworthy, as shown in trust function B in the above table, then the resulting value of the $Prov^{SN}$ expression is 2. If Betty chooses B as her model of trustworthiness, then she might reasonably interpret the resulting value as an indication that Bob's ID value of 6 is trustworthy. Had the value of the provenance expression evaluated to 0, Betty might have reasonably decided that she should not trust that Bob's ID was 6.

4.3   Example: Entity Resolution in MMP

In an earlier provenance model [Archer08], we formally defined and implemented an operator for entity resolution. The operator required that the user indicate the two tuples to be resolved. Then for each attribute where the values for the two tuples were different, the user was required to indicate which of the two values he or she preferred to retain in the resolved tuple. The provenance of the entity resolution was recorded in a history table in our earlier model. That model also included an "undo" operator that could reverse an entity resolution provided that none of the contributing attribute values had been changed in the interval between the original entity resolution operation and the undo operation. In MMP, an entity resolution can be implemented as a series of lower-level MMP operations. Consider an example schema: Employee(empNo, name, age, phone), and a relation C implementing an instance of this schema, and containing two tuples:

$$t_1 = <107, \text{"Joe"}, 25, 555\text{-}5555>, \text{the first tuple in relation C}$$
$$t_2 = <107, \text{"Joe"}, 27, 555\text{-}5555>, \text{the second tuple in relation C}$$

Suppose that the user wishes to resolve these tuples, and wishes to choose the value for age by selecting the value with the highest trust value. Suppose also that
$$Prov^{SN}((C, 1, age)) = X + W, \text{ and } Prov^{SN}((C, 2, age)) = X + Z$$
and that the trust function yields trust values as shown in the fourth column of the table above. (We omit the labels from this expression, for brevity.)

We can accomplish entity resolution for this case in MMP by the following series of operations, expressed in an informal syntax, which taken together comprise an MMP transaction. In the example, comments are prefaced by '//':

// begin transaction to resolve t1 and t2 from C into a new t3
// first, evaluate trust we have in the differing candidate attribute values
trustInTuple1 = ProvEval(C, t1, C_{stop} = ∅, T); // in our example, value is 2
trustInTuple2 = ProvEval(C, t2, C_{stop} = ∅, T); // in our example, value is 1
// next, formulate a new tuple in C, and return an identifier for it
tupleID =
Insert Tuple(C, (empNo, null, age, null, name, null, phone, null),null); // create new tuple
Paste Value (C, tupleID, empNo, C, t1, empNo); // empNo set by and has provenance from t1
Paste Value (C, tupleID, empNo, C, t2, empNo); // empNo also has provenance from t2
Paste Value (C, tupleID, phone, C, t1, phone); // as above, for phone attribute
Paste Value (C, tupleID, phone, C, t2, phone);
Paste Value (C, tupleID, name, C, t1, name); // as above, for name attribute
Paste Value (C, tupleID, name, C, t2, name); //
If (trustInTuple2 > trustInTuple1) // choose origin of age by using more trusted tuple
   Then Paste Value (C, tupleID, age, C, t2, age);
   Else Paste Value (C, tupleID, age, C, t1, age);
// now delete the original tuples, leaving the resolved tuple in their place
Drop Tuple (C, t1, null);
Drop Tuple (C, t2, null);
// end transaction

5   Related Work

Much of the work on models for provenance and relational data has focused on describing the connection from items (e.g., tuples) in a query answer to the items (e.g., tuples) in the input database from which it was derived. As an aid in contrasting such provenance models, we define the following distinguishing attributes. **History**. An *ancestry-only* model documents only the identity of data items contributing to a derived item. An *abstract* history model includes ancestry-only history as well as a representation of how the ancestors combined to form the derived item. A *full* history model provides enough information to fully reproduce the query result given query inputs. For example, a full history model might document the entire query text in addition to the source data for the query. **Eagerness**. We characterize provenance models by whether they compute and record provenance at the time an operation derives a result, or whether provenance is derived later, when a user wishes to inspect it. We call the former *eager* provenance and the latter *lazy* provenance. **Independence**. We classify provenance models by whether provenance is recorded as an annotation to data (including annotations stored in auxiliary relations), or has an independent existence in the model. We call the former *provenance-as-attribute* and the latter *provenance-as-entity*. **Granularity**. *Some-granularity* models record provenance for only some of the granularities of data supported by the data model, while *all-granularity* models support provenance for all granularities supported by the data model.

Cui and Widom [Cui00] address the problem of tracing data items in a data warehouse back to the source items from which they were derived. The resulting provenance model, called the *Lineage* model, is lazy, computing provenance by use of inverse queries run when users wish to trace provenance. The model is ancestry-only, recording only the set of tuples that causes a result tuple to appear. Lineage is a provenance-as-attribute model, recording provenance as an extra attribute for each tuple. In contrast, MMP is an eager, full-history, provenance-as-entity model. Because only provenance of tuples is recorded, Lineage is a some-granularity model, while MMP is an all-granularity model. Lineage also differs from MMP in that it computes provenance only for relational algebra operators (i.e., queries), while MMP additionally addresses DML and DDL operators.

Bhagwat et al. [Bhagwat04] present a general-purpose annotation-management system for relational databases. The system they describe acts as a provenance model when annotations consist of the identities of ancestor data. These annotations attach to each attribute value, rather than entire tuples. The model is thus a some-granularity, provenance-as-attribute model. Because the system is intended for general annotations, an implementation of the model could use any history approach. This model is eager, but addresses only provenance due to query operations.

Copy-Paste Database (CPDB) [Buneman06] defined the data curation setting. Curated databases in disciplines such as bioinformatics are typically maintained by significant manual correction, integration, and manipulation. Buneman noted that as a result, provenance information for such data is a key factor in assessing data quality. The CPDB provenance model was motivated by the provenance needs of users operating in such settings. Unlike other models in the literature, CPDB is a full-history model, although it only addresses DML operations, not queries or DDL operations. In work subsequent to CPDB, Buneman *et al.* developed a framework based on CPDB for managing provenance due to queries as well as data manipulations in a single model [Buneman08]. CPDB is an eager, provenance-as-attribute model. CPDB is unique among the models we consider in that, like MMP, it is an all-granularity model. CPDB does not address multiple insertions of identical data (nor tracking of multiple histories) as MMP does.

Trio supports both data uncertainty and provenance [Agrawal06]. We restrict our consideration of Trio to data operations without uncertainty. Trio is an eager, some-granularity, provenance-as-attribute model. Like Lineage, this provenance includes where data came from, but not what manipulations were done, nor who performed them: an ancestry-only model. Trio's language supports queries as well as data manipulation, but does not support multiple insertions as MMP does. Trio is the only current model besides MMP that retains deleted data. It is also the only current model that provides a provenance-specific built-in function, *Lineage()*, to help users in writing provenance-related queries.

Orchestra [Green07] is a system designed to allow sharing of data among peer databases. The provenance representation used in Orchestra expresses both ancestor data and a loose (algebraic) description of how data was derived, so we classify it as an abstract-history model. This representation uses semi-rings of polynomials [Green07b], similar to MMP provenance polynomials but not as expressive. In Orchestra, these polynomials are restricted so that there is no concept of derivations that include multiple operations applied over time. Because of this restriction, multiple insertions are not part of the Orchestra model, and there is no notion of multi-generation provenance in Orchestra. In contrast, MMP supports both of these capabilities.

The models discussed here are typical of models in the literature in that they specify how provenance is stored and how it is internally represented. MMP is a notable exception, specifying only what information is recorded and what its semantics are. MMP also specifies limits on how provenance may be manipulated. These differences lead us to categorize MMP as a conceptual provenance model, and the others as logical provenance models.

We evaluated the Lineage, Bhagwat, CPDB, Trio, and Orchestra models discussed above and discovered four gaps of interest that motivated our work on MMP: 1) these models do not model provenance resulting from a mix of DDL, DML, and query operations; 2) in each of these models, users must parse and interpret each provenance representation manually in order to select data or make other decisions based on provenance; 3) in each of these models, users must assemble multi-generation provenance manually before querying or browsing it; and 4) query languages used in implementations of these models are designed for relational data, and so are not well-suited to phrase queries over provenance. MMP addresses the first of these gaps by modeling provenance for all operations. MMP addresses gaps 2, 3, and 4 in several ways. First, MMP includes provenance graphs that show an intuitive representation of provenance that requires no user parsing or reconstruction. The MMP predicate language (described elsewhere) allows users to describe the characteristics of provenance that are required for their query, which MMP uses to compare against MMP-stored provenance information, so that users need not interpret nor parse provenance representations. The MMP model natively represents multiple-generation provenance, so that users need not manually assemble multiple generations of provenance information before using it.

6   ·Conclusions

MMP is a conceptual model for data and provenance in relational databases that addresses several shortcomings of other provenance models. MMP models data and provenance orthogonally, giving provenance first-class status. MMP models provenance at all levels of data granularity. MMP also allows for multiple insertions of identical data, allowing users to represent the case of data appearing in multiple sources. MMP also includes a Data Confidence Language that allows users to confirm or doubt values to record users' atomic judgments about the data. In this paper, we extend MMP to support potentially complex operations such as merging tuples, while capturing a complete record of provenance.

This paper contributes an overview of the MMP model and two extensions to support compound judgment operations. In our entity-resolution example, note that although the operation requires multiple primitive operations on the database, a single transaction in our extended MMP model associates all of these operators. Also note that the operations within the transaction are explicit about how attribute values are selected, because they reference immutable provenance state, fixed constants for trust valuation, and an explicit comparison of resulting trustworthiness to select attribute values. This combination of transactions and explicit evaluation of provenance is more expressive than our original MMP model in two ways. First, association of all primitive operations that comprise the complex operation makes the extent of the manipulations in the compound operation explicit in the model, where in MMP this information must be recorded outside the model. Second, decision criteria used in the compound operation are made explicit in the model, where in MMP these criteria are also not expressible.

Other work on MMP [Archer11] includes the definition of a logical model that supports the full MMP model without redundant storage embodied in the faces and provenance links. We proved that the effect of each MMP operation in the conceptual model is equivalent to the effect of the corresponding operation at the logical level. We demonstrated the existence of a surjective homomorphism between our provenance semi-ring, $Prov^{SN}$, and that of Green, $\mathbb{N}[X]$, to show that $Prov^{SN}$ is at least as expressive as $\mathbb{N}[X]$. We further showed that there can be no surjective mapping from $\mathbb{N}[X]$ to $Prov^{SN}$, due to the presence in $Prov^{SN}$ of variables representing operators, users, and timestamps, thus showing that $Prov^{SN}$ is more expressive. We classified provenance-related queries over relational data, and developed sample queries for each class, stated in the language of MMP and the language of one or more of the CPDB (in Datalog), Trio (in TriQL), and Orchestra (also in TriQL) models. We showed that MMP can express at least some queries in all classes of provenance-related queries we defined, while the other models we considered cannot express queries in all classes. We also evaluated the complexity of provenance-related queries by writing queries for MMP, CPDB, Trio, and Orchestra in eight of the classes of queries considered using Levitin's token count [Levitin86] as a metric for the complexity of queries. We found that queries written in Datalog for Buneman's model were uniformly more complex that those written for MMP by Levitin's metric and that queries for Trio and Green's model were comparable in complexity to those written for MMP.

There are several interesting questions that we intend to pursue with regard to MMP. For example, our choices for construction of provenance polynomials and their trust evaluation are by no means the only ones possible. We may also examine other semi-rings for polynomial evaluation. Users in a data curation setting may wish to represent multiple possible values for data when a single value is not clearly the correct one. We plan to explore the addition of multi-valued attribute values to MMP, and to study how our provenance model evolves with this addition. At present, trust (and other) evaluations of data in MMP are constrained to be viewed "one granularity at a time." For example, trust evaluation of tuples is done independently of trust evaluation of attribute values in tuples. We plan to explore ways to make such evaluations that take into account different evaluation results at varying granularities within the data. MMP currently models insertions from outside the relational structure by using tokens that represent external data sources. It may be that users insert data into an MMP instance from another MMP instance, in which case that inserted data may have associated provenance from its original MMP instance. We plan to explore how provenance inherited across multiple MMP instances can be meaningfully composed and evaluated.

References

[Agrawal06] Agrawal, P., Benjelloun, O., Das Sarma, A., Hayworth, C., Nabar, S., Sugihara, T., Widom, J.: Trio: a system for data, uncertainty, and lineage. In: Proceedings of the 32nd International Conference on Very Large Data Bases, VLDB 2006. VLDB Endowment (2006)

[Archer08] Archer, D.W., Delcambre, L.M.L.: Definition and Formalization of Entity Resolution Functions for Everyday Information Integration. In: Schewe, K.-D., Thalheim, B. (eds.) SDKB 2008. LNCS, vol. 4925, pp. 126–142. Springer, Heidelberg (2008)

[Archer10] Archer, D., Delcambre, L.: A Conceptual Model and Predicate Language for Data Selection and Projection Based on Provenance. In: Proceedings of the Second Workshop on the Theory and Practiceof Provenance (TaPP 2010), San Jose, CA (February 2010)

[Archer10] Archer, D.: Conceptual Modeling of Data with Provenance. PhD dissertation. Portland State University (2011)

[Bhagwat04] Bhagwat, D., Chiticariu, L., Tan, W., Vijayvargiya, G.: An annotation management system for relational databases.In Proceedings of the 30thInternational Conference on Very Large Data Bases, VLDB 2004. VLDB Endowment (2004)

[Buneman06] Buneman, P., Chapman, A., Cheney, J., Vansummeren, S.: A provenance model for manually curated data. In: Moreau, L., Foster, I. (eds.) IPAW 2006. LNCS, vol. 4145, pp. 162–170. Springer, Heidelberg (2006)

[Buneman08] Buneman, P., Cheney, J., Vansummeren, S.: On the expressivenesss of implicit provenance in query and update languages. ACM Transactions on Database Systems 33(4) (2008)

[Cui00] Cui, Y., Widom, J., Wiener, J.: Tracing the lineage of view data in a warehousing environment. ACM Transactions on Database Systems 25(2) (2000)

[Green07] Green, T., Karvounarakis, G., Taylor, N., Biton, O., Ives, Z., Tannen, V.: Orchestra: facilitating collaborative data sharing. In: SIGMOD 2007: Proceedings of the 2007 ACM SIGMOD International Conference on Management of Data. ACM, New York (2007)

[Green07b] Green, T., Karvounarakis, G., Tannen, V.: Provenance semirings. In: PODS 2007: Proceedings of the Twenty-Sixth ACM SIGMOD-SIGACTSIGART Symposium on Principles of Database Systems, ACM, New York (2007)

[Levitin86] Levitin, A.: How to measure size, and how not to. In: Proceedings of the Tenth COMPSAC Conference. IEEE Computer Society Press, Washington DC (1986)

An Abstract, Reusable, and Extensible
Programming Language Design Architecture*

Hassan Aït-Kaci

Université Claude Bernard Lyon 1
Villeurbanne, France
hassan.ait-kaci@univ-lyon1.fr

Abstract. There are a few basic computational concepts that are at the core of all programming languages. The exact elements making out such a set of concepts determine (1) the specific nature of the computational services such a language is designed for, (2) for what users it is intended, and (3) on what devices and in what environment it is to be used. It is therefore possible to propose a set of basic building blocks and operations thereon as combination procedures to enable programming software by specifying desired tasks using a tool-box of generic constructs and meta-operations. Syntax specified through LALR(k) grammar technology can be enhanced with greater recognizing power thanks to a simple augmentation of yacc technology. Upon this basis, a set of implementable formal operational semantics constructs may be simply designed and generated (syntax and semantics) *à la carte*, by simple combination of its desired features. The work presented here, and the tools derived from it, may be viewed as a tool box for generating language implementations with a desired set of features. It eases the automatic practical generation of programming language pioneered by Peter Landin's SECD Machine. What is overviewed constitutes a practical computational algebra extending the polymorphically typed λ-Calculus with object/classes and monoid comprehensions. This paper describes a few of the most salient parts of such a system, stressing most specifically any innovative features—formal syntax and semantics. It may be viewed as a high-level tour of a few reusable programming language design techniques prototyped in the form of a set of composable abstract machine constructs and operations.[1]

Keywords: Programming Language Design, Object-Oriented Programming, Bottom-up Parsing, LALR Parser Generation, Denotational Semantics, Operational Semantics, λ-Calculus, Polymorphic Types, Static/Dynamic Type Checking/Inference, Declarative Collections, Monoid Comprehensions, Intermediate Language, Abstract Machines.

This article is dedicated to Peter Buneman, a teacher and a friend—for sharing the fun! With fond memories of our Penn days and those Friday afternoon seminars in his office …

---

* Thanks to Val Tannen for his patience, Nabil Layaïda for his comments, and the anonymous referee for catching many glitches and giving good advice in general.

[1] Some of this material was presented as part of the author's keynote address at LDTA 2003 [1].

V. Tannen et al. (Eds.): Buneman Festschrift, LNCS 8000, pp. 112–166, 2013.
© Springer-Verlag Berlin Heidelberg 2013

The languages people use to communicate with computers differ in their intended aptitudes towards either a particular application area, or in a particular phase of computer use (high level programming, program assembly, job scheduling, *etc.*, ...). They also differ in physical appearance, and more important, in logical structure. The question arises, do the idiosyncrasies reflect basic logical properties of the situations that are being catered for? Or are they accidents of history and personal background that may be obscuring fruitful developments? This question is clearly important if we are trying to predict or influence language evolution.

To answer it we must think in terms, not of languages, but of families of languages. That is to say we must systematize their design so that a new language is a point chosen from a well-mapped space, rather than a laboriously devised construction.

PETER J. LANDIN—"The Next 700 Programming Languages" [2]

1   Introduction

1.1   Motivation—Programming Language Design?

Today, programming languages are designed more formally than they used to be fifty years ago. This is thanks to linguistic research that has led to syntactic science (begetting parser technology) and research in the formal semantics of programming constructs (begetting compiler technology—semantics-preserving translation from human-usable surface syntax to low-level instruction-based machine language). As in the case of a natural language, a grammar is used to control the formation of sentences (programs) that will be understood (interpreted/executed) according to the language's intended (denotational/operational) semantics. Design based on formal syntax and semantics can thus be made operational.

Designing a programming language is difficult because it requires being aware of all the overwhelmingly numerous consequences of the slightest design decision that may occur anytime during the lexical or syntactical analyses, and the static or dynamic semantics phases. To this, we must add the potentially high design costs investing in defining and implementing a new language. These costs affect not only time and effort of design and development, but also the quality of the end product—*viz.*, performance and reliability of the language being designed, not to mention how to justify, let alone guarantee, the correctness of the design's implementation [3].

Fortunately, there have been design tools to help in the process. So-called metacompilers have been used to great benefit to systematize the design and guarantee a higher quality of language implementation. The "*meta*" part actually applies to the lexical and syntactic phases of the language design. Even then, the metasyntactic tools are often restricted to specific classes of grammars and/or parsing algorithms. Still fewer propose tools for *abstract syntax*. Most that do confine the abstract syntax language to some form of idiosyncratic representation of an attributed tree language with some *ad hoc* attribute co-dependence interpretation. Even rarer are language design systems that propose abstract and reusable components in the form of expressions of a formal typed kernel calculus. It is such a system that this work proposes; it gives an essential overview of its design principle and the sort of services it has been designed to render.

This document describes the design of an abstract, reusable, and extensible, programming language architecture and its implementation in Java. What is described represents a generic basis insofar as these abstract and reusable constructs, and any well-typed compositions thereof, may be instantiated in various modular language configurations. It also offers a practical discipline for extending the framework with additional building blocks for new language features as per need. The first facet was the elaboration of $\mathfrak{J}acc$, an advanced system for syntax-directed compiler generation extending yacc technology [4].[2] A second facet was the design of a well-typed set of abstract-machine constructs complete enough to represent higher-order functional programming in the form of an object-oriented λ-Calculus, extended with *monoid comprehensions* [5,6,7,8]. A third facet could be the integration of logic-relational (from Logic Programming) and object-relational (from Database Programming) enabling LIFE-technology [9,10] and/or any other $\mathcal{CP}/\mathcal{LP}$ technology to cohabit.

What is described here is therefore a metadesign: it is the design of a design tool. The novelty of what is described here is both in the lexical/syntactical phase and in the typing/execution semantic phase.

The lexical and syntactic phases are innovative in many respects. In particular, they are conservative extensions considerably enhancing the conventional lex/yacc technology (or, similarly, flex/bison) meta-lexico-syntactical tools [4,11] with more efficient implementation algorithms [12] and recognizing power (*viz.*, overloaded grammar symbols, dynamic operator properties *à la* Prolog). This essentially gives $\mathfrak{J}acc$ the recognizing power of LALR(k) grammars, for any $k \geq 1$. Sections 2.1 and 2.2 give more details on that part of the system.

The interpretation is essentially the same approach as the one advocated by Landin for his Store-Environment-Code-Dump (SECD) machine [13] and optimzed by Luca Cardelli in his Functional Abstract Machine (FAM) [14].[3] The abstract machine we present here is but a systematic taking advantage of Java's object-oriented tool-set to put together a modular and extensible set of building blocks for language design. It is sufficiently powerful for expressing higher-order polymorphic object-oriented functional and/or   imperative   programming   languages.   This   includes   declarative

---

[2] See Section 2.1.

[3] Other formally derived abstract machines like the Categorical Abstract Machine (CAM) also led to variants of formal compilation of functional languages (*e.g.*, Caml). This approach was also adopted for the chemical metaphor formalizing concurrent computation as chemical reaction originally proposed by Banâtre and Le Métayer [15] and later adapted by Berry and Boudol to define their Chemical Abstract Machine (ChAM) [16]. The same also happened for Logic Programming [17].

collection-processing based on the concept of Monoid Comprehensions as used in object-oriented databases [5,6,7,8,18]. [4]

This machine was implemented and used by the author to generate several experimental 100%-java implementation of various language prototypes. Thus, what was actually implemented in this toolkit was done following a "by need" priority order. It is not so complete as to already encompass all the necessary building blocks needed for all known styles of programming and type semantics. It is meant as an open set of tools to be extended as the needs arise. For example, there is no support yet for $\mathcal{LP}$ [17], nor—more generally—$\mathcal{CLP}$ [25].

However, as limited as it may be, it already encompasses most of the basic familiar constructs from imperative and functional programming, including declarative aggregation (so-called "comprehensions"). Therefore, it is clearly impossible—not to say boring!—to cover all the nitty-gritty details of all the facets of the complete abtract machine generation system. This article is therefore organized as an informal stroll over the most interesting novel features or particularities of our design as it stands to date.

1.2   Our Approach—*Abstract* Programming Language Design

The approach we follow is that of compiling a specific relatively more sophisticated outer syntax into a simpler instruction-based "*machine*" language. However, for portability, this inner language is that of an "*abstract*" machine. In other words, it is just an intermediate language that can be either interpreted more efficiently on an emulator of that abstract machine, and/or be mapped to actual instruction-based assembly code of a specific machine more easily.

Thus, as for most compiled typed programming languages, there are actually several languages:

- a *surface language*—the syntax used by users to compose programs;

- a *kernel language*—the "essential" language into which the surface language is normalized;

- a *type language*—the language describing the types of expressions;

- an *intermediate language*—the language that is executable on an instruction-based abstract machine.

---

[4] As an example, we used our system to generate a prototype Algebraic Query Language (AQL v0.00) as a functional language augmented with a calculus of compehensions *à la* Fegaras-Maier [8], or *à la* Grust [18]. In other words, it is a complete query language, powerful enough to express most of ODMG's OQL, and thus many of its derivatives such as, *e.g.*, XQuery [19] and XPath [20], *etc.*, ... This version of AQL can be run both interactively and in batch mode. In the former case, a user can define top-level constructs and evaluate expressions. AQL v0.00 supports 2nd-order (ML-like) type polymorphism, automatic currying, associative arrays, multiple type overloading, dynamic operator overloading, as well as (polymorphic) type definition (both aliasing and hiding), classes and objects, and (of course) monoid homomorphisms and comprehensions (*N.B.*: no subtyping nor inheritance yet—but this is next on the agenda [21,22,23,24]).

Although we will not develop it into much detail in this paper, the Java execution backend for carrying out the operational semantics of the above *à la carte* design consists of:

– *An operational semantic language*—interpreting an abstract instruction set having effects on a set of runtime structures. The latter defining the state of an execution automaton. The objects operated on and stored in these structures are the basic data representation all surface language constructs.
– *A type-directed display manager*—maintaining a trace emulation of abstract machine code execution in relation to the source code it was generated from. This is also useful for debugging purposes while managing three sorted stacks (depending on the nature of Java data pushed on the various sorted stacks—`int`, `double`, or `Object`).[5]
– *A type-directed data reader*—management for reading three sorts of data (`int`, `double`, or `Object`).

The same applies for pragmatics as well:

– *Concrete vs. abstract error handling*—delegation of error reporting by inheritance along ⟨*design*⟩.`backend.Error.java` class hierarchy.[6]
– *Concrete vs. abstract vocabulary*—handling of errors according to the most specifically phrased error-handling messaging.

1.3   Organization of Paper

The rest of this document is organized as follows. Section 2 overviews original generic syntax-processing tools that have been conceived, implemented, and used to ease the experimental front-end development for language processing systems. Section 3 gives a high-level description of the architectural attributes of a set of kernel classes of programming language constructs and how they are processed for typing, compiling, and executing. Section 4 discusses the type system, which is made operational as a polymorphic type inference abstract machine enabling multiple-type overloading, type encapsulation, object-orientation, and type (un)boxing analysis. Section 5 sums up the essentials of how declarative iteration over collections may be specified using the notion of monoid homomorphism and comprehension as used in object-oriented databases

---

[5] This is essentiially a three-way SECD/FAM used to avoid systematically having to "box" into objects primitive Java values (*viz.*, of type `int` and `double`). This enables precious optimization that is particularly needed when dealing with variables of static polymorphic types but dynamically instantiated into `int` and `double` [26].

[6] Here and in what follows, we shall use the following abbreviated class path notation:
- "⟨*syntax*⟩." for "`hlt.language.syntax.`"
- "⟨*design*⟩." for "`hlt.language.design.`" and this latter package's sub-packages:
    * "⟨*kernel*⟩." for "⟨*design*⟩.`kernel.`"
    * "⟨*types*⟩." for "⟨*design*⟩.`types.`"
    * "⟨*instructions*⟩." for "⟨*design*⟩.`instructions.`"
    * "⟨*backend*⟩." for "⟨*design*⟩.`backend.`"
  when referring to actual classes' package paths (`hlt` stands for "hak's language tools.").

query languages to generate efficient collection-processing code. Section 6 concludes with a quick recapitulation of the contents and future perspectives.

In order to make this paper as self-contained as possible, the above overview of salient aspects of the system that has been implemented is followed by an Appendix of brief tutorials on essential key concepts and terminology this work relies upon, and/or extends.

2   Syntax Processing

2.1   𝔍acc—Just Another Compiler Compiler

At first sight, 𝔍acc may be seen as a "100% Pure Java" implementation of an LALR(1) parser generator [27] in the fashion of the well-known UNIX tool yacc—"yet another compiler compiler" [4]. However, 𝔍acc is much more than... *just another compiler compiler*: it extends yacc to enable the generation of flexible and efficient Java-based parsers and provides enhanced functionality not so commonly available in other similar systems.

The fact that 𝔍acc uses yacc's metasyntax makes it readily usable on most yacc grammars. Other Java-based parser generators all depart from yacc's format, requiring nontrivial metasyntactic preprocessing to be used on existing yacc grammars—which abound in the world, yacc being by far the most popular tool for parser generation. Importantly, 𝔍acc is programmed in pure Java—this makes it fully portable to all existing platforms, and immediately exploitable for web-based software applications.

𝔍acc further stands out among other known parser generators, whether Java-based or not, thanks to several additional features. The most notable are:

- 𝔍acc uses the most efficient algorithm known to date for its most critical computation (*viz.*, the propagation of LALR(1) lookahead sets). Traditional yacc implementations use the method originally developed by DeRemer and Penello [11]. 𝔍acc uses an improved method due to Park, Choe, and Chang [12], which drastically ameliorates the method of by DeRemer and Penello. To this author's best knowledge, no other Java-based metacompiler system implements the Park, Choe, and Chang method [28].

- 𝔍acc allows the user to define a complete class hierarchy of parse node classes (the objects pushed on the parse stack and that make up the parse tree: nonterminal and terminal symbols), along with any Java attributes to be used in semantic actions annotating grammar rules. All these attributes are accessible directly on any pseudo-variable associated with a grammar rule constituents (*i.e.*, $$, $1, $2, *etc.*).

- 𝔍acc makes use of all the well-known conveniences defining precedences and associativity associated to some terminal symbols for resolving parser conflicts that may arise. While such conflicts may in theory be eliminated for any LALR(1) grammar, such a grammar is rarely completely obtainable. In that case, yacc technology falls short of providing a safe parser for non-LALR grammar. Yet, 𝔍acc can accommodate any such eventual unresolved conflict using non-deterministic parse actions that may be tried and undone.

- Further still, Jacc can also tolerate non-deterministic tokens. In other words, the same token may be categorized as several distinct lexical units to be tried in turn. This allows, for example, parsing languages that use no reserved keywords (or more precisely, whose keywords may also be tokenized as identifiers, for instance).

- Better yet, Jacc allows dynamically (re-)definable operators in the style of the Prolog language (*i.e.*, at parse-time and run-time). This offers great flexibility for on-the-fly syntax customization, as well as a much greater recognition power, even where operator symbols may be overloaded (*i.e.*, specified to have several precedences and/or associativity for different arities).

- Jacc supports partial parsing. In other words, in a grammar, one may indicate any nonterminal as a parse root. Then, constructs from the corresponding sublanguage may be parsed independently from a reader stream or a string.

- Jacc automatically generates a full HTML documentation of a grammar as a set of interlinked files from annotated / * * . . . * / javadoc-style comments in the grammar file, including a navigatable pure grammar in "yacc form," obtained after removing all semantic and serialization annotations, leaving only the bare syntactic rules.

- Jacc may be directed to build a parse-tree automatically (for the concrete syntax, but also for a more implicit form which rids a concrete syntax tree of most of its useless information). By contrast, regular yacc necessitates that a programmer add explicit semantic actions for this purpose.

- Jacc supports a simple annotational scheme for automatic XML serialization of complex Abstract Syntax Trees (AST's) [29]. Grammar rules and non-punctuation terminal symbols (*i.e.*, any meaning-carrying tokens such as, e.g., identifiers, numbers, *etc.*) may be annotated with simple XML templates expressing their XML forms. Jacc may then use these templates to transform the Concrete Parse Tree (CST) into an AST of radically different structure, constructed as a jdom XML document.[7] This yields a convenient declarative specification of a tree transduction process guided by just a few simple annotations, where Jacc's "sensible" behavior on unannotated rules and terminals works "as expected." This greatly eases the task of retargeting the serialization of a language depending on variable or evolving XML vocabularies.

With Jacc, a grammar can be specified using the usual familiar yacc syntax with semantic actions specified as Java code. The format of the grammar file is essentially the same as that required by yacc, with some minor differences, and a few additional powerful features. Not using the additional features makes it essentially similar to the yacc format.

For the intrigued reader curious to know how one may combine dynamic operator with a static parser generator, Section 2.2 explains in some detail how Jacc extends yacc to support Prolog-style dynamic operators.

---

[7] http://www.jdom.org/

2.2   LR-Parsing with Dynamic Operators

In this section, we explain, justify, and specify the modifications that need to be made to a classical table-driven LALR(1) parser generator *à la* yacc [4]. For such a compiler generator to allow Prolog-style dynamic operators, it is necessary that it be adapted to account *statically* (*i.e.*, at compile-time) for runtime information. Indeed, in Prolog, operators may be declared either at compile-time or at runtime using the built-in predicate op/3.[8]

How 𝔍acc Enables Static LR-parsing with Dynamic Operators. In an LR-parser such as one generated by yacc, precedence and associativity information is no longer available at parse-time. It is used statically at parser generation-time to resolve potential conflicts in the parser's actions. Then, a fixed table of unambiguous actions is passed to drive the parser, which therefore always knows what to do in a given state for a given input token.

Thus, although they can recognize a much larger class of context-free languages, conventional shift-reduce parsers for LR grammars cannot accommodate parse-time ambiguity resolution. Although this makes parsing more efficient, it also forbids a parser generated by a yacc-like parser generator to support Prolog style operators.

In what follows, we propose to reorganize the structure of the implementation of a yacc-style parser generator to accommodate Prolog-style dynamic operators. We do so:

– increasing the user's convenience to define and use new syntax dynamically without changing the parser;
– adding new features while preserving the original yacc metasyntax;
– retaining the same efficiency as yacc-parsing for grammars which do not use dynamic operators;
– augmenting the recognizing power of bottom-up LALR parsing to languages that support dynamically (re)definable operators;
– making full use of the object-oriented capabilities of Java to allow the grammar specifier to tune the parser generation using user-defined classes and attributes.

Declaring Dynamic Operators. The first issue pertains to the way we may specify how dynamic operators are connected with the grammar's production rules. The command:

```
%dynamic op
```

is used to declare that the parser of the grammar being specified will allow defining, or redefining, dynamic operators of category op. The effect of this declaration is to create a non-terminal symbol named op that stands for this token category. Three implicit grammar rules are also defined:

```
op : 'op_' | '_op_' | '_op' ;
```

---

[8] See Appendix Section A for a quick review of Prolog-style dynamic operators.

which introduce, respectively, prefix, infix, and postfix, subcategories for operators of category op. These are terminal symbols standing as generic tokens that denote specific operators for each fixity. Specific operators on category op may be defined in the grammar specification as follows:

```
%op <operator> <specifier> <precedence>
```

For example,

```
%op '+' yfx 500
```

declares the symbol '+' to be an infix binary left-associative operator of category op, with binding tightness 500, just as in Prolog.

In addition, the generated parser defines the following method:

```
public final static void op ( String operator
                            , String specifier
                            , int precedence)
```

whose effect is to define, or redefine, an operator for the token category op dynamically using the given (Prolog-style) specifier and (Prolog-style) precedence. It is this method that can be invoked in a parser's semantic action at parse time, or by the runtime environment as a static method.

An operator's category name may be used in a grammar specification wherever an operator of that category is expected. Namely, it may be used in grammar rules such as:

```
expression : op expression
           | expression op
           | expression op expression
           ;
```

Using the non-terminal symbol op in a rule such as above allows operators of any fixity declared in the op category to appear where op appears. However, if an occurrence must be limited to an op of specific fixity only, then one may use:

– 'op_' for a prefix operator of category op;
– '_op' for a postfix operator of category op;
– '_op_' for an infix operator of category op.

For example, the above rules can be better restricted to:

```
expression : 'op_' expression
           | expression '_op'
           | expression '_op_' expression
           ;
```

A consequence of the above observations is that a major modification in the parser generator and the generic parser must also be made regarding the parser actions they generate for dynamic operators. A state may have contending actions on a given input.

Such a state is deemed conflictual if and only if the input creating the conflict is a dynamic operator, or if one of its conflicting actions is a reduction with a rule whose tag is a dynamic operator. All other states can be treated as usual, resolving potential conflicts using the conventional method based on precedence and associativity. Clearly, a dynamic operator token category does not have this information but delegates it to the specific token, which will be known only at parse time. At parser-construction time, a pseudo-action is generated for conflictual states which delays decision until parse time. It uses the state's table associating a set of actions with the token creating the conflict in this state. These sets of conflicting actions are thus recorded for each conflictual state.

When a token is identified and the current state is a conflictual state, which action to perform is determined by choosing in the action set associated to the state according to the same disambiguation rules followed by the static table construction but using the current precedence and associativity values of the specific operator being read. If a "reduce" action in the set involves a rule tagged with a dynamic operator, which precedence and associativity values to use for the rule are those of the specific operator tag for that rule, which can be obtained in the current stack. The stack offset of that operator will depend on which of the dynamic operator's rules is being considered.

Ambiguous Tokens. Note that in general, the tokenizer may return a set of possible tokens for a single operator. Consider for example the following grammar:

```
%token '!'
%dynamic op1
%op1 '!' yf 200
%dynamic op2
%op2 '!' yfx 500
%%
expression : expression1 _op1_ expression1
           | expression2 _op2
           | '!' expression
           ;
%%
```

For this grammar, the character '!' may be tokenized as either '!', 'op1', or 'op2'. The tokenizer can therefore be made to dispense with guaranteeing a token's lexical category. Looking up its token category tables, the parser then determines the set of admissible lexical categories for this token in the current state (*i.e.*, those for which it has an action defined). If more than one token remain in the set, a choice point for this state is created. Such a choice point records the current state of parsing for backtracking purposes. Namely, the grammar state, and the token set. The tokens are then tried in the order of the set, and upon error, backtracking resets the parser at the latest choice point deprived of the token that was chosen for it.

Note that the use of backtracking for token identification is not a guarantee of complete recovery. First, full backtracking is generally not a feasible nor desirable option as it would entail possibly keeping an entire input stream in memory as the buffer grows. The option is to keep only a *fixed-size buffer* and flush from the choice point stack any choice point that becomes stale when this buffer overflows. In effect, this enforces an automatic commit whenever a token choice is not invalidated within the time it takes to read further tokens as allowed by the buffer size.

Second, although backtracking restores the parser's state, it does not automatically undo the side effects that may have been performed by the execution of any semantic action encountered between the failure state and the restored state. If there are any, these must be undone manually. Thus, Jacc allows specifying undo actions to be executed when a rule is backtracked over.

The only limitation—shallow backtracking—is not serious, and in fact the choice-point stack's size can be specified arbitrarily large if need be. Moreover, any input that overruns the choice-point stack's default depth is in fact cleaning up space by getting rid of older and less-likely-to-be-used choice-points. Indeed, failure occurs generally shortly after a wrong choice has been made. We give separately a more detailed specification of the implementation of the shallow backtracking scheme that is adequate for this purpose.

Token Declarations. In order to declare tokens' attributes in yacc, one may use the commands %token, %right, %left, and %nonassoc. These commands also give the tokens they define a precedence level according to the order of declarations, tokens of equal precedence being declared in the same command. Since we wish to preserve compatibility with yacc's notations and conventions, we keep these commands to have the same effect. Therefore, these commands are used as usual to declare static tokens. However, we must explicate how the implicit precedence level of static token declarations may coexist with the explicit precedence information specified by the Prolog-like dynamic operator declarations.

We also wish to preserve compatibility with Prolog's conventions. Recall that the number argument in a Prolog 'op/3' declaration denotes the binding tightness of the operator, which is inversely related to parsing precedence. The range of these numbers is the interval $[1, 1200]$. To make this compatible with the foregoing yacc commands, the $\langle syntax \rangle$.Grammar.java class defines two constants:

```
static final int MIN_PRECEDENCE = 1;
static final int MAX_PRECEDENCE = 1200;
```

In order to have the binding tightness to be such that 1200 corresponds to minimum precedence and 1 to maximum precedence, we simply define the precedence level of binding tightness n to be $1200 - n + 1$. Thus, a declaration such as:

```
%op '+' yfx 500
```

assigns to binary '+' a precedence level of 701 (*viz.*, $1200 - 500 + 1$).

We also allow dynamic operators to be declared with the form:

```
%op <operator> <specifier>
```

leaving the precedence implicit, and defaulting to the precedence level effective at the command's execution time.

The first encountered token declaration with implicit precedence (*i.e.*, a conventional yacc token command or a two-argument dynamic operator command) uses the initial precedence level set to a default,[9] then increments it by a fixed increment. This increment is 10 by default, but the command:

```
%precstep <number>
```

may be used to set the increment to the given number. This command may be used several times. Each subsequent declaration with implicit precedence uses the current precedence level, then increments the precedence level by the current precedence increment. Any attempt to set a precedence level outside the $[1, 1200]$ range is ignored: the closest bound is used instead (*i.e.*, 1 if less and 1200 if more), and a warning is issued.

3 The Kernel Language

A language construct is said to be *primitive* (or *"built-in"*) if is not expressed in terms of other language constructs.[10] The kernel language is the set of primitive language constructs. It is sometimes also called the "desugared" language. This is because non-primitive constructs that are often-used combinations of primitive stuctures are both easier to use and read by human programmers. Hence, before being given any meaning, a program expressed using the "sugared" language syntax is first translated into its equivalent "desugared" form in the kernel language containing only primitive expressions.

3.1 Processing a Kernel Expression

Fig. 1 gives the complete processing diagram from reading a $\langle kernel \rangle$.Expression denoting a program to executing it.

Typically, upon being read, such a $\langle kernel \rangle$.Expression will be:

1. *"name-sanitized"*—in the context of a $\langle kernel \rangle$.Sanitizer to discriminate between local names and global names, and establish pointers from the local variable occurrences to the abstraction that introduces them, and from global names to entries in the global symbol table;
2. *type-checked*—in the context of a $\langle types \rangle$.TypeChecker to discover whether it has a type at all, or several possible ones (only expressions that have a unique unambiguous type are further processed);
3. *"sort-sanitized"*—in the context of a $\langle kernel \rangle$.Sanitizer to discriminate between those local variables that are of primitive Java types (int or double) or of Object type (this is necessary because the set-up means to use unboxed values of primitive types for efficiency reasons); this second "sanitization" phase is also used to compute offsets for local names (*i.e.*, so-called *de Bruijn indices*) for each of the three type sorts (int, double, Object);
4. *compiled*—in the context of a $\langle kernel \rangle$.Compiler to generate the sequence of instructions whose execution in an appropriate runtime environment will evaluate the expression;

---

[9] This value is a system constant called $\langle syntax \rangle$.Grammar.MIN_PRECEDENCE.

[10] This does not mean that it could not be. It just means that it is provided natively, either to ease oft-used syntax, and/or make it more efficient operationally.

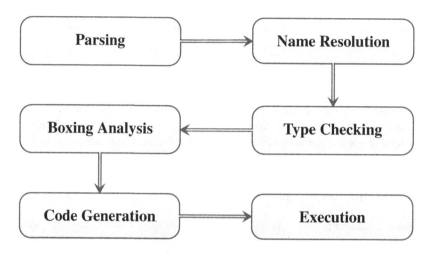

Fig. 1. Processing diagram

5. *executed*—in the context of a ⟨*backend*⟩.Runtime denoting the appropriate runtime environment in the context of which to execute its sequence of instructions.

The Syntax Sanitizer. A *sanitizer* is an object that "cleans up"—so to speak—an expression of any possibly remaining ambiguities as it is being parsed and further processed. There are two kinds of ambiguities that must be "sanitized:"

- after parsing, it must be determined which identifiers are the names of *local* variables *vs.* those of *global* variables;
- after type-checking, it must be determined the runtime sort of every abstraction parameter and use this to compute the local variable environment offsets of each local variable.[11]

Thus, a sanitizer is a discriminator of names and sorts.[12]

The Type Checker. The type checker is in fact a type inference machine that synthesizes missing type information by type unification. It may be (and often is) used as a type-checking automaton when types are (partially) present.

Each expression must specify its own ⟨*kernel*⟩.Expression.TypeCheck (⟨*types*⟩.TypeChecker) method that encodes its formal typing rule.

---

[11] These offsets are the so-called *de Bruijn* indices of λ-calculus [13]—Or rather, their sorted version.

[12] It has occurred to this author that the word "*sanitizer*" is perhaps a tad of a misnomer. Perhaps "*discriminator*" might have been a better choice. This also goes for the ⟨*kernel*⟩.Sanitizer.java class' method names (*i.e.*, discriminateNames and discriminateSorts rather than sanitizeNames and sanitizeSorts).

The Compiler. This is the class defining a compiler object. Such an object serves as the common compilation context shared by an ⟨*kernel*⟩.`Expression` and the subexpressions comprising it. Each type of expression representing a syntactic construct of the kernel language defines a ⟨*kernel*⟩.`Expression.compile(`⟨*kernel*⟩.`Compiler`) method that specifies the way the construct is to be compiled in the context of a given compiler. Such a compiler object consists of attributes and methods for generating straightline code which consists of a sequence of instructions, each of specific subtype of abstract type ⟨*instructions*⟩.`Instruction`, corresponding to a top-level expression and its subexpressions.

Upon completion of the compilation of a top-level expression, a resulting code array is extracted from the sequence of instructions, which may then be executed in the context of a ⟨*backend*⟩.`Runtime` object, or, in the case of a ⟨*kernel*⟩.`Definition`, be saved in the code array in the ⟨*kernel*⟩.`Definition`'s ⟨*kernel*⟩.`codeEntry()` field of type ⟨*types*⟩.`DefinedEntry`, which is an object that encapsulates its code entry point, and which may in turn then be used to access the defined symbol's code for execution.

Each expression construct of the kernel must therefore specify a compiling rule. Such a rule expresses how the abstract syntax construct maps into a straight-line code sequence.

In Appendix Section B, this process is illustrated in more detail on a few typical as well as less typical expressions.

4 Types

> We have illustrated a style of programming based on the use of rich type systems. This is not new in general, but the particularly rich type system we have described, based on type quantifiers and subtypes, extends the state of the art. This rich type structure can account for functional, imperative, algebraic, and object-oriented programming in a unified framework, and extends to programming in the large and, with care, to system programming.
>
> LUCA CARDELLI—"Typeful Programming" [30]

4.1 Type Language

We first define some basic terminology regarding the type system and operations on types.

Polymorphism. Here, by "*polymorphism*," we mean ML-polymorphism (*i.e.*, 2nd-order universal), with a few differences that will be explained along the way. The syntax of types is defined with a grammar such as:

[1] *Type*   ::= *SimpleType* | *TypeScheme*

[2] *SimpleType* ::= *BasicType* | *FunctionType* | *TypeParameter*

[3] *BasicType*   ::= $\mathfrak{Int}$ | $\mathfrak{Real}$ | $\mathfrak{Boolean}$ | ...

[4] *FunctionType*   ::= $SimpleType \rightarrow SimpleType$

[5] *TypeParameter* ::= α | α' | ... | β | β' | ...

[6] *TypeScheme*   ::= $\forall$ *TypeParameter* . *Type*

that ensures that universal type quantifiers occur only at the outset of a polymorphic type.[13]

Multiple Type Overloading. This is also often called *ad hoc* polymorphism. When enabled (the default), this allows a same identifier to have several unrelated types. Generally, it is restricted to names with functional types. However, since functions are first-class citizens, this restriction makes no sense, and therefore the default is to enable multiple type overloading for all types.

To this author's knowledge, there is no established prevailing technology for supporting *both* ML-polymorphic type inference and multiple type overloading. So here, as in a few other parts of this overall design, I have had to innovate. I essentially implemented a type proving logic using techniques from (Constraint) Logic Programming in order to handle the combination of types supportable by this architecture.

Currying. Currying is an operation that exploits the following mathematical isomorphism of types:[14]

$$T, T' \rightarrow T'' \simeq T \rightarrow (T' \rightarrow T'') \tag{1}$$

which can be generalized for a function type of any number of arguments to any of its multiple curried forms—*i.e.*, for all $k = 1, \ldots, n-1$:

$$T_1, \ldots, T_n \rightarrow T \simeq T_1, \ldots, T_k \rightarrow (T_{k+1}, \ldots, T_n \rightarrow T) \tag{2}$$

When function currying is enabled, this means that type-checking/inference must build this equational theory into the type unification rules in order to consider types equal modulo this isomorphism.

---

[13] Or more precisely that $\forall$ never occurs nested inside a function type arrow $\rightarrow$. This apparently innocuous detail ensures decidability of type inference. BTW, the *2nd* order comes from the fact that the quantifier applies to *type* parameters (as opposed to *1st* order, if it had applied to *value* parameters). The *universal* comes from $\forall$, of course.

[14] For the intrigued reader curious to know what deep connection there might be between functional types and Indian cooking, the answer is, *"None whatsoever!"* The word was coined after Prof. Haskell B. Curry's last name. Curry was one of the two mathematicians/logicians (along with Robert Feys) who conceived *Combinator Logic* and *Combinator Calculus*, and made extensive use of the isomorphism of Equation (1)—hence the folklore's use of the verb *to curry*—*(currying, curryed)*,— in French: *curryfier*—*(curryfication, curryfié)*, to mean transforming a function type of several arguments into that of a function of one argument. The homonymy is often amusingly mistaken for an exotic way of [un]spicing functions.

Standardizing. As a result of, *e.g.*, currying, the shape of a function type may change in the course of a type-checking/inference process. Type comparison may thus be tested on various structurally different, although syntactically congruent, forms of a same type. A type must therefore assume a canonical form in order to be compared. This is what *standardizing* a type does.

Standardizing is a two-phase operation that first *flattens* the domains of function types, then *renames* the type parameters. The flattening phase simply amounts to un-currying as much as possible by applying Equation (1) as a rewrite rule, although *backwards* (*i.e.*, from right to left) as long as it applies. The second phase (renaming) consists in making a consistent copy of all types reachable from a type's root.

Copying. Copying a type is simply taking a duplicate twin of the graph reachable from the type's root. Sharing of pointers coming from the fact that type parameters co-occur are recorded in a parameter substitution table (in our implementation, simply a `java.util.HashMap`) along the way, and thus consistent pointer sharing can be easily made effective.

Equality. Testing for equality must be done modulo a parameter substitution table (in our implementation, simply a `java.util.HashMap`) that records pointer equalities along the way, and thus equality up to parameter renaming can be easily made effective.

A tableless version of equality also exists for which each type parameter is considered equal only to itself.

Unifying. Unifying two types is the operation of filling in missing information (*i.e.*, type parameters) in each with existing information from the other by side-effecting (*i.e.*, binding) the missing information (*i.e.*, the type parameters) to point to the part of the existing information from the other type they should be equal to (*i.e.*, their values). Note that, like logical variables in Logic Programming, type parameters can be bound to one another and thus must be dereferenced to their values.

Boxing/Unboxing. The kernel language is polymorphically typed. Therefore, a function expression that has a polymorphic type must work for all instantiations of this type's type parameters into either primitive unboxed types (*e.g.*, $\mathfrak{Int}$, $\mathfrak{Real}$, *etc.*) or boxed types. The problem this poses is: how can we compile a polymorphic function into code that would correctly know what the actual runtime sorts of the function's runtime arguments and returned value are, *before the function type is actually instantiated into a (possibly monomorphic) type?*[15] This problem was addressed by Xavier Leroy and he proposed a solution, which has been implemented in the CAML compiler [26].[16] Leroy's method is based on the use of type annotation that enables a source-to-source

---

[15] The alternative would be either to compile distinct copies for all possible runtime sort instantiations (like, *e.g.*, C++ template functions), or compiling each specific instantiation as it is needed. The former is not acceptable because it tends to inflate the code space explosively. The latter can neither be envisaged because it goes against a few (rightfully) sacrosanct principles like separate compilation and abstract library interfacing—imagine having to recompile a library everytime you want to use it!

[16] See `http://caml.inria.fr/`

transformation. This source transformation is the automatic generation of *wrappers* and *unwrappers* for boxing and unboxing expressions whenever necessary. After that, compiling the transformed source as usual will be guaranteed to be correct on all types.

For our purpose, the main idea from Leroy's solution was adapted and improved so that:

- the type annotation and rules are greatly simplified;
- no source-to-source transformation is needed;
- un/wrappers generation is done at code-generation time.

This saves a great amount of space and time.

4.2 Type Processing

The type system consists of two complementary parts: a *static* and a *dynamic* part.[17] The former takes care of verifying all type constraints that are statically decidable (*i.e.*, before actually running the program). The latter pertains to type constraints that must wait until execution time to decide whether those (involving runtime values) may be decided. This is called dynamic type-checking and is best seen (and conceived) as an *incremental* extension of the static part.

A type is either a static type, or a dynamic type. A static type is a type that is checked before runtime by the type-checker. A dynamic type is a wrapper around a type that may need additional runtime information in order to be fully verified. Its static part must be (and is!) checked statically by the static type checker, but the compiler may complete this by issuing runtime tests at appropriate places in the code it generates; namely, when:

- binding abstraction parameters of this type in an application, or
- assigning to local and global variable of this type, or
- updating an array slot, a tuple component, or an object's field, of this type.

There are two kinds of dynamic types:

- Extensional types—defined with explicit extensions (either statically provided or dynamically computed runtime values):
  - `Set` extension type;
  - `Int` range extension type (close interval of integers);
  - `Real` range extension type (close interval of floating-point numbers).
  A special kind of set of `Int` type is used to define enumeration types (from actual symbol sets) through opaque type definitions.
- Intensional types—defined using any runtime Boolean condition to be checked at runtime, calls to which are tests generated statically; *e.g.*non-negative numbers (*i.e.*, `int+`, `double+`).

Static Types. The static type system is the part of the type system that is effective at compile-time.

---

[17] For the complete class hierarchy of types in the package $\langle design \rangle$.`types`, see Fig. 2.

Primitive Types

- Boxable types ($\mathfrak{Void}$, $\mathfrak{Int}$, $\mathfrak{Real}$, $\mathfrak{Char}$, and $\mathfrak{Boolean}$)
- Boxed types (*i.e.*, boxed versions of Boxable types or non-primitive types)

Non-primitive Types

- Built-in type constants (*e.g.*, $\mathfrak{String}$, *etc.*, ...)
- Type constructors
- Function types
- Tuple types:
  - Position tuple types
  - Named tuple types
- Array types:
  - 0-based int-indexed arrays
  - Int range-indexed arrays
  - Set-indexed arrays
  - Multidimensional arrays
- Collection types ($Set(\alpha)$, $Bag(\alpha)$, and $List(\alpha)$).
- Class types

The Class type This is the type of object structures. It declares an *interface* (or member type signature) for a class of objects and the members comprising its structure. It holds information for compiling field access and update, and enables specifying an *implementation* for methods manipulating objects of this type.

A class implementation uses the information declared in its interface. It is interpreted as follows: only non-method members—hereafter called *fields*—correspond to actual slots in an object structure that is an instance of the class and thus may be updated. On the other hand, all members (*i.e.*, both fields and method members) are defined as global *functions* whose first argument stands for the object itself (that may be referred to as 'this').

The syntax we shall use for a class definition is of the form:

$$\mathfrak{class}\ classname\ \{\ interface\ \}\ [\ \{\ implementation\}\ ] \qquad (3)$$

The *interface* block specifies the type signatures of the *members* (fields and methods) of the class and possibly initial values for fields. The *implementation* block is optional and gives the definition of (some or all of) the methods.

For example, one can declare a class to represent a simple counter as follows:

$$
\begin{aligned}
&\mathfrak{class}\ \text{Counter}\ \{\ \text{value} : \mathfrak{Int} = 1; \\
&\qquad\qquad\quad \mathfrak{method}\ \text{set} : \mathfrak{Int} \rightarrow \text{Counter}; \\
&\qquad\qquad\ \} \\
&\qquad\qquad\ \{\ \text{set}(\text{value} : \mathfrak{Int}) : \text{Counter}) \\
&\qquad\qquad\quad = (\text{this.value} = \text{value}); \\
&\qquad\qquad\ \}
\end{aligned} \qquad (4)
$$

The first block specifies the interface for the class type Counter defining two members: a field value of type $\mathfrak{Int}$ and a method set taking an argument of type $\mathfrak{Int}$

and returning a `Counter` object. It also specifies an initialization expression (1) for the `value` field. Specifying a field's initialization is optional—when missing, the field will be initialized to a null value of appropriate type: 0 for an $\mathfrak{Int}$, 0.0 for a $\mathfrak{Real}$, $\mathfrak{false}$ for a $\mathfrak{Boolean}$, $'\backslash 000'$ for a $\mathfrak{Char}$, " " for a $\mathfrak{String}$, $\mathfrak{void}$ for $\mathfrak{Void}$,[18] and null_T for any other type T. The implementation block for the `Counter` class defines the body of the `set` method. Note that a method's implementation can also be given outside the class declaration as a function whose first argument's type is the class. For example, we could have defined the `set` method of the class `Counter` as:

$$\mathfrak{def}\,\text{set}(x:\text{Counter},n:\mathfrak{Int}):\text{Counter}\;=\;(x.\text{value}=n); \qquad (5)$$

On the other hand, although a field is also semantically a function whose first argument's type is a class, it may *not* be defined outside its class. Defining a declared field outside a class declaration causes an error. This is because the code of a field is always fixed and defined to return the value of an object's slot corresponding to the field. Note however that one may define a unary function whose argument is a class type outside this class when it is not a declared field for this class. It will be understood as a *method* for the class (even though it takes no extra argument and may be invoked in "dot notation" without parentheses as a field is) and thus act as a "static field" for the class. Of course field updates using dot notation will not be allowed on these pseudo fields. However, they (like any global variable) may be (re)set using a global (re)definition at the top level, or a nested global assignment.

Note also that a field may be functional without being a method—the essential difference being that a field is part of the structure of every object instance of a class and thus may be updated within an object instance, while a method is common to all instances of a class and may not be updated within a particular instance, but only globally for all the class' instances.

Thus, everytime a `Counter` object is created with $\mathfrak{new}$, as in, for example:

$$c = \mathfrak{new}\;\text{Counter}; \qquad (6)$$

the slot that corresponds to the location of the `value` field will be initialized to the value 1 of type $\mathfrak{Int}$. Then, field and method invocation can be done using the familiar "dot notation;" *viz.*:

```
c.set(c.value + 2);
write(c.value);
```
$\qquad (7)$

This will set c's `value` field to 3 and print out this value. This code is exactly equivalent to:

```
set(c, value(c) + 2);
write(value(c));
```
$\qquad (8)$

Indeed, field and method invocation simply amounts to functional application. This scheme offers the advantage that an object's fields and methods may be manipulated

---

[18] Strictly speaking, a field of type $\mathfrak{Void}$ is useless since it can only have the unique value of this type (*i.e.*, $\mathfrak{void}$). Thus, a $\mathfrak{void}$ field should arguably be disallowed. On the other hand, allowing it is not semantically unsound and may be tolerated for the sake of uniformity.

as functions (*i.e.*, as first-class citizens) and no additional setup is needed for type-checking and/or type inference when it comes to objects.

Incidentally, some or all type information may be omitted while specifying a class's *implementation* (though not its *interface*) as long as non-ambiguous types may be inferred. Thus, the implementation block for class Counter in class definition (4) could be specified more simply as:

$$\{ \text{set}(n) = (\text{value} = n); \} \tag{9}$$

Declaring a class type and defining its implementation causes the following:

– the name of the class is entered with a new type for it in the type table (an object comprising symbol tables, of type ⟨*types*⟩.Tables.java; this ensures that its type definition links it to an appropriate ClassType object; namely, a class structure reprensented by an object of type ⟨*types*⟩.ClassInfo.java where the code entries for all its members' types are recorded;
– each field of a distinct type is assigned an offset in an array of slots (per sort);
– each method and field expression is name-sanitized, type-checked, and sort-sanitized after closing it into an abstraction taking this as first argument;
– each method definition is then compiled into a global definition, and each field is compiled into a global function corresponding to accessing its value from the appropriate offset;
– finally, each field's initialization expression is compiled and recorded in an object of type ClassType to be used at object creation time. An object may be created at run-time (using the *new* operator followed by a class name).

The Type System. Fig. 2 shows the hierarchy of Java classes representing the categories of types currently comprising the type system. The classes represented in boxes are abstract classes. There could be more, of course.

Structure of TypeChecker. An object of the class ⟨*types*⟩.TypeChecker.java is a backtracking prover that establishes various kinds of *goals*. The most common goal kind established by a type checker is a *typing goal*—but there are others.

A ⟨*types*⟩.TypingGoal object is a pair consisting of an expression and a type. Proving a typing goal amounts to unifying its expression component's type with its type component. Such goals are spawned by the type checking method of expressions as per their type checking rules.[19] Some globally defined symbols having multiple types, it is necessary to keep choices of these and backtrack to alternative types upon failure. Thus, a TypeChecker object maintains all the necessary structures for undoing the effects that happened since the last choice point. These effects are:

1. type variable binding,
2. function type currying,

---
[19] See Appendix Section B.

Class hierarchy of types in the package
hlt.language.design.types

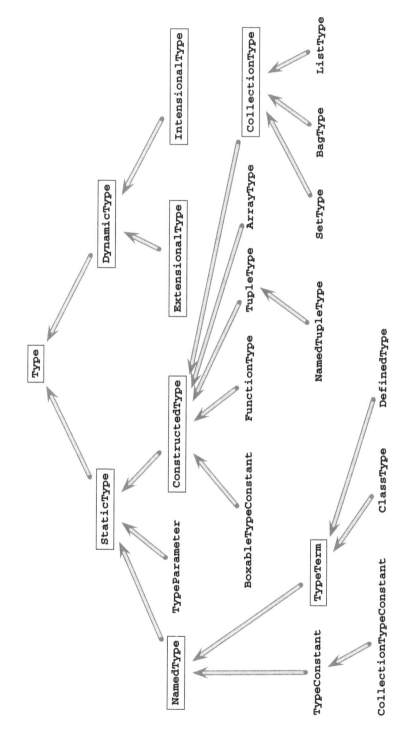

Fig. 2. The type system—Metaclass Hierarchy

3. application expression currying.

In addition, it is also necessary to remember all Goal objects that were proven since the last choice point in order to prove them anew upon backtracking to an alternative choice. This is necessary because the goals are spawned by calls to the typeCheck method of expressions that may be exited long before a failure occurs. Then, all the original typing goals that were spawned in the mean time since the current choice point's goal must be reestablished. In order for this to work, any choice points that were associated to these original goals must also be recovered. To enable this, when a choice point is created for a ⟨kernel⟩.Global symbol, choices are linked in the reverse order (i.e., ending in the original goal) to enable reinstating all choices that were tried for this goal. This amounts to the on-the-fly compiling of type-checking rules into "typing-goal" instructions that must be stored for potential retrial upon subsequent failure. Fig. 3 lists some typing goals making up the instruction set of the type inference abstract machine generated by the type checker.

- EmptyGoal
- TypingGoal
- UnifyGoal
- GlobalTypingGoal
- SubTypeGoal
- BaseTypeGoal
- ArrayIndexTypeGoal

- PruningGoal
- PushExitableGoal
- PopExitableGoal
- CheckExitableGoal
- ResiduatedGoal
- ShadowUnifyGoal
- UnifyBaseTypeGoal
- NoVoidTypeGoal

Fig. 3. Typing goals instruction set for the type inference abstract machine

In order to coordinate type proving in a common context, the same typechecker object is passed to all type checking and unification methods as an argument in order to record any effect in the appropriate trail.

To recapitulate, the structures of a ⟨types⟩.TypeChecker object are:

- a *goal stack* containing *goal* objects (e.g., ⟨types⟩.TypingGoal) that are yet to be proven;

- a *binding trail stack* containing type variables and boxing masks to reset to "unbound" upon backtracking;

- a *function type currying trail* containing 4-tuples of the form (function type, previous domains, previous range, previous boxing mask) for resetting the function type to the recorded domains, range, and mask upon backtracking;

- an *application currying trail* containing triples of the form (application type, previous function, previous arguments) for resetting the application to the recorded function and arguments upon backtracking;

- a *goal trail* containing ⟨types⟩.TypingGoal objects that have been proven since the last choice point, and must be reproven upon backtracking;

- a *choice-point stack* whose entries consists of:
  - a queue of `TypingGoalEntry` objects from where to constructs new `TypingGoal` objects to try upon failure;
  - pointers to all trails up to which to undo effects.

Type definitions Before we review dynamic types, we shall describe how one can define new types using existing types. Type definitions are provided both for (1) convenience of making programs more legible by giving terser "logical" names (or terms) to otherwise verbose type expressions, and (2) that of hiding information details of a type and making it act as a new type altogether. The former facility is that of providing *aliases* to types (exactly like a preprocessor's macros get expanded right away into their textual equivalents), while the latter offers the convenience of defining *new* types in terms of existing ones, but hiding this information. It follows from this distinction that a type alias is *always* structurally equivalent to its value (in fact an alias disappears as soon as it is read in, being parsed away into the structure defining it). By contrast, a defined type is *never* structurally equivalent to its value nor any other type—it is only equivalent to itself. To enable meaningful computation with a defined type, two meta-(de/con)structors are thus provided: one for explicitly *casting* a defined type into the type that defines it, and one explicitly seeing a type as a specified defined type (if such a defined type does exist and with this type as definition).

The class ⟨*types*⟩`.Tables.java` contains the symbol tables for global names and types. The name spaces of the identifiers denoting type and non-type (global or local) names (which are kept in the global symbol table) are disjoint—so there are no name conflicts between types and non-type identifiers.

The ⟨*types*⟩`.Tables.java.typeTable` variable contains the naming table for types and the ⟨*types*⟩`.Tables.java.symbolTable` variable contains the naming table for other (non-type) global names.

This section will overview some type-related data-structures starting from the class that manages symbols: ⟨*types*⟩`.Tables.java`. The names can be those of types and values. They are *global* names.[20] The type namespace is independent of the value namespace—*i.e.*, the same name can denote a value and a type.

Dynamic Types. Dynamic types are to be checked, if possible statically (at least their static part is), at least in two particular places of an expression. Namely,

- at assignment/update time; and,
- at (function) parameter-binding time.

This will ensure that the actual value placed in the slot expecting a certain type does respect additionnal constraints that may only be verified with some runtime values. Generally, as soon as a type's structure depends on a runtime value, is is necessarily a dynamic type. These are also often referred to as *dependent* types. For example, `array_of_size(int n)`, where n is the size of the array and is a runtime value. It

---

[20] At the moment, there is no name qualification or namespace management. When this service is provided, it will also be through the ⟨*types*⟩`.Tables.java` class.

denotes a "safe" array type depending on the array size that may be only computed at runtime.[21] From this, we require that a class implementing the `DynamicType` interface provides a method:

```
public boolean verifyCondition ()
```

that is invoked systematically by code generated for dynamically typed function parameters and for locations that are the target of updates (*i.e.*, array slot update, object field update, tuple field update) at compilation of abstractions and various assignment constructs. Of this class, three subclasses derive their properties:

– extensional types;
– Boolean-assertion types;
– non-negative number types.

We shall consider here a few such dynamic types (motivated esssentially by the typing needs of for OPL, or similar constraint languages [31]). Namely,

– extensional types;
– intensional types (*e.g.*, non-negative numbers)

An *extensional* type is a type whose elements are determined to be members of a predetermined and fixed extension (*i.e.*, any runtime value that denotes a collection—such as a set, an integer range, a floating-point number range, or an enumeration). Such types pose the additional problem of being usable at compile-time to restrict the domains of other variables. However, some of those variables' values may only fully be determined at runtime. These particular dynamic types have therefore a simple `verifyCondition()` method that is automatically run as soon as the extension is known. This method simply verifies that the element is a *bona fide* member of the extension, Otherwise, it relies on a more complicated scheme based on the notion of *contract*. Basically, a contract-based type is an extensional type that does not have an extension (as yet) but already carries the obligation that some particular individual constants be part of their extensions. Those elements constitute "contracts" that must be honored as soon as the type's extension becomes known (either positively—removing the honored contract; or, negatively—causing a type error).

Extensional types that have been included are set types, range types (integer and floating-point), and enumeration types. Other dynamic types could of course be added as needed (*e.g.*, lists, bags, *etc.*).

Intensional types can be accommodated by defining new opaque types—*e.g.*, in order to define non-negative numbers, we introduce a new (opaque) type `Nat` as a dynamically constrained `Int` type whose `verifyCondition` method ensures that only non-negative integer values may be used for this type.

5   Computing with Collections

There are two classes defined for such expressions: ⟨*kernel*⟩.`Homomorphism.java` and ⟨*kernel*⟩.`Comprehension.java`. These classes are based on the formal no-

---

[21] *e.g.*, *à la* Java arrays.

tion of monoid homomorphisms and comprehension as defined in query-language formalisms [5,6,7,8].[22]

These two classes of expressions use monoid homomorphisms as declarative iterators. Thus, henceforth, by *homomorphism* we mean specifically *monoid* homomorphism. For our purposes, a monoid is a set of data values or structures (*i.e.*, a data type) endowed with an associative binary operation and an identity element. Examples are given in Fig. 4. Monoid homomorphisms are quite useful for expressing a certain kind of iteration declaratively.

Type	Operation	Identity
$\mathfrak{Int}$	$+_{\mathfrak{Int}}$	0
$\mathfrak{Int}$	$*_{\mathfrak{Int}}$	1
$\mathfrak{Int}$	$\max_{\mathfrak{Int}}$	$-\infty_{\mathfrak{Int}}$
$\mathfrak{Int}$	$\min_{\mathfrak{Int}}$	$+\infty_{\mathfrak{Int}}$
$\mathfrak{Real}$	$+_{\mathfrak{Real}}$	0.0
$\mathfrak{Real}$	$*_{\mathfrak{Real}}$	1.0
$\mathfrak{Real}$	$\max_{\mathfrak{Real}}$	$-\infty_{\mathfrak{Real}}$
$\mathfrak{Real}$	$\min_{\mathfrak{Real}}$	$+\infty_{\mathfrak{Real}}$
$\mathfrak{Boolean}$	$\text{or}_{\mathfrak{Boolean}}$	$\mathfrak{false}$
$\mathfrak{Boolean}$	$\text{and}_{\mathfrak{Boolean}}$	$\mathfrak{true}$
set data structures	set union	the empty set $\{\}$
list data structures	list concatenation	the empty list $[]$
...		

Fig. 4. Examples of some familiar monoids

The class `Homomorphism` is the class of objects denoting (monoid) homomorphisms. An instance of such a class defines all the needed parameters for representing and iterating through a collection, applying a function to each element, accumulating the results along the way with an operation, and returning the end result. More precisely, it is the built-in version of the general computation scheme whose instance is the following "**hom**" functional, which may be formulated recursively, for the case of a list collection, as:

$$\begin{aligned}
\mathbf{hom}_\oplus^{\mathbb{1}_\oplus}(f)[] &= \mathbb{1}_\oplus \\
\mathbf{hom}_\oplus^{\mathbb{1}_\oplus}(f)[H|T] &= f(H) \oplus \mathbf{hom}_\oplus^{\mathbb{1}_\oplus}(f)T
\end{aligned} \tag{10}$$

Clearly, this scheme extends a function f to a homomorphism of monoids, from the monoid of lists to the monoid defined by $\langle \oplus, \mathbb{1}_\oplus \rangle$.

---

[22] See Appendix Section E for a refresher on monoid homomorphisms and comprehensions.

Thus, an object of this class denotes the result of applying such a homomorphic extension of a function (f) to an element of collection monoid (*i.e.*, a data structure such as a set, a list, or a bag), the image monoid being implicitly defined by the binary operation ($\oplus$)—also called the *accumulation* operation. It is made to work iteratively.

For technical reasons, we need to treat specially so-called *collection* homomorphisms; *i.e.*, those whose accumulation operation constructs a collection, such as a set. Although a collection homomorphism can conceptually be expressed with the general scheme, the function applied to an element of the collection will return a collection (*i.e.*, a *free* monoid) element, and the result of the homomorphism is then the result of tallying the partial collections coming from applying the function to each element into a final "concatenation."

Other (non-collection) homomorphisms are called *primitive* homomorphisms. For those, the function applied to all elements of the collection will return a *computed* element that may be directly composed with the other results. Thus, the difference between the two kinds of (collection or primitive) homomorphisms will appear in the typing and the code generated (collection homomorphism requiring an extra loop for tallying partial results into the final collection). It is easy to make the distinction between the two kinds of homomorphisms thanks to the type of the accumulation operation (see below).

Therefore, a *collection homomorphism* expression constructing a collection of type $coll(T)$ consists of:

- the collection iterated over—of type $coll'(T')$;
- the iterated function applied to each element—of type $T' \to coll(T)$; and,
- the operation "adding" an element to a collection—of type $T, coll(T) \to coll(T)$.

A *primitive homomorphism* computing a value of type T consists of:

- the collection iterated over—of type $coll'(T')$;
- the iterated function applied to each element—of type $T' \to T$; and,
- the monoid operation—of type $T, T \to T$.

Even though the scheme of computation for homomorphisms described above is correct, it is not often used, especially when the function already encapsulates the accumulation operation, as is always the case when the homomorphism comes from the desugaring of a *comprehension*—(see below). Then, such a homomorphism will directly side-effect the collection structure specified as the identity element with a function of the form $\text{fun } x \cdot x \oplus \mathbb{1}_\oplus$ (*i.e.*, adding element x to the collection) and dispense altogether with the need to accumulate intermediate results. We shall call those homomorphisms *in-place* homomorphisms. To distinguish them and enable the suppression of intermediate computations, a flag indicating that the homomorphism is to be computed in-place is provided. Both primitive and collection homomorphisms can be specified to be in-place. If nothing regarding in-place computation is specified for a homomorphism, the default behavior will depend on whether the homomorphism is collection (default is in-place), or primitive (default is *not* in-place). Methods to override the defaults are provided.

For an in-place homomorphism, the iterated function encapsulates the operation, which affects the identity element, which thus accumulates intermediate results and no further composition using the operation is needed. This is especially handy for collections that are often represented, for (space and time) efficiency reasons, by iteratable bulk structures constructed by allocating an empty structure that is filled in-place with elements using a built-in *"add"* method guaranteeing that the resulting data structure is canonical—*i.e.*, that it abides by the algebraic properties of its type of collection (*e.g.*, adding an element to a set will not create duplicates, *etc.*).

Although monoid homomorphisms are defined as expressions in the kernel, they are not meant to be represented directly in a surface syntax (although they could, but would lead to rather cumbersome and not very legible expressions). Rather, they are meant to be used for expressing higher-level expressions known as *monoid comprehensions*, which offer the advantage of the familar (set) comprehension notation used in mathematics, and can be translated into monoid homomorphisms to be type-checked and evaluated. This is what the kernel class `Comprehension` encapsulates, as it is defined relying on the class `Homomorpism`, exactly as its formal definition does.

A monoid comprehension is an expression of the form:

$$\langle \oplus, \mathbb{1}_\oplus \rangle \{ e \mid q_1, \ldots, q_n \} \tag{11}$$

where $\langle \oplus, \mathbb{1}_\oplus \rangle$ define a monoid, e is an expression, and the q_i's are *qualifiers*. A qualifier is either an expression e or a pair $x \leftarrow e$, where x is a variable and e is an expression. The sequence of qualifiers may also be empty. Such a monoid comprehension is just syntactic sugar that can be expressed in terms of homomorphisms as follows:

$$\langle \oplus, \mathbb{1}_\oplus \rangle \{ e \mid \} \quad\quad\quad \overset{\text{def}}{=} \ e \oplus \mathbb{1}_\oplus$$

$$\langle \oplus, \mathbb{1}_\oplus \rangle \{ e \mid x \leftarrow e', Q \} \overset{\text{def}}{=} \ \mathfrak{hom}_\oplus^{\mathbb{1}_\oplus} [\lambda x. \langle \oplus, \mathbb{1}_\oplus \rangle \{ e \mid Q \}](e') \tag{12}$$

$$\langle \oplus, \mathbb{1}_\oplus \rangle \{ e \mid c, Q \} \quad\quad \overset{\text{def}}{=} \ \mathfrak{if}\ c\ \mathfrak{then}\ \langle \oplus, \mathbb{1}_\oplus \rangle \{ e \mid Q \}\ \mathfrak{else}\ \mathbb{1}_\oplus$$

In other words, a comprehension is fully expressible in terms of compositions of homomorphims. Comprehensions are also interesting as they may be subject to transformations leading to more efficient evaluation than their simple "nested loops" operational semantics (by using "unnesting" techniques and using relational operations as implementation instructions [32,33]).

Although a monoid comprehension can be effectively computed using nested loops (*i.e.*, using a simple iteration semantics), such would be in general rather inefficient. Rather, an optimized implementation can be achieved by various syntactic transformation expressed as rewrite rules. Thus, the principal benefit of using monoid comprehensions is to formulate efficient optimizations on a simple and uniform general syntax of expressions irrespective of specific monoids [5,6,32,7,33]. All the attributes of the syntax of monoid comprehensions derived from monoid homomorphisms are represented in these type classes.

Thus, monoid comprehensions allow the formulation of "declarative iteration." Note the fact mentioned earlier that a homomorphism coming from the translation of a comprehension encapsulates the operation in its function. Thus, this is generally taken to advantage with operations that cause a side-effect on their second argument to enable an in-place homomorphism to dispense with unneeded intermediate computation.

6   Conclusion

6.1   Recapitulation

In this document we summarized the main characteristics of an abstract, reusable, and extensible programming language architecture, and its implementation in Java. We overviewed original generic syntax-processing tools that have been conceived, implemented, and used to ease the experimental front-end development for language processing systems. This consisted of Jacc, a flexible metacompiler all done in 100%-pure Java. We explained the machinery needed to extend LALR-parsing to enable dynamic operators à la Prolog. We gave a high-level description of the architectural attributes of a set of kernel classes of programming language constructs and how they are processed for typing, compiling, and executing. We presented our architecture general processing diagram taking a kernel expression into straightline abstract-machine code. We discussed a type system that is the basis for a polymorphic type inference abstract machine enabling multiple-type overloading, type encapsulation, object-orientation, and type (un)boxing analysis. We described the type language primitives and constructors, and how they were analyzed for efficient code generation and execution. We explained our implementation of type-checking and how execution of declarative iteration over collections may be specified using the notion of monoid homomorphism and comprehension as used in object-oriented database query languages to generate efficient collection-processing code.

For the sake of making this document self-contained, we append below a set of sections of tutorial nature giving background material and finer-point discussions regarding what was presented.

6.2   What's next?

This architecture offers a compromise between formal executable specification systems (e.g., [34,23]) and pragmatic needs for practical language prototyping backward compatible with popular existing tools (yacc, Java), while staying an *extensible* system—a *poor man's language kit?...* It enables fast and low-cost development of programming languages with basic and advanced features using familiar programming idioms like yacc and Java with a relatively high efficiency and confidence of correctness.

Importantly, it is *open* and favors *ease of extension* as well as *interoperability* with popular representation standards such as the W3C's. As mentioned several times, and made explicit in the title, this is work to be continued. Indeed, more tools and capabilities are to be added as this author's sees the need. The system has shown itself a practical and useful experimental tool. However, much more remains to be done (*e.g.*, namespace and access management, rule-based programming, logic programming, finer type logics, *etc.*, ...). Here are a few of the most immediate on our agenda.

- *Notation*—The next step is to extend Jacc by providing other structure-generating options besides XML, such as the JavaScript Object Notation (JSON)[23] and its

---

[23] http://www.json.org/

version for Linked Data (JSON-LD).[24] With this tool, it will then be easier to experiment using 𝔍𝔞𝔠𝔠 to generate RDF-triples (or variations thereof) as compilation schemes from high-level (*i.e.*, more legible and user-friendly) KR languages (such as, *e.g.*, $\mathcal{OSF}$ or LIFE syntax—or even higher level; *e.g.*, NL dialects).

- *Typing*—Truly polymorphic object-oriented subtyping *à la* Gesberg, *et al.* [21,22], or Satisfiability Modulo Theories *à la* Bierman *et al.* [23,24]. This is indeed a most desired set of type-analytical capabilities to enable subtyping and class inheritance in our type logic. The type-checking rules given for these systems are the best candidates to use for this objective.
- *Semantics*— The most ambitious next step in terms of semantics, would be to extend the current design with additional abstract meta-constructs for $\mathcal{LP}$ [17] and $\mathcal{CLP}$ [25] (and LIFE [9,10] in particular).
- *Pragmatics*—Not much has been said about the backend system.[25] Among the most desired to be done is a graphical front end based on Eclipse.[26] Wrapping all the backend tools and services in such a front-end would greatly help further meta-development.
- *Implementation*—Once abstracted into stable interfaces, any design may then be made more efficient where needed since implementation has thus been made independent. Attention may then be safely given to clever optimization of any type of algorithms used in the implementation of these interfaces, relying on time-tested techniques [35].

Appendix

In order to make this article self-contained, we include next a set of tutorials that overview essential background notions. Thus, this appendix consists of the following sections. Section A recalls the peculiar way that Prolog uses to enable changing the syntactic properties of its operators dynamically—*i.e.*, at run time. Section B describes how a few familiar programming language contructs may be specified as classes of objects and how these classes are processed in various syntax, typing, or execution contexts. Section C recounts notions on algebraic monoids. Section D is a reminder of the abstract syntax and type inference logic for a basic typed polymorphic λ-calculus with tupling. Section E presents OQL, an Object Query Language extending this basic λ-calculus into a monoid comprehension calculus dealing with collection data in a declarative manner thanks to monoid homomorphisms. Section F is a brief specification of the backend tooling needed to complete the system,

A Prolog-style Dynamic Operators

In Prolog, the built-in operator 'op/3' offers the user the means to declare or modify the syntax of some of its operators. For example, as will be explained below:

---

[24] http://json-ld.org/

[25] See Appendix Section F

[26] http://www.eclipse.org/

```
?- op(500,yfx,+).
```

declares the symbol '+' to be an infix binary left-associative operator with binding tightness 500. The second argument of the built-in predicate `op/3` is called the operator's *specifier*. It is a symbol that encodes three kinds of information concerning the operator; namely:

- arity (*unary* or *binary*),
- "fixity" (*prefix*, *infix*, or *postfix*),
- associativity (*left-*, *right-*, or *non-associative*).

The specifier is an identifier consisting of either two or three of the letters 'f', 'x', and 'y', which are interpreted as follows. The letter 'f' stands for the operator's position in an expression (its *fixity*), and the letters 'x' and 'y' stand for the arguments' positions. These letters are mnemonics for "*functor*," ('f') "*yes*," ('y') and "*no*" ('x'). A 'y' occurring on the left (resp., right) of 'f', means that the operator associates to the left (resp., right). An 'x' occurring on the left (resp., right) of 'f', means that the operator does not associate to the left (resp., right). Thus, the possible operator specifiers are shown in Table 1.[27]

Table 1. Mnemonic operator specifiers in Prolog

Specifier	Arity	Fixity	Associativity
fx	unary	prefix	non-associative
fy	unary	prefix	right-associative
xf	unary	postfix	non-associative
yf	unary	postfix	left-associative
xfx	binary	infix	non-associative
xfy	binary	infix	right-associative
yfx	binary	infix	left-associative

The binding tightness used by Prolog's 'op/3' works in fact as the opposite of the precedence level used in parsing: the smaller a Prolog operator's binding tightness measure is, the more it takes precedence for parsing. These binding tightness measures range inclusively from 1 (maximum precedence) to 1200 (minimum precedence).

The third argument of 'op/3' can be any syntactically well-formed Prolog functor. In particular, these need not be known as operator prior to runtime. Prolog's tokenizer only recognizes such a token as a functor. Thus, any functor, whether declared operator or not, can always be parsed as a prefix operator preceding a parenthesized comma-separated sequence of arguments. Whether it is a declared operator determines how it may be parsed otherwise. In Sicstus Prolog, for example:

---

[27] Note that 'yfy' is not allowed as an operator specifier because that would mean an ambiguous way of parsing the operator by associating either to the left or to the right.

```
| ?- X = 1 + 2 .
X = 1+2  ?
yes
| ?- X = +(1,2) .
X = 1+2  ?
yes
```

Prolog's parser can accommodate dynamic operators for two reasons:

1. The syntax of Prolog is completely uniform - there is only one syntactic construct: the first-order term. Even what appear to be punctuation symbols are in fact functors (e.g., ': -', ', ', '; ', etc., ...). Indeed, in Prolog everything is either a logical variable or a structure of the form $f(t_1, \ldots, t_n)$.
2. Prolog parser's is an operator-precedence parser where precedence and associativity information is kept as a dynamic structure.[28]

Operator-precedence parsing is a bottom-up shift-reduce method that works simply by shifting over the input looking for a handle in a sentential form being built on the stack, and reducing when such a handle is recognized. A handle is the substring of a sentential form whose right end is the leftmost operator whose following operator has smaller precedence, and whose left end is the rightmost operator to the left of this right-end operator (inclusive), whose preceding operator has smaller precedence. This substring includes any nonterminals on either ends. For example, if '∗' has higher precedence than '+', the handle in 'E + E ∗ E + E' is 'E ∗ E'.

Operator-precedence parsing is possible only for a very restricted class of grammars - the so-called "*Operator Grammars.*" A context-free grammar is an Operator Grammar if and only if no production's right-hand side is empty or contains two adjacent non-terminals. For example, the grammar:

```
E : 'id'  |  P E  |  E O E  |  '(' E ')' ;
P : '-' ;
O : '+'  |  '*'  |  '-'  |  '/' ;
```

is not an operator grammar. But the equivalent grammar:

```
E : 'id'  |  '-' E  |  E '+' E  |  E '*' E  |  E '-' E
  |  E '/' E  |  '(' E ')' ;
```

is. It is not difficult to see that a Prolog term can easily be recognized by an operator grammar. Namely,

```
T : 'var'  |  'fun'  |  'fun' '(' B ')'
  |  'fun' T  |  T 'fun'  |  T 'fun' T  |  '(' T ')' ;
B : T  |  T ',' B ;
```

which can thus easily accommodate dynamic operators.

---

[28] See "*the Dragon Book,*" [27]—Section 4.6, pp. 203–215.

B   Structure of Kernel Expressions

The class ⟨kernel⟩.Expression.java is the mother of all expressions in the kernel language. It specifies the prototypes of the methods that must be implemented by all expression subclasses. The subclasses of Expression are:

- Constant: constant (void, boolean, integer, real number, object);
- Abstraction: functional abstraction (à la λ-calculus);
- Application: functional application;
- Local: local name;
- Parameter: a function's formal parameter (really a pseudo-expression as it is not fully processed as a real expression and is used as a shared type information repository for all occurrences in a function's body of the variable it stands for);
- Global: global name;
- Dummy: temporary place holder in lieu of a name prior to being discriminated into a local or global one.
- Definition: definition of a global name with an expression defining it in a global store;
- IfThenElse: conditional;
- AndOr: non-strict Boolean conjunction and disjunction;
- Sequence: sequence of expressions (presumably with side-effects);
- Let: lexical scoping construct;
- Loop: conditional iteration construct;
- ExitWithValue: non-local function exit;
- Assignment: construct to set the value of a local or a global variable;
- NewArray: construct to create a new (multidimensional) array;
- ArraySlot: construct to access the element of an array;
- ArraySlotUpdate: construct to update the element of an array;
- Tuple: construct to create a new position-indexed tuple;
- NamedTuple: construct to create a new name-indexed tuple;
- TupleProjection: construct to access the component of a tuple;
- TupleUpdate: construct to update the component of a tuple;
- NewObject: construct to create a new object;
- DottedNotation: construct to emulate traditional object-oriented "dot" dereferencing notation;
- FieldUpdate: construct to update the value of an object's field;
- ArrayExtension: construct denoting a literal array;
- ArrayInitializer: construct denoting a syntactic convenience for specifying initialization of an array from an extension;
- Homomorphism: construct denoting a monoid homomorphism;
- Comprehension: construct denoting a monoid comprehension;

To illustrate the process, we next describe a few kernel constructs. A kernel expression description usually consist of some of the following items:

- ABSTRACT SYNTAX—describes the abstract syntax form of the kernel expression.

– OPERATIONAL SEMANTICS—for unfamiliar expressions, this describes informally the meaning of the expression. The notation $[\![e]\!]$, where e is an abstract syntax expression, denotes the (mathematical) semantic *denotation* of e. The notation $[\![T]\!]$, where T is a type, denotes the (mathematical) semantic *denotation* of T—namely, $[\![T]\!]$ is the set of all abstract denotations $[\![e]\!]$'s such that kernel expression e has type T.

– TYPING RULE—this describes more formally how a type should be verified or inferred using formal rules à la Plotkin's Structural Operational Semantics for typing the kernel expression, whose notation is briefly recalled as follows [36,37].
A *typing judgment* is a formula of the form $\Gamma \vdash e : T$, and is read as: "*under typing context Γ, expression e has type T.*"
In its simplest form, a *typing context* Γ is a function mapping the parameters of λ-abstractions to their types. In the formal presentation of an expression's typing rule, the context keeps the type binding under which the typing derivation has progressed up to applying the rule in which it occurs.
The notation $\Gamma[x : T]$ denotes the context defined from Γ as follows:

$$\Gamma[x : T](y) \ \overset{\text{def}}{=} \ \begin{cases} T & \text{if } y = x; \\ \Gamma(x) & \text{otherwise.} \end{cases} \tag{13}$$

A *typing rule* is a formula of the form:

$$\frac{J_1, \ldots, J_n}{J} \tag{14}$$

where J and the J_i's, $i = 0, \ldots, n$, $n \geq 0$, are typing judgments. This "fraction" notation expresses essentially an implication: when all the formulae of the rule's *premises* (the J_i's in the fraction's "numerator") hold, then the formula in the rule's *conclusion* (the fraction's "denominator") holds too. When $n = 0$, the rule has no premise—*i.e.*, the premise is tautologically *true* (*e.g.*, $0 = 0$)—the rule is called an *axiom* and is written with an empty "numerator."
A *conditional* typing rule is a typing rule of the form:

$$\frac{J_1, \ldots, J_n}{J} \ \text{if} \ c(J_1, \ldots, J_n) \tag{15}$$

where c is a Boolean metacondition involving the rule's judgments.
A typing rule (or axiom), whether or not in conditional form, is usually read backwards (*i.e.*, upwards) from the rule's *conclusion* (the bottom part, or "denominator") to the rule's *premises* (the top part, or "numerator"). Namely, the rule of the form:

$$\frac{\Gamma_1 \vdash e_1 : T_1, \ \ldots, \ \Gamma_n \vdash e_n : T_n}{\Gamma \vdash e : T} \tag{16}$$

is read thus:

"*The expression e has type T under typing context Γ* `if` *the expression e_1 has type T_1 under typing context Γ_1,* `and` *..., the expression e_n has type T_n under typing context Γ_n.*"

For example:

$$\frac{\Gamma \vdash c : \mathfrak{Boolean}, \; \Gamma \vdash e_1 : T, \; \Gamma \vdash e_2 : T}{\Gamma \vdash \text{if } c \text{ then } e_1 \text{ else } e_2 \; : \; T}$$

is read thus:

"*The expression* if c then e_1 else e_2 *has type T under typing context Γ* `if` *the expression c has type $\mathfrak{Boolean}$ under typing context Γ* `and` *if both expressions e_1 and e_2 have the same type T under the same typing context Γ.*"

With judgments spelled-out, a conditional typing rule (15) looks like:

$$\frac{\Gamma_1 \vdash e_1 : T_1, \; \ldots, \; \Gamma_n \vdash e_n : T_n}{\Gamma \vdash e : T} \quad \textit{if} \quad cond(\; \Gamma, \Gamma_1, \ldots, \Gamma_n, \qquad (17)$$
$$e, e_1, \ldots, e_n,$$
$$T, T_1, \ldots, T_n)$$

where "$cond(\Gamma, \Gamma_1, \ldots, \Gamma_n, e, e_1, \ldots, e_n, T, T_1, \ldots, T_n)$" is a Boolean meta-condition involving the contexts, expressions, and types. Such a rule is read thus:

"`if` *the meta-condition holds,* `then` *the expression e has type T under typing context Γ* `if` *the expression e_1 has type T_1 under typing context Γ_1,* `and` *..., the expression e_n has type T_n under typing context Γ_n.*"

An example of a conditional rule is that of abstractions that must take into account whether or not the abstraction is *exitable*—i.e., it may be exited non-locally:

$$\frac{\Gamma[x_1 : T_1] \cdots [x_n : T_n] \vdash e : T}{\Gamma \vdash \text{fun } x_1, \ldots, x_n \cdot e \; : \; T_1, \ldots, T_n \to T} \quad \textit{if} \quad \begin{array}{l} \text{fun } x_1, \ldots, x_n \cdot e \\ \text{is not exitable.} \end{array}$$

Similarly, a *typing axiom*:

$$\frac{}{\Gamma \vdash e : T} \qquad\qquad (18)$$

is read as: "*The expression e has type T under typing context Γ*" and a *conditional typing axiom* is a typing axiom of the form:

$$\frac{}{\Gamma \vdash e : T} \quad \textit{if} \quad c(\Gamma, e, T) \qquad (19)$$

where $c(\Gamma, e, T)$ is a Boolean meta-condition on typing context Γ, expression e, and type T and is read as, "`if` *the meta-condition $c(\Gamma, e, T)$ holds* `then` *the expression e has type T under typing context Γ.*"

– COMPILING RULE—describes the way the expression's components are mapped into a straightline sequence of instructions. The compiling rule for expression e is given as a function $compile[\![\_]\!]$ of the form:

$$compile[\![e]\!] = \begin{array}{l} \text{INSTRUCTION}_1 \\ \vdots \\ \text{INSTRUCTION}_n \end{array} \qquad (20)$$

The Constant Expression. Constants represents the built-in primitive (unconstructed) data elements of the kernel language.

– ABSTRACT SYNTAX A *Constant* expression is an atomic literal. Objects of class Constant denote literal constants: the integers (*e.g.*, -1, 0, 1, *etc.*), the real numbers (*e.g.*, -1.23, ..., 0.0, ..., 1.23, *etc.*), the characters (*e.g.*, $'a'$, $'b'$, $'@'$, $'\#'$, *etc.*), and the constants $\mathfrak{void}$, $\mathfrak{true}$, and $\mathfrak{false}$. The constant $\mathfrak{void}$ is of type $\mathfrak{Void}$, such that:

$$[\![\mathfrak{Void}]\!] \stackrel{\text{def}}{=} \{[\![\mathfrak{void}]\!]\}$$

and the constants:

$\mathfrak{true}$ and $\mathfrak{false}$ of type $\mathfrak{Boolean}$, such that:

$$[\![\mathfrak{Boolean}]\!] \stackrel{\text{def}}{=} \{[\![\mathfrak{false}]\!], [\![\mathfrak{true}]\!]\}.$$

Other built-in types are:

$$[\![\mathfrak{Int}]\!] \stackrel{\text{def}}{=} \mathbb{Z} = \{\ldots, [\![-1]\!], [\![0]\!], [\![1]\!], \ldots\}$$

$$[\![\mathfrak{Real}]\!] \stackrel{\text{def}}{=} \mathbb{R} = \{\ldots, [\![-1.23]\!], \ldots, [\![0.0]\!], \ldots, [\![1.23]\!], \ldots\}$$

$$[\![\mathfrak{Char}]\!] \stackrel{\text{def}}{=} \text{set of all Unicode characters}$$

$$[\![\mathfrak{String}]\!] \stackrel{\text{def}}{=} \text{set of all finite strings of Unicode characters.}$$

Thus, the Constant expression class is further subclassed into: Int, Real, Char, NewObject, and BuiltinObjectConstant, whose instances denote, respectively: integers, floating-point numbers, characters, new objects, and built-in object constants (*e.g.*, strings).

– TYPING RULE The typing rules for each kind of constant are:

$$[\text{void}] \quad \frac{}{\Gamma \vdash \mathfrak{void} : \mathfrak{Void}}$$

$$[\text{true}] \quad \frac{}{\Gamma \vdash \mathfrak{true} : \mathfrak{Boolean}}$$

$$[\text{false}] \quad \frac{}{\Gamma \vdash \mathfrak{false} : \mathfrak{Boolean}}$$

$$[\text{int}] \quad \frac{}{\Gamma \vdash n : \mathfrak{Int}} \qquad \textit{if } n \text{ is an integer} \tag{21}$$

$$[\text{real}] \quad \frac{}{\Gamma \vdash n : \mathfrak{Real}} \qquad \textit{if } n \text{ is a floating-point number}$$

$$[\text{char}] \quad \frac{}{\Gamma \vdash c : \mathfrak{Char}} \qquad \textit{if } c \text{ is a character}$$

$$[\text{string}] \quad \frac{}{\Gamma \vdash s : \mathfrak{String}} \qquad \textit{if } s \text{ is a string}$$

– COMPILING RULE Compiling a constant consists in pushing the value it denotes on the stack of corresponding sort.

$$[\text{void}] \quad \text{compile}[\![\mathfrak{void}]\!] = \text{No\_Op}$$

$$[\text{true}] \quad \text{compile}[\![\mathfrak{true}]\!] = \text{Push\_True}$$

$$[\text{false}] \quad \text{compile}[\![\mathfrak{false}]\!] = \text{Push\_False}$$

$$[\text{int}] \quad \text{compile}[\![n]\!] = \text{Push\_I } n \quad \textit{if } n \text{ is an integer} \tag{22}$$

$$[\text{real}] \quad \text{compile}[\![n]\!] = \text{Push\_R } n \quad \textit{if } n \text{ is a floating-point number}$$

$$[\text{char}] \quad \text{compile}[\![c]\!] = \text{Push\_I } c \quad \textit{if } c \text{ is a character}$$

$$[\text{string}] \quad \text{compile}[\![s]\!] = \text{Push\_O } s \quad \textit{if } s \text{ is a string}$$

The *Abstraction* Expression

– ABSTRACT SYNTAX This is the standard λ-calculus functional abstraction, possibly with multiple parameters. Rather than using the conventional λ notation, we write an abstraction as:

$$\mathfrak{fun} \; x_1, \ldots, x_n \; \cdot \; e \tag{23}$$

where the x_i's are *abstraction parameters*—identifiers denoting variables local to the expression e, the abstraction's *body*.

– TYPING RULE There are two cases to consider depending on whether the abstraction is or not *exitable*. An exitable abstraction is one that corresponds to a real source language's function from which a user may exit non-locally. Other (non-exitable) abstractions are those that are implicitly generated by syntactic desugaring of surface syntax. It is the responsibility of the parser to identify the two kinds of abstractions and mark as exitable all and only those abstractions that should be.

$$\frac{\Gamma[x_1 : T_1] \cdots [x_n : T_n] \vdash e : T}{\Gamma \vdash \mathsf{fun}\ x_1, \ldots, x_n \cdot e : T_1, \ldots, T_n \to T} \quad \textit{if}\ \ \begin{array}{l} \mathsf{fun}\ x_1, \ldots, x_n \cdot e \\ \text{is not exitable.} \end{array} \quad (24)$$

If the abstraction is exitable however, we must record it in the typing context. Namely, let $a = \mathsf{fun}\ x_1, \ldots, x_n \cdot e$; then:

$$\frac{\Gamma_{\aleph \leftarrow a}[x_1 : T_1] \cdots [x_n : T_n] \vdash e : T}{\Gamma \vdash a : T_1, \ldots, T_n \to T} \quad \textit{if}\ \ a \text{ is exitable} \quad (25)$$

where $\Gamma_{\aleph \leftarrow a}$ is the same context as Γ except that $\aleph_{\Gamma_{\aleph \leftarrow a}} \overset{\text{def}}{=} a$.

– COMPILING RULE Compiling an abtraction consists in compiling a flattened version of its body (uncurrying and computing parameters offsets), and then generating an instruction pushing a closure on the stack.

$$\mathsf{compile}[\![\mathsf{fun}\ x_1, \ldots, x_n \cdot e]\!] = \begin{array}{l} \mathsf{compile}[\![(\textit{flatten}(e), \textit{offsets}(x_1, \ldots, x_n)]\!] \\ \text{PUSH\_CLOSURE} \end{array} \quad (26)$$

The **Application** Expression

– ABSTRACT SYNTAX This is the familiar function call:

$$f(e_1, \ldots, e_n) \quad (27)$$

– TYPING RULE The type rule is as expected, modulo all potential un/currying that may be needed:

$$\frac{\Gamma \vdash e_1 : T_1, \ \cdots, \ \Gamma \vdash e_n : T_n, \ \ \Gamma \vdash f : T_1, \ldots, T_n \to T}{\Gamma \vdash f(e_1, \ldots, e_n) : T} \quad (28)$$

– COMPILING RULE

$$\mathsf{compile}[\![f(e_1, \ldots, e_n)]\!] = \begin{array}{l} \mathsf{compile}[\![e_n]\!] \\ \vdots \\ \mathsf{compile}[\![e_1]\!] \\ \mathsf{compile}[\![f]\!] \\ \text{APPLY} \end{array} \quad (29)$$

The IfThenElse Expression

- ABSTRACT SYNTAX This is the familiar conditional:

  if c then e_1 else e_2

- TYPING RULE

$$\frac{\Gamma \vdash c : \mathfrak{Boolean}, \ \Gamma \vdash e_1 : T, \ \Gamma \vdash e_2 : T}{\Gamma \vdash \text{if } c \text{ then } e_1 \text{ else } e_2 \ : \ T} \tag{30}$$

- COMPILING RULE

$$
\begin{aligned}
\text{compile}[\![\text{if } c \text{ then } e_1 \text{ else } e_2]\!] = \quad & \text{compile}[\![c]\!] \\
& \text{JUMP\_ON\_FALSE } jof \\
& \text{compile}[\![e_1]\!] \\
& \text{JUMP } jmp \\
jof : \ & \text{compile}[\![e_2]\!] \\
jmp : \ & \dots
\end{aligned} \tag{31}
$$

The AndOr Expression

- ABSTRACT SYNTAX

  e_1 and/or e_2

- TYPING RULE

$$\frac{\Gamma \vdash e_1 : \mathfrak{Boolean}, \ \Gamma \vdash e_2 : \mathfrak{Boolean}}{\Gamma \vdash e_1 \text{ and/or } e_2 : \mathfrak{Boolean}} \tag{32}$$

- COMPILING RULE

$$
\begin{aligned}
\text{compile}[\![e_1 \text{ and } e_2]\!] = \quad & \text{compile}[\![e_1]\!] \\
& \text{JUMP\_ON\_FALSE } jof \\
& \text{compile}[\![e_2]\!] \\
& \text{JUMP\_ON\_TRUE } jot \\
jof : \ & \text{PUSH\_FALSE} \\
& \text{JUMP } jmp \\
jot : \ & \text{PUSH\_TRUE} \\
jmp : \ & \dots
\end{aligned} \tag{33}
$$

$$
\begin{aligned}
\text{compile}[\![e_1 \text{ or } e_2]\!] = \quad & \text{compile}[\![e_1]\!] \\
& \text{JUMP\_ON\_TRUE } jot \\
& \text{compile}[\![e_2]\!] \\
& \text{JUMP\_ON\_FALSE } jof \\
jot : \ & \text{PUSH\_TRUE} \\
& \text{JUMP } jmp \\
jof : \ & \text{PUSH\_FALSE} \\
jmp : \ & \dots
\end{aligned} \tag{34}
$$

The **Sequence** Expression

– ABSTRACT SYNTAX

$$\{\, e_1;\, \ldots;\, e_n\, \}$$

– TYPING RULE

$$\frac{\Gamma \vdash e_1 : T_1,\; \ldots,\; \Gamma \vdash e_n : T_n}{\Gamma \vdash \{\, e_1;\, \ldots;\, e_n\, \} : T_n} \tag{35}$$

– COMPILING RULE

$$\begin{aligned}
\text{compile}[\![\{\, e_1;\, \ldots;\, e_n\, \}]\!] = \;&\text{compile}[\![e_1]\!] \\
&\text{POP\_sort}(e_1) \\
&\;\vdots \\
&\text{compile}[\![e_n]\!]
\end{aligned} \tag{36}$$

The **WhileDo** Expression

– ABSTRACT SYNTAX

$$\mathfrak{while}\; c\; \mathfrak{do}\; e \tag{37}$$

where c and e are expressions.

– TYPING RULE

$$\frac{\Gamma \vdash c : \mathfrak{Boolean},\; \Gamma \vdash e : T}{\Gamma \vdash \mathfrak{while}\; c\; \mathfrak{do}\; e : \mathfrak{Void}} \tag{38}$$

– COMPILING RULE

$$\begin{aligned}
\text{compile}[\![\mathfrak{while}\; c\; \mathfrak{do}\; e]\!] = \;&loop: \text{compile}[\![c]\!] \\
&\quad\; \text{JUMP\_ON\_FALSE}\; jof \\
&\quad\; \text{compile}[\![e]\!] \\
&\quad\; \text{JUMP}\; loop \\
&jof:
\end{aligned} \tag{39}$$

The **ExitWithValue** *Expression.* This is a primitive for so-called non-local exit, and may be used to express more complicated control structures such as exception handling.

- ABSTRACT SYNTAX

$$\text{e̞it ꭐitꞕ } v \qquad\qquad\qquad\qquad\qquad\qquad (40)$$

where v is an expression.

- OPERATIONAL SEMANTICS Normally, exiting from an abstraction is done simply by "falling off" (one of) the tip(s) of the expression tree of the abstraction's body. This operation is captured by the simple operational semantics of each of the three RETURN instructions. Namely, when executing a RETURN instruction, the runtime performs the following three-step procedure:
  1. it pops the result from its result stack;[29]
  2. it restores the latest saved runtime state (popped off the saved-state stack);
  3. it pushes the result popped in Step 1 onto the restored state's own result stack.
  Then, control follows up with the next instruction.
  However, it is also often desirable, under certain circumstances, that computation *not* be let to proceed further at its current level of nesting of *exitable* abstractions. Then, computation may be allowed to return right away from this current nesting (*i.e.*, as if having fallen off this level of exitable abstraction) when the conditions for this to happen are met. Exiting an abstraction thus must also return a specific value that may be a function of the context. This is what the kernel construction e̞it ꭐitꞕ v expresses. This kernel construction is provided in order to specify that the current local computation should terminate without further ado, and exit with the value denoted by the specified expression.

- TYPING RULE Now, there are several notions in the above paragraphs that need some clarification. For example, what an *"exitable"* abstraction is, and why worry about a dedicated construct in the kernel language for such a notion if it does nothing more than what is done by a RETURN instruction.
  First of all, from its very name e̞it ꭐitꞕ v assumes that computation has *entered* that from which it must *exit*. This is an *exitable* abstraction; that is, the latest λ-abstraction having the property of being *exitable*. Not all abstractions are exitable. For example, any abstraction that is generated as part of the target of some other kernel expression's syntacting sugar (*e.g.*, let $x_1 = e_1; \ldots; x_n = e_n;$ in e or $\langle \oplus, 1\!\!1_\oplus \rangle \{e \mid x_1 \leftarrow e_1, \ldots, x_n \leftarrow e_n\}$, and generally any construct that hide implicit abstractions within), will *not* be deemed exitable.
  Secondly, exiting with a value v means that the type T of v must be congruent with what the return type of the abstraction being exited is. In other words:

$$\frac{\Gamma \vdash \aleph_\Gamma : T' \to T, \ \Gamma \vdash v : T}{\Gamma \vdash \text{e̞it ꭐitꞕ } v \ : \ T} \qquad\qquad (41)$$

where $\aleph_\Gamma$ denotes the latest *exitable* abstraction in the context Γ.
The above scheme indicates the following necessities:

---

[29] Where *stack* here means "stack of *appropriate* runtime sort;" appropriate, that is, as per the instruction's runtime sort—*viz.*, ending in _I for INT, _R for REAL, or _O for OBJECT.

1. The typing rules for an abstraction deemed exitable must record in its typing context Γ the latest exitable abstraction, if any such exists; (if none does, a static semantics error is triggered to indicate that it is impossible to exit from anywhere before first entering somewhere).[30]

2. Congruently, the Apply instruction of an exitable closure must take care of chaining this exitable closure before it pushes a new state for it in the saved state stack of the runtime system with the last saved exitable closure, and mark the saved state as being exitable; dually, this exitable state stack must also be popped upon "falling off"—i.e., normally exiting—an exitable closure. That is, whenever an exitable state is restored.

3. New non-local return instructions NL_RETURN (for each runtime sort) must be defined like their corresponding RETURN instructions except that the runtime state to restore is the one popped out of the exitable state stack.

– COMPILING RULE

$$\text{compile}\,[\![\mathfrak{exit\ with}\ v]\!] = \begin{array}{l} \text{compile}\,[\![v]\!] \\ \text{NL\_RETURN\_}\textit{sort}(v) \end{array} \tag{42}$$

C Monoids

In this section, all notions and notations relating to monoids as they are used in this paper are recalled and justified.

Mathematically, a monoid is a non-empty set equipped with an associative internal binary operation and an identity element for this operation. Formally, let S be a set, $\star$ a function from $S \times S$ to S, and $\epsilon \in S$; then, $\langle S, \star, \epsilon \rangle$ is a monoid iff, for any x, y, z in S:

$$x \star (y \star z) = (x \star y) \star z \tag{43}$$

and

$$x \star \epsilon = \epsilon \star x = \epsilon. \tag{44}$$

Most familiar mathematical binary operations define monoids. For example, taking the set of natural numbers $\mathbb{N}$, and the set of boolean values $\mathbb{B} = \{\mathfrak{true}, \mathfrak{false}\}$, the following are monoids:

– $\langle \mathbb{N}, +, 0 \rangle$,
– $\langle \mathbb{N}, *, 1 \rangle$,
– $\langle \mathbb{N}, \max, 0 \rangle$,
– $\langle \mathbb{B}, \vee, \mathfrak{false} \rangle$,
– $\langle \mathbb{B}, \wedge, \mathfrak{true} \rangle$.

---

[30] This is why Typing Rule (25) needs to treat both kinds of abstractions.

The operations of these monoids are so familiar that they need not be explicated. For us, they have a "built -in" semantics that allows us to compute with them since primary school. Indeed, we shall refer to such readily interpreted monoids as *primitive monoids*.[31]

Note that the definition of a monoid does not preclude additional algebraic structure. Such structure may be specified by other equations augmenting the basic monoid equational theory given by the conjunction of equations (43) and (44). For example, all five monoids listed above are *commutative*; namely, they also obey equation (45):

$$x \star y = y \star x \tag{45}$$

for any x, y. In addition, the three last ones (*i.e.*, max, $\vee$, and $\wedge$) are also *idempotent*; namely, they also obey equation (46):

$$x \star x = x \tag{46}$$

for any x.

Not all monoids are primitive monoids. That is, one may define a monoid purely syntactically whose operation only builds a syntactic structure rather than being interpreted using some semantic computation. For example, linear lists have such a structure: the operation is list concatenation and builds a list out of two lists; its identity element is the empty list. A syntactic monoid may also have additional algebraic structure. For example, the monoid of bags is also defined as a commutative syntactic monoid with the disjunct union operation and the empty bag as identity. Or, the monoid of sets is a commutative and idempotent syntactic monoid with the union operation and the empty set as identity.

Because they are not interpreted, syntactic monoids pose a problem as far as representation of its elements is concerned. To illustrate this, let us consider an empty-theory algebraic structure; that is, one without any equations—not even associativity nor identity. Let us take such a structure with one binary operation $\star$ on, say, the natural numbers $\mathbb{N}$. Saying that $\star$ is a "syntactic" operation means that it constructs a syntactic term (*i.e.*, an expression tree) by composing two other syntactic terms. We thus can define the set $T_\star$ of $\star$-terms on some base set, say, the natural numbers, inductively as the limit $\cup_{n \geq 0} T_n$ where,

$$T_n \stackrel{\text{def}}{=} \begin{cases} \mathbb{N} & \text{if } n = 0 \\ \{t_1 \star t_2 \mid t_i \in T_{n-1}, i = 1, 2\} & \text{if } n > 0. \end{cases} \tag{47}$$

---

[31] We call these monoids "primitive" following the presentation of Fegaras and Maier [8] as it adheres to a more operational (as opposed to mathematical) approach more suitable to computer-scientists. Mathematically, however, these should be called "semantic" monoids since they are interpreted by the computation semantics of their operations. See Appendix Section E.1 for an overview of this formalism.

Clearly, the set $T_\star$ is well defined and so is the $\star$ operation over it. Indeed, $\star$ is a *bona fide* function from $T_\star \times T_\star$ to $T_\star$ mapping two terms t_1 and t_2 in $T_\star$ into a unique term in $T_\star$—namely, $t_1 \star t_2$. This is why $T_\star$ is called the *syntactic* algebra.[32]

Let us now assume that the $\star$ operation is associative—*i.e.*, that $\star$-terms verify Equation (43). Note that this equation defines a (syntactic) *congruence* on $T_\star$ which identifies terms such as, say, $1 \star (2 \star 3)$ and $(1 \star 2) \star 3$. In fact, for such an associative $\star$ operation, the set $T_\star$ defined in Equation (47) is not the appropriate domain. Rather, the right domain is the quotient set whose elements are (syntactic) congruence classes modulo associativity of $\star$. Therefore, this creates an ambiguity of representation of the syntactic structures.[33]

Similarly, more algebraic structure defined by larger equational theories induces coarser quotients of the empty-theory algebra by putting together in common congruence classes all the syntactic expressions that can be identified modulo the theory's equations. The more equations, the more ambiguous the syntactic structures of expressions. Mathematically, this poses no problem as one can always abstract away from individuals to congruence classes. However, operationally one must resort to some concrete artifact to obtain a unique representation for all members of the same congruence class. One way is to devise a *canonical* representation into which to transform all terms. For example, an associative operation could systematically "move" nested subtrees from its left argument to its right argument—in effect using Equation (43) as a one-way rewrite rule. However, while this is possible for some equational theories, it is not so in general—*e.g.*, take commutativity.[34]

From a programming standpoint (which is ours), we can abstract away from the ambiguity of canonical representations of syntactic monoid terms using a flat notation. For example, in LISP and Prolog, a list is seen as the (flat) sequence of its constituents. Typically, a programmer writes $[1, 2, 1]$ to represent the list whose elements are 1, 2 and 1 in this order, and does not care (nor need s/he be aware) of its concrete representation. A set—*i.e.*, a commutative idempotent syntactic monoid—is usually denoted by the usual mathematical notation $\{1, 2\}$, implicitly relying on disallowing duplicate elements, not minding the order in which the elements appear. A bag, or multiset—*i.e.*, a commutative but non-idempotent syntactic monoid—uses a similar notation, allowing duplicate elements but paying no heed to the order in wich they appear; *i.e.*, $\{\!\{1, 2, 1\}\!\}$ is the bag containing 1 twice, and 2 once.

---

[32] For a fixed set of base elements and operations (which constitute what is formally called a *signature*), the syntactic algebra is unique (up to isomorphism). This algebra is also called the *free*, or the *initial*, algebra for its signature.

[33] Note that this ambiguity never arises for semantic algebras whose operations are interpreted into a unique result.

[34] Such are important considerations in the field of *term rewriting* [38], where the problem of finding canonical term representations for equational theories was originally addressed by Donald Knuth and Peter Bendix in a seminal paper proposing a general effective method—the so-called Knuth-Bendix Completion Algorithm [39]. The problem, incidentally, is only semi-decidable. In other words, the Knuth-Bendix algorithm may diverge, although several interesting variations have been proposed for a wide extent of practical uses (see [38] for a good introduction and bibliography).

Syntactic monoids are quite useful for programming as they provide adquate data structures to represent collections of objects of a given type. Thus, we refer to them as *collection monoids*. Now, a definition such as Equation (47) for a syntactic monoid, although sound mathematically, is not quite adequate for programming purposes. This is because it defines the $\star$ operations on two distinct *types* of elements; namely, the base elements (here natural numbers) and constructed elements. In programming, it is desirable that operations be given a crisp type. A way to achieve this is by systematically "wrapping" each base element x into a term such as $x \star \epsilon$. This "wrapping" is achieve by associating to the monoid a function $\mathfrak{U}_\star$ from the base set into the monoid domain called its *unit injection*. For example, if $+\!\!+$ is the list monoid operation for concatenating two lists, $\mathfrak{U}_{+\!\!+}(x) = [x]$ and one may view the list $[a, b, c]$ as $[a] +\!\!+ [b] +\!\!+ [c]$. Similarly, the set $\{a, b, c\}$ is viewed as $\{a\} \cup \{b\} \cup \{c\}$, and the bag $\{\!\{a, b, c\}\!\}$ as $\{\!\{a\}\!\} \uplus \{\!\{b\}\!\} \uplus \{\!\{c\}\!\}$. Clearly, this bases the constructions on an isomorphic view of the base set rather than the base set itself, while using a uniform type for the monoid operator. Also, because the type of the base elements is irrelevant for the construction other than imposing the constraint that all such elements be of the same type, we present a collection monoid as a *polymorphic* data type. This justifies the formal view of monoids we give next using the programming notion of *polymorphic type*.

Because it is characterized by its operation $\oplus$, a monoid is often simply referred to as $\oplus$. Thus, a monoid operation is used as a subscript to denote its characteristic attributes. Namely, for a monoid $\oplus$,

- $\mathfrak{T}_\oplus$ is its type (*i.e.*, $\oplus : \mathfrak{T}_\oplus \times \mathfrak{T}_\oplus \to \mathfrak{T}_\oplus$),
- $\mathbb{1}_\oplus : \mathfrak{T}_\oplus$ is its identity element,
- $\Theta_\oplus$ is its equational theory (*i.e.*, a subset of the set $\{C, I\}$, where C stands for "commutative" and I for "idempotent");

and, if it is a collection monoid,

- $\mathfrak{C}_\oplus$ is its type constructor (*i.e.*, $\mathfrak{T}_\oplus = \mathfrak{C}_\oplus(\alpha)$),
- $\mathfrak{U}_\oplus : \alpha \to \mathfrak{C}_\oplus(\alpha)$ is its unit injection for any type variable α.

Examples of familiar monoids of both kinds are given in Table 2 in terms of the above characteristic attributes.[35]

D   The Typed Polymorphic λ-Calculus

We assume a set $\mathcal{C}$ of pregiven constants ususally denoted by $a, b \ldots$, and a countably infinite set of variable symbols $\mathcal{V}$ usually denoted by $x, y, \ldots$. The syntax of a term expression e of the λ-Calculus is given by the grammar shown in Fig. 5. We shall call $\mathfrak{T}_\Sigma$ the set of term expressions e defined by this grammar. These terms are also called *raw* term expressions.

---

[35] If the theory is $\{I\}$—*i.e.*, idempotent but not commutative—this defines yet another, though unfamiliar, type of collection monoid where there may be redundant elements but only if not adjacent.

Table 2. Attributes of a few common monoids

$\oplus$	$\mathfrak{T}_\oplus$	$\mathbb{1}_\oplus$	$\Theta_\oplus$
$+$	$\mathfrak{Int}$	0	$\{C\}$
$*$	$\mathfrak{Int}$	1	$\{C\}$
$\max$	$\mathfrak{Int}$	0	$\{C,I\}$
$\vee$	$\mathfrak{Boolean}$	$\mathfrak{false}$	$\{C,I\}$
$\wedge$	$\mathfrak{Boolean}$	$\mathfrak{true}$	$\{C,I\}$

$\oplus$	$\mathfrak{C}_\oplus$	$\mathfrak{T}_\oplus$	$\mathbb{1}_\oplus$	$\mathfrak{U}_\oplus(x)$	$\Theta_\oplus$
$\cup$	$\mathtt{set}$	$\mathtt{set}(\alpha)$	$\{\}$	$\{x\}$	$\{C,I\}$
$\uplus$	$\mathtt{bag}$	$\mathtt{bag}(\alpha)$	$\{\!\{\}\!\}$	$\{\!\{x\}\!\}$	$\{C\}$
$+\!+$	$\mathtt{list}$	$\mathtt{list}(\alpha)$	$[]$	$[x]$	$\emptyset$

Some primitive monoids   Familiar Collection monoids

$$
\begin{aligned}
e ::= \ &a \qquad (a \in \mathcal{C}) \ \text{constant}\\
\mid \ &x \qquad (x \in \mathcal{V}) \ \text{variable}\\
\mid \ &\lambda x.\, e \ (x \in \mathcal{V}) \ \text{abstraction}\\
\mid \ &e\, e \qquad\qquad\ \text{application}
\end{aligned}
$$

Fig. 5. Basic λ-Calculus Expressions

An abstraction $\lambda x.\, e$ defines a *lexical scope* for its *bound variable* x, whose extent is its *body* e. Thus, the notion of free occurrence of a variable in a term is defined as usual, and so is the operation $e_1[x \leftarrow e_2]$ of substituting a term e_2 for all the free occurrences of a variable x in a term e_1. Thus, a bound variable may be renamed to a new one in its scope without changing the abstraction.

The computation rule defined on λ-terms is the so-called β-reduction:

$$
(\lambda x.\, e_1)\, e_2 \ \longrightarrow \ e_1[x \leftarrow e_2]. \tag{48}
$$

We assume a set $\mathcal{B}$ of basic type symbols denoted by $A, B, \ldots$, and a countably infinite set of type variables $\mathcal{TV}$ denoted by $\alpha, \beta, \ldots$. The syntax of a type τ of the Typed Polymorphic λ-Calculus is given by the following grammar:

$$
\begin{aligned}
\tau ::= \ &A \qquad (A \in \mathcal{B}) \quad \text{basic type}\\
\mid \ &\alpha \qquad (\alpha \in \mathcal{TV}) \ \text{type variable}\\
\mid \ &\tau \to \tau \qquad\qquad \text{function type}
\end{aligned} \tag{49}
$$

We shall call $\mathfrak{T}$ the set of types τ defined by this grammar. A *monomorphic type* is a type that contains no variable types. Any type containing at least one variable type is called a *polymorphic type*.

The typing rules for the Typed Polymorphic λ-Calculus are given in Fig. 6. These rules can be readily translated into a Logic Programming language based on Horn-clauses such as Prolog, and used as an effective means to infer the types of expressions based on the Typed Polymorphic λ-Calculus.

The basic syntax of the Typed Polymorphic λ-Calculus may be extended with other operators and convenient data structures as long as typing rules for the new constructs

$$\frac{}{\Gamma \vdash a : \tau} \quad \text{if } \mathbf{type}(a) = \tau, \text{ for any type environment } \Gamma \text{ constant}$$

$$\frac{}{\Gamma \vdash x : \tau} \quad \text{if } \Gamma(x) = \tau \qquad\qquad\qquad \text{variable}$$

$$\frac{\Gamma[x : \tau_1] \vdash t : \tau_2}{\Gamma \vdash \lambda x.t : \tau_1 \to \tau_2} \qquad\qquad\qquad\qquad \text{abstraction}$$

$$\frac{\Gamma \vdash t_1 : \tau_1 \to \tau_2, \ \Gamma \vdash t_2 : \tau_1}{\Gamma \vdash t_1 \, t_2 : \tau_2} \qquad\qquad \text{application}$$

Fig. 6. Typing rules for the typed polymorphic λ-calculus

are provided. Typically, one provides at least the set $\mathbb{N}$ of integer constants and $\mathbb{B} = \{\mathsf{true}, \mathsf{false}\}$ of boolean constants, along with basic arithmetic and boolean operators, pairing (or tupling), a conditional operator, and a fix-point operator. The usual arithmetic and boolean operators are denoted by constant symbols (e.g., $+, *, -, /, \vee, \wedge$, etc.). Let $\mathbf{O}$ be this set.

The computation rules for these operators are based on their usual semantics as one might expect, modulo transforming the usual binary infix notation to a "curried" application. For example, $e_1 + e_2$ is implicitly taken to be the *application* $(+ \ e_1) \ e_2$. Note that this means that all such operators are implicitly "curried."[36]

For example, we may augment the grammar for the terms given in Fig. 5 with the addiional rules in Fig. 7.

$$
\begin{array}{lll}
e ::= \ \ldots & & \lambda\text{-calculus expression} \\
\quad | \ \langle e, \cdots, e \rangle & & \text{tupling} \\
\quad | \ e.n & (n \in \mathbb{N}) & \text{projection} \\
\quad | \ \text{if } e \text{ then } e \text{ else } e & & \text{conditional} \\
\quad | \ \text{fix } e & & \text{fixpoint}
\end{array}
$$

Fig. 7. Additional syntax for the extended λ-calculus (with Fig. 5)

---

[36] Recall that a curried form of an n-ary function f is obtained when f is applied to less arguments than it expects; i.e., $f(e_1, \ldots, e_k)$, for $1 \le k < n$. In the λ-calculus, this form is simply interpreted as the *abstraction* $\lambda x_1. \ldots \lambda x_{n-k}. f(e_1, \ldots, e_k, x_1, \ldots, x_{n-k})$. In their fully curried form, all n-ary functions can be seen as unary functions; indeed, with this interpretation of curried forms, it is clear that $f(e_1, \ldots, e_n) = (\ldots (f \ e_1) \ldots e_{n-1}) \ e_n$.

The computation rules for the other new constructs are:

$$\langle e_1, \cdots, e_k \rangle . i \longrightarrow \begin{cases} e_i & \text{if } 1 \leq i \leq k \\ \text{undefined} & \text{otherwise} \end{cases}$$

$$\text{if } e \text{ then } e_1 \text{ else } e_2 \longrightarrow \begin{cases} e_1 & \text{if } e = \text{true} \\ e_2 & \text{if } e = \text{false} \\ \text{undefined} & \text{otherwise} \end{cases} \tag{50}$$

$$\text{fix } e \longrightarrow e \ (\text{fix } e)$$

To account for the new constructs, the syntax of types is extended accordingly to:

$$\begin{array}{lll} \tau ::= \text{Int} \mid \text{Boolean} & & \text{basic type} \\ \quad \mid \alpha & (\alpha \in \mathcal{TV}) & \text{type variable} \\ \quad \mid \langle \tau, \cdots, \tau \rangle & & \text{tuple type} \\ \quad \mid \tau \to \tau & & \text{function type} \end{array} \tag{51}$$

We are given that $\text{type}(n) = \text{Int}$ for all $n \in \mathbb{N}$ and that $\text{type}(\text{true}) = \text{Boolean}$ and $\text{type}(\text{false}) = \text{Boolean}$. The (fully curried) types of the built-in operators are given similarly; namely, integer addition has type $\text{type}(+) = \text{Int} \to (\text{Int} \to \text{Int})$, Boolean disjunction has type $\text{type}(\vee) = \text{Boolean} \to (\text{Boolean} \to \text{Boolean})$, etc., ... The additional typing rules for this extended calculus are given in Fig. 8.

$$\frac{\Gamma \vdash t_1 : \tau_1, \ \cdots \ \Gamma \vdash t_k : \tau_k}{\Gamma \vdash \langle t_1, \cdots, t_k \rangle : \langle \tau_1, \cdots, \tau_k \rangle} \qquad \text{tupling}$$

$$\frac{\Gamma \vdash t : \langle \tau_1, \cdots, \tau_k \rangle}{\Gamma \vdash t.i : \tau_i} \ \text{if} \ 1 \leq i \leq k \qquad \text{tuple projection}$$

$$\frac{\Gamma \vdash t_1 : \text{Boolean}, \ \Gamma \vdash t_2 : \tau, \ \Gamma \vdash t_3 : \tau}{\Gamma \vdash \text{if } t_1 \text{ then } t_2 \text{ else } t_3 : \tau} \qquad \text{conditional}$$

$$\frac{\Gamma \vdash t : \tau \to \tau}{\Gamma \vdash \text{fix } t : \tau} \qquad \text{fixpoint}$$

Fig. 8. Additional typing rules for the extended typed polymorphic λ-calculus (with Fig. 6)

E   Object Query Language Formalisms

In this section, I review a formal syntax for processiong collections due to Peter Buneman *et al.* [5,6] and elaborated by Leonidas Fegaras and David Maier [8] using the notion of *Monoid Comprehensions*.

E.1 Monoid Homomorphisms and Comprehensions

The formalism presented here is based on [8] and assumes familiarity with the notions and notations summarized in Appendix Section C. I will use the programming view of monoids exposed there using the specific notation of monoid attributes, in particular for sets, bags, and lists. I will also assume basic familiarity with naive λ-calculus and associated typing as presented in Appendix Section D.

Monoid Homomorphisms. Because many operations and data structures are monoids, it is interesting to use the associated concepts as the computational building block of an essential calculus. In particular, iteration over collection types can be elegantly formulated as computing a *monoid homomorphism*. This notion coincides with the usual mathematical notion of homomorphism, albeit given here from an operational standpoint and biased toward collection monoids. Basically, a monoid homomorphism $\hom_{\oplus}^{\odot}$ maps a function f from a collection monoid $\oplus$ to *any* monoid $\odot$ by collecting all the f-images of elements of a $\oplus$-collection using the $\odot$ operation. For example, the expression $\hom_{+\!\!+}^{\cup}[\lambda x.\, x + 1]$ applied to the list $[1, 2, 1, 3, 2]$ returns the set $\{2, 3, 4\}$.[37]

In other words, the monoid homomorphism $\hom_{+\!\!+}^{\cup}$ of a function f applied to a list L corresponds to the following *loop* computation collecting the f-images of the list elements into a set (each f-image being a set):

```
result ← {};
foreach x in L do result ← result ∪ f(x);
return result;
```

This is formalized as follows:

Definition 1 (Monoid Homomorphism). *A Monoid Homomorphism $\hom_{\oplus}^{\odot}$ defines a mapping from a collection homomorphism $\oplus$ to any monoid $\odot$ such that $\Theta_{\oplus} \subseteq \Theta_{\odot}$ by:*

$$\hom_{\oplus}^{\odot}[f](\mathbb{1}_{\oplus}) \stackrel{def}{=} \mathbb{1}_{\odot}$$

$$\hom_{\oplus}^{\odot}[f](\mathfrak{U}_{\oplus}(x)) \stackrel{def}{=} f(x)$$

$$\hom_{\oplus}^{\odot}[f](x \oplus y) \stackrel{def}{=} \hom_{\oplus}^{\odot}[f](x) \odot \hom_{\oplus}^{\odot}[f](y)$$

for any function $f : \alpha \to \mathfrak{T}_{\odot}$, $x : \alpha$, and $y : \alpha$, where $\mathfrak{T}_{\oplus} = \mathfrak{C}_{\oplus}(\alpha)$.

Again, computationally, this amounts to executing the following iteration:

```
result ← 𝟙⊙;
foreach xi in 𝔘⊕(x1) ⊕ ··· ⊕ 𝔘⊕(xn) do result ← result ⊙ f(xi);
return result;
```

The reader may be puzzled by the condition $\Theta_{\oplus} \subseteq \Theta_{\odot}$ in Definition 1. It means that a monoid homomorphism may only be defined from a collection monoid to a monoid that has at least the same equational theory. In other words, one can only go from an

---

[37] See Table 2 for notation of a few common monoids.

empty theory monoid, to either a $\{C\}$-monoid or an $\{I\}$-monoid, or yet to a $\{C,I\}$-monoid. This requirement is due to an algebraic technicality, and relaxing it would cause a monoid homomorphism to be ill-defined. To see this, consider going from, say, a commutative-idempotent monoid to one that is commutative but not idempotent. Let us take, for example, $\hom_\cup^+$. Then, this entails:

$$1 = \hom_\cup^+[\lambda x.\,1](\{a\})$$
$$= \hom_\cup^+[\lambda x.\,1](\{a\} \cup \{a\})$$
$$= \hom_\cup^+[\lambda x.\,1](\{a\}) + \hom_\cup^+[\lambda x.\,1](\{a\})$$
$$= 1 + 1$$
$$= 2.$$

The reader may have noticed that this restriction has the unfortunate consequence of disallowing potentially useful computations, notable examples being computing the cardinality of a set, or converting a set into a list. However, this drawback can be easily overcome with a suitable modification of the third clause in Definition 1, and other expressions based on it, ensuring that anomalous cases such as the above are dealt with by appropriate tests.

It is important to note that, for the consistency of Definition 1, a non-idempotent monoid must actually be anti-idempotent, and a non-commutative monoid must be anti-commutative. Indeed, if $\oplus$ is non-idempotent as well as non-anti-idempotent (say, $x_0 \oplus x_0 = x_0$ for some x_0), then this entails:

$$\hom_\oplus^\odot[f](x_0) = \hom_\oplus^\odot[f](x_0 \oplus x_0)$$
$$= \hom_\oplus^\odot[f](x_0) \odot \hom_\oplus^\odot[f](x_0)$$

which is not necessarily true for non-idempotent $\odot$. A similar argument may be given for commutativity. This consistency condition is in fact not restrictive operationally as it is always verified (e.g., a list will not allow partial commutation of any of its element).

Here are a few familar functions expressed with well-defined monoid homomorphisms:

$$\texttt{length}(l) \quad = \hom_{+\!\!+}^+[\lambda x.\,1](l)$$
$$e \in s \quad = \hom_\cup^\vee[\lambda x.\,x = e](s)$$
$$s \times t \quad = \hom_\cup^\cup[\lambda x.\,\hom_\cup^\cup[\lambda y.\,\{\langle x,y\rangle\}](t)](s)$$
$$\texttt{map}(f,s) \quad = \hom_\cup^\cup[\lambda x.\,\{f(x)\}](s)$$
$$\texttt{filter}(p,s) = \hom_\cup^\cup[\lambda x.\,\text{if } p(x) \text{ then } \{x\} \text{ else } \{\}](s).$$

Monoid Comprehensions. The concept of monoid homomorphism is useful for expressing a formal semantics of iteration over collections. However, it is not very convenient as a programming construct. A natural notation for such a construct that is both conspicuous and can be expressed in terms of monoid homomorphisms is a *monoid comprehension*. This notion generalizes the familiar notation used for writing a set in comprehension (as opposed to writing it in extension) using a pattern and a formula describing its elements (as oppposed to listing all its elements). For example, the set comprehension $\{\langle x, x^2 \rangle \mid x \in \mathbb{N}, \exists n.x = 2n\}$ describes the set of pairs $\langle x, x^2 \rangle$ (the *pattern*), verifying the formula $x \in \mathbb{N}, \exists n.x = 2n$ (the *qualifier*).

This notation can be extended to any (primitive or collection) monoid $\oplus$. The syntax of a monoid comprehension is an expression of the form $\oplus\{e \parallel Q\}$ where e is an expression called the *head* of the comprehension, and Q is called its qualifier and is a sequence $q_1, \ldots, q_n$, $n \geq 0$, where each q_i is either:

- a *generator* of the form $x \leftarrow e$, where x is a variable and e is an expression; or,
- a *filter* ϕ which is a boolean condition.

In a monoid comprehension expression $\oplus\{e \parallel Q\}$, the monoid operation $\oplus$ is called the *accumulator*.

As for semantics, the meaning of a monoid comprehension is defined in terms of monoid homomorphisms.

Definition 2 (Monoid Comprehension). *The meaning of a monoid comprehension over a monoid $\oplus$ is defined inductively as follows:*

$$\oplus\{e \parallel \} \quad \overset{def}{=} \quad \begin{cases} \mathfrak{U}_\oplus(e) & \text{if } \oplus \text{ is a collection monoid} \\ e & \text{if } \oplus \text{ is a primitive monoid} \end{cases}$$

$$\oplus\{e \parallel x \leftarrow e', Q\} \overset{def}{=} \hom_\odot^\oplus[\lambda x. \oplus\{e \parallel Q\}](e')$$

$$\oplus\{e \parallel c, Q\} \overset{def}{=} \text{if } c \text{ then } \oplus\{e \parallel Q\} \text{ else } \mathbb{1}_\oplus$$

such that $e : \mathfrak{T}_\oplus$, $e' : \mathfrak{T}_\odot$, *and* $\odot$ *is a collection monoid.*

Note that although the input monoid $\oplus$ is explicit, each generator $x \leftarrow e'$ in the qualifier has an implicit collection monoid $\odot$ whose characteristics can be inferred with polymorphic typing rules.

Note that relational *joins* are immediately expressible as monoid comprehensions. Indeed, the join of two sets S and T using a function f and a predicate p is simply:

$$S \bowtie_p^f T \overset{def}{=} \cup\{f(x, y) \parallel x \leftarrow S, y \leftarrow T, p(x, y)\}. \tag{52}$$

Typically, a relational join will take f to be a record constructor. For example, if we write a record whose fields 1_i have values e_i for $i = 1, \ldots, n$, as $\langle 1_1 = e_1, \ldots, 1_n = e_n \rangle$, then a standard relational join can be obtained with, say, $f(x, y) = \langle name = y.name, age = 2 * x.age \rangle$, and $p(x, y)$ may be any condition such as $x.name = y.name, x.age \geq 18$.

Clearly, monoid comprehensions can immediately express queries using all usual relational operators (and, indeed, object queries as well) and most usual functions. For example,

$$\exists x \in s.e \quad \stackrel{\text{def}}{=} \quad \vee\{e \parallel x \leftarrow s\} \qquad \qquad \text{length}(s) \quad \stackrel{\text{def}}{=} \quad +\{1 \parallel x \leftarrow s\}$$

$$\forall x \in s.e \quad \stackrel{\text{def}}{=} \quad \wedge\{e \parallel x \leftarrow s\} \qquad \qquad \text{sum}(s) \quad \stackrel{\text{def}}{=} \quad +\{x \parallel x \leftarrow s\}$$

$$x \in s \quad \stackrel{\text{def}}{=} \quad \vee\{x = y \parallel y \leftarrow s\} \qquad \text{max}(s) \quad \stackrel{\text{def}}{=} \quad \text{max}\{x \parallel x \leftarrow s\}$$

$$s \cap t \quad \stackrel{\text{def}}{=} \quad \cup\{x \parallel x \leftarrow s, x \in t\} \qquad \text{filter}(p, s) \quad \stackrel{\text{def}}{=} \quad \cup\{x \parallel x \leftarrow s, p(x)\}$$

$$\text{count}(a, s) \quad \stackrel{\text{def}}{=} \quad +\{1 \parallel x \leftarrow s, x = a\} \qquad \text{flatten}(s) \quad \stackrel{\text{def}}{=} \quad \cup\{x \parallel t \leftarrow s, x \leftarrow t\}$$

Note that some of these functions will work only on appropriate types of their arguments. For example, the type of the argument of sum must be a non-idempotent monoid, and so must the type of the second argument of count. Thus, sum will add up the elements of a bag or a list, and count will tally the number of occurrences of an element in a bag or a list. Applying either sum or count to a set will be caught as a type error.

We are now in a position to propose a programming calculus using monoid comprehensions. Fig. 9 defines an abstract grammar for an expression e of the *Monoid Comprehension Calculus* and amounts to adding comprehensions to an extended Typed Polymorphic λ-Calculus. Fig. 10 gives the typing rules for this calculus.

$$
\begin{array}{lll}
e ::= \ldots & & \text{extended } \lambda\text{-calculus expression} \\
\mid \mathbb{1}_{\oplus} & & \text{monoid identity} \\
\mid \mathfrak{U}_{\oplus}(e) & & \text{monoid unit injection} \\
\mid e_1 \oplus e_2 & & \text{monoid composition} \\
\mid \oplus\{e \parallel Q\} & & \text{monoid comprehension}
\end{array}
$$

Fig. 9. Additional Syntax for the monoid comprehension calculus (with Fig. 7)

F   Backend System

Our generic backend system comprises classes for managing runtime events and objects, a display manager, and an error manager. As an example, we describe the organization of a runtime object.

The class $\langle backend \rangle$.Runtime.java defines what a runtime context consists of as an object of this class. Such an object serves as the common execution environment context shared by $\langle instructions \rangle$.Instruction objects being executed. It encapsulates a state of computtation that is effected by each instruction as it is executed in its context.

Thus, a $\langle backend \rangle$.Runtime.java object consists of attributes and structures that together define a state of computation, and methods that are used by instructions to effect this state as they are executed. Thus, each instruction subclass of $\langle instructions \rangle$.Instruction defines an execute($\langle backend \rangle$.Runtime) method

$$\frac{}{\Gamma \vdash \mathbb{1}_\oplus \ : \ \mathfrak{T}_\oplus} \qquad\qquad \mathbb{1}_\oplus \text{ monoid identity}$$

$$\frac{\Gamma \vdash e_1 \ : \ \mathfrak{T}_\oplus, \ \Gamma \vdash e_2 \ : \ \mathfrak{T}_\oplus}{\Gamma \vdash e_1 \oplus e_2 \ : \ \mathfrak{T}_\oplus} \qquad\qquad \oplus \text{ primitive monoid}$$

$$\frac{\Gamma \vdash e \ : \ \mathfrak{T}_\oplus}{\Gamma \vdash \oplus\{e \, \| \, \} \ : \ \mathfrak{T}_\oplus} \qquad\qquad \oplus \text{ primitive monoid}$$

$$\frac{\Gamma \vdash e \ : \ \tau}{\Gamma \vdash \mathfrak{U}_\oplus(e) \ : \ \mathfrak{C}_\oplus(\tau)} \qquad\qquad \oplus \text{ collection monoid}$$

$$\frac{\Gamma \vdash e_1 \ : \ \mathfrak{C}_\oplus(\tau), \ \Gamma \vdash e_2 \ : \ \mathfrak{C}_\oplus(\tau)}{\Gamma \vdash e_1 \oplus e_2 \ : \ \mathfrak{C}_\oplus(\tau)} \qquad\qquad \oplus \text{ collection monoid}$$

$$\frac{\Gamma \vdash e \ : \ \tau}{\Gamma \vdash \oplus\{e \, \| \, \} \ : \ \mathfrak{C}_\oplus(\tau)} \qquad\qquad \oplus \text{ collection monoid}$$

$$\frac{\Gamma \vdash e_2 \ : \ \mathfrak{C}_\odot(\tau_2), \ \Gamma[x:\tau_2] \vdash \oplus\{e_1 \, \| \, Q\} \ : \ \tau_1}{\Gamma \vdash \oplus\{e_1 \, \| \, x \, \leftarrow \, e_2, Q\} \ : \ \tau_1} \quad \textit{if} \ \ \Theta_\odot \subseteq \Theta_\oplus \ \text{subtheory}$$

$$\frac{\Gamma \vdash e_2 \ : \ \mathfrak{Boolean}, \ \Gamma \vdash \oplus\{e_1 \, \| \, Q\} \ : \ \tau}{\Gamma \vdash \oplus\{e_1 \, \| \, e_2, Q\} \ : \ \tau}$$

Fig. 10. Additional typing rules for the monoid comprehension calculus (with Fig. 6)

that specifies its operational semantics as a state transformation of its given runtime context.

Initiating execution of a $\langle backend \rangle$.Runtime.java object consists of setting its code array to a given instruction sequence, setting its instruction pointer _ip to its code's first instruction and repeatedly calling and invoking execute(this) on whatever instruction in the current code array for this Runtime.java object is currently at address _ip. The final state is reached when a flag indicating that it is so is set to true. Each instruction is responsible for appropriately setting the next state according to its semantics, including saving and restoring states, and (re)setting the code array and the various runtime registers pointing into the state's structures.

Runtime states encapsulated by objects in this class are essentially those of a stack automaton, specifically conceived to support the computations of a higher-order functional language with lexical closures—*i.e.*, a λ-Calculus machine—extended to support additional features—*e.g.*, assignment side-effects, objects, automatic currying... As such it may viewed as an optimized variant of Peter Landin's SECD machine [13]—in the same spirit as Luca Cardelli's Functional Abstract Machine (FAM) [14], although our design is quite different from Cardelli's in its structure and operations.

Because this is a Java implementation, in order to avoid the space and performance overhead of being confined to boxed values for primitive type computations, three concurrent sets of structures are maintained: in addition to those needed for boxed (Java object) values, two extra ones are used to support unboxed integer and floating-point values, respectively. The runtime operations performed by instructions on a $\langle back\text{-}end \rangle$.Runtime object are guaranteed to be type-safe in that each state is always such as it must be expected for the correct accessing and setting of values. Such a guarantee must be (and is!) provided by the ⟨*types*⟩.TypeChecker and the ⟨*kernel*⟩.Sanitizer, which ascertain all the conditions that must be met prior to having a ⟨*kernel*⟩.Compiler proceed to generating instructions which will safely act on the appropriate stacks and environments of the correct sort (integer, floating-point, or object).

Display manager objects and error manager objects are similarly organized.

References

1. Aït-Kaci, H.: An Abstract and Reusable Programming Language Architecture. Keynote presentation, LDTA 2003 (April 6, 2003)[38]
2. Landin, P.J.: The next 700 programming languages. Communications of the ACM 9(3), 157–166 (1966)[39]
3. Sethi, R.: Programming Languages—Concepts and Constructs, 2nd edn. Addison-Wesley, Reading (1996)
4. Johnson, S.: Yacc: Yet another compiler compiler. Computer Science Technical Report 32, AT&T Bell Labs, Murray Hill, NJ (1975); Reprinted in the 4.3BSD Unix Programmer's Manual, Supplementary Documents 1, PS1:15, UC Berkeley (1986)
5. Buneman, P., Libkin, L., Suciu, D., Tannen, V., Wong, L.: Comprehension syntax. ACM SIGMOD Record 23(1), 87–96 (1994) [40]
6. Buneman, P., Naqvi, S., Tannen, V., Wong, L.: Principles of programming with complex objects and collection types. Theoretical Computer Science 149(1), 3–48 (1995) [41]
7. Brodky, A., Segal, V.E., Chen, J., Exarkhopoulo, P.A.: The CCUBE system object-oriented database system. In: Ramakrishnan, R., Stuckey, P.J. (eds.) Constraints and Databases, pp. 245–277. Kluwer Academic Publishers, Norwell (1998); Special Issue on Constraints: An International Journal 2(3&4) (1997)
8. Fegaras, L., Maier, D.: Optimizing object queries using an effective calculus. ACM Transactions on Database Systems 25(4), 457–516 (2000) [42]
9. Aït-Kaci, H.: An introduction to LIFE—Programming with Logic, Inheritance, Functions, and Equations. In: Miller, D. (ed.) Proceedings of the International Symposium on Logic Programming, pp. 52–68. MIT Press (October 1993)
10. Aït-Kaci, H., Di Cosmo, R.: Compiling order-sorted feature term unification. PRL Technical Note 7, Digital Paris Research Laboratory, Rueil-Malmaison, France (December 1993)
11. DeRemer, F., Pennello, T.: Efficient computation of LALR(1) look-ahead sets. ACM Transactions on Programming Languages and Systems 4(4), 615–649 (1982) [43]
12. Park, J., Choe, K.M., Chang, C.: A new analysis of LALR formalisms. ACM Transactions on Programming Languages and Systems 7(1), 159–175 (1985) [44]
13. Landin, P.J.: The mechanical evaluation of expressions. Computer Journal 6(4), 308–320 (1963) [45]

---

[38] http://ldta.info/2003/

[39] http://www.thecorememory.com/Next_700.pdf

[40] http://www.acm.org/sigs/sigmod/record/issues/9403/
Comprehension.ps

[41] http://citeseerx.ist.psu.edu/viewdoc/summary?
doi=10.1.1.41.5516

[42] http://lambda.uta.edu/tods00.ps.gz

[43] http://dl.acm.org/citation.cfm?id=69622.357187

[44] http://dl.acm.org/citation.cfm?id=69622.357187

[45] http://www.cs.cmu.edu/ crary/819-f09/Landin64.pdf

14. Cardelli, L.: The functional abstract machine. Technical Report TR-107, AT&T Bell Laboratories, Murray Hill, New Jersey (May 1983) [46]
15. Banâtre, J.P., Le Métayer, D.: A new computational model and its discipline of programming. INRIA Technical Report 566, Institut National de Recherche en Informatique et Automatique, Le Chesnay, France (1986)
16. Berry, G., Boudol, G.: The chemical abstract machine. In: Proceedings of the 17th ACM SIGPLAN-SIGACT Symposium on Principles of Programming Languages, POPL 1990, pp. 81–94. ACM Press, New York (1990) [47]
17. Aït-Kaci, H.: Warren's Abstract Machine—A Tutorial Reconstruction. Logic Programming. MIT Press, Cambridge (1991)
18. Grust, T.: Monad comprehensions—a versatile representation for queries. In: Gray, P., Kerschberg, L., King, P., Poulovassilis, A. (eds.) The Functional Approach to Data Management: Modeling, Analyzing and Integrating Heterogeneous Data. Springer (September 2003) [48]
19. Bothner, P.: XQuery tutorial. Online tutorial [49]
20. Nic, M., Jirat, J.: XPath tutorial. Online tutorial [50]
21. Gesbert, N., Genevès, P., Layaïda, N.: Parametric polymorphism and semantic subtyping: the logical connection. In: Proceedings of the 16th ACM SIGPLAN International Conference on Functional Programming (ICFP 2011), Tokyo Japan, September 19-21, pp. 107–116. Association for Computing Machinery, New York (2011) [51]
22. Gesbert, N., Genevès, P., Layaïda, N.: Parametric polymorphism and semantic subtyping: the logical connection. SIGPLAN Notices 46(9) (September 2011); N.B.: full version of [21]
23. Bierman, G.M., Gordon, A.D., Hriʟcu, C., Langworthy, D.: Semantic subtyping with an SMT solver. In: Proceedings of the 15th ACM SIGPLAN International Conference on Functional Programmingm (ICFP 2010), Baltimore, MA USA, September 27-29, pp. 105–116. Association for Computing Machinery, New York (2010) [52]
24. Bierman, G.M., Gordon, A.D., Hriʟcu, C., Langworthy, D.: Semantic subtyping with an SMT solver. Journal of Functional Programming, 1–75 (2012); N.B.: full version of [23] [53]
25. Jaffar, J., Maher, M.J.: Constraint Logic Programming: A survey. Journal of Logic Programming 19/20, 503–581 (1994) [54]
26. Leroy, X.: Unboxed objects and polymorphic typing. In: Proceedings of the 19th Symposium on Principles of Programming Languages (POPL 1992), pp. 177–188. Association for Computing Machinary. ACM Press (1992) [55]
27. Aho, A.V., Sethi, R., Ullman, J.D.: Compilers—Principles, Techniques, and Tools. Addison-Wesley (1986)
28. Choe, K.M.: Personal communication. Korean Advanced Institute of Science and Technology, Seoul, South Korea (December 2000), choecompiler.kaist.ac.kr

---

[46] http://lucacardelli.name/Papers/FAM.pdf
[47] citeseerx.ist.psu.edu/viewdoc/summary?doi=10.1.1.127.3782
[48] http://www-db.in.tum.de/ grust/files/monad-comprehensions.pdf
[49] http://www.gnu.org/software/qexo/XQuery-Intro.html
[50] http://www.zvon.org/xxl/XPathTutorial/General/examples.html
[51] http://hal.inria.fr/inria-00585686/fr/
[52] http://research.microsoft.com/apps/pubs/?id=135577
[53] http://www-infsec.cs.uni-saarland.de/~hritcu/publications/dminor-jfp2012.pdf
[54] http://citeseer.ist.psu.edu/jaffar94constraint.html
[55] http://gallium.inria.fr/ xleroy/bibrefs/Leroy-unboxed.html

29. Aït-Kaci, H.: A generic XML-generating metacompiler. Part of the documentation of the $\mathfrak{Jacc}$package (July 2008)[56]
30. Cardelli, L.: Typeful programming. In: Neuhold, E.J., Paul, M. (eds.) Formal Description of Programming Concepts. Springer (1991)[57]
31. Hentenryck, P.: The OPL Optimization Programming Language. The MIT Press (1999)
32. Wong, L.: Querying Nested Collections. PhD thesis, University of Pennsylvania (Computer and Information Science) (1994)[58]
33. Fegaras, L.: An experimental optimizer for OQL. Technical Report TR-CSE-97-007, University of Texas at Arlington (May 1997)[59]
34. Visser, E.: Syntax Definition for Language Prototyping. PhD thesis, Faculteit Wiskunde, Informatics, Natuurkunde en Strenkunde, Universiteit van Amsterdam, Amsterdam, The Netherlands (September 1997)[60]
35. Aho, A.V., Hopcroft, J.E., Ullman, J.D.: The Design and Analysis of Computer Algorithms. Addison-Wesley, Reading (1974)
36. Plotkin, G.D.: A structural approach to operational semantics. Technical Report DAIMI FN-19, University of Århus, Århus, Denmark (1981) [61]
37. Plotkin, G.D.: A structural approach to operational semantics. Journal of Logic and Algebraic Programming 60-61, 17–139 (2004); N.B.: Published version of [36] [62]
38. Dershowitz, N.: A taste of rewrite systems. In: Lauer, P.E. (ed.) Functional Programming, Concurrency, Simulation and Automated Reasoning. LNCS, vol. 693, pp. 199–228. Springer, Heidelberg (1993) [63]
39. Knuth, D.E., Bendix, P.B.: Simple word problems in universal algebras. In: Leech, J. (ed.) Computational Problems in Abstract Algebra, pp. 263–297. Pergamon Press, Oxford (1970); Reprinted in Automatic Reasoning 2, pp. 342–276. Springer (1983)

---

[56] http://www.hassan-ait-kaci.net/jacc-xml.pdf

[57] http://lucacardelli.name/Papers/TypefulProg.A4.pdf

[58] ftp://ftp.cis.upenn.edu/pub/ircs/tr/94-09.ps.Z

[59] http://lambda.uta.edu/oqlopt.ps.gz

[60] http://eelcovisser.org/wiki/thesis

[61] http://citeseer.ist.psu.edu/673965.html

[62] http://homepages.inf.ed.ac.uk/gdp/publications/sos_jlap.pdf

[63] http://www-sal.cs.uiuc.edu/ nachum/papers/taste-fixed.ps.gz

A Discussion on Pricing Relational Data

Magdalena Balazinska, Bill Howe, Paraschos Koutris,
Dan Suciu, and Prasang Upadhyaya

University of Washington,
Seattle, USA

Abstract. There exists a growing market for structured data on the
Internet today, and this motivates a theoretical study of how relational
data should be priced. We advocate for a framework where the seller
defines a *pricing scheme*, by essentially stipulating the price of some
queries, and the buyer is allowed to purchase data expressed by any
query they wish: the system will derive the price automatically from
the pricing scheme. We show that, in order to understand pricing, one
needs to understand *determinacy* first. We also discuss some other open
problems in pricing relational data.

Keywords: relational databases, pricing.

1 Introduction

In the summer of 2007, Peter Buneman posed the following question to one of the
authors of this article. How should one set a price for data on the Internet? A lot
of data is freely available today, but for some data the production costs are quite
high, and it makes sense to charge for its usage in order to recover the production
costs. Peter's original motivation came from the IUPHAR database [1], a repository of receptor nomenclature and drug classifications contributed by a large
community of experts in the field. Observing that this data is extremely valuable
to pharmaceutical companies, Peter reasoned that one could recover some of the
costs of producing and maintaining the data by charging these pharmaceutical
companies a price for accessing it. Some technical developments resulting from
those initial discussions with Peter are available in a separate manuscript [7].

Today, Peter's question applies to a large number of datasets, both from the
scientific and commercial domains; increasingly, one finds data for sale on the
Internet. In fact, in recent years, one has witnessed the emergence of *marketplace services for data*, which are Websites whose purpose is to facilitate buying
and selling data. Examples of such data marketplaces are the Windows Azure
Marketplace [5], a data marketplace that contains over 100 data sources for sale,
Infochimps [10], which contains about 15,000 data sets for sale, and Xignite [17],
which sells financial data.

The database group at the University of Washington has started a research
project on data markets. Funded by a partnership between NSF and Microsoft,
the project plans to investigate several aspects of data markets, ranging from

V. Tannen et al. (Eds.): Buneman Festschrift, LNCS 8000, pp. 167–173, 2013.

systems issues arising from monitoring data usage for billing purposes, to understanding the principles of the interaction between data and prices [2,6,11]. In this paper, we outline our initial investigation into the latter: how to mix data and prices in a principled way. Our thinking was, in part, informed by those early discussions with Peter in 2007.

2   Of Versions and Views

On the surface, buying and selling data is not much different from buying and selling any other products. An agent produces the data and incurs some cost in doing so; the data has some value to a buyer; the seller and buyer agree on a price. This is a problem studied extensively by economists over centuries. However, as explained by Shapiro and Varian [16], digital goods, of which data sets are one instance, have unique characteristics that cause traditional pricing mechanisms to fail: they have a high and irrecoverable fixed cost (producing the data is expensive) and a very low variable cost (copying the data is almost free). The fixed and irrecoverable cost of data is quite distinct from that of physical goods. Shapiro and Varian illustrate this with a large airplane manufacturing company investing in a new factory: if the business plan turns sour, the company can still recover some of its investment by reselling the building and the manufacturing machinery. In contrast, if a company invests in acquiring detailed satellite data, and is undercut by a competitor selling similar data at a much lower price, it cannot recover anything from its now worthless satellite data. The low cost of copying digital goods further exacerbate the problem, allowing competitors to churn out copies in unrestricted quantities. The sharp skew towards fixed costs makes traditional cost-based pricing models inapplicable. This can lead either to fortunes for the producer (if she has no competition), or to total ruin.

Shapiro and Varian [16] argue that pricing on the Internet should be based on the value that a customer places on the information. They argue that *versioning* digital products is the solution to pricing digital goods. Even pricing traditional information products included some form of versioning. In the case of movies, the "new-release" version costs $12/person to watch, but renting the "DVD" version that comes out six month later costs $3/family; the two versions target two kinds of buyers, the must-see-it-now buyers willing to pay an extra price, and the price-conscious buyers who can wait six months.

The analog to versions in data markets are *views*. A view over a data instance is the same as a version of that instance. The view may contain only a subset of the data, or only some columns, or may contain information at a coarser granularity. All these can be seen as different versions of the digital product, and sold at different prices.

Consider, for example, a dataset stored in a single relation $R(x, y, z)$. The seller could set two price levels: a price p_1 for the entire dataset, and a price p_2 for an individual tuple. Presumably, the former price is much higher than the latter, $p_1 \gg p_2$. As a concrete example, it is possible today to buy either entire databases of curated business addresses [9] or to check the correctness of individual addresses [13]. This corresponds to two versions, one for the power customers, who need the entire dataset and are willing to pay a high price, and a second version for the occasional customer interested in only one or just a few records.

Dataset versions are commonly used today. For example, CustomLists.net [9] sells a database of 28.6 million American businesses for \$399. The price is only \$199 for a single state and it is only \$299 for the subset of American businesses that also have an email address. Such versions add significant flexibility, but what if a user wants some other subset of the data such as only large businesses with more than 1000 employees? Or businesses within 1 mile of a Home Depot? Or businesses in cities that experience frequent flooding? Today, buyers must either purchase supersets of the data they need or they must negotiate custom data products. AggData [4] is an example data seller that provides such custom solutions. Negotiating custom solutions, however, does not scale: If a human must look at each custom view and must price that view, possibly negotiating with the buyer, the total number of distinct views that can be priced is limited.

We envision a solution that allows the seller to assign a price to any possible view that the buyer may be willing to buy. This requires a study of how database views can be adorned with prices. We start with the following definition.

Definition 1. *Let D be a database instance. A pricing scheme for D is a set of view, price pairs:* $S = \{(V_1, p_1), \ldots, (V_k, p_k)\}$.

The data seller decides to create k "versions" of her digital product, defined by k views, and price each of them differently. The goal is to define some high-value views (for example, the entire dataset) to be sold to a few high rollers, yet define sufficiently many lower quality views that can be sold to a large number of customers. From these k views, the goal is to *automatically* derive the price of any other view V defined by the buyer. This is also the direction in which the initial discussion with Peter was heading in 2007: set the prices of some subsets, and infer automatically the prices of all other subsets [7].

An important problem that needs to be studied in pricing data is the choice of the view language in which we express the views $V_1, \ldots, V_k$ in Definition 1. This is non-trivial: we discuss here three dimensions of this problem, leaving a solution to future work.

Relational View. Any selections or projections should be available to the seller if she decides to set a price on that selection or projection. We argue that joins are needed too. For example, suppose the seller wants to set a certain price for the personal information of all CEO's of companies with a revenue $> \$10M$: this requires a semijoin of the CEO relation with the Company relation. In general, one can make the argument that the seller should be allowed to use *arbitrary relational views* to define versions of the data.

Increasing/Decreasing Accuracy. Decreasing the accuracy or adding noise to the data can produce a version that is less valuable, and, hence, can be sold at a lower price, to a larger number of buyers. For example, weather data for standard, city-wide weather forecast is virtually free, but detailed precipitation information required by commercial farmers can only be purchased at a cost. There is an interesting connection here to data privacy: private data is sold today at a price, but properly anonymized data is free. The converse is also true: by performing data cleaning, the seller may increase the value of her data product. *Views that add noise to the data* should be available to the seller to set prices.

User-defined Functions. The seller may own a domain specific algorithm for enhancing the data; by applying that function, the seller can produce new data that is more valuable than the raw data. For example, the seller may have a proprietary algorithm for image processing; by applying this function to all images in a collection it may produce a more valuable data set. Another example consists of a sophisticated data mining algorithm: the result of the data mining is much more valuable that the raw data itself. The seller should be able to define *views with user-defined functions*.

3   Arbitrage in Data Pricing

Consider a pricing scheme S given by Definition 1. Two problems may arise.

The first is consistency. One expects that every price point (V_i, p_i) will make sense. For example, it does not make sense to charge more for a single tuple than for the entire dataset. In similar spirit, if the entire relation R costs p_1 and a single tuple in R costs p_2, then it does not make sense to have $|R| \cdot p_2 < p_1$, or, else, no buyer will buy the entire dataset, but would instead buy one tuple at a time. We say that a pricing scheme $S = \{(V_1, p_1), \ldots, (V_k, p_k)\}$ is *consistent* if no view V_i can be obtained at a price lower than p_i by purchasing and combining some of the other views in S. The consistency problem is this: Given a pricing scheme S, check whether it is consistent.

The second problem is pricing a new view. Continuing the example where p_1 is the price for the entire data set and p_2 is the price for each individual record, how much should a buyer pay if she wants to buy half of the data records? On one hand she could buy the entire dataset and pay p_1, then retain only the half she needs. On the other hand, she could purchase one record at a time, and pay $|R| \cdot p_2/2$. Clearly, the buyer will choose whichever is cheaper. In general, the *price computation problem* is this: given a pricing scheme $S = \{(V_1, p_1), \ldots, (V_k, p_k)\}$ and a new view V (not necessarily mentioned in S), determine the cheapest way for a user to obtain V by purchasing views available in S.

Both problems are facets of *arbitrage*. Arbitrage occurs if the pricing scheme sets a price p for a view V (possibly a new view not explicitly priced by the seller), but a buyer has the option of answering V from $V_1, \ldots, V_m$ such that their combined price is less than p: not only can the buyer get away by paying less than p, but she could even profit by reselling V at a price lower than p, which is traditionally called *arbitrage*.

The key technical difficulty in studying arbitrage is determining when a buyer can answer a view V using the information in other views, say $V_1, \ldots V_m$. Let us write:

$$V_1, \ldots, V_m \twoheadrightarrow V \tag{1}$$

if V can be answered from the views $V_1, \ldots, V_m$. This is just a notation, not a formal definition; the intuition is that a buyer who needs the view V would rather purchase the views $V_1, \ldots, V_m$ and compute V, if these m views are cheaper than the price of V. We will discuss later how to define $\twoheadrightarrow$. Assuming that $\twoheadrightarrow$ is given, one can define both consistency and the price function.

Definition 2. *A* pricing scheme $S = \{(V_1, p_1), \ldots, (V_k, p_k)\}$ *is* consistent *if, whenever* $V_{i_1}, V_{i_2}, \ldots, V_{i_k} \twoheadrightarrow V_i$, *then* $p_i \leq p_{i_1} + p_{i_2} + \ldots + p_{i_k}$.
Given a view V and a pricing scheme $S = \{(V_1, p_1), \ldots, (V_k, p_k)\}$, let $S \twoheadrightarrow V$ indicate $\{V_1, V_2, \ldots, V_k\} \twoheadrightarrow V$. Then the price function *defined by S is*

$$p_S(V) = \min_{T \subseteq S, T \twoheadrightarrow V} \sum_{(V_i, p_i) \in T} p_i$$

In other words, S is consistent if a buyer cannot obtain V_i by paying less than p_i. Moreover, the price of an arbitrary view V is obtained by choosing the least expensive subset of S that can be used to answer V, where the price of $T \subseteq S$ is just the sum of the prices of the views it contains.

We can also formally express the property that a pricing function does not allow arbitrage.

Definition 3. *A* pricing function p *is* arbitrage-free *if, whenever* $V_1, \ldots, V_m \twoheadrightarrow V$, *then* $p(V) \leq \sum_{i=1}^m p(V_i)$.

Note that this definition does not assume any pricing scheme S; for example, the constant pricing function that assigns the same price to every view is arbitrage-free. On the other hand, if a pricing scheme S is given, then we seek an arbitrage-free pricing function p that agrees with S on all price points in S, in other words $p(V_i) = p_i$ for all $(V_i, p_i) \in S$. It is easy to see that, if such a function p exists, then S is consistent. We also proved recently [11] two interesting facts. Fix a pricing scheme S and consider the pricing function p_S defined in Definition 2. Then, assuming some some natural properties for $\twoheadrightarrow$: (1) p_S is arbitrage-free (even if S is inconsistent); and (2) S is consistent iff for every price point (V_i, p_i) is S, the following holds: $p_S(V_i) = p_i$.

We end this section with a discussion on the key technical difficulty of pricing: How should we define $\twoheadrightarrow$ in Equation 1? Database theoreticians have studied *query answering using views* for almost two decades, starting with Levy [12], and Abiteboul and Duschka [3]. More recently, Segoufin and Vianu [15] and Nash, Segoufin, and Vianu [14] have revisited the notion of query answering using information-content. Their formal definition of determinacy is equivalent to the following: $V_1, \ldots, V_m \twoheadrightarrow V$ if there exists a function f such that, for any database instance D, $f(V_1(D), \ldots, V_m(D)) = V(D)$. Let us call this definition of determinacy NSV. If one adopts NSV for pricing, then, given any pricing scheme S, the equation from Definition 2 extends it uniquely to a global pricing function p_S. We argue, however, that NSV is not the right notion for defining p_S, and therefore a different definition for $\twoheadrightarrow$ is needed in order to compute prices. Specifically:

- NSV is insensitive to the data instance. That means that the pricing function $p_S(V)$ depends only on the view V, and not on the database instance D. In practice, the database instance is also a variable, and should be considered as input to the pricing function. For example the seller may add more data to her raw dataset; as a consequence, she wants her pricing function to increase. The determinacy relation $\twoheadrightarrow$ should somehow depend on the database instance too. *Instance-based* determinacy has been much less studied in the literature; one such definition can be found in Calvanese *et al.* [8].
- Unfortunately, NSV is difficult to check: it is undecidable for unions of conjunctive queries, and its decidability is open for conjunctive queries [14]. This means that we do not have any practical means for computing the pricing function $p_S(V)$.
- NSV deals incorrectly with user-defined functions. For example, consider a view $V(x, f(y, z)) = R(x, y, z)$ that applies a proprietary user-defined function f to the attributes y and z. Naturally, the seller would like to charge more for V than for R, but R determines V, because, mathematically, one can compute V from R. NSV does not capture the fact that f is a proprietary function, which cannot be applied by the user interested in computing V from R.
- Noise and levels of accuracy are not captured by NSV either, because the latter is, in essence, a deterministic definition. We are not aware of any natural extension of the determinacy relation $\twoheadrightarrow$ that can deal with noise in the data.

To summarize, in order to understand the price of data one must understand the notion of determinacy first. NSV is an elegant definition for the latter, but it does not seem to be the right choice for setting prices.

4   Open Problems

Data markets motivate a new direction of research in database theory. While we have discussed the determinacy relation as the first step of this research, it is by far not the only one. Several other open problems exists, we briefly mention a few here.

Pricing Updates. The interaction between updates and prices is interesting. The seller expects its prices to increase once the data is updated (assuming tuples are being inserted), which seems to impose additional requirements on a pricing function. At a more practical level, one question is how to charge the buyer for incremental updates: if he already purchased data from the old version, he expects to pay a reduced price for the updates. Finally, it is unclear how consistency or arbitrage are affected by updates: if S is consistent, can it become inconsistent after an update?

Pricing Integrated Data. The interraction between multiple vendors affects the pricing function in interesting ways. For example, different vendors may add value in different ways to same data: the first vendor provides raw images, the second runs a proprietary face recognition algorithm, and the third integrates the extracted faces with a social network database, thus putting names on pictures. Each vendor adds some value to the data, by integrating it with her own dataset or her proprietary tools. It will be quite challenging to define pricing functions in such complex scenarios.

Pricing Competing Data Sources. There are often multiple vendors for quite similar data sources. For example, today one can buy data about businesses from several vendors. There are subtle relationships between these sources: some are more complete, others are more accurate, others are more up to date, while others yet are more reliable. Another major challenge is to understand how prices are affected by competing data sources.

References

1. http://www.iuphar-db.org/
2. The Data Eco$y$tem project: Data management and pricing in the cloud, http://data-pricing.cs.washington.edu/
3. Abiteboul, S., Duschka, O.M.: Complexity of answering queries using materialized views. In: PODS, pp. 254–263. ACM Press (1998)
4. http://www.aggdata.com/
5. https://datamarket.azure.com/
6. Balazinska, M., Howe, B., Suciu, D.: Data markets in the cloud: An opportunity for the database community. Proc. of the VLDB Endowment 4(12) (2011)
7. Buneman, P., Suciu, D.: Censoring and pricing data (manuscript, July 2007)
8. Calvanese, D., Giacomo, G.D., Lenzerini, M., Vardi, M.Y.: Lossless regular views. In: Popa, L. (ed.) PODS, pp. 247–258. ACM (2002)
9. http://www.customlists.net/
10. http://www.infochimps.com/
11. Koutris, P., Upadhyaya, P., Balazinska, M., Howe, B., Suciu, D.: Query-based data pricing. In: PODS 2012: Proceedings of the 31st Symposium on Principles of Database Systems of Data, Scottsdale, AZ, USA (2012)
12. Levy, A.Y., Mendelzon, A.O., Sagiv, Y., Srivastava, D.: Answering queries using views. In: PODS, pp. 95–104 (1995)
13. https://datamarket.azure.com/dataset/59a168b8-6d66-4f85-b000-38abcad310a2
14. Nash, A., Segoufin, L., Vianu, V.: Determinacy and rewriting of conjunctive queries using views: A progress report. In: Schwentick, T., Suciu, D. (eds.) ICDT 2007. LNCS, vol. 4353, pp. 59–73. Springer, Heidelberg (2006)
15. Segoufin, L., Vianu, V.: Views and queries: determinacy and rewriting. In: Li, C. (ed.) PODS, pp. 49–60. ACM (2005)
16. Shapiro, C., Varian, H.R.: Versioning: The smart way to sell information. Harvard Business Review 76, 106–114 (1998)
17. http://www.xignite.com/

Tractable Reasoning in Description Logics with Functionality Constraints

Andrea Calì[1,3], Georg Gottlob[2,3], and Andreas Pieris[2]

[1] Dept. of Computer Science and Inf. Syst., Birkbeck, University of London, UK
[2] Department of Computer Science, University of Oxford, UK
[3] Oxford-Man Institute of Quantitative Finance, University of Oxford, UK
andrea@dcs.bbk.ac.uk,
{georg.gottlob,andreas.pieris}@cs.ox.ac.uk

Abstract. Ontological query answering amounts to returning the answers to a query, that are logically entailed by the union of a set of membership assertions and an ontology, where the latter is a set of logical assertions. Ontological query answering has applications, for instance, in the Semantic Web and in semantic data integration. We propose as ontology language a new description logic, called $\mathsf{DLR}^{\pm}$, allowing for roles of arbitrary arity and role inclusion assertions with permutation, as well as functionality assertions, which generalizes the most widely-adopted tractable ontology languages. The interaction between functionality assertions and other constructs in ontology languages has been shown to lead easily to intractability and even undecidability. The absence of such interaction is characterized by *separability*, a semantic property which has been studied in different contexts. With the aim of finding expressive ontology languages that are also tractable, we give a precise characterization of separable $\mathsf{DLR}^{\pm}$ ontologies by providing a syntactic condition that is necessary and sufficient for separability. We also present an exhaustive complexity analysis of reasoning, here intended as conjunctive query answering and satisfiability checking, under separable $\mathsf{DLR}^{\pm}$ ontologies.

1 Introduction

An ontology is a set of logical sentences on a signature or schema; rather than enforcing constraints on instances (sets of facts) for the same signature, an ontology is to infer new knowledge from an instance. In particular, given a query q, an ontology $\mathcal{T}$, and an instance $\mathcal{A}$, the problem of *ontological query answering* amounts to provide the answers to q which are logically entailed by the theory $\mathcal{T} \cup \mathcal{A}$. Notice that we refer to the standard entailment, that is, entailment under arbitrary, not necessarily finite, models. Ontologies are also gaining importance in the area of databases, for example, in data integration [16], where *query answering* is the central issue. In such context, rather than on decidability issues, the focus is on scalability of query answering w.r.t. the data instance size.

Description Logics. *Description Logics (DLs)*, a popular ontology formalism, are decidable fragments of first-order logic, where predicates are *concepts* (classes of objects) and *roles* (binary relations on classes). In DLs, a knowledge base

V. Tannen et al. (Eds.): Buneman Festschrift, LNCS 8000, pp. 174–192, 2013.
© Springer-Verlag Berlin Heidelberg 2013

consists of a *TBox* (terminological component, that is, ontology assertions on concepts and roles) and an *ABox* (assertional component, i.e., ontology assertions on instances of concepts and roles); a TBox and an ABox can therefore be seen as a schema with constraints and a data instance for it, respectively. A central issue in DLs is the trade-off between expressive power and computational complexity of reasoning services. DL-based data-intensive applications have been gaining importance recently, therefore special attention is given to *data complexity* of query answering, that is, the complexity w.r.t. the data instance size, while all other inputs (query and ontology) are considered fixed.

Ontology Formalisms. The *DL-Lite* family [2,8,19] has the advantage of AC_0 data complexity of conjunctive query answering and of knowledge base satisfiability. We remind the reader that the low complexity class AC_0 is the complexity class of recognizing words in languages defined by constant-depth Boolean circuits with an unlimited fan-in AND and OR gates; it is strictly contained in LOGSPACE. This low complexity is due to *first-order rewritability (FO-rewritability)*, i.e., the possibility of answering every query q against a TBox $\mathcal{T}$ and an ABox $\mathcal{A}$ by rewriting q into a *first-order* query $q_{\mathcal{T}}$, which takes into account the TBox $\mathcal{T}$, and simply evaluating $q_{\mathcal{T}}$ over $\mathcal{A}$.

The well-known Entity-Relationship (ER) [12] model has recently gained importance in ontology specification, due to the fact that it is comprehensible to theorists and practitioners, while having good expressive power. The $ER^\pm$ family of ER-like languages [4], in particular, comprises several FO-rewritable ontology languages, which properly generalize the main languages of the DL-Lite family.

Another relevant, more general class of ontology languages, is the *Datalog$^\pm$* family, that is, a family of rule-based languages derived from Datalog (see, e.g., [3]) whose rules are (function-free) Horn rules, possibly with existentially quantified variables in the head, called *tuple-generating dependencies*, enriched with functionality constraints in the form of *equality-generating dependencies*, and *negative constraints*, a form of denial constraints.

Separability. A central issue in this context is the interaction between *functionality constraints* and the other constraints in the ontology. In general, functionality constraints impose a uniqueness of some sort; functional participation of instances of a set to a relation (e.g., in DLs or $ER^\pm$), or more general equality constraints (e.g., in Datalog$^\pm$). In all the aforementioned formalisms, the key notion that ensures FO-rewritability is *separability* [5]: an ontology $\mathcal{T}$ is separable if, for every query q and for every instance $\mathcal{A}$, assuming that the theory $\mathcal{T} \cup \mathcal{A}$ is satisfiable, the answers to q over $\mathcal{T} \cup \mathcal{A}$ coincide with the answers to q over $\mathcal{T}' \cup \mathcal{A}$, where $\mathcal{T}'$ is obtained from $\mathcal{T}$ by removing functionality constraints. In other words, in separable cases, if the theory is satisfiable, then the presence of functionality constraints does not play any role in query answering, and can therefore be ignored. Separability is normally enforced by a *syntactic* condition which prevents the functionality constraints from interacting with other constraints. Early separability conditions have been studied in [5,14] for inclusion and key dependencies, and, e.g., in [3] for tuple-generating and key dependencies.

Summary of Contributions. Studying efficient query answering under ontologies with functionality constraints, we tackle two fundamental challenges: *(i)* What language should we use for ontology modeling, so that it is expressive enough for applications? *(ii)* Under what (syntactic) conditions is a knowledge base in the chosen language separable? We aim at proposing a DL-based ontology formalism, which is at least as expressive as other well-established ontology formalisms, and to provide a separability condition that is as general as possible. The contributions of the paper can be summarized as follows.

1. We propose the DL $DLR^{\pm}$ with roles of arbitrary arity, which is equipped, among other constructs, with functionality constraints, role inclusions with arbitrary permutation of the arguments, and negative assertions (which prohibit certain existentially-quantified conjunctions of atoms to be true). $DLR^{\pm}$ is inspired by (and close to) the variant of the ER model studied in [4], and it is incomparable to the DL $\mathcal{DLR}$ of [9] (hence the symbol "$\pm$").

2. We exhibit a graph-based condition for separability of $DLR^{\pm}$ TBoxes; we define the DL *non-conflicting* $DLR^{\pm}$, called $NCDLR^{\pm}$, by means of a *syntactic* condition. Such condition is sufficient for all TBoxes, a result that is implicit in [4], where an analogous condition is proposed. In this paper, we prove that it is also necessary for those without negative assertions, and for those with negative assertions but which are *strongly consistent*, i.e., they admit at least one model where each concept and role is non-empty. We also investigate the complexity of deciding whether an $NCDLR^{\pm}$ TBox is strongly consistent (which is a natural property); in particular, we establish that this problem is PSPACE-complete.

3. We show that CQ answering is NP-complete in combined complexity for two variants of $NCDLR^{\pm}$. The first variant is obtained by prohibiting arbitrary permutations of arguments in role inclusions, and imposing the identity permutation, while the second one is obtained by assuming the arity of roles to be bounded by an integer constant.

4. Finally, we study the complexity of knowledge base satisfiability in $NCDLR^{\pm}$, and show that it is in AC$_0$ in data complexity. Moreover, we study the combined complexity, and we show that the problem is PSPACE-complete if we consider arbitrary $NCDLR^{\pm}$ knowledge bases, and coNP-complete if we restrict to the two variants mentioned above.

Notice that since $DLR^{\pm}$ is similar to the ER variant of [4], all our novel results can be straightforwardly ported to the formalism of [4].

2   Theoretical Background

As already said, DLs are logics that model the domain of interest in terms of *concepts*, representing sets of individuals, and *roles*, representing relations on sets of individuals. A DL knowledge base encodes subset relationships between concepts, subset relationships between roles, functional dependencies on roles, the membership of individuals to concepts, and the membership of tuples of individuals to roles. In this section, we introduce the DL $DLR^\pm$, inspired by an extended version of the ER model considered, e.g., in [7]. Typically, DLs are usable for binary roles only. However, the proposed formalism allows for n-ary roles as, for instance, the DL $\mathcal{DLR}$ proposed in [9], and the DLs of the DLR-Lite family [10], that is, an extension of the DL-Lite family to roles of arbitrary arity. Let us clarify that $DLR^\pm$ is incomparable to the aforementioned DLs (hence the symbol "$\pm$").

Syntax. Let $\mathbf{A}$, $\mathbf{R}$ and $\mathbf{I}$ be pairwise disjoint sets of atomic concepts, atomic roles of arbitrary arity and individuals, respectively. We write R/n to assert that the atomic role $R \in \mathbf{R}$ has arity $n \geqslant 2$. In the rest of the paper, let $[n]$ be the set $\{1,\ldots,n\}$, for an integer $n \geqslant 1$. A DL *knowledge base* $\mathcal{K} = \langle \mathcal{T},\mathcal{A}\rangle$, represents the domain of interest in terms of two parts, a TBox $\mathcal{T}$, specifying the intensional knowledge, and an ABox $\mathcal{A}$, specifying the extensional data. A $DLR^\pm$ TBox is a finite set of assertions which have one of the following forms; in the sequel, we assume that roles have arity $n \geqslant 2$, and also A and R (possibly with subscripts) to be atomic concepts and roles, respectively:

1. $A_1 \sqsubseteq A_2$;
2. $A \sqsubseteq \exists R[i]$, where $i \in [n]$;
3. $\exists R[i] \sqsubseteq A$, where $i \in [n]$;
4. $R_1[i_1,\ldots,i_n] \sqsubseteq R_2[j_1,\ldots,j_n]$, where $\{i_1,\ldots,i_n\} = \{j_1,\ldots,j_n\} = [n]$;
5. $\phi(\mathbf{X}) \sqsubseteq \bot$, where $\phi(\mathbf{X})$ is a conjunction of atoms of the form $A(X)$ and $R(X_1,\ldots,X_n)$;
6. (funct $R[i]$), where $i \in [n]$.

Assertions of the form $X \sqsubseteq Y$ are called *inclusion assertions*, while assertions of the form (funct $R[i]$) are called *functionality assertions*. We denote by $\text{sig}(\mathcal{T})$ the set of atomic concepts and roles in the TBox $\mathcal{T}$, and by $\text{arity}(\mathcal{T})$ the maximum arity over all roles in $\mathcal{T}$. An ABox is a finite set of membership assertions of the form $A(c)$ and $R(c_1,\ldots,c_n)$ stating that the individual $c \in \mathbf{I}$ is an instance of A, and the n-tuple $\langle c_1,\ldots,c_n\rangle \in \mathbf{I}^n$ of individuals is an instance of R, respectively.

Semantics. The semantics of a DL is given in terms of interpretations, where an interpretation $\mathcal{I} = \langle \Delta^\mathcal{I}, \cdot^\mathcal{I}\rangle$ consists of a non-empty *interpretation domain* $\Delta^\mathcal{I}$ and an *interpretation function* $\cdot^\mathcal{I}$. For the constructs of $DLR^\pm$ we have:

$$(\bot)^\mathcal{I} = \varnothing$$
$$A^\mathcal{I} \subseteq \Delta^\mathcal{I}$$
$$R^\mathcal{I} \subseteq (\Delta^\mathcal{I})^n$$
$$(\exists R[i])^\mathcal{I} = \{t_i \mid \langle t_1,\ldots,t_n\rangle \in R^\mathcal{I}\}$$
$$(R[i_1,\ldots,i_n])^\mathcal{I} = \{\langle t_{i_1},\ldots,t_{i_n}\rangle \mid \langle t_1,\ldots,t_n\rangle \in R^\mathcal{I}\}$$
$$(\phi(\mathbf{X}))^\mathcal{I} = \begin{cases} \{\langle\rangle\}, & \exists \mathbf{X}\,\phi(\mathbf{X}) \text{ is } true \text{ in } \mathcal{I} \\ \varnothing, & \exists \mathbf{X}\,\phi(\mathbf{X}) \text{ is } false \text{ in } \mathcal{I}. \end{cases}$$

$\mathcal{I}$ is a *model* of an inclusion assertion $X \sqsubseteq Y$ iff $X^\mathcal{I} \subseteq Y^\mathcal{I}$, while it is a model of a functionality assertion (funct $R[i]$) iff $\langle t_1,\ldots,t_{i-1},t_i,t_{i+1},\ldots,t_n\rangle \in R^\mathcal{I}$ and $\langle t'_1,\ldots,t'_{i-1},t_i,t'_{i+1},\ldots,t'_n\rangle \in R^\mathcal{I}$ implies $t_j = t'_j$, for each $j \in [n] \setminus \{i\}$.

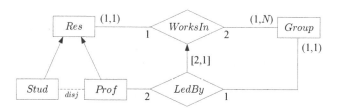

Fig. 1. Extended ER Schema

To specify the semantics of membership assertions, $\cdot^{\mathcal{I}}$ is extended to constants by assigning to each $c \in \mathbf{I}$ a distinct element $c^{\mathcal{I}} \in \Delta^{\mathcal{I}}$ (*unique name assumption*). $\mathcal{I}$ is a model of a membership assertion $A(c)$ (resp., $R(c_1, \ldots, c_n)$) iff $c^{\mathcal{I}} \in A^{\mathcal{I}}$ (resp., $\langle c_1^{\mathcal{I}}, \ldots, c_n^{\mathcal{I}} \rangle \in R^{\mathcal{I}}$).

Given an (inclusion, functionality or membership) assertion σ and an interpretation $\mathcal{I}$, we denote the fact that $\mathcal{I}$ is a model of σ by $\mathcal{I} \models \sigma$. A model of a TBox $\mathcal{T}$ (resp., an ABox $\mathcal{A}$) is an interpretation $\mathcal{I}$ such that $\mathcal{I} \models \sigma$, for each $\sigma \in \mathcal{T}$ (resp., $\sigma \in \mathcal{A}$). A model of a KB $\mathcal{K} = \langle \mathcal{T}, \mathcal{A} \rangle$ is an interpretation $\mathcal{I}$ such that $\mathcal{I} \models \mathcal{T}$ and $\mathcal{I} \models \mathcal{A}$; we write $\mathcal{I} \models \mathcal{K}$ if $\mathcal{I}$ is a model of $\mathcal{K}$. A KB $\mathcal{K}$ is *satisfiable* if it has at least one model; $\mathcal{K}$ is *unsatisfiable* if it has no model.

Example 1. Consider the DLR$^{\pm}$ TBox $\mathcal{T}$ constituted by

$$
\begin{array}{ll}
Prof \sqsubseteq Res & Group \sqsubseteq \exists LedBy[1] \\
Stud \sqsubseteq Res & (\text{funct } LedBy[1]) \\
Res \sqsubseteq \exists WorksIn[1] & \exists LedBy[2] \sqsubseteq Prof \\
(\text{funct } WorksIn[1]) & LedBy[1,2] \sqsubseteq WorksIn[2,1] \\
Group \sqsubseteq \exists WorksIn[2] & Prof(X), Stud(X) \sqsubseteq \bot.
\end{array}
$$

$\mathcal{T}$ asserts that professors and students, who are researchers, work in exactly one (mandatory and functional participation) research group, while research groups have at least one (but typically more than one) researcher. Moreover, research groups have exactly one leader who is himself a professor. Also, each professor works in the research group that (s)he leads. Finally, professors and students are disjoint sets. The ABox constituted by $Group(g)$, $LedBy(g,p)$ and $Professor(p)$, asserts that the individual g is a research group led by the professor p. ∎

It is easy to verify that DLR$^{\pm}$ is expressive enough to be able to capture an extended version of the ER model (see, e.g., [7]), which comprises is-a constraints among entities and relationships, functional and mandatory participation constraints, as well as disjointness among entities and relationships, and non-participation of an entity to a relationship. For instance, by adding to the TBox given in Example 1 the assertions $\exists WorksIn[1] \sqsubseteq Res$, $\exists WorksIn[2] \sqsubseteq Group$ and $\exists LedBy[1] \sqsubseteq Group$, what we obtain corresponds to the extended ER schema depicted in Figure 1, where the reader will recognize the familiar notation of Chen's ER model [12].

Conjunctive Queries. We now define queries over a KB. In this work, we focus on conjunctive queries. A *conjunctive query (CQ)* q of arity $n \geqslant 0$ over a KB $\mathcal{K}$ is an assertion of the form $p(\mathbf{X}) \leftarrow \phi(\mathbf{X}, \mathbf{Y})$, where $\phi(\mathbf{X}, \mathbf{Y})$ is a conjunction of atoms of the form $A(X)$ and $R(X_1, \ldots, X_m)$ with $A \in \mathbf{A}$, $R/m \in \mathbf{R}$ and $p \notin (\mathbf{A} \cup \mathbf{R})$ is an n-ary predicate. $\phi(\mathbf{X}, \mathbf{Y})$ is called the *body* of q, denoted as $body(q)$. A *Boolean CQ (BCQ)* is a CQ of arity zero. Given an interpretation $\mathcal{I}$, the *answer* to an n-ary CQ q of the form $p(\mathbf{X}) \leftarrow \phi(\mathbf{X}, \mathbf{Y})$ over $\mathcal{I}$, denoted as $q^{\mathcal{I}}$, is the set of all n-tuples $\mathbf{t}$ of domain elements such that, when assigning $\mathbf{t}$ to $\mathbf{X}$, the first-order formula $\exists \mathbf{Y}\, \phi(\mathbf{X}, \mathbf{Y})$ evaluates to *true* in $\mathcal{I}$. A BCQ has only the empty tuple $\langle \rangle$ as possible answer, in which case it is said that it has positive answer. Formally, a BCQ q has *positive* answer over $\mathcal{I}$, denoted as $\mathcal{I} \models q$, if $\langle \rangle \in q^{\mathcal{I}}$, or, equivalently, $q^{\mathcal{I}} \neq \varnothing$. We are now ready to define the notion of query answering over a KB. Given an n-ary CQ q and a KB $\mathcal{K}$, the *answer* to q w.r.t. $\mathcal{K}$, denoted as $ans(q, \mathcal{K})$, is the set of n-tuples $\mathbf{t}$ of constants appearing in $\mathcal{K}$ such that $\mathbf{t}^{\mathcal{M}} \in q^{\mathcal{M}}$, for every model $\mathcal{M}$ of $\mathcal{K}$. The answer to a BCQ q w.r.t. $\mathcal{K}$ is *positive*, denoted as $\mathcal{K} \models q$, if $\langle \rangle \in ans(q, \mathcal{K})$, or, equivalently, $ans(q, \mathcal{K}) \neq \varnothing$. Notice that, if $\mathcal{K}$ is unsatisfiable, then $ans(q, \mathcal{K})$ is trivially the set of all possible n-tuples of constants occurring in $\mathcal{K}$.

Reasoning Services. The reasoning services we are interested in are query answering over KBs and KB satisfiability. The decision problem CQAns is defined as follows: given a KB $\mathcal{K}$, an n-ary CQ q over $\mathcal{K}$, and an n-tuple $\mathbf{t}$ of constants in $\mathcal{K}$, decide whether $\mathbf{t} \in ans(q, \mathcal{K})$. If the given query is Boolean, then the above problem is called BCQAns. It is known that CQAns can be easily reduced to BCQAns (see, e.g., [13]), and thus CQAns and BCQAns are equivalent problems. Hence, for technical clarity, we focus on BCQAns. The decision problem KBSat associated to KB satisfiability is defined as follows: given a KB $\mathcal{K}$, decide whether $\mathcal{K}$ admits at least one model. Following Vardi's taxonomy [20], the *data complexity* of the above decision problems is calculated w.r.t. the size of the ABox only, while *combined complexity* w.r.t. the size of all inputs.

Canonical Interpretation. Using the *chase procedure* (see, e.g., [14,17]) we can construct the so-called *canonical interpretation* of a $\mathsf{DLR}^{\pm}$ KB constituted by *positive inclusions (PIs)*, that is, assertions of the form $X \sqsubseteq Y$, where $Y \neq \bot$. Notice that an assertion of the form $X \sqsubseteq \bot$ is called *negative inclusion (NI)*. The chase works on an ABox through the *chase rule*. We define a set $\mathbf{N}$ of labeled nulls, used as placeholders for unknown values. A lexicographic order is defined on $\mathbf{I} \cup \mathbf{N}$, such that every value of $\mathbf{N}$ follows all those in $\mathbf{I}$.

Definition 1. Consider an ABox $\mathcal{A}$, and a PI σ. The membership assertion α is defined as follows:

- If $\sigma = A_1 \sqsubseteq A_2$ and $A_1(c) \in \mathcal{A}$, then $\alpha = A_2(c)$.
- If $\sigma = A \sqsubseteq \exists R[i]$ and $A(c) \in \mathcal{A}$, then $\alpha = R(z_1, \ldots, z_{i-1}, c, z_{i+1}, \ldots, z_n)$, where each $z_i \in \mathbf{N}$ is a "fresh" labeled null not occurring in $\mathcal{A}$.
- If $\sigma = \exists R[i] \sqsubseteq A$ and $R(c_1, \ldots, c_n) \in \mathcal{A}$, then $\alpha = A(c_i)$.

- If $\sigma = R_1[i_1,\ldots,i_n] \sqsubseteq R_2[j_1,\ldots,j_n]$ and $R_1(\mathbf{t}_1) \in \mathcal{A}$, then $\alpha = R_2(\mathbf{t}_2)$, where $\langle \mathbf{t}_1[i_1],\ldots,\mathbf{t}_1[i_n]\rangle = \langle \mathbf{t}_2[j_1],\ldots,\mathbf{t}_2[j_n]\rangle$.
- If none of the above cases applies, then $\alpha = \epsilon$ (the empty assertion).

If $\alpha \neq \epsilon$, then σ is *applicable* to $\mathcal{A}$, and α is added to $\mathcal{A}$.   ■

Consider a DLR$^\pm$ KB $\mathcal{K} = \langle \mathcal{T}, \mathcal{A}\rangle$, where $\mathcal{T}$ contains only positive inclusions. The chase algorithm for $\mathcal{K}$ consists of an exhaustive application of the chase rule, which leads to a (possibly infinite) ABox, denoted as $chase(\mathcal{K})$. We assume that the chase algorithm is *fair*, i.e., each PI that must be applied during the construction of $chase(\mathcal{K})$ eventually it is applied. By exploiting the chase algorithm, we can define the central notion of the canonical interpretation of a KB.

Definition 2 (Canonical Interpretation). Let $\mathcal{K} = \langle \mathcal{T}, \mathcal{A}\rangle$ be a DLR$^\pm$ KB, where $\mathcal{T}$ contains only PIs. The *canonical interpretation* of $\mathcal{K}$, denoted $can(\mathcal{K})$, is defined as the interpretation $\langle \Delta^{can(\mathcal{K})}, \cdot^{can(\mathcal{K})}\rangle$, where:

- $\Delta^{can(\mathcal{K})}$ is the set of terms occurring in $chase(\mathcal{K})$,
- $t^{can(\mathcal{K})} = t$, for each term t occurring in $chase(\mathcal{K})$,
- $A^{can(\mathcal{K})} = \{t \mid A(t) \in chase(\mathcal{K})\}$, and
- $R^{can(\mathcal{K})} = \{\langle t_1,\ldots,t_n\rangle \mid R(t_1,\ldots,t_n) \in chase(\mathcal{K})\}$.   ■

Interestingly, the canonical interpretation of a KB $\mathcal{K} = \langle \mathcal{T}, \mathcal{A}\rangle$, where $\mathcal{T}$ contains only positive inclusions, is a *universal model* of $\mathcal{K}$, i.e., for every model $\mathcal{I}$ of $\mathcal{K}$, there exists a substitution $h : \Delta^{can(\mathcal{K})} \to \Delta^{\mathcal{I}}$ such that: *(i)* h is the identity on $\mathbf{I}$, *(ii)* if $t \in A^{can(\mathcal{K})}$, then $h(t) \in A^{\mathcal{I}}$, and *(iii)* if $\langle t_1,\ldots,t_n\rangle \in R^{can(\mathcal{K})}$, then $\langle h(t_1),\ldots,h(t_n)\rangle \in R^{\mathcal{I}}$. The substitution h is called a *homomorphism* from $can(\mathcal{K})$ to $\mathcal{I}$; the notion of homomorphism among sets of membership assertions can be defined analogously. By exploiting the above universality property, it is not difficult to show that the canonical interpretation of a KB is a very useful technical tool for BCQAns.

Theorem 1. *Consider a* DLR$^\pm$ *KB* $\mathcal{K} = \langle \mathcal{T}, \mathcal{A}\rangle$, *where* $\mathcal{T}$ *contains only positive inclusions. Then, for every BCQ* q *over* $\mathcal{K}$, $\mathcal{K} \models q$ *iff* $can(\mathcal{K}) \models q$.

3   Non-Conflicting Condition

In this section, we introduce a novel description logic, called *non-conflicting* DLR$^\pm$ (NCDLR$^\pm$), obtained by applying syntactic restrictions on the DL presented in the previous section. Intuitively, given an NCDLR$^\pm$ TBox $\mathcal{T}$, the inclusion and functionality assertions of $\mathcal{T}$ do not interact. This implies that answers to queries can be computed by considering the PIs only of $\mathcal{T}$, and ignoring the NIs and the functionality assertions, once it is known that the KB is satisfiable. This semantic property, whose definition is given below, is known as separability [5]. In the rest of the paper, for notational convenience, given a DLR$^\pm$ TBox $\mathcal{T}$, let $\mathcal{T}^+$ be the PIs of $\mathcal{T}$, $\mathcal{T}^-$ be the NIs of $\mathcal{T}$, and $\mathcal{T}^=$ be the functionality assertions of $\mathcal{T}$.

Definition 3 (Separability). A DLR$^\pm$ TBox $\mathcal{T}$ is said to be *separable* if, for every ABox $\mathcal{A}$, either $\mathcal{K} = \langle \mathcal{T}, \mathcal{A} \rangle$ is unsatisfiable or, for every BCQ q over $\mathcal{K}$, $\mathcal{K} \models q$ iff $\langle \mathcal{T}^+, \mathcal{A} \rangle \models q$. ∎

Notice that DLR$^\pm$ TBoxes are, in general, non-separable. Before defining formally NCDLR$^\pm$, we need some preliminary technical definitions.

Definition 4. The *dependency graph* for a DLR$^\pm$ TBox $\mathcal{T}$ is a directed multi-graph $\langle V, E, \lambda \rangle$, where V is the node set, E is the edge set, and λ is a labeling function $E \to \mathcal{T}^+$. For each atomic concept $A \in \mathbf{A}$ in $\mathcal{T}$ we have the node $A[1]$ which is called *concept node (c-node)*. For each atomic n-ary role $R \in \mathbf{R}$ in $\mathcal{T}$, and for each $i \in [n]$, we have the node $R[i]$ which is called *role node (r-node)*. If (funct $R[i]$) occurs in $\mathcal{T}$, then $R[i]$ is also a *functionality node (f-node)*. The edge set E is defined as follows. For each $\sigma \in \mathcal{T}^+$ of the form $A_1 \sqsubseteq A_2$, there exists an edge $(A_1[1], A_2[1])$ labeled by σ. For each $\sigma \in \mathcal{T}^+$ of the form $A \sqsubseteq \exists R[i]$, where R has arity n, there exists an edge $(A[1], R[i])$ labeled by σ, and also there exists a *special edge* $(A[1], R[j])$, for each $j \in [n] \setminus \{i\}$, labeled by σ. For each $\sigma \in \mathcal{T}^+$ of the form $\exists R[i] \sqsubseteq A$, there exists an edge $(R[i], A[1])$ labeled by σ. Finally, for each $\sigma \in \mathcal{T}^+$ of the form $R_1[i_1, \ldots, i_n] \sqsubseteq R_2[j_1, \ldots, j_n]$, and for each $k \in [n]$, there exists an edge $(R_1[i_k], R_2[j_k])$ labeled by σ. ∎

Intuitively, the non-special edges in a dependency graph G keep track of the fact that a term propagates from some concept or role to some other concept or role during the construction of the chase. The special edges keep track of the fact that the propagation of a term to some attribute of a role R, also creates a labeled null in all the other attributes of R. Consider now an edge e of G which is labeled by an assertion of the form $R_1[i_1, \ldots, i_n] \sqsubseteq R_2[j_1, \ldots, j_n]$. Roughly, the above assertion states that the i_k-th object of R_1 is the j_k-th object of R_2. This can be formally represented by the bijective function $f_e : [n] \to [n]$ defined as follows: for each $k \in [n]$, $f_e(i_k) = j_k$. We can now introduce the so-called *propagation function* associated to a cycle constituted by r-nodes of G. Intuitively, the propagation function associated to such a cycle C describes how terms are propagated during the construction of the chase due to C (hence the name "propagation" function).

Definition 5. Let G be the dependency graph for a DLR$^\pm$ TBox $\mathcal{T}$. Consider a cycle $C = v_1 v_2 \ldots v_m v_1$ of only r-nodes of G. The *propagation function* associated to C is the bijective function $g : [n] \to [n]$ defined as the composition $f_{e_m} \circ \ldots \circ f_{e_1}$, where $e_i = (v_i, v_{i+1})$, for each $i \in [m-1]$, and $e_m = (v_m, v_1)$. ∎

Example 2. Consider the DLR$^\pm$ TBox $\mathcal{T}$ constituted by

$$\begin{aligned}
\sigma_1 &: A \sqsubseteq \exists R_1[3] & \sigma_4 &: R_3[1,2,3] \sqsubseteq R_1[3,1,2] \\
\sigma_2 &: R_1[1,2,3] \sqsubseteq R_2[2,1,3] & \sigma_5 &: (\text{funct } R_3[1]). \\
\sigma_3 &: R_2[1,2,3] \sqsubseteq R_3[3,2,1]
\end{aligned}$$

The dependency graph G for $\mathcal{T}$ is depicted in Figure 2, where the f-nodes are shaded and the special edges are represented using dashed arrows. Clearly, the

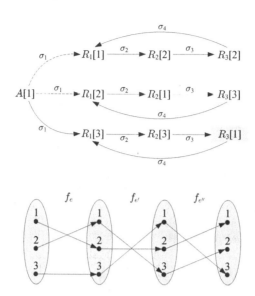

Fig. 2. The dependency graph G, and the propagation function associated to C

cycle $C = R_1[3]R_2[3]R_3[1]R_1[3]$ occurs in G. The propagation function associated to C, which is shown graphically in Figure 2, is the function $g = f_{e''} \circ f_{e'} \circ f_e$, where $e = (R_1[3], R_2[3])$, $e' = (R_2[3], R_3[1])$ and $e'' = (R_3[1], R_1[3])$; clearly, g is the identity on $\{1, 2, 3\}$. ∎

Having the notion of the dependency graph and the notion of the propagation function in place, we are now ready to give the formal definition of NCDLR$^\pm$.

Definition 6 (Non-Conflicting DLR$^\pm$). Let $\mathcal{T}$ be a DLR$^\pm$ TBox, and let G be the dependency graph for $\mathcal{T}$. $\mathcal{T}$ is *non-conflicting* if, for each path $v_1 v_2 \ldots v_m$, where $m \geqslant 2$, in G such that v_1 is a c-node, $v_2, \ldots, v_{m-1}$ are r-nodes, and v_m is an f-node, the following conditions are satisfied:

1. for each cycle C of only r-nodes going through v_m, the propagation function associated to C is the identity on $[n]$, where n is the arity of the role of v_m,
2. if $m \geqslant 3$ and (v_1, v_2) is non-special, then there exists a path of only r-nodes from v_m to v_2. ∎

Example 3. Consider the DLR$^\pm$ TBox $\mathcal{T}$ given in Example 2. Recall that the cycle $C = R_1[3]R_2[3]R_3[1]R_1[3]$, of only r-nodes, occurs in the dependency graph for $\mathcal{T}$. Since the propagation function associated to C is the identity on $\{1, 2, 3\}$, the first condition in the Definition 6 is satisfied. Furthermore, due to the existence of the edge $(R_3[1], R_1[3])$ in the dependency graph for $\mathcal{T}$, also the second condition is satisfied. Consequently, $\mathcal{T}$ is non-conflicting. ∎

The non-conflicting condition ensures separability, i.e., every NCDLR$^\pm$ TBox is separable. This result is implicit in [4], where a very similar condition on a variant of ER schemata is presented. Rather than presenting a complete proof, we explain intuitively why this result holds. The first condition in the Definition 6 guarantees that it is not possible to violate a functional assertion of the form (funct $R[i]$), during the construction of the chase, because of a cycle of only r-nodes (in the underlying dependency graph) that goes through the f-node $R[i]$. Now, a functional assertion (funct $R[i]$) may be violated, during the construction of the chase, due to a "bad" path of the form $v_1 v_2 \ldots v_m$, where $m \geqslant 3$, (v_1, v_2) is a non-special edge, v_1 is a c-node, $v_2, \ldots, v_m$ are r-nodes, and v_m is the f-node $R[i]$. Once (funct $R[i]$) is violated, one has to unify some terms in order to satisfy it. However, such a unification may generate new atoms. The existence of the "good" path of only r-nodes from the f-node $R[i]$ to v_2, which is ensured by the second condition in the Definition 6, guarantees that the new atoms mentioned above eventually will be obtained during the construction of the chase, even without considering (funct $R[i]$). We can now state our result.

Theorem 2. *Every* NCDLR$^\pm$ *TBox is separable.*

Characterizing Separability. An interesting question for DLR$^\pm$ TBoxes is whether the property of being non-conflicting it is also necessary for separability. As we establish below, the answer to this question is affirmative, providing that the set of negative inclusions is empty.

Theorem 3. *Consider a* DLR$^\pm$ *TBox* $\mathcal{T}$ *such that* $\mathcal{T}^- = \varnothing$. *If* $\mathcal{T}$ *is separable, then it is also non-conflicting.*

Proof (sketch). We can show that, if $\mathcal{T}$ is not non-conflicting, then it is always possible to construct an ABox $\mathcal{A}$ and a BCQ q such that $\langle \mathcal{T}, \mathcal{A} \rangle$ is satisfiable, and also $\langle \mathcal{T}, \mathcal{A} \rangle \models q$ but $\langle \mathcal{T}^+, \mathcal{A} \rangle \not\models q$. This implies that if $\mathcal{T}$ is not non-conflicting, then it is not separable, and the claim follows. □

Unfortunately, for DLR$^\pm$ TBoxes with a non-empty set of NIs, the property of being non-conflicting is not necessary for separability. For instance, it is not difficult to verify that the DLR$^\pm$ TBox $\{\exists R_1[1] \sqsubseteq A_1, A_2 \sqsubseteq \exists R_2[1], R_2[1,2] \sqsubseteq R_1[1,2], (\text{funct } R_1[1]), A_1(X), A_2(X) \sqsubseteq \bot\}$ is not non-conflicting but it is separable. We are interested to identify particular cases where, for DLR$^\pm$ TBoxes with a non-empty set of NIs, the non-conflicting condition is also necessary for separability. The argument to show that the TBox $\mathcal{T}$ given above is separable, it is heavily based on the fact that $A_2^\mathcal{I} = \varnothing$, for each model $\mathcal{I}$ of $\mathcal{T}$. This observation led us to conjecture that the non-conflicting property is necessary for separability if we consider *strongly consistent* TBoxes.

Definition 7 (Strong Consistency). A DLR$^\pm$ TBox $\mathcal{T}$ is said to be *strongly consistent* if there exists a (finite or infinite) interpretation $\mathcal{I}$ such that $\mathcal{I} \models \mathcal{T}$, and for each atomic concept A and role R in $\mathcal{T}$, $A^\mathcal{I} \neq \varnothing$ and $R^\mathcal{I} \neq \varnothing$. ∎

Let us now show that our conjecture holds.

Theorem 4. *Consider a strongly consistent* DLR$^\pm$ *TBox* $\mathcal{T}$. *If* $\mathcal{T}$ *is separable, then it is non-conflicting.*

Proof (sketch). The proof is analogous to that of Theorem 3, i.e., we can show that, if $\mathcal{T}$ is not non-conflicting, then it is always possible to construct an ABox $\mathcal{A}$ and a BCQ q such that $\langle \mathcal{T}, \mathcal{A} \rangle$ is satisfiable, and $\langle \mathcal{T}, \mathcal{A} \rangle \models q$ but $\langle \mathcal{T}^+, \mathcal{A} \rangle \not\models q$. Notice that membership assertions of the form $A(c)$ and $R(c_1, \ldots, c_n)$ occur in $\mathcal{A}$, where A is an atomic concept and R is an atomic role occurring in $\mathcal{T}$. Such an ABox always exists if we assume that there are no NIs in $\mathcal{T}$ (as in Theorem 3). However, if $\mathcal{T}^- \neq \varnothing$, then the existence of such an ABox is not guaranteed. The assumption that $\mathcal{T}$ is strongly consistent allows us always to construct such an ABox, even in the presence of NIs.   □

An interesting question concerns the computational complexity of deciding whether an NCDLR$^\pm$ TBox is strongly consistent. We show that this problem is PSPACE-complete. The desired lower bound is obtained by exploiting a decision problem, called *finite function generation*, denoted as FFG, introduced and studied in [15]: given a pair $\langle F, f \rangle$, where $F \cup \{f\}$ is a (finite) set of functions from a set to itself, decide whether f can be obtained by composing functions of F. It is known that FFG is PSPACE-complete, even for bijective functions.

Theorem 5. *The problem of deciding whether an* NCDLR$^\pm$ *TBox is strongly consistent is* PSPACE-*complete.*

Proof (sketch). Consider an NCDLR$^\pm$ TBox $\mathcal{T}$. It is possible to show that $\mathcal{T}$ is strongly consistent iff there exists an ABox $\mathcal{A}$ such that, for each atomic concept A and atomic role R in $\mathcal{T}$, $\mathcal{A}$ contains exactly one membership assertion of the form $A(c)$ and one of the form $R(c_1, \ldots, c_n)$, respectively, and $\langle \mathcal{T}, \mathcal{A} \rangle$ is satisfiable. Therefore, the problem under consideration can be solved by applying the following non-deterministic algorithm: guess an ABox $\mathcal{A}$ as described above, and if $\langle \mathcal{T}, \mathcal{A} \rangle$ is satisfiable, then *accept*; otherwise, *reject*. Clearly, the above algorithm runs in non-deterministic polynomial time with an oracle $\mathcal{C}$, where $\mathcal{C}$ is a complexity class powerful enough for deciding whether the KB $\langle \mathcal{T}, \mathcal{A} \rangle$ is satisfiable. As we shall see (Theorem 11), KBSat under NCDLR$^\pm$ TBoxes is feasible in PSPACE; since NP^{PSPACE} = PSPACE, the claim follows.

The PSPACE-hardness is established by a reduction from the complement of FFG. Let $\langle F, f \rangle$ be an instance of FFG, where $F = \{f_1, \ldots, f_m\}$ with $m \geqslant 1$; w.l.o.g. assume that $F \cup \{f\}$ is a set of bijective functions from $[n]$ to $[n]$, where $n \geqslant 2$. Let $\mathcal{T}$ be the NCDLR$^\pm$ TBox constituted by

$$A \sqsubseteq \exists R[1]$$
$$\{R[1, \ldots, n] \sqsubseteq R[f_i(1), \ldots, f_i(n)]\}_{i \in [m]}$$
$$R(X_1, \ldots, X_n), R(X_{f(1)}, \ldots, X_{f(n)}) \sqsubseteq \bot,$$

where A is an atomic concept and R is an n-ary atomic role. Clearly, the above construction can be carried out in polynomial time. Moreover, $\mathcal{T}$ is trivially non-conflicting since in the underlying dependency graph there is no f-node. It is easy to see that there exists an ABox $\mathcal{A}$ as described above iff the function f cannot be obtained by composing functions of F, and the claim follows.   □

Notice that if we consider $\mathsf{NCDLR}^{\pm}$ TBoxes where in inclusion assertions among roles only the identity permutation is used, or the arity of roles is bounded by an integer constant, then the problem of satisfiability is in coNP (Theorem 12). This implies that the algorithm proposed in the proof of Theorem 5 runs in $\mathrm{NP}^{\mathrm{coNP}}$, and thus the problem of deciding whether a TBox is strongly consistent is feasible in Σ_2^p. However, the exact complexity of the problem remains open.

4   Query Answering

In this section, we investigate the data and combined complexity of BCQAns under $\mathsf{NCDLR}^{\pm}$ KBs. Recall that the data complexity is calculated by considering only the ABox as part of the input, while the combined complexity by considering also the query and the TBox as part of the input.

Data Complexity. We show that our problem is in the highly tractable class AC_0 in data complexity. This is shown by establishing that $\mathsf{NCDLR}^{\pm}$ is first-order rewritable. To define formally first-order rewritable DLs, the so-called database interpretation of an ABox is needed.

Definition 8 (Database Interpretation). The *database interpretation* of an ABox $\mathcal{A}$, denoted $db(\mathcal{A})$, is defined as the interpretation $\langle \Delta^{db(\mathcal{A})}, \cdot^{db(\mathcal{A})} \rangle$, where:

- $\Delta^{db(\mathcal{A})}$ is the set of terms occurring in $\mathcal{A}$,
- $t^{db(\mathcal{A})} = t$, for each term t occurring in $\mathcal{A}$,
- $A^{db(\mathcal{A})} = \{t \mid A(t) \in \mathcal{A}\}$, and
- $R^{db(\mathcal{A})} = \{\langle t_1, \ldots, t_n \rangle \mid R(t_1, \ldots, t_n) \in \mathcal{A}\}$. ∎

Let us now define first-order rewritable DLs.

Definition 9 (First-Order Rewritability). A DL $\mathcal{L}$ is *first-order rewritable*, henceforth abbreviated as *FO-rewritable*, if for every TBox $\mathcal{T}$ expressed in $\mathcal{L}$, and for every BCQ q, it is possible to construct a (finite) first-order query $q_{\mathcal{T}}$ such that $\langle \mathcal{T}, \mathcal{A} \rangle \models q$ iff $db(\mathcal{A}) \models q_{\mathcal{T}}$, for every ABox $\mathcal{A}$. ∎

Notice that the notion of FO-rewritability was introduced in [8] under the name first-order reducibility.

Theorem 6. BCQAns *under* $\mathsf{NCDLR}^{\pm}$ *KBs is in* AC_0 *in data complexity.*

Proof (sketch). Consider an $\mathsf{NCDLR}^{\pm}$ TBox $\mathcal{T}$, and an ABox $\mathcal{A}$; let $\mathcal{K} = \langle \mathcal{T}, \mathcal{A} \rangle$. If $\mathcal{K}$ is unsatisfiable, then $\mathcal{K} \models q$, for every BCQ q over $\mathcal{K}$. Assume now that $\mathcal{K}$ is satisfiable. By Theorem 2, $\mathcal{K} \models q$ iff $\langle \mathcal{T}^+, \mathcal{A} \rangle \models q$, for every BCQ q over $\mathcal{K}$. It is not difficult to show that a (finite) first-order query q' can be constructed such that $\langle \mathcal{T}^+, \mathcal{A} \rangle \models q$ iff $db(A) \models q'$; in fact, this follows by observing that $\mathcal{T}^+$ is equivalent to a set of inclusions dependencies which are first-order rewritable [6]. Evaluating first-order queries is in AC_0 in data complexity [21]. The claim follows since, as we shall see (Theorem 10), the problem of deciding whether $\mathcal{K}$ is satisfiable is also in AC_0. □

Before we proceed further, we show that $\mathsf{DLR}^\pm$ is not FO-rewritable. This result descends straightforwardly from [4]; however, here we provide an alternative proof based on a simple complexity argument.

Lemma 1. $\mathsf{DLR}^\pm$ *is not FO-rewritable.*

Proof (sketch). Suppose that $\mathsf{DLR}^\pm$ is FO-rewritable, and thus BCQAns under $\mathsf{DLR}^\pm$ KBs is in AC_0 in data complexity. It can be shown that the same problem is PTIME-hard in data complexity, by a reduction from BCQAns under DL-Lite$_{core}^{\mathcal{HF}}$ KBs [2]. This implies that the complexity classes AC_0 and PTIME coincide which is a contradiction since $\mathrm{AC}_0 \subsetneq$ PTIME (see, e.g., [18]). Thus, $\mathsf{DLR}^\pm$ is not FO-rewritable. □

Combined Complexity. We now investigate the combined complexity of BCQAns under $\mathsf{NCDLR}^\pm$ KBs. In particular, we show that the problem under consideration is PSPACE-complete.

Theorem 7. BCQAns *under* $\mathsf{NCDLR}^\pm$ *KBs is* PSPACE-*complete in combined complexity.*

Proof (sketch). Consider an $\mathsf{NCDLR}^\pm$ TBox $\mathcal{T}$, and an ABox $\mathcal{A}$; let $\mathcal{K} = \langle \mathcal{T}, \mathcal{A} \rangle$. If $\mathcal{K}$ is unsatisfiable, then $\mathcal{K} \models q$, for every BCQ q over $\mathcal{K}$. Assume now that $\mathcal{K}$ is satisfiable. By Theorem 2, $\mathcal{K} \models q$ iff $\langle \mathcal{T}^+, \mathcal{A} \rangle \models q$, for every BCQ q over $\mathcal{K}$. Recall that the problem of deciding whether $\langle \mathcal{T}^+, \mathcal{A} \rangle \models q$ can be reduced to the problem of query answering under inclusion dependencies which is in PSPACE in combined complexity [14]. The desired upper bound follows since, as we shall see (Theorem 11), the problem of deciding whether $\mathcal{K}$ is satisfiable is in PSPACE. The PSPACE-hardness is established by a reduction from FFG. □

Interestingly, the combined complexity of query answering decreases to nondeterministic polynomial time if we consider the DLs obtained from $\mathsf{NCDLR}^\pm$ either by allowing only the *identity permutation* in inclusion assertions among roles, or by allowing only roles of *bounded arity*; the formal definitions follow.

Definition 10. A *non-conflicting* $\mathsf{DLR}_{id}^\pm$ ($\mathsf{NCDLR}_{id}^\pm$) TBox is an $\mathsf{NCDLR}^\pm$ TBox where all the inclusion assertions of the form $R_1[i_1, \ldots, i_n] \sqsubseteq R_2[j_1, \ldots, j_n]$, where $\{R_1, R_2\} \subseteq \mathbf{R}$, are such that $i_k = j_k$, for each $k \in [n]$. A *non-conflicting* $\mathsf{DLR}_{b}^\pm$ ($\mathsf{NCDLR}_{b}^\pm$) TBox is an $\mathsf{NCDLR}^\pm$ TBox where the arity of atomic roles is bounded by an integer constant. ∎

The NP-completeness of BCQAns under $\mathsf{NCDLR}_{b}^\pm$ KBs can be easily established by exploiting known results. In particular, as we shall see (Theorem 12), we can decide whether $\mathcal{K}$ is unsatisfiable in NP in combined complexity. Moreover, given an $\mathsf{NCDLR}_{b}^\pm$ TBox $\mathcal{T}$, $\mathcal{T}^+$ can be translated into a set of IDs where the arity is bounded; it is well-known that query answering under IDs, in the case of bounded arity, is in NP [14]. Finally, the desired lower bound follows immediately from the NP-hardness of query evaluation over relational databases [11].

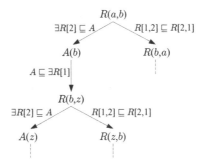

Fig. 3. The chase forest for $\mathcal{K}$; z is a labeled null of **N**

Theorem 8. BCQAns *under* NCDLR$_b^\pm$ *KBs is* NP-*complete in combined complexity.*

Let us now establish the NP-completeness of BCQAns under NCDLR$_{id}^\pm$ KBs. The desired lower bound is inherited from the NP-hardness of query evaluation over relational databases [11]. However, the desired upper bound does not follow from the fact that query answering under IDs, in the case of bounded arity, is in NP (as for NCDLR$_b^\pm$), since we have to deal with roles of unbounded arity. In order to establish the desired upper bound, several auxiliary technical notions and results are needed.

Definition 11. Consider a DLR$^\pm$ KB $\mathcal{K} = \langle \mathcal{T}, \mathcal{A} \rangle$. The *chase forest* for $\mathcal{K}$ is a directed graph $\langle V, E, \lambda \rangle$, where V is the node set, E is the edge set, and λ is a labeling function $E \to \mathcal{T}^+$. There exists a node for each membership assertion of $chase(\langle \mathcal{T}^+, \mathcal{A} \rangle)$. Also, for each pair of assertions α_1 and α_2 of $chase(\langle \mathcal{T}^+, \mathcal{A} \rangle)$, there exists an edge $e = (\alpha_1, \alpha_2)$, with $\lambda(e) = \sigma \in \mathcal{T}^+$, if α_2 is obtained from α_1 during the construction of the chase by a single-step application of σ. For an assertion $\alpha \in chase(\langle \mathcal{T}^+, \mathcal{A} \rangle)$, we denote by $subtree(\alpha)$ the subtree of the chase forest for $\mathcal{K}$ rooted at α.   ∎

Example 4. Consider the KB $\mathcal{K} = \langle \mathcal{T}, \mathcal{A} \rangle$, where

$$\mathcal{T} = \{\exists R[2] \sqsubseteq A, \ A \sqsubseteq \exists R[1], \ R[1,2] \sqsubseteq R[2,1]\}$$

and $\mathcal{A} = \{R(a,b)\}$ with $A \in \mathbf{A}$ and $R/2 \in \mathbf{R}$. An initial segment of the (infinite) chase forest for $\mathcal{K}$ is depicted in Figure 3.   ∎

We denote by $\delta(\alpha)$ the set of constants and nulls occurring in the membership assertion α. Given a finite set S of constants and nulls, two assertions α_1 and α_2 are *S-isomorphic*, denoted $\alpha_1 \simeq_S \alpha_2$, if there exists a bijection $h : \delta(\alpha_1) \to \delta(\alpha_2)$, such that h (resp., h^{-1}) is a homomorphism from α_1 to α_2 (resp., α_2 to α_1), and $h(X) = h^{-1}(X) = X$, for each $X \in S$. The notion of S-isomorphism naturally extends to pairs of subtrees of a chase forest. It is not difficult to show, by induction on the number of applications of the inclusion chase rule, that if two assertions are S-isomorphic, then their subtrees are also S-isomorphic.

Lemma 2. *Consider a* DLR$^{\pm}$ *KB* $\mathcal{K} = \langle \mathcal{T}, \mathcal{A} \rangle$. *If* $\alpha_1 \simeq_S \alpha_2$, *where* $\{\alpha_1, \alpha_2\} \subseteq$ *chase*$(\langle \mathcal{T}^+, \mathcal{A} \rangle)$, *then subtree*$(\alpha_1) \simeq_S$ *subtree*(α_2).

It is also possible to show that there exists an upper bound on the number of non-$\delta(\alpha)$-isomorphic assertions, where α is a membership assertion, that can be constructed during the chase. This result can be established by providing a combinatorial argument which exploits the fact that only the identity permutation can be employed in inclusion assertions among atomic roles.

Lemma 3. *Consider an* NCDLR$^{\pm}_{\mathsf{id}}$ *KB* $\mathcal{K} = \langle \mathcal{T}, \mathcal{A} \rangle$. *Let* $\alpha \in$ *chase*$(\langle \mathcal{T}^+, \mathcal{A} \rangle)$ *and* $S \subseteq$ *chase*$(\langle \mathcal{T}^+, \mathcal{A} \rangle)$ *such that, for each* $\alpha' \in S$, $\delta(\alpha') \subseteq \delta(\alpha) \cup \mathbf{N}$. *If* $|S| \geqslant |\mathsf{sig}(\mathcal{T})| \cdot ((\mathsf{arity}(\mathcal{T}))^2 + 2)$, *then* S *contains at least two* $\delta(\alpha)$-*isomorphic assertions.*

We can now establish that for query answering purposes it suffices to employ a "pseudo-canonical" interpretation, that is, an interpretation obtained by considering an initial finite segment of the chase up to a certain level which is polynomial w.r.t. the query and the TBox, and constant w.r.t. the ABox. For an assertion $\alpha \in$ *chase*$(\langle \mathcal{T}^+, \mathcal{A} \rangle)$, the *level* of α, denoted as *level*(α), is the number of inclusion chase rule applications that are needed to construct it. Let $can^k(\langle \mathcal{T}^+, \mathcal{A} \rangle)$ be the interpretation obtained by considering *chase*$^k(\langle \mathcal{T}^+, \mathcal{A} \rangle)$, that is, the set of assertions $\{\alpha \mid \alpha \in chase(\langle \mathcal{T}^+, \mathcal{A} \rangle)$ and *level*$(\alpha) \leqslant k\}$.

Lemma 4. *Consider an* NCDLR$^{\pm}_{\mathsf{id}}$ *KB* $\mathcal{K} = \langle \mathcal{T}, \mathcal{A} \rangle$ *and a BCQ* q *over* $\mathcal{K}$. *If* $can(\langle \mathcal{T}^+, \mathcal{A} \rangle) \models q$, *then* $can^k(\langle \mathcal{T}^+, \mathcal{A} \rangle) \models q$, *where* $k = |body(q)| \cdot |\mathsf{sig}(\mathcal{T})| \cdot ((\mathsf{arity}(\mathcal{T}))^2 + 2)$.

Proof. Since, by hypothesis, $can(\langle \mathcal{T}^+, \mathcal{A} \rangle) \models q$, it is easy to see that there exists a homomorphism h that maps $body(q)$ to *chase*$(\langle \mathcal{T}^+, \mathcal{A} \rangle)$. Let h be of this kind such that $level(h) = \sum_{\alpha \in body(q)} level(h(\alpha))$ is minimal. It suffices to show that $h(body(q))$ is contained in *chase*$^k(\langle \mathcal{T}^+, \mathcal{A} \rangle)$. Towards a contradiction, suppose that $h(body(q))$ is not contained in *chase*$^k(\langle \mathcal{T}^+, \mathcal{A} \rangle)$. Consider the tree T consisting of all atoms of $h(body(q))$ and their ancestors in the chase forest for $\mathcal{K}$. Since $h(body(q))$ is not contained in *chase*$^k(\langle \mathcal{T}^+, \mathcal{A} \rangle)$, a path $P = \alpha_1 \ldots \alpha_m$, where $m-1 > |\mathsf{sig}(\mathcal{T})| \cdot ((\mathsf{arity}(\mathcal{T}))^2 + 2)$ and $\{\alpha_2, \ldots, \alpha_{m-1}\} \cap h(body(q)) = \varnothing$, occurs in T. By Lemma 3, there are two $\delta(\alpha_1)$-isomorphic assertions β and γ on P. Lemma 2 implies that $subtree(\beta)$ and $subtree(\gamma)$ are $\delta(\alpha_1)$-isomorphic. Therefore, we can remove β and the path to γ, obtaining a path P' that is at least one edge shorter than P. Clearly, there exists a homomorphism μ that maps $subtree(\beta)$ to $subtree(\gamma)$. Then, the homomorphism $h' = \mu \circ h$ maps $body(q)$ to *chase*$(\langle \mathcal{T}^+, \mathcal{A} \rangle)$. Observe that $level(h') < level(h)$ which is a contradiction since h is such that $level(h)$ is minimal. We conclude that $h(body(q)) \subseteq chase^k(\langle \mathcal{T}^+, \mathcal{A} \rangle)$. $\square$

We are now ready to establish the desired complexity result.

Theorem 9. BCQAns *under* NCDLR$^{\pm}_{\mathsf{id}}$ *KBs is* NP-*complete in combined complexity.*

Proof (sketch). As already mentioned, the desired lower bound is obtained directly from the NP-hardness of query evaluation over relational databases [11]. Consider now an $\mathsf{NCDLR}_{\mathsf{id}}^{\pm}$ KB $\mathcal{K} = \langle \mathcal{T}, \mathcal{A} \rangle$ and a BCQ q over $\mathcal{K}$. By Theorem 2, we can decide whether $\mathcal{K} \models q$ by applying the following algorithm: if $\mathcal{K}$ is unsatisfiable or $\langle \mathcal{T}^+, \mathcal{A} \rangle \models q$, then *accept*; otherwise, *reject*. As we shall see (Theorem 12), we can decide whether $\mathcal{K}$ is unsatisfiable in NP in combined complexity. It remains to show that the problem of deciding whether $\langle \mathcal{T}^+, \mathcal{A} \rangle \models q$ is in NP in combined complexity. By Lemma 4, $\langle \mathcal{T}^+, \mathcal{A} \rangle \models q$ iff $can^k(\langle \mathcal{T}^+, \mathcal{A} \rangle) \models q$, where $k = |body(q)| \cdot |\mathsf{sig}(\mathcal{T})| \cdot ((\mathsf{arity}(\mathcal{T}))^2 + 2)$. Observe that, if $can^k(\langle \mathcal{T}^+, \mathcal{A} \rangle) \models q$, then q is entailed due to a finite part of $can^k(\langle \mathcal{T}^+, \mathcal{A} \rangle)$ of size at most $|body(q)| \cdot k$. To decide whether $can^k(\langle \mathcal{T}^+, \mathcal{A} \rangle) \models q$ we can construct non-deterministically a finite part P of $can^k(\langle \mathcal{T}^+, \mathcal{A} \rangle)$ of size at most $|body(q)| \cdot k$, and then check whether $P \models q$. Obviously, this is feasible in non-deterministic polynomial time, and the claim follows. $\qquad\square$

5   Knowledge Base Satisfiability

In this section, we investigate the data and combined complexity of KBSat under $\mathsf{NCDLR}^{\pm}$ KBs. Let us first establish an auxiliary technical lemma which states that unsatisfiability can be reduced to query answering. This lemma builds upon an analogous one in [4], from which it can be derived without difficulties; however, for the sake of completeness, we provide a proof sketch here, since several details are different from the case of [4]. We assume that the reader is familiar with the notion of *union of BCQs* (see, e.g., [1]).

Lemma 5. *Consider an* $\mathsf{NCDLR}^{\pm}$ *KB* $\mathcal{K} = \langle \mathcal{T}, \mathcal{A} \rangle$. *If* $\mathcal{T}$ *is fixed (resp., non-fixed), then we can construct an ABox* $\mathcal{A}'$ *and a union of BCQs* Q *in* AC_0 *(resp.,* PTIME*) such that* $\mathcal{K}$ *is unsatisfiable iff* $\langle \mathcal{T}^+, \mathcal{A}' \rangle \models Q$.

Proof (sketch). Let $\mathcal{A}'$ be the ABox obtained from $\mathcal{A}$ by adding a membership assertion $Neq(c_1, c_2)$, where Neq is an auxiliary binary role not occurring in $\mathcal{K}$, for each pair of distinct constants c_1 and c_2 in $\mathcal{A}$. The union of BCQs Q is constructed as follows. For every NI of the form $\phi(\mathbf{X}) \sqsubseteq \bot$ occurring in $\mathcal{T}^-$, add to Q the BCQ $p \leftarrow \phi(\mathbf{X})$. Moreover, for every functionality assertion of the form (funct $R[i]$) occurring in $\mathcal{T}^=$, where R is an n-ary role, add to Q the BCQ $p \leftarrow R(X_1, \ldots, X_{i-1}, Y, X_{i+1}, \ldots, X_n), R(Z_1, \ldots, Z_{i-1}, Y, Z_{i+1}, \ldots, Z_n), Neq(X_j, Y_j)$, for each $j \in [n] \setminus \{i\}$. We can show that $\mathcal{K}$ is unsatisfiable iff $\langle \mathcal{T}^+, \mathcal{A}' \rangle \models Q$. Suppose now that $\mathcal{T}$ is fixed, and let $C_{\mathcal{T}} = \mathsf{sig}(\mathcal{T}) \cap \mathbf{A}$ and $R_{\mathcal{T}} = \mathsf{sig}(\mathcal{T}) \cap \mathbf{R}$. The required membership assertions can be obtained by evaluating a first-order query, which depends only on $\mathcal{T}$, over $db(\mathcal{A})$. Evaluation of first-order queries is feasible in AC_0 in data complexity [21], and thus the required membership assertions can be constructed in AC_0 w.r.t. $\mathcal{A}$. Since Q depends only on $\mathcal{T}$ can be constructed in constant time. In the case of a non-fixed TBox, it is obvious that both $\mathcal{A}'$ and Q can be constructed in PTIME. In particular, the number of membership assertions in $\mathcal{A}'$ is at most n^2, where n is the number of constants in $\mathcal{A}$, while the number of BCQs in Q is at most $|\mathcal{T}^-| + \mathsf{arity}(\mathcal{T}) \cdot |\mathcal{T}^=|$. $\qquad\square$

In the sequel, given an $\mathsf{NCDLR}^\pm$ KB $\mathcal{K} = \langle \mathcal{T}, \mathcal{A} \rangle$, we will refer to the ABox $\mathcal{A}'$ and the union of BCQs Q, provided by Lemma 5, as $\mathcal{A}_\mathcal{K}$ and $Q_\mathcal{K}$, respectively.

Data Complexity. We are now ready to investigate the data complexity of KBSat under $\mathsf{NCDLR}^\pm$ KBs.

Theorem 10. KBSat *under* $\mathsf{NCDLR}^\pm$ *KBs is in* AC$_0$ *in data complexity.*

Proof. Let $\mathcal{K} = \langle \mathcal{T}, \mathcal{A} \rangle$ be an $\mathsf{NCDLR}^\pm$ KB. By Lemma 5, $\mathcal{K}$ is unsatisfiable iff $\langle \mathcal{T}^+, \mathcal{A}_\mathcal{K} \rangle \models Q_\mathcal{K}$. As already discussed in the proof of Theorem 6, the problem of deciding whether $\langle \mathcal{T}^+, \mathcal{A}_\mathcal{K} \rangle \models Q_\mathcal{K}$ is in AC$_0$ in data complexity. Since both $\mathcal{A}_\mathcal{K}$ and $Q_\mathcal{K}$ can be constructed in AC$_0$, the claim follows.   □

Combined Complexity. We now investigate the combined complexity of KBSat under $\mathsf{NCDLR}^\pm$ KBs. We establish that, in the general case, the problem under consideration is PSPACE-complete.

Theorem 11. KBSat *under* $\mathsf{NCDLR}^\pm$ *KBs is* PSPACE-*complete in combined complexity.*

Proof (sketch). By providing an argument similar to the one given in the proof of Theorem 10, we get that the problem of deciding whether an $\mathsf{NCDLR}^\pm$ KB is unsatisfiable is in PSPACE, and the desired upper bound follows. The PSPACE-hardness is established by a reduction from BCQAns under $\mathsf{NCDLR}^\pm$ KBs. Notice that the aforementioned problem remains PSPACE-hard even in the case of TBoxes which contain only PIs (implicit in the proof of Theorem 7). Consider a KB $\mathcal{K} = \langle \mathcal{T}, \mathcal{A} \rangle$, where both $\mathcal{T}^-$ and $\mathcal{T}^=$ are empty, and a BCQ q over $\mathcal{K}$ of the form $p \leftarrow \phi(\mathbf{X})$. Let $\mathcal{K}' = \langle \mathcal{T} \cup \{\phi(\mathbf{X}) \sqsubseteq \bot\}, \mathcal{A} \rangle$. It is easy to see that $\mathcal{K} \models q$ iff $\mathcal{K}'$ is unsatisfiable, and the claim follows.   □

The combined complexity of KBSat decreases if we restrict our attention on $\mathsf{NCDLR}^\pm_X$ KBs, where $X \in \{\mathsf{id}, \mathsf{b}\}$. By providing a proof similar to that of Theorem 11, and also by exploiting the fact that BCQAns under $\mathsf{NCDLR}^\pm_X$ KBs, where $X \in \{\mathsf{id}, \mathsf{b}\}$, is NP-complete we get the following result.

Theorem 12. KBSat *under* $\mathsf{NCDLR}^\pm_X$, *where* $X \in \{\mathsf{id}, \mathsf{b}\}$, *is* coNP-*complete in combined complexity.*

6   Conclusions

In this paper, we have presented the DL $\mathsf{DLR}^\pm$ with roles of arbitrary arity, which is equipped, among other constructs, with functionality constraints, role inclusions with arbitrary permutation of the arguments, and negative assertions. We have provided a syntactic condition which is necessary and sufficient for the separability of $\mathsf{DLR}^\pm$ TBoxes, thus identifying a fragment, which we call $\mathsf{NCDLR}^\pm$, which offers highly tractable (in data complexity) CQ answering and KB satisfiability. We have also investigated the combined complexity of reasoning in $\mathsf{NCDLR}^\pm$ (and variants of it).

Since $\mathsf{DLR}^{\pm}$ is very similar to the ER variant proposed in [4], called $\mathsf{ER}^{\pm}$, our result are straightforwardly applicable to $\mathsf{ER}^{\pm}$. It is also possible to show that every DL-Lite$_{\mathcal{F}}$ or DL-Lite$_{\mathcal{R}}$ TBox $\mathcal{T}$ can be transformed into an $\mathsf{NCDLR}^{\pm}$ TBox $\mathcal{T}'$ such that, for every ABox $\mathcal{A}$ and BCQ q, $\langle \mathcal{T}, \mathcal{A} \rangle \models q$ iff $\langle \mathcal{T}', \mathcal{A} \rangle \models q$. Moreover, the $\mathsf{NCDLR}^{\pm}$ TBox $\{R[1,2] \sqsubseteq R[2,1], (\mathsf{funct}\ R[1])\}$ cannot be expressed neither in DL-Lite$_{\mathcal{F}}$ nor in DL-Lite$_{\mathcal{R}}$. We can therefore state the result below.

Theorem 13. $\mathsf{NCDLR}^{\pm}$, *even with binary roles only, is strictly more expressive than DL-Lite$_X$, where $X \in \{\mathcal{F}, \mathcal{R}\}$.*

Finally, in this work we have considered arbitrary (finite or infinite) models. Determining the complexity of CQ answering and KB satisfiability under finite models only remains an open problem, and will be the subject of future research.

Acknowledgements. This research has received funding from the European Research Council under the European Community's Seventh Framework Programme (FP7/2007-2013) / ERC grant agreement DIADEM no. 246858.

References

1. Abiteboul, S., Hull, R., Vianu, V.: Foundations of Databases. Addison-Wesley (1995)
2. Artale, A., Calvanese, D., Kontchakov, R., Zakharyaschev, M.: The DL-Lite family and relations. J. Artif. Intell. Res. 36, 1–69 (2009)
3. Calì, A., Gottlob, G., Lukasiewicz, T., Marnette, B., Pieris, A.: Datalog+/-: A family of logical knowledge representation and query languages for new applications. In: Proc. of LICS, pp. 228–242 (2010)
4. Calì, A., Gottlob, G., Pieris, A.: Ontological query answering under expressive entity-relationship schemata. Inf. Syst. 37(4), 320–335 (2012)
5. Calì, A., Lembo, D., Rosati, R.: On the decidability and complexity of query answering over inconsistent and incomplete databases. In: Proc. of PODS, pp. 260–271 (2003)
6. Calì, A., Lembo, D., Rosati, R.: Query rewriting and answering under constraints in data integration systems. In: Proc. of IJCAI, pp. 16–21 (2003)
7. Calì, A., Martinenghi, D.: Querying incomplete data over extended ER schemata. TPLP 10(3), 291–329 (2010)
8. Calvanese, D., De Giacomo, G., Lembo, D., Lenzerini, M., Rosati, R.: Tractable reasoning and efficient query answering in description logics: The DL-lite family. J. Autom. Reasoning 39(3), 385–429 (2007)
9. Calvanese, D., De Giacomo, G., Lenzerini, M.: On the decidability of query containment under constraints. In: Proc. of PODS, pp. 149–158 (1998)
10. Calvanese, D., Giacomo, G.D., Lembo, D., Lenzerini, M., Rosati, R.: Data complexity of query answering in description logics. Artif. Intell. 195, 335–360 (2013)
11. Chandra, A.K., Merlin, P.M.: Optimal implementation of conjunctive queries in relational data bases. In: Proc. of STOCS, pp. 77–90 (1977)
12. Chen, P.P.: The Entity-Relationship model: Towards a unified view of data. ACM TODS 1(1), 124–131 (1976)

13. Glimm, B., Horrocks, I., Lutz, C., Sattler, U.: Conjunctive query answering for the description logic SHIQ. In: Proc. of IJCAI, pp. 399–404 (2007)
14. Johnson, D.S., Klug, A.C.: Testing containment of conjunctive queries under functional and inclusion dependencies. J. Comput. Syst. Sci. 28(1), 167–189 (1984)
15. Kozen, D.: Lower bounds for natural proof systems. In: Proc. of FOCS, pp. 254–266 (1977)
16. Lenzerini, M.: Data integration: A theoretical perspective. In: Proc. of PODS, pp. 233–246 (2002)
17. Maier, D., Mendelzon, A.O., Sagiv, Y.: Testing implications of data dependencies. ACM Trans. Database Syst. 4(4), 455–469 (1979)
18. Papadimitriou, C.H.: Computational Complexity. Addison-Wesley (1994)
19. Poggi, A., Lembo, D., Calvanese, D., De Giacomo, G., Lenzerini, M., Rosati, R.: Linking data to ontologies. J. Data Semantics 10, 133–173 (2008)
20. Vardi, M.Y.: The complexity of relational query languages. In: Proc. of STOC, pp. 137–146 (1982)
21. Vardi, M.Y.: On the complexity of bounded-variable queries. In: Proc. of PODS, pp. 266–276 (1995)

Toward a Theory of Self-explaining Computation

James Cheney[1], Umut A. Acar[2,3], and Roly Perera[1]

[1] University of Edinburgh
[2] Carnegie Mellon University
[3] INRIA-Rocquencourt

Abstract. Provenance techniques aim to increase the reliability of human judgments about data by making its origin and derivation process explicit. Originally motivated by the needs of scientific databases and scientific computation, provenance has also become a major issue for business and government data on the Web. However, so far provenance has been studied only in relatively restrictive settings: typically, for data stored in databases or scientific workflow systems, and processed by query or workflow languages of limited expressiveness. Long-term provenance solutions require an understanding of provenance in other settings, particularly the general-purpose programming or scripting languages that are used to glue different components such as databases, Web services and workflows together. Moreover, what is required is not only an account of mechanisms for recording provenance, but also a theory of what it means for provenance information to explain or justify a computation. In this paper, we begin to outline a such a theory of *self-explaining computation*. We introduce a model of provenance for a simple imperative language based on *operational derivations* and explore its properties.

1 Introduction

Scientific data (including both raw data and processed results) is now being published and shared online in unprecedented quantities. Understanding the significance, validity, or accuracy of this data depends on understanding its provenance. When data is not confined to a single user, system, or intended application, it is essential to make the origin, ownership history, processing steps, and context or assumptions about the data explicit, to avoid misinterpretation and aid reproducibility. Over the last decade, a wide variety of techniques aimed at addressing this *provenance problem* have been proposed, including new data formats [46,47] and mechanisms for generating provenance to accompany computations.

Buneman, Khanna and Tan's 2001 paper "Why and Where: A Characterization of Data Provenance" [9] was among the first publications to investigate the problem of provenance in database systems. Although provenance was studied earlier by Wang and Madnick [56], Woodruff and Stonebraker [59] and Cui et al. [20], Buneman et al. [9] has had greater influence (at least measured in terms of citations) than these other works. We conjecture that one reason for this is that Buneman et al. went beyond proposing mechanisms for provenance:

V. Tannen et al. (Eds.): Buneman Festschrift, LNCS 8000, pp. 193–216, 2013.

they also considered the question of the meaning of provenance. By considering and comparing two models, why-provenance and where-provenance, they made it clear that there might be many different models of provenance, with different advantages and disadvantages, and suitable for different applications.

Provenance techniques have since been studied in the context of databases [9,29], scientific workflow systems [43,7], operating systems [48], and inference systems [38] (including recent interest in the Semantic Web community, culminating in a W3C Working Group on Provenance [27,47]). In each of these contexts, there is a large design space for provenance mechanisms, yet at the same time there is not a clear consensus on the requirements or policies that these mechanisms ought to satisfy. Sometimes even the specifications of the techniques are unclear, or illustrated mainly through intuitive examples.

Instead, a wide variety of informal motivations have been cited, usually not accompanied by precise definitions or proofs of correctness. Such motivations include:

- To record a complete derivation of a program or inference process execution. [23,60,48]
- To guarantee repeatability, replayability or reproducibility. [23,45]
- To explain causal structure, history, influence or dependence. [40,17,13,15]
- To show where result data has been copied from, how result records were composed from input records, or why results were produced. [9,8,29,16]
- To validate a computation to ensure it is correct. [41]
- To diagnose and repair errors in computations involving components that are not believed to be reliable. [39]
- To facilitate efficient recomputation and comparison of computations, including recomputation from different inputs or in different computational environments. [23,5,17,29]

As of 2010, there were over 400 research papers on provenance in computer systems to date [44]. However, not all of them observe Lamport's rule "State the Problem Before Describing the Solution" [35]: instead, many present a proposed solution and then argue that it is a solution on its own terms, without making the problem it solves explicit. This state of affairs should be compared with the state of security research twenty-five years ago, when a wide variety of (often proprietary) security solutions were being proposed without a clear understanding of what problems they solved (or were meant to solve). In an influential essay, Good [28] argued that foundational understanding (theories and mathematical models) were necessary for computer security. We believe provenance research is in a similar state today: there are few formal models or crisp definitions of the requirements for provenance or proofs that actual techniques achieve their purported goals.

In previous work [17], we highlighted several hazards implicit in this state of affairs, which we called *provenance failures*. A provenance failure is a loss or risk exposed by failure to properly manage provenance: for example, losses due to outdated information in online trading [11] or due to inaccurate scientific results [42]. Government agencies may also view leaks as provenance failures [55], and as of this writing (June 2013), it is widely reported [30] that intelligence agencies are combining massive computing resources with unfettered access to metadata about phone calls and Internet use. Whether one views these developments as essential tools for fighting terrorism or unacceptable hazards to privacy and individual liberty, one cannot deny that the problems of protecting and securing metadata are becoming just as important as those for raw data.

Since 2009, there has been a major effort to define standards for provenance on the World Wide Web [47]. Provenance techniques are now being widely advocated as a basis for trusting online data and scientific results. However, if these techniques are not placed on a firm foundation, then this effort is doomed to failure: if the problems to be solved by provenance are not formulated precisely, then proposed solutions will, at best, provide a false sense of security.

For the purposes of this paper, we consider provenance to be any information, usually not already provided by the system, describing some aspect of a system's run-time behavior (or of data flowing through it). Our view is that general-purpose systems, including programming languages, should be equipped with general-purpose notions of provenance that are (a) clearly specified, (b) suitable for a variety of typical applications, and (c) equipped with a formal correctness property relating the behavior of the real system to the provenance description.

The first two criteria are relatively easy to satisfy. The aim of this paper is to bring the third requirement into focus and study it. Many of the commonly-stated requirements for provenance amount to a form of *explanation* that adequately accounts for the behavior of the system [22]. However, the precise sense in which some auxiliary data (which we call provenance) actually explains a computational process is seldom explicitly stated. In this paper, we begin to outline a theory of *self-explaining computation*, in which the semantics of provenance and its relationship to the conventional semantics of a programming language (or behavior of a system) are the objects of study.

What are the open questions that a theory of self-explaining computation should address? These are just a few possibilities:

1. If a system's actual behavior is described by explicit records, how do these constitute explanations? What are different appropriate definitions of explanation and how are they related?

2. Provenance can be recorded according to several different strategies, ranging from coarse-grained to fine-grained. Fine-grained provenance seems more useful or "complete" but can easily grow to dwarf the raw data. How can we understand and quantify the tradeoff between granularity and usefulness?

3. The full provenance record often includes far too much information to be useful. How can we extract subsets of this information that correctly approximates the full record?

4. Some provenance techniques (e.g. minimal witnesses in why-provenance) are *extensional*, or invariant with respect to a conventional semantics of the system, and others are *intensional*, meaning that their behavior can be different for conventionally-equivalent expressions (e.g. where-provenance). What are

the advantages and disadvantages of these different approaches? How can we justify intensional provenance semantics?

The behavior of computer systems can be described programmatically. The study of the semantics of programming languages has explored a large number of alternative approaches to defining the meaning of programs, ranging from *denotational* techniques [53] that interpret program text as an abstract, mathematical object such as a function, to *operational* techniques [50] that explain the behavior of complex program constructs via rules that describe how to evaluate a program step-by-step. We take the view that the theory of self-explaining computation should build on programming language semantics, in order to ensure that the specifications of provenance techniques are clear, and in order to facilitate formalization and proof of correctness properties.

We focus on an operational approach to provenance in the context of an imperative core-language **IMP** [57]. We explore the implications of taking a large-step operational derivation (that is, an explicit natural semantics proof tree [33]) as a form of provenance. We define a semantics for programs that produces both a standard result and an operational derivation tree, which we view as recording all of the information that could be relevant to understanding the program and how it executed (at the **IMP** level of abstraction).

We then consider the problem of *formalizing* some of the requirements above and *extracting* information from traces in order to meet these requirements. For example, we give a candidate definition of source locations (inspired by where-provenance [9]) and then show how this can be extracted from derivations. We also describe the use of derivations for a form of incremental computation (loosely inspired by self-adjusting computation [5]), in order to demonstrate that derivations are expressive enough to meet this strong requirement. We have made additional contributions since the first version of this paper was written [3,49], and we conclude with a discussion of these results and future steps.

2   Background

To illustrate our approach, we employ a simple imperative programming language **IMP** [57], augmented with pairs as a simple form of data structure. The syntax of **IMP** expressions $e \in$ Exp, commands $c \in$ Comm and values $v \in$ Val is as follows:

$$e ::= x \mid \texttt{let } x = e_1 \texttt{ in } e_2 \mid (e_1, e_2) \mid \texttt{fst}(e) \mid \texttt{snd}(e) \mid i \mid b \mid e_1 = e_2 \mid e_1 + e_2 \mid \cdots$$
$$c ::= \texttt{skip} \mid x := e \mid c_1; c_2 \mid \texttt{if } e \texttt{ then } c_1 \texttt{ else } c_2 \mid \texttt{while } e \texttt{ do } c$$
$$v ::= i \mid b \mid (v_1, v_2)$$

where $x \in$ Var denotes variables, $i \in \mathbb{Z}$ denotes integers, and $b \in \mathbb{B}$ denotes boolean values. We will also write $\oplus$ for an arbitrary binary operation, including $+$, $=$, and possibly others.

The meaning of expressions and commands is defined via operational semantics rules as shown in Figures 1 and 2. Our semantics is essentially a standard

$$\frac{}{\sigma, x \Downarrow \sigma(x)} \qquad \frac{\sigma, e_1 \Downarrow v_1 \quad \sigma[x := v_1], e_2 \Downarrow v_2}{\sigma, \texttt{let } x = e_1 \texttt{ in } e_2 \Downarrow v_2} \qquad \frac{i \in \mathbb{Z}}{\sigma, i \Downarrow i} \qquad \frac{\sigma, e_1 \Downarrow i_1 \quad \sigma, e_2 \Downarrow i_2}{\sigma, e_1 + e_2 \Downarrow i_1 + i_2}$$

$$\frac{\sigma, e_1 \Downarrow v_1 \quad \sigma, e_2 \Downarrow v_2}{\sigma, (e_1, e_2) \Downarrow (v_1, v_2)} \qquad \frac{\sigma, e \Downarrow (v_1, v_2)}{\sigma, \texttt{fst}(e) \Downarrow v_1} \qquad \frac{\sigma, e \Downarrow (v_1, v_2)}{\sigma, \texttt{snd}(e) \Downarrow v_1} \qquad \frac{b \in \{\texttt{true}, \texttt{false}\}}{\sigma, b \Downarrow b}$$

Fig. 1. Operational semantics derivation rules for **IMP** expressions

$$\frac{}{\sigma, \texttt{skip} \Downarrow \sigma} \qquad \frac{\sigma, e \Downarrow v}{\sigma, x := e \Downarrow \sigma[x := v]} \qquad \frac{\sigma, c_1 \Downarrow \sigma' \quad \sigma', c_2 \Downarrow \sigma''}{\sigma, c_1; c_2 \Downarrow \sigma''}$$

$$\frac{\sigma, e \Downarrow \texttt{true} \quad \sigma, c_1 \Downarrow \sigma'}{\sigma, \texttt{if } e \texttt{ then } c_1 \texttt{ else } c_2 \Downarrow \sigma'} \qquad \frac{\sigma, e \Downarrow \texttt{false} \quad \sigma, c_2 \Downarrow \sigma'}{\sigma, \texttt{if } e \texttt{ then } c_1 \texttt{ else } c_2 \Downarrow \sigma'}$$

$$\frac{\sigma, e \Downarrow \texttt{true} \quad \sigma, c \Downarrow \sigma' \quad \sigma', \texttt{while } e \texttt{ do } c \Downarrow \sigma''}{\sigma, \texttt{while } e \texttt{ do } c \Downarrow \sigma''} \qquad \frac{\sigma, e \Downarrow \texttt{false}}{\sigma, \texttt{while } e \texttt{ do } c \Downarrow \sigma}$$

Fig. 2. Operational semantics derivation rules for **IMP** commands

large-step operational semantics. We consider the set of *stores* Store = Var $\rightarrow$ Val and use functions $\sigma \in$ Store to store the values of variables. We write $[]$ for the empty store, $[x_1 := v_1, \ldots, x_n := v_n]$ for a store binding x_i to v_i, and $\sigma[x := v]$ for a store σ updated by replacing the value of x with v. More generally, we write $\sigma[\sigma']$ for σ updated with σ', that is, $\sigma[\sigma'](x) = \sigma'(x)$ if $x \in \text{dom}(\sigma')$ and $\sigma(x)$ otherwise.

In this paper, we view the derivations as explicit data structures, that is, as ordered, ranked trees with nodes labeled with *judgments* J. The judgments we will consider are:

$$J ::= \sigma, e \Downarrow v \mid \sigma, c \Downarrow \sigma'$$

The judgment $\sigma, e \Downarrow v$ indicates that an expression e evaluates to value v in store σ. The judgment $\sigma, c \Downarrow \sigma'$ indicates that a command c evaluates in store σ to store σ'.

The rules in Figures 1 and 2 thus essentially define construction rules for valid derivations. We write $D :: \sigma, e \Downarrow v$ to indicate that D is a valid derivation whose root is labeled with $\sigma, e \Downarrow v$. We may also write patterns of the form

$$\frac{D_1 \quad \cdots \quad D_n}{J}$$

to describe a valid derivation tree whose root is labeled with J and whose immediate subderivations are $D_1, \ldots, D_n$. Figure 3 shows three sample operational semantics derivations.

$$\frac{\overline{[x=4,y=2],x\Downarrow 4}\quad\overline{[x=4,y=2],2\Downarrow 2}}{\dfrac{[x=4,y=2],x=2\Downarrow\mathtt{false}}{[x=4,y=2],\mathtt{if}\ x=2\ \mathtt{then}\ x:=y*2\ \mathtt{else}\ y:=4\Downarrow[x=4,y=4]}\quad\overline{[x=4,y=2],y:=4\Downarrow[x=4,y=4]}}$$

$$\frac{\overline{[x=4,y=2],x\Downarrow 4}\quad\overline{[x=4,y=2],2\Downarrow 2}}{\dfrac{[x=4,y=2],x=2\Downarrow\mathtt{false}}{[x=4,y=2],\mathtt{if}\ x=2\ \mathtt{then}\ x:=y*2\ \mathtt{else}\ y:=x\Downarrow[x=4,y=4]}\quad\overline{[x=4,y=2],y:=x\Downarrow[x=4,y=4]}}$$

$$\frac{\overline{[x=3,y=2],x\Downarrow 3}\quad\overline{[x=3,y=2],2\Downarrow 2}}{\dfrac{[x=3,y=2],x=2\Downarrow\mathtt{false}}{[x=3,y=2],\mathtt{if}\ x=2\ \mathtt{then}\ x:=y*2\ \mathtt{else}\ y:=x\Downarrow[x=3,y=3]}\quad\overline{[x=3,y=2],y:=x\Downarrow[x=3,y=3]}}$$

Fig. 3. Example derivation trees

For illustration purposes, we also give the standard denotational semantics of **IMP** programs. Recall that a denotational semantics assigns to each program expression or command a mathematical meaning. Here, we interpret expressions e as functions $\mathcal{E}[\![e]\!]- :$ Store $\to$ Val$_\bot$ from stores to values, and commands c as functions $\mathcal{C}[\![c]\!]- :$ Store $\to$ Store$_\bot$. Here, we use the standard notation $S_\bot$ to abbreviate $S \uplus \{\bot\}$, that is, the set S augmented with a special "undefined" value $\bot$. One can equivalently think of the interpretations as partial functions Store $\rightharpoonup$ Val or Store $\rightharpoonup$ Store respectively. The denotational semantics is defined in Figures 4 and 5.

Theorem 1 ([57]). *The denotational and operational semantics are equivalent in the sense that:*

1. $\mathcal{E}[\![e]\!]\sigma = v$ *holds if and only if there exists a derivation D of $\sigma, e \Downarrow v$, and*
2. $\mathcal{C}[\![c]\!]\sigma = \sigma'$ *holds if and only if there exists a derivation D of $\sigma, c \Downarrow \sigma'$.*

The proof is standard, but in the interest of precision we exhibit functions that witness the forward direction by constructing explicit derivations. These are shown in Figures 6 and 7. The function $\mathcal{E}^{\mathcal{D}}[\![e]\!]\sigma$ yields a pair (D, v) of a derivation of $D :: \sigma, e \Downarrow v$ along with the actual value v. Likewise, the function $\mathcal{C}^{\mathcal{D}}[\![c]\!]\sigma$ yields a pair (D, σ'), where $D :: \sigma, c \Downarrow \sigma'$. (The second components of the respective return values, v and σ', are redundant, but this formulation makes the definition more uniform).

In the rest of this paper, we explore the consequences of viewing the derivation obtained by evaluating an **IMP** expression or command as a form of provenance in its own right.

2.1   A Note on the Overhead and Scale of Provenance Tracking

Our **IMP** language incorporates standard primitive operations found in most general-purpose programming languages, such as arithmetic and booleans. The

$$\mathcal{E}[\![e]\!] \; : \; \text{Store} \to \text{Val}$$

$$\mathcal{E}[\![x]\!]\sigma = \sigma(x)$$

$$\mathcal{E}[\![\texttt{let } x = e_1 \texttt{ in } e_2]\!]\sigma = \mathcal{E}[\![e_2]\!]\sigma[x := \mathcal{E}[\![e_1]\!]\sigma]$$

$$\mathcal{E}[\![i]\!]\sigma = i$$

$$\mathcal{E}[\![e_1 + e_2]\!]\sigma = \mathcal{E}[\![e_1]\!]\sigma + \mathcal{E}[\![e_2]\!]\sigma$$

$$\mathcal{E}[\![(e_1, e_2)]\!]\sigma = (\mathcal{E}[\![e_1]\!]\sigma, \mathcal{E}[\![e_2]\!]\sigma)$$

$$\mathcal{E}[\![\texttt{fst}(e)]\!]\sigma = v_1 \qquad (\mathcal{E}[\![e]\!]\sigma = (v_1, v_2))$$

$$\mathcal{E}[\![\texttt{snd}(e)]\!]\sigma = v_2 \qquad (\mathcal{E}[\![e]\!]\sigma = (v_1, v_2))$$

$$\mathcal{E}[\![b]\!]\sigma = b$$

$$\mathcal{E}[\![e_1 = e_2]\!]\sigma = \begin{cases} \texttt{true} & \mathcal{E}[\![e_1]\!]\sigma = \mathcal{E}[\![e_2]\!]\sigma \\ \texttt{false} & \mathcal{E}[\![e_1]\!]\sigma \neq \mathcal{E}[\![e_2]\!]\sigma \end{cases}$$

Fig. 4. Denotational semantics of expressions

$$\mathcal{C}[\![c]\!] \; : \; \text{Store} \to \text{Store}$$

$$\mathcal{C}[\![x := e]\!]\sigma = \sigma[x := \mathcal{E}[\![e]\!]\sigma]$$

$$\mathcal{C}[\![c_1; c_2]\!]\sigma = \mathcal{C}[\![c_2]\!](\mathcal{C}[\![c_1]\!]\sigma)$$

$$\mathcal{C}[\![\texttt{if } e \texttt{ then } c_1 \texttt{ else } c_2]\!]\sigma = \begin{cases} \mathcal{C}[\![c_1]\!]\sigma & \mathcal{E}[\![e]\!]\sigma = \texttt{true} \\ \mathcal{C}[\![c_2]\!]\sigma & \mathcal{E}[\![e]\!]\sigma = \texttt{false} \end{cases}$$

$$\mathcal{C}[\![\texttt{while } e \texttt{ do } c]\!]\sigma = \begin{cases} \mathcal{C}[\![\texttt{while } e \texttt{ do } c]\!](\mathcal{C}[\![c]\!]\sigma) & \mathcal{E}[\![e]\!]\sigma = \texttt{true} \\ \sigma & \mathcal{E}[\![e]\!]\sigma = \texttt{false} \end{cases}$$

Fig. 5. Denotational semantics of commands

derivation trace model we propose above could be prohibitively expensive in raw computational terms if we instrument the program to generating a new derivation step node for each primitive operation. Furthermore, the space needed for such a trace is likely to be large, in direct proportion to the running time.

In this paper we do not consider this practical aspect of provenance, which is obviously important. Our goal is to understand what information, in principle, one might consider as a "most precise" form of provenance, in order to understand what is lost by adopting more practical techniques. Moreover, it may be that the time and space overhead of naive derivation-trace provenance can be avoided, either through finding a more compact representation of the trace, or using standard compression techniques to compress the trace (which may have a lot of redundancy). Naturally, for a deterministic program, one such compressed representation is the original program itself plus its input: this requires no run-time or space overhead for provenance tracking, but requires completely

$$\mathcal{E}^{\mathcal{D}}[\![e]\!] \; : \; \text{Store} \to \text{Deriv} \times \text{Val}$$

$$\mathcal{E}^{\mathcal{D}}[\![x]\!]\sigma = \left(\overline{\sigma, x \Downarrow \sigma(x)}, \sigma(x)\right)$$

$$\mathcal{E}^{\mathcal{D}}[\![i]\!]\sigma = \left(\overline{\sigma, i \Downarrow i}, i\right)$$

$$\mathcal{E}^{\mathcal{D}}[\![b]\!]\sigma = \left(\overline{\sigma, b \Downarrow b}, b\right)$$

$$\mathcal{E}^{\mathcal{D}}[\![e_1 \oplus e_2]\!]\sigma = \text{let } (D_1, i_1) = \mathcal{E}^{\mathcal{D}}[\![e_1]\!]\sigma \text{ in}$$
$$\text{let } (D_2, i_2) = \mathcal{E}^{\mathcal{D}}[\![e_2]\!]\sigma \text{ in } \left(\frac{D_1 \quad D_2}{\sigma, e_1 \oplus e_2 \Downarrow i_1 \oplus i_2}, i_1 \oplus i_2\right)$$

$$\mathcal{E}^{\mathcal{D}}[\![\texttt{let } x = e_1 \texttt{ in } e_2]\!]\sigma = \text{let } (D_1, v_1) = \mathcal{E}^{\mathcal{D}}[\![e_1]\!]\sigma \text{ in}$$
$$\text{let } (D_2, v_2) = \mathcal{E}^{\mathcal{D}}[\![e_2]\!]\sigma[x := v_1] \text{ in } \left(\frac{D_1 \quad D_2}{\sigma, \texttt{let } x = e_1 \texttt{ in } e_2 \Downarrow v_2}, v_2\right)$$

$$\mathcal{E}^{\mathcal{D}}[\![(e_1, e_2)]\!]\sigma = \text{let } (D_1, v_1) = \mathcal{E}^{\mathcal{D}}[\![e_1]\!]\sigma \text{ in}$$
$$\text{let } (D_2, v_2) = \mathcal{E}^{\mathcal{D}}[\![e_2]\!]\sigma \text{ in } \left(\frac{D_1 \quad D_2}{\sigma, (e_1, e_2) \Downarrow (v_1, v_2)}, (v_1, v_2)\right)$$

$$\mathcal{E}^{\mathcal{D}}[\![\texttt{fst}(e)]\!]\sigma = \text{let } (D, (v_1, v_2)) = \mathcal{E}^{\mathcal{D}}[\![e]\!]\sigma \text{ in } \left(\frac{D}{\sigma, \texttt{fst}(e) \Downarrow v_1}, v_1\right)$$

$$\mathcal{E}^{\mathcal{D}}[\![\texttt{snd}(e)]\!]\sigma = \text{let } (D, (v_1, v_2)) = \mathcal{E}^{\mathcal{D}}[\![e]\!]\sigma \text{ in } \left(\frac{D}{\sigma, \texttt{snd}(e) \Downarrow v_2}, v_2\right)$$

Fig. 6. Extracting derivations for expressions

$$\mathcal{C}^{\mathcal{D}}[\![c]\!] \; : \; \text{Store} \to \text{Deriv} \times \text{Store}$$

$$\mathcal{C}^{\mathcal{D}}[\![x := e]\!]\sigma = \text{let } (D, v) = \mathcal{E}^{\mathcal{D}}[\![e]\!]\sigma \text{ in } \left(\frac{D}{\sigma, x := e \Downarrow \sigma[x := v]}, \sigma[x := v]\right)$$

$$\mathcal{C}^{\mathcal{D}}[\![c_1; c_2]\!]\sigma = \text{let } (D_1, \sigma') = \mathcal{C}^{\mathcal{D}}[\![c_1]\!]\sigma \text{ in}$$
$$\text{let } (D_2, \sigma'') = \mathcal{C}^{\mathcal{D}}[\![c_2]\!]\sigma' \text{ in } \left(\frac{D_1 \quad D_2}{\sigma, c_1; c_2 \Downarrow \sigma''}, \sigma''\right)$$

$$\mathcal{C}^{\mathcal{D}}[\![\texttt{if } e \texttt{ then } c_1 \texttt{ else } c_2]\!]\sigma = \text{let } (D, b) = \mathcal{E}^{\mathcal{D}}[\![e]\!]\sigma \text{ in}$$
$$\text{let } (D', \sigma') = \text{if } b \text{ then } \mathcal{C}^{\mathcal{D}}[\![c_1]\!]\sigma \text{ else } \mathcal{C}^{\mathcal{D}}[\![c_2]\!]\sigma \text{ in}$$
$$\left(\frac{D \quad D'}{\sigma, \texttt{if } e \texttt{ then } c_1 \texttt{ else } c_2 \Downarrow \sigma'}, \sigma'\right)$$

$$\mathcal{C}^{\mathcal{D}}[\![\texttt{while } e \texttt{ do } c]\!]\sigma = \text{let } (D, b) = \mathcal{E}^{\mathcal{D}}[\![e]\!]\sigma \text{ in}$$
$$\text{if } b$$
$$\text{then let } (D', \sigma') = \mathcal{C}^{\mathcal{D}}[\![c]\!]\sigma \text{ in}$$
$$\text{let } (D'', \sigma'') = \mathcal{C}^{\mathcal{D}}[\![\texttt{while } e \texttt{ do } c]\!]\sigma' \text{ in } \left(\frac{D \quad D' \quad D''}{\sigma, \texttt{while } e \texttt{ do } c \Downarrow \sigma''}, \sigma''\right)$$
$$\text{else } \left(\frac{D}{\sigma, \texttt{while } e \texttt{ do } c \Downarrow \sigma}, \sigma\right)$$

Fig. 7. Extracting derivations for commands

recomputing the program to perform provenance analysis. Exploring the tradeoff between time and space overhead of provenance tracking vs. provenance analysis is an important area for future work; here, we focus only on defining different provenance analyses in terms of derivation traces.

Another important observation about the overhead and scalabilty of our approach is that our approach is parametric over the primitive operations: they may be (as in our examples) fine-grained, machine arithmetic operations, but they could just as well be coarser-grained, macroscopic steps. Consider, for example, an alternative variant of **IMP** in which the primitive operations include entire external programs. In other words, instead of performing all of our numerically-intensive computation explicitly using **IMP**-level arithmetic, we can consider it as a scripting language for orchestrating larger computational steps that are treated as primitive operations from the point of view of **IMP**'s provenance records. Another interesting area for future work could be to understand how to combine efficient coarse-grained provenance with more-precise, on-demand fine-grained provenance tracking.

3   Finding Sources of Copied Data

As noted in the introduction, our goal is to use operational derivations as a starting point for formalizing various requirements on provenance. We start with the notion of where-provenance [9,8]. Essentially, where-provenance is intended to track the sources of data copied from the input of a computation to the output. We will define where-provenance for while-programs in two stages: first, we will define where-provenance for straight-line code, and then we will lift the definition to arbitrary programs by erasing derivations to straight-line programs.

Since we have been using abstract syntax trees for values and expression trees, it seems natural to employ *paths* that can be used to address parts of expressions and values. We write $\text{paths}(v)$ for the set of paths that are valid for a value. Specifically, $\text{paths} : \text{Val} \to \{1, 2\}^*$ is defined as:

$$\text{paths}(b) = \text{paths}(i) = \{\epsilon\}$$
$$\text{paths}((v_1, v_2)) = 1 \cdot \text{paths}(v_1) \cup 2 \cdot \text{paths}(v_2)$$

Here, if P is a set of paths, we write $i \cdot P$ for $\{i \cdot p \mid p \in P\}$. Similarly, we use paths of the form $x.p$ to point to parts of variable values in stores. We write $v[p]$ for the value located at path p in v, and we write $v[p := v']$ for the result of replacing the value at path p in v with v'. We extend these notations to environments and environment paths in the obvious way.

Now we first consider the problem of identifying the source path (if any) of a path in the result of an expression.

Definition 1. *Suppose $\mathcal{E}[\![e]\!]\sigma = v$ and $p \in \text{paths}(v)$. A source path q is a path such that $\sigma[q] = v[p]$ and for any v', we have if $\mathcal{E}[\![e]\!]\sigma[q := v'][p] = v'$.*

In other words, a source path q points to an input value $\sigma[q]$ that is a copy of the value $v[p]$ at result path p: if we change the input σ at q to v' then the change is mirrored at the output v'' at p. (Note that v'' may also differ at other places besides p; consider the expression (x, x).)

This definition of source path is based on the denotational semantics, and so for example two denotationally equivalent expressions such as $x + 0$ and x have the same source path behavior. Because of this, in general it appears difficult to determine source paths exactly: for example, if the primitive operations can encode Boolean formulas, then we can reduce the Boolean satisfiability problem to the problem of determining whether a Boolean variable is always an exact copy of a part of the input. With richer primitive operations such as arithmetic, determining whether source path relationships exist can become undecidable, reducing from Diophantine equation satisfiability.

Nevertheless, we can safely under-approximate the source paths of an expression, as shown in the $\mathsf{src}\,(e, p)$ function:

$$\mathsf{src} \;:\; \mathrm{Var} \times \mathrm{Path} \to \mathrm{Path}_\perp$$
$$\mathsf{src}\,(e, \perp) = \perp$$
$$\mathsf{src}\,(x, p) = x.p$$
$$\mathsf{src}\,(i, \epsilon) = \perp$$
$$\mathsf{src}\,(b, \epsilon) = \perp$$
$$\mathsf{src}\,(e_1 \oplus e_2, \epsilon) = \perp$$
$$\mathsf{src}\,((e_1, e_2), \epsilon) = \perp$$
$$\mathsf{src}\,((e_1, e_2), i \cdot p) = \mathsf{src}\,(e_i, p)$$
$$\mathsf{src}\,(\mathtt{fst}(e), p) = \mathsf{src}\,(e, 1 \cdot p)$$
$$\mathsf{src}\,(\mathtt{snd}(e), p) = \mathsf{src}\,(e, 2 \cdot p)$$
$$\mathsf{src}\,(\mathtt{let}\ x = e_1\ \mathtt{in}\ e_2, p) = \begin{cases} \mathsf{src}\,(e_1, q) & \text{if } \mathsf{src}\,(e_2, p) = x.q \\ \mathsf{src}\,(e_2, p) & \text{otherwise} \end{cases}$$

The cases for constants and primitive functions are obvious. For pair expressions, if the path is ϵ, then we return $\perp$ since the pair value was created by the pair expression. If the pair is $i \cdot p$ for some $i \in \{1, 2\}$, then we find the source of p in the appropriate subderivation. For projection operations $\mathtt{fst}$ or $\mathtt{snd}$, we find the source of $i \cdot p$ where $i = 1$ or $i = 2$ respectively. For $\mathtt{let}$-binding, we first find the source of p in the second subderivation. There are then two cases: either the source path is of the form $x.q$ where x was the bound variable, or it is $\perp$ or some other path $y.q$. In the first case, we find the source path of $x.q$ in e_1; in the second, we just return the source path we have already found (or $\perp$).

Theorem 2. *If $D :: \sigma, e \Downarrow v$ and $p \in \mathrm{paths}(v)$ and $\mathsf{src}\,(e, p) = q \neq \perp$ then q is a source path for p.*

Next, we consider commands. The definition of source path above extends naturally to *straight-line* code involving only sequential composition and assignment:

$$s ::= \mathtt{skip} \mid x := e \mid s_1; s_2$$

Again, source paths for commands can be extracted syntactically:

$$\text{src} \; : \; \text{Var} \times \text{Path} \to \text{Path}_\bot$$
$$\text{src}\,(s, \bot) = \bot$$
$$\text{src}\,(\texttt{skip}, x.p) = x.p$$
$$\text{src}\,(x := e, x.p) = \text{src}\,(e, p)$$
$$\text{src}\,(y := e, x.p) = x.p \qquad (x \neq y)$$
$$\text{src}\,(s_1; s_2, q) = \text{src}\,(s_1, \text{src}\,(s_2, q))$$

The idea is similar to where-provenance for expressions. The assignment command is handled similar to a let. Sequential composition is handled by composing src on subexpressions.

Theorem 3. *If $D :: \sigma, c \Downarrow \sigma'$ and $p \in \text{paths}(\sigma')$ and $\text{src}\,(c, p) = q \neq \bot$ then q is a source path for p.*

However, the above notion of source path does not transfer directly to commands with control-flow. For example, in a conditional if $x = 1$ then $y = x$ else $y = 2$ there is no source path for the value of y, even in the case where $x = 1$ and y seems to be copied from x. As a compromise, we consider a weaker notion, based on the idea of "freezing" the control-flow of a derivation to obtain a straight-line program.

$$\text{freeze}\left(\overline{\sigma, \texttt{skip} \Downarrow \sigma} \right) = \texttt{skip}$$

$$\text{freeze}\left(\frac{D}{\sigma, x := e \Downarrow \sigma'} \right) = x := e$$

$$\text{freeze}\left(\frac{D_1 \quad D_2}{\sigma, c_1; c_2 \Downarrow \sigma''} \right) = \text{freeze}\,(D_1)\,; \text{freeze}\,(D_2)$$

$$\text{freeze}\left(\frac{D \quad D'}{\sigma, \texttt{if } e \texttt{ then } c_1 \texttt{ else } c_2 \Downarrow \sigma'} \right) = \text{freeze}\,(D')$$

$$\text{freeze}\left(\frac{D :: \sigma, e \Downarrow \texttt{false}}{\sigma, \texttt{while } e \texttt{ do } c} \right) = \texttt{skip}$$

$$\text{freeze}\left(\frac{D :: \sigma, e \Downarrow \texttt{true} \quad D' \quad D''}{\sigma, \texttt{while } e \texttt{ do } c} \right) = \text{freeze}\,(D')\,; \text{freeze}\,(D'')$$

The function $\text{freeze}\,(D)$ gives a straight-line code approximation of the program based on its derivation. We have:

Theorem 4. *If $D :: \sigma, c \Downarrow \sigma'$ then $\sigma, \text{freeze}\,(D) \Downarrow \sigma'$.*

Note, however, that $\text{freeze}\,()$ is still an intensional concept: two derivations of equivalent programs on equal inputs need not have the same straight-line approximation, as illustrated by $D_1 :: [x := 1], \texttt{if } x = 1 \texttt{ then } x := 1 \texttt{ else skip} \Downarrow [x := 1]$ and $[x := 1], x \Downarrow [x := 1]$. Moreover, the above theorem does not uniquely characterize the behavior of freeze (); for example, an alternative definition that simply collects the assignments needed to map σ to σ' would also have the given property. Thus, freeze () represents an intuitive tradeoff between concreteness (avoiding control-flow) and faithfulness to the shape of the original derivation.

Given a derivation $D :: \sigma, e \Downarrow v$ and path p in the result value v, we can then define the source path of p in a general **IMP** program c as src (freeze (D), p).

Actually, very little of the derivation is needed to compute sources. Inspecting each rule, we never need to examine the input store of any judgment and we seldom need to inspect the return value: we only do this for `while`, and we could potentially avoid this by inferring whether the loop test holds from the structure of the subtree (i.e., a while-subderivation with only one child must correspond to a loop test that evaluates to false). So, in general, if we only want to extract source information then all we really need is the straight-line approximation of the derivation (i.e., freeze (D)), not the (usually much larger) full derivation with explicit store, expression, and value annotations. The straight-line approximation freeze (D) might be viewed as an interesting form of provenance in its own right. We can extract more than just source information from it; for example, we can determine whether an output value was computed by adding two inputs.

A straight-line program could also be viewed as a DAG, following many conventional approaches to provenance such as OPM [46]. Clearly, we could extract an OPM-style DAG from a straight-line program. Moreover, as argued by Cheney [13] and Moreau [45], provenance DAGs can be viewed as a model of computation for the purpose of analyzing the causality or reproducibility of the computation they represent. However, the DAG approximation corresponding to freeze (D) does not necessarily provide enough information for full recomputation. In the next section, we consider the related issue of using the derivation as a basis for efficient recomputation based on caching.

4   Dependence and Change Propagation

Another common motivation for provenance is to understand how parts of the result depend on intermediate computation steps or source data. The notion of dependence plays an important role in programming languages, particularly dependency tracking [1,2], information flow security [51] and change propagation [5,4]. As argued in [12,15], we believe that this is a good starting point for understanding how provenance should link results to the source data they depend on.

Analyzing dependence requires us to consider not just how an expression did evaluate but how its evaluation might change if the inputs were modified. If we expect provenance to explain the results, then what metric should we use to compare different explanations? We believe that an explanation should have *predictive value* in the sense that it can be used to effectively predict how the result might change if the inputs were modified. Of course, the original program also provides this ability, but full recomputation may involve redoing subcomputations where nothing has changed. Thus, a further requirement is that the explanation be concise in the sense that it avoids details of uninteresting parts of the computation that do not change.

Derivation trees already provide all of the information needed to predict the results of changes. In fact, for a deterministic language, the root judgment of a derivation tree already contains the whole program, and we can simply rerun this on any new input and compare the old derivation and result value with the new ones. However, we argue that this does not provide a satisfying explanation. Derivation trees are verbose and it is not easy to propagate changes through them. For example, in Figure 3 if we change the value of x from 4 to 3, the structure of the derivation does not change. A large number of parts of the derivation need to change, because there are many copies of the value of x in the store and return values. In some sense, all we really need to know about the result is that it is a copy of x, and the control flow depended on the fact that $x = 2$ was false. This gives us enough information to predict the result of any change to x that maintains the invariant $x \neq 2$.

To make this precise, consider the function $\mathcal{E}^{\Delta}(D, \delta)$ that takes a derivation D of $\sigma, e \Downarrow v$ and a partial environment δ and constructs the new value v' resulting from evaluating e on $\sigma[\delta]$. Here, δ is an environment that provides new values for some of the variables in σ. We write $\sigma[\delta]$ to indicate the environment that takes values $\delta(x)$ if $x \in \mathrm{dom}(\delta)$ and $\sigma(x)$ otherwise. We also consider an analogous function $\mathcal{C}^{\Delta}(D, \delta)$ that propagates changes through commands.

In Figure 8, we define functions $\mathcal{E}^{\Delta}(-, -) : \mathrm{Deriv} \times \mathrm{Store} \to \mathrm{Val}$ and $\mathcal{C}^{\Delta}(-.-) : \mathrm{Deriv} \times \mathrm{Store} \to \mathrm{Store}_{\perp}$ that attempt to reuse values cached in subderivations wherever possible. Specifically, whenever we can detect that the changed values in δ do not overlap with the free variables of an expression or command, we simply reuse the cached value (for an expression) or return δ (for a command). The following lemma shows that this is safe:

Lemma 1. *If* $\mathrm{dom}(\delta) \cap FV(e) = \emptyset$ *and* $\sigma, e \Downarrow v$ *then* $\sigma[\delta], e \Downarrow v$. *Moreover, if* $\mathrm{dom}(\delta) \cap FV(c) = \emptyset$ *and* $\sigma, c \Downarrow \sigma'$ *then* $\sigma[\delta], c \Downarrow \sigma'[\delta]$.

The first rule for expressions says that we can reuse a cached subexpression provided none of its variables have changed in value (that is, $FV(e) \cap \mathrm{dom}(\delta) = \emptyset$). The next few rules essentially just replay evaluation. The rule for `let` deserves discussion: essentially, we recompute the bound expression and compare its value with the previous value cached in the trace. If the values are equal, we recompute the body of the `let` using δ, otherwise, we add the new binding for x to δ. This makes it possible to use cached subderivations more often than if we always added x to δ.

For commands, the rules follow a similar pattern. The first rule indicates that it is safe to skip recomputation of a command whose free variables have not been changed. Assignment follows a pattern similar to `let`. However, we need to recompute subexpressions using the cached stores when the control flow changes, for example if the change affects the result of a conditional test. The rules for conditionals require re-starting evaluation when the control flow changes (we use the denotational semantics for brevity). For example, if a conditional

$$\mathcal{E}^{\Delta}\left(D :: \sigma, e \Downarrow v, \delta\right) = v \qquad (\mathrm{dom}(\delta) \cap FV(e) = \emptyset)$$

$$\mathcal{E}^{\Delta}\left(\overline{\sigma, x \Downarrow v}, \delta\right) = \delta(x) \quad (x \in \mathrm{dom}(\delta))$$

$$\mathcal{E}^{\Delta}\left(\frac{D_1 \quad D_2}{\sigma, e_1 \oplus e_2 \Downarrow v}, \delta\right) = \mathcal{E}^{\Delta}\left(D_1, \delta\right) \oplus \mathcal{E}^{\Delta}\left(D_2, \delta\right) \qquad (\oplus \in \{=, +, \ldots\})$$

$$\mathcal{E}^{\Delta}\left(\frac{D_1 \quad D_2}{\sigma, (e_1, e_2) \Downarrow (v_1, v_2)}, \delta\right) = \left(\mathcal{E}^{\Delta}\left(D_1, \delta\right), \mathcal{E}^{\Delta}\left(D_2, \delta\right)\right)$$

$$\mathcal{E}^{\Delta}\left(\frac{D}{\sigma, \mathtt{fst}(e) \Downarrow v}, \delta\right) = \mathrm{let}\ (v_1', v_2') = \mathcal{E}^{\Delta}\left(D, \delta\right)\ \mathrm{in}\ v_1'$$

$$\mathcal{E}^{\Delta}\left(\frac{D}{\sigma, \mathtt{snd}(e) \Downarrow v}, \delta\right) = \mathrm{let}\ (v_1', v_2') = \mathcal{E}^{\Delta}\left(D, \delta\right)\ \mathrm{in}\ v_2'$$

$$\mathcal{E}^{\Delta}\left(\frac{D_1 :: \sigma, e_1 \Downarrow v \quad D_2}{\sigma, \mathtt{let}\ x = e_1\ \mathtt{in}\ e_2}, \delta\right) = \begin{cases} \mathcal{E}^{\Delta}\left(D_2, \delta\right) & \left(\mathcal{E}^{\Delta}\left(D_1, \delta\right) = v\right) \\ \mathcal{E}^{\Delta}\left(D_2, \delta[x := \mathcal{E}^{\Delta}\left(D_1, \delta\right)]\right) & \text{otherwise} \end{cases}$$

Fig. 8. Update propagation for expressions

$$\mathcal{C}^{\Delta}\left(D :: \sigma, c \Downarrow \sigma', \delta\right) = \delta \qquad (\mathrm{dom}(\delta) \cap FV(c) = \emptyset)$$

$$\mathcal{C}^{\Delta}\left(\frac{D :: \sigma, e \Downarrow v}{\sigma, x := e \Downarrow \sigma'}, \delta\right) = \begin{cases} \delta & \left(\mathcal{E}^{\Delta}\left(D, \delta\right) = v\right) \\ \delta[x := \mathcal{E}^{\Delta}\left(D, \delta\right)] & \text{otherwise} \end{cases}$$

$$\mathcal{C}^{\Delta}\left(\frac{D_1 \quad D_2}{\sigma, c_1; c_2 \Downarrow \sigma'}, \delta\right) = \mathcal{C}^{\Delta}\left(D_2, \mathcal{C}^{\Delta}\left(D_1, \delta\right)\right)$$

$$\mathcal{C}^{\Delta}\left(\frac{D :: e \Downarrow \mathtt{true} \quad D_1}{\sigma, \mathtt{if}\ e\ \mathtt{then}\ c_1\ \mathtt{else}\ c_2 \Downarrow \sigma'}, \delta\right) = \mathrm{if}\ \mathcal{E}^{\Delta}\left(D, \delta\right)\ \mathrm{then}\ \mathcal{C}^{\Delta}\left(D_1, \delta\right)\ \mathrm{else}\ \mathcal{C}[\![c_2]\!](\sigma[\delta])$$

$$\mathcal{C}^{\Delta}\left(\frac{D :: \sigma, e \Downarrow \mathtt{false} \quad D_2}{\sigma, \mathtt{if}\ e\ \mathtt{then}\ c_1\ \mathtt{else}\ c_2 \Downarrow \sigma'}, \delta\right) = \mathrm{if}\ \mathcal{E}^{\Delta}\left(D, \delta\right)\ \mathrm{then}\ \mathcal{C}[\![c_1]\!](\sigma[\delta])\ \mathrm{else}\ \mathcal{C}^{\Delta}\left(D_2, \delta\right)$$

$$\mathcal{C}^{\Delta}\left(\frac{D :: \sigma, e \Downarrow \mathtt{true} \quad D' \quad D''}{\sigma, \mathtt{while}\ e\ \mathtt{do}\ c \Downarrow \sigma'}, \delta\right) = \mathrm{if}\ \mathcal{E}^{\Delta}\left(D, \delta\right)\ \mathrm{then}\ \mathcal{C}^{\Delta}\left(D'', \mathcal{C}^{\Delta}\left(D', \delta\right)\right)\ \mathrm{else}\ \delta$$

$$\mathcal{C}^{\Delta}\left(\frac{D :: \sigma, e \Downarrow \mathtt{false}}{\sigma, \mathtt{while}\ e\ \mathtt{do}\ c \Downarrow \sigma}, \delta\right) = \mathrm{if}\ \mathcal{E}^{\Delta}\left(D, \delta\right)\ \mathrm{then}\ \mathcal{C}[\![\mathtt{while}\ e\ \mathtt{do}\ c]\!](\sigma[\delta])\ \mathrm{else}\ \delta$$

Fig. 9. Update propagation for commands

test changes from true to false, then we cannot use the subderivation stored for the then-branch; we have to execute the else-branch "from scratch" using ordinary evaluation on the updated store $\sigma[\delta]$. Composition and `while` also follow predictable patterns; here, we use the denotational semantics for commands as shorthand for computing commands "from scratch".

Theorem 5. *If $D :: \sigma, e \Downarrow v$ then $\sigma[\delta], e \Downarrow \mathcal{E}^{\Delta}(D, \delta)$. Similarly, if $D :: \sigma, c \Downarrow \sigma'$ and $\sigma[\delta], c \Downarrow \sigma''$ then $\sigma'' = \sigma'[\mathcal{C}^{\Delta}(D, \delta)]$.*

Note that the second part needs to be stated carefully because there is no guarantee that recomputing a command on a changed input will terminate.

The correctness theorem above essentially states that the functions $\mathcal{E}^{\Delta}(-, -)$ and $\mathcal{C}^{\Delta}(-, -)$ can be used to correctly compute the updated result. We could go further, and augment these functions to calculate the new derivation as well, or the changed part of the derivation. The latter could serve as a rough measure of the amount of "work" needed to recompute; obviously, in many cases the changed part of the derivation will be much smaller than the whole derivation, just as the changed part of the store obtained by $\mathcal{C}^{\Delta}(-, -)$ can be smaller than the whole result store.

Propagating updates through computations efficiently is a subtle issue with a large, still-growing literature (particularly for self-adjusting computation in functional programming [5,4]). Our goal here is not to introduce a new approach to incremental recomputation that we claim will be more efficient, but only to establish a formal link between derivations-as-provenance and the notions of trace used in incremental recomputation. In particular, the $\mathcal{C}^{\Delta}(D, \delta)$ function highlights one qualitative difference between replaying the whole expression from scratch and derivation-based change propagation: only by recording some information about what happened in a previous run can we avoid fully recomputing each part of the program.

We could also push this idea further in several ways: we could allow finer-grained changes such as updates that change a specific path in a variable's value, not just the whole value; we could consider techniques for controlling the cost of caching by marking subexpressions with checkpointing annotations; we could improve the precision of update propagation for commands by static analysis of assignments; or we could incrementally recompute both the new value and its derivation (or the difference between derivations). Many of these ideas have already been explored in the context of self-adjusting computation, and it is intriguing to consider the possibility of unifying the notion of traces used in efficient self-adjusting computation systems with that needed for provenance.

5   Discussion

Pragmatic concerns, such as ease of use and extensibility, are often cited for employing operational semantics instead of denotational semantics. In particular, extensions such as nondeterminism, concurrency, additional type constructors, object-oriented features, and higher-order functions can be added to an operational semantics comparatively easily. Following the recipe in this paper, each such extension comes equipped with one or more standard notions of "operational derivation" which could be used as a form of provenance. However, the reality is not quite so simple: for example, adding sum types or collection types poses problems for our use of paths to address parts of result values. We discuss the ramifications of these extensions in the rest of this section.

5.1 Sum Types

Functional languages such as ML and Haskell support algebraic datatypes, based on type-theoretic *sum types*. The type $\tau_1 + \tau_2$ represents the disjoint union of types τ_1 and τ_2. Its introduction forms are injection functions $\text{inl} : \tau_1 \to \tau_1 + \tau_2$ and $\text{inr} : \tau_2 \to \tau_1 + \tau_2$, and its elimination form is a case construct that performs pattern matching.

$$e ::= \cdots \mid \text{inl}(e) \mid \text{inr}(e) \mid \textbf{case } e \textbf{ of } \{x.e_1 \mid y.e_2\}$$
$$v ::= \cdots \mid \text{inl}(v) \mid \text{inr}(v)$$

Sum types and the associated programming constructs can be handled similarly to booleans and conditionals:

$$\frac{\sigma, e \Downarrow v}{\sigma, \text{inl}(e) \Downarrow \text{inl}(v)} \qquad \frac{\sigma, e \Downarrow \text{inl}(v) \quad \sigma[x := v], e_1 \Downarrow v_1}{\sigma, \textbf{case } e \textbf{ of } \{x.e_1 \mid y.e_2\} \Downarrow v_1}$$

$$\frac{\sigma, e \Downarrow v}{\sigma, \text{inr}(e) \Downarrow \text{inr}(v)} \qquad \frac{\sigma, e \Downarrow \text{inr}(v) \quad \sigma[y := v], e_2 \Downarrow v_2}{\sigma, \textbf{case } e \textbf{ of } \{x.e_1 \mid y.e_2\} \Downarrow v_2}$$

Sum types complicate the issue of how to refer to parts of the input or output. A naive approach would simply be to add inl and inr as possible path steps, so that the path $1.\text{inl}.2$ refers to 42 in the value $(\text{inl}(17, 42), 0)$. However, this leads to problems with the definition of source path, since changes to the input might change the structure of the output in ways that invalidate paths involving inl or inr.

5.2 Higher-Order Functions and Other Control Abstractions

Modern programming languages increasingly support first-class higher-order functions, either explicitly (as in functional languages such as ML, Haskell, or Scheme, and more recently in object-oriented languages such as C#, Java or Scala), or implicitly via other constructs such as function objects or inner classes (available in older versions of Java).

$$e ::= \cdots \mid \lambda x.e \mid e_1\ e_2$$
$$v ::= \cdots \mid \langle \lambda x.e, \sigma \rangle$$

Here, $\langle \lambda x.e, \sigma \rangle$ is a *closure* packaging a function body up with the environment in which it was constructed. We extend the operational semantics as follows (in the standard way):

$$\frac{\sigma, e_1 \Downarrow \langle \lambda x.e, \sigma' \rangle \quad \sigma, e_2 \Downarrow v_2 \quad \sigma'[x := v_2], e \Downarrow v}{\sigma, e_1 \; e_2 \Downarrow v} \qquad \frac{}{\sigma, \lambda x.e \Downarrow \langle \lambda x.e, \sigma \rangle}$$

Higher-order functions pose a significant challenge to provenance tracking, because now the control flow (corresponding to the shape of the derivation tree) depends on evaluation: when evaluating a first-class function call, we first evaluate the function part to find the body of the function, which is in general not known until run time. Also, similarly to sums, it is difficult to use paths to refer to "parts" of closure values.

5.3 Collection Types

Now consider an extension to the language to permit simple collections (such as sets, lists, or bags), as in Nested Relational Calculus [10]:

$$e ::= \cdots \mid \emptyset \mid \{e\} \mid e_1 \cup e_2$$
$$v ::= \cdots \mid \emptyset \mid \{v_1, \ldots, v_n\}$$

The operational semantics of collection operations can be defined as follows:

$$\frac{}{\sigma, \emptyset \Downarrow \emptyset} \qquad \frac{\sigma, e_1 \Downarrow v_1 \quad \sigma, e_2 \Downarrow v_2}{\sigma, e_1 \cup e_2 \Downarrow v_1 \cup v_2} \qquad \frac{\sigma, e \Downarrow v}{\sigma, \{e\} \Downarrow \{v\}}$$

We could also add a set comprehension operation $\bigcup_{x \in e_0} e$ to obtain an expressive comprehension query language, but the problems we want to discuss do not require this. (Naturally, this would introduce additional complications due to variable binding).

The prospect of using paths to refer to parts of data structures is significantly complicated in the presence of collections, especially unordered collections. For lists, we have similar issues to those for sums. For sets, it is technically possible to refer to set elements via their values, although this can be unwieldy when sets are nested. But for multisets, paths are no longer sufficient to address each part of a value if we view multiset expressions as equal modulo reordering of elements.

As a simple example, consider a multiset expression $\{x - y\} \cup \{z + 1\}$ which evaluates to $\{1, 1\}$. If we want to ask for the provenance of one of the output elements, there is no location scheme for pure multiset values that lets us distinguish between the two copies of '1' in the output. This means that in order to support correct source tracking we need to impose some kind of location structure on multisets. Of course, we can avoid this problem in a simple way, by treating collection values as lists and using integer indices. However, this indexing approach becomes rather complex if we wish to propagate changes from the input to the output, because the paths are not stable with respect to changes that affect the sizes of subcollections.

For example, suppose we have an expression $\{a\} \cup x \cup \{d\}$. If we first evaluate it with $x = \{b\}$ then the result will be $\{a, b, d\}$ where $v[3] = d$. But if we update x to be $\{b, c\}$, then the result is $v' = \{a, b, c, d\}$, where $v'[3] = c$ and $v'[4] = d$. We would like to be able to say that changing x from $\{b\}$ to $\{b, c\}$ did not affect the d value at $v[3]$. Intuitively, the d value in $v[3]$ is the same as the d value at $v'[4]$, but they have different paths. Thus, we need to maintain a partial mapping $\{(1, 1), (3, 4)\}$ relating the paths in v to identical parts of v'. Now consider an expression such as $\{a\} \cup x \cup \{b\} \cup x \cup \{c\}$. If x is changed from $\{d\}$ to $\{d, e\}$, then we need to reindex both the b and c elements, that is, the partial mapping would be $\{(1, 1), (3, 4), (5, 7)\}$.

These examples illustrate that paths based on positional indices are not stable under changes to the input. Although indexing can be made to work using partial mappings, it is notationally heavy, and it seems much cleaner instead to use collections that maintain explicit, unique labels for their elements. These labels can be used in paths, and have two further advantages over indices: we can still treat labeled multisets as equivalent up to reordering, and we do not have to keep track of partial mappings among results. These advantages also hold for lists and sets, for which it is technically possible to use numbers or element values in paths instead of labels. On the other hand, using labels requires generating fresh labels for newly-created collections, which essentially makes the rules for creating collections nondeterministic, which in turn complicates matters for the same reason as other forms of nondeterminism. We are currently investigating this problem.

5.4   Nondeterminism

We model a simple form of nondeterminism by adding a coin-flip expression flip whose semantics is as follows:

$$\frac{}{\sigma, \texttt{flip} \Downarrow \texttt{true}} \qquad \frac{}{\sigma, \texttt{flip} \Downarrow \texttt{false}}$$

Obviously, nondeterminism makes it impossible to predict the result of a program or its derivation.

Nondeterminism has little impact on the source-location extraction function: a value constructed by flip simply has source $\bot$. However, nondeterminism has interesting consequences for the update-propagation semantics. Basically, the question is how we should deal with changes to computations involving flip. Should all coin flips that might affect the result of a computation be re-done? In this case, we would constrain the caching rules to apply only if e does not contain flip.

Or should we avoid this as much as possible, to try to preserve the structure of the derivation as much as we can? In this case, we would allow caching to reuse the results of coin-flips stored in the derivation. Only if a subexpression is re-evaluated (e.g. as the result of a control flow change) would new random coin flips be performed.

Either choice may be sensible, depending on the situation. If we want change propagation to simulate what actually happened as much as possible (e.g. to track down the source of an error), we would opt for the first design, reusing as many cached coin flips as possible. If we want change propagation to simulate all possible behaviors of the program, while reusing deterministic subcomputations, then we need the second semantics. If we interpret `flip` probabilistically instead of nondeterministically, there may be additional choices.

5.5   Arrays, References, Dynamic Allocation, and Concurrency

It is interesting to note that most approaches to provenance have focused on relatively high-level languages or abstractions such as database queries, scientific workflows, or operating system calls. In contrast, most work on program slicing [54], and much work on information flow in language-based security [51], has focused on small imperative languages similar to **IMP** extended with features such as arrays, references, and dynamic memory allocation. These features are, of course, still essential parts of programming most real-world systems written in C, C++, or Java, and are also present in many scripting or numerical computation languages used by scientists, such as Python, Matlab or R. Thus, to understand provenance in general, we will need to understand provenance for these features. Since these are exactly the features that tend to make program analysis, typechecking, and debugging difficult, we can predict with some confidence that they will pose challenges for provenance as well.

The approach taken in this paper should provide at least a starting point for understanding provenance in the presence of arrays, references or dynamic memory allocation. Concurrency may also be tackled using operational techniques. However, simply using some kind of derivation as a form of provenance leaves a lot of questions unanswered, especially in the case of concurrency: How can we efficiently record a full operational derivation? Is this even desirable in general, or can we formulate specifications that make it clear that we can make do with less? How can we recover a full operational derivation of a concurrent execution given that each concurrently-executing part only has access to part of the full derivation?

6   Related Work

There is some prior work discussing requirements or design philosophies for provenance systems (e.g. [32,37,39,31]). This work, like a great deal of work on provenance, has invoked informal motivations such as that provenance should identify data that are "relevant to", "caused" or "influenced" an output and provide "repeatability", "transparency", or "explanation". There has been little attempt to define these terms carefully or formally with respect to the semantics of the programs or systems being studied. As argued previously in some of our prior work [15,8,17], we believe that while these informal motivations are important, they are not enough on their own to explain what provenance is and why it is challenging to define, collect and manage it. There is a danger that different users and implementers may interpret these terms differently, leading to miscommunication and confusion. As was once common in computer security, there are many provenance mechanisms being designed without adequate understanding of the policies that they are meant to satisfy.

Some work on provenance in databases has considered whether certain forms of provenance can be extracted from others, including some negative results. For example, the semiring provenance model of Green et al. [29] can express some other models such as why-provenance and lineage, but cannot express where-provenance and vice versa (as discussed in [24,16]). However, the design space for techniques to track and manage provenance for data and computations that span databases, workflows, or general-purpose programming languages, remains largely unexplored. Our workshop paper [6] gives one approach to a unified model of provenance for database queries and workflows. A subsequent paper [3] investigates provenance extraction and security issues for a trace model for functional programs. We are interested in developing analogous techniques for database query languages, building on language-integrated query techniques [18].

In a previous paper [15], we identified a connection between dependence in information-flow security and provenance, and developed a new form of provenance based on dependence tracking. Our paper [17] explored connections to programming languages, security, incremental, and bidirectional computation research [1,5,25]. More recently, we have investigated foundations for provenance security [14], building on work by Chong [19]. We believe language-based provenance security to be a fruitful area for future work, possibly extending the derivation trace model in this paper.

Our recent work [3,49] considers traces and trace slicing for a pure, call-by-value calculus with product, sum and recursive types, and recursive functions, using a conventional large-step semantics; paths become unwieldy in this setting, and we adopt an alternative approach based on partial values. Other features such as exceptions, laziness, and first-class continuations (call/cc) pose similar, and possibly greater, challenges from the point of view of provenance. These challenges may require us to abandon the idea of using large-step derivations in favor of the small-step operational techniques typically used for these features [50].

Aside from a few papers on provenance techniques in concurrency calculi [52,21], the theory of self-explaining computation in the presence of computational effects, concurrency, or laziness is unexplored. General approaches to the denotational or operational semantics of effects [36,34] provide an intriguing starting point for the study of provenance in the presence of effects. Ideas from concurrency theory, particularly Winskel's *event structures* [58], may be a good place to start in understanding the meaning of provenance in concurrent or distributed settings.

7   Conclusions

To date, research on provenance has focused on particular classes of systems or computational models, such as databases, workflow management systems or operating systems. Real scientific data and processing pipelines are typically not confined to a single kind of system but instead use a combination of these systems as well as ad hoc programs written in general-purpose or scripting languages that glue these different systems together. We therefore argue here that provenance needs to be understood for general-purpose programming languages.

In this paper, we have proposed a simple (perhaps too simple) model of provenance in general-purpose programming language: the provenance trace of a computation is simply a full operational derivation, i.e. a "proof" that the program executed and produced a given value. This approach has both advantages and drawbacks. It seems reasonable to expect that we can extract any other form of provenance from such a trace: even in the presence of nondeterminism, the trace records all inputs, outputs and intermediate choices. Thus, we can extract other forms of provenance, such as source location information, as well as adapting traces to changes to the input. However, this generality (at least, if interpreted naively) comes at a high cost: the memory and processing overhead of storing such full traces for nontrivial programs appears prohibitive, strongly motivating compression or slicing techniques that can mitigate this cost while still providing detailed provenance. Another possible drawback, compared to, for example, the elegant semiring framework used in relational databases [29,24], is the absence of strong semantic properties that can be used to optimize programs in the presence of provenance.

Nevertheless, our contribution helps to frame the problem of provenance management in general-purpose languages, by proposing an idealized "most general" form of provenance that can be used to define and compare other, more practical techniques. Many other questions remain to be investigated in developing a theory of self-explaining computation, including:

- Can we compress or slice the full derivation trace efficiently enough to make it a practical approach? If not, what are the limits of efficient provenance for general-purpose programs?
- How can we extend derivation traces to handle complex features such as concurrency, side-effects or collections?
- Can we identify intermediate forms of provenance that retain a high degree of generality while remaining efficiently implementable?
- Can we develop an appropriate compositional model of provenance building on denotational semantics (and admitting standard program equivalences)?

Acknowledgments. Effort sponsored by the Air Force Office of Scientific Research, Air Force Material Command, USAF, under grant number FA8655-13-1-3006. The U.S Government is authorized to reproduce and distribute reprints for Governmental purpose notwithstanding any copyright notation thereon. Cheney is supported by a Royal Society University Research Fellowship, by the EU FP7 DIACHRON project, and EPSRC grant EP/K020218/1. Parts of this research were done while Acar and Perera were at Max-Planck Institute for Software Systems, Kaiserslautern, Germany, and while Perera was a PhD student at the University of Birmingham.

References

1. Abadi, M., Banerjee, A., Heintze, N., Riecke, J.G.: A core calculus of dependency. In: POPL, pp. 147–160. ACM Press (1999)
2. Abadi, M., Lampson, B., Lévy, J.-J.: Analysis and caching of dependencies. In: ICFP, pp. 83–91. ACM Press (1996)
3. Acar, U.A., Ahmed, A., Cheney, J., Perera, R.: A core calculus for provenance. In: Degano, P., Guttman, J.D. (eds.) POST 2012. LNCS, vol. 7215, pp. 410–429. Springer, Heidelberg (2012)
4. Acar, U.A., Blelloch, G.E., Blume, M., Harper, R., Tangwongsan, K.: An experimental analysis of self-adjusting computation. ACM Trans. Prog. Lang. Sys. 32(1), 3:1–3:53 (2009)
5. Acar, U.A., Blelloch, G.E., Harper, R.: Adaptive functional programming. ACM Trans. Program. Lang. Syst. 28(6), 990–1034 (2006)
6. Acar, U.A., Buneman, P., Cheney, J., Kwasnikowska, N., Van den Bussche, J., Vansummeren, S.: A graph model of data and workflow provenance. In: TAPP (2010), http://www.usenix.org/event/tapp10
7. Bowers, S., McPhillips, T.M., Riddle, S., Anand, M.K., Ludäescher, B.: Kepler/pPOD: Scientific workflow and provenance support for assembling the tree of life. In: Freire, et al. (eds.) [26], pp. 70–77.
8. Buneman, P., Cheney, J., Vansummeren, S.: On the expressiveness of implicit provenance in query and update languages. ACM Transactions on Database Systems 33(4), 28 (2008)
9. Buneman, P., Khanna, S., Tan, W.-C.: Why and where: A characterization of data provenance. In: Van den Bussche, J., Vianu, V. (eds.) ICDT 2001. LNCS, vol. 1973, pp. 316–330. Springer, Heidelberg (2000)
10. Buneman, P., Libkin, L., Suciu, D., Tannen, V., Wong, L.: Comprehension syntax. SIGMOD Record 23(1), 87–96 (1994)
11. Carey, S., Rogow, G.: UAL shares fall as old story surfaces online. Wall Street Journal (September 2008), http://online.wsj.com/article/SB122088673738010213.html
12. Cheney, J.: Program slicing and data provenance. IEEE Data Engineering Bulletin, 22–28 (December 2007) Invited paper
13. Cheney, J.: Causality and the semantics of provenance. In: Proceedings of the 2010 Workshop on Developments in Computational Models (2010)
14. Cheney, J.: A formal framework for provenance security. In: CSF, pp. 281–293. IEEE (2011)
15. Cheney, J., Ahmed, A., Acar, U.A.: Provenance as dependency analysis. Mathematical Structures in Computer Science 21(6), 1301–1337 (2011)
16. Cheney, J., Chiticariu, L., Tan, W.: Provenance in databases: Why, how, and where. Foundations and Trends in Databases 1(4), 379–474 (2009)
17. Cheney, J., Chong, S., Foster, N., Seltzer, M., Vansummeren, S.: Provenance: A future history. In: OOPSLA Companion (Onward! 2009), pp. 957–964 (2009)
18. Cheney, J., Lindley, S., Wadler, P.: A practical theory of language-integrated query. In: ICFP (to appear, 2013)
19. Chong, S.: Towards semantics for provenance security. In: Workshop on the Theory and Practice of Provenance (2009), Informal online proceedings, http://www.usenix.org/events/tapp09/
20. Cui, Y., Widom, J., Wiener, J.L.: Tracing the lineage of view data in a warehousing environment. ACM Trans. Database Syst. 25(2), 179–227 (2000)

21. Dezani-Ciancaglini, M., Horne, R., Sassone, V.: Tracing where and who provenance in linked data: A calculus. Theor. Comput. Sci. 464, 113–129 (2012)
22. Dourish, P.: Accounting for System Behaviour: Representation, Reflection and Resourceful Action. In: Computers and Design in Context, pp. 145–170. MIT Press (1997)
23. Foster, I., Vockler, J., Wilde, M., Zhao, Y.: Chimera: A virtual data system for representing, querying, and automating data derivation. In: SSDBM, pp. 1–10 (July 2002)
24. Foster, J.N., Green, T.J., Tannen, V.: Annotated XML: queries and provenance. In: PODS, pp. 271–280 (2008)
25. Foster, J.N., Greenwald, M.B., Moore, J.T., Pierce, B.C., Schmitt, A.: Combinators for bidirectional tree transformations: A linguistic approach to the view-update problem. ACM Trans. Program. Lang. Syst. 29(3), 17 (2007)
26. Freire, J., Koop, D., Moreau, L. (eds.): IPAW 2008. LNCS, vol. 5272. Springer, Heidelberg (2008)
27. Gil, Y., Cheney, J., Groth, P., Hartig, O., Miles, S., Moreau, L., da Silva, P.P., Coppens, S., Garijo, D., Gomez, J.M., Missier, P., Myers, J., Sahoo, S., Zhao, J.: Provenance XG final report (December 2010),
    http://www.w3.org/2005/Incubator/prov/XGR-prov-20101214/
28. Good, D.I.: The foundations of computer security: we need some (1986),
    http://www.ieee-security.org/CSFWweb/goodessay.html
29. Green, T.J., Karvounarakis, G., Tannen, V.: Provenance semirings. In: PODS, pp. 31–40. ACM (2007)
30. Greenwald, G., MacAskill, E.: NSA Prism program taps in to user data of Apple, Google and others. The Guardian (June 2013),
    http://www.guardian.co.uk/world/2013/jun/06/us-tech-giants-nsa-data
31. Groth, P., Gil, Y., Cheney, J., Miles, S.: Requirements for provenance on the web. International Journal of Digital Curation 7(1), 39–56 (2012)
32. Groth, P., Miles, S., Munroe, S.: Principles of high quality documentation for provenance: A philosophical discussion. In: Moreau, L., Foster, I. (eds.) IPAW 2006. LNCS, vol. 4145, pp. 278–286. Springer, Heidelberg (2006)
33. Kahn, G.: Natural semantics. In: Brandenburg, F.J., Wirsing, M., Vidal-Naquet, G. (eds.) STACS 1987. LNCS, vol. 247, pp. 22–39. Springer, Heidelberg (1987)
34. Kammar, O., Lindley, S., Oury, N.: Handlers in action. In: ICFP (to appear, 2013)
35. Lamport, L.: State the problem before describing the solution. SIGSOFT Softw. Eng. Notes 3, 26–26 (1978)
36. Levy, P.B.: Call-By-Push-Value: A Functional/Imperative Synthesis. Semantic Structures in Computation, vol. 2. Springer (2004)
37. Lynch, C.A.: When documents deceive: trust and provenance as new factors for information retrieval in a tangled web. J. Am. Soc. Inf. Sci. Technol. 52(1), 12–17 (2001)
38. McGuinness, D.L., Pinheiro da Silva, P.: Explaining answers from the semantic web: the inference web approach. Web Semant. 1, 397–413 (2004)
39. Miles, S., Groth, P., Branco, M., Moreau, L.: The requirements of using provenance in e-science experiments. Journal of Grid Computing 5, 1–25 (2007), doi:10.1007/s10723-006-9055-3
40. Miles, S., Groth, P.T., Munroe, S., Jiang, S., Assandri, T., Moreau, L.: Extracting causal graphs from an open provenance data model. Concurrency and Computation: Practice and Experience 20(5), 577–586 (2008)

41. Miles, S., Wong, S.C., Fang, W., Groth, P.T., Zauner, K.-P., Moreau, L.: Provenance-based validation of e-science experiments. J. Web Sem. 5(1), 28–38 (2007)
42. Miller, G.: A scientist's nightmare: Software problem leads to five retractions. Science 314(5807), 1856–1857 (2006)
43. Missier, P., Belhajjame, K., Zhao, J., Roos, M., Goble, C.A.: Data lineage model for Taverna workflows with lightweight annotation requirements. In: Freire, et al. (eds.), pp. 17–30
44. Moreau, L.: The foundations for provenance on the web. Foundations and Trends in Web Science 2(2-3), 99–241 (2010)
45. Moreau, L.: Provenance-based reproducibility in the semantic web. J. Web Sem. 9(2), 202–221 (2011)
46. Moreau, L., Clifford, B., Freire, J., Futrelle, J., Gil, Y., Groth, P.T., Kwasnikowska, N., Miles, S., Missier, P., Myers, J., Plale, B., Simmhan, Y., Stephan, E.G., den Bussche, J.V.: The open provenance model core specification (v1.1). Future Generation Comp. Syst. 27(6), 743–756 (2011)
47. Moreau, L., Missier, P. (eds.): PROV-DM: The PROV data model. W3C Recommendation (April 2013), http://www.w3.org/TR/2013/REC-prov-dm-20130430/
48. Muniswamy-Reddy, K.-K., Holland, D.A., Braun, U., Seltzer, M.: Provenance-aware storage systems. In: USENIX Annual Technical Conference, pp. 43–56. USENIX (June 2006)
49. Perera, R., Acar, U.A., Cheney, J., Levy, P.B.: Functional programs that explain their work. In: ICFP, pp. 365–376. ACM (2012)
50. Plotkin, G.D.: A structural approach to operational semantics. J. Log. Algebr. Program. 60-61, 17–139 (2004)
51. Sabelfeld, A., Myers, A.: Language-based information-flow security. IEEE Journal on Selected Areas in Communications 21(1), 5–19 (2003)
52. Souilah, I., Francalanza, A., Sassone, V.: A formal model of provenance in distributed systems. In: Workshop on the Theory and Practice of Provenance (2009)
53. Stoy, J.: Denotational Semantics: The Scott-Strachey Approach to Programming Language Semantics. MIT Press (1981)
54. Tip, F.: A survey of program slicing techniques. J. Prog. Lang. 3(3) (1995)
55. Varghese, S.: UK government gets bitten by Microsoft Word. Sydney Morning Herald (July 2003), http://www.smh.com.au/articles/2003/07/02/1056825430340.html
56. Wang, Y.R., Madnick, S.E.: A polygen model for heterogeneous database systems: The source tagging perspective. In: VLDB, pp. 519–538 (1990)
57. Winskel, G.: The Formal Semantics of Programming Languages: An Introduction. MIT Press (1993)
58. Winskel, G.: Events, causality and symmetry. Comput. J. 54(1), 42–57 (2011)
59. Woodruff, A., Stonebraker, M.: Supporting fine-grained data lineage in a database visualization environment. In: ICDE, pp. 91–102 (1997)
60. Zhao, Y., Wilde, M., Foster, I.: Applying the virtual data provenance model. In: Moreau, L., Foster, I. (eds.) IPAW 2006. LNCS, vol. 4145, pp. 148–161. Springer, Heidelberg (2006)

To Show or Not to Show
in Workflow Provenance

Susan B. Davidson, Sanjeev Khanna, and Tova Milo

Computer and Information Science Department
University of Pennsylvania, Philadelphia, PA, USA
School of Computer Science
Tel Aviv University, Israel
{susan,sanjeev}@cis.upenn.edu, milo@post.tau.ac.il

1   Introduction

Science has been revolutionized by the development and use of high-throughput technologies, which generate large amounts of experimental data. This data must then be analyzed to create knowledge, and for this scientists are increasingly turning to scientific workflow systems. Scientific workflow systems not only help conceptualize and visualize the analysis process, but enable the sharing and reuse of subworkflows between analysis processes by maintaining repositories of workflows.

Once a workflow has been designed it will be executed many times, generating a large amount of "in-silico" experimental data which must also be managed by the system. To help users understand how this data was generated, tools for capturing provenance are being developed in systems such as myGrid/Taverna, Kepler and VisTrails. By maintaining *provenance* information about the sequence of processing steps (module executions) used to produce a data item, as well as the parameter settings and intermediate data items passed between module executions, the validity and reliability of data can be better understood and results can be made reproducible. In particular, users can ask queries over this provenance information such as: "What were the input data and parameter settings for BLAST (a particular processing step) in this workflow execution?" (direct provenance information), "What downstream data was affected by this particular data?" (direct and transitive provenance information), "Does this data depend directly or indirectly on that data?" (a reachability query), or "In how many executions of this workflow was the alternative BLAST chosen to implement the alignment search?" (an aggregate query over all executions of a particular workflow).

However, as observed in our previous work [6,5], authors/owners of workflows may wish to keep some of this provenance information private. For example, intermediate *data* within an execution may contain sensitive information, such as the social security number, a medical record, or financial information about an individual. Although users with the appropriate level of access may be allowed to see such confidential data, making it available to all users through a workflow

V. Tannen et al. (Eds.): Buneman Festschrift, LNCS 8000, pp. 217–226, 2013.

repository, even for scientific purposes, is an unacceptable breach of privacy. Beyond data privacy, a *module* itself may be proprietary, and hiding its description may not be enough: users without the appropriate level of access should not be able to *infer* its behavior if they are allowed to see the inputs and outputs of the module. Finally, details of how certain modules in the workflow are connected may be proprietary, and therefore showing how data is passed between modules may reveal too much of the *structure* of the workflow. **There is thus an inherent tradeoff between the utility of the information shown in response to a search/query and the privacy guarantees that authors/owners desire.**

In this paper, we discuss the issues associated with and our recent progress on *module* and *structural* privacy. We start in Section 2 by giving a model of workflow provenance, and reviewing our approach to *module* privacy. We follow in Section 3 by discussing ideas related to *structural* privacy. We conclude in Section 4.

2   Module Privacy

Module privacy assumes that the structure of the workflow is known, but that the functionality of certain *private* modules is unknown and should not be revealed through the visible provenance information. In contrast, the names and behavior of *public* modules may be completely known by users. Public modules are the norm in workflows, since users typically want to know what a module does and whether or not it is behaving correctly. However, private modules may arise when software has been developed at a significant cost to the owner; while the owner may be willing to share their software for use, possibly for a fee, they do not want it pirated and reproduced. In such cases, the software is typically certified by trusted third parties (e.g., as is the case for the software controlling your car).

We start our discussion of module privacy by providing a simple model of workflow provenance as a relational table, and discussing the approach we take to module privacy. We then highlight our initial results for workflows in which all modules are private (*all-private* workflows) and workflows in which there is a mixture of public and private modules (*public/private* workflows).

2.1   Provenance as a Relation

Workflow provenance is defined as a "depends-on" relationship between output data, and the module, input data and parameters that produced the output data. It is typically represented as a graph. For simplicity, in this section we will assume that the workflow specification is a rooted directed acyclic graph (DAG) in which the nodes are modules and edges denote potential dataflow. In an execution, *all* modules are executed and data flows on all edges, i.e., there is no looping or alternation. Thus the specification also defines the structure of the execution, and we can represent provenance as a database table (*relation*), in which the attributes represent the names of data edges in the workflow specification and a row represents the values of data flowing over the edges in an execution of the workflow.

For example, consider the specification in Figure 1 (to the left), in which there are three modules represented as boxes (m_1, m_2 and m_3), and seven data edges (a_1, ..., a_7). Data a_1 and a_2 are initial input to the workflow and a_6 and a_7 are final input. Data a_3,..., a_5 are intermediate data; note that a_4 is input to both m_2 and m_3 and indicates *data sharing*. In this example, all data is boolean, and the complete provenance relation for this workflow can be found in the table to the right. Since each module is a *function*, functional dependencies are defined from each module's input to its output (far right).

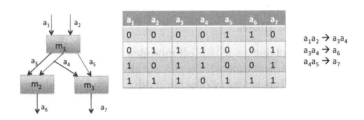

Fig. 1. Sample Workflow Specification and Provenance Relation

2.2   Privacy Approach

We start by observing that if complete provenance information is given for multiple executions of a workflow on different initial inputs, then partial or complete functionality of modules may be revealed. For example, in the provenance relation in Figure 1 the functionality of module m_1 is completely revealed since all possible inputs are shown (a_1, a_2) along with the output for each input (a_3,..,a_5).

The approach that we take in [4] is to *hide a carefully chosen subset of intermediate data*, thereby limiting the amount of provenance data shown to the user and guaranteeing some desired level of privacy. Formally, we define a module m to be Γ-private iff for every input x to m, the output value $m(x)$ is indistinguishable from $\Gamma - 1$ other possible values w.r.t. the visible data.

For example, if we hide a_2 and a_4 in the provenance relation in Figure 1, then 4-privacy is achieved for m_1. Taking the input (x) as a vector (a_1, a_2) and the output $m_1(x)$ as a vector (a_3, a_4, a_5), $m_1(0,0)$ could be (0,0,1), (0,1,1), (1,0,0) or (1,1,0); the same holds for $m_1(0,1)$. Similarly, $m_1(1,0)$ and $m_1(1,1)$ could be (1,0,0), (1,1,0), (1,0,1) or (1,1,1).

We assume that a certain level of privacy is desired for the workflow as a whole (e.g., $\Gamma = 4$), and that the *owner* of each (private) module specifies the subsets of attributes (*safe* sets) whose hiding guarantees Γ-privacy when the module is executed in isolation (*standalone* privacy).[1] The safe sets may represent both

---

[1] We also study the communication and computation complexity of finding these subsets in [4].

input and output data. The workflow *designer* must then decide which attributes to hide in the provenance relation for the workflow so as to guarantee Γ-privacy for each individual private module (the *workflow secure-view* problem). The same data is then hidden over *all* executions of the workflow, i.e., users are presented a view of the workflow provenance relation which is a projection over the visible (non-hidden) attributes.

Note that there may be several safe sets for each private module, each of which guarantees its Γ-privacy. Furthermore, each data item in the workflow may have a different value to users in terms of provenance, represented as a "cost". In the associated workflow secure-view *optimization* problem, the goal is therefore to minimize the cost of the hidden provenance data (i.e., maximize the value of the visible data) while guaranteeing Γ-privacy for each private module.

2.3   All-Private Workflows

In [4] we studied the setting in which *all* modules in the workflow are private. Although the privacy of a module within the workflow is inherently linked to the workflow topology and functionality of other modules, we were able to show that module privacy in all-private workflows is *compositional*, i.e., ensuring the standalone privacy of each module guarantees its privacy when placed in a workflow. Thus any set of attributes chosen to hide in the workflow provenance relation that includes at least one safe set for each private module guarantees its privacy in the workflow setting. The workflow secure-view problem was shown to be NP-hard in the number of attributes in the relation R, which may be very large. However, under a natural restriction, the problem is approximable to within a logarithmic factor in poly-time.

Returning to the example in Figure 1, let $\Gamma = 4$, $\{a_4, a_6\}$ be a safe set for m_2 and $\{a_4, a_5\}$ be a safe set for m_3. Then hiding $\{a_2, a_4, a_5, a_6\}$ in the provenance relation for the sample workflow guarantees 4-privacy for m_1, m_2 and m_3 and is therefore a solution to the workflow secure-view problem. (Whether or not it is optimal depends on additional information, i.e., the costs of the attributes and the set of all safe sets for m_1, m_2 and m_3).

2.4   Public/Private Networks

We have also studied the setting in which only some of the modules in a workflow are private and the rest are public, and here compositionality does not hold. For example, consider the workflow in Figure 2 in which the middle module (m_2) is private whereas the upstream and downstream modules, m_1 and m_3, are public *identity* modules. Certainly, hiding all the data associated with private module m_2 (indicated by the "X" on edges) would guarantee standalone privacy for any Γ. However, the hidden data is exposed by the input to m_1 and output of m_3.

It is therefore necessary to hide additional information in the workflow in order to guarantee Γ-privacy for private modules. One idea is to *privatize* certain public modules, i.e., to hide their name and function, an approach that we pursued in [4]. Returning to our example, if m_1 and m_3 were privatized then hiding the input

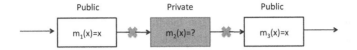

Fig. 2. Public/Private Example

to and output of m_2 would now suffice. However, since much is known about public modules it may be possible to infer the names of privatized modules by the types of inputs/outputs, the structure of the network, or other available information.

Another idea is to *propagate* hiding through public modules. Returning to our example, if the input to m_2 were hidden then the input to m_1 would also be hidden (*upward* propagation), although the user would still know that m_1 were the equality function. Similarly, if the output of m_2 were hidden then the output of m_3 would also be hidden (*downward* propagation); again, the user would still know that m_3 was the equality function. While in this example things appear to be simple, several technically challenging issues must be addressed when employing such a propagation model in the general case: 1) whether to propagate hiding upward (e.g., to m_1) or downward (e.g., to m_3); 2) how far to propagate data hiding; and 3) which data of public modules must be hidden. Overall the goal is the same as in the all-private secure view problem: guaranteeing that the functionality of private modules is not revealed while minimizing the amount of hidden data.

In recent work [3], we have focussed on *downward* propagation and have obtained the following strong results: For a special class of common workflows, *single (private)-predecessor workflows*, or simply *single-predecessor workflows* (which include the common tree and chain workflows), taking a safe set for each private module augmented with specially chosen input/output data of public modules in their *public closure* (modules reachable up to a successor private module) that is rendered *upstream-downstream safe* by the data hiding[2] and hiding the union of data in the augmented solutions for each private module will ensure Γ-workflow privacy for all private modules. Furthermore, for tree-structured or chain workflows (which are common in practice), the minimum cost such solution can be found in poly-time; for other types of single-predecessor workflows, the problem is NP-complete in the number of modules in the public closure. We also show that single-predecessor workflows is the largest class of workflows for which propagation of data hiding only within the public closure suffices.

In contrast to single-predecessor workflows, for *general* workflows, hiding data within a public closure of each private module no longer suffices; data hiding must continue through other private modules to the entire downstream workflow.

---

[2] *Downstream* safety ensures that if two tuples look the same on the visible input, then they look the same on the visible output; *upstream* safety ensures that if two tuples look the same on the visible output, then they look the same on the visible input.

In return, the data hiding requirement for public modules is somewhat weaker here: hiding must only ensure that the module is *downstream-safe*, which typically involves fewer input/output data than upstream-downstream-safety.

Discussion. In this work, we have adopted the notion of ℓ-diversity[12] to define Γ-privacy for modules. However, ℓ-diversity is susceptible to attack when the user has background knowledge [9,10]. *Differential privacy* [7,8] gives a much stronger privacy guarantee. Originally proposed for *statistical databases* and *aggregate queries*, differential privacy requires that the output distribution is *almost* invariant to the inclusion of any particular record. However, it is well-known that no *deterministic* algorithm can guarantee differential privacy, and the standard approach of including random noise is not suitable for our purposes — provenance queries are typically not aggregate queries, and we need the output views to be consistent (e.g., the same module must map the same input to the same output in all executions of the workflow). It is possible that the *Exponential Mechanism* [13], which implements differential privacy in non-numeric domains, can be applied to our problem by suitably defining the feasible output space. However, our initial research shows that even if we ignore the time complexity of implementing this mechanism, the utility guarantee provided is often trivial due to the nature of provenance queries. Defining an appropriate notion of differential privacy for module functionality with respect to provenance queries remains an interesting open problem.

In the next section, we explore the use of differential privacy for hiding *structural* information about a workflow execution.

3   Structural Privacy

The goal of structural privacy is to keep information about the structure of an execution private. For example, we may wish to keep private the information that some module M contributes to the generation of a data item d, output by another module M', or we may wish to keep private all details of some *subworkflow* of the workflow. Alternatively, we may assume that the workflow specification and therefore its structure is known, but that an execution may take only some of the paths in the specification (a departure from our model of the previous section). In this case, we may wish to hide details of a particular *execution*, i.e., which set of paths in the workflow specification were taken during the execution.

We start by discussing structural privacy as it relates to connections and subworkflows, and introduce hierarchical workflow specifications. We then discuss structural privacy as it relates to execution paths, and pursue an approach based on differential privacy.

3.1   Hiding Connections and Subworkflows

Our approach to module privacy in the previous section was to present a *view* of provenance information to users. However, we assumed that users knew the structure of the specification and therefore that data was passed between two module executions, even if they did not know *what value* the data had. Returning to the example in Figure 1, users would know that data was passed $m_1 \longrightarrow m_2$ and $m_2 \longrightarrow m_3$, and that therefore a_7 depends on a_1 via m_1, even if they cannot see the actual data flowing over the edges. In structural privacy, we may wish to keep such dependencies private.

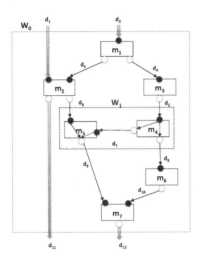

Fig. 3. Hierarchical Workflow Specification

For example, consider the sample workflow in Figure 3, in which modules now have input ports (dark circles) and output ports (white circles), and input/output to the workflow as a whole is indicated by thick edges. Now suppose that we wish to keep certain connections private, for example, the connection between m_4 and m_5. One possible approach is to *delete* edges and vertices from the specification that is seen by the user so as to eliminate all paths from m_4 to m_5, e.g., in this example to delete the edge d_7. However, by doing so, we may hide additional provenance information that does not need be hidden, e.g., the existence of a path from m_3 to m_5. Another approach is to use *clustering*, where certain modules are hidden in a composite module so that modules and edges contained in the new composite module are no longer visible to the user. Returning to our example, we could cluster m_4 and m_5 into a single composite module (indicated by the dotted box labeled W_1). However, if we still assume that all outputs depend on all outputs, we may now infer incorrect provenance information. In our example, since d_8 is an output of W_1, the assumption is that it depends on d_6, which is input to W_1. There is also now a path from m_2 to m_7. This is called an *unsound view* in [11,2]. Both the deletion and clustering approaches yield challenging optimization problems: guaranteeing an adequate level of privacy while preserving soundness and minimizing unnecessary loss of information.

Note that the clustering approach builds on a *hierarchical* model of workflows, i.e., one in which composite modules may themselves expand to subworkflows. For example, in Figure 3 the *root* workflow is W_0, which expands to a subworkflow consisting of modules m_1, m_2, m_3, W_1, m_6 and m_7, and dataflow edges $d_1,...,$ d_6, $d_8,...,d_{12}$. W_1 is a composite module and itself expands to a subworkflow consisting of m_4, m_5 and the edge d_7; the inputs to W_1 are d_5 and d_6, and its outputs are d_8, d_9. In our work [1], we model hierarchical workflows as *graph grammars* in which composite modules expand to one or more subworkflows via *production rules*. This also allows recursion and alternation to be modeled. *Views* of workflow specifications are then defined to allow users to expand only a subset of the production rules. One such view in our example would be to allow the expansion of W_0 but disallow that of W_1. Furthermore, we allow *fine-grained* dependencies between the inputs and outputs of a module to be captured by explicitly modeling the dependencies between input/output ports. These dependencies can also be specified for composite modules, which can be used to avoid the problem of unsound views. Returning to our example, suppose that m_4 and m_5 had full dependencies between their inputs and outputs, as shown by the dotted lines within the module boxes. Then the dependencies specified for W_1 could be that d_9 depends on both inputs, d_5 and d_6, but that d_8 depends only on d_5.

3.2   Hiding Execution Paths

We now turn to the problem of hiding which paths were taken during an execution of the workflow. The motivation for this is that in some applications, a breach of privacy may occur merely by revealing information about the actual sequence of executed modules even when all data is hidden. For example, the set of diagnostic tests conducted on a patient reveals information about her medical condition even when the results of these tests are kept private. We focus here on applications where a user is familiar with the structure of the entire workflow, but for which an execution of a workflow may take only some of the paths represented in the specification. The goal is to reveal *aggregate statistics* for the set of all workflow executions while keeping private the details about which modules were executed in a particular execution.

We again assume that the workflow is given by a DAG, where the nodes correspond to modules and the edges correspond to potential dataflow. A *valid execution* of a workflow is a set of paths from the root, representing the modules that were executed and the actual data that was passed between module executions.

The structure of an execution of the workflow is represented by a boolean vector in $\{0,1\}^N$, where N is the number of modules in the workflow, indicating the set of modules that were executed. Given a set of executions of the workflow, we would like to publish the values X_m representing the number of executions in which a particular module m was involved. Unfortunately, publishing the exact value of X_m for every module m may compromise privacy in certain situations. For example, if the value of X_m for a module m that is executed only if a patient has a particular medical condition changes after inclusion of a new patient's record, it can be inferred that the patient is suffering from that condition. This example exhibits a breach of differential privacy (discussed at the end of the previous section), which requires that the output distribution changes only nominally with the inclusion/deletion of a single record. Our goal, therefore, is to output a sequence of estimates for $\langle X_m \rangle$ that is ϵ-*differentially private* for a given privacy-parameter ϵ.

We also observe that additional constraints may be imposed by the workflow structure. For instance, a control structure (conditional `if-then-else` module) imposes the restriction that only one of its children in the workflow graph can be executed. The solution returned by our mechanism must be *consistent* with such restrictions (e.g., the count of a conditional module in the published answer should be sum of the counts of its children). It is not difficult to show that if a workflow consists of only conditional modules, then privacy and consistency can be simultaneously guaranteed with $O(Nh/\epsilon)$ error in the L_1-accuracy of the counts returned, where N is the number of modules and h is the longest path in the workflow. Our ongoing work aims at extending this initial observation to a comprehensive understanding of the interplay between structural privacy and accuracy for general workflows.

4   Conclusions

The ability to capture, manage and query workflow provenance is increasingly important for scientific as well as business applications. In this paper we discussed the problem of providing useful answers to provenance queries while ensuring that privacy concerns are met. Specifically, we have focused on *module* and *structural* privacy and discussed issues associated with our recent progress in these two directions.

We addressed the problem of preserving module privacy in workflows by providing a view of provenance information in which the input-to-output mapping of private modules remains hidden. As the examples in this paper show, the workflow-privacy of a module critically depends on the structure (connection patterns) of the workflow, the behavior/functionality of other modules in the workflow, and the selection of hidden attributes. We formalized the tradeoff between the utility of the provided provenance information and the privacy it guarantees for modules, and studied the related optimization problems.

For structural privacy we consider two approaches. The first, targeted at reachability queries, is based on fine grained hierarchical workflow specifications as well as the definition of privacy-preserving views over them. The second, targeted at aggregate queries, employs differential privacy. Our ongoing work aims at extending these results to develop a comprehensive understanding of the interplay between structural privacy and accuracy for general workflows. Determining whether differential privacy is applicable also for module privacy is of particular interest here. Finally, the design of efficient query evaluation algorithms in this context is a challenging research direction.

References

1. Bao, Z., Davidson, S., Milo, T.: View-adaptive labeling for fine-grained workflows (submitted)
2. Biton, O., Davidson, S.B., Khanna, S., Roy, S.: Optimizing user views for workflows. In: ICDT 2009: Proceedings of the 12th International Conference on Database Theory, pp. 310–323 (2009)
3. Davidson, S., Milo, T., Roy, S.: A propagation model for provenance views of public/private workflows (submitted)
4. Davidson, S.B., Khanna, S., Milo, T., Panigrahi, D., Roy, S.: Provenance views for module privacy. In: Proceedings of the 30th ACM SIGMOD-SIGACT-SIGART Symposium on Principles of Database Systems, pp. 175–186 (2011)
5. Davidson, S.B., Khanna, S., Roy, S., Stoyanovich, J., Tannen, V., Chen, Y.: On provenance and privacy. In: ICDT, pp. 3–10 (2011)
6. Davidson, S.B., Khanna, S., Tannen, V., Roy, S., Chen, Y., Milo, T., Stoyanovich, J.: Enabling privacy in provenance-aware workflow systems. In: CIDR, pp. 215–218 (2011), http://www.crdrdb.org
7. Dwork, C.: Differential privacy: A survey of results. In: Agrawal, M., Du, D.-Z., Duan, Z., Li, A. (eds.) TAMC 2008. LNCS, vol. 4978, pp. 1–19. Springer, Heidelberg (2008)
8. Dwork, C.: The differential privacy frontier (Extended abstract). In: Reingold, O. (ed.) TCC 2009. LNCS, vol. 5444, pp. 496–502. Springer, Heidelberg (2009)
9. Ganta, S.R., Kasiviswanathan, S.P., Smith, A.: Composition attacks and auxiliary information in data privacy. In: Proceeding of the 14th ACM SIGKDD International Conference on Knowledge Discovery and Data Mining, KDD 2008, pp. 265–273. ACM, New York (2008)
10. Kifer, D.: Attacks on privacy and de Finetti's theorem. In: SIGMOD Conference, pp. 127–138 (2009)
11. Liu, Z., Davidson, S.B., Chen, Y.: Generating sound workflow views for correct provenance analysis. ACM Trans. Database Syst. 36(1), 6 (2011)
12. Machanavajjhala, A., Kifer, D., Gehrke, J., Venkitasubramaniam, M.: L-diversity: Privacy beyond k-anonymity. ACM Trans. Knowl. Discov. Data 1(1), 3 (2007)
13. McSherry, F., Talwar, K.: Mechanism design via differential privacy. In: Proceedings of the 48th Annual IEEE Symposium on Foundations of Computer Science, pp. 94–103. IEEE Computer Society, Washington, DC (2007)

Provenance-Directed Chase&Backchase

Alin Deutsch and Richard Hull

[1] University of California, San Diego
[2] IBM Watson Research Center

Abstract. The Chase&Backchase algorithm for rewriting queries using views is based on constructing a canonical rewriting candidate called a universal plan (during the chase phase), then chasing its exponentially many subqueries in search for minimal rewritings (during the backchase phase). We show that the backchase phase can be sped up significantly if we instrument the standard chase to maintain provenance information. The particular provenance flavor required is known as minimal why-provenance in the literature, and it can be computed by exploiting the analogy between a chase step execution and query evaluation.

1 Chase&Backchase

The Chase&Backchase ($\mathcal{C}\&\mathcal{B}$) is an algorithm for rewriting queries using views while exploiting integrity constraints. It was introduced in [DPT99] for queries and views expressed as conjunctive queries (CQ) and integrity constraints expressed as embedded dependencies [AHV95] ([DPT99] extends the $\mathcal{C}\&\mathcal{B}$ to conjunctive queries over complex-valued and OO data models, not treated here).

The $\mathcal{C}\&\mathcal{B}$ algorithm is based on expressing the view definitions as a set $\mathcal{V}$ of embedded dependencies, then chasing with these as well as with the integrity constraints $\mathcal{I}$. Let us denote the result of chasing a query Q with a set of embedded dependencies $\mathcal{D}$ as $Q^{\mathcal{D}}$. [1] The $\mathcal{C}\&\mathcal{B}$ algorithm proceeds in two phases:

Chase: The input query Q is chased with the view constraints $\mathcal{V}$ and integrity constraints $\mathcal{I}$, to obtain a chase result $Q^{\mathcal{V}\cup\mathcal{I}}$. Next, the subquery U of $Q^{\mathcal{V}\cup\mathcal{I}}$ is produced by restricting $Q^{\mathcal{V}\cup\mathcal{I}}$ to the vocabulary of views. U is called the *universal plan U*.

Backchase: The subqueries of the universal plan U are checked for equivalence (under $\mathcal{I}$ and $\mathcal{V}$) to Q, and all equivalent subqueries are output (as long as they are minimal, i.e. contain no subqueries that are already equivalent to Q).

---

[1] We confine ourselves here to the case when the chase terminates, thus yielding a finite result. It is well-known that this result is not necessarily unique, as it depends on the non-deterministic choices made during the chase sequence among simultaeneously applicable chase steps. However, the result is unique up to homomorphic equivalence [AHV95], which suffices for our purposes. We will therefore refer to "the" chase result in the remainder of this paper.

V. Tannen et al. (Eds.): Buneman Festschrift, LNCS 8000, pp. 227–236, 2013.
© Springer-Verlag Berlin Heidelberg 2013

The equivalence check involves chasing each subquery sq "back" to Q (more precisely, checking that Q has a containment mapping into $sq^{\mathcal{V} \cup \mathcal{I}}$).

We illustrate the $\mathcal{C}\&\mathcal{B}$ algorithm on the following running example (for simplicity, without integrity constraints).

Example 1.1. *Consider the query*

$$Q(x) : -R(x, w, y), S(y, z), T(z, u)$$

and assume that the following views have been defined:

$$V_R(x, y) : - R(x, w, y)$$
$$V_S(y, z) : - S(y, z)$$
$$V_{RS}(x, z) : - R(x, w, y), S(y, z)$$
$$V_T(z, u) : - T(z, u)$$

It is easy to see that

$$R_1(x) : - V_R(x, y), V_S(y, z), V_T(z, u)$$
$$R_2(x) : - V_{RS}(x, z), V_T(z, u)$$

are equivalent rewritings of Q using the views. Also, each rewriting is minimal, in the sense that no atom of its definition can be removed while preserving equivalence to Q.

To find these rewritings, the $\mathcal{C}\&\mathcal{B}$ algorithm prescribes capturing the view definitions by a set $\mathcal{V}$ of embedded dependencies. These are obtained canonically by stating the inclusion (in both directions) between the result of the query defining each view and the view's extent. For the example, $\mathcal{V}$ is the following set of dependencies (as usual in the literature, free variables are to be read as universally quantified):

$$c_{V_R} : R(x, w, y) \rightarrow V_R(x, y)$$
$$b_{V_R} : V_R(x, y) \rightarrow \exists w \; R(x, w, y)$$

$$c_{V_S} : S(y, z) \rightarrow V_S(y, z)$$
$$b_{V_S} : V_S(y, z) \rightarrow S(y, z)$$

$$c_{V_{RS}} : R(x, w, y) \wedge S(y, z) \rightarrow V_{RS}(x, z)$$
$$b_{V_{RS}} : V_{RS}(x, z) \rightarrow \exists w, y \; R(x, w, y) \wedge S(y, z)$$

$$c_{V_T} : T(z, u) \rightarrow V_T(z, u)$$
$$b_{V_T} : V_T(z, u) \rightarrow T(z, u)$$

The Chase Phase. *When chasing Q with $\mathcal{V}$, the only chase steps that apply involve $c_{V_R}, c_{V_S}, c_{V_T}, c_{V_{RS}}$, yielding chase result*

$$Q^{\mathcal{V}}(x) : -R(x, w, y), S(y, z), T(z, u), V_R(x, y), V_S(y, z), V_T(z, u), V_{RS}(x, z).$$

The restriction of $Q^{\mathcal{V}}$ to the schema of the views yields the universal plan

$$U(x) : -V_R(x, y), V_S(y, z), V_T(z, u), V_{RS}(x, z).$$

The Backchase Phase. *In this phase, the subqueries of U are inspected. Notice that R_1, R_2 above are among them.*

We illustrate only for the suqbquery of U corresponding to R_2. To show that R_2 is equivalent to Q, we chase R_2 with $\mathcal{V}$ and we search for a containment mapping from Q into $R_2^{\mathcal{V}}$. The only applicable chase steps involve $b_{V_{RS}}, b_{V_T}$, yielding the result

$$R_2^{\mathcal{V}}(x) : -V_{RS}(x, z), V_T(z, u), R(x, w, y), S(y, z), T(z, u).$$

Since the identity mapping on variables is a containment mapping from Q to $R_2^{\mathcal{V}}$, R_2 is equivalent to Q, and thus a rewriting. R_2 is moreover minimal, since none of its subqueries is a rewriting of Q (the backchase checks this). R_2 is therefore output by the $\mathcal{C}\&\mathcal{B}$ algorithm.

R_1 is discovered analogously.

It turns out that there are no other minimal rewritings of Q. The backchase phase determines this by systematically checking the other subqueries of U, but discarding them as not being equivalent to Q, or not being minimal. For instance, the subquery

$$sq(x) : -V_R(x, u), V_T(z, u)$$

is not a rewriting of Q, and the subquery

$$sq'(x) : -V_S(y, z), V_T(z, u), V_{RS}(x, z)$$

is a rewriting but is not minimal.

Completeness of the $\mathcal{C}\&\mathcal{B}$ Algorithm. The fact that rewritings R_1 and R_2 in Example 1.1 are discovered among the subqueries of U is not accidental. In [DPT99], it was shown that all minimal rewritings of Q are (isomorphic to) subqueries of U, in the absence of integrity constraints. The result was extended to the presence of integrity constraints expressed as embedded dependencies as long as the chase with them terminates (Theorem 1 in [DT03b]; the proof can be found in [Deu02]; see also [DPT06]). The result was further extended to queries and views expressed as unions of conjunctive queries, and disjunctive embedded dependencies [DT03b, Deu02].

Implementation of $\mathcal{C}\&\mathcal{B}$ Rewriting. The first $\mathcal{C}\&\mathcal{B}$ implementation is described in [PDST00], where the backchase phase is identified as the performance bottleneck. This is expected, since exponentially many subqueries of the universal plan are checked for equivalence with the original query, and each equivalence check involves a chase. While [DPT99] shows that this brute-force search is optimal from a complexity-theoretic point of view, [PDST00] concerns itself with practical feasibility and proposes techniques for pruning the search while preserving completeness. Essentially, these boil down to enumerating subqueries of the universal plan U in a bottom-up fashion, starting with all single-atom subqueries, next with two-atom subqueries, etc. Since the backchase searches for minimal rewritings, this bottom-up strategy allows pruning the equivalence check for all subqueries sq of U that already include a rewriting as subquery, since all such sq are non-minimal. In Example 1.1, subquery sq' would be pruned this way.

Even with bottom-up pruning, exponentially many subqueries remain to be chased in the worst case. In practice, this worst case occurs often, for instance when there is no rewriting of the query using the views. In this case the pruning never kicks in and all possible subqueries of U need to be checked. To deal with this case, [PDST00] proposes first checking that Q has a rewriting, before even starting the subquery enumeration. This check is performed as follows.

A corollary of the completeness of the $\mathcal{C\&B}$ algorithm states that Q has a rewriting using the views if and only if it has a containment mapping into $U' = U^{\mathcal{V} \cup \mathcal{I}}$, i.e. into the result of chasing the universal plan U with the dependencies in $\mathcal{V}$ and $\mathcal{I}$. In practical implementations (e.g. in [PDST00]), the existence of a containment mapping from Q into U' is checked by treating U' as a small symbolic database instance (known as "canonical" instance in the literature [AHV95]), and evaluating Q over it. This amounts to computing the set of *all* containment mappings from Q into U', and checking its non-emptiness.

Example 1.2. *Revisiting Example 1.1, a possible chase sequence of U with $\mathcal{V}$ involves, in order, chase steps with b_{RS}, b_R, b_S and b_T, yielding*

$$U^{\mathcal{V}}(x) : - V_R(x,y), V_S(y,z), V_T(z,u), V_{RS}(x,z),$$
$$R(x,w_1,y), S(y,z), T(z,u), R(x,w_2,y_2), S(y_2,z).$$

If we evaluate Q over the canonical instance of $U^{\mathcal{V}}$, we obtain the containment mappings $h_1 = \{x \mapsto x, y \mapsto y, w \mapsto w_1, z \mapsto z, u \mapsto u\}$ and $h_2 = \{x \mapsto x, y \mapsto y_2, w \mapsto w_2, z \mapsto z, u \mapsto u\}$. Therefore, U is a (redundant) rewriting of Q, and it makes sense to start inspecting its subqueries in search of minimal rewritings.

[PDST00], and the follow-up work in [DT03a] show that the effort of chasing U itself is in practice comparable to that of chasing any subquery of U, since the chase can be made particularly fast by implementing it as query evaluation over a canonical database of toy dimensions. The rewriting existence check is therefore shown to be well worth the effort: it bounds the overhead to an exponential fraction of the backchase runtime and yields up to exponential speedup (realized whenever there is no rewriting).

[PDST00] also presents a suite of techniques which further prune the search, when instead of all minimal rewritings one only seeks a cheapest rewriting according to a cost estimator. This setting is relevant in query optimization. It is shown how cost estimation can be interleaved with the bottom-up backchase. If the cost model satisfies reasonable assumptions like monotonicity, the resulting algorithm is shown to preserve the guarantee of finding a cheapest rewriting while pruning all subqueries whose cost exceeds the best found so far, even without chasing them to check if they are rewritings. In this paper we do not concern ourselves with cost-based pruning, focusing on enumeration of all minimal rewritings.

2   Provenance-Directed $\mathcal{C}\&\mathcal{B}$

The remainder of this paper shows that significantly more can be done to prune the search for all minimal rewritings while preserving completeness, assuming that the chase procedure used in the backchase phase is instrumented to maintain provenance information.

Intuitively, the original backchase enumerates the subqueries of the universal plan U in a bottom-up fashion and chases each of them in isolation from the others, to determine equivalence to the input query Q. This leads to *redundant chasing* of the atoms occurring in common within distinct subqueries of U. It also leads to *fruitless chasing* when the chosen subquery ends up not being equivalent to Q.

Example 2.1. *In our running example, the bottom-up backchase search prunes all strict superqueries of R_1, R_2 except U. This leads to pruning subqueries $V_R \wedge V_{RS} \wedge V_T$ and $V_S \wedge V_{RS} \wedge V_T$.[2]*

In addition, the backchase will prune those subqueries that do not contain the universal plan's head variables, as only safe rewritings are of interest (e.g. it will prune V_S, and $V_S \wedge V_T$).

However, the backchase still carries out fruitless chases of the following 7 subqueries of U

$$V_R, V_{RS},$$
$$V_R \wedge V_S, V_R \wedge V_T, V_R \wedge V_{RS}, V_S \wedge V_{RS},$$
$$V_R \wedge V_S \wedge V_{RS}$$

only to determine that none of them are rewritings of Q.

One might wonder why the backchase won't more aggressively prune away all subqueries that don't even mention all relations mentioned by Q. In our example, this would immediately dismiss all 7 subqueries listed above. Note that this aggressive pruning is unsafe in general, in the sense of compromising completeness of the backchase. Indeed, if the set of constraints includes tuple-generating dependencies (such as foreign key constraints), the minimal rewritings do not

---

[2] To avoid clutter, in the running example we specify universal plan subqueries by mentioning only the view names of involved atoms. This is not ambiguous since U contains no distinct atoms with the same view name. We also omit the specification of the distinguished variables, as these are in all cases (x).

necessarily mention all relations mentioned by the query. It is easy to construct such examples: for instance, assume that the second component of S is a foreign key referencing the first component of T. Then subqueries $V_R \wedge V_S$ and V_{RS} are minimal rewritings that would be missed by the aggressive pruning.

Notice how, across rewritings R_1 and R_2, the common V_T atom is chased redundantly multiple times (once when chasing U, then again when chasing R_1, and also when chasing R_2, and in the fruitless chases of the three above-listed subqueries involving V_T).

Our aim is to minimize both fruitless and redundant chasing.

The solution we propose starts from the observation that, while chasing the universal plan U to check the existence of a rewriting, we simltaneously chase all of its subqueries, though not in isolation as in original backchase, but collectively. This collective chase will duplicate all chase steps of the isolated chases, possibly enabling strictly more chase steps that result from the interaction between simultaneous chases of the subqueries. More formally, the nature of the chase implies the following fact:

Fact 1. *The union of the results of chasing each subquery of U in isolation maps homomorphically into the result of chasing U itself.*

Fact 1 follows immediately from the fact that all chase steps that fire on an isolated subquery of U also fire on its isomorphic copy in U.

Now note that each containment mapping image i of Q in U' must have been introduced because of the presence of certain atoms in U (which induce a subquery of U). But by Fact 1 above, those subqueries of U who do not contribute to the creation of an image of Q even when chased collectively with the other subqueries, will certainly not do so when chased in isolation. Therefore, they cannot be rewritings of Q. Our goal is to dismiss these subqueries immediately, without chasing them in isolation, thus saving the effort when compared to the original backchase. As it turns out, we can do even better than that, avoiding the redundant effort across isolated chases of the remaining subqueries.

To this end, we propose a new backchase strategy that keeps track of the provenance of each atom a in U', where the *provenance* of a gives the set(s) of view atoms from U whose chasing led to the introduction of a into U'. This provenance information enables us to run Q over the canonical instance of U', identify each image i of Q into U', and trace it back to the subquery sq of U that is responsible for the creation of i during the chase of U. The search for rewriting candidates thus confines itself to the set of provenances of the images of Q into U'. This set is significantly smaller than the set of all subqueries of U. Indeed, in most cases we have encountered in practice, the backchase was exploring a large fraction of the exponentially many subqueries of U, even when there were only very few minimal rewritings.

Example 2.2. *We illustrate by revisiting Example 1.2. We show again $U^{\mathcal{V}}$, this time annotating the atoms of $U^{\mathcal{V}}$ with their provenance in terms of the view atoms in U. Since U contains no two atoms using the same view name, we drop* *the variables from the provenance annotation, to avoid clutter. The provenance annotations appear as superscripts.*

$$U^{\mathcal{V}}(x) :- \overbrace{V_R(x,y)}^{V_R}, \overbrace{V_S(y,z)}^{V_S}, \overbrace{V_T(z,u)}^{V_T}, \overbrace{V_{RS}(x,z)}^{V_{RS}},$$
$$\overbrace{R(x,w_1,y)}^{V_R}, \overbrace{S(y,z)}^{V_S}, \overbrace{T(z,u)}^{V_T}, \overbrace{R(x,w_2,y_2)}^{V_{RS}}, \overbrace{S(y_2,z)}^{V_{RS}}.$$

Note that the view atoms in $U^{\mathcal{V}}$ are annotated with themselves, as they are not introduced by chasing, but instead inherited directly from U. The R, S, T atoms in $U^{\mathcal{V}}$ are introduced by the chase, for instance the first R atom stems from chasing $V_R(x,y)$ with view dependency b_{V_R}, while the second R atom stems from chasing $V_{RS}(x,z)$ with $b_{V_{RS}}$.

Recall from Example 1.2 that Q has precisely two containment mapping images into $U^{\mathcal{V}}$: one given by h_1, comprising the T atom and the first R and S atoms, and another given by h_2, comprising the T atom and the second R and S atoms. The provenance of the first image of Q is $V_R \wedge V_S \wedge V_T$, which corresponds to rewriting R_1 in Example 1.1, while the provenance of the second image is $V_T \wedge V_{RS}$, corresponding to rewriting R_2 in the running example.

Notice how by computing the containment mappings of Q into $U^{\mathcal{V}}$ (a step that is already carried out in the original $\mathcal{C}\&\mathcal{B}$ algorithm), we immediately identify the two rewritings of Q, saving the fruitless individual chases of the subqueries listed in Example 2.1.

Also notice how, across the two remaining subqueries, R_1 and R_2, the common V_T atom is only chased once and for all when chasing U, saving the redundant chasing that would have resulted from chasing R_1 and R_2 in isolation (as prescribed by the original backchase).

2.1   Provenance-Aware Chase

We next detail the notion of provenance formula and how to instrument the chase to keep book of provenance information. We call the resulting chase *provenance-aware*. The proposed bookkeeping exploits the analogy between chase step application and query evaluation, with the chase-maintained provenance paralleling the *minimal why-provenance* flavor introduced for query evaluation in [BKT01].[3]

Intuitively, the provenance of an atom a is meant to specify the universal plan subqueries whose chase constructs atom a. This information is captured in the form of expressions obtained by starting with universal plan atoms as terms and combining them using logical conjunction and disjunction. To define the provenance of an atom in the chase result, we introduce some notation first. Given an atom a, its provenance formula is denoted as $\pi(a)$. For set/conjunction of atoms A, the provenance is the logical conjunction of the provenances of A's elements: $\pi(A) = \bigwedge_{a \in A} \pi(a)$.

---

[3] This analogy is already exploited in the original $\mathcal{C}\&\mathcal{B}$ implementation, to speed up standard chase step evaluation.

We define the provenance-aware chase only for embedded dependencies corresponding to tuple-generating dependencies (tgds), i.e. dependencies in which the conclusion of the implication contains no equality atoms [AHV95]. This leaves out equality-generating dependencies (egds) which we do not treat here for simplicity sake. Notice that all dependencies in $\mathcal{V}$ are tgds, and in general tgds can express such integrity constraints as inclusion dependencies and beyond, but cannot express key constraints and functional dependencies in general.

Provenance-Aware Chase Step. The provenance-aware chase of the universal plan builds provenance formulae inductively as follows:

- For each atom a of the universal plan U, let $\pi(a) = a$.
- Let ρ be an instance. Let d be a tgd of the form

$$d : \; premise(\bar{x}) \to \exists \bar{y} \; conclusion(\bar{x}, \bar{y})$$

where *premise* and *conclusion* are conjunctions of relational atoms and $\bar{x}$, $\bar{y}$ are vectors of variables. Let h be a homomorphism from *premise* into ρ.
We say that the chase step of ρ with d under h *does not apply* if there is an extension $\bar{h}$ of h to a homomorphism from *conclusion* into ρ, such that $\pi(h(premise))$ implies $\pi(\bar{h}(conclusion))$.
If the chase step does apply, then it yields ρ' obtained from ρ by adding new atoms precisely as the standard chase would, and annotating each of them with $\pi(h(premise))$. If ρ already contains atom a with provenance p_1, and the chase step introduces atom a with provenance p_2, this is represented in ρ' by keeping a single copy of a, with provenance $p_1 \vee p_2$.

Note that the provenance-aware chase constructs atoms just like the standard chase, but annotates them with provenance formulae, and has a more refined step applicability test. In the standard chase a step with tgd d under homomorpism h does not apply when the conclusion is already witnessed by atoms in ρ. In contrast, in the provenance-aware chase, we need to further make sure that these witness atoms of d's conclusion stem from the same view atoms whose chase yielded the image under h of d's premise.

Also note that the provenance formulae use logical conjunction and disjunction with their expected properties such as commutativity, distributivit, idempotence and absorption. This corresponds to the minimal why-provenance of [BKT01] and is a particular case of a provenance semiring [GKT07].

2.2 Provenance-Directed Backchase

Once the universal plan U is provenance-aware-chased into result U', it is easy to "read off" the subqueries of U (if any) that chase into results that accommodate containment mappings from Q. These subqueries are rewritings of Q using the views.

To find them, we simply run Q over U' to compute all containment mappings from former to latter. We denote their set with $\mathcal{H}$. For each containment mapping

$h \in \mathcal{H}$, the provenance information of Q's image under h, $\pi(h(Q))$, gives the subquery of U whose chase led to this image (and therefore is a rewriting of Q). Let us denote this set of rewritings as $\mathcal{R} = \{\pi(h(Q)) \mid h \in \mathcal{H}\}$. It can be shown that set $\mathcal{R}$ contains all minimal rewritings of Q using the views, but it may also contain some non-minimal rewritings. These are easily identified, as they contain as subquery some other rewriting from $\mathcal{R}$. The provenance-directed backchase purges these rewritings from $\mathcal{R}$ and returns the result.

The above processing can be equivalently cast in terms relating to querying provenance-annotated databases:

The provenance-directed backchase consists in running Q over the canonical instance of U' while keeping track of the *minimal why-provenance* [BKT01] of the result. The provenance of the tuple corresponding to Q's distinguished variables corresponds straightforwardly to subqueries of U, all of which are returned.

Example 2.3. *Recalling Example 2.2, the provenance of tuple (x) in the answer of Q over $U^{\mathcal{V}}$ is $(V_R \wedge V_S \wedge V_T) \vee (V_{RS} \wedge V_T)$, which is minimal (neither conjunct contains the other). Each of the conjuncts corresponds to a rewriting of Q: the first to R_2, the second to R_1.*

2.3   Putting It All Together

We summarize the provenance-aware $\mathcal{C\&B}$ below.

algorithm $\mathcal{C\&B}_{\mathbf{V}}^{\mathcal{I}}$
params: set $\mathbf{V}$ of CQ views, captured using set $\mathcal{V}$ of tgds,
    set $\mathcal{I}$ of integrity constraints expressed as tgds with terminating chase

input: CQ query Q,
output: all minimal CQ rewritings of Q using views from $\mathbf{V}$ under $\mathcal{I}$

//chase phase:
1. compute universal plan U
 by standard-chasing Q with $\mathcal{V} \cup \mathcal{I}$ and keeping only view atoms

//provenance-directed backchase phase:
2. compute U' by provenance-aware-chasing U with $\mathcal{V} \cup \mathcal{I}$
3. run Q over U', computing the
 minimal why-provenance of the tuple corresponding to Q's head variables.
4. return the subqueries of U defined by this provenance.

We can show that the directed backchase preserves completeness:

Theorem 2.1. *If the set of integrity constraints $\mathcal{I}$ consists of tgds only (with terminating chase), then the provenance-directed $\mathcal{C\&B}$ is sound and complete. That is, $\mathcal{C\&B}_{\mathbf{V}}^{\mathcal{I}}$ finds all and only the minimal rewritings of the input query using the views $\mathbf{V}$ under $\mathcal{I}$.*

3   Conclusion

Chase step execution is in essence query evaluation, and therefore there is a natural way to extend the standard chase to be provenance-aware. This exention is particulary useful when the chase is employed within the $C\&B$ algorithm for rewriting queries using views. By using provenance-aware chasing during the $C\&B$'s backchase phase, we can directly "read" the rewritings from the result of chasing back the universal plan U, thus saving the effort of running isolated chases for exponentially many subqueries of U.

Note that instrumenting the standard chase to keep provenance information introduces ovehead at runtime. We expect this overhead to be negligible, being more than made up for by the performance savings over the standard backchase. Definitive confirmation requires experimental evaluation, which we leave for future work.

Acknowledgement. This work is dedicated to Peter Buneman. Both the $C\&B$ project and the provenance project starting with [BKT01] originated in Penn's Database Lab. At the time, Peter was playing a key leadership role in the lab, and the first author was a graduate student educating himself on the chase by reading the chapter in [AHV95] written by the second author.

References

[AHV95]   Abiteboul, S., Hull, R., Vianu, V.: Foundations of Databases. Addison-Wesley (1995)

[BKT01]   Buneman, P., Khanna, S., Tan, W.-C.: Why and where: A characterization of data provenance. In: Van den Bussche, J., Vianu, V. (eds.) ICDT 2001. LNCS, vol. 1973, pp. 316–330. Springer, Heidelberg (2000)

[Deu02]   Deutsch, A.: XML Query Reformulation Over Mixed and Redundant Storage. PhD thesis, University of Pennsylvania (2002)

[DPT99]   Deutsch, A., Popa, L., Tannen, V.: Physical data independence, constraints, and optimization with universal plans. In: VLDB, pp. 459–470 (1999)

[DPT06]   Deutsch, A., Popa, L., Tannen, V.: Query reformulation with constraints. SIGMOD Record 35(1), 65–73 (2006)

[DT03a]   Deutsch, A., Tannen, V.: Mars: A system for publishing xml from mixed and redundant storage. In: VLDB, pp. 201–212 (2003)

[DT03b]   Deutsch, A., Tannen, V.: Reformulation of XML queries and constraints. In: Calvanese, D., Lenzerini, M., Motwani, R. (eds.) ICDT 2003. LNCS, vol. 2572, pp. 225–238. Springer, Heidelberg (2002)

[GKT07]   Green, T.J., Karvounarakis, G., Tannen, V.: Provenance semirings. In: PODS, pp. 31–40 (2007)

[PDST00]   Popa, L., Deutsch, A., Sahuguet, A., Tannen, V.: A chase too far? In: ACM SIGMOD Conference, pp. 273–284 (2000)

Data Quality Problems beyond Consistency and Deduplication

Wenfei Fan[1], Floris Geerts[2], Shuai Ma[3], Nan Tang[4], and Wenyuan Yu[1]

[1] University of Edinburgh, UK
wenfei@inf.ed.ac.uk, wenyuan.yu@ed.ac.uk
[2] University of Antwerp, Belgium
floris.geerts@ua.ac.be
[3] SKLSDE Lab, Beihang University, China
mashuai@buaa.edu.cn
[4] Qatar Computing Research Institute, Qatar
ntang@qf.org.qa

Abstract. Recent work on data quality has primarily focused on data repairing algorithms for improving data consistency and record matching methods for data deduplication. This paper accentuates several other challenging issues that are essential to developing data cleaning systems, namely, error correction with performance guarantees, unification of data repairing and record matching, relative information completeness, and data currency. We provide an overview of recent advances in the study of these issues, and advocate the need for developing a logical framework for a uniform treatment of these issues.

1 Introduction

Data quality has been a longstanding line of research for decades [20]. It is estimated that dirty data costs US companies alone 600 billion dollars each year [9]. With this comes the need for data cleaning systems to improve data quality, and to add accuracy and value to business processes. As an example, data cleaning tools deliver "an overall business value of more than 600 million GBP" each year at BT [31]. In light of this, the market for data cleaning systems is growing at 17% annually, substantially outpacing the 7% average of other IT segments [21].

There has been a host of work on data quality. Recent work has primarily focused on two central issues:

- *Recording matching*: to identify tuples that refer to the same real-world entity [10], for data deduplication.
- *Data repairing*: to find a repair (database) that is consistent *w.r.t.* integrity constraints and minimally differs from the original data, by detecting and fixing (semantic) errors, to improve data consistency [1].

Most data cleaning systems on the market support record matching, *e.g.*, ETL tools (extraction, transformation, loading; see [24] for a survey). Some prototype systems also provide a data repairing functionality [3,6,28,37].

V. Tannen et al. (Eds.): Buneman Festschrift, LNCS 8000, pp. 237–249, 2013.
© Springer-Verlag Berlin Heidelberg 2013

There are other data quality issues that are not limited to algorithms for record matching or data repairing, but are also essential to developing practical data cleaning systems. Unfortunately, these issues have not received much attention from the research community. In particular, we highlight the following.

(1) Certain fixes. Prior data repairing methods are typically heuristic. They attempt to fix all the errors in the data, but do not guarantee that the generated fixes are correct. Worse still, new errors may be introduced when trying to repair the data. In practice, we often want to find *certain fixes*, *i.e.*, fixes that are guaranteed to be correct, although we might not be able to fix *all* the errors in the data. The need for certain fixes is particularly evident when repairing critical data, *e.g.*, medical data, in which a seemingly minor error may mean life or death.

(2) Unification of data repairing and record matching. Data repairing and record matching are typically treated as independent processes. However, the two processes often interact with each other: repairing helps us identify matches, and vice versa. This suggests that we unify repairing and matching by interleaving their operations.

(3) Information completeness. A data cleaning system should be able to tell us, given a database D and a query Q, whether D has complete information to answer Q. If the information is missing from D, the answer to Q in D is hardly sensible. Information completeness is as important as data consistency and deduplication. Indeed, pieces of information perceived as being needed for clinical decisions were missing from 13.6% to 81% of the time [29]. Traditionally we deal with this issue by adopting either the Closed World Assumption (CWA) or the Open World Assumption (OWA). However, real-life databases are often neither entirely closed-world nor entirely open-world. This asks for a revision of the CWA, OWA and the model of information completeness.

(4) Data currency. The quality of data in a real-life database quickly degenerates over time. It is estimated that "2% of records in a customer file become obsolete in one month" [9]. That is, in a database of 500 000 customer records, 10 000 records may go stale per month, 120 000 records per year, and within two years about 50% of all the records may be obsolete. As a result, we often find that multiple values of the same entity reside in a database, which were *once correct, i.e.*, they were true values of the entity at some time, but most of them have become *obsolete* and *inaccurate*. This highlights the need for studying *data currency*, to identify the current values of entities in a database, and to answer queries with the current values.

This paper aims to bring attention to these issues. We present an overview of recent work on these four issues (in Sections 2– 5, respectively). We argue that these issues interact with each other and also interact with data repairing and record matching; they should be uniformly treated in a logical framework (Section 6). We refer to the monograph [15] for a more complete treatment of these issues.

	FN	LN	AC	phn	type	str	city	zip	item	when	where
t_1:	Bob	Brady	020	079172485	2	null	Edi	EH7 4AH	CD	7pm, 28/08/2010	UK
t_2:	Max	Smith	131	6884593	1	5 Oak St	Ldn	EH8 9HL	CD	06/11/2009	UK
t_3:	Mark	Smith	131	6884563	1	null	Edi	null	DVD	1pm, 06/11/2009	US

(a) Example input tuples t_1 and t_2

	FN	LN	AC	Hphn	Mphn	str	city	zip	gender
s_1:	Robert	Brady	131	6682845	079172485	51 Elm Row	Edi	EH7 4AH	M
s_2:	Mark	Smith	131	6884563	075568485	5 Oak St	Edi	EH8 9HL	M

(b) Example master relation D_m

Fig. 1. Example input tuples and master relation

2 Certain Fixes Instead of Heuristics Repairs

Data repairing detects and fixes errors by using integrity constraints, such that data conflicts and errors emerge as violations of the constraints. A variety of constraints have been studied for data repairing, such as denial constraints [3], traditional functional and inclusion dependencies [1], and conditional dependencies [4, 6, 16, 37].

Integrity constraints are capable of detecting whether the data is dirty, *i.e.*, the presence of errors in the data. However, they do not tell us which attributes of a tuple have errors and how we should correct the errors.

Example 1: Consider an input tuple t_1 given in Fig. 1(a). It specifies a transaction record (tran) of a credit card: an item purchased at place where and time when, by a UK customer who is identified by name (FN, LN), phone number (area code AC and phone phn) and address (street str, city, zip code). Here phn is either home phone or mobile phone, indicated by type (1 or 2, respectively). It is known that when AC is 020, city should be London (Ldn), and when AC is 131, city must be Edinburgh (Edi). This semantics of the data can be expressed as conditional functional dependencies (CFDs [16]). The CFDs detect that tuple t_1 is *inconsistent*: $t_1[AC] = 020$ but $t_1[city] = Edi$. However, they do not tell us which of $t_1[AC]$ and $t_1[city]$ is wrong, and to what value it should be changed.

In light of this, prior data repairing methods are *heuristic*: they do not guarantee to find correct fixes in data repairing. Worse still, they may introduce new errors when trying to repair the data. Indeed, the correct values of $t_1[AC, city]$ are (131, Edi). Nevertheless, all of the prior methods may opt to change $t_1[city]$ to Ldn; this does not fix the erroneous attribute $t_1[AC]$ and worse still, messes up the correct attribute $t[city]$. □

In practice it is often necessary to guarantee each fix to be *certain*, *i.e.*, assured correct (validated). This can done by using master data and editing rules. *Master data (a.k.a. reference data)* is a single repository of high-quality data that provides various applications in an enterprise with a synchronized, consistent view of its core business entities [27]. It is increasingly common for enterprises to maintain master data. *Editing rules* tell us which attributes of a tuple are wrong and what values from master data they should take, provided that some attributes are validated. As opposed to integrity constraints, they specify updates and have a *dynamic* semantics.

Example 2: A master relation D_m is shown in Fig. 1(b). Each tuple in D_m specifies a UK credit card holder (card) in terms of the name, home phone (Hphn), mobile phone (Mphn), address and gender. Consider the following editing rules:

- eR$_1$: for an input tuple t, if there exists a master tuple s in D_m such that $s[\mathsf{zip}] = t[\mathsf{zip}]$, then t should be updated by $t[\mathsf{AC, str, city}] := s[\mathsf{AC, str, city}]$, provided that $t[\mathsf{zip}]$ is validated (*e.g.*, assured by the users).
- eR$_2$: if $t[\mathsf{type}] = 2$ (indicating mobile phone) and if there exists a master tuple s with $s[\mathsf{phn}] = t[\mathsf{Mphn}]$, then $t[\mathsf{FN, LN}] := s[\mathsf{FN, LN}]$, as long as $t[\mathsf{phn, type}]$ are already validated.

When $t_1[\mathsf{zip}]$ is assured correct, eR$_1$ *corrects* attribute $t_1[\mathsf{AC}]$ and enriches $t_1[\mathsf{str}]$ by taking values from master data $s_1[\mathsf{AC, str}]$. Note that when the editing rule and $t_1[\mathsf{zip}]$ are validated, the fix to $t_1[\mathsf{AC}]$ is certainly correct. Similarly, when $t_1[\mathsf{Mphn, type}]$ are validated, eR$_2$ *standardizes* $t_1[\mathsf{FN}]$ by changing Bob to Robert.   □

Certain Fixes. More specifically, we define certain fixes as follows (see [19] for details). Consider an input tuple t and a set Z of attributes such that $t[Z]$ is validated. We use $t \rightarrow_{(\varphi, t_m, Z)} t'$ to denote that tuple t' is obtained from t by means of updates specified in an editing rule φ with a master tuple t_m. We denote by $\mathsf{ext}(Z, \varphi, t_m)$ the *validated region* of t', which includes attributes in Z and the attributes updated by φ with t_m.

Given a set Θ of editing rules and master data D_m, we say that a tuple t' is a *fix* of t by (Θ, D_m), denoted by $t \rightarrow^*_{(\Theta, D_m, Z)} t'$, if there exists a finite sequence $t_0 = t, t_1, \ldots, t_k = t'$ of tuples, and for each $i \in [1, k]$, there exists an editing rule $\varphi_i \in \Theta$ and a master tuple $t_{m_i} \in D_m$ such that (a) $t_{i-1} \rightarrow_{(\varphi_i, t_{m_i}, Z_{i-1})} t_i$, where $Z_i = \mathsf{ext}(Z_{i-1}, \varphi_i, t_{m_{i-1}})$; (b) $t_i[Z] = t[Z]$; and (c) for all $\varphi \in \Theta$ and $t_m \in D_m$, $t' \rightarrow_{(\varphi, t_m, Z_m)} t'$. Intuitively, (a) each step of the correcting process is justified; (b) $t[Z]$ is validated and hence, remains unchanged; and (c) t' is a fixpoint and cannot be further updated, *i.e.*, the changes incurred to t by (Θ, D_m) are "maximum".

We say that t has a *certain fix* by (Θ, D_m) *w.r.t.* Z if there exists a *unique* t' such that $t \rightarrow^*_{(\Theta, D_m, Z)} t'$.

Given a set Θ of editing rules and master data D_m, one can monitor input tuples and find their certain fixes. For each tuple t, the user may assure that a (possible empty) set $t[Z]$ of attributes is correct. There is an algorithm that, given Z, iteratively employs Θ and D_m to find a certain fix for as many attributes in t as possible. The correctness of the fix is guaranteed by master data and editing rules. As opposed to data repairing, we do not stress fixing all the attributes of t by requiring the users to validate a large region $t[Z]$. Nevertheless, when the users opt to find a certain fix for the entire t, there is an algorithm that, given Z, identifies a *minimal* set Z' of attributes such that when $t[Z \cup Z']$ is validated, a certain fix for t is warranted [19]. One can recommend $t[Z']$ to the users for validating, and the users may respond with more validated attributes (not necessarily $t[Z']$). From these an interactive process readily follows that proceeds until all the attributes of t are validated.

Fundamental Problems. There are several important problems associated with certain fixes. Consider tuples of a relation schema R. One problem is to determine, given a set Θ of editing rules, master data D_m, and a set Z of attributes of schema R, whether for all tuples t of R, if $t[Z]$ is validated then t has a certain fix by (Θ, D_m). In other words, it is to determine whether Θ and D_m have conflicts. Another problem is to find, given Θ and D_m, a minimal set Z of attributes such that for all tuples t of schema R, if $t[Z]$ is validated then all the attributes of t can be validated by (Θ, D_m). Intuitively, it is to find a minimal region for the users to validate. It is shown that these are intractable [19], but efficient heuristic algorithms have been developed for these problems.

3   Interaction between Repairing and Record Matching

Current data cleaning systems typically treat data repairing and record matching as separate processes, executed consecutively one after another. In practice, the two processes often interact with each other, as illustrated below.

Example 3: Consider the transaction records of Fig. 1(a) and master data for credit card holders given in Fig. 1(b), referred to as tran and card tuples, respectively. Following [11,16], we use CFDs [16] φ_1–φ_2 to specify the consistency of the tran data, and a *matching dependency* (MD) [11] ψ as a rule for matching tran records and card tuples:

φ_1: tran($[AC = 131] \rightarrow [city = Edi]$),
φ_2: tran($[type = 1, city, phn] \rightarrow [str, AC, zip]$),
ψ: tran[LN, city, str, zip] = card[LN, city, str, zip] $\wedge$ tran[FN] $\approx$ card[FN]
$\wedge$ tran[type] $= 1 \rightarrow$ tran[FN, phn] $\rightleftharpoons$ card[FN, Hphn]

Here (1) CFD φ_1 asserts that if the area code is 131, the city must be Edi; (2) CFD φ_2 states that when type $= 1$ (*i.e.,* phn is mobile phone), city and home phone uniquely determine street, area code and zip code; and (3) MD ψ assures that for any tran record t and any card tuple, if they have the same last name and address, and if their first names are *similar*, then their home phone and FN attributes can be identified (when $t[type] = 1$).

Consider tuples t_2 and t_3 in Fig. 1(a). One suspects that the two refer to the same person. If so, then these records show that the same person made purchases in the UK and in the US at about the same time (taking into account the 5-hour time difference between the two countries), indicating that a fraud has likely been committed.

Observe that t_2 and t_3 are quite different in their FN, city, str, zip and phn attributes. No rule allows us to identify the two directly. Nonetheless, they can be matched by *interleaved* matching and repairing operations:

(a) get a repair t_2' of t_2 such that $t_2'[city] = Edi$ by applying CFD φ_1 to t_2;

(b) match t_2' with master tuple s_2, to which MD ψ can be applied; as a result of the matching operation, get a repair t_2'' of t_2 by correcting $t_2''[phn]$ with the master data $s_2[Hphn] = 6884563$;

(c) find a repair t_3' of t_3 by applying CFD φ_2 to t_2'' and t_3: since t_2'' and t_3 agree on their city and phn attributes and $t_2''[\text{type}] = t_3[\text{type}] = 1$, φ_2 can be applied. This allows us to enrich $t_3[\text{str}]$ and fix $t_3[\text{zip}]$ by taking corresponding values from t_2'', which have been confirmed correct with the master data in step (b).

Note that t_2'' and t_3' agree on every attribute in connection with personal information. It is evident that they indeed refer to the same person; hence a fraud. Observe that not only repairing helps matching (*e.g.*, from step (a) to (b)), but matching also helps us repair the data (*e.g.*, step (c) is doable only after the matching in (b)).   □

Unification. The example tells us the following. (1) When taken together, record matching and data repairing perform much better than being treated as separate processes. (2) To make practical use of their interaction, matching and repairing operations should be *interleaved*, rather than executing the two processes one after another. Unifying matching and repairing, we state the data cleaning problem as follows.

Given a database D, master data D_m, integrity constraints Σ and matching rules Γ, the *data cleaning problem* is to find a repair D_r of D such that (a) D_r is *consistent* (*i.e.*, satisfying Σ), (b) no more tuples in D_r can be *matched* to master tuples in D_m by matching rules of Γ, and (c) D_r minimally differs from the original data D.

The interaction between repairing and matching has been observed in, *e.g.*, [8, 18, 36]. Here, [8, 36] investigate record matching in the presence of error data, and suggest to integrate matching and data merge/fusion. In [18], a rule-based framework is proposed in which CFDs and MDs are both treated as *cleaning rules*. These rules tell us how to fix errors by updating the data, and allow us to interleave repairing and matching operations. Based on these rules, algorithms have been developed to clean data, in the presence or in the absence of master data. It has been shown that by unifying repairing and matching, these algorithms substantially improve the accuracy of repairing and matching taken as separate processes [18].

Fundamental Problems. When integrity constraints (for data repairing) and matching rules (for record matching) are taken together, the classical consistency and implication problems for constraints need to be revisited. These issues are investigated for CFDs and MDs in [18], which shows that these problems remain to be NP-complete and coNP-complete, respectively, the same as their counterparts for CFDs alone.

There are two fundamental questions about rule-based data cleaning. The *termination problem* is to decide whether a cleaning process stops, *i.e.*, it reaches a *fixpoint*, such that no more rules can be applied. The *determinism problem* asks whether all terminating cleaning processes end up with the same repair, *i.e.*, all of them reach a *unique* fixpoint. When CFDs and MDs are treated as cleaning rules, both problems are PSPACE-complete [18].

4   Relative Information Completeness

Given a database D and a query Q, we want to know whether a complete answer to Q can be found in D. Traditional work on this issue adopts either the CWA or the OWA. The CWA assumes that a database contains all the tuples representing real-world entities, but the *values* of some attributes in those tuples are possibly *missing*. The OWA assumes that *tuples* may also be *missing* [35]. As remarked earlier, few real-life databases are closed-world. Under the OWA, one can often expect few sensible queries to find complete answers.

Databases in real world are often neither entirely closed-world nor entirely open-world. This is particularly evident in the presence of master data. Master data of an enterprise contains complete information about the enterprise in certain aspects, *e.g.*, employees and projects, and can be regarded as a closed-world database. Meanwhile a number of other databases may be in use in the enterprise. On one hand, these databases may not be complete, *e.g.*, some sale transactions may be missing. On the other hand, certain parts of the databases are *constrained by* the master data, *e.g.*, employees. In other words, these databases are *partially closed*.

Example 4: Consider a company that maintains DCust(cid, name, AC, phn), a master data relation consisting of all its domestic customers, in which a tuple (c, n, a, p) specifies the id c, name n, area code a and phone number p of a customer. In addition, the company also has databases (a) Cust(cid, name, CC, AC, phn) of all customers of the company, domestic (with country code CC = 01) or international; and (b) Supt(eid, dept, cid), indicating that employee eid in dept supports customer cid. Neither Cust nor Supt is part of the master data.

Consider query Q_1 posed on Supt to find all the customers in NJ with AC = 908 who are supported by the employee with eid = e_0. The query may *not* get a complete answer since some tuples may be missing from Supt. However, if Q_1 returns all NJ customers with AC = 908 found in master data DCust, then we can safely conclude that Supt is complete for Q_1 and hence, there is no need to add more tuples to Supt to answer Q_1.

Now consider a query Q_2 to find *all* customers supported by e_0. Note that the international customers of Cust are not constrained by master data. As a result, we are not able to tell whether any Supt tuples in connection with e_0 are missing. Worse still, we do not even know what tuples should be added to Supt to make the answer to Q_2 in Supt complete. Nevertheless, if we know that (eid → dept, cid) is a functional dependency (FD) on Supt, then we can also conclude that the answer to Q_2 in Supt is complete as long as it is nonempty.   □

Relative Information Completeness. A practical data cleaning system should be able to decide whether a database has complete information to answer a query. To this end, as shown by the example, we need a model to specify partially closed databases. There has been a host of work on incomplete information, notably representation systems (*e.g.*, c-tables, v-tables [23, 25]) and models for missing tuples [22, 26, 30] (see [35] for a survey). However, the prior work neither considers master data nor studies the question mentioned above.

Given a database D and master data D_m, we specify a set V of *containment constraints* [13]. A containment constraint is of the form $q(D) \subseteq p(D_m)$, where q is a query posed on D, and p is a simple projection query on D_m. Intuitively, the part of D that is constrained by V is bounded by D_m, while the rest is open-world. We refer to a database D that satisfies V as a *partially closed* database *w.r.t.* (D_m, V). A database D' is a *partially closed extension* of D if $D \subseteq D'$ and D is partially closed *w.r.t.* (D_m, V) itself.

A partially closed database D is said to be *complete for a query Q relative to* (D_m, V) if for all partially closed extensions D' of D *w.r.t.* (D_m, V), $Q(D') = Q(D)$. That is, there is no need for adding new tuples to D, since they either violate the containment constraints, or do not change the answer to Q. In other words, D already contains complete information necessary for answering Q (see [12, 13] for details).

Fundamental Problems. One problem is to determine, given a query Q, master data D_m, a set V of containment constraints, and a partially closed database D *w.r.t.* (D_m, V), whether D is complete for Q relatively to (D_m, V). Another problem is to decide, given Q, D_m and V, whether there exists a partially closed database D that is complete for Q relatively to (D_m, V). The analyses of these problems help us identify what data should be collected in order to answer a query. These problems are investigated in [12, 13]. As indicated by Example 4, the complexity of these problems varies depending on different queries and containment constraints [12, 13].

5 Data Currency

A data cleaning system should support data currency analysis: among multiple (possibly obsolete) values of an entity, it is to identify the latest value of the entity, and to answer queries using the latest values only. The question of data currency would be trivial if all data values carried valid timestamps. In practice, however, timestamps are often unavailable or imprecise [38]. Add to this the complication that data values are often copied or imported from other sources [2, 7], which may not support a uniform scheme of timestamps.

Not all is lost. It is often possible to deduce currency orders from the semantics of the data. Moreover, data copied from other sources inherit currency orders in those sources. Taken together, these often allow us to deduce sufficient current values of the data to answer certain queries, as illustrated below.

Example 5: Consider two relations of a company shown in Fig. 2. Each Emp tuple is an employee record with name, address (country, zip code, street), salary and marital status. A Dept tuple specifies the name, manager and budget of a department. Records in these relations may be stale, and do not carry timestamps. Here tuples t_1, t_2 and t_3 refer to the same employee Mary, while t_4 does not refer to Mary. Consider the following queries posed on these relations.

(1) Query Q_1 is to find Mary's current salary. No timestamps are available for

	FN	LN	country	zip	street	salary	status
t_1:	Mary	Smith	UK	OX1 3QD	2 Small St	50k	single
t_2:	Mary	Dupont	UK	EB21 5FX	10 Elm Ave	50k	married
t_3:	Mary	Dupont	UK	EH9 1SU	6 Main St	80k	married
t_4:	Bob	Luth	UK	DB9 FJ8	8 Cowan St	80k	married

(a) Relation Emp

	dname	mgrFN	mgrLN	mgrAddr	budget
s_1:	R&D	Mary	Smith	2 Small St, OX1 3QD, UK	6500k
s_2:	R&D	Mary	Smith	2 Small St, OX1 3QD, UK	7000k
s_3:	R&D	Mary	Dupont	6 Main St,EH9 1SU, UK	6000k
s_4:	R&D	Ed	Luth	8 Cowan St, DB9 FJ8, UK	6000k

(b) Relation Dept

Fig. 2. A company database

us to tell which of 50k or 80k is more current. However, we may know that the salary of each employee in the company does *not* decrease, as commonly found in the real world. This yields currency orders $t_1 \prec_{salary} t_3$ and $t_2 \prec_{salary} t_3$, *i.e.*, t_3 is *more current* than t_1 and t_2 in *attribute* salary; in other words, t_3[salary] is more current than both t_1[salary] and t_2[salary]. Hence the answer to Q_1 is 80k.

(2) Query Q_2 is to find Mary's current last name. We can no longer answer Q_2 as above. Nonetheless, we may know the following: (a) marital status can only change from single to married and from married to divorced; but not from married to single; and (b) Emp tuples with the most current marital status also contain the most current last name. Therefore, $t_1 \prec_{LN} t_2$ and $t_1 \prec_{LN} t_3$, and the answer to Q_2 is Dupont.

(3) Query Q_3 is to find Mary's current address. We may know that Emp tuples with the most current salary contain the most current address. From this and (1) above, we know that the answer to Q_3 is "6 Main St".

(4) Finally, query Q_4 is to find the current budget of department R&D. Again no timestamps are available for us to evaluate the query. However, we may know the following: (a) Dept tuples s_1 and s_2 have copied their mgrAddr values from t_1[street, zip, county] in Emp; similarly, s_3 has copied from t_3, and s_4 from t_4; and (b) in Dept, tuples with the most current address also have the most current budget. Taken together, these tell us that $s_1 \prec_{budget} s_3$ and $s_2 \prec_{budget} s_3$. Observe that we do not know which budget in s_3 or s_4 is more current. Nevertheless, in either case the most current budget is 6000k, and hence it is the answer to Q_4.

□

Modeling Data Currency. To study data currency we need to specify currency orders on data values in the absence of timestamps but in the presence of copy relationships. Such a model is recently proposed in [17].

(1) To model partially available currency information in a database D, it assumes a currency order $\prec_A$ for each attribute A, such that for tuples t_1 and t_2 in D that represent the same real-world entity, $t_1 \prec_A t_2$ indicates that t_2 is more up-to-date than t_1 in the A attribute value.

(2) It uses denial constraints [1] to express currency relationships derived from the semantics of the data. For instance, all the currency relations we have seen in Example 5 can be expressed as denial constraints.

(3) A copy function from a data source to another is defined in terms of a partial mapping that preserves the currency order in the source. Based on these, one can define *consistent completions* D^c of D, which extend $\prec_A$ in D to a total order on all tuples pertaining to the same entity, such that D^c satisfies the denial constraints and constraints imposed by the copy functions.

One can construct from D^c the *current tuple* for each entity w.r.t. $\prec_A$, which contains the entity's most current A value for each attribute A. This yields the *current instance* of D^c consisting of only the current tuples of the entities in D, from which currency orders can be removed. In light of this, one can compute *certain current answers* of a query Q in D, *i.e.*, tuples that are the answers to Q in *all* consistent completions D^c of D (see [17] for details).

The study of data currency is related to temporal databases, which assume the availability of timestamps (see [32] for a survey). Also related is the line of work on querying indefinite data (see, *e.g.*, [34]), which considers data that is linearly ordered but only provides a partial order, but does not evaluate queries using current instances. Algorithms for discovering copy dependencies and functions are developed in [2,7].

Fundamental Problems. Given a database D on which partial currency orders, denial constraints and copy functions $\bar{\rho}$ are defined, we want to determine (1) whether a value is more up-to-date than another, and (2) whether a tuple is a certain current answer to a query. In addition, about copy functions $\bar{\rho}$, we want to determine (3) whether $\bar{\rho}$ is *currency preserving* for a query Q, *i.e.*, no matter how we extend $\bar{\rho}$ by copying more values of those entities in D, the certain current answers to Q in D remain unchanged; and (4) whether $\bar{\rho}$ can be extended to be currency preserving for Q. These problems have been studied in [17] for different queries.

6   Open Research Issues

It is evident that functionalities for handling these issues should logically become part of a data cleaning system. We envisage that a data cleaning system should be able not only to detect data inconsistencies and duplicates, but it should also be able to compute certain fixes that are guaranteed correct. Moreover, it should also be able to improve data currency and information completeness, beyond data consistency and deduplication. Indeed, we naturally want data quality management to tell us whether the answers to our queries in a database are trustable or not. This requires that we take data consistency, currency and information completeness together, as illustrated in the example below.

Example 6: Consider the relation Emp shown in Fig. 2, and a master relation EmpHistory consisting of *all* the historical information of its employees, as shown in Fig. 3. Each EmpHistory tuple is an employee record with name, address

	FN	LN	country	zip	street	phone	grade	salary	status
r_1:	Mary	Smith	UK	OX1 3QD	2 Small St	66757574	10	50k	single
r_2:	Mary	Dupont	UK	EB21 5FX	10 Elm Ave	66757574	10	50k	married
r_3:	Mary	Dupont	UK	EH9 1SU	6 Main St	66757574	11	80k	married
r_4:	Bob	Luth	UK	DB9 FJ8	8 Cowan St	46357642	11	80k	married
r_5:	Bob	Luth	UK	DB9 FJ8	8 Cowan St	46357642	12	100k	married

Fig. 3. Relation EmpHistory

(country, zip code, street), phone, grade, salary and marital status. Two constant CFDs are posed on relations Emp and EmpHistory: φ_1 : Emp([country = UK, zip = "EH9 1SU"] → [street = "6 Main St"]), and φ_2 : Emp([country =UK, zip = "DB9 FJ8"] → [street = "8 Crown St"]), where φ_1 states that in the UK, if one's zip code is "EH9 1SU", its street should be "6 Main St"; similarly, φ_2 states that in the UK, if one's zip code is "DB9 FJ8", its street should be "8 Crown St".

(1) Query Q_1 is to find Mary's current salary. Recall from Example 5(1) that Mary's most current salary is derived to be 80k, drawn from tuple t_3 in relation Emp. Observe the following: (a) t_3 is consistent as it satisfies the CFDs. (b) Mary's salary information gathered in relation Emp is complete *w.r.t.* EmpHistory, since it contains all Mary's employment records in EmpHistory table. Hence we can trust that the answer to Q_1 is 80k, since the data is consistent and the information about Mary is complete.

(2) Query Q_2 is to find Bob's current salary. The only record about Bob in Emp is t_4. Note that t_4 is consistent since it satisfies the CFDs. The answer to Q_2 is 55K in Emp. However, the information about Bob is not complete: there are more records about Bob in EmpHistory, with higher salaries. In other words, relation Emp alone is not sufficient to answer Q_2 correctly. Hence we cannot trust 55K to be the answer to Q_2.

This example demonstrates that to determine whether our queries can be answered correctly, all of data consistency, data currency and information completeness have to be taken into account.   □

No matter how important, however, we are not aware of any data cleaning system that supports functionalities to handle all these central data quality issues. The study of these issues is still in its infancy, and it has raised as many questions as it has answered. Below we highlight some of the open issues.

Certain fixes. One question is how to find certain fixes in the absence of master data. Another question concerns methods for discovering editing rules. Indeed, it is unrealistic to rely solely on human experts to design editing rules via an expensive and long manual process. It is likely, however, that editing rules can be deduced from master data and constraints such as CFDs and MDs, for which discovery algorithms are already in place [5, 33].

Relative information completeness and data currency. While the fundamental problems for these issues have been studied, efficient algorithms have yet to be developed and incorporated into data cleaning systems.

A uniform logical framework. To answer a query using a database D, one naturally wants D to be both complete and consistent for Q, and moreover, does not contain duplicates and stale data. In addition, there are intimate connections between these issues. (1) Improving data completeness provides us with more information to repair and match the data, and conversely, data repairing and record matching help us enrich the data as shown in Example 2. (2) Identifying the current value of an entity helps resolve data inconsistencies and duplication, and repairing and matching help us remove obsolete data. (3) Data currency is essentially to deal with missing temporal information, and hence can naturally capitalize on techniques for relative information completeness such as containment constraints and master data. All these highlight the need for developing a uniform framework to handle certain fixes, data repairing, record matching, relative information completeness and data currency. The framework should support the interaction of these processes, to improve the accuracy of data cleaning.

It is both natural and feasible to develop such a framework based on constraints and master data (see *e.g.,* [14] for a initial attempt in this direction). Indeed, (1) constraints are typically used to capture inconsistencies (*e.g.,* [1,4,16]). (2) Record matching rules [11] and editing rules [19] can be expressed as dynamic constraints. (3) It is shown [13] that constraints for data consistency, such as denial constraints [1] and conditional dependencies [4,16], are expressible as simple containment constraints studied for relative information completeness. As a result, we can assure that only consistent and partially closed databases are considered by enforcing containment constraints. (4) It suffices to express data currency commonly found in practice as denial constraints [17], the same class of constraints for data consistency. (5) As remarked earlier, master data has proved effective in dealing with each and every of these issues.

References

1. Arenas, M., Bertossi, L.E., Chomicki, J.: Consistent query answers in inconsistent databases. TPLP 3(4-5), 393–424 (2003)
2. Berti-Equille, L., Sarma, A.D., Dong, X., Marian, A., Srivastava, D.: Sailing the information ocean with awareness of currents: Discovery and application of source dependence. In: CIDR (2009)
3. Bohannon, P., Fan, W., Flaster, M., Rastogi, R.: A cost-based model and effective heuristic for repairing constraints by value modification. In: SIGMOD (2005)
4. Bravo, L., Fan, W., Ma, S.: Extending dependencies with conditions. In: VLDB (2007)
5. Chiang, F., Miller, R.: Discovering data quality rules. PVLDB 1(1) (2008)
6. Cong, G., Fan, W., Geerts, F., Jia, X., Ma, S.: Improving data quality: Consistency and accuracy. In: VLDB (2007)
7. Dong, X., Berti-Equille, L., Srivastava, D.: Truth discovery and copying detection in a dynamic world. In: VLDB (2009)
8. Dong, X., Halevy, A., Madhavan, J.: Reference reconciliation in complex information spaces. In: SIGMOD (2005)
9. Eckerson, W.W.: Data quality and the bottom line: Achieving business success through a commitment to high quality data. The Data Warehousing Institute (2002)

10. Elmagarmid, A., Ipeirotis, P., Verykios, V.: Duplicate record detection: A survey. TKDE 19(1), 1–16 (2007)
11. Fan, W., Gao, H., Jia, X., Li, J., Ma, S.: Dynamic constraints for record matching. VLDB J. 20(4), 495–520 (2011)
12. Fan, W., Geerts, F.: Capturing missing tuples and missing values. In: PODS (2010)
13. Fan, W., Geerts, F.: Relative information completeness. TODS 35(4) (2010)
14. Fan, W., Geerts, F.: Uniform dependency language for improving data quality. IEEE Data Eng. Bull. 34(3), 34–42 (2011)
15. Fan, W., Geerts, F.: Foundations of Data Quality Management. Synthesis Lectures on Data Management. Morgan & Claypool Publishers (2012)
16. Fan, W., Geerts, F., Jia, X., Kementsietsidis, A.: Conditional functional dependencies for capturing data inconsistencies. TODS 33(2) (2008)
17. Fan, W., Geerts, F., Wijsen, J.: Determining the currency of data. In: PODS (2011)
18. Fan, W., Li, J., Ma, S., Tang, N., Yu, W.: Interaction between record matching and data repairing. In: SIGMOD (2011)
19. Fan, W., Li, J., Ma, S., Tang, N., Yu, W.: Towards certain fixes with editing rules and master data. VLDB J. 21(2), 213–238 (2012)
20. Fellegi, I., Holt, D.: A systematic approach to automatic edit and imputation. J. American Statistical Association 71(353), 17–35 (1976)
21. Gartner. Forecast: Data quality tools, worldwide, 2006-2011. Technical report, Gartner (2007)
22. Gottlob, G., Zicari, R.: Closed world databases opened through null values. In: VLDB (1988)
23. Grahne, G.: The Problem of Incomplete Information in Relational Databases. Springer (1991)
24. Herzog, T.N., Scheuren, F.J., Winkler, W.E.: Data Quality and Record Linkage Techniques. Springer (2009)
25. Imieliński, T., Lipski Jr., W.: Incomplete information in relational databases. JACM 31(4) (1984)
26. Levy, A.Y.: Obtaining complete answers from incomplete databases. In: VLDB (1996)
27. Loshin, D.: Master Data Management. Knowledge Integrity, Inc. (2009)
28. Mayfield, C., Neville, J., Prabhakar, S.: ERACER: a database approach for statistical inference and data cleaning. In: SIGMOD (2010)
29. Miller, D.W., et al.: Missing prenatal records at a birth center: A communication problem quantified. In: AMIA Annu. Symp. Proc. (2005)
30. Motro, A.: Integrity = validity + completeness. TODS 14(4) (1989)
31. Otto, B., Weber, K.: From health checks to the seven sisters: The data quality journey at BT (September 2009) BT TR-BE HSG/CC CDQ/8
32. Snodgrass, R.T.: Developing Time-Oriented Database Applications in SQL. Morgan Kaufmann (1999)
33. Song, S., Chen, L.: Discovering matching dependencies. In: CIKM (2009)
34. van der Meyden, R.: The complexity of querying indefinite data about linearly ordered domains. JCSS 54(1) (1997)
35. van der Meyden, R.: Logical approaches to incomplete information: A survey. In: Chomicki, J., Saake, G. (eds.) Logics for Databases and Information Systems. Kluwer (1998)
36. Weis, M., Naumann, F.: Dogmatix tracks down duplicates in XML. In: SIGMOD (2005)
37. Yakout, M., Elmagarmid, A.K., Neville, J., Ouzzani, M., Ilyas, I.F.: Guided data repair. PVLDB 4(1) (2011)
38. Zhang, H., Diao, Y., Immerman, N.: Recognizing patterns in streams with imprecise timestamps. In: VLDB (2010)

Hitting Buneman Circles

Michael Paul Fourman

School of Informatics, The University of Edinburgh
Michael.Fourman@ed.ac.uk

Abstract. We discuss Peter Buneman's suggestion that a fibre connection to the internet — a hub — should be available within every circle enclosing a population of at least 2,000 people (a b-circle). This poses the problem of finding a small set, H, of hubs, such that *every* b-circle contains a hub. We show that a greedy algorithm does not lead to an optimal set of hubs. Instead it models market forces, which are naturally greedy. An unfettered market will exploit the most profitable communities and, just like a greedy algorithm, leave gaps that it is uneconomic to fill. We describe a geometric heuristic for the discovery of efficient hub placements satisfying a purely combinatorial analogue of Buneman's criterion, and apply it to illustrate the inherent inefficiency of gap-funding in a market-led broadband policy.

Keywords: hitting set, approximation algorithm, facilities location, broadband, market forces, gap funding.

1 Introduction

In Scotland, as elsewhere, many communities are too far from an optical connection to the internet to allow them to benefit from the low-latency, high-bandwidth, symmetric internet connections that will soon be routine in metropolitan areas.

This work arose from the Royal Society of Edinburgh's Digital Scotland inquiry [8]. It was easy for the inquiry to decide that Scotland should have enough "fibred points of presence" (FPOPs, or *hubs*) to provide every community in the country with adequate backhaul.

Quantifying where these should be and where the fibre should be laid, without embarking on detailed infrastructure planning, was more difficult. Our diagram shows the areas served by a collection of hubs satisfying a simple, but ingenious criterion, suggested by Peter Buneman. Such provision

V. Tannen et al. (Eds.): Buneman Festschrift, LNCS 8000, pp. 250–258, 2013.

would allow every substantial community in Scotland to access next generation broadband.

The population of Scotland, and other countries, is not randomly distributed. Most people live in relatively dense clusters, many of which are widely separated. Because communities are hard to identify objectively, it is difficult to specify an equitable policy for the provision of a fibre backhaul connection — a *hub* — to every community. Buneman's criterion,

> *"Draw any circle (I mean any) on a map of Scotland. If that circle contains more than 2000 people, then the circle must also contain a fibre point-of-presence."*[1]

was adopted as the key recommendation of the Digital Scotland report, intended to ensure that every community will have access to Scotland's digital infrastructure. The rationale for this recommendation is that the aggregate bandwidth demand from a population of this size will, at peak times, exceed the capacity of a copper or wireless backhaul connection[2].

The Digital Scotland report assumes that a population of 2,000 corresponds to approximately 800 premises, and that a copper or wireless backhaul connection is limited to ~ 512 Mb/s. With these assumptions, the available bandwidth per subscriber is at most ~ 16 Mb/s, at a contention ratio[3] of 25 : 1.

To a first approximation, the bandwidth available for a communication channel is proportional to the frequency of the carrier signal. Since the electromagnetic frequencies used for optical signals are around 10^5 times those used for electrical or wireless communications, fibre can carry correspondingly higher bandwidths. Thus, a single fibre could provide the entire population of the UK with more bandwidth *per caput* than a wireless or copper channel can deliver to a community of 2,000.

Once a community has access to backhaul there are many technologies available for the creation of a local access network — striking examples are given by the Tegola network developed by Peter and colleagues [1], and other projects it has inspired.

The Buneman criterion provides a novel approach to facilities location, in that it analyses the infrastructure requirements for distribution of a utility good, rather than the more usual focus on placement for profit.

The methods introduced here should also have application in areas other than backhaul provision. For example, to find solutions to the wireless base-station placement problem that, unlike much earlier work (see e.g. [5]), impose limits on the number of clients served by each base station. Such constraints are increasingly relevant as contention for spectrum increases.

---

[1] Personal communication, 2010.

[2] A *backhaul connection* is the essential link from a local access network to the internet.

[3] Backhaul is typically provisioned on the assumption that most subscribers will be idle most of the time. Contention is the ratio of the total number of subscribers to the number that can be served concurrently, at the advertised bandwidth.

2   Discussion

Buneman circles *(b-circles)* are those circles on the map of Scotland that include a settled population of at least 2,000 individuals. Every b-circle should include a hub. The beauty of Buneman's criterion is that *any* collection of 2,000 or more individuals (we call such a collection *substantial*) may be viewed as a community, and thus every substantial community is guaranteed at least one fibre hub within any circumscribing circle. Each individual will belong to many such communities.

We now set out a mathematical context for discussion of this criterion. To begin, let S (Scotland) be a bounded subset of the plane, $\mathbb{R}^2$.

Definition 1. *A population distribution is a finite measure, π on S.*
We identify two special cases:
A population *is the counting measure on a finite set of points $P \subseteq S$.*
A census *is a discrete measure, given by a finite set of census points, $A \subseteq S$, together with a count $\pi(a) > 0$ of the population ascribed to each $a \in A$.*

It is often helpful to think of a population as a sample from the probability distribution associated with a more abstract population distribution, and a census as the result of aggregating a population to a (relatively) small number of census points. Throughout this paper, we assume a given population distribution, π, and speak of $\pi(C)$ as the *population* of $C \subseteq S$.

The data used for the Digital Scotland analysis of backhaul requirements is a census, derived from postcode data by multiplying the number of residential addresses for each postcode by a factor of 2.5 inhabitants per household.

Definition 2. *A Buneman circle is a disc, D, with population $\pi(D) \geqslant k$ (hereinafter, a b-circle).*[4]
We write $\mathcal{B}_x$ for the minimal-radius b-circle centred at x, and $\beta(x)$ for the radius of this circle — the b-radius of x.

Buneman computed the b-circle $\mathcal{B}_p$ for every one of the 196,273 postcodes, p, in Scotland. The calculated b-radii range from 84 metres (AB25 1FE, a high-rise in Aberdeen) to 55 kilometres (ZE2 9JU, the Fair Isle). Buneman's computation places the data in a k-d tree, and then uses standard k-nearest neighbour queries and binary search to determine $\beta(x)$ for any point x. For UK postcode data, k-d trees provide adequate performance on standard hardware. See [4] for a recent review of other methods, suitable for massive data sets.

Recall that any set which includes least one element in every set in a collection X is called a *hitting set* for X. The Digital Scotland recommendation stipulates that the hubs should form a hitting set for the collection of *all* b-circles. Dually, for each potential hub location, h we can consider its *client set* $\mathcal{C}_h = \{x \mid h \in \mathcal{B}_x\}$. Clearly,

$$H \text{ is a hitting set for } \{\mathcal{B}_x \mid x \in \mathbb{R}^2\} \text{ iff } \{\mathcal{C}_h \mid h \in H\} \text{ covers } \mathbb{R}^2.$$

---

[4] For the purposes of this note, k can be considered to be a fixed integer, substantially smaller than the total population, $\pi(S)$.

3   Properties and Anomalies

Lemma 1. β *is uniformly continuous.* $\mathcal{C}_h$ *is star-convex.*

Proof. Given two points, x, y, we claim that $|\beta(x) - \beta(y)| \leqslant |x - y|$. It suffices to show that $\beta(y) \geqslant \beta(x) - |x - y|$.

The result then follows by symmetry.

Observe that $\forall r, z. \ \pi(D_{r,z}) < k$ iff $r < \beta(z)$ (where $D_{r,z}$ is the disc of radius r centred at z).

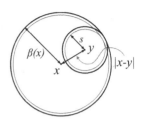

For $y \in \mathcal{B}_x$, suppose $s < \beta(x) - |x - y|$, then,

$$s + |x - y| < \beta(x), \text{ and}$$

$$D_{s,y} \subseteq D_{s+|x-y|,x}$$

$$\text{so } \pi(D_{s,y}) \leqslant \pi(D_{s+|x-y|,x}) < k.$$

$$\text{Thus, } s < \beta(y).$$

The same construction also shows that $\mathcal{C}_h$ is star-convex. If $x \in \mathcal{C}_h$ (equivalently, if $h \in \mathcal{B}_x$) and y lies on the radius (of length $\beta(x)$) from x through h, then $|y - h| \leqslant \beta(y)$, so $y \in \mathcal{C}_h$. □

Buneman's intention [personal communication] was universal provision: that a "circle drawn on the map of Scotland" really should include *any* circle — *"even one centred in Newfoundland"* — on an infinitely extended map. We call this the *strong Buneman criterion*.

Interactions between the geometry of circles and a discrete population can be surprising. One consequence of the strong criterion is that there must be hubs near the boundaries of $\mathcal{S}$. For any $\varepsilon > 0$ and any half-plane H with $\pi(H) \geqslant k$ we must place a hub within ε of H — since b-circles with arbitrarily distant centres must be hit. In specially coincidental cases, $\mathcal{B}_x$ may have an arbitrarily large population — for example, if P contains a large number of individuals all on a circle, such as the shores of a circular loch. In general, a population will be in general position — a sample from a distribution almost certainly will — but a census is certainly not. If we take a community, $C \subseteq \mathcal{S}$, even one of the form $\mathcal{B}_x$, then the circumcircle of the population of C may contain many more individuals than does C.

Clearly, the Buneman criterion is satisfied if *every* disc $\mathcal{B}_x$ contains a hub. However, this set of discs is infinite, and so is the set of possible hub locations.

We have not attempted to produce hub sets satisying the strong criterion. Instead, we weaken the condition, by interpreting a "circle drawn on the map of Scotland" to mean a disc $D_{r,x}$ whose centre, $x \in \text{supp}(\pi)$, belongs to the support of π — we call this the *egocentric* interpretation. For a discrete population, or census, this simply means that x ranges over the sample points, so we now have only finitely many $(O(n))$ circles to hit.

This replaces universal provision with egocentric guarantees. Wherever you live in Scotland, your nearest hub should be among your 800 nearest neighbours. It is also natural to strengthen the criterion by requiring that hubs should be built only in habitable regions — so we look for a hitting set that is also contained in $\text{supp}(\pi)$.

A more appealing, but less tractable, community-focussed guarantee would stipulate that for every substantial community $C \subseteq \mathcal{S}$ the circumcircle of C should contain a hub. A substantial community distributed around the shores of a circular loch would then be guaranteed a loch-side hub — or a floating one — whereas the egocentric criterion might only place hubs well inland.

Nevertheless, in the interest of tractability, and because we are not aware of a need for a community-centric guarantee arising in practice, we use the egocentric version, with hubs located in populated sites. Let $P = \text{supp}(\pi)$. For $p \in P$ we define

$$\mathcal{N}_p = \mathcal{B}_p \cap P \qquad \mathcal{K}_p = \mathcal{C}_p \cap P$$

$H \subseteq P$ is a hitting set for $\{\mathcal{N}_p \mid p \in P\}$ iff $\{\mathcal{K}_h \mid h \in H\}$ covers P.

We want to find small hitting sets, H, such that $\{\mathcal{K}_h \mid h \in H\}$ covers P. For a discrete population distribution, this is a purely combinatorial problem.

4   Selecting Hubs

Standard approaches to the hitting-set problem include a naïve greedy algorithm and linear programming relaxation (LPR) (see [10], Ch. 1). We tried both on Buneman's postcode data. They did not perform well. A geometrically-motivated heuristic produces much better results.

We used various types of synthetic data, as well as the postcode data, to understand why these approaches fail and to evaluate alternative methods. These data sets included:

- a uniform lattice of n^2 points in the unit square,
- samples of size n^2 drawn from the uniform distribution on the unit square,
- samples of size n^2 drawn from the bivariate normal distribution $\mathcal{N}_2(\mathbf{0}, \mathbf{1})$.

The randomised examples are chosen to model the kinds of local variation (and in some areas local uniformity) that we see in our population data. Uniform density across a region with a sharp boundary is often seen near a coastline, and a unimodal peak characterises many isolated communities.

Consider covering a uniform $n \times n$ square lattice with discs containing k lattice points.. Take $k = n$ and let $n \to \infty$, then, away from the boundary, we approach the well-known geometric problem of covering the plane with uniform discs. The familiar regular hexagonal cover always gives a baseline solution (which may sometimes be improved upon by exploiting quantisation gaps in the lattice).

The greedy algorithm first chooses a maximal disjoint set of circles, and then fills in the gaps, normally producing a sub-baseline solution. LPR uses randomised rounding to derive a cover from a non-integral solution to an integer linear program (ILP) expressing the constraints. Away from the boundary, our problem is regular. Solution of the LP relaxation gives equal weight to indistinguishable candidates, and so provides no useful information — randomised rounding amounts to random selection.

A geometric heuristic: Our heuristic is initially designed to produce good solutions for the uniform lattice, where we are guided by a clear geometric picture. We find that, with a minor modification described below, it also performs well on randomised and real-life data.

Consider the continuous limiting case of a uniform population distribution extending infinitely. The b-radius is uniform. Without loss, assume that $\beta(x) = 1$. We write $\mathcal{B}_x$ for the b-circle $D_{1,x}$ of x, and note that each client set is also a unit disc $\mathcal{C}_h = D_{1,h}$. For this idealised setting, we want to produce a regular hexagonal covering of the plane by discs $\mathcal{C}_h$, using an algorithm that only has access to the combinatorial relationship $x \in \mathcal{C}_h$ or, equivalently, $h \in \mathcal{B}_x$.

Suppose we have already placed two hubs, a, b, which are (by magic) $\sqrt{3}$ apart. What discs might we add to extend our cover?

It is clear that we need to cover the uncovered points near the intersections of our two circles. We identify these as points that are hard to cover.

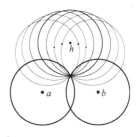

We write U for the set of uncovered points. In general, a point p can be covered by any disc C_h centred at $h \in \mathcal{B}_p$, but we can characterise the particular points we want to identify if we only consider discs with uncovered centres, $h \in \mathcal{B}_p \cap U$. For p near a covering circle, many points in $\mathcal{B}_p$ are already covered by that circle. For uncovered points, $p \in U$, near to *both* circles few points in $\mathcal{B}_p$ remain uncovered.

For uncovered points, p, near a cusp where the two circles meet $\mathcal{B}_p \cap U$ is smaller than it is for uncovered points further from the cusp — the points nearer the cusp are harder to cover. So, we say that, 'covering p is hard', if p is not yet covered and there are few uncovered h such that $h \in \mathcal{B}_p$ (or, equivalently, $p \in C_h$) (the fewer, the harder). Then we restrict our attention, temporarily, to those h that cover the hardest p, and from these select, greedily, an h such that C_h covers as many uncovered q as possible.

The diagram shows our two original discs, with centres a, b, together with a few of the potential C_h we have to consider — with their centres, h, sized to indicate the relative size of $C_h \cap U$. The candidate covering circles, C_h, shown all cover all uncovered points in a neighbourhood of the upper cusp. Choosing greedily from among these candidates selects the central one, because it includes the largest uncovered area.

If we start from our magical initial configuration and repeat this procedure indefinitely we will incrementally generate the regular covering of the plane. If we start instead from a pair of discs that overlap, but have less than the magic separation, what then? Our new circle, centred at h, includes the hard to reach points and passes through one intersection of the original two circles. It is placed symmetrically with respect to the originals. If the angle between the two original radii is θ, then the angle between the new radius and either original is

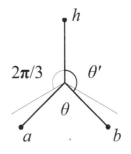

$$\theta' = \theta + (2\pi/3 - \theta)/2.$$

The same formula applies if we start with two discs marginally too far apart. So, as we iterate our construction, successive values of θ approach the ideal value, $2\pi/3$. This explains how our algorithm adapts to variations in population density, and why it produces reasonable solutions for our synthetic data.

In the next section we transfer this idea to our discrete setting and report on our real-world application.

5   An Algorithm

We use the heuristic introduced above to select new hubs, while keeping track of the set U of uncovered sites.

Iteration: One step of the algorithm consists of choosing a site, p, to cover; choosing a hub, $h \in \mathcal{N}_p$, so that $\mathcal{K}_h$ will cover p (we will say, 'h covers p') ; then updating U. We take such steps until U is empty.

First, for each uncovered p, the set of uncovered candidates that would cover it is given by $N(p) = U \cap \mathcal{N}_p$. The difficulty of covering $p \in U$ is given by the reciprocal of the number of uncovered sites potentially available to cover it $d(p) = 1/|N(p)|$. For $q \notin U$ set $d(q) = 0$. We will cover some p of maximal difficulty, chosen from the set $M = \{p|d(p) = \max_{q \in U} d(q)\}$.

Second, we must choose h from $\bigcup_{p \in M} \mathcal{N}_p$. For the purely geometric version of our problem described in the previous section, a greedy selection, based solely on maximising the number of newly covered sites, will choose the 'correct' hub for each p. For the discrete version of the problem, we find that quantisation introduces enough noise to perturb this effect: a purely greedy choice will often leave a hard-to-cover site that can only be inefficiently covered. To overcome this effect, we again favour choices that cover difficult sites, using $d(q)^2$ as a measure of the value of covering q.[5] So, we choose a hub, $h \in \bigcup_{p \in M} \mathcal{N}_p$, to maximize $\sum_{q \in \mathcal{K}_h} d(q)^2$. Finally, we remove $\mathcal{K}_h$ from U.

Initialisation: We can start our procedure with an empty collection of hubs, and every site uncovered, or with an arbitrary collection of hubs, with the sites already covered computed accordingly. In the geometric setting, starting from an empty set of hubs, the initial moves introduce two tangential circles, then a third circle centred at their meeting point. To produce a uniform cover we could use a few iterations to produce a pair with near-perfect separation, and only then start to produce our cover. In practice, we have found that this does not give perceptibly improved results on noisy data.

Completion: Once all sites are covered, we may find that a handful (typically $\ll 1\%$) of client sets in our chosen covering are double-covered: some chosen hubs have been rendered redundant by later choices. As long as any such remain, we prune one, and so eventually arrive at an irredundant cover.

6   Results

The picture illustrates a covering, H, of a sample of 40,000 points drawn from a 2D Gaussian, with $k = 200$, by showing the convex hull of each $\mathcal{K}_h$ for $h \in H$.

First, we used synthetic data to develop and tune our heuristic. The uniform hexagonal cover of the plane by discs has a multiplicity of $\frac{2\pi}{3\sqrt{3}} \approx 1.21$. We take this as a baseline against which we compare the efficiency of our coverings.

We used random samples of 40,000 points, from normal and uniform distributions, to compare the use of different exponents, w, in our measure, $d(q)^w$, of the value of covering q. The table below shows the multiplicities of typical covers.

w	0	1	2	3	4
2D Gaussian	1.48	1.45	1.36	1.35	1.4
Uniform	1.45	1.375	1.315	1.35	1.35

As discussed earlier our population data can be modelled informally as a mix of synthetic data from these two distributions. This justifies the choice of a quadratic exponent for our hardness measure. Pragmatically, we find that it gives lower multiplicities (smaller covers), on our data, than other small integer values.

---

[5] We have no principled justification for the quadratic exponent used here. It was chosen following the experimentation described in our results.

Applying the same algorithm to Buneman's circles for Scotland, we obtain a cover with 4,224 hubs. However, a further relaxation of the Buneman criterion, to guarantee that every b-circle includes some site with a hub within 500 metres of it, dramatically reduces the number of hubs we require. We implement this relaxation by simply adding any site within 500m of a site in $\mathcal{N}_x$ to $\mathcal{N}_x$. This clearly has the greatest effect in the most densely populated areas. The diagram on our title page of this article depicts the convex hull of $\mathcal{K}_h$ for each of the resulting collection of 1,652 hubs.

A naïve greedy algorithm, applied to this relaxed problem, produces a cover with 1,803 hubs. For the sake of comparison, we have run a less naïve greedy algorithm on the same data. For this, we modified the code to omit the first part of each step (restricting our choice to hubs that cover the hardest sites), so at each step we consider every site not yet used as a potential hubs, then make a greedy choice favouring hubs that cover difficult sites. With a quadratic weighting, this gave a cover with 1,734 hubs.

We have shown that a greedy algorithm does not lead to an optimal cover. Market forces, however, are greedy. An unfettered market will exploit the most profitable communities and, just like the greedy algorithm, leave gaps that it is uneconomic to fill. Our next experiment suggests that market-led greed, which will focus initial investment on the most compact communities, is even less efficient than naïve greed, which looks for hubs that serve as many premises as possible, even if these premises are thinly spread.

Scotland's current broadband policy, developed in consultation with the incumbent supplier, is to provide next generation access to over 80% of the population by 2015. Roughly 72% of Scotland's postcodes have b-radii $\leqslant 700m$. We call these *compact* communities. They account for just over 80% of Scotland's residential addresses.

We have run our algorithm to find a set of hubs that will serve just these compact communities, to try to model the likely impact of government policy. Our algorithm produces 1,092 hubs that cover these communities. If we then rerun the algorithm to cover all the communities not served by these 1,092 hubs, we find we need a further 707 hubs to complete the job. So, *in toto* this two-step approach would require over 10% more than the 1,652 hubs in our one-step plan for universal provision; and public support would be required for 707 hubs — over 25% more than the gap of 560 between our 1,652 requirement and the 1,092 financed by the market.

Clearly, what we have just sketched is a very simplistic, indeed over-simplistic, model of the complex planning and investment decisions negotiated between government and incumbent. Nevertheless, we believe that even this simple model captures a key challenge that policy-makers face in trying to ensure universal provision while being committed to a gap-funding policy that waits for gaps in market-driven provision to appear, before intervening to fill them.

Market-led provision is, by definition and design, greedy, and thus becomes inefficient beyond a certain point. Where it will not deliver universal provision, *post hoc* gap-filling will be inefficient.

7   Related Work

The idea of using distance to nearest neighbours to study the spatial distribution of populations is not new. Clark and Evans [2] use distance to nearest neighbour to study how the distributions exhibited by populations of living organisms differ from a Poisson ideal. Loftsgaarden and Quesenberry ([6]) introduce the key idea of using distance to k^{th}-nearest event for density estimation. In Smoothed Particle Hydrodynamics (SPH) [7] "the mass of each point is distributed according to a smoothing function W whose size adapts to the local value of the density of points." For the visualisation of galaxies Colberg ([3]) uses a grid-based adaptation of SPH. The Delaunay Triangulation Field Estimator (DTFE) introduced by Schaap and van der Weygaert ([9]), takes a Delaunay triangulation, and then considers the n-simplices incident at a point as a natural neighbourhood of that point. These examples are not exhaustive, but this brief list gives some idea of the range of applications where related ideas have been considered.

Buneman's insight that we could use this estimator of local density as a basis for the provisioning of a rate-limited resource appears to be novel. We hope his ideas may find further application in some of these other domains.

References

1. Bernardi, G., Buneman, P., Marina, M.K.: Tegola tiered mesh network testbed in rural Scotland. In: WiNS-DR 2008: Proceedings of the 2008 ACM Workshop on Wireless Networks and Systems for Developing Regions, pp. 9–16. ACM (September 2008), http://dl.acm.org/citation.cfm?id=1410067

2. Clark, P.J., Evans, F.C.: Distance to nearest neighbor as a measure of spatial relationships in populations. Ecology 35(4), 445–453 (1954), http://www.jstor.org/stable/10.2307/1931034

3. Colberg, J.: Parallel Supercomputer Simulations of Cosmic Evolution. PhD thesis, Ludwig-Maximilians-Universität München (1999), http://edoc.ub.uni-muenchen.de/272/1/Colberg_Joerg.pdf

4. Connor, M., Kumar, P.: Fast construction of k-nearest neighbor graphs for point clouds. IEEE Transactions on Visualization and Computer Graphics 16(4), 599–608 (2009), http://compgeom.com/~piyush/papers/tvcg_stann.pdf

5. Lev-Tov, N., Peleg, D.: Exact algorithms and approximation schemes for base station placement problems. In: Penttonen, M., Meineche Schmidt, E. (eds.) SWAT 2002. LNCS, vol. 2368, pp. 90–99. Springer, Heidelberg (2002), http://dl.acm.org/citation.cfm?id=645901.672620

6. Loftsgaarden, D.O., Quesenberry, C.P.: A nonparametric estimate of a multivariate density function. Annals of Mathematical Statistics 36(3), 1049–1051 (1965), http://projecteuclid.org/DPubS/Repository/1.0/
Disseminate?view=body&id=pdf_1&handle=euclid.aoms/1177700079

7. Monaghan, J.J.: Smoothed particle hydrodynamics. Annual Review of Astronomy and Astrophysics 30, 543–574 (1992), http://www.annualreviews.org/doi/pdf/10.1146/annurev.aa.30.090192.002551

8. The Royal Society of Edinburgh. Digital Scotland (October 2010)

9. Schaap, W.E., van der Weygaert, R.: Continuous fields and discrete samples: reconstruction through delaunay tessellations. Astron. Astrophys. 363, L29–L32 (2000), http://www.astro.rug.nl/~weygaert/tim1publication/dtfeaaletter.pdf

10. Williamson, D.P., Shmoys, D.B.: The design of approximation algorithms. Cambridge University Press (June 2011), http://www.designofapproxalgs.com/book.pdf

Looking at the World Thru Colored Glasses

Floris Geerts[1], Anastasios Kementsietsidis[2], and Heiko Müller[3]

[1] ADReM Research Group, University of Antwerp, Antwerpen, Belgium
`floris.geerts@ua.ac.be`
[2] IBM Research - Thomas J. Watson Research Ctr, Hawthorne, NY, USA
`akement@us.ibm.com`
[3] Intelligent Sensing and Systems Laboratory, CSIRO, Hobart, Australia
`heiko.mueller@csiro.au`

Abstract. There are two central issues in the curation of (scientific) databases: annotation management and archiving. Both issues have been addressed by the Edinburgh database group and led to the MONDRIAN annotation management system and the XArch archiving system, respectively. In this paper, we present an application of MONDRIAN to represent and query the history of evolving databases. We show how the annotation model and query language underlying MONDRIAN not only allows to answer queries about how individual data values change over time, but also allows to capture and query structural changes that occur in a database over time, beyond the querying functionalities that XArch currently offers.

1 Introduction

In recent years, one has seen a vast increase in the number of curated databases. This is particularly true for databases that originate from scientific research and from governmental agencies. Common examples include IUPHARDB, the official database of the IUPHAR Committee on Receptor Nomenclature and Drug Classification [2], and the CIA World Factbook, a comprehensive resource of demographic data [1], among others.

Annotations play an important role in database curation. Indeed, the curation process usually involves manual collection, verification, and aggregation of existing data sources by a dedicated group of curators. Annotations can, for example, represent opinions of curators about the quality of data or suggested changes, record information about the provenance of data, as well as indicate temporal information with regards to the validity of data. In general, annotations can be regarded as additions to the core data for which there is no dedicated place within the database schema. The importance of annotations has been recognized by several research efforts in which the problems of maintaining and querying annotated databases have been addressed [7,3,13,14,20,9,16].

Equally important in the curation process is the ability to store, manipulate and query different versions of the data. Indeed, it is common that curated data evolves and gets updated at a regular pace and proper archiving of the data is

V. Tannen et al. (Eds.): Buneman Festschrift, LNCS 8000, pp. 259–272, 2013.
© Springer-Verlag Berlin Heidelberg 2013

required [4]. Furthermore, users want to query the history of the data, rather than simply querying a single old version of the data. A prime example of this is the CIA World Factbook [1] where queries like "How did the population of China change over the past 15 years?" are common[1]. To deal with these challenges, different approaches and systems for archiving and querying data have been developed in recent years [6,19,8,18,21].

In this paper we marry two ideas, both developed when the authors were doing time in the database group in Edinburgh. The first idea concerns the modeling of annotated databases by means of colors, to represent the annotations, and blocks, to represent the data items to which the colors are associated. The resulting annotation management system, MONDRIAN, was reported in [13,12]. The second idea concerns the archiving of data by means of keys and XML. More specifically, in the XARCH system [19], different versions of an evolving database are merged into a single well-defined hierarchical data format. Furthermore, temporal information is stored as annotations of elements in the archive. The goal of this paper is to show that by modeling time-stamped XML as so-called color relations in the MONDRIAN system, and by using the corresponding color algebra as query language, we obtain a flexible mechanism to store, manipulate and query annotated historical data. Using the CIA World Factbook as an example, we show that this approach enables to answer queries over archives that XARCH currently cannot answer.

The remainder of this paper is structured as follows: We review the MONDRIAN annotation management system in Section 2. In Section 3, we describe the archiving system XARCH. Finally, in Section 4 we combine both systems to represent and query annotated evolving databases.

2   The MONDRIAN Annotation System

Most existing approaches for annotation management deal with annotations of individual values or records [7,3,13,14,20,9,16]. In many cases, however, it is of importance to be able to annotate sets of values. In data integration, for example, one wants to use annotations to provide evidence for the correctness of associations between values. Likewise, it is often important to group and annotate values that have a semantic or temporal relationship. We illustrate how the MONDRIAN annotation system models such complex annotations by means of the following example:

Example 1. Consider the relations in Fig. 1(a)-(c) taken from the CIA World Factbook of 2011. The relations list for each country (a) the highest-valued imported products; (b) the most important import trading partners; and (c) the highest-valued exported products. Figure 1(d) shows an integrated relation in which countries are associated with their trading partners and corresponding imported products. Annotations in this relation represent evidence for associations,

---

[1] This query is one of Peter Buneman's favorite queries. Others include the shoe and hat size of individuals, which are outside the scope of this paper.

country	imports
Brazil	Chemical prod.
Brazil	Electronics
Chile	Chemicals
Chile	Electrical equip.
Chile	Vehicles

country	partner
Brazil	S. Korea
Brazil	US
Chile	Germany
Chile	S. Korea
Chile	US

country	exports
Germany	Chemicals
Germany	Motor vehicles
Korea, South	Motor vehicles
Korea, South	Semiconductors
United States	Organic chemicals

(a) Imported products   (b) Import trading partners   (c) Exported products

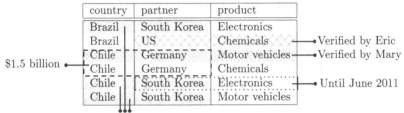

country	partner	product
Brazil	South Korea	Electronics
Brazil	US	Chemicals
Chile	Germany	Motor vehicles
Chile	Germany	Chemicals
Chile	South Korea	Electronics
Chile	South Korea	Motor vehicles

$1.5 billion

Verified by Eric
Verified by Mary
Until June 2011

S. Korea = Korea, South = South Korea

(d) Integrated relation of imported products

Fig. 1. Three relations (a), (b) and (c) on imports and exports taken from the CIA World Factbook (2011) and their integrated relation (d)

assumptions that were made during the integration process, as well as temporal information. Annotations are shown in the form of color blocks. Here, a block is a set of values for which an annotation exists. Colors are used to represent annotations for this block. In the figure, we also show the semantics of each color. For example, the ⠿ -colored block in the fifth tuple is valid "Until June 2011". In the first and the last two tuples one block indicates that the association between *Brazil* (and *Chile* resp.) and *South Korea* is based on the assumption that the names *S. Korea, Korea, South,* and *South Korea* all represent the same country. As another example, the block in the third tuple indicates that the association has been verified by curator Eric. Note that not all annotations are shown (e.g., US and United States are regarded the same as well). □

Complex annotations like those shown in the previous example pose interesting challenges in terms of how they can be implemented on top of existing database management systems (DBMS). In MONDRIAN, a simple albeit efficient relational representation of color databases (i.e., databases that contain color blocks) was proposed. In a nutshell, the relation schemas are first extended with so-called block attributes, one for each attribute in the original schema; and second, a single color attribute (*col*) is attached to each relation. If A is an attribute in the original schema, we denote by A^b its corresponding block attribute. Intuitively, if a tuple t has a block covering attribute A, then A^b will be set to 1. Otherwise, the A^b-attribute of the tuple t is set to 0. Similarly, if t has a block of a certain color, then this color is simply recorded in its *col*-attribute. More specifically, let R be a relation consisting attributes $A_1, \ldots, A_n$. For any

country	partner	product	country^b	partner^b	product^b	col
Brazil	South Korea	Electronics	1	1	0	
Brazil	US	Chemicals	0	1	1	
Chile	Germany	Motor vehicles	1	1	1	
Chile	Germany	Motor vehicles	1	1	0	
Chile	Germany	Chemicals	1	1	0	
Chile	South Korea	Electronics	0	1	1	
Chile	South Korea	Electronics	1	1	0	
Chile	South Korea	Motor vehicles	1	1	0	

Fig. 2. Relational encoding of the color relation shown in Fig. 1(d)

relation scheme R, we define the relation scheme $\bar{R} = R \cup \{A_1^b, \ldots, A_n^b\} \cup \{col\}$. Note that $\bar{R}$ is the schema of the relational representation of the color databases. More generally, to every color block database schema $\mathcal{S}$ we can associate the relational database schema $\bar{\mathcal{S}}$ which has precisely the same relation variables, but when relation variable x has relation scheme R in $\mathcal{S}$, then x has relation scheme $\bar{R}$ in $\bar{\mathcal{S}}$.

Example 2. Consider the color relation shown in Fig. 1(d). The corresponding relational representation is shown in Fig. 2. In this figure, the colors represent the annotations as given in Fig. 1(d). □

The advantage of the relational encoding used by MONDRIAN is that it requires a minimal restructuring of the existing schema. Indeed, although the representation shown in Fig. 2 requires the addition of new attributes (for blocks and colors), one can equivalently work with a representation in which separate tables for blocks and colors are present. These are then linked by means of tuple, block and color identifiers as is common practice in DBMSs. In addition, annotations of the database imposes minimum overhead in terms of space [13]. Several indexing methods, such as bitmaps [17] and multi-dimensional indexes [10], are in place to better support the presence of color blocks in databases.

In addition to supporting complex annotations, MONDRIAN provides a query interface in which color blocks are treated as first-class citizens. More specifically, a color algebra was introduced in [13] that allows the user to focus on the annotated data, without knowing how these annotations are modeled in the underlying relational database system. More specifically, the color algebra, or CA for short, consists of the following operators:

- **Projection** (π_X^{col}): which behaves like a standard projection on the data part and simply inherits all color blocks, restricted to the attributes in X;
- **Lower and Upper Block Selection** (Π_X^L, Π_X^U): which simply select all tuples and their color blocks covering all attributes in X (lower), or cover only attributes in X (upper);
- **Color Selection** (Σ_γ): which selects all tuples that contain a color block of color γ;
- **Selection** ($\sigma_{A=B}$): which behaves like the standard selection on the data part and simply copies all color blocks in the selected tuples;

Table 1. Simulation of CA by conjunctive queries (CQ). If X is a set of attributes, then X^b denotes its corresponding set of block attributes. Furthermore, in the case of the tuple join, $x \bowtie y$, the letter R (S) refers to the relation scheme of the color block relation x (y), f (resp. g) renames the common block attributes A_i^b in $R \cap S$ to attributes of the form C_i^b (resp. D_i^b), and finally, **or** is the truth table of disjunction in which the third attribute contains the result of the union of the bits in first two attributes. The latter is needed to combine all blocks in the joined tuples.

CA	$\mapsto$	CQ
$\pi_X^{col}(x)$	$\mapsto$	$\pi_{X \cup X^b \cup \{col\}}(x)$
$\Pi_X^L(x)$	$\mapsto$	$\sigma_{\bigwedge_{A \in X} A^b = 1}(x)$
$\Pi_X^U(x)$	$\mapsto$	$\sigma_{\bigwedge_{A \notin X} A^b = 0}(x)$
$\Sigma_\gamma(x)$	$\mapsto$	$\sigma_{col = \gamma}(x)$
$\sigma_{A=B}(x)$	$\mapsto$	$\sigma_{A=B}(x)$
$x \cup y$	$\mapsto$	$x \cup y$
$\rho_{A/B}(x)$	$\mapsto$	$\rho_{A/B}(\rho_{A^b/B^b}(x))$
$x \bowtie y$	$\mapsto$	$\pi_{R \cup S \cup R^b \cup S^b \cup \{col\}}(\rho_f(x)) \bowtie \rho_g(\rho_{col/col'}(y))) \bowtie_{i=1}^p \mathbf{or}(C_i^b, D_i^b, A_i^p))$
		$\cup$ Same expression but with the roles of x and y reversed.
$x \boxtimes y$	$\mapsto$	$x \bowtie y$
$\rightleftarrows_B^A(x)$	$\mapsto$	$\rho_{A^b/B^b}(x)$

- **Union** ($\cup$): which behaves like the standard union on the data part and simply copies color blocks in the tuples in the component relations;
- **Block Join** ($\boxtimes$): which joins tuples together that agree on the data part *and* share the same color block on common attributes;
- **Tuple Join** ($\bowtie$): which joins tuples together that agree on the data part, irregardless of any color blocks that may be present;
- **Renaming** ($\rho_{A/B}$): which simply renames attributes; and finally
- **Block Switch** ($\rightleftarrows_B^A$): which switches color blocks involving covering attribute A by blocks involving attribute B.

Note that none of these operators access the color blocks explicitly. Indeed, their semantics does not rely on the relational representation used to model color databases. However, to make the semantics more precise we provide a translation from the operators in CA to conjunctive queries (CQ) over the relational representation described earlier (Table 1).

Example 3. Consider again the color relation shown in Fig. 1(d). Suppose that we want to find all the tuples that have a block of color *"Verified by Mary"*, or concern the country *Brazil*. Also, assume that we are only interested in keeping the $\{country, partner\}$ attributes from these tuples. Then, the CA expression

$$e = \pi_{country, partner}^{col}((\Sigma_{\text{"Verified by Mary"}}(r)) \cup (\sigma_{country = \text{"Brazil"}}(r)))$$

returns the desired result. As another example, asking for all the tuples that have an annotation of the attribute *product* can be simply expressed in CA by means of

country	partner	country^b	partner^b	col
Brazil	South Korea	1	1	
Brazil	US	0	1	
Chile	Germany	1	1	

country	partner	
Brazil	South Korea	
Brazil	US	Verified by Eric
Chile	Germany	Verified by Mary

S. Korea = Korea, South = South Korea

(a) Relational representation of result   (b) Color result relation

Fig. 3. Query result as relational representation (a); and color relation (b)

$\Pi^L_{product}(r)$. When interested in all tuples that involve annotations exactly covering *country, partner*, then the CA expressions $\Pi^L_{country,partner}(\Pi^U_{country,partner}(r))$ would give the desired result. We refer to [13] for more examples.   □

The MONDRIAN system leverages the translation given in Table 1 by translating the user's CA query into a CQ query on the underlying relational representation. Once the result of the CQ query is obtained, it is converted again into a color relation that is given to the user. We refer to [12] for more details of the MONDRIAN system. It is noteworthy to point out that the evaluation of CA expressions, by means of the intermediate translation step to the underlying RDBMS, is comparable in terms of query execution time when compared to its unannotated version [13].

Example 4. Consider the CA expression e from the previous example. To evaluate e on the color relation shown in Fig. 1(d), MONDRIAN first translates e into a CQ query q_e as specified by Table 1. It is readily verified that q_e equals

$$\pi_{country,partner,country^b,partner^b,col}(\sigma_{col=\text{"Verified by Mary"}}(\bar{r})\cup\sigma_{country=\text{"Brazil"}}(\bar{r}))),$$

where $\bar{r}$ denotes the schema r extended with block and color attributes. The CQ query q_e is then executed on the relational representation shown in Fig. 2. The result of the q_e and the corresponding color relation is shown in Fig. 3.   □

We conclude the description of the MONDRIAN system by stating that CA (on color databases) has the same expressive power as CQ (over relational representations of color databases), even though CA does not access color blocks explicitly. Observe that Table 1 implies that for every CA-expression over $\mathcal{S}$, there exists an equivalent CQ-expression over $\bar{\mathcal{S}}$. The converse is also true:

Theorem 1 ([13]). *For every conjunctive query over $\bar{\mathcal{S}}$ whose result relation scheme is of the form $\bar{R}$ for some relation scheme R, there exists an equivalent CA expression over $\mathcal{S}$.*

As final remark, we note that in the setting that blocks cover all the attributes, and thus only the colors matter, Theorem 1 is shown to hold even in the presence of negation [11].

3   The XARCH Archiving System

Curated databases are predominantly kept in well-organized hierarchical data formats. These data formats are often equipped with a key structure that provides a canonical identification for each element in the hierarchical data. For instance, a key for an element can be taken as the combination of the path in which the element occurs together with the values of some of its sub-elements. Buneman et al. [6] developed an archiving approach that takes advantage of such keys to maintain multiple versions of an evolving curated databases. The archiving system XARCH implements an extended version of the original approach that allows archiving databases of arbitrary size [15]. More specifically, in XARCH, multiple snapshots of an evolving database are merged into a single archive. Corresponding elements in different snapshots are identified based on their key values and stored only once in the resulting archive. Each snapshot is then given a unique identifier and each element is annotated with a timestamp that represents the sequence of snapshots in which the particular element was contained in. Archives in XARCH are currently stored as XML documents. We next provide a high-level description of the archiving process by means of the following example and refer to [6,15] for more details.

Example 5. Consider the following two (XML) entries from two releases of the CIA Factbook in 1992 (left) and 1998 (right). These entries concern the number of airports in Kazakhstan:

```
                                      <country>
                                          <name>Kazakhstan</name>
<country>                                 <category>
    <name>Kazakhstan</name>                   <name>Transportation</name>
    <category>                                <property>
        <name>Communications</name>               <name>Air Transport</name>
        <property>                                <subprop>
            <name>Airports</name>                     <name>Airports</value>
            <value>NA</value>                         <value>10</value>
        </property>                               </subprop>
    </category>                               </property>
<country>                                 </category>
                                      </country>
```

In order to compare, merge and archive these two entries, a key specification is required to tell what the corresponding elements are in these two releases. The keys relevant for this fragment of the CIA Factbook are as follows:

$$k_1 = (\text{/country}, \{\text{name}\})$$
$$k_2 = (\text{/country/name}, \{\})$$
$$k_3 = (\text{/country/category}, \{\text{name}\})$$
$$k_4 = (\text{/country/category/name}, \{\})$$
$$k_5 = (\text{/country/category/property}, \{\text{name}\})$$
$$k_6 = (\text{/country/category/property/name}, \{\})$$
$$k_7 = (\text{/country/category/property/value}, \{\})$$
$$k_8 = (\text{/country/category/property/subprop}, \{\text{name}\})$$
$$k_9 = (\text{/country/category/property/subprop/name}, \{\})$$
$$k_{10} = (\text{/country/category/property/subprop/value}, \{\})$$

We provide the formal definition of keys below. The archiver will merge corresponding nodes in both entries, in a top-down manner, starting from the country nodes. The key k_1 specifies that elements nodes of type country are uniquely specified by the value of their name child node. Clearly, in order for this to make sense /country/name nodes should carry a unique value and have no further nodes below them (they are frontier nodes). For the two entries given above, "Kazakhstan" is the key for both country nodes and thus both nodes correspond to the same country. As a consequence, they will be merged in the archive. The resulting country node has timestamps $\{1992, 1998\}$. The key k_2 specifies that nodes of type name are identified by their own value. Again, the archiver merges both name nodes and the corresponding timestamps are inherited from its parent country node. As another example, k_3 says that category nodes are again identified by the value of their name child node. In the archive, we thus have two distinct nodes for the entries above, one for "Communications" (with timestamp $\{1992\}$) and one for "Transportation" (with timestamp $\{1998\}$). Proceeding along this way, until all nodes are processed, we obtain a timestamped XML documents that contains both entries. In case that more versions are available, the archiver will sequentially add each version to the archive computed so far. Figure 4 shows a minor modification of part of our current archive of the CIA World Factbook that contains the annual releases of the Factbook from 1992 to 2002. We only show the information related to the number of airports in Kazakhstan over these years. In the figure, element nodes are shown in square boxes together with their label (in angle brackets) and their key value (in square brackets). Timestamps are shown as edge labels. Note that elements (or edges) without an explicit timestamp inherit the timestamp of their parent. The two entries from 1992 and 1998 are embedded in the archive and are highlighted by bold edges. As already mentioned, frontier nodes that are used as key values, e. g., /country/name, can have only one text node as their child since objects are identified based on this value. Thus, the key value for each country is the value of this text node. Other frontier nodes, e. g., /country/category/property/value, may have multiple text nodes as children, each with a different (disjoint) timestamp. Indeed, these nodes are not used as key for any node and may have multiple values.   □

More formally, an archive $\mathcal{A}$ is a tree with two types of nodes: (i) element nodes, and (ii) text nodes. Only element nodes may occur as internal nodes. In addition, each element node has a label and a key value. Element keys are defined using key constraints. Here, we consider only a limited form of key constraints and refer to [5,6] for an extended definition and for further details. A key specification K is a set of key definitions $k = (p, q)$, where p is an absolute path of element labels and q is a set of element labels. The key definition specifies for each element e reachable by path p how the key value is derived from the subtree of e. If q is empty then $key(e) = \bot$. Otherwise, $key(e)$ is an array of values; one for each the children of e reachable by path p/ℓ, for $\ell \in q$. Elements whose values are used as key values are called *key path values*. Note that (i) there has to be exactly one child of e for each label $\ell \in q$, and (ii) this child is a frontier node, i. e., it does not have other element nodes as children. All element keys are relative keys, i. e., the key identifies an element among its siblings (with the same label).

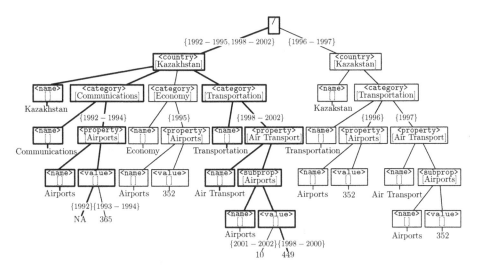

Fig. 4. Part of the archive of the CIA World Factbook (1992–2002)

Moreover, the concatenation of key values along the path from the root to an element e forms an absolute key for e. Let T denote the set of snapshot identifiers. Each node $n \in \mathcal{A}$ has a timestamp $time(n) \subseteq T$ that represents the set of snapshots that node was present in. Timestamps satisfy the following property: if a node n is a descendant of a node m in $\mathcal{A}$, then $time(n) \subseteq time(m)$. Since changes to databases are largely accretive and an element is likely to exist for a long time, we compactly represent its timestamp using time intervals rather than a sequence of version numbers. As illustrated in the previous example, the timestamps are assigned when merging different versions of the data.

Merging different snapshots into a single archive has several advantages: (i) any specific snapshot is retrievable from the archive in a single pass over the data, (ii) the storage space required is comparable to that of delta-based approaches that keep a sequence of records of changes between pairs of consecutive versions, (iii) tracking object history is easy. XARCH implements a query language (XAQL) for retrieval of individual database snapshots as well as queries over the history of data. The query language XAQL has a SQL-like syntax and it uses a restricted form of XPath expressions to filter output elements.

Example 6. The following XAQL query returns the name and population of European countries between years 2000 and 2008 in our current archive of the CIA World Factbook:

```
SELECT $c/name, $c/category[name ='People']/property[name ='Population']/value
FROM $c IN archive('CIAWFB')/country
VERSION 2000-2008
WHERE $c/category[name ='Geography']/property[name = 'Map references']/value = 'Europe'    □
```

XARCH has been successfully used to maintain the history of several curated databases. While the archiving approach generally works very well, it does make the critical assumption that the structure of the archived database remains unchanged. This restriction, however, is almost certainly to become an issue when archiving over a long period of time.

Figure 4 shows a typical problem the archiver currently faces, that is, the change of (absolute) key values. Over the history of the Factbook, the information about the total number of airports in Kazakhstan (referred to as *Kazakstan* in 1996 and 1997) was first located under category *Communications*, then under category *Economy* and 1996 moved to category *Transportation*. In 1997, the Factbook started to group information about the airports, heliports, and airlines (not shown in Figure 4) as sub-properties under a new property *Air Transport*. Due to the change in its absolute key value the archiver maintains different elements at different levels of the tree about the number of airports in Kazakhstan. While this redundancy causes a slight storage overhead, a more severe problem occurs when querying the archive. Indeed, the same information can now be found under different paths in different snapshots.

As another example, more recently, the Factbook renamed category *People* into *People and Society*. Thus, the query shown in Example 6 would return an empty result for the more recent snapshots in our archive. Making matters worse, the population of China can now be found under different paths in the history of the Factbook. XAQL queries in XARCH are currently not able to handle such changes. That is, in order to retrieve to full history of the population of China one would have to issue two separate queries and manually merge the results. Moreover, XARCH currently does not provide any mechanism to maintain information about different key values for the same element. In the following, we show how MONDRIAN can be used to maintain and query historic data in the presence of key value changes.

4   Mondrianizing XARCH

We start by showing that an archive in XARCH is a special form of a color database where timestamps are represented as color blocks. That is, we can turn any archive into a color relation. Annotations in such a relation have temporal semantics, i.e., they represent the snapshots in which a data value was valid. Then, the color algebra can be used for temporal queries over the history of data. We can use additional annotations to capture the semantic relationships of different elements in an archive, and use this to better answer queries over the history of data. In comparison to XAQL this gives us (a) a formal query language, and (b) the ability to query data under key value changes.

Consider an archive $\mathcal{A}$ following key specification K. For simplicity, assume that for all key definitions $(p,q) \in K$, q is either empty or contains exactly one label. When transforming $\mathcal{A}$ into a color database we generate a single color relation with schema $\overline{R^k} = \{A_1, \ldots, A_n\} \cup \{A_1^b, \ldots, A_n^b\} \cup \{col\}$. The schema $\overline{R^k}$ has exactly one attribute A_i for each key definition $(p,q) \in K$ where p does not identify a key path value. That is, if $p = p_1/\ell$ then $(p_1, \{\ell\})$ is not in K. We use Ψ to denote the mapping from path p in the key definition to the corresponding attribute $A_i \in \overline{R^k}$. Figure 5(a) shows the mapping Ψ for the archive in Figure 4, while Figures 5(b) and (c) show the schema of the generated relation $\overline{R^k}$. For convenience, in our implementation we split $\overline{R^k}$ into two relations (as mentioned in Section 2), one relation for storing the archive raw data and another for storing just the annotations.

We now turn our attention on how to compute the instances shown in the figures and concentrate first on the raw data. Let r^k be in general the instance for schema R^k. We create one tuple in r^k for each text node n in $\mathcal{A}$ that is not a child of a key path value. Let $value(n)$ denote the text value of n and let $<e_1, \ldots, e_m>$ denote the sequence of elements on the path to n. Furthermore, let $path(e)$ denote the path of element e. Then, for the text node n, we create a tuple t where for each $e \in <e_1, \ldots, e_{m-1}>$ we set $t[\Psi(path(e))] = key(e)$ and for e_m we set $t[\Psi(path(e_m))] = value(n)$. For attributes $A \in R^k$ where no element e with $\Psi(path(e)) = A$ exists in $<e_1, \ldots, e_m>$, we set $t[A] = \perp$. Figure 5(b) shows an instance r^k for the archive in Figure 4.

We next consider the creation of colors and blocks. For each of the tuples t in r^k and each snapshot identifier s in $time(e)$ with e the text element that warranted the creation of t in r^k, we create one tuple $\overline{r^k}$ with $t[col]$ representing the snapshot identifier s. This sets the color of the tuples. For the blocks, we set $t[A_i^b] = 1$, for $1 \leq i < m$ if $s \in time(e_i)$. Likewise, for A_m^b we use the timestamp of text node n to decide the value of $t[A_m^b]$. We illustrate the above construction by means of the following example.

Example 7. The instance $\overline{r^k}$ of $\overline{R^k}$ corresponding the CIA Factbook fragment shown in Figure 4 consists of the raw data instance shown in Figure 5(b) together with colored blocks represented by the first 11 tuples in Figure 5(c). For example, there are two blocks for the tuple with $tid = 3$ of Figure 5(b), since the corresponding path is present in both 1994 and 1995. Similarly, there are three blocks for the tuple with $tid = 6$ for the years 1998, 1999 and 2000.   □

In our example the timestamp of every internal node equals the union of timestamps of its children. This is not true in general, however. For example, in any snapshot of the CIA World Factbook a country may have a category without property elements or a property value without a text node child. Note that the key path values for a node, however, always have to exists, i.e., there are no missing values in element keys. To ensure that our transformation of an archive into a color relation is lossless we have to create a tuple in r^k for every element e whose timestamp contains snapshot identifiers that are not contained in the timestamp of any of e's children. We set tuple values according to the sequence of elements on the path to e. That is, for every snapshot identifier $s \in time(e)$ that does not appear in any of the timestamps of the children of e we create one tuple $\overline{r^k}$ such that $t[col]$ represents s.

The advantage of modeling archives by means of color relations is that one can annotate the archived data, beyond the encoding of timestamps, at no additional cost.

tid	co^b	ca^b	pr^b	prv^b	sp^b	spv^b	col
1	1	1	1	1	0	0	1992
2	1	1	1	1	0	0	1993
3	1	1	1	1	0	0	1994
3	1	1	1	1	0	0	1995
4	1	1	1	1	0	0	1996
5	1	1	1	0	1	1	1997
6	1	1	1	0	1	1	1998
6	1	1	1	0	1	1	1999
6	1	1	1	0	1	1	2000
7	1	1	1	0	1	1	2001
7	1	1	1	0	1	1	2002
1	1	1	1	1	0	0	KZ
2	1	1	1	1	0	0	KZ
3	1	1	1	1	0	0	KZ
4	1	1	1	1	0	0	KZ
5	1	1	1	0	1	1	KZ
6	1	1	1	0	1	1	KZ
7	1	1	1	0	1	1	KZ
2	0	0	0	1	0	0	APNo
3	0	0	0	1	0	0	APNo
4	0	0	0	1	0	0	APNo
5	0	0	0	0	0	1	APNo
6	0	0	0	0	0	1	APNo
7	0	0	0	0	0	1	APNo

/country	→ co
/country/category	→ ca
/country/category/property	→ pr
/country/category/property/value	→ prv
/country/category/property/subprop	→ sp
/country/category/property/subprop/value	→ spv

(a) Mapping Ψ of element paths to attributes

(c) Encoding of timestamps and semantics using colors/blocks

tid	co	ca	pr	prv	sp	spv
1	Kazakhstan	Communications	Airports	NA	⊥	⊥
2	Kazakhstan	Communications	Airports	365	⊥	⊥
3	Kazakhstan	Economy	Airports	352	⊥	⊥
4	Kazakstan	Transportation	Airports	352	⊥	⊥
5	Kazakstan	Transportation	Air Transport	⊥	Airports	352
6	Kazakhstan	Transportation	Air Transport	⊥	Airports	10
7	Kazakhstan	Transportation	Air Transport	⊥	Airports	449

(b) An archive relation for the number of airports in Kazakhstan

Fig. 5. A representation of archives in MONDRIAN

Example 8. For example, we already mentioned that there are (at least) two spellings, namely *Kazakstan* and *Kazakhstan*, for the same country. With colors and blocks, we alleviate such issues by introducing a new color *KZ* that corresponds to the ISO 3166 country code for this country. Then, we use this color to define 7 blocks that cover each of the tuples in Figure 5(b). Another *semantic* annotation can be used to denote that, in spite of the structural differences, all tuples in Figure 5(b) actually represent information about the number of airports in Kazakhstan. For that, we can use a new color *APNo* (for Airport Number) to create a block for each column (it can be a different column for each tuple) that is used to store the number of airports. The last six tuples in Figure 5(c) define these blocks. Notice that for the tuple with $tid=1$ in Figure 5(b) there is no block with color *APNo* in Figure 5(c) since the number of airports is not available (NA).   □

We conclude this section by showing that the color algebra allows for the querying of the archived data beyond current capabilities of XAQL.

Example 9. We can use CA to query the annotated relation with timestamps. The following CA query retrieves the tuples between 1995 and 1997.

$$\Sigma_{\text{``1995''}}\left(r^k\right) \cup \Sigma_{\text{``1996''}}\left(r^k\right) \cup \Sigma_{\text{``1997''}}\left(r^k\right)$$

Notice that while the blocks annotate different columns in different tuples, this difference is not visible in the query itself. This is unlike the XARCH system where structural differences manifest themselves in the query expression. With this in place, the following simple CA expression retrieves all the different spellings of the country's name:

$$\pi_{co}(\Sigma_{\text{``KZ''}}(r^k))$$

Notice that this query is not expressible in the XARCH system since unless we know explicitly the different spellings, we cannot identify the relevant parts of the tree that refer to this country (and not another one). As another example, the following CA expression retrieves all the tuples for which the number of airports in Kazakhstan is stored in the *prv* column:

$$\Sigma_{\text{``KZ''}}(\Pi_{prv}^{U}(r^k))$$

The query returns the tuples with $tid=2$, $tid=3$ and $tid=4$. Again, notice that we retrieve these numbers for different spellings of the country's name, and for values that are located at different paths of the corresponding tree in the XARCH system.   □

All combined, this shows that MONDRIAN naturally allows for the modeling of curated evolving data and that the color algebra provides an elegant way to pose historical queries. The current paper provides only a proof-of-concept of our approach. We leave the experimental validation to future work.

References

1. https://www.cia.gov/library/publications/the-world-factbook/index.html
2. http://www.iuphar-db.org
3. Bhagwat, D., Chiticariu, L., Tan, W.C., Vijayvargiya, G.: An annotation management system for relational databases. In: Proceedings of the 30th International Conference on Very Large Data Bases (VLDB), pp. 900–911 (2004)
4. Buneman, P., Cheney, J., Tan, W.C., Vansummeren, S.: Curated databases. In: Proceedings of the 27th Symposium on Principles of Database Systems (PODS), pp. 1–12 (2008)
5. Buneman, P., Davidson, S., Fan, W., Hara, C., Tan, W.C.: Keys for xml. In: Proceedings of the 10th International Conference on World Wide Web (WWW), pp. 201–210 (2001)
6. Buneman, P., Khanna, S., Tajima, K., Tan, W.C.: Archiving scientific data. ACM Trans. Database Syst. 29(1), 2–42 (2004)
7. Buneman, P., Khanna, S., Tan, W.C.: On propagation of deletions and annotations through views. In: Proceedings of the 21st Symposium on Principles of Database Systems (PODS), pp. 150–158 (2002)
8. Curino, C.A., Moon, H.J., Zaniolo, C.: Graceful database schema evolution: the prism workbench. Proc. VLDB Endow. 1(1), 761–772 (2008)
9. Eltabakh, M.Y., Aref, W.G., Elmagarmid, A.K., Ouzzani, M., Silva, Y.N.: Supporting annotations on relations. In: Proceedings of 12th International Conference on Extending Database Technology (EDBT), pp. 379–390 (2009)
10. Eltabakh, M.Y., Ouzzani, M., Aref, W.G., Elmagarmid, A.K., Laura-Silva, Y., Arshad, M.U., Salt, D., Baxter, I.: Managing biological data using bdbms. In: Proceedings of the 25th International Conference on Data Engineering (ICDE), pp. 1600–1603 (2008)
11. Geerts, F., den Bussche, J.V.: Relational completeness of query languages for annotated databases. J. Comput. Syst. Sci. 77(3), 491–504 (2011)

12. Geerts, F., Kementsietsidis, A., Milano, D.: *i*MONDRIAN: A visual tool to annotate and query scientific databases. In: Ioannidis, Y., et al. (eds.) EDBT 2006. LNCS, vol. 3896, pp. 1168–1171. Springer, Heidelberg (2006)
13. Geerts, F., Kementsietsidis, A., Milano, D.: Mondrian: Annotating and querying databases through colors and blocks. In: Proceedings of the 22nd International Conference on Data Engineering, ICDE (2006)
14. Green, T.J., Karvounarakis, G., Tannen, V.: Provenance semirings. In: Proceedings of the 26th Symposium on Principles of Database Systems (PODS), pp. 31–40 (2007)
15. Koltsidas, I., Müller, H., Viglas, S.D.: Sorting hierarchical data in external memory for archiving. Proc. VLDB Endow. 1(1), 1205–1216 (2008)
16. Kostylev, E., Buneman, P.: Combining dependent annotations for relational algebra. In: Proceedings of the 15th International Conference on Database Theory, ICDT (2012)
17. Mavromatis, M.: Indexing in the MONDRIAN annotation management system. Master's thesis, University of Edinburgh, United Kingdom (2006)
18. Moon, H.J., Curino, C.A., Deutsch, A., Hou, C.Y., Zaniolo, C.: Managing and querying transaction-time databases under schema evolution. Proc. VLDB Endow. 1(1), 882–895 (2008)
19. Müller, H., Buneman, P., Koltsidas, I.: Xarch: archiving scientific and reference data. In: Proceedings of the ACM SIGMOD International Conference on Management of Data (SIGMOD), pp. 1295–1298 (2008)
20. Srivastava, D., Velegrakis, Y.: Intensional associations between data and metadata. In: Proceedings of the ACM SIGMOD International Conference on Management of Data (SIGMOD), pp. 401–412 (2007)
21. Wang, H.(W.), Liu, R., Theodoratos, D., Wu, X.: Efficient storage and temporal query evaluation in hierarchical data archiving systems. In: Bayard Cushing, J., French, J., Bowers, S. (eds.) SSDBM 2011. LNCS, vol. 6809, pp. 109–128. Springer, Heidelberg (2011)

Static Analysis and Query Answering
for Incomplete Data Trees with Constraints

Amélie Gheerbrant[1,2], Leonid Libkin[1], and Juan Reutter[1,3]

[1] School of Informatics, University of Edinburgh
[2] LIAFA (Université Paris Diderot - Paris 7 & CNRS)
[3] Department of Computer Science, Pontificia Universidad Catolica de Chile

Abstract. Data trees serve as an abstraction of XML documents: in such trees, every node comes with a label from a finite alphabet, as well as a data value from an infinite set. Incomplete data trees model XML documents with incomplete information; they may include both structural incompleteness and incompleteness of data. Here we study two basic problems for incomplete data trees under typical constraints such as keys and foreign keys. The first problem is consistency of specifications of incomplete data trees. We show that many of recently established results on consistency of constraints and schema descriptions can be transferred to the consistency of incomplete tree specifications without any increase in complexity. After that we examine query answering over incomplete data trees under constraints, and show that tractable bounds can be recovered under key constraints, but are lost under foreign keys.

1 Introduction

In this paper we examine two basic problems about XML documents with incomplete information: namely their consistency (or satisfiability), and query answering. The first problem asks whether a description of an incomplete document is consistent, under some schema restrictions: that is, whether a completion satisfying the schema requirement exists. The second problem is to find certain answers, i.e., answers independent of a particular interpretation of missing features of the incomplete document. These are standard data management problems and they have been studied extensively, in particular in the context of incomplete XML documents. Our *main contribution* here is to study them when the schema description contains constraints commonly found in databases, such as keys and foreign keys.

Traditional XML schema descriptions, such as DTDs, can be subsumed by the power of tree automata [22]; such automata operate on trees labeled with letters from a finite alphabet. Constraints such as keys and foreign keys, on the other hand, talk about *data* in XML documents. Since data values typically come from infinite domain (e.g., numbers, or strings), they cannot be captured by traditional automata.

The interplay between finiteness of the description of the structure of XML document and the infinite domains of data such document carry has been a central theme in XML research. A typical object of investigation is the abstraction

V. Tannen et al. (Eds.): Buneman Festschrift, LNCS 8000, pp. 273–290, 2013.

of XML documents known as *data trees*: these are finitely-labeled trees that can carry data from an infinite set. Now we apply some of the developed techniques to the study of such data trees with incomplete information. In the rest of the introduction, we explain briefly what incomplete data trees are, and the two main problems we study.

Incomplete XML Documents. We follow a general approach to incompleteness in XML described in [3]. In relational databases, incompleteness is usually modeled via null values, which may appear in place of constants. In XML, due to its more complex structure, two other types of incompleteness may appear:

- structural incompleteness: precise relationships between some nodes may not be known (for instance, we may know that one node is a descendant of another without knowing the full path between them);
- labeling incompleteness: some node labels can be replaced by wildcards, indicating that the exact label is not known at present.

Consistency Problem. For usual XML documents with incomplete information, the consistency problem asks whether such an incomplete description t can represent a complete tree T satisfying some schema constraints, typically expressed by a tree automaton $\mathcal{A}$. Most versions of this problem range from tractable to being NP-complete [3].

A different type of consistency problems often arises in the study of *static analysis* of XML. A typical formulation is as follows: we are given some schema information, say an automaton $\mathcal{A}$, and some constraints Δ involving data values (e.g., keys, foreign keys). The question is whether there is an XML document that conforms to the schema (is accepted by $\mathcal{A}$) and satisfies Δ.

Simplest versions of this problem (for Δ containing unary keys and foreign keys, for instance) are known to be NP-complete [13], but by now many other variations exist, e.g., [2,6,7,8,12,23,24]. Reasoning tasks can be of varying complexity, starting from NP and going up to high but elementary [2,7] or extremely high (e.g., non-primitive-recursive [14,15]) and even undecidable (e.g., binary keys and foreign keys [13]).

Our consistency problem is different from a pure static analysis, as it takes an incomplete data tree t as an input, together with the static information such as $\mathcal{A}$ and Δ. Our result on the consistency problem is that, under mild assumptions, the complexity of static analysis tasks for complete XML documents applies to the analysis of incomplete documents. In other words, we show how incomplete documents can be added into static analysis tasks without any increase in computational complexity. Note of course that an incomplete tree t can be encoded as an automaton, so in principle static analysis can be extended to handle data. However, an automaton encoding t may well be of exponential size in t, and to prove our result we need to find a way around this exponential blow up.

Query Answering. The standard approach to answering queries over databases with incomplete information is to look for *certain answers*, i.e., answers independent of how particular incomplete features are interpreted. Here we look at analogs of (unions of) conjunctive queries for XML. In the relational case, these can be evaluated in polynomial time [18], but in the XML case, their complexity can range from polynomial time to CONP-complete [3]. However, it was shown in [3] that their complexity drops back to polynomial time in the case of *rigid* trees, that do not allow any structural incompleteness. This is true without constraints, but the relational case teaches us that constraints are likely to change the complexity of query answering [10].

We show here that this is true in the XML case too: when we allow just a single unary inclusion constraint, finding certain answers over rigid trees jumps to CONP-complete, but with keys it stays in polynomial time.

Organization. In Section 2 we describe data trees and integrity constraints. In Section 3 we describe the model of incomplete XML documents (or data trees). In Section 4 we study the consistency problem, and in Section 5 we present our results on query answering.

2   Preliminaries

Data Trees and Automata. To describe data trees, we assume

- a countably infinite set $\mathcal{C}$ of possible data values (notation $\mathcal{C}$ stands for "constants"; later we shall extend data trees to domains that contain both constants and nulls), and
- a countably infinite set $\mathcal{L}$ of node labels (element types). We shall normally denote labels by lowercase Greek letters.

A data tree over a finite alphabet $\Sigma \subset \mathcal{L}$ is a 2-sorted structure

$$T = \langle D, A, \downarrow, \rightarrow, (P_\alpha)_{\alpha \in \Sigma}, \rho \rangle, \tag{1}$$

where

- D is a finite unranked tree domain, i.e., a prefix-closed subset of $\mathbb{N}^*$ such that $w \cdot i \in D$ implies $w \cdot j \in D$ for $j < i$;
- $\downarrow$ and $\rightarrow$ are the child and next-sibling relations, for which we shall use, as is common, the infix notation: $w \downarrow w \cdot i$ whenever $w \cdot i \in D$, and $w \cdot i \rightarrow w \cdot (i+1)$ whenever $w \cdot (i + 1) \in D$;
- each P_α is the set of elements of D labeled α (of course we require that these partition D);
- $A \subset \mathcal{C}$ is a finite set of data values; and
- $\rho : D \rightarrow A$ assigns to each node $w \in D$ a data value.

We refer to D as the *domain* of T, and denote it by $\mathrm{dom}(T)$, and to A as the *active domain* (of data values) of T and denote it by $\mathrm{adom}(T)$. We always assume that A has precisely the elements of $\mathcal{C}$ used in T, i.e., if $v \in A$ then there is a node w such that $v = \rho(w)$. We denote by $V_\alpha(T)$ the set of all data values assigned to α-nodes by ρ. That is, $V_\alpha(T) = \{\rho(w) \mid P_\alpha(w) \text{ holds}\}$.

We shall denote the transitive closure of $\downarrow$ by $\Downarrow$ and the transitive closure of $\rightarrow$ by $\Rightarrow$.

An *unranked tree automaton* [26] over Σ is a tuple $\mathcal{A} = (Q, \Sigma, \delta, F)$, where Q is a finite set of states, $F \subseteq Q$ is the set of final states, and $\delta : Q \times \Sigma \rightarrow 2^{Q^*}$ is a transition function. We require all $\delta(q, \alpha)$'s to be regular languages over alphabet Q, for all $q \in Q$ and $\alpha \in \Sigma$.

A *run* of $\mathcal{A}$ over a tree T is a function $\tau_{\mathcal{A}} : \mathrm{dom}(T) \rightarrow Q$, such that for each node w that is labeled α and has k children $w \cdot 0, \ldots, w \cdot (k-1)$, the word $\tau_{\mathcal{A}}(w \cdot 0) \cdots \tau_{\mathcal{A}}(w \cdot (k-1))$ belongs to the language of $\delta(\tau_{\mathcal{A}}(w), \alpha)$. In particular, if w is a leaf, then the empty word belongs to $\delta(\tau_{\mathcal{A}}(w), \alpha)$. A run is accepting if $\tau_{\mathcal{A}}(\epsilon) \in F$, that is, if the root of T is assigned a final state. As customary, we denote the language of all trees accepted by $\mathcal{A}$ by $L(\mathcal{A})$.

XML Integrity Constraints. We consider keys, inclusion constraints and foreign keys as our basic integrity constraints. They are the most common constraints in relational databases, and are common in XML as well, as many documents are generated from databases. Moreover, these sets of constraints are similar to, but more general than XML ID/IDREF specifications, and can be used to model most of the key/keyref specifications of XML Schema used in practice [20,19]. Here we only deal with constraints specified with element types rather than those specified by paths, as is done, for instance, in [2,9].

Let $\Sigma \subset \mathcal{L}$. Then a *basic XML constraint* over Σ is one of the following:

- A *key* constraint $key(\alpha)$, where $\alpha \in \Sigma$. An XML tree T satisfies $key(\alpha)$, denoted by $T \models key(\alpha)$ iff for every distinct α-nodes n and n' in T, we have $\rho(n) \neq \rho(n')$, i.e., the data values on n and n' are different.
- An *inclusion constraint* $\alpha_1 \subseteq \alpha_2$, where $\alpha_1, \alpha_2 \in \Sigma$. This constraint is satisfied, i.e., $T \models \alpha_1 \subseteq \alpha_2$, iff $V_{\alpha_1}(T) \subseteq V_{\alpha_2}(T)$.
- A *foreign key*. A combination of an inclusion constraint and a key constraint, namely $\alpha_1 \subseteq_{\mathrm{FK}} \alpha_2$ holds iff $\alpha_1 \subseteq \alpha_2$ and $key(\alpha_2)$ both hold.

3   XML with Incomplete Information

To define incomplete XML documents, we assume a countably infinite supply of null values (or variables) $\mathcal{V}$. Following [3,16], incompleteness can appear in documents in the following ways.

- Data-values incompleteness. This is the same as incompleteness in relational models: some data values could be replaced by nulls.
- Labeling incompleteness. Instead of a known label, some nodes can be labeled with a wildcard.
- Structural incompleteness. Some of the structure of the document may not be known (e.g., we can use descendant edges in addition to child edges, or following-sibling edges instead of next-sibling).

This can be captured as follows. An *incomplete data tree* over Σ is a 2-sorted structure

$$t = \langle N, V, \downarrow, \Downarrow, \rightarrow, \Rightarrow, (P_\alpha)_{\alpha \in \Sigma}, \rho \rangle, \tag{2}$$

where

- N is a set of nodes, and V is a set of values from $\mathcal{C} \cup \mathcal{V}$;
- $\downarrow, \Downarrow, \rightarrow, \Rightarrow$ are binary relations on N;
- P_α's are disjoint subsets of N; and
- ρ is a function from N to V.

As before, $\text{dom}(t)$ refers to N, and $\text{adom}(t)$ to V. We now distinguish between $\text{adom}_c(t)$, which refers to elements of $\mathcal{C}$ in $\text{adom}(t)$, and $\text{adom}_\perp(t)$, which refers to elements of $\mathcal{V}$ in $\text{adom}(t)$.

These represent incompleteness in XML as follows:

- elements of $\mathcal{V}$ are the usual null values;
- P_α's do not necessarily cover all of N; those nodes in N not assigned a label can be thought of as labeled with a wildcard;
- structural incompleteness is captured by relations $\downarrow, \rightarrow, \Downarrow, \Rightarrow$ which could be arbitrary. For example, we may know that $w \Downarrow w'$ without knowing anything about the path between the two.

Rigid Trees. An incomplete tree $t = \langle N, V, \downarrow, \Downarrow, \rightarrow, \Rightarrow, (P_\alpha)_{\alpha \in \Sigma}, \rho \rangle$ is called *rigid* [3] if its pure "structural part", i.e., $t_0 = \langle N, \downarrow, \rightarrow, (P_\alpha)_{\alpha \in \Sigma} \rangle$ is a labeled unranked tree with wildcards. That is, N is an unranked tree domain, the P_α's are disjoint subsets of N, and for nodes n, n' we have

- $n \downarrow n'$ iff $n' = n \cdot i$ for some $i \in \mathbb{N}$;
- $n \rightarrow n'$ iff $n = w \cdot i$ and $n' = w \cdot (i + 1)$ for some $w \in \mathbb{N}^*$ and $i \in \mathbb{N}$.

In other words, in rigid trees we do not permit any structural incompleteness regarding the axes $\downarrow, \rightarrow, \Downarrow,$ and $\Rightarrow$ (the axes $\Downarrow$ and $\Rightarrow$ will always be interpreted as the transitive closures of $\downarrow$ and $\rightarrow$ respectively). The only allowed types of incompleteness are nulls for data values, and wildcards.

Semantics. As is common with incomplete information, we define semantics via homomorphisms $h : t \rightarrow T$ from an incomplete data tree t to a complete data tree T. A *homomorphism*

$$h : \langle N, V, \downarrow, \Downarrow, \rightarrow, \Rightarrow, (P_\alpha)_{\alpha \in \Sigma}, \rho \rangle \longrightarrow \langle D, A, \downarrow, \rightarrow, (P_\alpha)_{\alpha \in \Sigma'}, \rho \rangle,$$

where $\Sigma \subseteq \Sigma'$, is a map from $N \cup V$ to $D \cup A$ such that

- $h(n) \in D$ if $n \in N$ and $h(v) \in A$ if $v \in V$;
- if wRw' in t, then $h(w)Rh(w')$ in T, when R is one of $\downarrow, \rightarrow, \Downarrow, \Rightarrow$;
- if $w \in P_\alpha$ in t, then $h(w) \in P_\alpha$ in T, for each $\alpha \in \Sigma$;
- $h(c) = c$ whenever $c \in \mathcal{C}$; and
- $h(\rho(w)) = \rho(h(w))$ for each $w \in N$.

Not that homomorphisms are not injective, i.e. two nodes in N can be mapped to the same node in D. To allow such a situation where two nodes might represent the same information is standard in incomplete information. The semantics of an incomplete tree t is the set of all complete trees T that it has a homomorphism into:

$$[\![t]\!] \;=\; \{T \mid \text{there exists a homomorphism } h : t \to T\}.$$

4   Consistency

In this section we consider the consistency problem for XML incomplete descriptions in the presence of integrity constraints of various forms. More formally, let **I** be a class of XML integrity constraints. We consider the following problem:

> PROBLEM: INCTREE-CONSISTENCY(**I**)
> INPUT: an incomplete tree t,
>   a tree automaton $\mathcal{A}$;
>   a set Δ of constraints in **I**.
> QUESTION: is there a tree $T \in [\![t]\!]$ so that $T \in L(\mathcal{A})$ and $T \models \Delta$?

4.1   Consistency with Respect to Automata and Constraints

As already mentioned, satisfiability (or consistency) questions arise often in the XML setting, and substantial progress has been made on solving pure static analysis problems, i.e., those not involving data. In fact, many decidable formalisms are known for XML schemas, specified by automata, and constraints or queries [2,6,7,8,11,12,13,21,23,24]. The complexity of such reasoning problems usually ranges from NP-complete (since Boolean satisfiability can easily be encoded) to a stack of exponentials and beyond (e.g., non-primitive-recursive [14,15], or even undecidable [7,13]).

Many of such static analysis problems studied in the XML context can be abstracted as follows. Let again **I** be a class of XML integrity constraints. The problem we deal with now is:

> PROBLEM: AUTOMATA-CONSISTENCY(**I**)
> INPUT: A tree automaton $\mathcal{A}$,
>   a set Δ of constraints in **I**.
> QUESTION: is there a tree T so that $T \in L(\mathcal{A})$ and $T \models \Delta$?

For constraints that we deal with here, [13] tells us that AUTOMATA-CONSISTENCY($\mathcal{K} + \mathcal{IC}$) is NP-complete, where $\mathcal{K} + \mathcal{IC}$ is the class of keys and inclusion constraints. These results have been extended to more powerful constraints (and automata as well). For instance, [12] looked at *linear data constraints* and *set constraints*, that essentially extend basic XML constraints with the full power of linear equations; these generalize keys and foreign keys. A different approach was considered in [2], where constraints involving regular expressions were studied, and results extended for constraints that do not hold in the entire XML document, but in subsets of it. Multiple papers deal with constraints provided by XPath expressions (e.g., [7,8,11,24]) or more complex models of automata (e.g., [6]).

Naturally, any lower bound for AUTOMATA-CONSISTENCY($\mathbf{I}$) applies directly as a lower bound for INCTREE-CONSISTENCY($\mathbf{I}$), since one can easily construct incomplete trees that represent the entire universe of XML trees (e.g., a single root-node). This implies, for example, that INCTREE-CONSISTENCY($\mathcal{K} + \mathcal{IC}$) is NP-hard.

What about the upper bounds? We show in the next section that most known upper bounds for different versions of AUTOMATA-CONSISTENCY continue to hold if we add incomplete trees into the mix, as one can reason about incomplete trees for free, provided the AUTOMATA-CONSISTENCY does not trivialize. Essentially, this says that we can transfer known results on static reasoning about XML to reasoning about incomplete trees: those come for free.

4.2 General Upper Bound

To achieve the transfer of complexity results from AUTOMATA-CONSISTENCY to INCTREE-CONSISTENCY, we need to impose some mild conditions on the former. The first is that its complexity should not be too low. The second and third state that systems of constraints must have some degree of uniformity (for instance, they should not be tied to just one alphabet, or a particular data value). And the last condition states that they should be extendable with constraints that admit modest reasoning complexity. We now formalize these requirements and demonstrate that many instances of AUTOMATA-CONSISTENCY satisfy them.

Complexity. Most reasoning tasks involving schema and constraints are at least NP-hard (e.g., even the simple case of DTDs and unary keys and inclusion constraints is such [13]). Hence, we shall require that the complexity class to which AUTOMATA-CONSISTENCY belongs be closed under NP-reductions.

A complexity class $\mathbf{C}$ is *closed under* NP-*reductions* if whenever we have languages $A, B \subseteq \Gamma^*$ such that $B \in \mathbf{C}$ and there is a polynomial-time computable function $f : \Gamma^* \times \Gamma^* \to \Gamma^*$ and a polynomial p such that for each $x \in \Gamma^*$ we have $x \in A$ iff $f(y, x) \in B$ for some $y \in \Gamma^*$ of size at most $p(|x|)$, then $A \in \mathbf{C}$.

Most complexity classes above NP that allow nondterministic guesses rather trivially satisfy this condition.

Alphabet Extensions. A class $\mathbf{I}$ allows for *alphabet extension* if the following holds. Let Σ and Σ' be alphabets of labels, and let γ be a surjective map $\Sigma' \to \Sigma$. Then for every set Δ of constraints over Σ one can construct, in polynomial time, a set Δ' of constraints over Σ' such that a tree T' over Σ' satisfies Δ' iff its projection T to Σ satisfies Δ.

Constraint Extensions. Following [13,12], we introduce set and linear constraints as follows. Fix variables x_α, V_α and $|V_\alpha|$, for each $\alpha \in \Sigma$. The interpretation of x_α is $\#_\alpha(T)$, the number of α-nodes in T; and the interpretation of V_α and $|V_\alpha|$ is, respectively, $V_\alpha(T)$ and $|V_\alpha(T)|$, the set of data values found in α nodes in T, and the cardinality of this set. We shall assume that the complexity of AUTOMATA-CONSISTENCY(**I**) does not change if **I** is expanded with the following: linear constraints over variables x_α and $|V_\alpha|$, and set constraints of form $V_\alpha = V_{\alpha_1} \cap \cdots \cap V_{\alpha_p}$, or $V_\alpha \cap V_{\alpha'} = \emptyset$.

We call a class of constraints *feasible* if it is generic (i.e., invariant under permutations of the domain of data values) and satisfies the alphabet-extension and the constraint-extension conditions above.

While these conditions (with the exception of the standard notion of genericity) may look restrictive, they are not: in fact, they apply to a large number of constraints. For instance, they apply to the following.

- Classes of keys, inclusion constraints, and foreign keys. Indeed, it is well known that these can be stated as linear and set constraints introduced above [13], and the complexity of such constraints is in NP [12]. In fact many other constraints could be for free added too, e.g., *denial* constraints, stating that $V_\alpha(T) \cap V_{\alpha'}(T) = \emptyset$ for $\alpha \neq \alpha'$.
- Extensions of keys and inclusion constraints specified by properties of nodes. For instance, instead of $key(\alpha)$, one can state a condition $key(\phi)$, where ϕ is a formula with one free variable over the language of unranked trees. We only require that ϕ be definable in MSO. For instance, ϕ could be an XPath node formula. The meaning of such a constraint is that all nodes satisfying ϕ have different data values. Such constraints include many constraints considered, for instance, in [2,9]. Their good properties easily follow from [12].
- Classes of constraints expressed by [25]. Such automata are closed under adding set and linear constraints, and they capture many existing models of constraints over data trees (e.g., those expressible in 2-variable logic).

Now we can state our transfer result.

Theorem 1. *Let* **C** *be a complexity class that is closed under* NP-*reductions, and* **I** *a feasible class of integrity constraints. If* AUTOMATA-CONSISTENCY(**I**) *is in* **C***, then so is* INCTREE-CONSISTENCY(**I**)

Proof. Let **I** and **C** be as stated in the theorem. Since by the assumption **C** is closed under NP-reductions, it suffices to show that INCTREE-CONSISTENCY(**I**) is NP-reducible to AUTOMATA-CONSISTENCY(**I**).

To that extent, let t, $\mathcal{A}$ and $\Delta \in$ **I** be arbitrary inputs of INCTREE-CONSISTENCY(**I**). The basic idea behind the reduction is to construct a tree automaton $\mathcal{A}_t$ whose language is exactly $[\![t]\!]$, in which case one trivially has that AUTOMATA-CONSISTENCY(**I**) accepts on inputs $\mathcal{A} \times \mathcal{A}_T$ and Δ if and only if INCTREE-CONSISTENCY(**I**) accepts on inputs t, $\mathcal{A}$ and Δ.

Unfortunately, it is not difficult to show that $\mathcal{A}_t$ might be exponential in the size of t. In order to avoid the exponential blowup, we use the fact that we can *guess* with no cost (since **C** is closed under NP-reductions), and guess first an *intermediate* structure describing only the information about $[\![t]\!]$ that is enough to show consistency. We denote these structures as *tree skeletons*, which we define next.

Tree skeletons are defined just as XML trees, with the difference that instead of the child relation we can use either $\downarrow$ or $\downarrow^+$, and instead of next sibling relation one can use either $\rightarrow$ or $\rightarrow^+$. As expected, $\downarrow^+$ and $\rightarrow^+$ are interpreted as *strict* descendant and *strict* following sibling, respectively. More formally, we define a tree skeleton as a structure $sk = \langle D, A, \downarrow, \downarrow^+, \rightarrow, \rightarrow^+, (P_\alpha)_{\alpha \in \Sigma}, \rho \rangle$, where D is an unranked tree domain, the relations $\downarrow, \downarrow^+, \rightarrow, \rightarrow^+$, are binary, and relations P_α's are unary, and the following are satisfied:

1. Every node w in D can have at most one $\downarrow^+$-child (i.e., at most one w' such that $w \downarrow^+ w'$ holds), and
2. No node w in D can have $\downarrow$-children and $\downarrow^+$-children at the same time (i.e., there could be no nodes w', w'' so that $w \downarrow w'$ and $w \downarrow^+ w''$ hold).

We define the notion of a homomorphism h from a skeleton to a tree T so that they preserve all relations, i.e., if $w \downarrow^+ w'$ in the skeleton, then $h(w')$ is a strict descendant of $h(w)$ in T, and so on. With this, the semantics of tree skeletons is defined using homomorphisms:

$$[\![sk]\!] = \{T \mid \text{there exists a homomorphism } sk \rightarrow T\}.$$

The following lemma captures the intuition that tree skeleton, while possibly exponentially smaller than trees, carry enough information to solve the consistency problem.

Lemma 1. *There exists a polynomial p with the following properties. Let t be an incomplete tree, T a data tree in $[\![t]\!]$, and S a subset of nodes in T. Then, there exists a skeleton sk of size at most $p(|t| + |S|)$ such that*

1. *$T \in [\![sk]\!]$,*
2. *$[\![sk]\!] \subseteq [\![t]\!]$, and*
3. *for each α-node in S with data value c, there is at least one α-node in sk with data value c.*

Proof sketch: Since $T \in [\![t]\!]$, there is a homomorphism from t to T. The skeleton sk is constructed by marking in T all nodes in S, as well as all nodes in T that witness the homomorphism from t to T. From these marked nodes one can construct a tree-shaped skeleton by subsequently adding the least common ancestor of every pair of nodes that are not a direct descendant of a marked node, and adding first and last siblings if these are not already marked. It is not difficult, but rather cumbersome, to show that this construction can be done in polynomial time, and satisfies the desired properties.   □

Let sk be a tree skeleton over Σ. Our next task is to define an automaton that corresponds, at least in some extent, to the set of trees represented by sk.

Recall that we denote the active domain (of data values) by adom(sk), and let $\perp$ be a fresh value not in $\mathcal{C}$. We now show how to construct from sk and $\perp$ an unranked tree automaton $A_{(sk,\perp)} = (Q, (\Sigma \times (\text{adom}(sk) \cup \{\perp\})), \{q_f\}, \delta)$, where Q and δ are defined inductively. We start with $Q = \{q_f\} \cup \{q_n \mid n \in D\}$, and the following transitions in δ:

- $(q_f, (\alpha, \perp)) \to q_f^*$, for each α in Σ

Next, for each $n \in D$, we add extra states and transitions to $A_{(sk,\perp)}$, according to the following conditions:

- If n is a leaf, add to δ the transition $(q_n, (\alpha, \rho(n))) \to q_f^*$.
- Else, if n has a (single) child $n \cdot 0$ such that $n \downarrow^+ n \cdot 0$ holds in the skeleton, then add to Q a fresh state q, and add to δ the transitions $(q_n, (\alpha, \rho(n))) \to q_f^* \cdot q \cdot q_f^*$, and $(q, (\alpha', \perp)) \to q_f^* \cdot (q \mid q_{n \cdot 0}) \cdot q_f^*$, for each α' in Σ.
- Finally, if n has k children $n \cdot 0, \ldots, n \cdot (k-1)$ under relation $\downarrow$, assume that the children are ordered as $n \cdot 0 \; \theta_1 \; n \cdot 1 \; \theta_2 \; \ldots \; \theta_{k-1} \; n \cdot (k-1)$, where each θ_i is either $\to$ or $\to^+$. Add to δ the transition

$$(q_n, (\alpha, \rho(n))) \to q_f^* \cdot q_{n \cdot 0} \cdot r_1 \cdot q_{n \cdot 1} \cdot r_2 \; \cdots \; r_{k-1} \cdot q_{n \cdot (k-1)} \cdot q_f^*,$$

where each r_j is ϵ if θ_j is $\to$, or q_f^* if θ_j is $\to^+$.

The intuition is that every tree in the language of $A_{(sk,\perp)}$ represents to some extent a set of trees in $[\![sk]\!]$. The data values used in sk are represented with labels of the form (α, c), for some α in Σ and c in $\mathcal{C}$, and nodes in which the data value is not important to witness the membership in $[\![sk]\!]$ are labeled with $(\alpha', \perp)$, for α' in Σ.

More formally, given a tree T over $\Sigma \times (V \cup \{\perp\})$, we say that a tree T' over Σ is a *data projection* of T into Σ if T' can be formed from T by replacing each node in T labeled with (α, c) for a node labeled α with data value c, and every node labeled with $(\alpha', \perp)$ in T for a node labeled α' and a data value $a \in \mathcal{C}$. The following is straightforward from the construction:

Lemma 2. *Let sk be a tree skeleton over Σ with active domain* adom(sk), *and let $\perp$ be a fresh data value not in $\mathcal{C}$. A tree T over Σ belongs to $[\![sk]\!]$ if and only if there is a tree T' over $\Sigma \times (V \cup \{\perp\})$ that is accepted by $A_{(sk,\perp)}$, and such that T is a data projection of T' over Σ.*

In other words, the set of data projections over Σ of all trees accepted by $A_{(sk,\perp)}$ corresponds precisely to the set of trees in $[\![sk]\!]$. We now have all the ingredients to state our NP-reduction for consistency.

Checking for Consistency:

Consider an arbitrary incomplete tree t, a tree automaton A over Σ and a set Δ of constraints.

First, perform the following operations:

1. Guess a tree skeleton sk such that $[\![sk]\!] \subseteq [\![t]\!]$.

2. Let adom(sk) be all data values that are mentioned in sk, and let $\perp$ a fresh data value not used in $\mathcal{C}$.
3. Define the alphabet $\Sigma \times (\text{adom}(sk) \cup \{\perp\})$ and consider its projection to Σ. Due to feasibility, construct, in polynomial time, the set Δ' of constraints over trees over $\Sigma \times (\text{adom}(sk) \cup \{\perp\})$ so that such a tree satisfies Δ' iff its Σ-projection satisfies Δ.
4. Construct the following set of constraints Γ:
   - For each $c \in \text{adom}(sk)$ and $\alpha \in \Sigma$ such that there is at least one (α, c)-labeled node in sk, add the constraint $|V_{(\alpha,c)}| = 1$ to Γ.
   - For each $c \in \text{adom}(sk)$ and $\alpha \in \Sigma$, if sk does not contain a node labeled α with data value c, then add the constraint $V_{(\alpha,c)} = \emptyset$.
   - Moreover, for each pair of values c, c' in adom(sk) and each $\alpha \in \Sigma$, such that there are nodes labeled with α and α' with data value c in sk, add the constraints $V_{(\alpha,c)} = V_{(\alpha',c)}$ to Γ.
   - Finally, for each $\alpha, \alpha' \in \Sigma$ and distinct values $c, c' \in \text{adom}(sk) \cup \{\perp\}$, add the constraints $V_{(\alpha,c)} \cap V_{(\alpha',c')} = \emptyset$ to Γ.
5. Build an automaton $A^{(\text{adom}(sk),\perp)}$ from A by replacing every transition of form $(q, \alpha) \to L$ with the transitions $(q, (\alpha, c)) \to L$ for each $c \in \text{adom}(sk) \cup \{\perp\}$.
6. Finally, check whether $(A^{(\text{adom}(sk),\perp)} \times A_{(sk,\perp)}), (\Delta' \cup \Gamma)$ is consistent. This of course is possibile due to the feasibility assumption, with the same complexity.

Correctness and Soundness.

We need to prove that (A, t, Δ) is consistent if and only if there exists a skeleton sk, with $[\![sk]\!] \subseteq [\![t]\!]$, and such that $(A^{(\text{adom}(sk),\perp)} \times A_{(sk,\perp)}), (\Delta' \cup \Gamma)$ is consistent.

($\Rightarrow$): Let sk be a skeleton such that $[\![sk]\!] \subseteq [\![t]\!]$, and $(A^{(\text{adom}(sk),\perp)} \times A_{(sk,\perp)})$, $(\Delta' \cup \Gamma)$ is consistent, and let T be the tree over $\Sigma \times (\text{adom}(sk) \cup \{\perp\})$ that witnesses the consistency.

Let $f : \text{adom}(T) \to (\text{adom}(T) \cup \text{adom}(sk))$ be the following renaming of data values: For each data value $d \in \text{adom}(T)$, if there is an (α, c)-node in T with data value d, then $f(d) = c$; and otherwise $f(d) = d$. Notice then that f is an injection. Indeed, since T is consistent with Γ, it satisfies the constraints $V_{(\alpha,c)} = V_{(\alpha',c)}$ and $V_{(\alpha,c)} \cap V_{(\alpha',c')} = \emptyset$, and $|V_{(\alpha,c)}| = 1$, for each $\alpha, \alpha' \in \Sigma$ and distinct $c, c' \in (\text{adom}(sk) \cup \{\perp\})$. Thus, all (α, c)-nodes, for any $\alpha \in \Sigma$, share the same, single data value, which is at the same time not used anywhere else in T.

Next we prove that the data projection $f(T)'$ of $f(T)$ over Σ is consistent with Δ, A and t. From the construction of $A^{(\text{adom}(sk),\perp)}$, it is obvious that $f(T)'$ is in the language of A. Furthermore, from feasibility of $\mathbf{I}$ we have that $f(T)$ is consistent with Δ', and that its data projection $f(T)'$ is consistent with Δ. Finally, since T is in the language of $A_{(sk,\perp)}$, so is $f(T)$, and then by Lemma 2 we have that $f(T)'$ belongs to $[\![sk]\!]$, which by the assumption that $[\![sk]\!] \subseteq [\![t]\!]$ entails that $f(T)'$ belongs to $[\![t]\!]$.

($\Leftarrow$): Assume that (A, t, Δ) is consistent, and let T be a tree witnessing the consistency, with h a homomorphism from t to T. Construct a set S of nodes from T as follows. If n is in the image of h, then add n to S. Moreover, for each α-node n in S with data value c, and for each $\alpha' \in \Sigma$ such that T has at least one α'-labeled node with data value c, add one of these nodes to S. By Lemma 1, there is a skeleton sk containing all nodes in S, such that $T \in [\![sk]\!]$ and such that $[\![sk]\!] \subseteq [\![t]\!]$. Let $\perp$ be a value not in $\mathcal{C}$.

We now construct a tree T' over the alphabet $\Sigma \times (\mathrm{adom}(sk) \cup \{\perp\})$ that is a witness for the consistency of $(A^{(\mathrm{adom}(sk), \perp)} \times A_{(sk, \perp)}), (\Delta' \cup \Gamma)$. This is done as follows. Replace each α-node in T with data value $c \in \mathrm{adom}(sk)$ with a (α, c)-labeled node with data value c, and each α-node in T with data value not in $\mathrm{adom}(sk)$ with a $(\alpha, \perp)$-labeled node with the same original data value. By construction, it is not difficult to see that T' is consistent with Γ. Moreover, from feasibility of $\mathbf{I}$ we obtain that T' is consistent with Δ'. Third, given that T is a data projection of T' over Σ, by Lemma 2 we have that T' belongs to the language of $A_{(sk, \perp)}$. Finally, it is straightforward to see that T' is in the language of $A^{(\mathrm{adom}(sk), \perp)}$, which finishes the proof.

Membership in C: A simple inspection on the reduction reveals that steps (3), (4) and (5) can be performed in polynomial time with respect to sk, A, Σ and Δ. Furthermore, from Lemma 1 and the above remarks we have that there always exists a skeleton sk of polynomial size with respect to t that suffices for the correctness of the reduction. This shows that the problem INCTREE-CONSISTENCY($\mathbf{I}$) is NP-reducible to AUTOMATA-CONSISTENCY($\mathbf{I}$). The theorem follows from the assumption that $\mathbf{C}$ is closed under NP-reductions.

From Theorem 1 and the results from [13] we immediately obtain tight complexity bounds for INCTREE-CONSISTENCY($\mathcal{K} + \mathcal{IC}$), where $\mathcal{K} + \mathcal{IC}$ is the class of basic XML constraints (keys and foreign keys).

Corollary 1. INCTREE-CONSISTENCY($\mathcal{K} + \mathcal{IC}$) *is* NP-*complete.*

In fact, any class of constraints expressible with linear and set constraints (e.g., denial constraints) can be added for free, without changing the complexity bound.

4.3   A Tractable Case

The fact that AUTOMATA-CONSISTENCY($\mathcal{K} + \mathcal{IC}$) is already NP-hard rules out any possibility of finding tractable classes for INCTREE-CONSISTENCY problem without extra restrictions. Following [4], one can look at the consistency problems without tree automata, in which case, given a set Δ of constraints and an incomplete tree t, we ask for a $T \in [\![t]\!]$ so that $T \models \Delta$. It is not difficult to adapt the results in [4] to obtain the following.

Theorem 2. *Without automata in the input,* INCTREE-CONSISTENCY($\mathcal{K} + \mathcal{IC}$) *can be solved in* PTIME *for rigid incomplete data trees, but remains* NP-*hard for arbitrary incomplete data trees.*

5 Query Answering

As is common in the scenarios when one needs to compute certain answers (by means of intersection) [18,3], we look at queries that can only output tuples of data values. The queries will be essentially unions of conjunctive queries over XML trees; however, to avoid the clumsiness of a two-sorted presentation, we follow the standard approach and define them via *patterns*.

An example of a pattern is

$$\alpha(x)/[\beta(x) \to \gamma(1), \delta(y) \to \gamma(x)].$$

When evaluated on a tree T, it collects all instantiations of variables x and y so that a tree has an α-node whose data value is x, together with a β-child with the same data value x whose next sibling is a γ-node with data value 1, and a δ-child with data value y whose next sibling is a γ-node with data value x.

Formally, patterns are given by the grammar:

$$\pi := \alpha(\bar{z}) \mid \alpha(\bar{z})/[\mu, \ldots, \mu] \mid \alpha(\bar{z})//[\mu, \ldots, \mu] \mid \alpha(\bar{z})/[\mu, \ldots, \mu]//[\mu, \ldots, \mu]$$
$$\mu := \pi \mid \pi \rightsquigarrow \ldots \rightsquigarrow \pi$$

where each $\rightsquigarrow$ is either $\to$ or $\Rightarrow$.

Semantics. We define the semantics of a pattern with respect to an XML tree $T = \langle D, A, \downarrow, \to, (P_\alpha)_{\alpha \in \Sigma}, \rho \rangle$, a node w, and a valuation ν for variables $\bar{x}$ in $\mathcal{C}$:

- $(T, w, \nu) \models \alpha(\bar{z})/[\mu_1, \ldots, \mu_n]//[\mu'_1, \ldots, \mu'_k]$ if $w \in P_\alpha$ (whenever α is a Σ-letter), $\rho(w) = \nu(\bar{z})$, and there exist n children $w_1, \ldots, w_n$ of w such that $(T, w_i, \nu) \models \mu_i$ for each $i \le n$, and there exist k descendants $w'_1, \ldots, w'_k$ of w such that $(T, w'_i, \nu) \models \mu'_i$ for each $i \le k$.
- $(T, w, \nu) \models \pi_1 \rightsquigarrow \ldots \rightsquigarrow \pi_m$ if there is a sequence of nodes $w = w_1, \ldots, w_m$ so that $(T, w_i, \nu) \models \pi_i$ for each $i \le m$ and $w_i \to w_{i+1}$ whenever the ith $\rightsquigarrow$ is $\to$, and $w_i \Rightarrow w_{i+1}$ whenever the ith $\rightsquigarrow$ is $\Rightarrow$.

We write $\pi(\bar{x})$ if $\bar{x}$ is a tuple of all the variables mentioned in π. Also, to simplify notation, we shall write $\alpha(\bar{x})/\beta(\bar{y})$ instead of the more formal $\alpha(\bar{x})/[\beta(\bar{y})]$. Finally, we write $(T, w) \models \pi(\bar{a})$ if $(T, w, \nu) \models \pi(\bar{x})$ where ν assigns values $\bar{a}$ to variables $\bar{x}$.

Pattern-Based XML Queries. We now define XML analogs of unions of conjunctive queries based on patterns. First, we need a class of *conjunctive queries* (essentially defined in [1,5,17]): these are obtained by closing patterns under conjunction and existential quantification of variables:

$$q(\bar{x}) \;=\; \exists \bar{y}_1 \ldots \bar{y}_n \; \pi_1(\bar{x}, \bar{y}_1) \land \ldots \land \pi_n(\bar{x}, \bar{y}_n)$$

The semantics is defined as follows. Given a tree T and a valuation $\bar{a}$ for variables $\bar{x}$, we have $T \models q(\bar{a})$ if there exist tuples $\bar{b}_1, \ldots, \bar{b}_n$ of data values and nodes $w_1, \ldots, w_n$ in T so that $(T, w_i) \models \pi_i(\bar{a}, \bar{b}_i)$ for every $i \le n$. We define $\mathrm{UCQ}_{\mathrm{XML}}$ as queries of the form $q_1(\bar{x}) \cup \ldots \cup q_m(\bar{x})$, where each q_i is a conjunctive query.

Example. Consider the query

$$q_1(x) := \exists y, z \; \alpha(x)/[\beta(y) \to \gamma(z)]$$
$$\vee$$
$$\exists y \; \alpha(x)//\delta(y)$$

It selects data values x found in α-labeled nodes which either have two consecutive children labeled β and γ, or a descendant labeled δ.

Certain Answers. Since queries in languages introduced above produce sets of tuples of data values, we can define the usual notion of certain answers for evaluating them over incomplete documents. That is, for a query Q and an incomplete tree t, we let

$$certain_{\mathcal{A}}^{\Delta}(Q(\bar{x}), t) \;=\; \bigcap \Big\{ Q(T) \;\mid\; T \in [\![t]\!], \; T \in L(\mathcal{A}) \text{ and } T \models \Delta \Big\}.$$

We study data complexity of certain answers (where Q, $\mathcal{A}$ and Δ are fixed).

PROBLEM: $certain_{\mathcal{A}}^{\Delta}(Q)$
INPUT: an incomplete data tree t and a tuple $\bar{a}$ of size $|\bar{x}|$
QUESTION: does $\bar{a}$ belong to $certain_{\mathcal{A}}^{\Delta}(Q(\bar{x}), t)$?

We also consider variations of the problem when the automaton $\mathcal{A}$, the constraints Δ, or both are missing from the parameters, referring to them as $certain_{\mathcal{A}}$, $certain^{\Delta}$, and just $certain$. Note that $certain(Q(\bar{x}), t) = \bigcap \{Q(T) \mid T \in [\![t]\!]\}$ is the standard notion of certain answers, without constraints and schemas.

5.1   General Upper Bound

Theorem 3. *For every query $Q(\bar{x}) \in \mathrm{UCQ_{XML}}$, tree automaton $\mathcal{A}$ and a set Δ of keys, foreign keys and inclusion constraints, the problem $certain_{\mathcal{A}}^{\Delta}(Q)$ is in* CONP.

Proof sketch: From [3], we know that $certain_{\mathcal{A}}(Q)$ is in CONP. We first briefly recall the idea behind this upper bound and then explain how to extend the proof to account for an additional set Δ of constraints. The standard way to obtain an upper bound for a query Q (say, Boolean for this sketch) over t is to prove that if $certain(Q, t)$ is false, then there is $T \in [\![t]\!]$ with some specific size bounds in t such that $T \models \neg Q$.

Our starting point here is as follows: suppose we have $T \in [\![t]\!]$ such that $T \models \neg Q$ and $T \in L(\mathcal{A})$. For the sketch, assume that $Q = q_1 \vee \ldots \vee q_n$, where each q_i is a conjunctive query; that is, $T \models \neg q_i$ for each $i \leq n$. Take a homomorphism $h : t \to T$, and add to the image of h all nodes which are least common ancestors of nodes in the image, plus the root. We call it the skeleton. Via careful renaming of some occurrences of data values in the tree and using a reasoning on types, the main argument of the proof consists of pruning long vertical and horizontal paths in T in order to obtain a tree which contains every node in the skeleton of T and hence still belongs to $[\![t]\!]$, while it also agrees with T on all the q_is, is still accepted by $\mathcal{A}$ and is of polynomial size in t.

This proof can be extended as follows. Since we only have unary constraints in Δ, we first chase their relational representation, i.e., constraints applied to unary relations U_α corresponding to labels α. The form of constraints implies that they are weakly acyclic, and hence the chase terminates in polynomial time and produces a set of tuples of the form $U_\alpha(x)$ where x is either a data value or a null. To each of these tuples, we associate a new single node pattern labeled $L(x)$. We then form the union of all these structures with the incomplete tree t and call this new structure t^Δ. Note that labels, nulls and constants might occur both in t and in some of the single nodes patterns in t^Δ. At this point if t^Δ still does not satisfy some of the constraints in Δ (e.g. some key constraints) we simply conclude that the certain answer is vacuously true. Otherwise, assume $\text{certain}_{\mathcal{A}}^{\Delta}(Q(\bar{x}), t)$ is false. Then there is $T \in [\![t^\Delta]\!]$ such that T is accepted by $\mathcal{A}$, T satisfies Δ and $T \models \neg Q$. The only difference with the proof for $\text{certain}_{\mathcal{A}}(Q(\bar{x}), t)$ is that instead of taking a homomorphism $h : t \to T$, we now consider a homomorphism $h : t^\Delta \to T$ and generate the corresponding skeleton. The remainder of the proof is as in [3]. $\qquad\square$

5.2   Rigid Trees

It was shown in [3] that on rigid trees, the problem $\text{certain}(Q)$ becomes tractable as certain answers can be computed by naïve evaluation. Recall that a rigid tree is a tree in which no structural information is missing; that is, the only types of missing information are nulls and wildcards. In the following we show that on rigid trees $\text{certain}_\Delta(Q)$ can become CONP-hard as soon as Δ contains even a single inclusion constraint, but remains tractable if Δ only contains keys.

CONP-**Hardness.**

Theorem 4. *There exists a query $Q(\bar{x})$ in UCQ_{XML} and a set of constraints Δ containing one single inclusion constraint such that the problem $\text{certain}_\Delta(Q)$ is CONP-hard even over rigid incomplete data trees.*

Proof. The proof is by reduction from non 3-colorability. Let $G = \langle V, E \rangle$ be a directed graph, with the set of vertices $V = \{v_1, \ldots, v_n\}$ and the set of edges $E = \{e_1, \ldots, e_m\}$, where each edge e_i is a pair (v_1^i, v_2^i) of vertices from V. We show how to build a rigid incomplete data tree t from G and give a fixed Boolean query $q \in \text{UCQ}_{\text{XML}}$ and a fixed inclusion constraint Δ such that $\text{certain}_\Delta(Q, t)$ evaluates to *true* if and only if G is not 3-colorable.

We use *root*, C, G and E as labels and *red*, *blue*, *green* and a as data values. We use $v_1, \ldots, v_n$ as null values and construct t as follows. The root, labeled *root(a)* has four linearly ordered children:

– the first one labeled $C(red)$,

- the second one labeled $C(blue)$,
- the third one labeled $C(green)$,
- the last one labeled $G(a)$.

The three first children of the root are leaves, but its last $G(a)$-labeled child has m linearly ordered $G(a)$-labeled children where for every $i \leq m$ the following holds:

- the ith child has two ordered children, the first one is labeled $E(v_1^i)$ and the second one is labeled $E(v_2^i)$.

Now we let $\Delta = \{E \subseteq C\}$ and $Q = q_1 \vee q_2 \vee q_3 \vee q_4$, where:

$$q_1 = \exists x\ root(a)/G(a)/G(a)[E(x) \to E(x)]$$
$$q_2 = \exists x \exists y \exists z \exists v \exists w\ root(a)/[\_(x) \to \_(y) \to \_(z) \to \_(v) \to \_(w)]$$
$$q_3 = \exists x\ root(a)/G(a)//C(x)$$
$$q_4 = \exists x \exists y\ root(a)/C(x)/\_(y)$$

We show that $certain_\Delta(Q, t)$ evaluates to $true$ if and only if G is not 3-colorable.

Assume first that G is 3-colorable and let $c : V \to \{red, blue, green\}$ be a 3-coloring of G. We construct a complete tree $T \in [\![t]\!]$ such that $T \models \Delta$ and $T \not\models Q$ by simply replacing every null value v_i occurring in t with $c(v_i)$. Since T is a homomorphic image of t, it does not satisfy any of the queries q_2, q_3, q_4. Also, since c is a 3-coloring of G, we have that $T \not\models q_1$ and so $T \not\models Q$. It follows that $certain_\Delta(Q, t)$ evaluates to $false$.

Now assume that $certain_\Delta(Q, t)$ evaluates to $false$. Then there exists a tree $T \in [\![t]\!]$ such that $T \models \Delta$ and $T \not\models Q$. As $T \in [\![t]\!]$, there is a homomorphism $h : t \to T$. Since $T \not\models q_i$ for every $2 \leq i \leq 4$, it follows that T only contains three C-labeled nodes, which carry respectively one of the three data values red, $blue$, $green$. Also as T satisfies the constraint $E \subseteq C$, every E-labeled node carries one of the data values red, $blue$, $green$. As $T \not\models q_1$, the homomorphism h gives a 3-coloring of G.

Tractable Upper Bounds.

Theorem 5. *For every query* $Q \in \mathrm{UCQ_{XML}}$ *and set* Δ *of keys, the problem* $certain_\Delta(Q)$ *is in* PTIME, *when restricted to rigid incomplete data trees.*

The tractability of $certain_\Delta(Q)$ follows directly from the proof of tractability of $certain(Q)$ on rigid trees in [3]. There is only one additional step, in which we first check whether $t \models \Delta$. By Theorem 2, this can be done in polynomial time in the size of t. If $t \not\models \Delta$, then it is clear that Δ will not be satisfied by any completion of t and we conclude that the certain answers is vacuously $true$. Otherwise $t \models \Delta$ and we go on with evaluating Q on t using naïve evaluation, exactly as in [3].

Acknowledgment. Work partially supported by EPSRC grant G049165 and FET-Open Project FoX, grant agreement 233599. It was done while all authors were at the University of Edinburgh.

References

1. Arenas, M., Fan, W., Libkin, L.: On the complexity of verifying consistency of XML specifications. SIAM J. Comput. 38, 841–880 (2008)
2. Arenas, M., Libkin, L.: XML data exchange: consistency and query answering. Journal of the ACM 55, 2 (2008)
3. Barceló, P., Libkin, L., Poggi, A., Sirangelo, C.: XML with incomplete information. Journal of the ACM 58, 1 (2010)
4. Barceló, P., Libkin, L., Reutter, J.: On incomplete XML documents with integrity constraints. In: AMW 2010 (2010)
5. Björklund, H., Martens, W., Schwentick, T.: Conjunctive query containment over trees. J. Comput. Syst. Sci. 77(3), 450–472 (2011)
6. Bojanczyk, M.: Automata for data words and data trees. In: RTA 2010, pp. 1–4 (2010)
7. Bojanczyk, M., David, C., Muscholl, A., Schwentick, T., Segoufin, L.: Two-variable logic on data words. ACM Trans. Comput. Log. 12(4), 27 (2011)
8. Bojanczyk, M., Lasota, S.: An extension of data automata that captures XPath. Logical Methods in Computer Science 8(1) (2012)
9. Buneman, P., Davidson, S., Fan, W., Hara, C., Tan, W.-C.: Keys for XML. Computer Networks 39(5), 473–487 (2002)
10. Calì, A., Lembo, D., Rosati, R.: On the decidability and complexity of query answering over inconsistent and incomplete databases. In: PODS 2003, pp. 260–271 (2003)
11. Calvanese, D., De Giacomo, G., Lenzerini, M., Vardi, M.Y.: Regular XPath: constraints, query containment and view-based answering for XML documents. In: LID (2008)
12. David, C., Libkin, L., Tan, T.: Efficient reasoning about data trees via integer linear programming. ACM TODS 37(3), 19 (2012)
13. Fan, W., Libkin, L.: On XML integrity constraints in the presence of DTDs. Journal of the ACM 49, 368–406 (2002)
14. Figueira, D.: Forward-XPath and extended register automata on data-trees. In: ICDT 2010, pp. 231–241 (2010)
15. Figueira, D.: Bottom-up automata on data trees and vertical XPath. In: STACS 2011, pp. 93–104 (2011)
16. Gheerbrant, A., Libkin, L., Tan, T.: On the complexity of query answering over incomplete XML documents. In: ICDT 2012, pp. 169–181 (2012)
17. Gottlob, G., Koch, C., Schulz, K.: Conjunctive queries over trees. Journal of the ACM 53(2), 238–272 (2006)
18. Imieliński, T., Lipski, W.: Incomplete information in relational databases. Journal of the ACM 31(4), 761–791 (1984)
19. Jan Bex, G., Neven, F., Van den Bussche, J.: DTD versus XML Schema: A Practical Study. In: WEBDB 2004, pp. 79–84 (2004)
20. Laender, A., Moro, M., Nascimento, C., Martins, P.: An X-Ray on Web-Available XML Schemas. SIGMOD Record 38(1), 37–42 (2009)
21. Libkin, L., Sirangelo, C.: Reasoning about XML with temporal logics and automata. J. Applied Logic 8(2), 210–232 (2010)
22. Martens, W., Neven, F., Schwentick, T.: Simple off the shelf abstractions for XML schema. SIGMOD Record 36(3), 15–22 (2007)

23. Segoufin, L.: Automata and logics for words and trees over an infinite alphabet. In: Ésik, Z. (ed.) CSL 2006. LNCS, vol. 4207, pp. 41–57. Springer, Heidelberg (2006)
24. Segoufin, L.: Static analysis of XML processing with data values. SIGMOD Record 36(1), 31–38 (2007)
25. Tan, T.: An automata model for trees with ordered data values. In: LICS 2012 (2012)
26. Thatcher, J.W.: Characterizing derivation trees of context-free grammars through a generalization of finite automata theory. JCSS 1, 317–322 (1967)

Using SQL for Efficient Generation and Querying of Provenance Information

Boris Glavic[1], Renée J. Miller[2], and Gustavo Alonso[3]

[1] Illinois Institute of Technology
bglavic@iit.edu
[2] University of Toronto
miller@cs.toronto.edu
[3] ETH Zurich
alonso@inf.ethz.ch

Abstract. In applications such as data warehousing or data exchange, the ability to efficiently generate and query provenance information is crucial to understand the origin of data. In this chapter, we review some of the main contributions of Perm, a DBMS that generates different types of provenance information for complex SQL queries (including nested and correlated subqueries and aggregation). The two key ideas behind Perm are representing data and its provenance together in a single relation and relying on query rewrites to generate this representation. Through this, Perm supports fully integrated, on-demand provenance generation and querying using SQL. Since Perm rewrites a query requesting provenance into a regular SQL query and generates easily optimizable SQL code, its performance greatly benefits from the query optimization techniques provided by the underlying DBMS.

1 Introduction

Peter Buneman was one of the first to recognize the importance of data provenance. With co-authors Khanna and Tan, he introduced the seminal models of *Why*- and *Where*-provenance [7]. Provenance, information about the creation process or the origin of data, can be used to debug queries and clean data in data warehouses, to understand and correct complex data integration transformations, for auditing, and to understand the value of data in curated databases. Provenance generation has also been used as a supporting technology for exchanging updates between heterogeneous databases [21], to provide access control based on the origin of data [31], and in modeling uncertainty in databases [35].

While provenance has many applications, these applications often place very high requirements on a provenance management system to be useful in practice. In this chapter, we overview the contributions of the *Perm* provenance management system [17]. *Perm* was designed as a scalable system for the generation and querying of provenance information over relational data. To understand the requirements for such a system, we begin with an example and then consider the foundations in provenance research on which *Perm* builds.

V. Tannen et al. (Eds.): Buneman Festschrift, LNCS 8000, pp. 291–320, 2013.

Customer

	SSN	name	age
u_1	1	Gert	34
u_2	2	Waltraud	65
u_3	3	Joe	19

Purchase

	month	desc	amount	creditc	import
p_1	Jan	starbucks	12	4059	1
p_2	Jan	grandson	3100	1234	1
p_3	Jan	rent	7000	1235	1
p_4	Feb	rent	7000	1235	1
p_5	Feb	tvshop	399	9999	2
p_6	Feb	starbucks	5	9999	2

Creditcard

	number	company	owner	limit
c_1	4059	VISA	1	4000
c_2	3066	MASTER	2	2000
c_3	1234	VISA	2	3000
c_4	1235	VISA	3	10000
c_5	9999	AE	3	400

Imports

	id	employee	company	date
i_1	1	Daniel	VISA	10.06.2000
i_2	2	Petra	AE	06.06.2000

Fig. 1. Example Database

Example 1 (Running Example). The example database shown in Figure 1 stores credit card information: customers, their credit cards, purchases made with credit cards (Purchase), and from which external database (recorded in the company attribute) a batch of purchase tuples was imported, when and by whom (Imports). For convenience, we show an identifier for each tuple in the instance (e.g., p_2). The query q shown in Figure 2 returns the months during which customers with at least two credit cards exceeded their credit limit on some card. To understand from which inputs of q the result tuple t_2 (Joe,Feb) is derived, a user needs access to the data provenance of the query and the ability to query this information. For example, a user may be interested in knowing if some of these over-drafts are caused by suspiciously low credit card limits. This question can be answered by running a query over the provenance of q to retrieve tuples in the result of q that depend on credit card tuples with low limit values (i.e., these credit card tuples belong to the data provenance of the tuples to be returned). Alternatively, if the user realizes that some names are spelled incorrectly in the query result, she needs to understand where the name attribute values in the query result have been copied from to trace this error. This requires access to a different type of provenance that tracks the copying of information instead of which inputs caused a tuple to appear in the query result.

1.1   Requirements for Provenance Systems

The example and discussion above motivates four requirements for relational provenance systems. **(Requirement 1)** Support different types of provenance with sound semantics. Information from different provenance types is often needed to best understand the data and how it has been transformed. We would consider a provenance type to have sound semantics, if it provably captures our intuitive understanding of provenance. For example, the provenance of a query

```
SELECT DISTINCT name, month
FROM
        (SELECT month, creditc, SUM(amount) AS total
        FROM purchase p
        GROUP BY month, creditc) AS monthly,
        customer c,
        creditcard cc
WHERE p.cc = cc.number
        AND cc.owner = c.id
        AND total > cc.limit
        AND c.id IN (SELECT cc2.owner
                     FROM creditcard cc2
                     GROUP BY cc2.id
                     HAVING count(*) > 1)
```

Query Result

	name	month
t_1	Waltraud	Jan
t_2	Joe	Feb

Fig. 2. Example Query

result should be sufficient to derive this result through the query. (**Requirement 2**) Support provenance generation for SQL including complex features such as nested subqueries and aggregation. The example query is relatively simple in comparison with queries used in data warehouse applications. A system must support a large subset of SQL to be useful in practice. (**Requirement 3**) Support complex queries over provenance information. Provenance is difficult to interpret without the ability to extract parts of interest. For instance, even identifying for which tuples the provenance is interesting requires query support to be feasible for large databases. Generally, users will want to use queries to specify the characteristics of what provenance they want to see. Many interesting questions that can be answered using provenance data require the use of advanced SQL-like features such as aggregation over the provenance. For example, *Which over-drafts are based on a large number of small purchases (high count, but low average amount)?* (**Requirement 4**) Support efficient generation and querying of provenance for large database instances. Provenance can easily outgrow the size of the database for complex queries. Unless a user explicitly requests *all* the provenance, the system should efficiently generate only provenance that satisfies the user's request (by combining provenance generation with a user's query over the provenance). In our example, if a user is only interested in over-drafts due to low credit limits (a query on provenance), then the system should not generate provenance for all over-drafts.

1.2   State of the Art

The tremendous amount of work on relational provenance brings us close, but not all the way, to achieve these requirements. We present the state-of-the-art along the four dimensions introduced above and discuss how Perm has contributed to each.

(1) **Support for Different Types of Provenance.** The largest body of work on relational provenance is on semantics. We have a rich literature on different semantics, along with a rich literature comparing these semantics and analyzing when they are useful [10]. *Data provenance*, which represents dependencies between a query's output and input data, has been categorized based on the type of dependency that is modeled. *Why*-provenance, intuitively, models which input tuples are used to create an output tuple, though there are different ways to formalize this notion. Types of *Why*-provenance are the original *Why*-provenance as pioneered by Buneman et al. [7], *Lineage* proposed by Cui et al. [12], and *PI-CS* (Perm Influence contribution semantics) the original provenance semantics supported by Perm [16]. *Where*-provenance models where values in an output tuple are copied from. Types of *Where*-provenance include the *Where*-provenance introduced by Buneman et al. [7] and the *C-CS* semantics (Copy contribution semantics) of Perm [16]. *How*-provenance augments *Why*-provenance with information about how input tuples are used to create an output tuple. *Provenance polynomials* [22,24] and later versions of the *Trio* [35] provenance model can be classified as *How*-provenance. Provenance polynomials are the most general form of annotation in the framework of Green et al. [22] that defines the positive relational algebra for relations annotated with elements from a semiring (called K-relations). Thus, provenance polynomials generalize all provenance semantics that can be modeled as semirings such as the original Why-provenance and the Trio-model [23]. Foster et al. [14] use the semiring model to annotate unordered XML data and compute provenance for XQuery. Through an XML encoding of annotated relations and XQuery encoding of relational algebra this approach provides a type of attribute granularity *Where*-provenance. The semiring model has been extended for aggregation [4] and several extensions for set difference have been proposed [3,20,15]. Recently, Kostylev et al. [29] studied data annotated with more than one type of annotation within this framework. Several other data provenance types have been presented in the literature that do not fall directly under these categories. For example, causality-based provenance [30,9], types inspired by program analysis [1,8], and *transformation provenance* [19] (which operators of a query contribute to a result). Most provenance systems implement one type of provenance. *DBNotes* [11,5,33] is an annotation management system that uses Where-provenance [7] to propagate annotations. *Trio* [35] is a database system with support for uncertainty and provenance. Boolean formulas over tuple variables are used as provenance. Lineage was implemented in the *WHIPS* data-warehouse prototype [12]. The update-exchange system *Orchestra* [21] uses provenance polynomials to record the provenance of updates exchanged between peers. In principle, Orchestra also supports Why-provenance and the model of Trio, because these provenance types can be extracted from provenance polynomials. Green provides a provenance hierarchy showing how this extraction can be achieved [23].

Perm's Contribution. To the best of our knowledge, Perm is the first system to support a representative set of provenance semantics including the relational adaptation of the *Where*-provenance [10] as defined by Buneman et al. [7], provenance polynomials [22], and new types of *Why, Where,* and *How* (defined further throughout this chapter) that include a new form of transformation provenance [19]. In contrast to Orchestra, generation of these provenance types is supported natively instead of deriving them from a more expressive provenance model. This enables us to use type-specific optimizations during provenance generation for more efficient execution. Perm also supports propagating user-defined annotations based on Why semantics.

(2) Support for Provenance Generation for Complex SQL. DBNotes supports the SQL equivalent of unions of conjunctive queries (set-semantics) [11,5]. WHIPS computes Lineage for ASPJ (aggregate-select-project-join queries) and set operations (union, intersection and set difference) [12]. Lineage was defined for set-semantics, but extensions for bag-semantics were discussed by the authors. Trio supports ASPJ queries with set operations though the released prototype has stricter limitations (e.g., single aggregation in a query) [35]. Orchestra supports union of SPJ queries and is the only approach to support recursion [21]. However, the semiring model used by Orchestra has also been extended for aggregation [4]. In contrast to the Lineage and Perm Why-provenance models, which only record provenance for each result tuple of an aggregation, this extension of the semirings model attaches provenance to each aggregated value. This has the advantage of enabling deletion propagation, but results in increased provenance size and a more complex provenance model.

Perm's Contribution. Like WHIPS, Perm supports ASPJ queries and set operations. Perm is the first provenance system to support nested and correlated subqueries.

(3) Support for Complex Queries over Provenance Information. Most systems do not represent provenance relationally. To query provenance, they provide special query languages over their provenance data model. The query language of DBNotes, *pSQL* [11,5], provides some support for querying annotations (provenance) which is equivalent to being able to pose SPJ queries with unions on the provenance. Orchestra supports *ProQL* [25], a query language for the graph representation of provenance polynomials for relations derived though schema mappings. ProQL queries return a subgraph of the input based on path expressions used in the query and optionally evaluate the provenance polynomial of a tuple in a certain semiring, i.e., change the type of annotations attached to tuples.[1] The language does not support aggregation directly. However, some types of aggregation can be simulated using semiring evaluations. *TriQL* [34], the query language of Trio, has a conditional language construct that evaluates to true if tuples from two specified relations are connected by lineage. WHIPS [12] does not introduce a new query language for provenance. SQL queries can be used to query provenance generated by the system. However, the system represents provenance as a list of relations which makes querying this information more complicated. WHIPS does not associate data with its provenance.

---

[1] This feature can be used to derive other provenance types from the polynomials.

Perm's Contribution. Perm uses a relational representation for provenance that models the connection between a query result tuple and its provenance. Hence, Perm supports full SQL for querying data associated with provenance.

(4) **Support for Large Databases.** DBNotes [5] stores provenance annotations for a relation in additional attributes that are added to the schema of this relation. The system generates provenance during the execution of a pSQL query. Such a query is translated into a single SQL query over a relational encoding of annotated relations. This allows the system to rely on a DBMS to optimize the execution. However, the SQL query results have to be post-processed to transform them into DBNotes's data model which introduces a potential performance bottleneck. A query in Orchestra's query language ProQL [25] is implemented by running several queries over a materialized relational encoding of a provenance graph. Orchestra produces provenance during update-exchange. Update-exchange and provenance generation is expressed in datalog extended with skolem functions and implemented in a Java middleware which evaluates the datalog rules over a relational DBMS. Even though some care is taked to avoid shipping data between Java and the DBMS, using several SQL queries to implement a single ProQL query and full materialization of provenance information limits the scalability of the approach. Trio [2] generates provenance eagerly during query execution. The system materializes the results of each query and creates a separate relation to store its provenance as a mapping between input and output tuple identifiers. Trio is implemented as a Python middleware and a set of PostgreSQL UDFs (user-defined functions). WHIPS [12] implements provenance generation as stored procedures that split a query q into subexpressions and execute one or more SQL queries to retrieve the Lineage of each segment. This separation into multiple queries limits the space of possible optimizations that the underlying DBMS can apply.

Perm's Contribution. Provenance generation in Perm is on-demand, meaning that Perm supports simple SQL language extensions (SQL-PLE) to let a user specify when (and what) provenance to compute. In Perm, a query over provenance information would usually include a subquery that generates the provenance. Thus, provenance generation and querying are entangled within a single SQL-PLE query that is rewritten by the system into a single SQL query. This approach allows us to take full advantage of the optimizer of the underlying DBMS. For SQL queries without nesting, we have shown experimentally that the optimizer can (and does) significantly improve the performance of provenance queries by, e.g., pushing selections over provenance data into the provenance generation. For nested subqueries, we present a set of novel un-nesting and de-correlation optimizations tailored for provenance generation.

In summary, given the maturity of data provenance models, with Perm we sought to build upon the state-of-the-art in provenance systems to provide a complete relational provenance management system that supports efficient querying and generation of provenance. Our approach focuses on robust SQL support (including correlated subqueries) and full support for querying provenance using SQL. Approaches that generate and store the complete provenance of a query

Semantics	Category	Granularity
PI-CS	Data (Why)	Tuple
C-CS	Data (Where)	Tuple
Transformation Provenance	Transformation	Algebra Operator
Where	Data (Where)	Attribute Value
Polynomials	Data (How)	Tuple

Fig. 3. Supported Provenance Types

during execution incur large storage costs and runtime overheads, and, thus may not be applicable to large databases and/or complex queries. We call such approaches *exhaustive* to distinguish them from approaches that only generate provenance *on-demand*. The main innovation of Perm is to represent a query's result and provenance in a single relation which is generated on-demand by rewriting the original query into a query producing this representation. In the remainder of this chapter, we overview how this simple idea enabled the development of a robust relational provenance system that achieves the advances towards all four requirements we have presented.

We give an end-to-end overview of our approach in Section 2. Afterwards, we present three of the provenance types supported by Perm in detail and discuss how they were implemented within the system (Sections 3 to 5). For each provenance type, we present the formal definition, the algebraic (and SQL) rewrites used to generate its relational representation, and present some of the optimizations that can be applied in a provenance system like Perm.

2   The Perm Approach

We now present an overview of the Perm system focusing on its relational provenance representation (Section 2.1), query rewrite techniques (Section 2.2), and SQL language extensions (Section 2.3). Perm represents provenance information as relations generated and queried on-demand using standard SQL queries. If the users requests one of the provenance types supported by Perm for a query q using the SQL-PLE language extension, the system transforms q into an SQL query that returns the provenance of q in addition to the regular results of q. Perm supports the provenance types shown in Figure 3. The initial version supporting *PI-CS* provenance (*Perm Influence contribution semantics*, a form of *Why*-provenance) for ASPJ queries and set operations was introduced by Glavic and Alonso [17] and later extended for nested and correlated subqueries [18]. *Transformation* provenance, provenance that models which operators of a query influence a query results, was introduced in *TRAMP* [19], an extension of Perm for debugging data exchange scenarios. In this chapter, we also present *Copy contribution semantics*, a *Where*-provenance type supported by Perm, and several optimizations for PI-CS [16]. To demonstrate the flexibility of our approach we have also implemented the original Where-provenance [7] and provenance polynomials [22] in Perm. As mentioned in the introduction, provenance polyno-

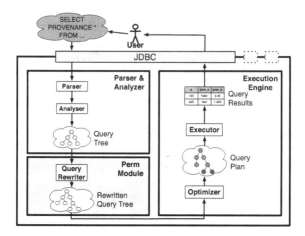

Fig. 4. *Perm* Architecture

mials generalize several other provenance semantics. We will discuss how PI-CS relates to this model in Section 3.6.

Perm is implemented as a modified PostgreSQL engine, extending its SQL dialect with provenance features. Provenance generation in Perm is light-weight and lazy: no provenance is generated unless explicitly requested. Thus, if the provenance features of Perm are not used, the system behaves like a normal Postgres server - clients will observe no overhead in runtime [2] or storage space. Figure 4 shows the architecture of the system. The parser and analyzer module of PostgreSQL (extended to recognize SQL-PLE) parse incoming SQL queries and transform them into an internal tree representation. The output of the analyzer module is passed to the *Perm* rewrite module. This module implements the query rewrite rules as transformations on query trees. The rewritten query tree produced by the *Perm* module is handed over to the original Postgres optimizer. From the optimizer's point of view the input it retrieves is a regular SQL query.

2.1   Provenance Representation

Perm represents the provenance of a query q as a single relation that contains both the original query results of q and its provenance. Provenance information is attached to a query result tuple by extending the tuple with additional attributes that are used to store provenance information. Regular result tuples are duplicated if necessary to represent the complete provenance.

Data Provenance: PI-CS and C-CS, the two data provenance semantics developed for Perm, represent provenance as so-called witness lists. A witness-list for a query is a list of input tuples that were used together to derive an output tuple; one from each input relation of the query (leaves of the algebra tree) or the special value $\perp$ which indicates that no tuple from the relation at this leaf of

---

[2] Except for an additional traversal of the query tree to search for SQL-PLE constructs.

the tree contributed to the output tuple. The relational representation of PI-CS and C-CS appends all attributes from the relations accessed by the query to the query's result schema. The additional attributes in the provenance representation are used to extend a result tuple with all tuples from one of its witness lists. Thus, tuples with more than one witness list in their provenance are duplicated and each duplicate is paired with the relational encoding of one witness list. To distinguish between regular result attributes and provenance attributes, the later are identified by a prefix and the name of the relation they are derived from (adding a distinguishing identifier for relations that are accessed more than once by the query). The special value $\perp$ used in witness lists is modeled as NULL values in the representation.

Transformation Provenance: Transformation provenance models which parts of a query (that is, which operator) contributed to an output tuple. Provenance is represented as a single attribute of either type text or XML that stores the SQL string of the query (or an XML representation thereof) with the transformation provenance modeled as tags (<NOT>...</NOT>) that surround parts of the query that did not contribute to a result tuple. We have introduced the XML representation to enable query access to transformation provenance (using the XSLT support of PostgreSQL).

Example 2 (Provenance Representation). Consider the query shown in Figure 5 evaluated over the example database and its PI-CS and transformation provenance. The provenance attribute names for PI-CS are given in a separate table to simplify the exposition. Tuple t_2 in the result of the query was derived by joining tuple u_2 with tuples c_2 and c_3. Thus, the PI-CS provenance of tuple t_2 consists of two witness lists $< u_2, c_2, \perp >$ and $< u_2, c_3, \perp >$. These are represented as two tuples in the relational representation by duplicating t_2 and pairing each duplicate with the tuples from one of the witness lists. Tuple t_1 is derived from the left input of the union without any influence from its right input. Therefore, the right input is enclosed in a NOT tag in the transformation provenance of t_1.

The provenance representation used in Perm has several advantages. (1) Provenance is represented as a standard relation, that can be stored as a view or queried using SQL. Even more important, the system can often avoid generating provenance that will be filtered out in later stages of a query using the DBMS optimizer (see Section 2.2). (2) Representing data provenance as complete tuples and directly associating a query's regular result data with its provenance allows a user to understand how they relate to each other and enables queries that make use of this information.

However, these advantages come at the price of verbosity and in some cases loosing the ability to run queries over the regular results. The verbosity is usually unproblematic, because the user can run queries over this information to extract parts of interest and instruct the system to only use certain attributes as provenance instead of complete input tuples. The duplication of regular result tuples is necessary to be able to pair them with their complete provenance, but it may restrict the execution of normal queries over this relation (i.e., result tuple multiplicities may be different from the multiplicities of the original

```
(SELECT name
FROM customer c JOIN creditcard cc
     ON (c.ssn = cc.owner))
UNION
(SELECT employee FROM imports);
```

Query Result

name
t_1	Gert
t_2	Waltraud
t_3	Joe
t_4	Daniel
t_5	Petra

PI-CS Provenance

	customer			creditcard				imports			
	name	p_1	p_2	p_3	p_4	p_5	p_6	p_7	p_8	p_9	p_{10}	p_{11}
t_1	Gert	1	Gert	34	4059	VISA	1	4000				
t_2	Waltraud	2	Waltraud	65	3066	MASTER	2	2000				
t_2	Waltraud	2	Waltraud	65	1234	VISA	2	3000				
t_3	Joe	3	Joe	19	1235	VISA	3	10000				
t_3	Joe	3	Joe	19	9999	AE	3	400				
t_4	Daniel								1	Daniel	VISA	10.06.2000
t_5	Petra								2	Petra	AE	06.06.2000

Attribute Names

alias	attribute name
p_1	prov_customer_ssn
p_2	prov_customer_name
p_3	prov_customer_age
p_4	prov_creditcard_number
p_5	prov_creditcard_company
p_6	prov_creditcard_owner
p_7	prov_creditcard_limit
p_8	prov_imports_id
p_9	prov_imports_employee
p_{10}	prov_imports_company
p_{11}	prov_imports_added

Transformation Provenance

	name	trans_prov
t_1	Gert	SELECT c.name FROM customer c JOIN creditcard cc ON c.ssn = cc.owner UNION <NOT>SELECT imports.employee FROM imports </NOT>

Fig. 5. Provenance Representation

query). However, the original result multiplicities can be reconstructed from the provenance and input multiplicities if needed.

2.2 On-demand Provenance Generation Using Query Rewrites

The research underlying Perm has demonstrated that SQL is powerful enough to express the computation of provenance for a large subset of queries expressible in SQL. The approach supports aggregations, set operations, nested or correlated subqueries, and user-defined functions. We do not support non-deterministic functions that return different results for the same input in the scope of one query. For example, a random number generator is a non-deterministic function.

Requesting the provenance of a query q through the system's SQL extensions (see Section 2.3) instructs Perm to rewrite q into a standard SQL query that returns one type of provenance for q using the provenance representation introduced in Section 2.1. The query rewrites for each provenance type were developed following the process shown in Figure 6. (1) We state a provenance type's semantics as a declarative definition and define a relational representation. This approach was chosen because correctness criteria one would intuitively expect to hold for provenance are easily stated declaratively. For instance, for data prove-

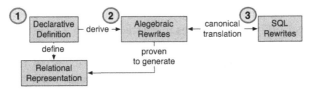

Fig. 6. SQL Rewrite Development Process

nance, the provenance of a tuple t from the result of a query q should contain sufficient information to produce the tuple t. (2) From the declarative definition we derive algebraic rewrites which transform a query into a provenance-generating query and prove their correctness. (3) A canonical translation is applied to translate the algebraic rewrites into SQL rewrites.

The seamless integration of provenance generation as an SQL language feature has many advantages. We can provide full SQL query support for provenance information (Requirement 3). The rewrite rules are unaware of how the provenance attributes of their input were produced. Thus, they can be used to propagate provenance information that was created manually or by another provenance management system. A query over provenance data is implemented as a regular SQL query with a subquery that implements the provenance generation. Thus, we fully utilize the DBMS optimizer to speed up provenance computation by, e.g., pushing selections and projections applied by a query into the provenance generation (Requirement 4). Since optimizing provenance generation is still in its infancy, this is a feasible approach for efficient provenance generation and querying (e.g., we can efficiently compute the PI-CS provenance of the TCP-H benchmark queries for a 1GB TCP-H instance [16]).

2.3   SQL Language Extension

The *provenance language extension* (SQL-PLE) of Perm enriches SQL with additional keywords to request provenance, control how far to trace provenance, and to inform the system about existing provenance information. The keyword PROVENANCE is employed in the SELECT clause of a query q to instruct *Perm* to compute the provenance of q. An optional ON CONTRIBUTION modifier is used to choose the provenance type that is produced (PI-CS is the default). For example, the query below returns the PI-CS provenance of the query from Figure 2.

```
SELECT PROVENANCE DISTINCT name , month
FROM (SELECT month, creditc , SUM(amount) AS total
    . . .
```

Note that all original SQL features provided by PostgreSQL are not affected by the language extension, and even more important, they can be used in combination with provenance computation. Given the provenance representation of Perm this enables complex queries that filter provenance based on properties of the input tuples in the provenance, the results of the query, or both. This type of query functionality generalizes what has been called *backward* (track the provenance of an output) and *forward* (which outputs have a certain input in their provenance) provenance queries in related work [6,27,26].

Example 3 (Querying Provenance). Assume the user expected the running example query to return less credit over-drafts. Her assumption is that some over-drafts are caused by credit card limits which have been recorded too low. The user runs the following query to determine which over-drafts are caused by (have tuples in their provenance with) suspiciously low credit card limits (say $500):

```
SELECT *
FROM (SELECT PROVENANCE DISTINCT name, month
      . . .
      HAVING count(*) > 1)) AS orig
WHERE prov_creditcard_limit < 500;
```

The default behavior is to generate the provenance of a complete query by tracing which tuples in a query's output are affected by which tuples in the query's input. Perm also supports limiting the provenance generation to parts of a query to trace the effect of intermediate query results instead of the input relations. The keyword BASERELATION is appended to an item in the FROM clause to limit how far back the provenance is traced.

Example 4 (Limit Provenance Generation). Retrieving the full provenance of the running example query may return a large number of tuples, because each aggregated monthly amount (subquery monthly) can depend on a large number of individual purchases. Questions like the one from Example 3 can be answered without information about the influence of each individual purchase tuple. The user can mark the subquery monthly with the BASERELATION keyword to only investigate the effect of the aggregated monthly amounts.

```
SELECT PROVENANCE DISTINCT name, month
FROM (SELECT month, creditc, SUM(amount) AS total
      FROM purchase p
      GROUP BY month, creditc) BASERELATION AS monthly,
      . . .
```

Perm can handle existing provenance information that was not produced by the system itself as long as (1) it is stored in additional attributes of tuples following the representation used by Perm and (2) the system is made aware of which attributes store provenance information (by appending the keyword PROVENANCE followed by a list of attribute names to the FROM-clause item).

Example 5 (External Provenance). The imports relation from the running example stores from which data sources each purchase tuple is imported. This is a type of provenance information for the purchase relation. Joining the imports relation with the purchase relation and using the PROVENANCE keyword in the FROM clause, the user makes Perm aware of the existence of the additional provenance data. The system will treat this provenance in the same way as provenance generated by the system itself. The modified example query is shown below.

```
SELECT PROVENANCE DISTINCT name, month
FROM (SELECT month, creditc, SUM(amount) AS total
     FROM (SELECT *
          FROM purchase, imports
          WHERE id = import
          ) PROVENANCE (employee, company, date) AS p
     GROUP BY month, creditc) AS monthly,
     ...
```

3   Perm Influence Contribution Semantics (PI-CS)

This and the following sections discuss the provenance types supported by Perm in more depth. Recall that we follow the process shown in Figure 6 to develop provenance semantics that are implemented as SQL query rewrites. The PI-CS provenance semantics was developed based on Lineage [12]. Lineage defines provenance for single operators declaratively. This definition is extended for queries with more than one operator by assuming transitivity. Lineage represents the provenance of a tuple t from the result of a query q as a list of relations; each element in the list is a subset of one input relation of the query. PI-CS also uses a declarative per-operator definition and transitivity, but represents provenance as witness-lists, defines a relational representation (see Section 2.1), and extends the declarative definition of the semantics with additional constraints to handle outer-joins, set difference, and nested subqueries correctly. For the proofs of the theorems we present in this section see Glavic [16].

3.1   Background and Notation

Before discussing the details of PI-CS, we present the relational algebra variant used in Perm and introduce notational conventions. The algebra (shown in Figure 7) is an extended relational algebra that operates on bags (multi-sets). We use t^n to denote that tuple t has the multiplicity n (number of duplicates) with the convention that a tuple with multiplicity smaller than one is not present in a relation. Let q be a query. We use $[[q]]$ (and sometimes Q) to denote the result of evaluating q and $\mathbf{Q}$ to denote its schema (the same notation is used for relations). The projection of a tuple t on a list A of attributes (or expressions) is denoted as $t.A$. Projection (Π) projects its input on a list of expressions over attributes, constants, functions and renaming (represented by $a \rightarrow b$). Selection (σ), joins ($\bowtie, \bar{\bowtie}, \ldots$), and set operations are defined as usual. Duplicate elimination (δ) returns the input relation with all tuple multiplicities set to one. Aggregation (α) groups its input on a list G of grouping expressions and computes the aggregation functions from list agg for each group. Here B_i denotes the list of input attributes for aggregation function agg_i. Each result tuple of an aggregation contains the grouping expression values and the aggregation function results (res_i) for one group. The value $null$ is represented as ε and we write $null(q)$ for a tuple of null-values with schema $\mathbf{Q}$. Due to space limitations we do

$$[[\Pi_A(q)]] = \{t^n \mid n = \sum_{u^m \in Q \wedge u.A=t} m\} \qquad\qquad [[\sigma_C(q)]] = \{t^n \mid t^n \in Q \wedge t \models C\}$$

$$[[\alpha_{G,agg}(q)]] = \{(t.G, res_1, \ldots, res_m)^1 \mid t^n \in Q \wedge \underset{i \in \{1,m\}}{\forall} : res_i = agg_i(\Pi_{B_i}(\sigma_{G=t.G}(q)))\}$$

$$[[q_1 \bowtie_C q_2)]] = \{(t_1 \blacktriangleright t_2)^{n \times m} \mid t_1{}^n \in Q_1 \wedge t_2{}^m \in Q_2 \wedge (t_1 \blacktriangleright t_2) \models C\}$$

$$[[q_1 \rightthreetimes\!\!\bowtie_C q_2]] = \{(t_1 \blacktriangleright t_2)^{n \times m} \mid t_1{}^n \in Q_1 \wedge t_2{}^m \in Q_2\}$$
$$\cup \{(t_1 \blacktriangleright null(q_2))^n \mid t_1{}^n \in Q_1 \wedge (\nexists t_2 \in Q_2 : (t_1 \blacktriangleright t_2) \models C)\}$$

$$[[q_1 \cup q_2]] = \{t^{n+m} \mid t^n \in Q_1 \wedge t^m \in Q_2\} \quad [[q_1 \cap q_2]] = \{t^{min(n,m)} \mid t^n \in Q_1 \wedge t^m \in Q_2\}$$

$$[[q_1 - q_2]] = \{t^{n-m} \mid t^n \in Q_1 \wedge t^m \in Q_2\} \quad [[\delta(q)]] = \{t^1 \mid t^n \in Q\}$$

Fig. 7. Algebra

not include the algebra for nested subqueries [18], but instead present an example. The SQL query SELECT * FROM R WHERE R.a IN (SELECT b FROM S) can be written as σ_a IN $\Pi_b(S)(R)$. We use $< e_1, \ldots, e_n >$ to denote a list with elements e_1 to e_n and $l_1 \blacktriangleright l_2$ to denote the concatenation of lists l_1 and l_2.

3.2 Declarative Definition

We start by stating the properties of PI-CS as a declarative definition and define a relational representation for this provenance type. The declarative definition allows us to directly state the properties we expect to hold for PI-CS. The PI-CS provenance for a result tuple of a query q is a subset of the multiset of *potential witness lists* for q - a set with all possible combinations of input tuples from the query and the special value $\bot$. Recall from Section 2.1 that $\bot$ denotes that no tuple from a specified relation participates in a witness list.

Definition 1 (Potential Witness Lists). *For a query q with inputs $q_1, \ldots, q_n$ the bag $\mathcal{W}(q)$ of potential witness lists for q is defined as:*

$$\mathcal{W}(q) = \{< t_1, \ldots, t_n >^{m_1 \times \ldots \times m_n} \mid \underset{i \in \{1,n\}}{\forall} : t_i^{m_i} \in Q_i \vee (t_i = \bot \wedge m_i = 1)\}$$

We use $w[i]$ to denote the ith component (tuple) of a witness list w. A witness list w' subsumes a witness list w ($w \prec w'$) iff w can be derived from w' by replacing some tuples with $\bot$: $(\forall i : w[i] = w'[i] \vee w[i] = \bot) \wedge (\exists i : w'[i] \neq \bot \wedge w[i] = \bot)$.

The declarative definition for PI-CS defines the provenance of a tuple t from the result of a single algebra operator op as a subset of $\mathcal{W}(op)$ that fulfills the following four conditions. (1) Evaluating op over the provenance of t returns t.[3] This guarantees that the provenance of t is sufficient to produce t. (2) Each witness list w in the provenance contributes to the result, that is, evaluating the operator over w returns a non-empty result. (3) Subsumed witness lists are excluded from the provenance. This condition is necessary to produce precise

---

[3] Glavic [16] defines a semantics for query evaluation over sets of witness lists.

provenance for outer-joins and set union. (4) The provenance is the maximal multi-set with these properties, meaning that no witness lists that contribute to t are left out. The provenance of a query is defined by recursively applying the per-operator definition to each operator of the query.

Definition 2 (Declarative Definition of PI-CS). *Let op be an algebra operator with inputs* $q_1, \ldots, q_n$ *and* t *a tuple in the result of op* ($t^x \in [[op]]$). *A multi-set* $P \subseteq \mathcal{W}(op)$ *is the PI-CS provenance* $PI(op, t)$ *of* t *iff:*

$$[[op(P)]] = \{t^x\} \tag{1}$$
$$\forall w \in P : [[op(w)]] \neq \emptyset \tag{2}$$
$$\neg \exists w, w' \in P : w \prec w' \tag{3}$$
$$\neg \exists P \subset P' \subseteq \mathcal{W}(q) : P' \models (1), (2), (3) \tag{4}$$

The PI-CS provenance $PI(q, t)$ *of a tuple* t *from the result of a query* q *is defined by transitivity over* $PI(op, t)$ *for each operator op in* q.

For simplicity, we left out additional conditions applied in the definition to handle nested subqueries and adapted the definition slightly (without changing its semantics) [16]. We define the relational representation of the PI-CS provenance for a query q which combines each tuple t in Q with all witness lists in $PI(q, t)$.

Definition 3 (Relational Representation). *The relational representation* Q^{PI} *for the PI-CS provenance of a query* q *is defined as:*

$$Q^{PI} = \{(t \blacktriangleright w[1]' \blacktriangleright \ldots \blacktriangleright w[n]')^m \mid t^p \in Q \wedge w^m \in PI(q, t)\}$$
$$w[i]' = \begin{cases} w[i] & \text{if } w[i] \neq \perp \\ null(q_i) & \text{else} \end{cases}$$

3.3 A Compositional Semantics

The declarative definition does not provide a direct way to compute provenance except for the brute force method of evaluating the conditions of the definition for each provenance candidate (subset of $\mathcal{W}(q)$). A more algorithmic approach is needed to simplify the development and correctness proofs for the algebraic rewrites. We derive compositional rules that define the provenance of an algebra operator based on the provenance of its inputs and prove that these rules are equivalent to the declarative definition of PI-CS.

Definition 4 (Compositional Semantics for PI-CS). *Figure 8 shows a compositional definition of PI-CS. Here* $\perp(q)$ *denotes a witness list for* q *with* $\perp$ *values only.*

Note that we omitted the rules for right and full outer-join and for nested subqueries [16]. The following theorem states the equivalence between the declarative definition and the compositional rules.

$$PI(R,t) = \{< t >^n | \ t^n \in R\}$$
$$PI(\sigma_C(q_1),t) = PI(q_1,t)$$
$$PI(\Pi_A(q_1),t) = \{w^n \ | \ w^n \in PI(q_1,u) \wedge u.A = t\}$$
$$PI(\alpha_{G,agg}(q_1),t) = \{w^n \ | \ w^n \in PI(q_1,u) \wedge u.G = t.G\} \cup \{<\perp>| \ Q_1 = \emptyset \wedge | \ G \ | = 0\}$$
$$PI(q_1 \bowtie_C q_2,t) = \{(w_1 \blacktriangleright w_2)^{n \times m} \ | \ w_1^n \in PI(q_1,t.\mathbf{Q_1}) \wedge w_2^m \in PI(q_2,t.\mathbf{Q_2})\}$$
$$PI(q_1 \ ⊐\!\!\!\bowtie_C q_2,t) = \begin{cases} \{(w \blacktriangleright \perp (q_2))^n \ | \ w^n \in PI(q_1,t.\mathbf{Q_1})\} & \text{if } t \not\models C \\ PI(q_1 \bowtie_C q_2,t) & \text{else} \end{cases}$$
$$PI(q_1 \cup q_2,t) = \{(w \blacktriangleright \perp (q_2))^n \ | \ w^n \in PI(q_1,t)\} \cup \{(\perp (q_1) \blacktriangleright w)^n \ | \ w^n \in PI(q_2,t)\}$$
$$PI(q_1 \cap q_2,t) = \{(w_1 \blacktriangleright w_2)^{n \times m} \ | \ w^n \in PI(q_1,t) \wedge w_2^m \in PI(q_2,t)\}$$
$$PI(q_1 - q_2,t) = \{(w \blacktriangleright \perp (q_2))^n \ | \ w^n \in PI(q_1,t)\}$$

Fig. 8. Compositional Semantics of PI-CS

Theorem 1 (Equivalence with Declarative Semantics). *The declarative and compositional definitions of PI-CS are equivalent.*

Example 6. Consider the query from Figure 5 expressed in relational algebra as $q = \Pi_{name}(customer \bowtie_{ssn=owner} creditcard) \cup \Pi_{employee}(imports)$. Recall from Example 2 that the PI-CS provenance of tuple t_2 is $\{< u_2, c_2, \perp >, < u_2, c_3, \perp >\}$.

3.4   Algebraic Rewrites

Based on the compositional semantics we developed algebraic rewrite rules that generate the relational representation of PI-CS by propagating provenance tuples through the rewritten query. These rewrite rules are defined for single algebra operators and are applied recursively to rewrite a query. Each rule modifies both the structure of the algebra expression and an auxiliary data structure called the provenance attribute list. The provenance attribute list is the schema for the relational representation of a witness list (attributes storing provenance information). Using single operator rules allows us to support user created provenance information as long as it uses the same provenance representation as Perm and to limit provenance generation to parts of a query (see Example 4).

Definition 5 (Algebraic Rewrite Rules for PI-CS). *Let q be a query. The algebraic rewrite rules for PI-CS shown in Figure 7 transform q into a query q^+ that returns the relational representation of the PI-CS provenance for q. $\mathcal{P}(q^+)$ denotes the list of provenance attributes for query q^+, $P(R)$ is the list of provenance attribute names for relation R, and $=_\epsilon$ is an equality comparison operator that considers null values to be equal.*

Consider the rewrite rules for join (R6) and aggregation (R4) as an example of how these rules work. The rewrite rule for join rewrites the left and right input of the join and applies a projection to the result to achieve the correct

Structural Rewrite

$$q = R: \qquad q^+ = \Pi_{\mathbf{R}, \mathbf{R} \to P(\mathbf{R})}(R) \qquad\qquad \textbf{(R1)}$$

$$q = \sigma_C(q_1): \qquad q^+ = \sigma_C(q_1{}^+) \qquad\qquad \textbf{(R2)}$$

$$q = \Pi_A(q_1): \qquad q^+ = \Pi_{A, \mathcal{P}(q^+)}(q_1{}^+) \qquad\qquad \textbf{(R3)}$$

$$q = \alpha_{G, agg}(q_1): \quad q^+ = \Pi_{G, agg, \mathcal{P}(q^+)}(\alpha_{G, agg}(q_1) \; \sqsupset\!\bowtie_{G = \epsilon X} \; \Pi_{G \to X, \mathcal{P}(q_1{}^+)}(q_1{}^+)) \quad \textbf{(R4)}$$

$$q = \delta(q_1): \qquad q^+ = q_1^+ \qquad\qquad \textbf{(R5)}$$

$$q = q_1 \bowtie_C q_2: \qquad\qquad q^+ = \Pi_{\mathbf{Q_1}, \mathbf{Q_2}, \mathcal{P}(q^+)}(q_1{}^+ \bowtie_C q_2{}^+) \qquad \textbf{(R6)}$$

$$q = q_1 \sqsupset\!\bowtie_C q_2: \qquad\qquad q^+ = \Pi_{\mathbf{Q_1}, \mathbf{Q_2}, \mathcal{P}(q^+)}(q_1{}^+ \sqsupset\!\bowtie_C q_2{}^+) \qquad \textbf{(R7)}$$

$$q = q_1 \cup q_2: \quad q^+ = (q_1{}^+ \times null(\mathcal{P}(q_2{}^+))) \cup (\Pi_{\mathbf{Q_1}, \mathcal{P}(q^+)}(q_2{}^+ \times null(\mathcal{P}(q_1{}^+)))) \quad \textbf{(R8)}$$

$$q = q_1 \cap q_2: \quad q^+ = \Pi_{\mathbf{Q_1}, \mathcal{P}(q^+)}(\delta(q_1 \cap q_2) \bowtie_{\mathbf{Q_1} = \epsilon X} \Pi_{\mathbf{Q_1} \to X, \mathcal{P}(q_1{}^+)}(q_1{}^+) \qquad \textbf{(R9)}$$

$$\bowtie_{\mathbf{Q_1} = \epsilon Y} \Pi_{\mathbf{Q_2} \to Y, \mathcal{P}(q_2{}^+)}(q_2{}^+))$$

$$q = q_1 - q_2: \quad q^+ = \Pi_{\mathbf{Q_1}, \mathcal{P}(q^+)}(\delta(q_1 - q_2) \bowtie_{\mathbf{Q_1} = \epsilon X} \Pi_{\mathbf{Q_1} \to X, \mathcal{P}(q_1{}^+)}(q_1{}^+) \qquad \textbf{(R10)}$$

$$\times null(\mathcal{P}(q_2{}^+)))$$

Provenance Attribute List Rewrite

$$\mathcal{P}(q^+) = \begin{cases} \mathcal{P}(q_1{}^+) & \text{if } q = \sigma_C(q_1) \mid \Pi_A(q_1) \mid \alpha_{G, agg}(q_1) \mid \delta(q_1) \\ P(R) & \text{if } q = R \\ \mathcal{P}(q_1{}^+) \blacktriangleright \mathcal{P}(q_2{}^+) & \text{else} \end{cases}$$

Fig. 9. *PI-CS* Algebraic Rewrite Rules

QB   **QB$^+$**

```
SELECT A                    SELECT A, P(q^+)
FROM  q_1 ... q_n     →      FROM  q_1^+ ... q_n^+
WHERE  C                     WHERE  C;
```

Fig. 10. SQL Query Block Rewrite

ordering between regular result attributes and provenance attributes. The list of provenance attributes for a rewritten join is the concatenation of the provenance attribute lists of its input. The rewrite rule for aggregation joins the original aggregation with the rewritten input on the group-by attributes. As can be seen in Figure 8, the provenance of an output tuple t from an aggregation contains the witness lists for all tuples from the input that have the same group-by attribute values as t, as precisely these tuples were used to compute t. The provenance attribute list for an aggregation is the provenance attribute list of its input. We refer the interested reader to Glavic [16] for detailed descriptions of the these rewrites. We presented a generic rewrite strategy [18] (called the *Gen* strategy) applicable for all types of nested subqueries by generating $\mathcal{W}(q)$ for the nested subquery using a cross product and filtering out tuples that do not belong to the provenance using additional nested subqueries and correlation. The following theorem states the correctness of the rewrite rules for PI-CS.

Theorem 2 (Rewrite Rules Correctness). *Given a query q, the query q^+ derived after Definition 5 generates the PI-CS provenance of q: $Q^+ = Q^{PI}$*

3.5 SQL Rewrites

In a final step, the algebraic rewrites are translated into SQL rewrites. First, we define a canonical translation between SQL queries and relational algebra expressions. We then classify types of SQL query blocks based on the algebra operators used in their translation. Finally, we develop an SQL rewrite rule for each of these block types. A block is translated into a relational algebra expression q, rewritten into expression q^+, and then q^+ is translated back into SQL. The SQL rewrite rule is then inferred from the original and rewritten SQL query.

Example 7 (SQL Rewrite Rules for PI-CS). Consider an SPJ (select-project-join) query block without aggregations as shown on the left of Figure 10. Such a query block is translated into an algebra expression q that is a list of joins followed by a selection and a projection. Applying the algebraic rewrites, then pulling and merging projections, we derive a rewritten expression q^+ which can be translated back into a single query block (shown as QB^+ in Figure 10).

3.6 Relationship with Provenance Polynomials

Recall from the introduction that the provenance polynomials introduced by Green et al. [22] generalize several other provenance semantics for positive relational algebra (USPJ queries). A natural question to ask is how PI-CS is related to this model. In contrast to Why-provenance [7], the PI-CS provenance of a tuple can not be derived from its provenance polynomial. The reason is that the structure of a witness list depends on the structure of the algebra expression q and this structure is not encoded in a provenance polynomial. However, the provenance polynomial of a tuple can be derived from its PI-CS provenance. Note that a polynomial can be written as a sum of products (called monomials). We transform the PI-CS provenance of a tuple t into a provenance polynomial by turning each witness list into a monomial and summing up the monomials for all witness lists of t.

Theorem 3 (Derive Provenance Polynomials from PI-CS). *Let $\mathbb{N}[X](q,t)$ denote the provenance polynomial for a tuple t in the result of a query q derived using the algebra with annotation propagation from Green et al. [22]. There exists a surjective function h from bags of witness lists to provenance polynomials so that for every positive relational algebra expression q and tuple $t \in Q$ the following holds:*

$$h(PI(q,t)) = \mathbb{N}[X](q,t)$$

There exists no function h' such that $h'(\mathbb{N}[X](q,t)) = PI(q,t)$ for every such q and t.

Proof. We construct such a function by deriving a monomial from a witness list w by multiplying all tuples from w (ignoring $\perp$ values) and summing up the monomials for all witness lists of a tuple. The equivalence of $h(PI(q,t))$ to $\mathbb{N}[X]$ can be proven by induction over the structure of an algebra expression.

$$h(PI(q,t)) = \sum_{w^m \in PI(q,t)} \left(\prod_{i \in \{1,n\} \wedge w[i] \neq \perp} w[i] \right)$$

The non-existence of h' is disproven by contradiction (see [19] for a similar proof).

Example 8. Reconsider the query q from Example 6. The result tuple t_2 was derived by joining the customer tuple u_2 with the credit card tuples c_2 and c_3. Thus, the PI-CS provenance of t_2 is $\{< u_2, c_2, \perp >, < u_2, c_3, \perp >\}$. The result of $h(PI(q,t))$ is $u_2 \times c_2 + u_2 \times c_3$, the provenance polynomial for t_2.

As mentioned before, the extension of provenance polynomials for aggregation stores provenance for individual aggregated values. The provenance attached to an attribute value by this model encapsulates both the influence of input tuples and the computation of the aggregation function result. Thus, it is not surprising that this type of provenance can not be derived from the PI-CS provenance. Similarly, some extensions of semiring provenance for set difference are more informative than PI-CS with regard to this operation [15,3,15]. Whereas PI-CS only considers the left input of a set difference to contribute to the result, m-semirings [15] capture the positive influence of the right input in cases such as $q = R - (S - T)$. [4]

3.7   Optimizations

The rewrites implemented in Perm use several optimizations to speed up the execution of provenance queries. For queries without nested subqueries a standard DBMS optimizer will carry out most of the possible optimizations for us, e.g., by pushing down selections over provenance data into the provenance generation. For nested subqueries, the Gen strategy (see Section 3.4) leads to very complex nested subqueries that are hard to de-correlate and un-nest. Such unnesting is necessary to avoid cross-products in the outer query. Therefore, most of the optimizations for PI-CS target this type of query. Glavic and Alonso [18] presented two simple un-nesting strategies to optimize provenance computation for specific types of nested subqueries. The current version of Perm [16] extends this approach and applies a wide range of un-nesting and de-correlation techniques inspired by approaches for optimizing regular nested queries. For instance, we de-correlate correlated aggregation subqueries by using group-by and joins, and inject the outer-query block into a nested subquery to de-correlate universally quantified subqueries (ALL) with inequality predicates [28,13,32]. New de-correlation strategies can be applied in provenance computation that are not applicable to regular queries. For instance, under certain circumstances a correlated existentially quantified subquery (EXISTS) can be rewritten into a join without the need to eliminate duplicates as would be required for regular queries. Rewrite strategies are chosen heuristically, because at the level we apply the query rewrites we do not have access to cost estimates. We always prefer un-nesting and de-correlation techniques to other types of rewrites. This is a reasonable heuristic for provenance computation because avoiding the Gen strategy is almost always beneficial. Experimental results indicate that this heuristic can drastically improve performance [16].

3.8   Query Rewrite Example

We now demonstrate how Perm computes the provenance of the running example query (Figure 2) as specified in Example 4. Recall that the user decided to limit provenance generation to not trace into subquery monthly. The result of the SQL rewrites applied by Perm for this query is shown in Figure 11. The SELECT clause contains additional attributes to store the relational provenance representation. For simple relation accesses (customer and creditcard relations in the FROM clause of the outer query) these attributes are just renamed versions of the attributes of these relations (e.g., c.ssn AS prov_customer_ssn). The same applies for the monthly subquery, because the user has instructed Perm to limit

---

[4] In this example, a tuple t from relation T can contribute to a result tuple, because it may cause a tuple s from S to not appear in the result of $(S - T)$ which in turn causes a tuple r from R to be in the result of q.

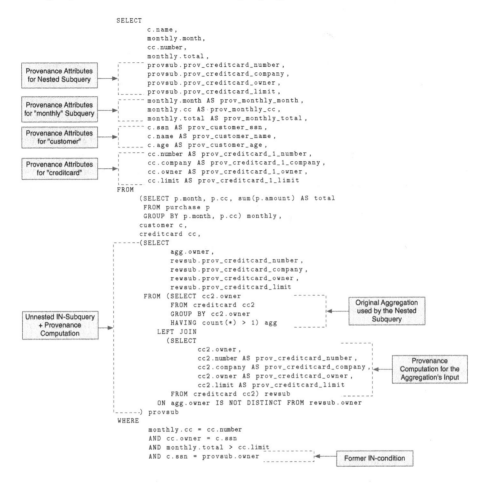

Fig. 11. Rewritten SQL query

provenance generation to the results of this subquery using the BASERELATION keyword. Recall that the original query used an IN-subquery in the WHERE clause. This subquery was un-nested by turning it into a FROM clause subquery that implements both the selection condition containing the subquery and the provenance computation for this subquery. The IN condition has been translated into a simple selection condition (see Figure 11). The provenance computation for this subquery is realized by applying the rewrite rule for aggregation (joining the original aggregation with its rewritten input).

4   Copy Contribution Semantics (C-CS)

Copy contribution semantics (C-CS) is a restriction of PI-CS to input tuples that are copied (partially) to a result tuple. This is similar to Where-provenance [7,5]

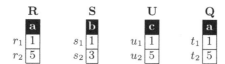

Fig. 12. C-CS Example

except that we track copying at tuple granularity instead of attribute value granularity. Perm supports four variants of this provenance semantics based on the distinction of whether to consider equality conditions as an implicit form of copying values and the distinction between partially and completely copied tuples. We limit the discussion to the variant that takes partial and implicit copying into account. For the other variants and correctness theorems see Glavic [16]. Intuitively, it is apparent that the set of input tuples that have been copied to a tuple t is a subset of the tuples that contributed to t. Thus, it is reasonable to derive C-CS from PI-CS by filtering out tuples from the PI-CS witness lists that have not been copied to the output.

Example 9 (PI-CS vs. C-CS). Consider the query $q = \Pi_a(R \bowtie_{a<b} S) \cup U$ evaluated over the database instance shown in Figure 12. The PI-CS provenance of result tuple t_1 is $\{< r_1, s_2, \bot >, < \bot, \bot, u_1 >\}$. The a attribute value of t_1 has been copied from the a attribute of tuple r_1 and the c attribute of tuple u_1. Tuple s_2 was joined with tuple r_1 to produce t_1, but did not contribute any values to the result. Therefore, the C-CS provenance of t_1 is $\{< r_1, \bot, \bot >, < \bot, \bot, u_1 >\}$.

We use data structures called copy-maps to determine which tuples from a PI-CS witness list should be removed to form the corresponding witness list for C-CS. This data structures model from which attributes each result attribute of a query is copied. Formally, a copy-map is a function that maps an algebra expression q, one attribute a from one of its input relations, a result tuple t, and one witness list w in $PI(q,t)$ to the set of result attributes to which a is copied with respect to t and w. Copy-maps are defined recursively for all operators of the algebra in a similar fashion as the compositional semantics for PI-CS. Reconsider tuple t_1 from Example 9 as an example of why it is necessary to include a witness list as an input parameter for copy maps. The two witness lists in $PI(q,t_1)$ exhibit different copy behavior. According to the first witness list, the result attribute a is copied from the a attribute of tuple r_1. According to the second witness list, the result attribute a is copied from tuple u_1.

Definition 6 (C-CS and Copy-Map). *The C-CS provenance $C(q,t)$ of a tuple t from the result of a query q is a multiset of witness lists defined as follows (the copy-map $\mathcal{CM}(q,a,w,t)$ is defined in Figure 13).*

$$C(q,t) = \{\hat{w}^n \mid w^n \in PI(q,t)\}$$

$$\hat{w}[i] = \begin{cases} w[i] & if \exists a \in \mathbf{Q_i} : \mathcal{CM}(q,a,w,t) \neq \emptyset \\ \bot & else \end{cases}$$

$$CM(R, a, w, t) = \{a\}$$
$$CM(\sigma_C(q_1), a, w, t) = CM(q_1, a, w, t) \cup$$
$$\{x \mid \exists y : (x = y) \in C \wedge t \models (x = y) \wedge y \in CM(q_1, a, w, t)\}$$
$$CM(\Pi_A(q_1), a, w, t) = \{x \mid (x \in CM(q_1, a, w, y) \wedge x \in A \wedge y.A = t)\}$$
$$\cup \{x \mid (b \to x) \in A \wedge b \in CM(q_1, a, w, y) \wedge y.A = t)\}$$
$$\cup \{x \mid if\ (C)\ then\ (x)\ else\ (e) \in A \wedge x \in CM(q_1, a, w, y)$$
$$\wedge y.A = t \wedge y \models C)\}$$
$$\cup \{x \mid if\ (C)\ then\ (e)\ else\ (x) \in A \wedge x \in CM(q_1, a, w, y)$$
$$\wedge y.A = t \wedge y \not\models C)\}$$
$$CM(q_1 \bowtie_C q_2, a, w, t) = CM(q_1, a, w[q_1], t.\mathbf{Q_1}) \cup CM(q_2, a, w[q_2], t.\mathbf{Q_2})$$
$$\cup \{x \mid \exists y : (x = y) \in C \wedge w \models (x = y)$$
$$\wedge (y \in CM(q_1, a, w[q_1], t.\mathbf{Q_1}) \vee y \in CM(q_2, a, w[q_2], t.\mathbf{Q_2}))\}$$

Fig. 13. Copy-Map Definition

We use $w[q_1]$ to denote the part of a witness list corresponding to subquery q_1.

As an example, consider the copy-map definition for projection. For a tuple t and one of its witness lists w, the value of an attribute a has been copied to a result attribute x if one of the following holds: (1) x is in the copy map of a for a tuple from the input of the projection that has been projected on t (first line); (2) the same applies for an attribute b that has been renamed to x (second line); or (3) the projection contains an if-then-else expression (CASE in SQL) with x being the result expression for either the "then" respective "else" branch and the condition is fulfilled respective not fulfilled (third and fourth line).

4.1   Algebraic Rewrites

We use the fact that C-CS is defined as filtering out parts from PI-CS witness lists to develop rewrite rules for this provenance type. We first apply modified versions of the PI-CS rewrite rules to generate a rewritten query q^{C+}. These rules use additional projections expressions, called *copy expressions*, to iteratively build a relational encoding of the copy-map for the query. Afterwards, a final projection is added to the rewritten query to conditionally replace provenance attribute values with null values based on the copy expression information. The relational encoding of a copy map is a list of set valued attributes. Each of these attributes is used to store the result of a copy-map for one input attribute a ($CM(q, a, t, w)$). Conditional projection expressions (if-then-else in algebra or CASE in SQL) are used whenever the inclusion of an output attribute into the copy-map is conditional. The final projection determines for each input relation if at least one attribute from this relation has been copied to the output (for the current tuple and witness list) using a disjunction of comparisons between copy expressions and the empty-set. If this expression evaluates to false, the provenance attributes for this input relation are replaced with null values.

$$CM(R) = \underset{a \in \mathbf{R}}{\blacktriangleright} \{a\} \to \mathcal{C}(a)$$

$$CM(\sigma_C(q_1)) = \underset{a \in \mathcal{B}(q_1)}{\blacktriangleright} (\mathcal{C}^*(q_1, a) \cup \mathcal{C}(a)) \to \mathcal{C}(a)$$

$$CM(q_1 \bowtie_C q_2) = \underset{a \in \mathcal{B}(q_1)}{\blacktriangleright} (\mathcal{C}^*(q_1, a) \cup \mathcal{C}(a)) \to \mathcal{C}(a) \underset{a \in \mathcal{B}(q_2)}{\blacktriangleright} (\mathcal{C}^*(q_2, a) \cup \mathcal{C}(a)) \to \mathcal{C}(a)$$

$$\mathcal{C}^*(q, a) = \underset{x \in \mathbf{Q} \wedge ((x=y) \in C \vee (y=x) \in C)}{\bigcup} \quad if \ ((x = y) \wedge x \in \mathcal{C}(a)) \ then \ (\{y\}) \ else \ (\emptyset)$$

$$CM(\alpha_{G,agg}(q_1)) = \underset{a \in \mathcal{B}(q_1)}{\blacktriangleright} (\mathcal{C}(a) \cap G) \to \mathcal{C}(a)$$

$$CM(\Pi_A(q_1)) = \underset{a \in \mathcal{B}(q_1)}{\blacktriangleright} \left(\underset{x \in A}{\bigcup} \mathcal{C}^*(a, x) \to \mathcal{C}(a) \right)$$

$$\mathcal{C}^*(a, x) = \begin{cases} \{x\} \cap \mathcal{C}(a) & \text{for } x \in \mathbf{Q_1} \\ if \ (C) \ then \ (\{y\} \cap \mathcal{C}(a)) \ else \ (\emptyset) & \text{for } x = \ if \ (C) \ then \ (y) \ else \ (e) \\ if \ (C) \ then \ (\emptyset) \ else \ (\{y\} \cap \mathcal{C}(a)) & \text{for } x = \ if \ (C) \ then \ (e) \ else \ (y) \\ if \ (y \in \mathcal{C}(a)) \ then \ (\{z\}) \ else \ (\emptyset) & \text{for } x = (y \to z) \\ \emptyset & \text{else} \end{cases}$$

Fig. 14. C-CS Copy Expressions

Definition 7 (C-CS Rewrite Rules). *Let $\mathcal{B}(q)$ denote the list of all attributes from the relations accessed by query q. A query q is rewritten into a provenance generating query q^C according to C-CS as shown below. Query q^C uses projection expressions $\mathcal{P}^*(q^{C+})$ to filter out tuples from witness lists over a rewritten version q^{C+} of q.*

$$q^C = \Pi_{\mathbf{Q}, \mathcal{P}^*(q^{C+})}(q^{C+})$$

$$\mathcal{P}^*(q^{C+}) = \underset{a \in \mathcal{B}(q)}{\blacktriangleright} \ if \ (\mathcal{C}^+(a)) \ then \ (P(a)) \ else \ (\varepsilon) \to P(a)$$

$$\mathcal{C}^+(a) = (\mathcal{C}(b_1) \neq \emptyset \vee \ldots \vee \mathcal{C}(b_x) \neq \emptyset) \ for \ a \in \mathbf{Q_j} = (b_1, \ldots, b_x)$$

Each of the adapted PI-CS rewrites adds the copy expressions to the rewritten query. We present the rule for projection as an example:

$$q = \Pi_A(q_1): \qquad\qquad q^{C+} = \Pi_{A, \mathcal{P}(q^{C+}), CM(q)}(q_1{}^{C+})$$

The copy expressions $CM(q)$ for a query q are defined in Figure 14.

4.2 Optimizations

Generating the C-CS provenance of a query q requires the generation of copy-expressions in addition to generating the PI-CS provenance of q. However, for a wide range of algebra expressions the query that generates *C-CS* can be simplified based on the following observations. *Instance Independent Copy Expressions:*

```
SELECT PROVENANCE ON CONTRIBUTION (COPY PARTIAL TRANSITIVE)
        CASE
                WHEN r.a < 20 THEN r.a
                ELSE s.c
        END AS cleana,
        CASE
                WHEN r.b < 30 THEN r.b
                ELSE s.c
        END AS cleanb
FROM r NATURAL JOIN s;
```

	R				**S**				**Q**	
	id| **a**	**b**		**id**	**c**			**cleana**	**cleanb**
r_1	1	1	40	s_1	1	10	t_1	1	10
r_2	2	51	60	s_2	2	20	t_2	20	20

```
SELECT
        CASE
                WHEN r.a < 20 THEN r.a
                ELSE s.c
        END AS cleana,
        CASE
                WHEN r.b < 30 THEN r.b
                ELSE s.c
        END AS cleanb,
        ...
        CASE
                WHEN NOT biteq(bitor(
                  CASE
                        WHEN NOT (r.a < 20) THEN B'0010' ELSE B'0000'
                  END,
                  CASE
                        WHEN NOT (r.b < 30) THEN B'0001' ELSE B'0000'
                  END), B'0000')
                THEN s.c
                ELSE NULL
          END AS prov_s_c
FROM
    r NATURAL JOIN s
```

Fig. 15. Example C-CS SQL Rewrite

Often, we can deduce that some conditional clauses used in copy expressions evaluate to a constant result independent of the data. For example, this holds for projections without conditional expressions. We identify and evaluate constant copy expressions at query compile time to avoid unnecessary computations at run-time. *Omit Rewrite*: If the provenance attributes for an input relation are guaranteed to be ε, it is not necessary to compute any provenance for this relation. Thus, we can avoid rewriting a sub-expression if it exclusively accesses input relations with this property.

Example 10 (C-CS Optimizations). Consider the query $q = \Pi_a(R \bowtie_{a<b} S)$ evaluated over the instance from Figure 12. The single attribute of each result tuple of q is copied from the a attribute of a tuple from relation R. Therefore, we can apply the original PI-CS rewrites to relation R and avoid rewriting S at all.

4.3   SQL Rewrites

The translation of the algebraic C-CS rewrite rules into SQL rewrites is analogous to the translation for PI-CS except for modeling copy expressions and filtering provenance attributes in the outermost projection. An efficient way to model the set-valued attributes used in the copy expressions are bit-arrays (natively supported by PostgreSQL). The copy-expressions for all attributes of one input relation are represented as a single bit-array using n bits (where n is the number of query result attributes) to represent the result set for each attribute. UDFs are used to speed up common operations on the bit-array type.[5]

Example 11 (Example SQL Rewrite). The query shown in Figure 15 removes outlier values (values outside some predefined bound) from a relation R by replacing them with a per-id default value from a relation S. This kind of query is similar to queries used in data cleaning or fusion. The user can request the C-CS provenance of this query to understand from where the values in the result are copied (Figure 15 shows an excerpt of the rewritten query). Consider the expression that determines the value for the provenance attribute prov_S_c. A bit-array of length four is constructed to store which of the two result attributes are copied from which of the two attributes of relation S. The construction consists of an outer bitwise-or and inner conditional construction of bit-arrays. For example, if the condition $R.a < 20$ holds, then attribute $S.c$ is copied to the first result attribute (0010). Similar, if $R.b < 30$ holds, then $S.c$ is copied to the second result attribute (0001). The outer-most CASE construct checks whether at least one attribute from relation S has been copied to one of the result attributes, i.e., if the constructed bit-array is not equal to a sequence of zeros (0000).

5   Transformation Provenance

Transformation provenance models what parts of a transformation contribute to a result tuple [19]. We represent the transformation provenance of a query q

---

[5] For a DBMS without support for a bit-array datatype or UDFs, we could simulate a bit-array as a list of boolean attributes.

using annotated algebra trees for q. For a result tuple t and a witness list w in PI(q,t), the transformation provenance includes an annotated algebra tree for q with 1 and 0 annotations on the operators. A 1 indicates this operator on w influences t, a 0 indicates it does not.

Definition 8 (Annotated Algebra Tree). *An annotated algebra tree for a query q is a pair $(Tree_q, \theta)$ where $Tree_q = (V, E)$ is a tree that contains a node for each algebra operator used in q and $\theta : V \to \{0,1\}$ is a function that associates each operator in the tree with an annotation from $\{0,1\}$. We define a preorder on the nodes to give each node an identifier (and to order the children of binary operators). Let $I(op)$ denote the identifier assigned to node op.*

We define transformation provenance based on PI-CS provenance. Intuitively, each witness list in the PI-CS provenance of a tuple t represents one evaluation of an algebra expression q. For one witness list, each part of the algebra expression has either contributed to the result of evaluating q on w or not. We represent the transformation provenance as a set of annotated algebra trees of q with one member per witness list w. PI-CS provenance is used to decide whether an operator op in q is annotated with 0 or 1. If evaluating the subtree sub_{op} under op on w results in the empty set $(sub_{op}(w) = \emptyset)$, then op has contributed nothing to the result t and should not be included in the transformation provenance.

Definition 9 (Transformation provenance). *The transformation provenance $\mathcal{T}(q, t)$ of a tuple t in the result of a query q is a set of annotated trees defined as:*
$$\mathcal{T}(q, t) = \{(Tree_q, \theta_w) \mid w \in PI(q, t)\}$$

$$\theta_w(op) = \begin{cases} 0 \ if \ sub_{op}(w) = \emptyset \\ 1 \ else \end{cases}$$

5.1 Algebraic Rewrites

Transformation provenance is defined by evaluating subexpressions of a query over the PI-CS provenance. However, we have shown that it is possible to generate the transformation provenance of a query without instantiating its PI-CS provenance. The rewrite rules for transformation provenance rewrite a query q into a query q^T adding an additional attribute $\mathcal{T}$ to its schema that is used to store transformation provenance information. Recall that the *transformation provenance* of a result tuple t is a set of annotated algebra trees (one tree per witness list w). The elements of this set represents the same algebra tree with different annotation functions θ_w. Therefore, we can factor out the tree and store only the annotation functions. Each value of attribute $\mathcal{T}$ stores θ_w for one witness-list w of t (represented as the set of operators that carry a 1-annotation).

Each *transformation* provenance rewrite rule computes a new set of annotations from the annotation sets of the rewritten inputs of the operator. Fig. 16 presents the rewrite rules for some algebra operators (see Glavic [16] for the remaining operators). The rewrite rule for a base relation access adds the singleton annotation set for the operator $\{I(R)\}$ as the value for attribute $\mathcal{T}$ to all result

$$
\begin{aligned}
q = R: &\quad q^T = \Pi_{\mathbf{R}, \mathcal{T}(q^T) \to \mathcal{T}}(R) &\quad \mathcal{T}(q^T) = \{R\} \\
q = \sigma_C(q_1): &\quad q^T = \Pi_{\mathbf{Q_1}, \mathcal{T}(q^T) \to \mathcal{T}}(\sigma_C(q_1^T)) &\quad \mathcal{T}(q^T) = \{\sigma_c(q_1)\} \cup \mathbf{Q_1}.\mathcal{T} \\
q = \Pi_A(q_1): &\quad q^T = \Pi_{A, \mathcal{T}(q^T) \to \mathcal{T}}(q_1^T) &\quad \mathcal{T}(q^T) = \{\Pi_A(q_1)\} \cup \mathbf{Q_1}.\mathcal{T} \\
q = q_1 \cup q_2: &\quad q^T = \Pi_{\mathbf{Q_1}, \mathcal{T}(q^T) \to \mathcal{T}}(q_1^T \cup q_2^T) &\quad \mathcal{T}(q^T) = \{q_1 \cup q_2\} \cup \mathbf{Q_1}.\mathcal{T}
\end{aligned}
$$

Fig. 16. Transformation Provenance Rewrite Rules

tuples. A selection is rewritten by applying the unmodified selection and then adding the identifier of the selection to the annotation set. The rewrite rules for projection and union work analogously.

5.2   SQL Rewrites and Optimizations

We represent an annotation set as a bit-array in the SQL rewrites, because its space requirements are low, and the union operation used frequently in the rewrite rules is efficient (bit-wise disjunction). Similar to C-CS, we can precompute the transformation provenance for a sub-expression if it is independent of the input and avoid rewriting this sub-expression. To provide a useful *transformation* provenance representation to the user the bit-vector representation is transformed into either SQL text with markup or XML (chosen by using the keyword *TRANSSQL* or *TRANSXML* to trigger provenance computation) by applying a UDF f_{SQL} or f_{XML} in the outermost projection of the rewritten query.[6] The SQL representation encloses parts of the original query text with <NOT> and </NOT> to indicate which parts do not belong to the *transformation* provenance. The XML representation is a hierarchical representation of the query that models each clause as an XML element.

6   Conclusions

We presented an overview of the Perm approach for integrating efficient on-demand provenance support in relational databases and discussed its contributions with respect to the requirements for a provenance system outlined in Section 1. Perm stands out for using a pure relational representation of provenance information which is generated and queried by executing standard SQL queries, thus, taking full advantage of the DBMS optimizer. We demonstrated the flexibility of the approach by implementing several provenance types including Where-provenance and provenance polynomials. The Perm approach enables a wide range of optimizations such as using algebraic equivalences to develop more efficient rewrites (used to optimize nested subqueries for PI-CS),

---

[6] UDFs are used to increase performance. In principle, the CASE construct and string concatenation are sufficient for producing these representations.

static analysis of queries to avoid unnecessary generation of provenance information (used for C-CS and transformation provenance), and DBMS specific optimizations using specialized data types (mainly used for C-CS, transformation provenance, and the provenance polynomial implementation). Perm provides a platform for exploring advanced topics such as provenance-aware physical operators, cost-based optimization for provenance generation, provenance compression and summarization, and provenance of updates. In addition to these topics, we plan to extend the approach to support provenance for complete transactions.

References

1. Acar, U., Buneman, P., Cheney, J., van den Bussche, J., Kwasnikowska, N., Vansummeren, S.: A graph model of data and workflow provenance. In: TaPP (2010)
2. Agrawal, P., Benjelloun, O., Das Sarma, A., Hayworth, C., Nabar, S.U., Sugihara, T., Widom, J.: Trio: A System for Data, Uncertainty, and Lineage. In: VLDB, pp. 1151–1154 (2006)
3. Amsterdamer, Y., Deutch, D., Tannen, V.: On the Limitations of Provenance for Queries with Difference. In: TaPP (2011)
4. Amsterdamer, Y., Deutch, D., Tannen, V.: Provenance for Aggregate Queries. In: PODS, pp. 153–164 (2011)
5. Bhagwat, D., Chiticariu, L., Tan, W.-C., Vijayvargiya, G.: An Annotation Management System for Relational Databases. VLDB Journal 14(4), 373–396 (2005)
6. Bose, R., Frew, J.: Lineage retrieval for scientific data processing: A survey. ACM Computing Surveys 37(1), 1–28 (2005)
7. Buneman, P., Khanna, S., Tan, W.-C.: Why and Where: A Characterization of Data Provenance. In: Van den Bussche, J., Vianu, V. (eds.) ICDT 2001. LNCS, vol. 1973, pp. 316–330. Springer, Heidelberg (2000)
8. Cheney, J.: Program Slicing and Data Provenance. IEEE Data Engineering Bulletin 30(4), 22–28 (2007)
9. Cheney, J.: Causality and the Semantics of Provenance. In: DCM, pp. 63–74 (2010)
10. Cheney, J., Chiticariu, L., Tan, W.-C.: Provenance in Databases: Why, How, and Where. Foundations and Trends in Databases 1(4), 379–474 (2009)
11. Chiticariu, L., Tan, W.-C., Vijayvargiya, G.: DBNotes: a Post-it System for Relational Databases based on Provenance. In: SIGMOD, pp. 942–944 (2005)
12. Cui, Y., Widom, J., Wiener, J.L.: Tracing the Lineage of View Data in a Warehousing Environment. TODS 25(2), 179–227 (2000)
13. Dayal, U.: Of Nests and Trees: A Unified Approach to Processing Queries That Contain Nested Subqueries, Aggregates, and Quantifiers. In: VLDB, pp. 197–208 (1987)
14. Foster, J.N., Green, T.J., Tannen, V.: Annotated XML: Queries and Provenance. In: PODS, pp. 271–280 (2008)
15. Geerts, F., Poggi, A.: On database query languages for K-relations. Journal of Applied Logic 8(2), 173–185 (2010)
16. Glavic, B.: Perm: Efficient Provenance Support for Relational Databases. PhD thesis, University of Zurich (2010)
17. Glavic, B., Alonso, G.: Perm: Processing Provenance and Data on the same Data Model through Query Rewriting. In: ICDE, pp. 174–185 (2009)

18. Glavic, B., Alonso, G.: Provenance for Nested Subqueries. In: EDBT, pp. 982–993 (2009)
19. Glavic, B., Alonso, G., Miller, R.J., Haas, L.M.: TRAMP: Understanding the Behavior of Schema Mappings through Provenance. In: VLDB, pp. 1314–1325 (2010)
20. Green, T.J., Ives, Z.G., Tannen, V.: Reconcilable Differences. In: ICDT, pp. 212–224 (2009)
21. Green, T.J., Karvounarakis, G., Ives, Z.G., Tannen, V.: Update Exchange with Mappings and Provenance. In: VLDB, pp. 675–686 (2007)
22. Green, T.J., Karvounarakis, G., Tannen, V.: Provenance Semirings. In: PODS, pp. 31–40 (2007)
23. Green, T.J.: Containment of conjunctive queries on annotated relations. Theory of Computing Systems 49(2), 429–459 (2011)
24. Karvounarakis, G., Green, T.J.: Semiring-Annotated Data: Queries and Provenance. SIGMOD Record 41(3), 5–14 (2012)
25. Karvounarakis, G., Ives, Z.G., Tannen, V.: Querying data provenance. In: SIGMOD, pp. 951–962 (2010)
26. Kementsietsidis, A., Wang, M.: On the Efficiency of Provenance Queries. In: ICDE, pp. 1223–1226 (2009)
27. Kementsietsidis, A., Wang, M.: Provenance Query Evaluation: What's so Special about it? In: CIKM, pp. 681–690 (2009)
28. Kim, W.: On Optimizing an SQL-like Nested Query. TODS 7(3), 443–469 (1982)
29. Kostylev, E.V., Buneman, P.: Combining dependent annotations for relational algebra. In: ICDT, pp. 196–207 (2012)
30. Meliou, A., Gatterbauer, W., Moore, K.F., Suciu, D.: The Complexity of Causality and Responsibility for Query Answers and non-Answers. PVLDB 4(1), 34–45 (2010)
31. Park, J., Nguyen, D., Sandhu, R.: A provenance-based access control model. In: PST, pp. 137–144. IEEE (2012)
32. Seshadri, P., Pirahesh, H., Leung, T.Y.C.: Complex Query Decorrelation. In: ICDE, pp. 450–458 (1996)
33. Tan, W.-C.: Containment of Relational Queries with Annotation Propagation. In: DBPL, pp. 37–53 (2003)
34. Widom, J.: Trio: A System for Managing Data, Uncertainty, and Lineage. In: Managing and Mining Uncertain Data, pp. 113–148 (2008)
35. Widom, J., Theobald, M., Das Sarma, A.: Exploiting Lineage for Confidence Computation in Uncertain and Probabilistic Databases. In: ICDE, pp. 1023–1032 (2008)

Bounds and Algorithms for Joins via Fractional Edge Covers

Martin Grohe

RWTH Aachen University
`grohe@informatik.rwth-aachen.de`

1   Introduction

Among the operations of relational algebra, the join operation tends to be the most costly. There is a wealth of research in the database literature devoted to efficient join processing. Short of fully computing the result of a join or a sequence of joins (we use the term *join query* in the following), in many applications it is also important to get good bounds on the size of the result.

A relatively new idea exploits the structure of the join query to obtain nontrivial bounds on the size of the result and to design algorithms computing the result in time linear in the estimated size of the result. These bounds are based on a combinatorial parameter known as *fractional edge cover number* of the query. The purpose of this paper is to explain this idea and give a survey of the results based on it.

Consider the natural-join query

$$Q = R_1 \bowtie \ldots \bowtie R_m.$$

Given a database instance D of schema $\{R_1, \ldots, R_m\}$, we want to bound the size of the query answer $Q(D)$ in terms of the sizes $N_i := |R_i(D)|$ of the input relations. As a start, suppose that there is a relation R_i that contains all attributes appearing in the query. Then, trivially, the size of the query answer is bounded by the size of the relation: $|Q(D)| \leq N_i$. Suppose next that, instead of one relation that contains all attributes, we have relations $R_{i_1}, \ldots, R_{i_k}$ that together contain all attributes. Then $|Q(D)| \leq \prod_{j=1}^{k} N_{i_j}$. We call $R_{i_1}, \ldots, R_{i_k}$ an *edge cover* of Q. Now we can try to find the edge cover that gives us the best bound. We can express this as an integer linear program in the variables $x_1, \ldots, x_m$, where $x_i = 1$ expresses that R_i is in the edge cover. Suppose that the attributes appearing in Q are $A_1, \ldots, A_n$.

$$\text{minimise} \quad \sum_i x_i \log N_i, \tag{1}$$

$$\text{where} \quad \sum_{\substack{i \text{ such that } A_j \\ \text{attribute of } R_i}} x_i \geq 1 \qquad \text{for } j = 1, \ldots, n \tag{2}$$

$$x_i \in \{0, 1\} \qquad \text{for } i = 1, \ldots, m. \tag{3}$$

V. Tannen et al. (Eds.): Buneman Festschrift, LNCS 8000, pp. 321–338, 2013.
© Springer-Verlag Berlin Heidelberg 2013

Then for every solution $\boldsymbol{x} = (x_1, \ldots, x_m) \in \{0,1\}^m$ of this integer linear program, we have

$$|Q(D)| \leq \prod_{i=1}^{m} N_i^{x_i} = 2^{\sum_i x_i \log N_i}. \tag{4}$$

We call the value $\rho(Q, D) = \sum_i x_i \log N_i$ of an optimal solution of the integer linear program the *edge cover number* of Q in D.

So — we have found a complicated way to state a trivial observation. It is hard to imagine, though, how we can obtain nontrivial bounds on the size of the query answer if we just know the query and the size of the input relations. Surprisingly, there are such bounds. Let us look at the LP relaxation of the integer linear program (1)–(3), where we replace the integrality constraints $x_i \in \{0,1\}$ by the inequalities

$$0 \leq x_i \qquad \text{for } i = 1, \ldots, m. \tag{5}$$

(There is no need to add inequalities $x_i \leq 1$, because in an optimal solution it never makes sense to let $x_i > 1$.) We call a rational solution $\boldsymbol{x} = (x_1, \ldots, x_m) \in \mathbb{Q}^m$ to this linear program a *fractional edge cover* of Q. We call the value $\rho^*(Q, D) := \sum_i x_i \log N_i$ of an optimal solution $\boldsymbol{x}$ to the linear program the *fractional edge cover number* of Q in D. It turns out that the bound (4) remains valid for fractional edge covers and that it is actually tight.

Theorem 1 (Grohe and Marx [6], Atserias, Grohe, and Marx [1]). *Let Q be a join query. Then for every database instance D,*

$$|Q(D)| \leq 2^{\rho^*(Q,D)}.$$

Furthermore, there are arbitrarily large database instances D such that $|Q(D)| = 2^{\rho^*(Q,D)}$.

It is neither obvious why this theorem should hold nor why it is an improvement over the trivial bound (4) for the (integral) edge cover number. I will try to answer both questions with the following examples. In a way, these examples form the core of the whole paper.

1.1 Examples

We give two examples. The first illustrates the main idea of the upper bound of Theorem 1. The second shows that the fractional edge cover number of Q in D may be substantially smaller than the edge cover number.

Example 1. Let us consider the query

$$Q(A, B, C) = R(A, B) \bowtie S(B, C) \bowtie T(C, A)$$

with attributes A, B, C and relation schemas $R = R(A, B)$, $S = S(B, C)$, and $T = T(C, A)$. Let D be a database instance of this schema, and let $N_R := |R(D)|$,

$N_S := |S(D)|$, and $N_T := |T(D)|$. We want to give an upper bound on the size $N_Q := |Q(D)|$ of the query answer.

The linear program associated with Q and D looks as follows:

$$\text{minimise } x_R \log N_R + x_S \log N_S + x_T \log N_T,$$
$$\text{where } x_R + x_T \geq 1$$
$$x_R + x_S \geq 1$$
$$x_S + x_T \geq 1$$
$$x_R, x_S, x_T \geq 0.$$

Observe that $x_R = x_S = x_T = 1/2$ is a feasible solution to this linear program. It is an optimal solution if $N_R = N_S = N_T$. We shall prove that

$$N_Q \leq 2^{(1/2)\log N_R + (1/2)\log N_S + (1/2)\log N_T} = \sqrt{N_R \cdot N_S \cdot N_T}. \qquad (6)$$

It is worth thinking about how to prove this bound for a minute. The special case where D is an undirected graph and $R = S = T$ is the edge relation may be most intuitive. In this special case, Q asks for all triangles in the graph, and (6) says that there are at most $M^{3/2}$ triangles, where $M := N_R = N_S = N_T$ is the number of edges of the graph. (This bound on the number of triangles appeared in [2]; the slightly better bound $(2M)^{3/2}/6$ can be found in [7]). Even in this special case, I see no obvious direct proof for the bound.

In our proof, we take an information theoretic approach. We ask how many bits we need on average to describe a tuple chosen from $Q(D)$ uniformly at random. To be clear what is meant here, let us describe this as a two-player game: suppose that player (P) wants to inform player (M) about the outcome of an experiment where a tuple $(a, b, c) \in Q(D)$ was drawn uniformly at random. Both players know the query Q and the database D and thus the query answer $Q(D)$ in advance, but only (P) knows the outcome (a, b, c) of the experiment. The players may agree on a coding system that allows (P) to transmit (a, b, c) using as few bits as possible on average. For example, they may use a Huffman code. The quantity "average number of bits" we look for is essentially the *entropy* $H(X_Q)$ of a random variable X_Q that, for all $(a, b, c) \in Q(D)$, takes value (a, b, c) with probability $1/N_Q$.[1] As the distribution is uniform, the best the two players can do is number the tuples in $Q(D)$ in advance and then have (P) send the number corresponding to (a, b, c) in binary. This essentially shows that $H(X_Q) = \log N_Q$.

We now give a different protocol that yields an estimate of $H(X_Q)$ in terms of $H(X_R)$, $H(X_S)$, and $H(X_T)$, where X_R is the random variable that picks an element $(a, b) \in R(D)$ uniformly at random and X_S, X_T are defined similarly. The same argument that showed $H(X_Q) = \log N_Q$ shows that $H(X_R) = \log N_R$ and $H(X_S) = \log N_S$ and $H(X_T) = \log N_T$.

Here is the protocol. (P) transmits the tuple $(a, b, c) \in Q(D)$ in three steps. In the first step, he transmits a using an optimal coding system for the projection

---

[1] To be precise, we have $H(X_Q) \leq$ expected number of transmitted bits of an optimal coding system $< H(X_Q) + 1$. This is Shannon's famous Source Coding Theorem [9].

of X_A on the first component. The distribution of the projected random variable is known as the marginal distribution; note that it is not necessarily uniform, because some elements a may be contained in more tuples $(a, b, c) \in Q(D)$ than others. In the second step, (P) transmits b, taking into account that (M) already knows a. He uses an optimal coding system for the random variable that picks a b such that (a, b) can be extended to a tuple $(a, b, c) \in Q(D)$ with a distribution that takes the number of such extensions into account. In the third step, (P) transmits c, taking into account that (M) already knows a, b, and using an optimal coding system for the random variable that picks a c such that $(a, b, c) \in Q(D)$. More formally, we write X_Q as a triple (X_A, X_B, X_C) of random variables describing the first, second, and third component of the tuple. As indicated above, the random variables X_A, X_B, X_C are not uniformly distributed. And of course they are not independent. The protocol is based on the fact that

$$H(X_Q) = H(X_A) + H(X_B \mid X_A) + H(X_C \mid X_A, X_B).$$

Here the *conditional entropy* $H(X_B \mid X_A)$ of "X_B given X_A" is essentially the average, taken over all a, of the average number of bits transmitted with an optimal coding system for b given a. The conditional entropy $H(X_C \mid X_A, X_B)$ of "X_C given X_A and X_B" has a similar meaning.

Based on the fact that the uniform distribution on a domain always has the highest entropy (because there are no clever coding systems that exploit imbalances in the distribution), we make a few crucial observations:

(i) $H(X_A) + H(X_A \mid X_B) = H(X_A, X_B) \leq H(X_R)$,
   because transmitting (a, b) such that there is a c with $(a, b, c) \in Q(D)$ requires fewer bits than transmitting an arbitrary $(a, b) \in R(D)$ chosen uniformly at random;

(ii) $H(X_B \mid X_A) + H(X_C \mid X_A, X_B) \leq H(X_B) + H(X_C \mid X_B) = H(X_B, X_C) \leq H(X_S)$,
   where for the first inequality we note that dropping information can only increase the entropy and for the second inequality we argue as in (i).

(iii) $H(X_A) + H(X_C \mid X_A, X_B) \leq H(X_A) + H(X_C \mid X_A) = H(X_A, X_C) \leq H(X_T)$.

Putting things together, we see that

$$\begin{aligned}
2 \log N_Q &= 2H(X_Q) \\
&= 2\big(H(X_A) + H(X_B \mid X_A) + H(X_C \mid X_A, X_B)\big) \\
&= \big(H(X_A) + H(X_B \mid X_A)\big) + \big(H(X_B \mid X_A) + H(X_C \mid X_A, X_B)\big) \\
&\quad + \big(H(X_A) + H(X_C \mid X_A, X_B)\big) \\
&\leq H(X_R) + H(X_S) + H(X_T) \\
&= \log N_R + \log N_S + \log N_T.
\end{aligned}$$

This implies (6).

A formal treatment of the arguments given in Example 1, including definitions of entropy and conditional entropy, can be found in Section 2.

Example 2 ([6]). Let $m \in \mathbb{N}^+$ be even, and let $n := \binom{m}{m/2}$. For every $m/2$-element subset $s \subseteq [m] := \{1, \ldots, m\}$, let $A(s)$ be an attribute, and for every $i \in [m]$, let R_i be a relation schema with attributes $A(s)$ for all s that contain i. Let $Q := R_1 \bowtie \ldots \bowtie R_m$, and let D be a database instance with $|R_i(D)| = N$ for all $i \in [m]$. Then

$$\rho^*(Q, D) \leq 2 \log N,$$

because $\boldsymbol{x} = (x_1, \ldots, x_m)$ with $x_i := 2/m$ is a solution for the linear program (1), (2), and (5).

On the other hand,

$$\rho(Q, D) \geq (m/2 + 1) \log N.$$

To see this, let $\boldsymbol{x} = (x_1, \ldots, x_m) \in \{0, 1\}^m$ be a solution to the integer linear program (1)–(3). Then at most $m/2 - 1$ of the x_is are 0, because otherwise there is a set $s \subseteq [m]$ such that $|s| = m/2$ and $x_i = 0$ for all $i \in s$, and then equation (2) is violated for the index j of the attribute $A(s)$. Thus at least $(m/2 + 1)$ of the x_is are 1, and we have $\sum_i x_i \log N \geq (m/2 + 1) \log N$.

1.2   Algorithms

It was shown in [6] that there is an algorithm computing the result of a join query Q in a database D of size N in time

$$O\bigl(N + M \cdot 2^{\rho^*(Q,D)}\bigr), \tag{7}$$

where $M := \max_R |R(D)|$ is the maximum size of a relation of D. Here we are mainly concerned with data complexity and ignore a small polynomial factor in terms of the query size. It was observed in [1] that for every join query Q there is a *join-project plan* (i.e., a relational-algebra expression equivalent to the query that uses only joins and projections) that can be executed in time (7). Furthermore, it was shown that there are queries Q such that every *join plan* for Q has an execution time that is worse by a factor $O(N^{\log |Q|})$.

Ngo et al. [7] found an algorithm for answering join queries that avoids the factor M in the running time (7) and is thus worst-case optimal.

Theorem 2 (Ngo, Porat, Ré, and Rudra [7]). *There is an algorithm for answering a join query Q in a database D of size N in time*

$$O\bigl(N + 2^{\rho^*(Q,D)}\bigr). \tag{8}$$

Recently, Veldhuizen [11] gave a simpler algorithm for answering join queries that achieves essentially the same running time

Interestingly, Ngo et al. [7] also showed that the running time (8) cannot be achieved by executing a join-project plan for the query.

1.3   Further Results

Gottlob, Lee, and Valiant [5,4] extended Theorem 1 from join queries to conjunctive queries. They obtained similar bounds in a setting that involves key dependencies. These were extended by Valiant and Valiant [10,4] to a a setting with arbitrary functional dependencies.

In a completely different direction, Atserias et al. [1] also considered an average case scenario (all results described so far were worst-case results). In the average case model, the size of the query answer is governed by a different combinatorial parameter of the query, the *maximum density*. Contrasting the worst-case results, it was shown that for every query there is a join plan whose execution is almost always optimal (in a precise probabilistic sense).

1.4   The Rest of This Paper

In Section 2, we give a proof of Theorem 1. In Section 3 we discuss extensions to conjunctive queries. Finally, in Section 4, we sketch the simple algorithm for answering join queries with running time (7) and discuss query plans.

1.5   Notation

We denote by $\mathbb{R}$, $\mathbb{Q}$, $\mathbb{Z}$, $\mathbb{N}$, $\mathbb{N}^+$ the reals, rationals, integers, nonnegative integers, and positive integers, respectively. For every $n \in \mathbb{N}$ we let $[n] := \{1, \ldots, n\}$.

2   Bounds for Join Queries

2.1   Entropy and Shearer's Lemma

Random variables are mappings defined on some probability space. We only consider finite probability spaces. For each element $a \in \mathrm{rg}(X)$ of the range of a random variable X we have a probability $\Pr(X = a)$; this defines a probability distribution on the range. We allow arbitrary ranges for random variables (and not just real numbers). In our applications, the ranges will be sets of tuples of a database instance. If we have random variables X, Y with ranges A, B, respectively, then we may form a new random variable (X, Y) with range $A \times B$ by letting $\Pr((X, Y) = (a, b)) := \Pr(X = a, Y = b)$ (the comma in probabilities means conjunction). Conversely, if we have a random variable Z with range $A \times B$, then we may decompose it into two random variables X, Y with ranges A, B, respectively, such that $Z = (X, Y)$. We have $\Pr(X = a) = \sum_{b \in B} \Pr(Z = (a, b))$ and $\Pr(Y = b) = \sum_{a \in A} \Pr(Z = (a, b))$.

In the following, let X, Y be random variables with ranges A, B, respectively. The *entropy* of X is

$$H(X) := \sum_{a \in A} \Pr(X = a) \log \frac{1}{\Pr(X = a)}.$$

In Section 1.1, we interpreted $H(X)$ as the expected number of bits needed to encode a randomly chosen value of X with an optimal coding system. A more immediate interpretation that also gives a good intuition (at least qualitatively) is to think of $H(X)$ as a measure for the *uncertainty* of X. If there is an $a \in A$ such that $\Pr(X = a) = 1$ then there is no uncertainty, and we have $H(X) = 0$. On the other hand, if X is uniformly distributed, i.e., $\Pr(X = a) = 1/|A|$ for all $a \in A$, then we have $H(X) = \log |A|$. It is easy to see that this is the maximum entropy that a random variable X with range A may have, that is,

$$H(X) \leq \log |A| \tag{9}$$

for all X with $\mathrm{rg}(X) = A$.

The *joint entropy* $H(X, Y)$ of X and Y is the entropy of (X, Y), i.e.,

$$H(X, Y) = \sum_{a \in A, b \in B} \Pr(X = a, Y = b) \log \frac{1}{\Pr(X = a, Y = b)}.$$

For $b \in B$ with $\Pr(Y = b) \neq 0$, the *conditional probability* of $X = a$ given $Y = b$ is defined as $\Pr(X = a \mid Y = b) := \frac{Pr(X=a, Y=b)}{Pr(Y=b)}$, and the *conditional entropy* of X given $Y = b$ is

$$H(X \mid Y = b) := \sum_{a \in A} \Pr(X = a \mid Y = b) \log \frac{1}{\Pr(X = a \mid Y = b)}.$$

Finally, the *conditional entropy* of X given Y is

$$H(X \mid Y) := \sum_{b \in B} \Pr(Y = b) \cdot H(X \mid Y = b)$$

$$= \sum_{b \in B} \Pr(Y = b) \cdot \sum_{a \in A} \Pr(X = a \mid Y = b) \log \frac{1}{\Pr(X = a \mid Y = b)}.$$

A straightforward calculation shows that

$$H(X, Y) = H(X) + H(Y|X). \tag{10}$$

Indeed,

$$H(X, Y) = \sum_{a \in A, b \in B} \Pr(X = a, Y = b) \log \frac{1}{\Pr(X = a, Y = b)}$$

$$= \sum_{a \in A} \Pr(X = a) \sum_{b \in B} \Pr(Y = b \mid X = a) \left(\log \frac{1}{\Pr(X = a)} + \log \frac{1}{\Pr(Y = b \mid X = a)} \right)$$

$$= \sum_{a \in A} \Pr(X = a) \log \frac{1}{\Pr(X = a)} \sum_{b \in B} \Pr(Y = b \mid X = a)$$

$$+ \sum_{a \in A} \Pr(X = a) \sum_{b \in B} \Pr(Y = b \mid X = a) \log \frac{1}{\Pr(Y = b \mid X = a)}$$

$$= H(X) + H(Y \mid X),$$

where the last equality holds because $\sum_{b \in B} \Pr(Y = b \mid X = a) = 1$.

It is slightly more difficult to prove that

$$H(X \mid Y) \le H(X). \tag{11}$$

Intuitively, this is clear because the uncertainty about X can only decrease with the additional information $Y = b$. A formal proof uses Jensen's inequality.

The definitions and equations (10) and (11) can easily be generalised to more than two random variables. In particular, for random variables $X_1, \ldots, X_n$,

$$H(X_1, \ldots, X_n) = H(X_1) + H(X_2 \mid X_1) + H(X_3 \mid X_1, X_2) \tag{12}$$
$$+ \ldots + H(X_n \mid X_1, \ldots, X_{n-1}),$$

and for all $J \subseteq [n]$

$$H(X \mid X_1, \ldots, X_n) \le H(X \mid (X_j : j \in J)). \tag{13}$$

The following lemma first appeared in [3]. Our formulation and proof of the lemma are from [8].

Lemma 1 (Shearer's Lemma). *Let I be a finite set, and for each $i \in I$, let X_i be a random variable. For each $J \subseteq I$, let $X_J := (X_j : j \in J)$. Let $\mathcal{J} \subseteq 2^I$ be a multiset of subsets of I such that each $i \in I$ appears in at least q members of $\mathcal{J}$. Then*

$$H(X_I) \le \frac{1}{q} \sum_{J \in \mathcal{J}} H(X_J).$$

Proof. Let $<$ be an arbitrary linear order on I. By (12), for every $J \subseteq I$ we have

$$H(X_J) = \sum_{j \in J} H(X_j \mid (X_i : i \in J \text{ with } i < j)).$$

Thus

$$\sum_{J \in \mathcal{J}} H(X_J) = \sum_{J \in \mathcal{J}} \sum_{j \in J} H(X_j \mid (X_i : i \in J \text{ with } i < j))$$

$$\ge \sum_{J \in \mathcal{J}} \sum_{j \in J} H(X_j \mid (X_i : i \in I \text{ with } i < j)) \qquad \text{by (13)}$$

$$\ge q \cdot \sum_{j \in I} H(X_j \mid (X_i : i \in I \text{ with } i < j)) \qquad \begin{array}{l}\text{because every } j \text{ ap-}\\ \text{pears in at least } q \text{ sets}\\ J \in \mathcal{J}\end{array}$$

$$= q \cdot H(X_I).$$

□

2.2   Proof of the Upper Bound

Consider a join query

$$Q = R_1 \bowtie \ldots \bowtie R_m.$$

Suppose that the attributes of Q are $A_1, \ldots, A_n$. For each $i \in [m]$, let J_i be the set of all $j \in [n]$ such that A_j is an attribute of R_i. Let D be a database instance of schema $\{R_1, \ldots, R_m\}$. For all $i \in [m]$, let $N_i := |R_i(D)|$. Let $L(Q, N_1, \ldots, N_m)$ be the linear program

$$\text{minimise} \quad \sum_{i \in [m]} x_i \log N_i, \tag{14}$$

$$\text{where} \quad \sum_{\substack{i \in [m] \text{ with } j \in J_i}} x_i \geq 1 \qquad \text{for all } j \in [n] \tag{15}$$

$$x_i \geq 0 \qquad \text{for all } i \in [m]. \tag{16}$$

(This is precisely the linear program from the introduction, which we repeat for the reader's convenience.) Let $\boldsymbol{x} = (x_1, \ldots, x_m) \in \mathbb{Q}^m$ be a rational solution to $L(Q, N_1, \ldots, N_m)$. We shall prove that

$$|Q(D)| \leq 2^{\sum_{i \in [m]} x_i \log N_i}. \tag{17}$$

This will imply the upper bound of Theorem 1.

Let $p_1, \ldots, p_m \in \mathbb{N}$ such that $x_i = p_i/q$ for all i. Let $\mathcal{J}$ be a collection of subsets of $[n]$ that contains p_i copies of J_i, for each $i \in [m]$. Then every $j \in [n]$ occurs in at least q sets in $\mathcal{J}$, because

$$\sum_{\substack{i \in [m] \text{ with } j \in J_i}} p_i = q \cdot \sum_{\substack{i \in [m] \text{ with } j \in J_i}} x_i \geq q$$

by (15).

Without loss of generality we assume that $Q(D) \neq \emptyset$; otherwise (17) is trivial. Let $X = (X_1, \ldots, X_n)$ be uniformly distributed over $Q(D)$. Then

$$\log |Q(D)| = H(X)$$

$$\leq \frac{1}{q} \cdot \sum_{i=1}^{m} p_i \cdot H(X_j \mid j \in J_i) \qquad \text{by Shearer's Lemma}$$

$$\leq \sum_{i=1}^{m} x_i \log N_i.$$

This implies (17). $\qquad\qquad\square$

Remark 1. The proof of the upper bound of Theorem 1 through Shearer's Lemma is inherently nonconstructive. As a by-product of their algorithm for answering join queries (see Theorem 2), Ngo et al. [7] gave a constructive (but far more complicated) proof of the upper bound.

2.3   LP Duality and Proof of the Lower Bound

Let Q, $R_1, \ldots, R_m$, $A_1, \ldots, A_n$, and $J_1, \ldots, J_m$ be as in the previous subsection, and let $N_1, \ldots, N_m \in \mathbb{N}^+$ be arbitrary. The *dual* of the linear program

$L(Q, N_1, \ldots, N_m)$ is the following linear program $D(Q, N_1, \ldots, N_m)$ in the variables $y_1, \ldots, y_n$.

$$\text{maximise} \sum_{j=1}^{n} y_j, \tag{18}$$

$$\text{where} \sum_{j \in J_i} y_j \leq \log N_i \qquad \text{for all } i \in [m] \tag{19}$$

$$y_j \geq 0 \qquad \text{for all } j \in [n]. \tag{20}$$

By linear programming duality, for all solutions $(x_1, \ldots, x_m)$ to $L(Q, N_1, \ldots, N_m)$ and $(y_1, \ldots, y_n)$ to $D(Q, N_1, \ldots, N_m)$ we have

$$\sum_{i=1}^{m} x_i \log N_i \geq \sum_{j=1}^{n} y_j,$$

with equality if both solutions are optimal.

Now suppose that all the N_i are powers of 2, say, $N_i = 2^{L_i}$ for some $L_i \in \mathbb{N}$. Then all coefficients of $D(Q, N_1, \ldots, N_m)$ are integers, and hence there exists an optimal rational solution. Let $(y_1, \ldots, y_n) \in \mathbb{Q}^n$ be such an optimal solution. Let $p_1, \ldots, p_n, q \in \mathbb{N}$ such that $y_j = p_j/q$. Observe that $(p_1, \ldots, p_n)$ is an optimal solution to the linear program $D(Q, N_1^q, \ldots, N_m^q)$. We shall construct a database instance D with $|R_i(D)| = N_i^q$ and

$$|Q(D)| = 2^{\sum_{j=1}^{n} p_j} = 2^{\rho^*(Q,D)}. \tag{21}$$

This will imply the lower bound of Theorem 1.

To define the instance D, for every $i \in [m]$, we first define a relation $R_i'(D)$ to be the set of all tuples t such that for all $j \in J_i$ the projection $\pi_{A_j}(t)$ is in $[2^{p_j}]$. (So $R_i'(D)$ is the cartesian product of the sets $[2^{p_j}]$, for $j \in J_i$, if we forget about the names of the attributes.) Then

$$|R_i'(D)| = \prod_{j \in J_i} 2^{p_j} = 2^{\sum_{j \in J_i} p_j} \leq 2^{q \log N_i} = N_i^q.$$

We choose $R_i(D) \supseteq R_i'(D)$ with $|R_i(D)| = N_i^q$ arbitrarily. Then $Q(D)$ contains all tuples t such that for all $j \in [n]$ the projection $\pi_{A_j}(t)$ is in $[2^{p_j}]$. Hence

$$|Q(D)| \geq \prod_{j=1}^{n} 2^{p_j} = 2^{\sum_{j=1}^{n} p_j} = 2^{\rho^*(Q,D)}.$$

Actually, we must have equality here because we already know that $|Q(D)| \leq 2^{\rho^*(Q,D)}$. $\qquad \square$

Remark 2. It would be nicer if for all $N_1, \ldots, N_q \in \mathbb{N}^+$ we could construct a database instance D with $R_i(D) = N_i$ and $|Q(D)| = 2^{\rho^*(Q,D)}$. We cannot always do that. However, it was proved in [1] that we can always construct an instance D with $R_i(D) = N_i$ and $|Q(D)| \geq 2^{\rho^*(Q,D)-n}$. In general, this is best possible.

2.4   Bounds Depending on the Query Only

The bounds of Theorem 1 depend on the sizes of the individual relations in the database. Obviously, any reasonable estimate on the size of the query answer should depend on the size of the database, but maybe we only have an estimate of the size of the whole database instead of the sizes of the individual relations. In this situation, we can use the database size as an upper bound on the size of all relations.

Observe that if $N_i = N$ for all $i \in [m]$, then an optimal solution $\boldsymbol{x}$ to the linear program $L(Q, N, \ldots, N)$ no longer depends on N (only its value does). We let $L(Q)$ be the linear program obtained from $L(Q, N, \ldots, N)$ by replacing the cost function (14) by $\sum_{i \in [m]} x_i$ and let $\rho^*(Q)$ be the optimal value of this linear program. Then $\rho^*(Q) = \rho^*(Q, D) / \log N$ for all database instances D with $|R_i(D)| = N$ for all $i \in [m]$. Observe that in the dual $D(Q)$ of $L(Q)$ we replace inequalities (19) by $\sum_{j \in J_i} y_j \leq 1$.

Defining the size $||D||$ of a database instance D as the sum $\sum_{i \in [m]} |R_i(D)|$ of the sizes of all relations, we obtain the following corollary to Theorem 1.

Corollary 1. *Let Q be a join query. Then for every database instance D*

$$|Q(D)| \leq ||D||^{\rho^*(Q)}.$$

Furthermore, for every $N \in \mathbb{N}$ there is a database instance D of size $||D|| \geq N$ such that $|Q(D)| \geq (||D||/m)^{\rho^*(Q)}$.

3   Conjunctive Queries

In this section, we extend the bounds of Theorem 1 to conjunctive queries.

3.1   Projections of Join Queries

We start by considering conjunctive queries of the following special form:

$$P(B_1, \ldots, B_k) = \pi_{B_1, \ldots, B_k} Q(A_1, \ldots, A_n), \tag{22}$$

where $Q(A_1, \ldots, A_n)$ is a join query and $B_1, \ldots, B_k \in \{A_1, \ldots, A_n\}$. Here $\pi_{B_1, \ldots, B_k}$ is a projection operator. We allow k to be 0, in which case the query is Boolean.

Consider a conjunctive query P of the form (22). Without loss of generality we assume that $B_j = A_j$ for all $j \in [k]$. Suppose that $Q = R_1 \bowtie \ldots \bowtie R_m$ as before, and let J_i be the set of indices of the attributes of R_i. Let $N_1, \ldots, N_m \in \mathbb{N}^+$. We try to bound the size $P(D)$ of the query answer in a database instance D with $|R_i(D)| = N_i$. We modify our linear programs $L(Q, N_1, \ldots, N_m)$ and $D(Q, N_1, \ldots, N_m)$, essentially ignoring the attributes that are "projected out".

The primal linear program $L(P, N_1, \ldots, N_m)$ is defined as follows.

$$\text{minimise} \quad \sum_{i \in [m]} x_i \log N_i, \tag{23}$$

$$\text{where} \quad \sum_{\substack{i \in [m] \text{ with } j \in J_i}} x_i \geq 1 \qquad \text{for all } j \in [k] \tag{24}$$

$$x_i \geq 0 \qquad \text{for all } i \in [m]. \tag{25}$$

This linear program has the following dual $D(P, N_1, \ldots, N_m)$.

$$\text{maximise} \quad \sum_{j=1}^{k} y_j, \tag{26}$$

$$\text{where} \quad \sum_{j \in J_i \cap [k]} y_j \leq \log N_i \qquad \text{for all } i \in [m] \tag{27}$$

$$y_j \geq 0 \qquad \text{for all } j \in [k]. \tag{28}$$

For a database instance D with $|R_i(D)| = N_i$, let $\rho^*(P, D)$ be the value of the optimal solution to the linear programs. As an easy consequence of Theorem 1, we obtain the following bounds for projections of join queries.

Corollary 2. *Let P be a conjunctive query of the form* (22)*. Then for every database instance D,*

$$|P(D)| \leq 2^{\rho^*(P,D)}.$$

Furthermore, there are arbitrarily large database instances D such that $|P(D)| = 2^{\rho^*(P,D)}$.

Proof. Let P, Q, $R_1, \ldots, R_m$, $A_1, \ldots, A_n$, $B_j = A_j$ for $j \in [k]$, and $J_1, \ldots, J_m$ be as above.

For every $i \in [m]$, let R_i' be a relation schema with attributes A_j for $j \in J_i \cap [k]$, and let $Q' := R_1' \bowtie \ldots \bowtie R_m'$. For every database instance D of schema $\{R_1, \ldots, R_m\}$, let D' be the instance of schema $\{R_1', \ldots, R_m'\}$ with $R_i'(D') := \pi_{A_1, \ldots, A_k} R_i(D)$. Then $P(D) \subseteq Q'(D')$. Observe that for all $N_1, \ldots, N_m \in \mathbb{N}^+$ we have $L(Q', N_1, \ldots, N_m) = L(P, N_1, \ldots, N_m)$.

For the upper bound, let D be a database instance with $|R_i(D)| =: N_i$. Then by Theorem 1, we have

$$|P(D)| \leq |Q'(D')| \leq 2^{\rho^*(Q', D')}.$$

Here $\rho^*(Q', D')$ is the optimal value of the linear program $L(Q', N_1', \ldots, N_m')$, where $N_i' := |R_i'(D')| \leq N_i$. As the linear programs $L(Q', N_1', \ldots, N_m')$ and $L(Q', N_1, \ldots, N_m) = L(P, N_1, \ldots, N_m)$ only differ in their cost functions (23), we have $\rho^*(Q', D') \leq \rho^*(P, D)$.

For the lower bound, we observe that for every database instance D' of schema $\{R_1', \ldots, R_m'\}$ we can construct an instance D of schema $\{R_1, \ldots, R_m\}$ such that $|P(D)| = |Q'(D')|$ and $|R_i(D)| = |R_i'(D')|$ for all $i \in [m]$. We simply choose a default value, say 1, and extend all tuples $t \in R_i'(D')$ by letting $t(A) := 1$ for all attributes of R_i not in $\{A_1, \dots, A_k\}$. Then the lower bound follows from the lower bound of Theorem 1. □

Remark 3. As we did in Section 2.4, Gottlob, Lee, and Valiant [5,4] state their bounds in terms of the query only. For a conjunctive query P as above, they look at the dual linear program $D(P)$:

$$\text{maximise} \quad \sum_{j=1}^{k} y_j,$$

$$\text{where} \quad \sum_{j \in J_i \cap [k]} y_j \leq 1 \qquad \text{for all } i \in [m]$$

$$y_j \geq 0 \qquad \text{for all } j \in [k].$$

They interpret rational solutions $\boldsymbol{y} = (y_1, \dots, y_k)$ of $D(P)$ as colourings of the query in the following sense.

A *valid colouring* C of P assigns to each $j \in [k]$ (or to the attribute A_j) a finite set $C(j)$ of colours in such a way that $C(j) \neq \emptyset$ for at least one $j \in [k]$. The *value* of a colouring C is

$$v(C) := \frac{\left| \bigcup_{j \in [k]} C(j) \right|}{\max_{i \in [m]} \left| \bigcup_{j \in J_i \cap [k]} C(j) \right|}.$$

The *colouring number* of P is defined to be the maximum of the values of all its valid colourings. We will see that this maximum always exists and is equal to the value of the linear program $D(P)$.

Let C be a valid colouring of P. Without loss of generality, we may assume that $C(j) \cap C(j') = \emptyset$ for all $j \neq j' \in [k]$, because if a colour appears in $C(j) \cap C(j')$ then dropping this colour from one of the sets gives a colouring with the same or a better value. Let $q := \max_{i \in [m]} \left| \bigcup_{j \in J_i \cap [k]} C(j) \right|$. For $j \in [k]$, let $p_j := |C(j)|$ and $y_j := p_j / q$. Then $(y_1, \dots, y_k)$ is a solution of $D(Q)$ of value $\sum_{j=1}^{k} y_j = v(C)$.

Conversely, let $(y_1, \dots, y_k) \in \mathbb{Q}^k$ be a rational solution of $D(Q)$ such that $\sum_{j \in J_i \cap [k]} = 1$ for some $i \in [m]$. Clearly, an optimal solution has this property. Suppose that $y_j = p_j / q$ for all $j \in [k]$. We define a valid colouring by letting $C(j)$ be a set of p_j fresh colours (so that $C(1), \dots, C(k)$ are mutually disjoint). Then $v(C) = \sum_{j=1}^{k} y_j$.

As $D(Q)$ has integer coefficients, there is an optimal rational solution, and it yields a colouring of optimal value.

Th purpose of viewing solutions of the dual linear program as colourings in this way is that it yields a natural extension to the setting with functional dependencies.

3.2   Arbitrary Conjunctive Queries

We view a general conjunctive query as an expression

$$C(\bar{X}) \leftarrow R_1(\bar{X}_1), \ldots, R_m(\bar{X}_m), \tag{29}$$

where $R_1, \ldots, R_m$ are (not necessarily distinct) relation names of arities $k_1, \ldots, k_m$, respectively, and $\bar{X}, \bar{X}_i$ are tuples of not necessarily distinct variables of lengths $k, k_1, \ldots, k_m$, respectively, such that all variables appearing in $\bar{X}$ also appear in some $\bar{X}_i$. Without loss of generality we assume that the set of all variables appearing in the query C is $\{X_1, \ldots, X_n\}$, where $X_1, \ldots, X_n$ are pairwise distinct, and that $\bar{X} = (X_1, \ldots, X_k)$. (We can do this because it does not affect the size of the query answer if we repeat variables in the head $C(\bar{X})$.) For each $i \in [m]$, let $J_i \subseteq [n]$ be the set of indices of the variables appearing in $\bar{X}_i$.

For a database instance D of schema $\{R_1, \ldots, R_m\}$, the query answer $C(D)$ is the set of all k-tuples $(a_1, \ldots, a_k)$ that can be extended to an n-tuple $\bar{a} = (a_1, \ldots, a_n)$ such that for each $i \in [m]$ the projection of $\bar{a}$ to the indices of the variables in $\bar{X}_i$ (in the right order) is in $R_i(D)$.

Note that the variables play the role the attributes played so far. Projections of join queries, as considered in the previous subsection, correspond to the case that the relations $R_1, \ldots, R_m$ are pairwise distinct and that for each $i \in [m]$ the variables appearing in $\bar{X}_i$ are pairwise distinct.

For all $N_1, \ldots, N_m \in \mathbb{N}^+$, we define the following linear program $L(C, N_1, \ldots, N_m)$.

$$\text{minimise} \quad \sum_{i \in [m]} x_i \log N_i, \tag{30}$$

$$\text{where} \quad \sum_{i \in [m] \text{ with } j \in J_i} x_i \geq 1 \qquad \text{for all } j \in [k] \tag{31}$$

$$x_i \geq 0 \qquad \text{for all } i \in [m]. \tag{32}$$

Note that if the relations $R_1, \ldots, R_m$ are pairwise distinct and for each $i \in [m]$ the variables appearing in $\bar{X}_i$ are pairwise distinct, then this is precisely the linear program (23)–(25) defined in the previous subsection.

We let $\rho^*(C, N_1, \ldots, N_m)$ be the value of an optimal solution of $L(C, N_1, \ldots, N_m)$. The following lemma is an easy consequence of Corollary 2.

Lemma 2. *Let C be a conjunctive query of the form (29) such that $R_1, \ldots, R_m$ are pairwise distinct. Then for all $N_1, \ldots, N_m \in \mathbb{N}^+$ and all database instances D of schema $\{R_1, \ldots, R_m\}$ with $|R_i(D)| \leq N_i$,*

$$|C(D)| \leq 2^{\rho^*(C, N_1, \ldots, N_m)}.$$

Furthermore, there are arbitrarily large $N_1, \ldots, N_m \in \mathbb{N}^+$ and databases instances D with $|R_i(D)| = N_i$ such that $|C(D)| = 2^{\rho^*(C, N_1, \ldots, N_m)}$.

Proof. For every $i \in [m]$, let $\ell_i := |J_i|$. Then obviously we have $\ell_i \leq k_i$, where equality holds if the variables in $\bar{X}_i$ are distinct. For each $i \in [m]$, we let $R_i^{\neq}$

be a fresh ℓ_i-ary relation symbol. We let $\bar{X}_i^{\neq}$ be the ℓ_i-tuple of variables that contains the same variables as $\bar{X}_i$, but without repetitions, in the order of their first appearance in $\bar{X}_i$. We let

$$C^{\neq}(\bar{X}) \leftarrow R_1^{\neq}(\bar{X}_1^{\neq}), \ldots, R_m^{\neq}(\bar{X}_m^{\neq}),$$

Then $C^{\neq}(\bar{X})$ is a projection of a join query of the type considered in the previous subsection.

For every database instance D of schema $\{R_1, \ldots, R_m\}$ we define an instance $D^{\neq}$ of schema $\{R_1^{\neq}, \ldots, R_m^{\neq}\}$ by letting $R_i^{\neq}(D)$ be the set of all $\bar{X}_i^{\neq}$-tuples obtained from $\bar{X}_i$-tuples in $R_i(D)$. To make this precise, suppose that $\bar{X}_i = (X(i,1), \ldots, X(i,k_i))$, where of course each $X(i,j)$ is an element of $\{X_1, \ldots, X_n\}$. Let $J(1), \ldots, J(\ell_i)$ be the partition of $[k_i]$ such that $X(i,j) = X(i,j')$ for all $p \in [\ell_i]$ and $j, j' \in J(p)$, and $X(i,j) \neq X(i,j')$ for all $p \neq p' \in [\ell_i]$ and $j \in J(p), j' \in J(p')$. For each $p \in [\ell_i]$, let $j(p)$ be the minimum of $J(p)$. Without loss of generality we assume that $j(1) < j(2) < \ldots < j(\ell_i)$. Then $\bar{X}_i^{\neq} = (X(i,j(1)), \ldots, X(i,j(\ell_i)))$. Now we let $R_i^{\neq}(D)$ be the set of all ℓ_i-tuples $(a^{\neq}(1), \ldots, a^{\neq}(\ell_i))$ such that there is a k_i-tuple $(a(1), \ldots, a(k_i)) \in R_i(D)$ with $a(j) = a^{\neq}(p)$ for all $p \in [\ell_i], j \in J(p)$. It is immediate from the definitions that $C(D) = C^{\neq}(D^{\neq})$ and $|R_i(D)| \geq |R_i^{\neq}(D)|$.

Now the upper bound follows from Corollary 2 and the observation that

$$L(C, N_1, \ldots, N_m) = L(C^{\neq}, N_1, \ldots, N_m).$$

To prove the lower bound, we start with an instance D' of schema $\{R_1^{\neq}, \ldots, R_m^{\neq}\}$ with sufficiently large $N_i := |R_i^{\neq}(D')|$ such that

$$|C^{\neq}(D')| = 2^{\rho^*(C^{\neq},D')} = 2^{\rho^*(C^{\neq},N_1,\ldots,N_m)} = 2^{\rho^*(C,N_1,\ldots,N_m)}.$$

It is easy to construct an instance D of schema $\{R_1, \ldots, R_m\}$ such that $D' = D^{\neq}$ and $|R_i(D)| = |R_i^{\neq}(D')| = N_i$ for all $i \in [m]$. Then we have $|C(D)| = |C^{\neq}(D')| = 2^{\rho^*(C,N_1,\ldots,N_m)}$. $\qquad\qquad\square$

For general conjunctive queries, we obtain a slightly weaker lower bound that takes into account the multiplicities with which the relations appear in the query: the inequalities $|R_i(D)| \leq N_i$ are replaced by (33).

Theorem 3 (Gottlob, Lee, Valiant [5,4]). *Let C be a conjunctive query of the form (29). Then for all $N_1, \ldots, N_m \in \mathbb{N}^+$ and all database instances D of schema $\{R_1, \ldots, R_m\}$ with $|R_i(D)| \leq N_i$,*

$$|C(D)| \leq 2^{\rho^*(C,N_1,\ldots,N_m)}.$$

Furthermore, there are arbitrarily large $N_1, \ldots, N_m \in \mathbb{N}^+$ and databases instances D with

$$|R_i(D)| \leq \sum_{\substack{j \in [m] \\ \text{with } R_j = R_i}} N_j \qquad (33)$$

for all $i \in [m]$ such that $|C(D)| \geq 2^{\rho^*(C,N_1,\ldots,N_m)}$.

Proof. For every $i \in [m]$, let R'_i be a fresh k_i-ary relation name, and let

$$C'(\bar{X}) \leftarrow R'_1(\bar{X}_i), \ldots, R'_m(\bar{X}_m).$$

Observe that for all $N_1, \ldots, N_m \in \mathbb{N}^+$ we have $L(C, N_1, \ldots, N_m) = L(C', N_1, \ldots, N_m)$.

For every database instance D of schema $\{R_1, \ldots, R_m\}$, let D' be the instance of schema $\{R'_1, \ldots, R'_m\}$ with $R'_i(D') := R_i(D)$. Then $C(D) = C'(D')$. As all relations appearing in C' are distinct, the upper bound follows directly from Lemma 2.

To prove the lower bound, we choose a database instance D' of schema $\{R'_1, \ldots, R'_m\}$ for sufficiently large $N_i := |R'_i(D')|$ such that

$$|C'(D')| = 2^{\rho^*(C', N_1, \ldots, N_m)} = 2^{\rho^*(C, N_1, \ldots, N_m)}.$$

Such a D' exists by Lemma 2. We define an instance $D_\cup$ of schema $\{R_1, \ldots, R_m\}$ by letting

$$R_i(D_\cup) := \bigcup_{\substack{j \in [m] \\ \text{with } R_j = R_i}} R'_j(D').$$

Obviously, $D_\cup$ satisfies (33), and we have $C(D_\cup) \supseteq C'(D')$ and hence $|C(D_\cup)| \geq |C'(D')| \geq 2^{\rho^*(C, N_1, \ldots, N_m)}$. □

As for join queries (see Corollary 1), it is easy to formulate a version of the theorem where the bounds only depend on the size of the database instance and the query and not on the sizes of the individual relations. This is how Gottlob et al. [5] originally phrased their theorem.

4 Query Plans

A *query plan* for a query Q is an expression φ in the relational algebra, using (binary) join operators, projection operators, and possibly other relational algebra operators, such that $Q(D) = \varphi(D)$ for every database instance D. A query plan is a *join plan* if the only operator it uses is the join operator, and it is a *join-project plan* if it only uses joins and projections. A *subplan* of a query plan is defined in the natural way; all nodes of the parse tree of the plan correspond to subplans. *Executing* a query plan φ in a database instance means computing $\psi(D)$ for all subplans ψ, until finally $\varphi(D)$ is computed. As all relational algebra operations can be implemented with a running time linear in the size of the input(s) plus the output, the time it takes to execute a query plan is linear in the size of the maximal intermediate result.

Obviously, for every join query there is a join plan. However, it may happen that the intermediate results of the executions of all possible join plans for a query are substantially larger than the final result.

Example 3. Recall the query $Q := R \bowtie S \bowtie T$ of Example 1. Every join plan for Q contains either $R \bowtie S$ or $R \bowtie T$ or $S \bowtie T$ as a subplan, and in a database instance D with $R(D) = S(D) = T(D) = N$ it may happen that $|(R \bowtie S)(D)|, |(R \bowtie T)(D)|, |(S \bowtie T)(D)| = \Theta(N^2)$, whereas we have seen in Example 1 that $|Q(D)| \leq N^{3/2}$.

The query of Example 2 is underlying the following theorem.

Theorem 4 ([1]). *There are arbitrarily large join queries Q and databases D such that $\rho^*(Q) \leq 2$ and every join plan for Q has a subplan ψ with $|\psi(D)| \geq ||D||^{\Omega(\log |Q|)}$.*

Thus join plans may lead to relatively inefficient algorithms for answering join queries. Join-project plans, on the other hand, are almost optimal.

Theorem 5 ([1]). *For every join query Q there is a join-project plan φ such that for every subplan ψ of φ and a every database instance D,*

$$|\psi(D)| \leq 2^{\rho^*(Q,D)} \cdot M,$$

where M is the maximum size of the projection of a relation in D to a single attribute.

Proof. Let $Q = R_1 \bowtie \ldots \bowtie R_m$. As always, suppose that the attributes of Q are $A_1, \ldots, A_n$, and let J_i be the set of indices of the attributes of R_i. The idea is to evaluate Q by iteratively computing the projections $\pi_{A_1,\ldots,A_j} Q(D)$, for $j = 1, \ldots, n$.
We let

$$\varphi_1 := \Big(\cdots \big((\pi_{A_1}(R_1) \bowtie \varphi_{A_1}(R_2)) \bowtie \pi_{A_1}(R_3) \big) \bowtie \ldots \bowtie \pi_{A_1}(R_m) \Big),$$

and for $j = 1, \ldots, n-1$,

$$\varphi_{j+1} := \Big(\cdots \big((\varphi_j \bowtie \pi_{A_1,\ldots,A_{j+1}}(R_1)) \bowtie \pi_{A_1,\ldots,A_{j+1}}(R_2) \big) \bowtie \ldots \bowtie \pi_{A_1,\ldots,A_{j+1}}(R_m) \Big).$$

Either by a direct argument or by an application of the upper bound of Corollary 2, it is easy to see that the plan $\varphi := \varphi_n$ has the desired properties. The crucial observation is that

$$\big| (\varphi_j \bowtie \pi_{A_1,\ldots,A_{j+1}}(R_1))(D) \big| \leq \big| \varphi_j(D) \times \pi_{A_{j+1}} R_1(D) \big| \leq 2^{\rho^*(Q,D)} \cdot M,$$

because $\pi_{A_{j+1}} R_1(D) \leq M$ and for the conjunctive query $P_j := \pi_{A_1,\ldots,A_j} R_1 \bowtie \ldots \bowtie R_m$, for which φ_j is a query plan, we have $\rho^*(P_j, D) \leq \rho^*(Q, D)$ and thus $|\varphi_j(D)| = |P_j(D)| \leq 2^{\rho^*(P_j,D)} \leq 2^{\rho^*(Q,D)}$ by Corollary 2. □

The execution of the join-project plan of Theorem 5 leads to an algorithm answering Q in time $O(2^{\rho^*(Q,D)} \cdot M)$ (ignoring a small polynomial factor depending on Q). We remind the reader of the algorithm of Theorem 2, which avoids the factor M in the running time. Ngo et al. [7] showed that a running time of $O(2^{\rho^*(Q,D)})$ cannot be achieved with the execution of a join-project plan.

References

1. Atserias, A., Grohe, M., Marx, D.: Size bounds and query plans for relational joins. In: Proceedings of the 49th Annual IEEE Symposium on Foundations of Computer Science, pp. 739–748 (2008)
2. Chiba, N., Nishizeki, T.: Arboricity and subgraph listing algorithms. SIAM Journal on Computing 14, 210–223 (1985)
3. Chung, F., Frank, P., Graham, R., Shearer, J.: Some intersection theorems for ordered sets and graphs. Journal of Combinatorial Theory, Series A 43, 23–37 (1986)
4. Gottlob, G., Lee, S.T., Valiant, G., Valiant, P.: Size and treewidth bounds for conjunctive queries. Journal of the ACM 59(3) (2012)
5. Gottlob, G., Lee, S.T., Valiant, G.J.: Size and treewidth bounds for conjunctive queries. In: Proceedings of the 28th ACM Symposium on Principles of Database Systems, pp. 45–54 (2009)
6. Grohe, M., Marx, D.: Constraint solving via fractional edge covers. In: Proceedings of the 17th Annual ACM-SIAM Symposium on Discrete Algorithms, pp. 289–298 (2006)
7. Ngo, H.Q., Porat, E., Ré, C., Rudra, A.: Worst-case optimal join algorithms. In: Proceedings of the 31st ACM Symposium on Principles of Database Systems (2012)
8. Radhakrishnan, J.: Entropy and counting. In: Misra, J.C. (ed.) Computational Mathematics, Modelling and Algorithms. Narosa Pub. House (2003)
9. Shannon, C.E.: A mathematical theory of communication. The Bell System Technical Journal 27, 379–423, 623–656 (1948)
10. Valiant, G., Valiant, P.: Size bounds for conjunctive queries with general functional dependencies. Arxiv preprint arXiv:0909.2030 (2009)
11. Veldhuizen, T.L.: Leapfrog triejoin: A worst-case optimal join algorithm. arXiv e-print archive arXiv:1210.0481 (2012), http://arxiv.org/abs/1210.0481

Incremental Data Fusion
Based on Provenance Information

Carmem Satie Hara[1], Cristina Dutra de Aguiar Ciferri[2],
and Ricardo Rodrigues Ciferri[3]

[1] Universidade Federal do Paraná – Curitiba, PR, Brazil
carmem@inf.ufpr.br
[2] Universidade de São Paulo – São Carlos, SP, Brazil
cdac@icmc.usp.br
[3] Universidade Federal de São Carlos – São Carlos, SP, Brazil
ricardo@dc.ufscar.br

Abstract. Data fusion is the process of combining multiple representations of the same object, extracted from several external sources, into a single and clean representation. It is usually the last step of an integration process, which is executed after the schema matching and the entity identification steps. More specifically, data fusion aims at solving attribute value conflicts based on user-defined rules. Although there exist several approaches in the literature for fusing data, few of them focus on optimizing the process when new versions of the sources become available. In this paper, we propose a model for incremental data fusion. Our approach is based on storing provenance information in the form of a sequence of operations. These operations reflect the last fusion rules applied on the imported data. By keeping both the original source value and the new fused data in the operations repository, we are able to reliably detect source value updates, and propagate them to the fusion process, which reapplies previously defined rules whenever it is possible. This approach reduces the number of data items affected by source updates and minimizes the amount of user manual intervention in future fusion processes.

1 Introduction

The huge amount of data available nowadays and the need to integrate data imported from several external sources continue to be a challenge to the database community. Although data integration has been investigated for several years, there is no single solution that suits all applications.

The integration process involves both schema and instance level integration. At the instance level, the integration process comprises two major problems [28]: entity identification ambiguity and attribute value conflict. Entity identification refers to the problem of identifying overlapping data in different sources. It has been the purpose of extensive research on the relational [24], entity-relationship [23], and XML [27] data models. Attribute value conflict refers to the problem of

V. Tannen et al. (Eds.): Buneman Festschrift, LNCS 8000, pp. 339–365, 2013.

two or more sources containing information on the same entity or attribute, but with conflicting values. The process of combining several representations of one real world object into a single, consistent and clean representation is the goal of *data fusion* [7], which is the focus of this paper.

Data fusion is based on a set of strategies that determine how value conflicts are solved. A survey of existing approaches for data fusion can be found in [7]. As an example, when integrating several external sources, one can define that a conflict on a given numerical attribute should be solved by computing the average from the values provided by the sources. The data resulting from the fusion process can be stored in a local database for answering queries based on clean, mediated data. However, if no additional information is kept in the local database other than the fused value, when one of the data sources updates its value, all the other sources will have to be accessed again in order to apply the same fusion strategy. One approach for avoiding this is to keep the data provenance [11,12]; that is, copies of the original values provided from the sources and the strategy applied to obtain the value stored in the database. Following this approach, the focus of this paper is on provenance-based data fusion.

In our system, provenance information is kept by mapping the application of fusion strategies to sequences of simple insert-remove-edit-copy operations. This resembles the works on manually curated data [8,9], in which the system keeps a *log* of operations that the user undertakes in order to clean imported data. Although we consider a similar set of operations, in our system operations do not keep track of the user's actions, but keep the original source values and coordinate them with the local database. By keeping the original values, we are able to reliably detect source updates and propagate them to the local database. The problem of updating a database based on changes to an independently maintained source has recently been referred to as data coordination [22].

In this paper we propose a fusion system for XML which supports incremental updates based on provenance information. We assume that external sources have been previously processed for identifying entities, producing fully keyed documents. Our fusion approach is based on user-defined rules, which are stored in a *rule base*. Moreover, provenance information is kept in an *operations repository* that consists of simple operations that coordinate external sources with the local database. The operations repository along with the rule base allows incremental updates on the local database and minimizes the amount of user intervention in future fusion processes.

1.1 A Motivating Example

Consider two sources, s_1 and s_2, containing data on the same paper, but that disagree on the values reported for its attributes as depicted in Figures 1(a) and 1(b). In this example, we identify that **paper** information provided by s_1 and s_2 refers to the same publication because they coincide on their values for **title** and **year**. That is, **title** and **year** are the keys for **paper**. In order to generate a database with fused data, the user provides high-level *fusion rules* for deciding how value conflicts should be solved. As an example, the user can define that conflicts on paper's author names should be solved as follows: first, choose the value reported by the majority of the sources; if the conflict cannot be solved then consider the one reported from the most trustful source. Since in our example we only have two sources, the first strategy cannot be applied. Then, considering that we rely more on source s_1 than on s_2, the value stored in the database for the paper's first author is John, and the second author Jack, based on the values reported by s_1. Similarly, we can define that the database should contain the average number reported for citationQty based on all the sources. In this case, the resulting value stored in the database is citationQty: 9. The conflict on city is solved by *manually* choosing the value Philadelphia, reported by s_2. These results are stored in the mediated database, as shown in Figure 1(d).

When a new version of source s_1 or s_2 is uploaded, or new sources are integrated to the database, these fusion rules can be automatically reapplied, and only *new* conflicts are presented to the user in the fusion process. As an example, consider that a new version for s_1 is uploaded with a value 12 for citationQty. Given that the average number of citations, considering s_1 and s_2 is now 10, the database is updated with this value. Now consider that values from a third source s_3 is integrated to the database. If s_3 also contains values for the same paper, and reports Jack as its first author and John as the second, then the first strategy defined on the previous fusion process can be applied for updating the database with the values reported by the majority of the sources. That is, the name of the first author is updated to Jack, and the second to John, based on the values reported by s_2 and s_3.

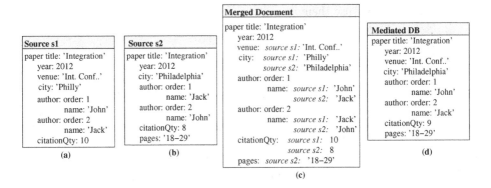

Fig. 1. Integration of two conflicting sources

Our fusion system offers all the aforementioned functionality, and also allows the mediated database to be used as an integrated repository of curated data according to the users' decisions.

This paper builds on three previous works from the authors. The first proposes a system for XML data fusion, which allows the definition of data cleaning rules for solving value conflicts detected during the integration process [14]. The second presents a model for reapplying user's decisions in subsequent integration processes when data is manually curated by insert-remove-edit-copy operations that are stored in an operations repository [33]. At last, the third work introduces a data model for XML instance level integration that helps the resolution of value attribute conflicts by explicitly representing them in a merged document [26]. Here, we consider our previous works in the same setting. However, we focus on *mapping* fusion strategies to sequences of simple operations, and *reapplying* previous rules for incrementally updating the mediated database when new sources are uploaded or when sources are updated. The purpose of the system is to minimize the amount of user input in future fusion processes.

1.2 Organization

The paper is organized as follows. Section 2 describes preliminary definitions. Section 3 introduces the architecture of our fusion system, followed by the definition of our data model in Section 4. Section 5 details the modules that compose the system. Related work are presented in Section 6, and Section 7 concludes the paper.

2 Preliminary Definitions

Before describing the components of our data fusion system, we present definitions for XML keys (Section 2.1), strategies for data fusion (Section 2.2), and basic operations (Section 2.3). These notions have been previously proposed in the literature and we use them as building blocks in our system.

2.1 XML Keys

An XML document is typically modeled as a node-labeled tree T, which can be depicted in a directory style representation as illustrated in Figures 1(a) and 1(b). We assume that each XML tree has a distinct identifier, such as s_1 and s_2, which denotes its source. We refer to attribute and element nodes as *objects* throughout the article. Moreover, we say that an object is *simple* if it corresponds to a text element or an attribute, and *complex* otherwise.

Following the syntax proposed in [10], we define an XML key as *(context-path, (target-path, {key-paths}))*, where the values of the *key-paths* uniquely identify nodes reached following a *target-path* in the context of each subtree defined by the *context-path*.

Example 1. Given the XML trees depicted in Figures 1(a) and 1(b), the following key definitions allow us to uniquely identify a single node in each of the trees.

- k_1 : $(\epsilon, (paper, \{title, year\}))$: in the context of the entire document (ϵ denotes the root), a **paper** is identified by its **title** and **year** of publication;

- k_2 : $(paper, (author, \{order\}))$: within the context of any subtree rooted at a paper node, an author is identified by its order;
- k_3 : $(paper, (citationQty, \{\}))$: within the context of any subtree rooted at a paper node, there exists at most one citationQty element; that is, it is identified by an empty set of values. Similarly, we can define uniqueness constraints for venue, city, pages and author name as follows: k_4 : $(paper, (venue, \{\}))$ and k_5 : $(paper, (city, \{\}))$ and k_6 : $(paper, (pages, \{\}))$ and k_7 : $(paper/author, (name, \{\}))$.

Observe that based on the key definitions, it is possible to generate a path expression for obtaining a node using key values as filters. As an example, based on k_1, we can obtain a (single) paper node from the trees in Figures 1(a) and 1(b) using the expression $/paper[title='Integration'$ and $year='2012']$ and the first author with the expression $/paper[title='Integration'$ and $year='2012']$ $/author[order='1']$. Thus, these path expressions can be considered as the nodes' *keys* or *object identifiers*. We refer to nodes reached by key paths, such as *title* and *year* as *key nodes*.

2.2   Strategies for Data Fusion

There are a number of strategies proposed in the literature for solving value conflicts [6,36,16,13,17]. Here, we consider a set of strategies based on those proposed in [6]. We describe the ones that are used in this article below. However, the set of strategies can be much larger, with little impact on our fusion approach, as discussed in Section 6.

Trust Your Friends (TYF). This strategy is based on a reliability criterion. The user assigns a confidence rate for each source, and a value conflict is solved by choosing the one provided by the source with the highest confidence rate.

Meet In The Middle (MIM). This is a strategy to mediate the conflict by generating a new value that is a compromise among all conflicting values, e.g., an average of all conflicting numeric values.

Cry With The Wolves (CWW). This strategy is defined for choosing the value reported by the majority of sources.

Choose a Value (CAV). In this strategy the user manually chooses one value among those reported from the sources.

Pass It On (PIO). This is a non-resolving strategy. Although in most cases the user wants a single value for each data item, for some items she may want to postpone the decision for a future fusion process.

Observe that there are high-level strategies such as TYF, MIM, and CWW, and also value-based strategies such as CAV. In our approach, we reapply only high-level strategies on subsequent fusion processes without any user intervention. As an example, the conflict on citationQty described in Section 1.1 has been solved by computing the average value from all the ones reported from the sources (MIM strategy). This strategy can continue to be applied in future fusion processes, by taking into consideration the value updates and values uploaded from new sources.

However, this is not the case for value-based strategies. As an example, consider the conflict on `city` between sources s_1 and s_2 depicted in Figure 1(a) and (b). If the user manually chooses the value 'Philadelphia' reported by s_2 using the CAV strategy, we can assume that she will continue to do so as long as the sources keep providing the same values. Once one of them, say s_1, modifies its value to 'Philadelphia, PA', it is not clear whether the decision of choosing the value reported from s_2 over s_1 is correct, and thus the strategy cannot be reapplied. Otherwise, inconsistencies would be introduced in the database without the user's consent.

2.3   Basic Operations

There are a number of definitions for basic operations on XML data, but here we adopt the ones proposed by [33]. Four operations are considered: *edit, copy, insert*, and *remove*. *Edit* is an unary operation that operates on simple objects and has the effect of modifying the object by assigning a value either provided by the user, or generated by the system as the result of an aggregate function. *Copy*, on the other hand, takes the value of a simple object provided from one source, for copying it to a second source. *Insert* and *remove* are operations on complex objects. *Insert* is a binary operation that creates a new object in one source, based on an object already stored in another source. In the newly created object, the identifiers are filled in with values obtained from the keys of the original object. Finally, *remove* is an unary operation that deletes an object from a source, based on its key.

Regarding the integration process, there are several methodologies for database integration. Here, we adopt a binary ladder strategy [2], in which we first analyze a first source, then analyze a second source by identifying its inconsistencies and managing them with regard to the first source, then analyze a third source by identifying its inconsistencies and managing them with regard to the first and second sources, and so on. Furthermore, as stated in Section 1, we assume that external sources have been previously processed for identifying entities, producing fully keyed documents. We adopt concepts that are similar to the notion of "insertion-friendly" set of keys defined in [10]. With insertion-friendly keys, one can unambiguously determine the position in the tree in which new elements should be inserted.

3   System Architecture

Our approach for tackling the problem of incrementally fusing XML data is based on keeping a repository of operations reflecting the user's decisions and data provenance, along with a rule base. That is, user-defined high-level fusion rules are stored in a *rule base*. The application of a strategy on a data item is mapped to a sequence of basic operations that are stored in the *operations repository*.

The architecture of the system is depicted in Figure 2. We consider the existence of several XML sources $s_1, \ldots s_n$, that have been previously transformed to documents that follow the database schema. That is, we assume that any structural discrepancies among sources have been solved by a schema integrator prior to the fusion process. Moreover, we use key values as a means for *entity identification*. More specifically, whenever two elements from distinct sources are used to populate the same database element, based on their key values, they are considered to refer to the same entity in the real world. Thus, whenever their attribute values differ, we conclude that there is an *attribute value conflict* that should be solved.

The system is based on three modules: *fusion, validation,* and *update.* Data from each source is uploaded to the database separately by the *update* module. This module is responsible for checking whether imported elements already exist in the database, and if there are attribute value conflicts among them. If so, these attribute values are combined into a single representation in a *merged document.* In a *merged document,* data imported from several sources are combined whenever they are mapped to an object that coincide on their key values. Moreover, it explicit represents value conflicts among sources, along with the provenance for each value.

As an example, consider the source documents depicted in Figures 1(a) and 1(b) and the key definitions in Example 1. In the merged document, `paper` elements imported from sources s_1 and s_2 are combined because their `title` and `year` key elements coincide, revealing value conflicts on their `citationQty` and `city` values. Similarly, they disagree on who are the first and second authors of the paper. The resulting merged document, in which values of non-key simple objects are associated with their provenance, is depicted in Figure 1(c).

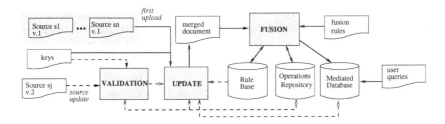

Fig. 2. Incremental fusion based on provenance

Value conflicts are solved by the *fusion* module based on user-defined *fusion rules.* Fusion rules are stored in a *rule base.* They may be defined in the context of a single element or on a larger context involving multiple elements. Thus, if a newly detected conflict is within the context of an existing rule then the conflict can be automatically solved without any manual user intervention. As the result of applying a rule to a conflict, a value is written in the *mediated database,* which consists of fused data. That is, there exists at most one value associated with any element in the database. Since it contains no value conflicts, user queries are processed based on data stored in the mediated database.

In order to be able to reapply the same decisions in future fusion processes, applications of the rules are mapped to sequences of basic operations that are kept in the *operations repository*. Similar to database log files, these operations contain not only the new value of the data item, but also the original source values. As an example, consider the conflict on `citationQty` depicted in Figure 1(c). As a result of the application of the *Meet in the Middle* strategy, value 9 for the paper's `citationQty` is written in the mediated database, and the following sequence of basic operations is stored in the operations repository: (i) edit the mediated database (`db`) to 9; (ii) copy from `db` to s_1, modifying its value from 10 to 9; and (iii) copy from `db` to s_2, updating it from 8 to 9.

We use the notion of *validation* for determining when the effects of the operations in the repository are identical to the ones already executed in previous fusion processes. Intuitively, we would like to ensure a strict reproduction of the user's decisions, guaranteeing that the same rules defined by the user to decide previous conflicts will be applied to solve conflicts on the same object in the future. In the example above, if in new versions of s_1 and s_2 their values for `citationQty` remain unchanged, the operations on both sources are considered *valid*, since they continue to update 10 to 9 in s_1 and 8 to 9 in s_2. However, if one of them updates its value, say s_1 updates it to 12, then the operation on s_1 that maps 10 to 9 is *invalid* since the original value recorded in the operation does not match the value reported by the new version. As a result, the *update* module includes `citationQty` and the values reported by s_1 and s_2 in the merged document generated as input to a *fusion* process.

In the new fusion process, for every conflict in the merged document, it is checked whether there exists a high-level fusion rule already defined for the object. If this is the case, the conflict is solved, and both the mediated database and the operations repository are updated. In our running example, the value for `citationQty` in the mediated database is updated to 10, and the sequence of operations in the repository is replaced with new ones that reflect the new value recorded in the database. On the other hand, if there exists no fusion rules, or the existing strategy is value-based then a new decision is requested from the user. Intuitively, if a sequence of operations is *valid* there is no need for re-executing them because their effects are already recorded in the system. *Invalid* operations indicate source updates, and they can be solved without user intervention if high-level fusion rules have been defined on the conflicting objects.

4   Data Model

In this section we present the structure of the data involved in our fusion system: merged document (Section 4.1), rule base (Section 4.2), and operations repository (Section 4.3). We also define how fusion rules should be mapped to the operations repository (Section 4.4).

4.1   Merged Document

There are three categories of XML documents in our system: data source, merged document, and mediated database. They all follow the same schema which satisfies the following constraint: every element in the schema is associated with a key that determines how the element is identified in the context of its parent, based solely on its simple components. As an example, the set of keys in Example 1 is insertion-friendly for all the XML documents in Figure 1 given that every object is either keyed by a set of simple objects, such as `paper` objects, or they are unique in the context of their parent, such as `citationQty` and `name`.

A merged document differs from the source and mediated database on the contents of its simple objects. Instead of having text values, the merged document contains a set of pairs *(sourceId, value)* for every non-key simple object. Intuitively, a merged document combines into a single node all the values extracted from a set of sources that are identified by the same key. Discrepancies among these values indicate a conflict that is solved by fusing them into a single value, which in turn is stored in the mediated database.

Definition 1. *Given a set of sources S and a set $\mathcal{K}$ of insertion-friendly XML keys, we define a **merged document** T_m as an XML tree with a set of nodes V, such that a leaf node $v \in V$ is either: (a) a key node, which contains a single text value; or (b) a non-key node containing a set of pairs (sourceId, value), where sourceId is the identifier of a source $s \in S$ and value is extracted from a node in s that has the same key that identifies v in T_m according to $\mathcal{K}$.*

An example of a merged document is illustrated in Figure 1(c). Given a merged document T_m and a key k, we define a function `value`(T_m, k) to return the set of pairs associated with the node v with key k in T_m. We define a similar function on sources and the mediated database to return the text value associated with a simple object.

4.2   Rule Base

Given that a merged document explicitly represents value conflicts, we need a means for defining how these conflicts are solved. In our system, this is accomplished by user-defined fusion rules, stored in the *rule base*.

Definition 2. *A fusion rule is a pair $\langle \sigma, \Sigma \rangle$, where*
   (1) σ is a path expression representing the context covered by the strategy;
   (2) Σ is a non empty list of strategies for handling value conflicts on nodes reached by the context path σ.

The context of a rule is defined by a path expression σ and therefore it may cover not only a single element or attribute node, but also a *set* of nodes reached by following σ. Furthermore, a rule may define a *list* of strategies for solving a conflict. Thus, if the first strategy is not able to single out a value for a given data item, the following strategies are considered one by one until either the end of the list is reached or the conflict is solved.

Example 2. Consider the value conflicts on paper's `citationQty` and author names depicted in Figure 1(c). The fusion rules described in Section 1.1 can be defined as follows.

– ⟨*/paper[title='Integration' and year='2012']/citationQty, [MIM]* ⟩
– ⟨*/paper[title='Integration' and year='2012']/author/name, [CWW, TYF]*⟩

The first rule determines that conflicts on `citationQty` for the paper identified by '`Integration`' as its `title` and '2012' as its `year`, is solved by the *Meet in the Middle (MIM)* strategy. That is, the average value is computed, considering the imported values from all sources. The second rule defines that for any `author` of the same `paper`, `name` conflicts are solved by first finding the value reported by the majority of the sources (*Cry With the Wolves - CWW* strategy). If the strategy does not single out a value then *Trust Your Friends (TYF)* strategy is applied. Assuming that the confidence rate of s_1 is higher than s_2, the value reported from s_1 is chosen over that from s_2.

Observe that rules are defined in a context defined by a path expression. Thus, if conflicts on `citationQty` of all papers are to be solved by the MIM strategy, we could define a rule with a larger context as follows: ⟨*/paper/citationQty, [MIM]*⟩. That is, conflicts on any node reached by the path */paper/citationQty* are solved using the same strategy. Besides the notion of rule context, in our previous work, we introduce the notion of a *valid* set of rules, based on the concept of rule overriding. That is, inspired by object-oriented concepts, when the context of a rule is contained in the context of another, we choose to apply the one most specific to the node that presents a value conflict. As an example, we can define a *general* rule for solving conflicts on author `names` as ⟨*/paper/author/name, [TYF]*⟩, which can be overrid by a rule that is specific for 2012 papers: ⟨*/paper[year='2012']/author/name, [CWW]*⟩.

4.3 Operations Repository

One of the main goals of our proposed system is the ability to reapply user's decisions in future fusion processes. Our approach to reach this goal is to map the application of fusion strategies to sequences of basic operations that are stored in the *operations repository*.

Definition 3. *An operations repository is a list of records, grouped into blocks, where each record refers to a basic operation with the following attributes:*

– `bId`: *sequential number that identifies a list of records; given two `bId`s b_1 and b_2, $b_1 < b_2$ if b_1 has been executed before b_2;*
– `objId`: *key value that uniquely identifies an object on which the operation is executed;*
– `op`: *the operation can be an object insertion (`in`), removal (`rm`), or a simple object value edition (`ed`) or copy (`cp`);*

- origin: *source from which the operation obtains an object (or value) to be inserted (or copied) to another source. It is set to* null *for removal and edit operations;*
- target: *source updated by the operation;*
- prevVal: *target object value overwritten by operations edit and copy;*
- newVal: *new target object value.*

In the sequence we present an example of a block of operations that results from the application of a fusion strategy.

Example 3. Consider the rule defined for attribute citationQty in our running example. Its value is set to 9 in the mediated database when sources s_1 and s_2 are uploaded based on the MIM strategy. In the operations repository we store one edit operation in order to modify the mediated database (db) value to 9, followed by two copy operations from db to s_1 and s_2, as illustrated in Figure 3.

bId	objId	op	orig	target	prevVal	newVal
14	paper[..]/citationQty	ed	null	db	10	9
14	paper[..]/citationQty	cp	db	s1	10	9
14	paper[..]/citationQty	cp	db	s2	8	9

Fig. 3. A block of operations resulting from the *Meet in the Middle* strategy

Observe that the operations keep the original value reported by the sources in the prevVal field. Thus, when new sources are uploaded or if one of the sources updates the value, the system can continue to compute the average. For instance, consider the situation described in Section 1.1, in which a new version for s_1 is uploaded with the value 12 for citationQty. If the value uploaded from s_2 were not kept in the operations repository, we would be unable to compute the new average value of 10.

Observe also that the three operations belong to the same block, indicated by the same block identifier (bId: 14). This is because in the validation process each operation involving the uploaded source is analyzed to check whether the value in the current version matches the value recorded in the operation. Consider again the update from 10 to 12 on s_1's citationQty and the operations in Figure 3. The first copy operation from db to s_1 is *invalid,* since the value of prevVal is 10, while the new version reports 12. However, not only this operation should be considered invalid, but the whole block, since it reflects the application of a fusion strategy. Moreover, the reapplication of the MIM strategy affects not only the value of s_1, but all the other sources and the db. Thus, a block is considered *invalid* if it contains an invalid operation. In other words, validation is an operation-based process, but once an operation is found invalid, the whole block in which it is contained is considered invalid.

4.4   Mapping Fusion Rules to Operations

In this section we present details on how the application of a fusion strategy is recorded as a block of operations in the repository. First, observe that as the result of a rule application either: (a) a rule successfully singles out a value for an object that presented a conflict or (b) the user decides to postpone the decision on how to solve it for future fusion processes (*Pass it on* - PIO strategy).

In case (a) the block of operations has the following structure. First, an operation for modifying the value in the mediated database (db) is generated followed by a sequence of operations to copy this value to each of the sources that provide values for the same object. Observe that there are basically two types of strategies for solving a conflict: choose one value among the conflicting ones, such as strategies TYF, CWW, and CAV, or generate a new value, such as strategy MIM. An example of a block generated from the application of the MIM strategy is presented in Figure 3, in which we modify the value of db using an edit operation. However, when the strategy chooses one of the values provided from a source s_i, instead of an edit operation, we generate a copy operation from s_i to db. As an example, if the conflict on citationQty described in Example 3 is solved by choosing the value provided by s_1 over s_2, we generate a block with two operations: a copy from s_1 to db followed by a copy from db to s_2.

In case (b), in which the user decides to postpone the fusion decision, we keep the values provided by the sources in the operations repository, by modifying them to a null value using an edit operation. Since the actual value remains unknown, no value is recorded in the mediated database. Consider again the conflict on citationQty. If the user applies the PIO strategy, two edit operations are recorded in the repository: from 10 (as prevVal) to null on s_1, and from 8 to null on s_2.

An algorithm for generating a block of operations is given in Figure 4. Procedure insBlockOp takes as input five parameters: the *strategy* that has been applied to solve the conflict; the key *objId* of the object with conflicting values; a set *allVal* of pairs *(sourceId, val)* with the values reported from the sources, which may include a pair *(db, val)* if the mediated database already contains a value for the node; the value *finalVal* that results from the application of the *strategy*; and the source identification *valSource* that provides *finalVal*. After obtaining a new block identification *bId* (Line 1), the procedure keeps in *dbPrevVal* the previous value stored in the mediated database (Lines 2 to 4). Lines 7 to 9 considers the case when the strategy is PIO, generating a block of operations to edit the value of each source to null. The case when a final value for solving the conflict has been determined is considered in Lines 11 to 17. A valSource with null value indicates that a new value, not extracted from the sources have been generated to solve the conflict. In this case, an edit operation is generated (Lines 11 and 12); otherwise, we generate a copy operation (Lines 14 and 15). In the sequence, copy operations from the database to all remaining sources are recorded in the same block (Lines 16 to 17).

Procedure insBlockOp can be executed in $O(|S|)$ time, where $|S|$ denotes the number of input sources. To see this, observe that the set *allVal* is of size

---

Procedure `insBlockOp` *(strategy, objId, allVal, finalVal, valSource)*
Input: *strategy* applied to solve the value conflict, *objId* of the node,
      allVal: a set of pairs *(sourceId, val)*,
      finalVal: the value recorded in the mediated DB,
      valSource: the sourceId that provided *finalVal*

1.   *bId:=* **new**(*block*);   {generates a new bId}
2.   **if** there exists a pair *(db, v′)* in *allVal* **then**
3.   *dbPrevVal:=* $v′$*;*
4.   remove *(db, v′)* from *allVal;*
5.   **else**
6.   *dbPrevVal:=* `null`*;*
7.   **if** *strategy* is 'PIO' **then**
8.   **for** each *(sourceId, val)* in *allVal* **do**
9.   `insOpRep(`[*bId, objId,* 'ed', `null`, *sourceId, val,* `null`]`)`;
10. **else**
11.   **if** *valSource* is `null` **then** {the strategy created a new value}
12.   `insOpRep(`[*bId, objId,* 'ed', `null`, 'db', *dbPrevVal, finalVal*]`)`;
13.   **else**   {the strategy chose a reported value}
14.   `insOpRep(`[*bId, objId,* 'cp', *valSource,* 'db', *dbPrevVal, finalVal*]`)`;
15.   remove *(valSource, finalVal)* from *allVal;*
16.   **for** all pairs *(sourceId, val)* in *allVal* **do**
17.   `insOpRep(`[*bId, objId,* 'cp', 'db', *sourceId, val, finalVal*]`)`;

Fig. 4. Algorithm for inserting a block of operations

$O(|S|)$ since it contains at most one element for each source. Thus, checking containment in the set (Line 2) and removal from the set (Lines 4 and 15) takes $O(|S|)$ time. Lines 8-9 and 16-17 also take $O(|S|)$ time since procedure `insOpRep` takes constant time for writing a record at the end of operations repository file.

One advantage of keeping the operations repository is the feedback the system can give back to the sources. That is, after the fusion process, we can easily generate a sequence of operations for making any source s_i consistent with the mediated database simply by selecting the operations in which the `target` is s_i. Considering again the contents of the operation repository in Figure 3, a feedback for s_1 consists of the first copy operation, while for s_2 it contains the second copy operation.

5 System Modules

Given the data model presented in the previous section, we are now ready to describe the functionality of the fusion, validate, and update modules that compose our system.

5.1 Fusion Module

The major goal of the fusion module is to generate a *mediated database* resulting from the fusion of data imported from several sources. The input to the fusion module is a *merged document* and a set of user-defined *fusion rules*. Besides generating the mediated database, rules are stored in the *rule base*, and the *operations repository* is updated in order to reflect to last fusion operations that produced the values stored in the database.

Figure 5 presents an algorithm for the fusion module. **Clean** is a recursive function that traverses a merged document in post-order. Observe that in a merged document, all value conflicts are in the leaves. Thus, when processing internal nodes, the algorithm only calls the **clean** function recursively in order to collect the set of source identifiers that populate its descendants. This is because the provenance of the uploaded values in the merged document are recorded only on the set of pairs *(sourceId, val)* associated with the leaves. Thus, given *obj*, an internal node in a merged document, there exists a correspondent node in a source if it contributes with at least a value for one of the *obj*'s descendants. For each of these sources, we generate an insert operation in the operations repository by invoking the procedure **insObjOpRep** (Lines 1 to 7). In this procedure, for each *sourceId* in the set, it checks whether an insertion operation for the source already exists, and if not a new one is recorded.

When processing a simple non-key object, the function first obtains its set of pairs *(sourceId, val)* and its set of value providers by calling **getValues** and **getSourceIds**, respectively (Lines 9 and 10). If all sources agree on the reported value, it is simply stored in the mediated database and a block of operations is generated in the operations repository (Lines 11 to 14). Otherwise, we first look if there exists already a fusion rule defined for the node (Line 16) and check whether the conflict can be solved calling procedure **applyRule**. Observe that **applyRule** only reapplies high-level strategies such as TYF, MIM, and TYF. If the existing strategy is value-based, such as CAV, then it is removed from the rule base, without solving the conflict. Thus, if the conflict persists, the definition of a new rule is requested from the user (Lines 21 to 26), which is stored in the rule base (Line 23). If after this process, the conflict still persists, we conclude that the user chooses not the solve it at the moment. Thus, we record a PIO strategy for the node in the rule base, and remove the node from the database if it exists. The fusion decision is also recorded in the operations repository by invoking the **insBlockOp** procedure (Line 33). It is worth noticing that by allowing the user to postpone the fusion decision, it is possible to upload several sources to the system before making any decision on how to solve the conflicts. That is, although we consider a binary ladder integration approach in which sources are uploaded to the system one-by-one, the cleansing decisions are not necessarily made considering one new source at a time. It is also worth noticing that human input are valuable and should be used whenever possible. Therefore, we designed our system so that we notify users when previous changes have been invalidated and allow them to give suggestions on how these changes might be managed.

Algorithm *clean* can be executed in $O(|T|^3|R||S|)$ time, where $|T|$ is the size of the merged document, $|R|$ is the size of the rule base and $|S|$ is the number of sources. Observe that each node in the tree is processed once. For internal nodes, procedure **insObjOpRep** is invoked to determine whether the collected

---

Function clean (*obj*)
Input: *obj*: an object with key *objId* in a merged document *mergedDoc*
Output: *setsIds*: set of sourceIds that populate an *obj*'s descendant in *mergedDoc*

1. **if** *obj* is an internal node **then**
2.   *setsIds*:= *{}*;
3.   **for** all *obj*'s children *c* **do**
4.   **if** *c* is not a key object **then**
5.   *setsIds*:= *setsIds* ∪ **clean**(*c*);
6.   **insObjOpRep**(*objId*, *setsIds*);
7.   **return** *setsIds*;
8. **else**
9.   *allVal*:= **getValues**(*objId*); {return set of pairs *(sourceId, val)*}
10.   *setsIds*:= **getSourceIds**(*allVal*);
11.   **if** all sources provide the same value *v* **then**
12.   **updateDB**(*objId*, *v*);
13.   *sourceFinalVal*:= smallest *sourceId* in *setsIds*;
14.   **insBlockOp**(**null**, *objId*, *allVal*, *v*, *sourceFinalVal*);
15.   **else**
16.   *rule*:= **getRule**(*objId*); {obtain list of strategies [*r1*, ..., *rn*] from rule base}
17.   *solved*:= **false**;
18.   **while** not *solved* and *rule* not empty **do**
19.   *r*:= **extractFirst**(*rule*);
20.   *solved*:= **applyRule**(*r*, *allVal*, *finalVal*, *sourceFinalVal*);
21.   **if** not *solved* **then**   {request new rule from the user}
22.   *newRule*:= **getNewRule**(*objId*) from user input;
23.   **storeRuleBase**(*newRule*);
24.   **while** not solved and *newRule* not empty **do**
25.   *r*:= **extractFirst**(*newRule*);
26.   *solved*:= **applyRule**(*r*, *allVal*, *finalVal*, *sourceFinalVal*);
27.   **if** not *solved* **then**
28.   *r*:= 'PIO';
29.   *finalVal*:= **null**;
30.   **remDB**(*objId*);
31.   **else**
32.   **updateDB**(*objId*, *finalVal*);
33.   **insBlockOp**(*r*, *objId*, *allVal*, *finalVal*, *sourceFinalVal*);
34.   **return** *setsIds*;

Fig. 5. Algorithm clean

sourceIds have already been inserted in the operations repository. This takes a single traversal of the operations repository, which is of size $O(|T| * |S|)$, since each node in the tree may have at most one record for each source in the set S. For leaves, on the other hand, the execution of **getValues**, **getSourceIds**, and also for checking whether all sources agree on their values take $O(|S|)$ time, given that each leaf may have at most one value for each source. If all sources agree, procedures **updateDB** and **insBlockOp** procedures are invoked, which takes $O(|T|)$ and $O(|S|)$ time, respectively. The existence of value conflicts among sources requires the application of a rule. Function `getRule` can be executed in $O(|R| * |T|^2)$ time. Each rule is considered once, and the path expression σ in the rule is evaluated on T to check whether it contains the cleaning node. This is executed in $(|T| * |\sigma|)$ time [18] which is $O(|T|^2)$. Once the rule to be applied is singled out, each of its strategies are applied by calling `applyRule`, which can be executed in time $O(|S|)$ since the rules require scanning through the values provided by each source. The execution time for getting a new rule require the same time as the application of a new rule, in addition to storing it in the rule base, which takes $O(1)$ given that the rule is written at the end of the file. Updates on the database in lines 30 and 32 takes $O(|T|)$, while the insertion of a new block of operations in line 33 is $O(|S|)$. Thus, the entire algorithm is $O(|T| * (((|T| * |S|) + |S| + (|T| + |S|) + (|R| * |T|^2 + |S| + |T| + |S|)))$, which is $O(|T|^3|S||R|)$.

Example 4. Consider again our running example. Suppose that first, source s_1 is uploaded to the mediated database. Observe that for the first uploaded source s_1, the merged document is almost identical to the source, but with the non-key leaves annotated with the provenance of the single element in the set $\{(s_1, val)\}$. Since there are no conflicts, algorithm `clean` generates a document identical to s_1 in the mediated database and records these operations in the operations repository. The contents of the operations repository at this point is illustrated in Figure 6. Observe that the insertion operations (blocks 4, 6, and 8) have been generated by procedure `insObjOpRep`, while the remaining blocks are recorded by `insBlockOp`.

bId	objId	op	orig	target	prevVal	newVal
1	paper[..]/venue	cp	s1	db	null	'Int. Conf..'
2	paper[..]/city	cp	s1	db	null	'Philly'
3	paper[..]/author[order='1']/name	cp	s1	db	null	'John'
4	paper[..]/author[order='1']	in	s1	db		
5	paper[..]/author[order='2']/name	cp	s1	db	null	'Jack'
6	paper[..]/author[order='2']	in	s1	db		
7	paper[..]/citationQty	cp	s1	db	null	'10'
8	paper[title='Int..]	in	s1	db		

Fig. 6. Operations repository after upload of source s_1

If in the sequence s_2 is uploaded, the contents of the operations repository are modified as presented by Figure 7. New operations are generated for s_2's internal nodes (blocks 11, 13, and 16) but not for s_1, because they have already been generated during s_1's upload. Since value conflicts have been detected on `city`, author `names`, and `citationQty`, new blocks reflecting the user's decisions are recorded (blocks 9, 10, 12, and 14). Observe also that previously existing blocks involving these objects are removed from the repository (blocks 2, 3, 5, and 7). These removals are executed by the update module, which is based on the validation process, described in the next section.

bId	objId	op	orig	target	prevVal	newVal
1	paper[..]/venue	cp	s1	db	null	'Int. Conf..'
~~2~~	~~paper[..]/city~~	~~cp~~	~~s1~~	~~db~~	~~null~~	~~'Philly'~~
~~3~~	~~paper[..]/author[order='1']/name~~	~~cp~~	~~s1~~	~~db~~	~~null~~	~~'John'~~
4	paper[..]/author[order='1']	in	s1	db		
~~5~~	~~paper[..]/author[order='2']/name~~	~~cp~~	~~s1~~	~~db~~	~~null~~	~~'Jack'~~
6	paper[..]/author[order='2']	in	s1	db		
~~7~~	~~paper[..]/citationQty~~	~~cp~~	~~s1~~	~~db~~	~~null~~	~~'10'~~
8	paper[title='Int..']	in	s1	db		
9	paper[..]/city	cp	s2	db	'Philly'	'Philadelphia'
9	paper[..]/city	cp	db	s1	'Philly'	'Philadelphia'
10	paper[..]/author[order='1']/name	cp	s1	db	'John'	'John'
10	paper[..]/author[order='1']/name	cp	db	s2	'Jack'	'John'
11	paper[..]/author[order='1']	in	s2	db		
12	paper[..]/author[order='2']/name	cp	s1	db	'Jack'	'Jack'
12	paper[..]/author[order='2']/name	cp	db	s2	'John'	'Jack'
13	paper[..]/author[order='2']	in	s2	db		
14	paper[..]/citationQty	ed	null	db	10	9
14	paper[..]/citationQty	cp	db	s1	10	9
14	paper[..]/citationQty	cp	db	s2	8	9
15	paper[..]/pages	cp	s2	db	null	'18-29'
16	paper[title='Int..']	in	s2	db		

Fig. 7. Operations repository after upload of source s_2

5.2 Validation Module

The main goal of the validation module is to determine whether the execution of the operations in the repository have the same effect if executed on new versions of the sources. That is, if a new version presents no updates then all operations on the source are *valid* and thus there is no need for reexecuting them. On the other hand, an *invalid* operation indicates a source update which requires the object to go through a new fusion process. By selecting objects involved in invalid operations, the validation process can substantially reduce the volume of data considered in subsequent fusion processes. The validation module is also responsible for detecting removals and insertions in the source.

An algorithm for the validation module is presented in Figure 8. It takes as input an XML tree provided by a source identified by sId, and produces as output three sets, all of them containing *objIds*: *invalidUpdate* for invalid operations due to source value updates, *invalidRem* for invalid operations due to removals in the source, and *newObjIds* for elements inserted in the new version. First, we initialize the set *newObjIds* with the keys of all nodes in the document s, and the remaining sets as empty (Lines 1 to 3). Then each block in the operations repository is examined. Observe that blocks consist of operations on the same object and there exists at most one operation involving each source, but multiple operations involving the mediated database. Recall that a block is considered invalid if it contains at least one invalid operation. Thus, when validating a

---

Function `validate` (s)
Input: s: an XML tree with a new version for data source sId
Output: invalidUpdate: objIds for invalid operations due to updates,
                invalidRem: objIds for invalid operations due to removals
                newObjIds: objIds of elements inserted in the new version

1. newObjIds:= set of all objIds in s;
2. invalidUpdate:= {};
3. invalidRem:= {};
4. **for** each block b in the operations repository **do**
5.   **for** each record r in b **do**
6.   **if** r.origin == sId or r.target == sId **then**
7.   **if** r.objId is not in newObjIds **then**
8.   insert r.objId in invalidRem;
9.   **else**
10.   remove r.objId from newObjIds;
11.   **if** (r.op == 'cp' or r.op == 'ed') and
                        ((r.origin == sId and **value**(s, r.objId) <> r.newVal) or
                        (r.target == sId and **value**(s, r.objId) <> r.prevVal)) **then**
12.   insert r.objId in invalidUpdate;
13. **return** (invalidUpdate, invalidRem, newObjIds);

Fig. 8. Algorithm for validating operations

block, we first check whether there exists an operation involving sId. If so, either the object continues to be provided by the source or it has been removed. In the latter case, we consider the operation invalid and insert the objId in the invalidRem set (Lines 7 and 8). In the former case, since the object has already been provided in a previous version, we remove it from newObjIds (Line 10). Moreover, the algorithm checks if the value provided in the new version remains unchanged. Recall that in an operation record, `newValue` refers to the value provided by the `origin` source to update the `target` source, while `prevValue` refers to the value previously stored in `target`. Thus, we consider an operation invalid either if it contains sId as the `origin` and the value provided by the new version disagrees with the operation's `newValue` attribute or if it contains sId as the `target` and the provided value disagrees with the `prevValue` attribute (Lines 11 and 12). Recall that function `value` (s, objId) is responsible for extracting the value associated with the node with key objId in the document s.

Function `validate` can be executed in $O(|T|^2|S|)$ time. To see this, observe that the number of blocks in the operations repository is the number of nodes in the database T, and that each block contains at most $|S|$ records, one for each source. When processing a record in the repository, we have to check whether the object is in the set newObjIds, which is of size $O(|T|)$ and possibly obtain its value in the database, which takes $O(|T|)$ time. Thus, the time complexity of the algorithm is $O(|T| * |S| * |T|)$.

Example 5. As an example, consider the new version for source s_1 (referred to as $s_1.v_2$) presented in Figure 9(a) and the operations repository in Figure 7.

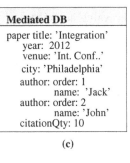

Source s1 – new version
paper title: 'Integration' year: 2012 venue: 'Int. Conf..' city: 'Philly' author: order: 1   name: 'Jack' citationQty: 12 pages: '1–10'

(a)

Merged Document

paper title: 'Integration'
year: 2012
author: order: 1
    name: *source s1:* 'Jack'
               source s2: 'Jack'
author: order: 2
    name: *source s2:* 'John'
citationQty: *source s1:* 12
               source s2:   8
pages: *source s1:* '1–10'
            source s2: '18–29'

(b)

Mediated DB

paper title: 'Integration'
year: 2012
venue: 'Int. Conf..'
city: 'Philadelphia'
author: order: 1
    name: 'Jack'
author: order: 2
    name: 'John'
citationQty: 10

(c)

Fig. 9. Upload of s_1's new version

The operation in the block with bId:1 is valid because s_1 is the origin and the value in newVal coincides with the value in the new version $s_1.v_2$. The insertion operation in block 4 is also valid because there exists a node with the same key for the author with order:1 in $s_1.v_2$. However, the insertion in block 6 is invalid because there exists no author with order:2 in $s_1.v_2$ and thus this object is inserted in the *invalidRem* set. The next block containing an invalid operation is the one with bId:10. The first operation in this block has s_1 as the origin but the value in newVal (*'John'*) disagrees with the value in $s_1.v_2$. Thus, the object is inserted in the *invalidUpdate* set. After processing all the operations in the repository, the only remaining object in the *newOb-jIds* is */paper[..]/pages* given that it is the only new object in the new version. The final contents of the other two sets are: *{/paper[..]/author[order='1']/name, paper[..]/citationQty}* for *invalidUpdate*, and *{/paper[..]/author[order='2'], /pa-per[..]/author[order='2']/name}* for the set *invalidRem*.

The sets resulting from the validate module are then given as input to the update module, which is responsible for generating a merged document with conflicts involving the updated objects.

5.3   Update Module

The goal of the update module is twofold. First, it generates a merged document which explicitly represents conflicts involving elements in a new source or in elements updated in a new version of a source. This document is the input to the fusion process described in Section 5.1. Second, it removes from the operations repository blocks containing invalid operations.

An algorithm for the update module is given in Figure 10. Function update takes as input a new version of a source *sId*, represented by an XML tree, and the three sets generated by the validate function and processes each of them as follows. First, observe that *objIds* in the *invalidUpdate* set are always simple elements since they are the ones that contain associated values. Thus, we simply remove the block of operations involving the object from the operations repository, and an element in the merged document is generated substituting the value associated with sId by the one provided by its new version (Lines 2 to 6). Observe that function extractValues receives a list of operation records, and returns a set of pairs *(sourceId, value)*, where *value* consists of the original value provided by *sourceId*. That is, if in the operation record *sourceId* is the origin then *value* is extracted from the newValue attribute; otherwise, it is extracted from prevValue. Moreover, procedure insMerged*(mergedDoc, objId, allVal)* inserts an element n identified by *objId* in *mergedDoc* and all the elements in the path from the root to n if they do not exist. The values for n are obtained from the set of pairs in *allVal*, except the pair associated with the source 'db'. The sets *invalidRem* and *newObjIds* are processed similarly (Lines 7 to 18, and 19 to 24, respectively). Observe, however, that when an object is removed from the new version, we must check if sId was the only source that provided it. If this is the case, we also have to remove it from the mediated database (Lines 11 and 16).

The update module may be invoked both after a validation process or for the first upload of a new source. For new sources, function update is called with both *invalidUpdate* and *invalidRem* as empty sets, and *newObjIds* containing the set of all *objIds* in the new document.

Function update can be executed in $O(|T|^2|S|)$ time. Observe that each object in the source is either in the set *invalidUpdate*, *invalidRem*, or *newObjIds*. For each of them, the operations repository, of size $O(|T| * |S|)$ is traversed once in order to be updated, and either the database or the merged document, both of size $|T|$, has to be updated. These operations require a single traversal on the tree. Thus the entire function is $O(|T| * (|T||S| + |T|))$, which is $O(|T|^2|S|)$.

Example 6. Consider again the contents of the sets of updated *objIds* in Example 5 and the operations repository in Figure 7. Based on the contents of *invalidUpdate*, block 10 (on paper[..]/author[order='1']/name and block 14 (on paper[..]/citationQty are removed from the repository and elements in the merged document are inserted with the original values provided by source s_2 and the values in the new version of s_1, as depicted in Figure 9(b). Similarly, based on the contents of *invalidRem*, block 6 (on paper[..]/author[order='2']) is removed from the repository. Observe that in this case, the corresponding object is not removed from the database because the repository still contains an insertion operation based on the author list provided by s_2. Moreover, block 12 is removed, with operations on paper[..]/author[order='2']/name, and an element is generated in the merged document, containing only the value provided by s_2. Given that the set *newObjIds* contains a single element paper[..]/pages, block 15 is removed from the repository, and the value provided by s_2 extracted from the operation is combined with the new element inserted in s_1. The resulting merged document is presented in Figure 9(b). Observe that elements venue and city, which remained unchanged in the new version are not inserted in the merged document since their operations remain valid.

Considering only the fusion rules presented in Example 2, value conflicts on elements citationQty and author name can be solved without any manual inter-

Function update *(s, invalidUpdate, invalidRem, newObjIds)*
Input: *s:* an XML tree provided by source *sId*
        invalidUpdate, invalidRem, newObjIds: sets of *objIds* of updates on *s*
Output: *mergedDoc:* updated values in *s* combined with values from other sources

1.   *mergedDoc:=* ϵ;
2. **for** each *objId* in *invalidUpdate* **do**
3.   *newVal:=* **value**(*s, objId*);
4.   extract block *b* involving *objId* from the operations repository;
5.   *allVal:=* **extractValues**(b) $-$ *{(sId, _)}* $\cup$ *{(sId, newVal)}*;
6.   **insMerged**(*mergedDoc, objId, allVal*);
7. **for** each *objId* in *invalidRem* **do**
8.   **if** *objId* refers to an internal node **then**
9.   remove [_ , *objId, 'in', sId, 'db', null, null*] from the operations repository;
10.   **if** there exists no other operation on *objId* in the operations repository **then**
11.   **remDB**(*objId*);
12.   **else**
13.   extract block *b* involving *objId* from the operations repository;
14.   *allVal:=* **extractValues**(b) $-$ *{(sId, _)}*;
15.   **if** *allVal* is empty **then**
16.   **remDB**(*objId*);
17.   **else**
18.   **insMerged**(*mergedDoc, objId, allVal*);
19. **for** each *objId* in *newObjIds* **do**
20.   **if** object with key *objId* is a simple object **then**
21.   *newVal:=* **value**(*s, objId*);
22.   extract block *b* involving *objId* from the operations repository;
23.   *allVal:=* **extractValues**(*b*) $\cup$ *{(sId, newVal)}*;
24.   **insMerged**(*mergedDoc, objId, allVal*);
25. **return** *mergedDoc*;

Fig. 10. Algorithm for the update module

vention, but not on **pages**. Thus, the fusion module requests a new rule from the user. If she decides to postpone the decision then the system sets the strategy to be PIO. The resulting mediated database is presented in Figure 9(c) and the final contents of the operations repository is given in Figure 11. Here we do not show the removed blocks, but only the ones that remained from the previous snapshot and the new blocks, which are above and below the dashed line, respectively.

Although the complexity of the algorithms in the paper had been presented in terms of the input size, the complexity of an incremental algorithm can also be measured in terms of the size of changes in the input and output, which represents the updating costs that are inherent to the incremental problem itself. With this respect, an incremental algorithm is said to be bounded if its cost can be expressed as a function of the size of changes. Intuitively, the algorithm is bounded if it processes only the subset of data input and output that change [29]. Recall that the goal of function **validate** is to determine which objects have been changed. That is, $|changed| = |invalidUpdate| +$

bId	objId	op	orig	target	prevVal	newVal
1	paper[..]/venue	cp	s1	db	null	'Int. Conf..'
4	paper[..]/author[order='1']	in	s1	db		
8	paper[title='Int..]	in	s1	db		
9	paper[..]/city	cp	s2	db	'Philly'	'Philadelphia'
9	paper[..]/city	cp	db	s1	'Philly'	'Philadelphia'
11	paper[..]/author[order='1']	in	s2	db		
13	paper[..]/author[order='2']	in	s2	db		
16	paper[title='Int..]	in	s2	db		
17	paper[..]/author[order='1']/name	cp	s1	db	'John'	'Jack'
17	paper[..]/author[order='1']/name	cp	db	s2	'Jack'	'Jack'
18	paper[..]/author[order='2']/name	cp	s2	db	'Jack'	'John'
19	paper[..]/citationQty	ed	null	db	9	10
19	paper[..]/citationQty	cp	db	s1	12	10
19	paper[..]/citationQty	cp	db	s2	8	10
20	paper[..]/pages	ed	null	s1	'1-10'	null
20	paper[..]/pages	ed	null	s2	'18-29'	null

Fig. 11. Operations Repository after upload of s_1's new version

$|invalidRem| + |newObjIds|$. Moreover, these changes affect the value of these objects in the mediated database and the corresponding records in the operations repository. Given that the merged document T is built based on these records, $|affected| = |T|$. The extraction of these records from the operations repository and the update of the mediated database can be done in time defined as a function of $|affected|$ if there exists an appropriate index structure on the *objId* both on the operations repository and the mediated database. Similarly, in order to bound the time complexity of the *clear* function to $|affected|$ we need an auxiliary structure to get the fusion rule defined on each object affected by the changes in the source new version.

6   Related Work

Data integration and cleaning have been studied extensively by the database community [4,7]. Most of previous works consider data on relational format, but recently it has been stressed the need for investigating the problem of solving conflicts on semi-structured data. XClean [34] is a system that allows declarative and modular specification of a cleaning process. It consists of a declarative language with operators that cover not only the fusion process, but also entity identification and combination of values that refer to the same object. The main goal is to provide a modular system that can be easily extended with new operators. Potter's Wheel [30] follow a cleaning strategy based on a set of operations to transform data, such as *format, drop, copy, merge, split, divide, fold* and *select*. However, instead of storing the result of a data transformation, the sources are stored along with the definition of the transformation. The transformation is applied on-the-fly whenever a consistent and clean information is required. Hummer [5] and Fusionplex [25] are systems that focus on the fusion process.

Hummer proposes an extension for SQL with fusion functions that can be applied to attributes in the query result. Fusionplex is also a strategy-based system in which conflicts are solved based both on metadata such as timestamp, cost, accuracy, and availability, and value-based strategies. However, none of these systems focus on incremental updates on fused data when sources are updated, which is the goal of our work.

There are a number of strategies for data fusion proposed in the literature [6,36,16,13,17], and a survey can be found in [7]. The strategies we described in Section 2.2 and used throughout the paper were introduced in [6]. However, extending our system with new strategies have little impact on our incremental update approach. First, observe that as a result of the application of a strategy, one of the following sequence of operations is recorded: *(case 1)* a copy operation from a source to the mediated database and several copy operations from the mediated database to each remaining source; and *(case 2)* an edit operation in the mediated database and several copy operations from the mediated database to each source. In the work described in [36], given a large number of facts that correspond to conflicting information obtained from several websites, it applies an iterative method to infer the trustworthiness of websites and to determine the confidence of facts based on the inferred trustworthiness. Solomon [16] is a system that can detect copying between sources and measure the quality of sources based on the intuition that copying may change the sources' quality. It applies the results to solve data conflicts and to decide true values of entities. In [13], it is proposed a model for determining the relative accuracy of attributes. Based on accuracy rules and an inference system, this work determines whenever possible a unique entity whose attributes are composed of the most accurate values from all conflicting attributes from the same real world object. If there is not enough information to generate a complete entity, the work computes the top-k candidate entities based on a preference model. Another work that focus on determining a unique entity whose attributes are consistent and store the most current value is described in [17]. The conflict resolution is solved by specifying data currency in terms of a partial currency order and currency constraints, and by enforcing data consistence with conditional functional dependencies. Based on the results produced by the aforementioned strategies, the user can solve a value conflict by choosing the most trustworthy fact, the most appropriate true value, the most appropriate top-k candidate entity, or by simply agreeing with the result returned by the strategy. As the value that is chosen to solve a value conflict is always obtained from a given source, our system can be extended to consider these strategies recording their results in the operations repository following *case 1*.

Regarding provenance-based integration systems that have been proposed in the literature, the ELIT (Exploration and LIneage Tracing) system [32] focuses on the lineage tracing problem in mediator-based integration systems. It collects information related to provenance during query processing in order to use this information to identify the data in the heterogeneous sources that contributed to a query answer. In Trio [3,35], data provenance is used to estimate the quality of imported data. Similar to our approach, the system stores values of the same piece of data imported from external sources. However, these value conflicts are solved by attaching confidence rates to values. But ELIT and Trio differ from our work on how provenance is applied in the integration process. Differently from our work, neither ELIT nor Trio store provenance on data transformations, which in our system are based on fusion rules and, therefore, they cannot be used to reapply previous fusion decisions.

Two systems that follow the operation-based approach, i.e., keep track of provenance related to data and transformations based on operations, are CPDB (Copy-Paste DataBase) [8,9] and CHIME (Capturing Human Intension Metadata with Entities) [1]. The main goal of CPDB is to manage provenance for manually curated databases, as defined by its authors as follows. "Given a definition of the complete and correct history of a database as it evolves over time, the goal of CPDB is to store sufficient provenance information to be able to answer queries about the history given only the provenance information and the final database state(s)". Also, Buneman et al. [8] investigate four techniques for storing provenance information, named naive provenance, transactional provenance, hierarchical provenance e transactional-hierarchical provenance. These techniques are aimed to reduce the provenance storage size, by defining different levels of details, from a higher level of detail (i.e., naive provenance) to a lower level of detail (i.e., transactional-hierarchical provenance). On the other hand, in CHIME the user first integrates heterogeneous sources into a single relation using as a basis a set of operations. These operations are collected automatically and store the data used in the integration, as well as which data is correct. Then, the user may query this integrated relation to extract information about the data collected in order to perform data audit. Our model differs from CPDB and CHIME on its purpose. We aim at reapplying fusion decisions in subsequent source uploads, while this feature is not supported neither by CPDB nor CHIME.

Orchestra [21] is a system for sharing structured data that is collaboratively authored by a large community of users. It models the exchange of data among sites as update exchange among peers, which is subject to transformations through schema mappings. Also, it employs data provenance for enforcing trust policies that are used to solve conflicts and for performing update exchange incrementally. Panda [19,20] is a generic framework for selectively update the output of a data-oriented workflow. That is, the user selects the data items she wants to update, and the system traces back their origin in the workflow in order to recompute their current values. The application of a fusion rule can be considered a data transformation in the Panda setting. However, Orchestra and Panda are based on specific characteristics that differs them from our work. Orchestra requires that each source provides its updates (delta) since the last integration process, while our approach does not require delta files, and has a much richer set of conflict solving rules. Panda is generic for any data transformation, and although one of its goals is similar to the idea of reapplying previous decisions (defined as workflows) in subsequent ones, it does not provide details on how the reapplication can be applied for data fusion processes, which is the focus of this paper.

Data provenance has also been used in the literature to support Extract-Transform-Load (ETL) processes in data warehousing environments (e.g., [15,31]). However, the use of provenance is typically to store metadata that allows one to trace the data origin and transformations, and not at incremental application of the transformations.

Finally, incremental updates on a database based on source updates has been recently referred to as data coordination [22]. However, the approach proposed in [22] differs from ours on how updates on the sources are detected. While we rely on the operations validation process, [22] proposes a materialization of the source data followed by an algorithm for detecting the differences with a new version. To the best of our knowledge, our approach is the first to apply an operation-based provenance model in the context of data fusion processes.

7   Conclusion

In this paper we presented a system that tackles the problem of incrementally updating a database populated with fused data provided by external sources. The approach is based on storing the data provenance in an operations repository that consists of records that contain both the original and new values. Since the operations coordinate the database with the sources, they can be used to provide feedback to the sources with the results of the fusion process. We proposed a validation process, which reliably determines whether a source updated an object provided in previous processes. When an update is identified, the value is combined with the values provided from other sources, extracted from the operations repository, in order to go through a new fusion process. By filtering out the objects that remained unchanged in new versions, and reapplying previously defined fusion rules, we can substantially minimize the need for manual user intervention in future fusion processes.

We intend to extend the XFusion [14] tool with the functionality presented in this paper and run some experiments in order to determine the efficacy of the proposed approach. Efficient storage and index structures to support the operations repository is also a topic for future investigation. In this paper, we adopt the where-provenance model [12], by keeping the origin of each data item that contributed to a value stored in the database, and the fusion rule that originated the final value. We can extend the proposed model by keeping all the source updates, so that it would be possible to obtain historical data by tracing back what have been the updates since their first upload to the system. Another line of investigation consists of extending the proposed framework for allowing update operations directly on the mediated database with operations logged in the operations repository. That is, the mediated database would combine imported data with local generated data. We intend to investigate how these direct operations impact those resulting from the application of fusion rules, possibly extending previous results [33] with characterizations of transitive and overlapping operations. We also plan to extend our system with the data fusion strategies surveyed in Section 6.

Acknowledgement. This work has been supported by the following Brazilian research agencies: CNPq, FAPESP, CAPES, RNP, and FINEP.

References

1. Archer, D.W., Delcambre, L.M.L., Maier, D.: A framework for fine-grained data integration and curation, with provenance, in a dataspace. In: Proceedings of the 1st Workshop on the Theory and Practice of Provenance, pp. 1–10 (2009)
2. Batini, C., Lenzerini, M., Navathe, S.B.: Comparative analysis of methodologies for database schema integration. ACM Computing Surveys 18(4) (December 1986)
3. Benjelloun, O., Sarma, A.D., Hayworth, C., Widom, J.: An introduction to ULDBs and the Trio system. IEEE Data Engineering Bulletin 29(1), 5–16 (2006)
4. Bhattacharya, I., Getoor, L.: Collective entity resolution in relational data. IEEE Data Engineering Bulletin 29(2), 4–12 (2006)
5. Bilke, A., Bleiholder, J., Naumann, F., Böhm, C., Weis, M.: Automatic data fusion with hummer. In: Proceedings of the 31st VLDB Conference, pp. 1251–1254 (2005)
6. Bleiholder, J., Naumann, F.: Conflict handling strategies in an integrated information system. In: Proceedings of the International Workshop on Information Integration on the Web, IIWeb (2006)
7. Bleiholder, J., Naumann, F.: Data fusion. ACM Computing Survey 41(1), 1–41 (2008)
8. Buneman, P., Chapman, A., Cheney, J.: Provenance management in curated databases. In: SIGMOD 2006: Proceedings of the 2006 ACM SIGMOD International Conference on Management of Data, pp. 539–550 (2006)
9. Buneman, P., Chapman, A., Cheney, J., Vansummeren, S.: A provenance model for manually curated data. In: Moreau, L., Foster, I. (eds.) IPAW 2006. LNCS, vol. 4145, pp. 162–170. Springer, Heidelberg (2006)
10. Buneman, P., Davidson, S., Fan, W., Hara, C., Tan, W.C.: Keys for XML. Computer Networks 39(5), 473–487 (2002)
11. Buneman, P., Khanna, S., Tan, W.-C.: Data provenance: Some basic issues. In: Kapoor, S., Prasad, S. (eds.) FST TCS 2000. LNCS, vol. 1974, pp. 87–93. Springer, Heidelberg (2000)
12. Buneman, P., Khanna, S., Tan, W.-C.: Why and where: A characterization of data provenance. In: Van den Bussche, J., Vianu, V. (eds.) ICDT 2001. LNCS, vol. 1973, pp. 316–330. Springer, Heidelberg (2000)
13. Cao, Y., Fan, W., Yu, W.: Determining the relative accuracy of attributes. In: SIGMOD 2013: Proceedings of the ACM SIGMOD International Conference on Management of Data, pp. 565–576 (2013)
14. Cecchin, F., de Aguiar Ciferri, C.D., Hara, C.S.: XML data fusion. In: Bach Pedersen, T., Mohania, M.K., Tjoa, A.M. (eds.) DAWAK 2010. LNCS, vol. 6263, pp. 297–308. Springer, Heidelberg (2010)
15. Cui, Y., Widom, J.: Lineage tracing for general data warehouse transformations. The VLDB Journal 12(1), 41–58 (2003)
16. Dong, X., Berti-Equille, L., Hu, Y., Srivastava, D.: SOLOMON: Seeking the truth via copying detection. PVLDB 3(2), 1617–1620 (2010)
17. Fan, W., Geerts, F., Tang, N., Yu, W.: Inferring data currency and consistency for conflict resolution. In: ICDE 2013: Proceedings of the IEEE International Conference on Data Engineering, pp. 470–481 (2013)
18. Gottlob, G., Koch, C., Pichler, R.: Efficient algorithms for processing xpath queries. In: VLDB 2002: Proceedings of the 28th International Conference on Very Large Data Bases, pp. 95–106 (2002)

19. Ikeda, R., Widom, J.: Panda: A system for provenance and data. IEEE Data Engineering Bulletin 33(3), 42–49 (2010)
20. Ikeda, R., Salihoglu, S., Widom, J.: Provenance-based refresh in data-oriented workflows. In: Proceedings of the 20th ACM International Conference on Information and Knowledge Management, CIKM 2011, pp. 1659–1668. ACM, New York (2011), http://doi.acm.org/10.1145/2063576.2063816
21. Ives, Z.G., Green, T.J., Karvounarakis, G., Taylor, N.E., Tannen, V., Talukdar, P.P., Jacob, M., Pereira, F.: The Orchestra collaborative data sharing system. SIGMOD Record 37(3), 26–32 (2008)
22. Lawrence, M., Pottinger, R., Staub-French, S.: Data coordination: Supporting contingent updates. Proceedings of the VLDB Endowment 4(11), 831–842 (2011)
23. Menestrina, D., Benjelloun, O., Garcia-Molina, H.: Generic entity resolution with data confidences. In: Proceedings of the International VLDB Workshop on Clean Databases, Seoul, Korea (2006)
24. Lim, E.P., Srivastava, J., Prabhakar, S., Richardson, J.: Entity identification in database integration. Information Sciences 89(1) (1996)
25. Motro, A., Anokhin, P.: Fusionplex: resolution of data inconsistencies in the integration of heterogeneous information sources. Information Fusion 7(2), 176–196 (2006)
26. do Nascimento, A.M., Hara, C.S.: A model for XML instance level integration. In: SBBD 2008: Proceedings of the 23rd Brazilian Symposium on Databases, pp. 46–60 (2008)
27. Poggi, A., Abiteboul, S.: XML data integration with identification. In: Bierman, G., Koch, C. (eds.) DBPL 2005. LNCS, vol. 3774, pp. 106–121. Springer, Heidelberg (2005)
28. Prabhakar, S., Richardson, J., Srivastava, J., Lim, E.P.: Instance-level integration in federated autonomous databases. In: Hawaiian Conference for System Science (1993)
29. Ramalingam, G., Reps, T.W.: An incremental algorithm for a generalization of the shortest-path problem. Journal of Algorithms 21(2), 267–305 (1996)
30. Raman, V., Hellerstein, J.M.: Potter's wheel: An interactive data cleaning system. In: VLDB 2001: Proceedings of the 27th International Conference on Very Large Data Bases, pp. 381–390 (2001)
31. Sellis, T.K., Skoutas, D., Simitsis, A., Vassiliadis, P.: Data provenance in ETL scenarios. In: Proceedings of the 1st Workshop on Principles of Provenance, pp. 1–3 (2007)
32. Shiri, N., Taghizadeh-Azari, A.: Lineage tracing in mediator-based information integration systems. In: Ramos, F.F., Larios Rosillo, V., Unger, H. (eds.) ISSADS 2005. LNCS, vol. 3563, pp. 267–282. Springer, Heidelberg (2005)
33. Tomazela, B., Hara, C.S., Ciferri, R.R., Ciferri, C.D.A.: Empowering integration processes with data provenance. Data & Knowledge Engineering 86, 102–123 (2013)
34. Weis, M., Manolescu, I.: Declarative XML data cleaning with XClean. In: Krogstie, J., Opdahl, A.L., Sindre, G. (eds.) CAiSE 2007 and WES 2007. LNCS, vol. 4495, pp. 96–110. Springer, Heidelberg (2007)
35. Widom, J.: Trio: A system for data, uncertainty, and lineage. In: Aggarwal, C. (ed.) Managing and Mining Uncertain Data, ch. 5. Springer (2009)
36. Yin, X., Han, J., Yu, P.S.: Truth discovery with multiple conflicting information providers on the web. IEEE Transactions on Knowledge and Data Engineering 20(6), 796–808 (2008)

Provenance for Linked Data[*]

Grigoris Karvounarakis[1], Irini Fundulaki[2,**], and Vassilis Christophides[3]

[1] LogicBlox and ICS-FORTH
[2] ICS-FORTH
[3] ICS-FORTH and Univ. of Crete

Abstract. Assessing the *quality of linked data* currently published on the Web is a crucial need of various data-intensive applications. Extensive work on similar applications for relational data and queries has shown that *data provenance* can be used in order to compute trustworthiness, reputation and reliability of query results, based on the source data and query operators involved in their derivation. In particular, *abstract provenance models* can be employed to record information about source data and query operators during query evaluation, and later be used e.g., to assess trust for individual query results. In this paper, we investigate the extent to which relational provenance models can be leveraged for capturing the provenance of SPARQL queries over linked data, and identify their limitations. To overcome these limitations, we advocate the need for new provenance models that capture the full expressive power of SPARQL, and can be used to support assessment of various forms of data quality for linked data manipulated declaratively by such queries.

1 Introduction

Recently, the W3C Linked Open Data (LOD) Initiative[1] has boosted the publication and interlinkage of massive amounts of scientific, corporate, government and crowd-sourced data sets on the emerging *Data Web* for open access, as RDF data [27] queried with the SPARQL query language [30]. Open data published according to the Linked Data Paradigm [23] are essentially transforming the Web from a document publishing-only environment into a *global data space* where yesterday's passive readers have become *active data aggregators* and *generators* themselves. In this setting, linked open data are freely *exchanged, integrated,* and *materialized* in distributed repositories accessible through SPARQL endpoints[2]. Understanding how an RDF triple was created or where it was copied from, is crucial to assess the *data quality* and strengthen *data accountability* (see W3C Provenance Incubator Group Requirements[3]). This functionality essentially calls

---

[*] An earlier version of this paper appeared in IEEE Internet Computing 15(1): 31-39, 2011.
[**] Visiting Researcher at CWI.
[1] www.w3.org/standards/semanticweb/data
[2] www.w3.org/wiki/SparqlEndpoints
[3] www.w3.org/2005/Incubator/prov/wiki/User_Requirements

V. Tannen et al. (Eds.): Buneman Festschrift, LNCS 8000, pp. 366–381, 2013.
© Springer-Verlag Berlin Heidelberg 2013

for representing and reasoning on the *provenance* of replicated and incomplete sets of RDF triples manipulated by SPARQL queries worldwide.

For instance, in the case of *trust assessment* [3] the trustworthiness of query results is determined based on the trustworthiness of source datasets from which they were derived. For simple *Boolean trust* assessment we only need to determine which output data should be trusted. For *ranked trust* assessment we need to choose the most trusted among competing evidence from diverse sources. Additionally, for *uncertain* and *fuzzy* data sets, the probabilities of query results are derived based on the probabilities associated with the original data [26]. In all these cases, the goal is to compute appropriate *annotations* for query results that reflect data quality, based on the annotations of source data. If source annotations were static and common for all users, this computation could be done together with the query evaluation [13,31]. However, in general, different users may have different beliefs about the *trustworthiness*, *reputation* or *reliability* of the source RDF triples, and these beliefs may change over time, even when the relationship of query results with the source data remains unchanged. For this reason, an alternative approach is to use *abstract provenance models* to capture this relationship along with the query operators that combined source data to derive query results. This information can be recorded [21] in the hosting repository when the data is imported, and used to compute appropriate annotations for different applications and users at a later time [25].

Unlike most of the related work in the *Semantic Web* (see W3C Provenance Incubator Group State of the Art[4]), in this paper, we focus on *data provenance* in the style of [8,20], i.e. provenance in the result of *declarative queries*. This is different from *workflow* provenance [14] [11] which typically describes procedural data processing, and where operations are usually treated as black boxes due to their complexity. Moreover, we are interested in *implicit* provenance [5] of queries that only manipulate data and are oblivious about the possible annotations thereof. Implicit provenance captures the abstract structure and properties of query operators and can, thus, be used for various annotation computations [25,4]. This is in contrast to work on *explicit* provenance [5], as well as on RDF named graphs [7]) where queries can also manipulate source annotations and specify explicitly the annotation of the query results. Consequently, the resulting annotations can be arbitrary and may not reflect the structure and characteristics of the query operators, as actually needed to support alternative annotation computations. Finally, [12] has studied implicit data provenance for a SPARQL fragment that is close to the positive relational algebra. In this paper, we take a first step in specifying an abstract provenance model for arbitrary SPARQL expressions. In particular, we:

- present the basic characteristics of abstract provenance models and argue on the benefits of using those to compute annotations for various applications on Semantic Web data (Section 3).

---

[4] www.w3.org/2005/Incubator/prov/wiki/State_of_the_Art_Report

- review representative abstract provenance models for relational queries that can be used to capture the provenance of a positive SPARQL fragment over linked open data (Section 5).
- identify the limitations of these models for capturing the provenance of certain SPARQL operators (Section 6). The main challenges stem from the SPARQL OPTIONAL operator, which is crucial for dealing with the incompleteness of linked open data but – as we explain later – cannot be handled by relational provenance models. For this reason, we advocate the need for new provenance models for SPARQL queries.

2 Motivating Example

Let us consider the following example of Linked Open Data (LOD) that motivates our study of provenance. Assume that we are interested in aggregating through SPARQL queries RDF triples [27] regarding Points of Interest (POI) and cafes-restaurants published in the LOD Cloud[5] and store them locally in a repository. Figure 1 illustrates a snapshot of such repository with RDF triples (asserting the fact that *subject* resource is associated with *object* through *property*) inspired by the LinkedGeoData project[6] aiming to enrich the Web of Data with spatial information originating from various independent contributors and knowledge bases (as OpenStreetMap[7]).

Triple Set T			
S	**P**	**O**	**Contributor**
Starbucks	lgdo:type	Cafe	http://linkedgeodata.org/users/John (c_1)
Starbucks	geo:branchLoc	53rd St	http://linkedgeodata.org/users/Alice (c_2)
MoMA	geo:address	53rd St	http://linkedgeodata.org/users/James (c_3)

Fig. 1. A repository with RDF triples from LinkedGeoData, with information about the contributor of each triple

In our example a set of RDF triples is stored in a single relational table, using attributes **S**, **P** and **O** to represent the *subject*, *predicate* and *object* of a triple. To capture the origin of each individual RDF triple we employ a fourth column stating its contributor. In a typical data sharing setting, such provenance information is fundamental in order to assess the trustworthiness, reputation or reliability of integrated data. For example, a particular user may only trust a subset of the contributors (*Boolean trust*), or may have different levels of trust for different contributors (*ranked trust*). In both cases, the goal is to determine some trust score for SPARQL query results, based on trust scores of source data and how they were combined through queries to derive each result.

---

[5] lod-cloud.net

[6] linkedgeodata.org

[7] www.openstreetmap.org

For example, given the information in Figure 1, Peter may write a SPARQL query looking for cafes located on the same street as MoMA.[8] If Peter trusts all contributors completely, then he will conclude that there is a `Starbucks` store on the same street as `MoMA`. However, if, for instance, he does not trust Alice and does not take data she has contributed into account, then he will not be able to reach this conclusion. To simplify the presentation, in the rest of the paper we consider that provenance tokens (e.g., c_1, c_2, etc.) are associated to the actual contributors depicted in Figure 1 and use those tokens later on to create compact provenance expressions of SPARQL query results. Note that identifiers similar to our tokens are actually used in real systems to minimize the provenance storage space overhead.

3 Requirements for Abstract Provenance Models

In order to support computations such as the trust assessment in the example above, a common approach in the relational world is to *annotate* query results with expressions capturing information about source data and query operators involved in their derivation, i.e., information about the *provenance* of query results. If one is only interested in computing one of the kind of result annotations (e.g., Boolean trust), and the related annotations of source data are static (e.g., we know in advance which users are trusted and which are not), then it is possible to extend query answering to compute these annotations when data is imported through queries and materialized. However, in the Web of Data:

- different applications may need to assess various dimensions of data quality (such as Boolean or ranked trust) of the same linked open datasets;
- different users may have individual perceptions, that may change over time, regarding the data quality of the same linked open datasets;
- data annotations typically have to be computed for only a (possibly small) subset of the linked open datasets stored locally;
- source linked open data imported into the repository may be unavailable when one tries to assess their quality.

As already investigated in the relational world [22,21,25], it appears to be quite beneficial in such expressive settings to capture the common parts of such annotation computations by recording *abstract provenance information* when data is imported through queries and evaluate them on demand for materializing specific data annotations along with query results. It should be also stressed that various other computations, ranging from computing probabilistic event expressions [15] to Boolean expressions dealing with incompleteness or uncertainty [24], or to tuple multiplicities [28], can also be computed in a similar manner [22]. Our goal is to determine whether there are abstract provenance models for SPARQL queries over RDF data that can similarly record sufficient

---

[8] We show later in the paper how to express such queries in SPARQL.

information to support such expressive annotation computations on the Web of Data.

The granularity of the provenance information about source LOD on which these computations are based typically depends on the main constructs of the data model. For instance, relational provenance models consider *sets of attributes* [6,17], individual *tuples* [4,22,6,9,19] or even entire *relations* [6]. For SPARQL queries and RDF data, we consider the case where source triples are annotated with information about their contributors abstracted using provenance tokens (such as in the example of Figure 1).

For some settings, just knowing the set of source RDF triples that are involved in their derivation may be sufficient. However, to make e.g., trust judgements such as the ones presented in Section 2, more detailed information is needed. In particular, we should be able to assert whether relevant source triples provide alternative justifications for a query result, or if all of them need to be trusted in order for the result to be trusted. For instance, in our motivating example all three contributors need to be trusted in order to reach the conclusion that there is a cafe on the same street as MoMA. On the other hand, for a query such as "is there any information about businesses on 53rd St", information from Alice and John is complementary, i.e., trusting one of them is sufficient to obtain a positive answer. Thus, for applications such as trust assessment, we need more detailed *provenance expressions*, that – in addition to provenance tokens – also record some information about how they were combined through *query operators* to derive each query result, thereby storing information on *how* input triples were combined to produce the result in question.

Ideally, one would like to design an abstract provenance model that accommodates all the needs of users and applications consuming LOD. However, there is often a tradeoff between the expressiveness of provenance models [20] and the cost for storing and manipulating the corresponding provenance expressions [25]. As a result, whenever we need to support only a subset of the above requirements, it may be desirable to employ less-informative abstract provenance models for which the resulting provenance expressions can typically be stored and manipulated more efficiently.

4   Capturing the Provenance of SPARQL Queries

Before embarking towards our goal of designing abstract provenance models for SPARQL, we briefly overview the SPARQL query semantics. To leverage the amount of work on relational provenance models, we identify the SPARQL operators whose semantics are similar to relational algebra operators and explain how popular relational provenance models can be adapted to capture their provenance. Finally, we focus on SPARQL operators, whose semantics cannot be captured by the existing relational provenance models, raising the need for new provenance models capturing SPARQL queries computation.

4.1   SPARQL in a Nutshell

SPARQL presentation in this section is based on the algebra presented in [29,2]. This algebra employs triple patterns for binding variables to values in the dataset having the form (x, y, z), where x, y, z can be constants or variables (prefixed with "?") on the *subject*, *predicate* and *object* positions. A set of pairs (*variable, value*), i.e. the SPARQL analog of the relational *valuation*, is called a *mapping*. For instance, the pattern $(?x, ?y, \texttt{Cafe})$ only matches triples whose *object* has the value $\texttt{Cafe}$ and the result of matching it to the first triple of T (Table (a) in Figure 3), is the mapping $\{(?x, \texttt{Starbucks}), (?y, \texttt{lgdo:type})\}$ indicating that variables $?x$, $?y$ are bound to values $\texttt{Starbucks}$ and $\texttt{lgdo:type}$, respectively. The evaluation of a triple pattern on a set of triples is a bag of *mappings*, i.e. a set of *mappings* along with a cardinality function, that associates every mapping of the set with an integer. To simplify the presentation, we will use the tabular representation of the mapping bags shown in Figure 2, where each column corresponds to a variable in the mappings.

The SPARQL algebra is comprised of: a) the unary operators σ (filtering) and π (projection) capturing the SPARQL constructs FILTER and SELECT, respectively and b) the binary operators, $\cup$, $\bowtie$, $\bowtie\!\!\!\!\!\bowtie$ capturing the SPARQL constructs UNION, AND, and OPTIONAL, respectively.

Filtering on the triple positions specifies the subset of mappings for which some variable has a specific constant value (literal or URI). For instance, let Ω (Table (a) of Figure 2) denote the evaluation of $(?x, ?y, ?z)$ over T. Then, $\sigma_{?y=\text{"lgdo:type"}}(\Omega)$ contains only the mapping $\{(?x, \texttt{Starbucks}), (?y, \texttt{lgdo:type}), (?z, \texttt{Cafe})\}$.

Projection specifies the subset of variables in mappings to be returned in the query result. For example, $\Omega_1 = \pi_{?x, ?y}(\sigma_{?z=\text{"53}^{\text{rd}}\text{ St"}}(\Omega))$ is the bag of mappings obtained from projecting the variables $?x$, $?y$ of $\sigma_{?z=\text{"53}^{\text{rd}}\text{ St"}}(\Omega)$ (Table (b) of Figure 2). Similarly, Ω_2 in Table (c) of Figure 2 denotes the result of query $\pi_{?y, ?z}(\sigma_{?x=\text{"Starbucks"}}(\Omega))$. To simplify the presentation, we employ symbols μ_i in Figure 2 to identify individual mappings.

Unlike relational union that is defined on relations of the same schema, the union operation ($\cup$) of the SPARQL algebra can be applied on bags of mappings defined for different variables. In such cases, the result may include mappings with unbound variables, denoted by "-" in Table (e) of Figure 2 (in SQL that would be a *null* value) that shows the result of $\Omega_1 \cup \Omega_2$.

In order to define the semantics of the join operator ($\bowtie$), SPARQL algebra relies on a notion of *compatible mappings*. Two mappings are considered *compatible* if they agree on their *common* variables. The $\bowtie$ output for two compatible input mappings is a mapping whose set of variables is the union of their bound variables. For each variable in the output, its value is the same as in the corresponding input mapping(s). It is worth noticing that in contrast to relational algebra where a null value in an attribute makes any join condition fail, unbound variables in SPARQL do not affect the compatibility of mappings. Table (f) of

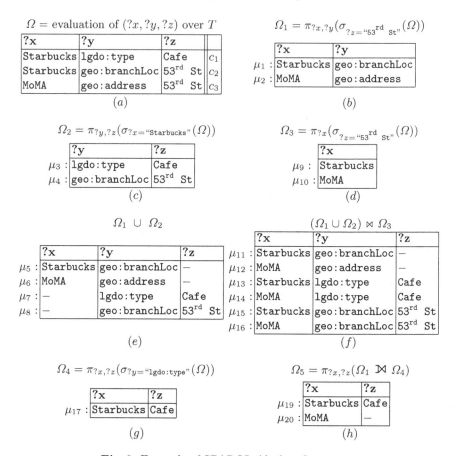

Fig. 2. Example of SPARQL Algebra Operators

Figure 2 shows the result of $(\Omega_1 \cup \Omega_2) \bowtie \Omega_3$ where $\Omega_1 \cup \Omega_2$ is shown in Table (e), while Ω_3 in Table (d). Note that, although $?x$ is unbound in μ_7, SPARQL considers μ_7 to be compatible with μ_9 and μ_{10}, for which $?x$ is bound.

Finally, the application of the optional operator ($\bowtie$) on two mapping bags Ω_l and Ω_r returns the mappings contained in the result of $\Omega_l \bowtie \Omega_r$, as well as all mappings from Ω_l that are not compatible with any mapping in Ω_r. In this manner, $\bowtie$ is reminiscent of the left outer join operator of the relational algebra. As shown in [29,2], the following algebraic equivalence holds:

$$\Omega_l \bowtie \Omega_r = (\Omega_l \bowtie \Omega_r) \cup (\Omega_l \setminus \Omega_r) \tag{1}$$

Figure 2 illustrates the result of $\Omega_1 \bowtie \Omega_4$ in Table (h), where Ω_1 is shown in Table (b) and Ω_4 in Table (g). For instance, μ_{19} is in the result because of the join between μ_1 and μ_{17}, while μ_{20} appears in the result because μ_2 belongs to Ω_1 and is not compatible with μ_{17}. We denote with $\Omega_l \setminus \Omega_r$ the mappings of Ω_l that are not compatible with any Ω_r mapping; for instance, $\Omega_1 \setminus \Omega_4 = \{\mu_2\}$.

We should stress that there are some subtle differences between the "\" operator of [29,2] and the relational minus operator (denoted "−" below). The former checks mappings (that may have different schemas) for compatibility, while the latter only compares tuples (of the same schema) for equality. Clearly, compatibility between mappings is an 1–n relationship, i.e. a mapping of Ω_l may be compatible with many mappings of Ω_r, while equality between tuples is an 1–1 relationship. Consider for instance, the relational query $R_l - R_r$. A tuple of R_l relation can be equal to at most one tuple of R_r. As a consequence, the existence of multiple copies of a mapping in Ω_l and Ω_r does not affect the cardinality of that mapping in the result: if a mapping μ has cardinality m in Ω_l and there is one compatible mapping with cardinality n in Ω_r, μ will have cardinality 0 in the result, i.e., it will not appear in it. On the contrary, in the relational context, if a tuple t has cardinality m in relation R_l and n in R_r, then the cardinality of t in $R_l - R_r$, is $m - n$, if $m > n$, and 0, otherwise.

5   Provenance Models for Positive SPARQL

From the previous discussion, there is a clear analogy among the SPARQL algebra operators for projection (π), filter (σ), join ($\bowtie$) and union ($\cup$) with the corresponding operators of the positive relational algebra and thus we refer to the fragment of SPARQL consisting only the above operators as *positive* SPARQL. In this Section we investigate whether provenance models for the positive fragment of the relational algebra can be also applied to unions of conjunctive SPARQL queries, despite their subtle differences.

An obvious difference between them lies in the fact that relational algebra operates on tuples, while SPARQL algebra operates on mappings. However, this is easily handled by associating mappings that are returned by triple patterns with the provenance tokens of the triples they were obtained from. Moreover, SPARQL algebra adopts *bag semantics* by default, although set semantics can be enforced through the use of the operator DISTINCT. Among relational provenance models, only *how*-provenance can be used to compute correct result multiplicities under bag semantics [22], while all models can handle set semantics. Finally, the differences (mentioned in Section 4.1) between SPARQL and relational algebra for the $\cup$ and $\bowtie$ operators do not affect the provenance of output mappings. As a consequence, all abstract provenance models for positive relational algebra from the literature [9,6,19,4,22] can be also applied to positive SPARQL under set semantics, while one of them (*how*-provenance [22]) can be used when bag semantics is needed. We briefly recall the main features of three representative provenance models below, while also highlighting their differences in terms of their ability to support annotation computations such as the ones we described earlier.

Consider the query $Q(\Omega) = \pi_{?y,?z}(\pi_{?x,?y}(\Omega) \bowtie \pi_{?x,?z}(\Omega) \cup \pi_{?y,?z}(\Omega) \bowtie \pi_{?x,?z}(\Omega))$, where Ω is the mapping set shown in Figure 2, where the annotation for each mapping has been obtained from the corresponding source triple annotations. From this point on, and for ease of readability we will be referring

$$\pi_{?x,?y}(\Omega) \bowtie \pi_{?x,?z}(\Omega)$$

	?x	?y	?z	Why-prov.	How-prov.
μ_a :	Starbucks	lgdo:type	Cafe	$\{\{c_1\}\}$	$c_1 \odot c_1$
μ_b :	Starbucks	lgdo:type	53rd St	$\{\{c_1,c_2\}\}$	$c_1 \odot c_2$
μ_c :	Starbucks	geo:branchLoc	Cafe	$\{\{c_1,c_2\}\}$	$c_1 \odot c_2$
μ_d :	Starbucks	geo:branchLoc	53rd St	$\{\{c_2\}\}$	$c_2 \odot c_2$
μ_e :	MoMA	geo:address	53rd St	$\{\{c_3\}\}$	$c_3 \odot c_3$

(a)

$$\pi_{?y,?z}(\Omega) \bowtie \pi_{?x,?z}(\Omega)$$

	?x	?y	?z	Why-prov.	How-prov.
μ_f :	Starbucks	lgdo:type	Cafe	$\{\{c_1\}\}$	$c_1 \odot c_1$
μ_g :	Starbucks	geo:branchLoc	53rd St	$\{\{c_2\}\}$	$c_2 \odot c_2$
μ_h :	Starbucks	geo:address	53rd St	$\{\{c_2,c_3\}\}$	$c_2 \odot c_3$
μ_i :	MoMA	geo:branchLoc	53rd St	$\{\{c_2,c_3\}\}$	$c_2 \odot c_3$
μ_j :	MoMA	geo:address	53rd St	$\{\{c_3\}\}$	$c_3 \odot c_3$

(b)

$$Q(\Omega) = \pi_{?y,?z}(\pi_{?x,?y}(\Omega) \bowtie \pi_{?x,?z}(\Omega) \cup \pi_{?y,?z}(\Omega) \bowtie \pi_{?x,?z}(\Omega))$$

	?y	?z	Why-prov.	How-provenance
μ_k	lgdo:type	Cafe	$\{\{c_1\}\}$	$(c_1 \odot c_1) \oplus (c_1 \odot c_1)$
μ_l	lgdo:type	53rd St	$\{\{c_1,c_2\}\}$	$c_1 \odot c_2$
μ_m	geo:branchLoc	Cafe	$\{\{c_1,c_2\}\}$	$c_1 \odot c_2$
μ_n	geo:branchLoc	53rd St	$\{\{c_2\},\{c_2,c_3\}\}$	$(c_2 \odot c_2) \oplus (c_2 \odot c_2) \oplus (c_2 \odot c_3)$
μ_o	geo:address	53rd St	$\{\{c_3\},\{c_2,c_3\}\}$	$(c_3 \odot c_3) \oplus (c_3 \odot c_3) \oplus (c_2 \odot c_3)$

(c)

Fig. 3. *Why*-provenance and *how*-provenance of positive SPARQL queries over Ω

to mappings obtained from the evaluation of SPARQL queries as tuples. Recall that, after the initial variable binding of triple patterns, all SPARQL operators produce and consume sets of mappings.

Figure 3 illustrates the result of $Q(\Omega)$, annotated with provenance expressions from two relational provenance models. To simplify understanding, we first show the results of two subqueries of $Q(\Omega)$ in Figure 3(a) and (b), before combining them to produce the final result in Figure 3(c). In this example, we do not show provenance expressions for some other relational provenance models (e.g., *lineage* [9], *Trio*-lineage [4], *Perm* [19]) due to space constraints, but we mention later how these models compare to the presented ones, in terms of expressiveness.

To highlight the main characteristics and differences of the relational provenance models selected for our study (see the corresponding columns of Figure 3(a)-(c)), we will focus on the provenance of the last tuple $\mu_o = (\text{geo:address}, 53^{rd} \text{ St})$ in the result of $Q(\Omega)$ which was produced by three derivations (involving mappings). One is obtained as a projection of $\mu_e = (\text{MoMA}, \text{geo:address}, 53^{rd} \text{ St})$ from subquery $\pi_{?x,?y}(\Omega) \bowtie \pi_{?x,?z}(\Omega)$ (Figure 3(a)) and the other two as projections on the results of subquery $\pi_{?y,?z}(\Omega) \bowtie \pi_{?x,?z}(\Omega)$ (μ_h and μ_j in Figure 3(b)).

The *lineage* [9] of a tuple in the result of a query is the set of (provenance tokens of) source tuples that were involved *in some derivation* of that result tuple. The *why*-provenance [6] encodes all the different derivations of a tuple in the query result by storing a set of provenance tokens *for each derivation*, thus yielding a *sets of sets of provenance tokens*. In our example, derivations producing μ_e and μ_j only involve c_3, so they are both represented by the same set ($\{c_3\}$), whereas μ_h is derived by joining the mappings annotated with c_3 and c_2, and thus its why-provenance is $\{c_2,c_3\}$. As shown in Figure 3(c) the why-provenance of (geo:address, 53rd St) in the result of $Q(\Omega)$ is the union of these sets. Intuitively, each inner set represents one or more derivations that involve the same source data, while multiple tokens in an inner set, such as $\{c_2,c_3\}$, indicate a join between the corresponding tuples. On the other hand, lineage uses a single set to represent all derivations, i.e., the lineage of (geo:address, 53rd St) in the result of $Q(\Omega)$ would be $\{c_2,c_3\}$.

The provenance model of *Perm* [19] is very similar to why-provenance for positive queries (its main difference is that it captures a form of relational negation). *Trio*-lineage [4] extends the model of why-provenance by also recording information about different ways in which the same set of source tuples contributes in the query result, resulting in a *bag* of sets of tokens, each of which corresponds to one derivation. For instance, the Trio-lineage of (geo:address, 53rd St) in the result of $Q(\Omega)$ would be $\{\{c_3\},\{c_3\},\{c_2,c_3\}\}$.

Finally, *how*-provenance [22] encodes not only the union and join operators, but also the *number of times a tuple participates in a join*. To this end, it employs the abstract binary operator $\oplus$ to encode union and projection and $\odot$ to encode join. In our example the source triple (MoMA, geo:address, 53rd St), annotated with c_3 participates twice in the derivation of each of μ_e and μ_j and, thus, the how-provenance of each is $c_3 \odot c_3$. The derivation μ_h involves a join between the source triples (MoMA, geo:address, 53rd St) and (Starbucks, geo:branchLoc, 53rd St), annotated with c_3 and c_2 respectively, resulting in the provenance expression $c_2 \odot c_3$. Thus, as shown in last column of Figure 3, the how-provenance of (geo:address,53rd St) is $(c_3 \odot c_3) \oplus (c_3 \odot c_3) \oplus (c_2 \odot c_3)$. *How*-provenance is more informative than all other relational provenance models described above [20]. In fact, as shown in [22], it is *universal* for all provenance models (such as the aforementioned ones) that can be expressed as semirings.

5.1 Using Provenance to Assess Data Quality

As we explained above, some provenance models capture more information than others, at the expense of producing more complex provenance expressions. However, this additional complexity is necessary for various applications involving assessment of data quality [21,25,22,20]. In the rest of this paper, we focus on two such applications, namely Boolean and ranked trust assessment, to illustrate such differences in expressiveness requirements.

5.1.1 Boolean Trust Assessment

In this case we are interested in determining which tuples in the result of a query should be trusted or not, based on the trustworthiness of the source tuples.

If a tuple has a single derivation, involving joins among various source tuples, this derivation is considered trusted if all contributing source tuples are trusted. For tuples with multiple derivations, they are trusted if at least one of their derivations is trusted. This is equivalent to answering the query over the subset of the input data that is trusted [21,22]: a tuple will be returned in the result if and only if there is at least one derivation for it involving only trusted tuples.

Alternatively, if the provenance expressions have been computed and stored during the original query evaluation, they can be used to assess on demand the trustworthiness of tuples in the result of this query. The first step in this process involves assigning truth values to provenance tokens (*true* for trusted vs. *false* for untrusted tuples). For instance, in the example of Figure 3, suppose that Peter trusts triples that were contributed by John and James (i.e. assigns *true* to c_1 and c_3), but not by Alice (i.e. assigns *false* to c_2). Then, he can determine whether to trust (geo:address, 53rd St) in the query result e.g., by taking its *why*-provenance (or any of the more expressive provenance models), i.e. $\{\{c_3\},\{c_2,c_3\}\}$ and evaluating it as a Boolean expression. This can be achieved by interpreting inner sets as conjunctions (i.e., a set is *true* if all its members are *true*) and the outer set as a disjunction (i.e., it evaluates to *true* if at least one inner set evaluates to *true*). Thus Peter can conclude that (geo:address, 53rd St) should be trusted, because there exists a derivation (namely $\{c_3\}$), for which all tokens correspond to trusted source tuples (i.e., have the value *true*). Note that, for instance, lineage does not contain enough information for this kind of computation, since we cannot use it to determine if there is a derivation for (geo:address, 53rd St) that does not involve the source tuple annotated by c_2.

5.1.2   Ranked Trust Assessment

In *ranked trust* assessment [25], every source tuple is associated with a *rank*, i.e., a natural number that denotes how trusted it is. In particular, 0 is the rank of the most trusted tuples, while ∞ indicates tuples that are completely untrusted. If a tuple has multiple derivations, as a result of a union or projection operator in the query, the rank of the output tuple is the minimum rank among all derivations, i.e. that of the most trusted derivation. In the case of a join, the rank of the resulting tuple is the sum of the ranks of the input tuples. For instance, let $c_1 = 1$, $c_2 = 2$, $c_3 = 3$. Then, we can use *how*-provenance expressions to compute the rank of e.g., (geo:address, 53rd St), by substituting the provenance tokens with their values, and using min and $+$ in the place of the abstract operators $\oplus$ (union) and $\odot$ (join), respectively, and evaluating the resulting expression as follows: $min(min(c_3 + c_3, c_3 + c_3), c_2 + c_3) = min(min(3 + 3, 3 + 3), 2 + 3) = min(6, 5) = 5$. If we had employed a less expressive model for our ranked trust assessment, we would have computed an incorrect rank for (geo:address, 53rd St). For instance, consider the Trio-lineage of (geo:address, 53rd St) ($\{\{c_3\},\{c_3\},\{c_2,c_3\}\}$). If we use $+$ to combine ranks in inner sets, and min for the outer set, the evaluation would yield $min(min(c_3, c_3), c_2 + c_3) = min(min(3, 3), 2 + 3) = min(3, 5) = 3$. The reason

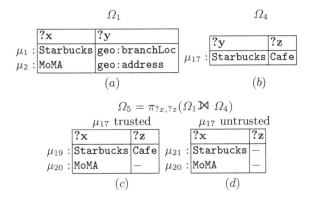

Fig. 4. Example of Boolean Trust

for the incorrect result is that Trio-lineage does not record the fact that e.g., c_3 was involved in some derivations of (geo:address, 53rd St) twice.

We conclude that Trio-lineage, as well as less expressive provenance models such as lineage, why-provenance and Perm, are not expressive enough to support ranked trust assessment, as well as that ranked trust assessment requires a more expressive provenance model than Boolean trust assessment.

6   Towards Models for Capturing SPARQL Provenance

In the previous section, we explained how relational provenance models can be adapted to capture the provenance of positive SPARQL queries. However, these models are not sufficient to capture provenance of algebraic expressions involving the ⋈ SPARQL operator. This is because ⋈ involves a form of negation (see the use of "\" in expression (1) in Section 4), while most of the aforementioned models capture the provenance of positive queries. We illustrate the challenges posed by ⋈ through an example of Boolean trust assessment explained previously[9]

Recall that, in order to compute the set of trusted mappings in the result of a SPARQL algebraic expression, we can evaluate it on the subsets of input mapping sets that include only the trusted mappings. Returning to our original example of Figure 1, assume that Peter trusts all contributors, and wants to determine whether to trust the results of the query $\Omega_5 = \pi_{?x,?z}(\Omega_1 \bowtie \Omega_4)$. As we can see in Figure 2(h) this query essentially looks for businesses located on 53rd St, and returns them, along with their type, if specified. In this case, it is easy to check that all μ_1, μ_2, μ_{17} are trusted, and thus the trusted mappings in the result of the query are as shown in Figure 4(c). Indeed, μ_{19} belongs to the result as it can be derived from two compatible and trusted mappings, μ_1 and

---

[9] The semantics of trust assessment in our example is taken by *tSPARQL* (trdf.sourceforge.net/documents/tsparql.pdf), if we apply the EnsureTrust operator to filter out untrusted mappings from input mapping sets (by setting the lower (l) and upper (u) bounds to *true*).

μ_{17}, while μ_{20} is trusted because μ_2 is trusted in Ω_1 and is not compatible with any trusted mapping of Ω_4.

On the other hand, if Peter trusts Alice and James, but not John, it is easy to check that this implies μ_1 and μ_2 are trusted, while μ_{17} is not. Thus, the expected result is what we would get from applying the $\bowtie$ operator between Ω_1 in Figure 4(a) and an empty Ω_4. Then, according to the semantics of $\bowtie$, the trusted mappings in the result of this query would be as shown in Figure 4(d). In particular, μ_{21} appears in this result as trusted, because μ_1 is not compatible with any trusted mapping in Ω_4.

When using abstract provenance models for computations such as the one in the example above, we need to materialize provenance expressions over provenance tokens during query evaluation, without depending on the particular values that those tokens may take for specific annotation computations. Thus, to handle cases such as in the example above, an abstract provenance model would need to associate appropriate provenance expressions with both μ_{19} and μ_{21}, even though they cannot both appear in the result of the same annotation computation (e.g., they can never both be trusted at the same time). Unfortunately, none of the existing relational provenance models [8,20] meets this requirement.

Among those models, *Perm* captures some form of negation in relational algebra, but does not record sufficient information for enabling annotation computations such as the Boolean trust assessment in the example above. More precisely, Perm records the reason why μ_{20} exists in the result, i.e. that μ_2 is not compatible with μ_{17}. However, it does not encode any provenance expression for μ_{21}. Thus, when μ_{17} is untrusted, it has no way to infer that μ_{21} should appear in the result as trusted.

M-semirings [18] is a recent extension of *how*-provenance for capturing the relational minus operator. To this end, it defines an additional abstract operator, denoted by $\ominus$. To compute provenance expressions for our running example, the m-semiring model would employ equation (1) for Ω_5. The provenance expressions for mappings in Ω_5 are computed in the same manner as in the case of *how*-provenance. For example, the provenance of μ_{19} is $c_1 \odot c_3$, where c_1 (resp. c_3) is the provenance of μ_1 (resp. μ_{17}) in Ω_1 (resp. Ω_4). The $\ominus$ operator is employed to compute the provenance of mappings in $\Omega_1 \setminus \Omega_4$. In particular, the provenance of μ_{20} is $c_2 \ominus 0$, where c_2 is the provenance of μ_2 in Ω_1, while 0 denotes that μ_2 does not belong to Ω_4. According to the formal properties of $\ominus$, $c_2 \ominus 0 = c_2$. Moreover, the provenance of μ_{21} is $c_1 \ominus c_3$. Consequently, in the case that μ_{17} is untrusted, m-semirings infer that μ_{21} should appear in the result as trusted. However, m-semirings follow the semantics of relational minus, which differs from the semantics of $\setminus$ in SPARQL algebra. Suppose, for instance, that Ω_4 had an additional mapping $\mu_{22} = \{(?y, b), (?z, e)\}$, that is compatible with μ_1. Then μ_{21} would appear in the result as trusted (as shown in Table (d) of Figure 4), only if *both* μ_{17} and μ_{22} were untrusted. However, the m-semiring expression for μ_{21} can only encode a single mapping of Ω_4 in the "negative" part of its provenance expression (i.e., on the right of the $\ominus$ operator).

Recently, Damasio et al. [10] proposed an approach that employs m-semirings to capture the semantics of SPARQL query answering over annotated RDF. This approach does not use the $\ominus$ operator to capture the semantics of SPARQL difference directly, but instead encodes SPARQL difference through a complex relational expression involving joins, relational set difference and duplicate elimination. Then, they use (m, δ)-semirings which are m-semirings extended with a duplicate elimination operator δ, as introduced in [18]. However, the resulting annotations reflect this complex encoding of SPARQL difference and thus do not provide a very intuitive description of the actual operations in the original query (e.g., in contrast to how-provenance expressions for relational queries). Moreover, both (m, δ)-semirings and m-semirings have the same deficiency, in terms of their suitability as the foundation for a provenance model: their universal structure does not allow for a simple representation of its elements and is completely symbolic and not amenable to algebraic manipulation. For instance, because of this difficulty, Damasio et al. [10] resort to a simpler model in order to compute trust annotations, by fixing the duplicate elimination function δ. However, as a result, they disregard all (m, δ)-semirings with a more complex δ for such computations.

Finally, Amsterdamer et.al. [1] obtained an alternative semantics for relational difference based on their semantics for queries with *aggregation* on annotated relations, through an encoding of difference using aggregation. Interestingly, the semantics of the difference defined in this manner seems similar to the semantics of SPARQL difference. However, similarly to the case of Damasio et al. [10], the resulting annotations reflect the encoding of difference through aggregation, instead of the actual operators in a SPARQL query. Moreover, Amsterdamer et.al. [1] do not propose a universal object that could be used as the provenance model for queries with difference under these semantics.

We conclude that a new provenance model is needed in order to cope with the $\bowtie$ operator. In this model, provenance expressions should be recorded even for some mappings that do not appear in the un-annotated result of a query involving the $\bowtie$ operator, such as μ_{21} in Ω_5 in the example of Figure 4(c). Note that a similar need arises if we want to support such annotation computations over relational queries involving left (or right) outer joins. However, such a new provenance model for SPARQL cannot be based on techniques used in relational provenance models to deal with relational minus, due to the differences (see also section 4.1) between the SPARQL algebra operator "\" and the relational minus. In particular, the provenance expression of a mapping should encode information about *all* compatible mappings in the right-hand mapping set, while in the relational case it suffices to encode information about a single tuple in the right-hand relation. Finally, the provenance expression for the \ operator should conform to SPARQL semantics for cardinalities of the corresponding mappings, as explained in Section 4.1.

To address this need, in a recent paper with Geerts [16] we propose a new algebraic structure for capturing the semantics of SPARQL difference, and define *spm-semirings*, an extension of semirings with a new operation that has a universal structure and provides a concise representation of the provenance of RDF data and SPARQL queries involved.

7   Conclusions

In this paper, we investigated the extent to which relational provenance models can be leveraged for SPARQL queries over linked open data. More specifically, we discussed how implicit provenance information of SPARQL query results can be used to compute annotations reflecting various dimensions of linked data quality, such as Boolean and ranked trust. We have identified a SPARQL fragment for which provenance models for positive relational queries can be leveraged, despite the subtle differences between the semantics of SPARQL and relational algebra operators. Finally, we have highlighted the limitations of relational provenance models for capturing the semantics of the SPARQL OPTIONAL operator. This is mainly due to the semantic discrepancies between the SPARQL algebra operator "\" and the relational minus operator. For this reason, we have advocated the need for a new abstract provenance model capturing the full expresiveness of SPARQL. We are currently working on the formalization of this model.

Acknowledgments. Work partially supported by the NoE *APARSEN* (Alliance Permanent Access to the Records of Science in Europe, FP7, Proj. No 269977).

References

1. Amsterdamer, Y., Deutch, D., Tannen, V.: Provenance for Aggregate Queries. In: PODS (2011)
2. Arenas, M., Pérez, J.: Querying Semantic Web Data with SPARQL. In: PODS (2011)
3. Artz, D., Gil, Y.: A Survey of Trust in Computer Science and the Semantic Web. Web Semantics 5(2) (2007)
4. Benjelloun, O., Sarma, A.D., Halevy, A.Y., Widom, J.: ULDBs: Databases with Uncertainty and Lineage. In: VLDB (2006)
5. Buneman, P., Cheney, J., Vansummeren, S.: On the Expressiveness of Implicit Provenance in Query and Update Languages. ACM TODS 33(4) (2008)
6. Buneman, P., Khanna, S., Tan, W.-C.: Why and Where: A Characterization of Data Provenance. In: Van den Bussche, J., Vianu, V. (eds.) ICDT 2001. LNCS, vol. 1973, pp. 316–330. Springer, Heidelberg (2000)
7. Carroll, J.J., Bizer, C., Hayes, P.J., Stickler, P.: Named Graphs. Web Semantics 3(4) (2005)
8. Cheney, J., Chiticariu, L., Tan, W.C.: Provenance in Databases: Why, Where and How. Foundations and Trends in Databases 1(4) (2009)
9. Cui, Y., Widom, J.: Lineage Tracing for General Data Warehouse Transformations. In: VLDB (2001)
10. Damásio, C.V., Analyti, A., Antoniou, G.: Provenance for SPARQL queries. In: Cudré-Mauroux, P., et al. (eds.) ISWC 2012, Part I. LNCS, vol. 7649, pp. 625–640. Springer, Heidelberg (2012)

11. Davidson, S.B., Freire, J.: Provenance and scientific workflows: challenges and opportunities. In: SIGMOD (2008)
12. Dividino, R., Sizov, S., Staab, S., Schueler, B.: Querying for Provenance, Trust, Uncertainty and other Meta Knowledge in RDF. Web Semantics 7(3) (2009)
13. Flouris, G., Fundulaki, I., Pediaditis, P., Theoharis, Y., Christophides, V.: Coloring RDF Triples to Capture Provenance. In: Bernstein, A., Karger, D.R., Heath, T., Feigenbaum, L., Maynard, D., Motta, E., Thirunarayan, K. (eds.) ISWC 2009. LNCS, vol. 5823, pp. 196–212. Springer, Heidelberg (2009)
14. Freire, J., Koop, D., Santos, E., Silva, C.T.: Provenance for Computational Tasks: A Survey. CiSE 10(3) (2008)
15. Fuhr, N., Rölleke, T.: A Probabilistic Relational Algebra for the Integration of Information Retrieval and Database Systems. ACM TOIS 14(1) (1997)
16. Geerts, F., Karvounarakis, G., Christophides, V., Fundulaki, I.: Algebraic Structures for Capturing the Provenance of SPARQL Queries (submitted for publication)
17. Geerts, F., Kementsietsidis, A., Milano, D.: MONDRIAN: Annotating and Querying Databases through Colors and Blocks. In: ICDE (2006)
18. Geerts, F., Poggi, A.: On Database Query Languages for K-Relations. Applied Logic 8(2) (2010)
19. Glavic, B., Alonso, G.: Perm: Processing Provenance and Data on the Same Data Model through Query Rewriting. In: ICDE (2009)
20. Green, T.J.: Containment of Conjunctive Queries on Annotated Relations. Theory of Computing Systems 49(2) (2011)
21. Green, T.J., Karvounarakis, G., Ives, Z.G., Tannen, V.: Update Exchange with Mappings and Provenance. In: VLDB (2007)
22. Green, T.J., Karvounarakis, G., Tannen, V.: Provenance Semirings. In: PODS (2007)
23. Heath, T., Bizer, C.: Linked Data: Evolving the Web into a Global Data Space. Synthesis Lectures on the Semantic Web. Morgan & Claypool Publishers (2011)
24. Imielinski, T., Lipski, W.: Incomplete Information in Relational Databases. JACM 31(4) (1984)
25. Karvounarakis, G., Ives, Z.G., Tannen, V.: Querying Data Provenance. In: SIGMOD (2010)
26. Lian, X., Chen, L.: Efficient Query Answering in Probabilistic RDF graphs. In: SIGMOD, pp. 157–168. ACM (2011)
27. Manola, F., Miller, E., McBride, B.: RDF Primer (February 2004), http://www.w3.org/TR/rdf-primer
28. Mumick, I.S., Shmueli, O.: Finiteness Properties of Database Queries. In: ADC (1993)
29. Pérez, J., Arenas, M., Gutierrez, C.: Semantics and Complexity of SPARQL. ACM TODS 34(3) (2009)
30. Prud'hommeaux, E., Seaborne, A.: SPARQL Query Language for RDF (January 2008), http://www.w3.org/TR/rdf-sparql-query
31. Udrea, O., Recupero, D.R., Subrahmanian, V.S.: Annotated RDF. ACM Trans. Comput. Logic 11(2), 10:1–10:41 (2010)

First-Order Provenance Games

Sven Köhler[1], Bertram Ludäscher[1], and Daniel Zinn[2]

[1] Dept. of Computer Science, University of California, Davis
{svkoehler,ludaesch}@ucdavis.edu
[2] LogicBlox, Inc.
daniel.zinn@logicblox.com

Abstract. We propose a new model of provenance, based on a game-theoretic approach to query evaluation. First, we study games G in their own right, and ask how to explain that a position x in G is won, lost, or drawn. The resulting notion of *game provenance* is closely related to winning strategies, and excludes from provenance all "bad moves", i.e., those which unnecessarily allow the opponent to improve the outcome of a play. In this way, the value of a position is determined by its game provenance. We then define *provenance games* by viewing the evaluation of a first-order query as a game between two players who argue whether a tuple is in the query answer. For $\mathcal{RA}^+$ queries, we show that game provenance is equivalent to the most general semiring of provenance polynomials $\mathbb{N}[X]$. Variants of our game yield other known semirings. However, unlike semiring provenance, game provenance also provides a "built-in" way to handle negation and thus to answer *why-not* questions: In (provenance) games, the reason why x is *not* won, is the same as why x is *lost* or *drawn* (the latter is possible for games with draws). Since first-order provenance games are draw-free, they yield a new provenance model that combines *how-* and *why-not* provenance.

1 Introduction

A number of provenance models have been developed in recent years that aim at explaining why and how tuples in a query result $Q(D)$ are related to tuples in the input database D (see [5,16] for recent surveys). Motivated by applications in data warehousing, Cui *et al.* [6] defined a notion of data *lineage* to trace backward which tuples in D contributed to the result. Buneman *et al.* [4] refined and formalized new forms of *why-* and *where*-provenance, and introduced a notion of (minimal) witness basis to do so. Later, Green *et al.* [14] proposed a form of *how*-provenance through *provenance semirings* that emerged as an elegant, unifying framework for provenance. For $\mathcal{RA}^+$ (positive relational algebra) queries, provenance semirings form a hierarchy [11], with *provenance polynomials* $\mathbb{N}[X]$ as the most informative semiring at the top (i.e., providing the most detailed account *how* a result was derived), and other semirings with "coarser" provenance information below, e.g., *Boolean provenance polynomials* $\mathbb{B}[X]$ [11], *Trio* provenance [3], *why*-provenance [4], and *lineage* [6]. The key idea of the unifying framework is to annotate each tuple in the input database D with an element from a semiring K and then propagate K-annotations through query evaluation. Semiring-style provenance support has been added to practical systems, e.g., ORCHESTRA [13] and LogicBlox [15]. However, the semiring approach does not extend easily to negation and other non-monotonic constructs, thus spawning further research [10,12,1,2].

V. Tannen et al. (Eds.): Buneman Festschrift, LNCS 8000, pp. 382–399, 2013.

In this paper, we take a fresh look at provenance by employing *games*. Game theory has a long history and many applications, e.g., in logic, computer science, biology, and economics. The first formal theorem in the theory of games was published by Ernst Zermelo exactly 100 years ago [21].[1] In 1928, von Neumann's paper "*Zur Theorie der Gesellschaftsspiele*" [17] marked the beginning of game theory as a field. In it he asks (and answers) the question of how a player should move to achieve a good outcome. We employ such "good" moves to define a natural notion of provenance for games G, which we call *game provenance* $\Gamma (= \Gamma_G)$, and which is thus closely related to *winning strategies*. The crux is that by considering only "good" moves while ignoring "bad" ones, one can get a game-theoretic explanation for why a position is won, lost, or drawn, respectively. By viewing query evaluation as a game, we can then apply game provenance to obtain an elegant new provenance approach we call *provenance games*.

Game Plan. In Section 2 we introduce basic concepts and terminology for games G and show how to solve them using a form of backward induction. We then discuss the regular structure inherent in solved games G^γ and use it to define our notion of game provenance Γ. The solved positions imply a labeling of moves as "good" or "bad", which we use to define the game provenance $\Gamma(x)$ of position x as the subgraph of G, reachable from x without "bad" moves. The value of a position is determined by its game provenance, and it captures why and how a position is won, lost, or drawn.

In Section 3 we propose to apply game provenance to first-order (FO) queries in Datalog$^\neg$ form, by viewing the evaluation of query Q on database D as a game $G_{Q,D}$. By construction, our *provenance games* yield the standard semantics for FO queries. For positive relational queries $\mathcal{RA}^+$, game provenance $\Gamma_{Q,D}$ is equivalent to the most general semiring of provenance polynomials $\mathbb{N}[X]$. Variations of the provenance game yield other semirings, e.g., $\mathsf{Trio}(X)$. While provenance games are equivalent to provenance semirings for positive queries, the former also handles negation seamlessly, as complementary claims and negation are inherent in games. Provenance games can thus also answer *why-not* questions easily: The explanation for why x is *not* won is the same as why x is lost (or drawn, for games that are not draw-free). Since provenance games are always draw-free for first-order queries, we obtain a simple and elegant provenance model for FO that combines how-provenance and why-not provenance. In Section 4 we conclude and suggest some future work.

2   Games

We consider games as graphs $G = (V, M)$, where two players move alternately between *positions* V along the edges (*moves*) $M \subseteq V \times V$. We assume that G is finite, i.e., $|V| < \infty$,[2] but game graphs can have cycles and thus still may result in infinite plays. Each $v_0 \in V$ defines a game $G^{v_0} = (V, M, v_0)$ starting at v_0. A *play* $\pi \ (=\pi_{v_0})$ of G^{v_0} is a (finite or infinite) sequence of edges

$$v_0 \to v_1 \to v_2 \to \cdots \tag{π}$$

---

[1] Some confusion prevails about Zermelo's theorem, but it is all sorted out in [18].

[2] Many game-theoretic notions and results carry over to the transfinite case; cf. [7].

where for all $i = 0, 1, 2, \ldots$ the edge $v_i \to v_{i+1}$ is a move $(v_i, v_{i+1}) \in M$. A play π is *complete*, either if it is infinite, or if it ends after $n = |\pi|$ moves in a sink of the game graph. The player who cannot move loses the play, while the previous player (who made the last possible move) wins it. If $|\pi| = 2k + 1$, that is, $\pi =$

$$v_0 \xrightarrow{\text{I}} v_1 \xrightarrow{\text{II}} v_2 \xrightarrow{\text{I}} \cdots \xrightarrow{\text{II}} v_{2k} \xrightarrow{\text{I}} v_{2k+1} \qquad \text{(I moves last)}$$

then v_o is *won* (for I) in π. Conversely, if II moves last, then $|\pi| = 2k$ for some $\pi =$

$$v_0 \xrightarrow{\text{I}} v_1 \xrightarrow{\text{II}} v_2 \xrightarrow{\text{I}} \cdots \xrightarrow{\text{II}} v_{2k} \qquad \text{(II moves last)}$$

so v_o is *lost* (for I) in π, because II wins the play. A play π of infinite length is a *draw* (in *finite* games G, this means that M must have a cycle).

The Value of a Position: Playing Optimally. Assume v_0 is won in π, i.e., $|\pi| = 2k+1$ moves were played, starting with player I at v_0, then II got stuck at a sink, so I won. But what if II made a "bad move" along the way in π, i.e., missed an opportunity to win or at least draw? Then although I won this play π, I may not be able to *force* a win, if II avoids bad moves and plays optimally. We are not interested in plays π that involve bad moves. To determine the *value* of a position (i.e., independent of a particular play π), we consider plays where the opponents play optimal (or at least "good enough") so that the best possible outcome is guaranteed. More formally, we define:

A *strategy* is a partial mapping $S : V \to V$ with $S \subseteq M$. Position v_0 is *won for player* I in (at most) n moves, if there is a strategy S_{I}, such that for all strategies S_{II}, there is a number $j = 2k + 1 \le n$ such that $v_j = S_{\text{I}} \circ (S_{\text{II}} \circ S_{\text{I}})^k (v_0)$ is defined, but $S_{\text{II}}(v_j)$ is not: II cannot move. In this case, S_{I} is a *winning strategy* for I at v_0. Conversely, v_0 is *won for player* II in (at most) n moves, if there is a strategy S_{II}, such that for all strategies S_{I}, there is a number $j = 2k \le n$ such that $v_j = (S_{\text{II}} \circ S_{\text{I}})^k (v_0)$ is defined, but $S_{\text{I}}(v_j)$ is not: I cannot move. Finally, the *value* of v_0 is *won* (*lost*) if it is won for player I (player II). If v_0 is neither won nor lost, its value is *drawn*, so neither I nor II can force a win from v_0, but both can avoid losing via an infinite play.

2.1 Solving Games: Labeling Nodes

Let $G = (V, M)$ be the game in Figure 1(a). How can we *solve* G, i.e., determine whether the value of $x \in V$ is won, lost, or drawn? We represent the value of x using a node labeling $\gamma : V \to \{\text{W}, \text{L}, \text{D}\}$ and write $G^\gamma = (V, M, \gamma)$ to denote a solved game.

The following Datalog$^\neg$ query, consisting of a single rule, solves games:

$$\text{win}(X) :- \text{move}(X, Y), \neg\text{win}(Y) \qquad (Q_G)$$

Q_G says that position x is won in G if there is a move to position y, where y is not won. For non-stratified Datalog$^\neg$ programs like Q_G (having recursion through negation), the three-valued *well-founded model* $\mathcal{W}$ [20] provides the desired answer:

Proposition 1 (Q_G Solves Games). *Let* $P := (Q_G \cup \text{move})$ *be the Datalog$^\neg$ query* Q_G *plus finitely many "*move*" facts, representing a game* $G = (V, M)$*. For all* $x \in V$*:*

$$\mathcal{W}_P(\text{win}(x)) = \left\{ \begin{array}{l} \text{true} \\ \text{false} \\ \text{undef} \end{array} \right\} \quad \Leftrightarrow \quad \gamma(x) = \left\{ \begin{array}{l} \text{W} \\ \text{L} \\ \text{D} \end{array} \right\}.$$

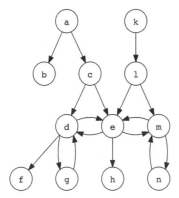
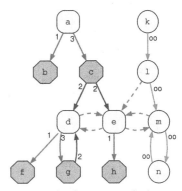

(a) What are the "good moves", e.g., in position e? Is e won (or lost, or drawn), and if so how?

(b) The solved game reveals the answer: move e→h is winning; the moves e→d and e→m are not.

Fig. 1. Position values in game G (left) are revealed by the solved game $G^\gamma = (V, M, \gamma)$ on the right: positions are *won* (green boxes), *lost* (red octagons), or *drawn* (yellow circles). This separates provenance-relevant moves (solid, colored arcs), from irrelevant "bad" ones (dashed, gray). The length ℓ of a move $x \xrightarrow{\ell} y$ indicates how quickly one can force a win, or how long one can delay a loss, using that move.

When implemented via an alternating fixpoint [19], one obtains an increasing sequence of underestimates $U_1 \subseteq U_2 \subseteq \ldots$ converging to the true atoms U^ω from below, and a decreasing sequence of overestimates $O_1 \supseteq O_2 \supseteq \ldots$ converging to O^ω, the union of true or undefined atoms from above. Any remaining atoms in the "gap" have the third truth-value (undef). For the game query Q_G above, U^ω contains the won positions V^W; the "gap" (if any) $O^\omega \setminus U^\omega$ contains the drawn positions V^D; and the atoms in the complement of O^ω (i.e., which are neither true nor undefined) are the lost positions V^L.

To solve G directly, consider, e.g., the three moves e→d, e→h, and e→m in Fig. 1(a). The move e→h is clearly winning, as it forces the opponent into a sink. However, the status of the moves e→d and e→m is unclear unless the game has been solved. Fig. 1(b) depicts the solved game G^γ. The set of positions is a disjoint union $V = V^W \dot\cup V^L \dot\cup V^D$.

To obtain G^γ, proceed as follows: First, find all *sinks* x, i.e., nodes for which the set of *followers* $F(x) = \{y \mid (x, y) \in M\}$ is empty. These positions are immediately lost and colored red: $V_0^L = \{x \in V \mid F(x) = \emptyset\}$. In our example, $V_0^L = \{b, f, h\}$. We then find all nodes x for which there is *some* y with $(x, y) \in M$ such that $y \in V_0^L$. These positions are won and colored green; here: $V_1^W = \{a, d, e\}$. We then find the unlabeled nodes x for which *all* followers $y \in F(x)$ are already won (i.e., colored green). Since the player moving from that position can only move to a position that is won for the opponent, those x are also *lost* and added to V_2^L. In our example $V_2^L = \{c, g\}$. We now iterate the above steps until there is no more change. One can show that $V_1^W \subseteq V_3^W \subseteq V_5^W \cdots$ converges to the won positions V^W, whereas $V_0^L \subseteq V_2^L \subseteq V_4^L \cdots$ converges to the lost positions V^L; the drawn positions are $V^D := V \setminus (V^W \cup V^L)$.

Algorithm 1. Compute solution $G^\gamma = (V, M, \gamma)$

$V^W := \emptyset$;   // Initially we don't know any won positions
$V^L := \{x \in V \mid \mathsf{F}(x) = \emptyset\}$;   // ... but all sinks are lost ...
$\text{len}(x) := 0$ for all $x \in V^L$;   // ... immediately: their length is 0.
repeat
    for $x \in V \setminus (V^W \cup V^L)$ **do**
        $F^L := \mathsf{F}(x) \cap V^L$; $F^W := \mathsf{F}(x) \cap V^W$;
        if $F^L \neq \emptyset$ **then**
            $V^W := V^W \cup \{x\}$;   // **some** $y \in \mathsf{F}(x)$ is lost, so x is **won**
            $\text{len}(x) := 1 + \min\{\text{len}(y) \mid y \in F^L\}$;   // shortest win
        if $\mathsf{F}(x) = F^W$ **then**
            $V^L := V^L \cup \{x\}$;   // **all** $y \in \mathsf{F}(x)$ are won, so x is **lost**
            $\text{len}(x) := 1 + \max\{\text{len}(y) \mid y \in F^W\}$;   // longest delay
until V^W and V^L *change no more*;
$V^D := V \setminus (V^W \cup V^L)$;   // remaining positions are now draws
$\text{len}(x) := \infty$ for all $x \in V^D$;   // ... and can be delayed forever
$\gamma(x) := \mathsf{W}/\mathsf{L}/\mathsf{D}$ for all $x \in V^W/V^L/V^D$, respectively.

Algorithm 1 depicts the details of a simple, round-based approach to solve games. In it, we also compute the *length* of a position, which adds further information to a solved game G^γ, i.e., how quickly one can win (starting from green nodes), or how long one can delay losing (starting from red nodes). In Fig. 1, the (delay) length of f is 0, since f is a sink and no move is possible. In contrast, the (win) length of d is 1: the next player moving wins by moving to f. For g, the (delay) length is 2, since the player can move to d, but the opponent can then move to f. So g is lost in 2 moves.

Remark. As described, Algorithm 1 proceeds in *rounds* to determine the value of positions, i.e., in each round i, *all* newly won positions, and *all* newly lost positions are determined. This could be used, e.g., to simplify the computation of the length of a position ($\text{len}(x)$ can be derived from the first round in which the value of x becomes known). On the other hand, this is not strictly necessary: one can replace the **for**-loop ranging over all unlabeled nodes by a non-deterministic **pick** of any unlabeled node. As long as we pick nodes in a fair manner, the non-deterministic version will also converge to the correct result, while allowing more flexibility during evaluation [22].

2.2 Game Provenance: Labeling Edges

We return to our original question: why is $x \in V$ won, lost, or drawn? We would like to define a suitable notion of *game provenance* $\Gamma(x)$ that is similar in spirit to the how-provenance devised for positive queries [14], but that works for games and explains the value (won, lost, or drawn) of x. Some desiderata of game provenance are immediate: First, only nodes *reachable* from x can influence the outcome at x, i.e., only nodes and edges in the transitive closure $\mathsf{F}^+(x)$. Thus, one expects $\Gamma(x)$ to depend only on

	y *won* (W)	y *drawn* (D)	y *lost* (L)
x *won* (W)	*bad*	*bad*	g: *winning*
x *drawn* (D)	*bad*	y: *drawing*	*n/a*
x *lost* (L)	r: *delaying*	*n/a*	*n/a*

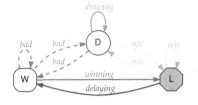

Fig. 2. Depending on node labels, moves $x \to y$ are either *winning* (or *green*) (W $\overset{g}{\rightsquigarrow}$ L), *delaying* (or *red*) (L $\overset{r}{\rightsquigarrow}$ W), or *drawing* (or *yellow*) (D $\overset{y}{\rightsquigarrow}$ D). All other moves are either *bad* (allowing the opponent to improve the outcome), or non-existent (*n/a*): e.g., if x is lost, then there are only delaying moves (i.e., ending in won positions y for the opponent).

$\mathsf{F}^+(x)$. In addition, one expects the value $\gamma(x)$ of position x to be independent of "bad moves", i.e., which give the opponent a better outcome than necessary. We use a partial edge-labeling function λ to distinguish different types of moves.

Definition 1 (Edge Labels). Let $G^\gamma = (V, M, \gamma)$ be a solved game. The edge-labeling $\lambda : V \times V \to \{\mathsf{g}, \mathsf{r}, \mathsf{y}\}$ defines a color for a subset of edges from M as shown in Fig. 2.□

In Figure 2 we use $\gamma(x)$ and $\gamma(y)$, i.e., node labels W, D, and L of moves $(x, y) \in M$ to derive an appropriate edge label. This allows us to distinguish provenance-relevant ("good") moves (*winning*, *drawing*, or *delaying*), from irrelevant (*bad*) moves. The latter are excluded from game provenance:

Definition 2 (Game Provenance). Let $G^\gamma = (V, M, \gamma)$ be a solved game. The *game provenance* $\Gamma(=\Gamma_G)$ is the λ-colored subgraph of G^γ. For $x \in V$, we define $\Gamma(x)$ as the subgraph of Γ, reachable via λ edges.   □

Consider the solved game on the right in Fig. 1. Since bad (dashed) edges are excluded, the game provenance consists of two disconnected subgraphs: (i) The bipartite "red-green" subgraph, which is draw-free, i.e., every position is either won or lost, and (ii) the "yellow" subgraph, representing the drawn positions.

The figure also reveals that solved games G^γ and thus game provenance Γ have a nice, regular structure. The following is immediate from the underlying game-theoretic semantics of G.

Theorem 1 (Provenance Structure). *Let* $G^\gamma = (G, M, \gamma)$ *be a solved game,* Γ *its edge-labeled provenance graph. The game provenance* Γ *has a regular structure:*

$$\Gamma(x) = \begin{cases} M_{\mathsf{g}.(\mathsf{r}.\mathsf{g})^*}(x) \; ; \textit{if } x \textit{ is won} \\ M_{(\mathsf{r}.\mathsf{g})^*}(x) \quad ; \textit{if } x \textit{ is lost} \\ M_{\mathsf{y}^+}(x) \qquad ; \textit{if } x \textit{ is drawn} \end{cases}$$

Here, for a regular expression R, and a node $x \in V$, the expression $M_R(x)$ denotes a subset of labeled edges of M, i.e., for which there is a path π in Γ whose labels match the expression R. As we shall see below, for positive queries, the bipartite structure of won and lost nodes nicely corresponds to the structure of provenance polynomials [16].

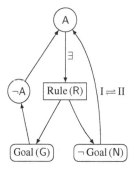

Move	Claim made by making the move
$A \overset{\exists}{\leadsto} R$	"A is true: it's the head of this instance of R."
$R \leadsto G$	"Positive goal $g_k(=A')$ in your rule body fails!"
$G \leadsto \neg A$	"No! Its negation $\neg A'$ fails and A' is true."
$\neg A \leadsto A$	"No: atom A' fails! I dare you to prove it."
$R \leadsto N$	"Negative goal $\neg A'$ in the rule body fails."
$N \leadsto A$	"No: $\neg A'$ succeeds, but A' fails."

Fig. 3. Move types of the query evaluation game (left) and implicit claims made (right). Moving along an edge, a player aims to verify a claim, thereby refuting the opponent. Initially, player I is a verifier, trying to prove A, while II tries to spoil this attempt and refute it. Roles are swapped (I $\rightleftharpoons$ II) when moving through a negated goal (R$\leadsto$N$\leadsto$A).

3   Provenance Games

The game semantics (avoiding bad moves) yields a natural model of provenance. We now apply this notion to queries expressed using non-recursive Datalog$^\neg$ rules. Any first-order query $\varphi(\bar{x})$ on input database D can be expressed as a non-recursive Datalog$^\neg$ program Q_φ with a distinguished relation ans $\in idb(Q_\varphi)$ [3] such that evaluating Q_φ with input D under the stratified semantics[4] agrees with the result of $\varphi(\bar{x})$. In the following we use $Q(D)$ to denote the result of evaluating Q on input D.

3.1   Query Evaluation Games

Query evaluation of $Q(D)$ can be seen as a game between players I and II who argue whether an atom $A \in Q(D)$ is true. The argumentation structure is stylized in Fig. 3. There are three classes of positions in the game as shown on the left of Figure 3:

- Relation nodes—depicted as circles,
- Rule nodes—depicted as rectangles, and
- Goal nodes—depicted as rectangles with rounded corners.

Both relation nodes and goal nodes can be positive or negative.

Usually, an evaluation game starts with I claiming that a ground atom $A(x)$ is true. That is she starts the game in a relation node for A. To substantiate her claim she moves to a rule that has A as a head atom and specifies constants for the remaining existentially quantified variables in the body of the rule. Now, II tries to reject the validity of the rule by selecting a goal atom (e.g., B) in its body that he thinks is not satisfied (e.g., II moves to the goal node for B). I then moves to a negated relation node for this goal (eg, a node $\neg B$), claiming the goal is true because its negation is false. From here,

---

[3] The arity of ans matches that of $\varphi(\bar{x})$.

[4] which coincides with the well-founded semantics on non-recursive Datalog$^\neg$

II moves to the relation node B, questioning I's claim that B is true. The game then continues in the same way. Note that the graph on the left of in Fig. 3 is a schema-level description. When one cycle (relation$\leadsto$rule$\leadsto$goal$\leadsto\neg$relation$\leadsto$relation) is complete, the actual fact that is argued about has changed (e.g., from A to B). If II selects a negated goal (e.g., $\neg C$) in the body of a rule then player I moves directly from the negated goal node to the relation node for C. This essentially switches the roles of I and II since now player II has to argue for a relation node C.

We now demonstrate the general argumentation scheme for a concrete Datalog$^{\neg}$ program Q_{neg}. The program Q_{neg} consists of a single rule r_1:

$$r_1: \quad \text{A}(X) :- \underbrace{\text{B}(X,Y)}_{g_1}, \underbrace{\neg\text{C}(Y)}_{g_2} \qquad\qquad (Q_{\text{neg}})$$

The game diagram for Q_{neg} is shown in Fig. 4a. Player I starts in a relation node $A(x)$ to prove that $\text{A}(x) \in Q(D)$. In her first move, she picks the rule r_1 together with bindings for all existentially quantified variables in r_1; essentially picking a ground instance $r_1(x,y)$ such that the variable X is bound to the desired x. She claims the rule body is satisfied. If this is not the case, II can falsify the claim by selecting a *goal* from the body, i.e., either $g_1^1(x,y)$, thus making a counter-claim that $\text{B}(x,y)$ is false, or $g_1^2(y)$, claiming instead that $C(y)$ is true. *Positive case,* e.g., II moved to $g_1^1(x,y)$. Player I will move from $g_1^1(x,y)$ to $\neg B(x,y)$, from which II will move to $B(x,y)$. In this node, there is an edge for player I if and only if $B(x,y) \in D$, that is if there is a trivial, bodyless rule $r_B(x,y)$ representing this fact. Thus, I wins the game if $B(x,y) \in D$ and II wins if $B(x,y) \notin D$. *Negative case,* e.g., II just moved to $g_1^2(y)$. Player I moves to $C(y)$. Here, II loses and I wins if $C(y) \notin D$; II wins the argument if $C(y) \in D$ by moving to the trivial rule node, forcing I to lose.

Construction of Evaluation Game Graph. We create a game in which the constants are also encoded within the game positions. In Fig. 4b, we provide Datalog rules that define the move relation M of the evaluation game $G_{Q_{\text{neg}},D}$ for Q_{neg} with an input database D. Here, d is a relation that contains the active domain of Q_{neg} and D.

For each ground atom, we create a postive and a negative relation node. We use Skolem functions to create "node identifiers". E.g., for a ground atom $\text{S}(a_1, \ldots, a_n)$ we use $f_S(a_1, \ldots, a_n)$ for its positive relation nodes and $f_{\neg S}(a_1, \ldots, a_n)$ for its negative relation node. The first three rules in Fig. 4b create an edge from the negative to the positive node.[5]

Furthermore, we create a *rule node* for each rule r_i in the ground program with a unique identifier $f_{r_i}(X_1, \ldots, X_n)$ including the rule number and the assignments of variables found in the rule's body to constants. For simplicity, we alphabetically order variables and provide the constants in this order. There is an edge from the ground head atom to the ground rule node (cf. Fig. 4b first line of middle block). For example, the skolem function $f_{r_1}(a,b)$ encodes the whole rule body $r1 : [B(a,b), \neg C(b)]$.

Then, we add moves from rule node r_i to its goal nodes g_i^j. Goal nodes are identified by the rule number i they occur in, their positions j within the body, and the bound

---

[5] The use of Skolems is for convenience only. We could instead use constants and increase the arity of relations accordingly, or even avoid constants [8,9].

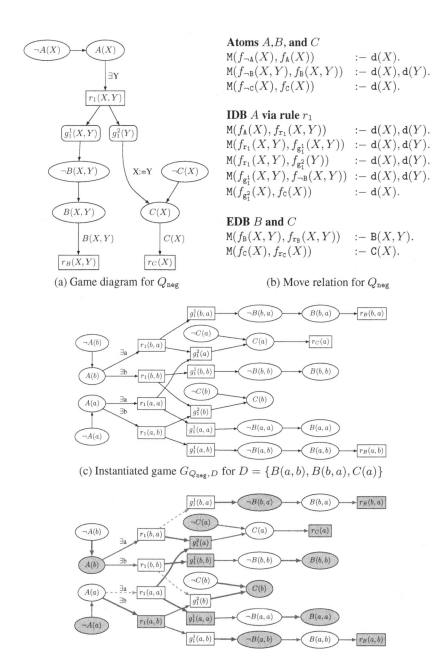

Atoms A, B, and C

$$M(f_{\neg A}(X), f_A(X)) \qquad :- d(X).$$
$$M(f_{\neg B}(X,Y), f_B(X,Y)) \quad :- d(X), d(Y).$$
$$M(f_{\neg C}(X), f_C(X)) \qquad :- d(X).$$

IDB A via rule r_1

$$M(f_A(X), f_{r_1}(X,Y)) \qquad :- d(X), d(Y).$$
$$M(f_{r_1}(X,Y), f_{g_1^1}(X,Y)) \quad :- d(X), d(Y).$$
$$M(f_{r_1}(X,Y), f_{g_1^2}(Y)) \qquad :- d(X), d(Y).$$
$$M(f_{g_1^1}(X,Y), f_{\neg B}(X,Y)) \quad :- d(X), d(Y).$$
$$M(f_{g_1^2}(X), f_C(X)) \qquad :- d(X).$$

EDB B and C

$$M(f_B(X,Y), f_{r_B}(X,Y)) \quad :- B(X,Y).$$
$$M(f_C(X), f_{r_C}(X)) \qquad :- C(X).$$

(a) Game diagram for Q_{neg} (b) Move relation for Q_{neg}

(c) Instantiated game $G_{Q_{neg},D}$ for $D = \{B(a,b), B(b,a), C(a)\}$

(d) Solved game $G^\gamma_{Q_{neg},D}$ for $D = \{B(a,b), B(b,a), C(a)\}$. Lost positions are (dark) red; won positions are (light) green. Provenance edges are solid; bad moves are depicted via dashed lines.

Fig. 4. Game diagram, and provenance game for $Q_{neg} := A(X) :- B(X,Y), \neg C(Y)$

constants. (cf. lines 2 and 3 of middle block). From positive (negative) goal nodes, we move to negative (positive) relation nodes keeping the bound constants fixed (cf. lines 4 and 5 of middle block). Finally, for edb relations, we add an edge from the positive relation node $R(\bar{c})$ to a rule node $f_{r_R}(\bar{c})$ iff $R(\bar{c}) \in D$. This ensures that a player reaching the relation node $R(\bar{c})$ wins iff $R(\bar{c}) \in D$. In Fig. 4c the game graph for Q_{neg} with input database $D = \{B(a,b), B(b,a), C(a)\}$ is shown. The solved game is shown in Fig. 4d. Here, we see that I has a winning strategy for e.g., $A(a)$, $B(b,a)$, and $C(a)$.

Acyclicity of FO Games. For FO queries, represented by non-recursive Datalog⁻ programs, no relation node is reachable from itself and the resulting game graph is acyclic.

Theorem 2 (FO Provenance Game). *Consider a first-order query φ in the form of a non-recursive Datalog⁻ program Q_φ with output relation* ans *and input database facts D. Let $G^\gamma_{Q_\varphi,D} = (V, M, \gamma)$ be the solved game. Then:*

1. $G^\gamma_{Q_\varphi,D}$ is draw-free.

$$2. \ Q_\varphi(\, \text{ans}(\bar{x})\,) = \begin{Bmatrix} \text{true} \\ \text{false} \end{Bmatrix} \Leftrightarrow \gamma(\, f_{\text{ans}}(\bar{x})\,) = \begin{Bmatrix} \text{W} \\ \text{L} \end{Bmatrix}$$

Sketch. It is easy to see that one can associate with every non-recursive Datalog⁻ program Q and input D an evaluation game graph $G_{Q,D}$ together with a solved game $G^\gamma_{Q,D}$. Since the game graph is acyclic, the solved game will not contain any drawn positions. This can easily be verified by an induction of how Algorithm 1 behaves on graphs without cycles. Further, by construction, $G^\gamma_{Q,D}$ models query evaluation of $Q(D)$. □

3.2 Relationship with Provenance Polynomials – How-Provenance for $\mathcal{RA}^+$

Game graphs are constructed to preserve provenance information available in program and database. It turns out that for positive Datalog programs Q they generate semiring provenance polynomials as defined in [14,16] for atoms $A(\bar{x}) \in Q(D)$.

Semiring Provenance Polynomials. Semiring provenance [14,16] attaches provenance information to EDB and IDB facts. The provenance information are elements of a commutative semiring K. A commutative semiring is an algebraic structure with two distinct associative and commutative operations "+" and "×". During query evaluation, result facts are annotated with elements from K that are created by combining the provenance information from input facts. For example, in the join R(a, b) :− S(a, b), T(a) with S(a, b) being annotated with $p_1 \in K$ and T(a) being annotated with $p_2 \in K$, the result fact R(a, b) will be annotated with $p_1 \times p_2$. Intuitively, "×" is used to combine provenance information of *joint* use of input facts, whereas "+" is used for alternative use of input facts.

Depending on the concrete semiring used, different (provenance) information is propagated during query evaluation. The *most informative*[6] semiring is the *positive algebra*

---

[6] In the sense that for any other semiring K', there exists a semiring homomorphism $\mathcal{H} : \mathbb{N}[X] \rightarrow K'$. This has important implications in practice [14,16].

provenance semiring $\mathbb{N}[X]$ [14,16] whose elements are polynomials with variables from a set X and coefficients from $\mathbb{N}$. The operators "$\times$" and "$+$" in $\mathbb{N}[X]$ are the usual addition and multiplication of polynomials. Usually, facts from the input database D are annotate by variables from a set X. Formally, we use $\mathcal{P}^{\mathbb{N}[X]}$ as a function that maps a ground atom to its provenance annotation in $\mathbb{N}[X]$.

Obtaining Semiring Polynomials from Game Provenance. Consider only positive programs, and fix an atom $A(\bar{x})$ with $A(\bar{x}) \in Q(D)$. The provenance graph $\Gamma_{Q,D}(f_{\mathtt{A}}(\bar{x})) = (V, M, \gamma)$ for $A(\bar{x})$ can easily be transformed into an operator tree for a provenance polynomial. The operator tree is represented as a DAG $G^{\Omega}(A(\bar{x}))$ in which common sub-expressions are re-used. $G^{\Omega}(A(\bar{x})) = (V', M', \delta)$ has nodes V', edges M', and node labels δ. For a fixed $A(\bar{x})$, the structures of Γ and G^{Ω} coincide, that is $V = V'$ and $M = M'$. The labeling function δ maps inner nodes to either "$+$" or "$\times$", denoting n-ary versions of the semiring operators. Leaf nodes in game provenance graphs correspond to atoms over the EDB schema. We here only assign elements from K to leaf nodes of the form $f_{\mathtt{r_R}}(\bar{x})$. Formally, the labeling function δ is defined as follows:

$$\delta(v) = \begin{cases} \mathcal{P}^{\mathbb{N}[X]}(A(\bar{x})) & \text{if } \mathsf{F}(v) = \emptyset \text{ and } v = f_{\mathtt{r_A}}(\bar{x}) \\ \text{``}\times\text{''} & \text{if } \mathsf{F}(v) \neq \emptyset \text{ and } \gamma(v) = \mathsf{L} \\ \text{``}+\text{''} & \text{if } \mathsf{F}(v) \neq \emptyset \text{ and } \gamma(v) = \mathsf{W} \end{cases} \quad (1)$$

We use Ω to denote the transformation of obtaining $G^{\Omega}(A(\bar{x}))$ from $\Gamma_{Q,D}(f_{\mathtt{A}}(\bar{x}))$. The provenance semiring polynomial of fact $A(\bar{x})$ is now explicit in $G^{\Omega}(A(\bar{x}))$. An inner node "$+$" (or "$\times$") with n children represents an n-ary version of $+$ (or $\times$) from the semiring. Since the semiring operators are associative and commutative, their n-ary versions are well-defined.

Proposition 2. *For positive Q, and $A(\bar{x}) \in Q(D)$, all leaves in $\Gamma_{Q,D}(A(\bar{x}))$ are of type $f_{\mathtt{r_B}}(X, Y)$; thus the labeling described above is complete.*

Sketch. For positive programs, positive relation nodes are reachable from other positive relation nodes over a path of length four as shown on the left side of Fig. 3. For an atom $A(\bar{x}) \in Q(D)$, all reachable rule nodes are lost and all reachable goal nodes are won.□

The following theorem relates semiring provenance polynomials to the provenance expressions we obtain in G^{Ω}:

Theorem 3. *Let $\Gamma_{Q,D}$ be the game provenance of an $\mathcal{RA}^{+}$ query Q (in the form of a positive, non-recursive Datalog program) over database D. Then $\Gamma_{Q,D}$ represents the provenance polynomials $\mathbb{N}[X]$ as follows: for all $A(\bar{x}) \in Q(D)$,*

$$\Omega \circ \Gamma_{Q,D}(f_{\mathtt{A}}(\bar{x})) \equiv \mathcal{P}_{Q,D}^{\mathbb{N}[X]}(A(\bar{x})).$$

Sketch. Our game graph construction is an extension of the graph presented in Section 4.2 of [16]. Rule nodes correspond to the join nodes presented in [16]. Named goal nodes can be seen as labels on the edges between (goal) tuple nodes and join nodes and allow us to identify at which position a tuple was used in the body. For a detailed proof, please refer to Appendix A.
□

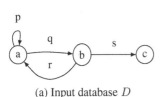

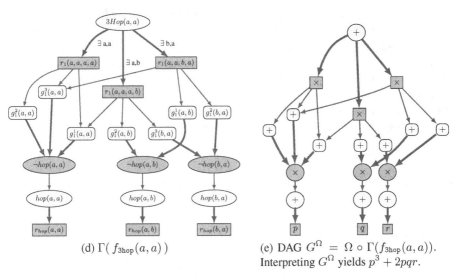

(a) Input database D

(b) Labels δ for leaf nodes of $\Gamma_{Q_{3\text{Hop}},D}$.

(c) Provenance for inner relation nodes of $\Gamma_{Q_{3\text{Hop}},D}$.

(d) $\Gamma(\,f_{3\text{hop}}(a,a)\,)$

(e) DAG $G^{\Omega} = \Omega \circ \Gamma(f_{3\text{hop}}(a,a))$. Interpreting G^{Ω} yields $p^3 + 2pqr$.

Fig. 5. Input graph for program $Q_{3\text{Hop}}$ in (a) using edge labeling according to (b). Game provenance $\Gamma_{Q_{3\text{Hop}},D}$ for the query $3\text{Hop}(\mathsf{a},\mathsf{a})$ on input database of (a) is shown in (d). When labeling leaf nodes according to (b), lost inner nodes by "×", and won inner nodes by "+" then the operator DAG G^{Ω} shown in (e) is created. This DAG represents the semiring-provenance polynomial for the query $3\text{Hop}(\mathsf{a},\mathsf{a})$ shown in (c) and [16].

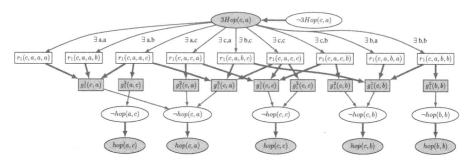

Fig. 6. Why-not provenance for 3Hop(c, a) using provenance games

Example 3hop from [16]. Consider the 3Hop query $Q_{3\text{Hop}}$ used in Figure 7 of [16]:

$$r_1: \quad 3\text{Hop}(X, Y) :- \text{hop}(X, Z_1), \text{hop}(Z_1, Z_2), \text{hop}(Z_2, Y).$$

The query uses an input database consisting of a single binary EDB relation hop representing a directed graph. It asks for pairs of nodes that are reachable via exactly three edges(=*hops*). An input database D and $\mathcal{P}_{Q_{3\text{Hop}},D}^{\mathbb{N}[X]}$ annotations of $Q_{3\text{Hop}}$ are shown in Fig. 5b. Figure 5d shows the game provenance $\Gamma(f_{3\text{Hop}}(a, a))$ of fact 3Hop(a, a). Positive won relation nodes indicate the existence of the corresponding fact in $Q_{3Hop}(D)$. To obtain the provenance polynomial of fact $f_{3\text{Hop}}(a, a)$, we apply Ω to $\Gamma(f_{3\text{Hop}}(a, a))$ as shown in Fig. 5e: we replace inner won nodes by "×", inner lost nodes by "+", and leaf nodes by their respective annotations from K as given in Fig. 5b and [16]. The so relabeled graph encodes the provenance equation

$$\Omega \circ \Gamma_{Q_{3\text{Hop}},D}(f_{3\text{Hop}}(a, a)) = (p \times p \times p) + (p \times q \times r) + (p \times q \times r) = p^3 + 2pqr$$

which is equivalent to the annotation of provenance semiring polynomials as shown in Fig. 5c and [16].

3.3 Why-Not Game Provenance for $\mathcal{RA}^+$

Game provenance also yields meaningful explanations for *why-not* questions. Consider for example the query $Q_{3\text{Hop}}$ and its input database D. The atom 3Hop(c, a) is not in $Q_{3\text{Hop}}(D)$ and we want to get an explanation why. Figure 6 shows the game provenance $\Gamma_{Q_{3\text{Hop}},D}(f_{\neg 3\text{Hop}}(c, a))$ of the missing fact 3Hop(c, a). The lost relation node 3Hop(c, a) indicates that player I will lose the argument that tries to show that 3Hop(c, a) $\in Q_{3Hop}(D)$. The game provenance explains why: Any ground instantiation of rule r_1 will be winning node for player II. Consider, e.g., moving to $r_1(c, a, a, a)$ which represents the rule instantiation for $X/c, Y/a, Z_1/a, Z_2/a$. Player II wins the game here by questioning that the first goal $g_1^1(c, a)$ is satisfied. And indeed, player I will move from $g_1^1(c, a)$ to $\neg\text{hop}(c, a)$; II to hop(c, a). Now, I loses the game since hop(c, a) $\notin D$ and thus there is no move out of hop(c, a). We also see that another rule instantiation $X/c, Y/a, Z_1/a, Z_2/b$ fails for the same reason: the missing hop(c, a). The instantiation $X/c, Y/a, Z_1/b, Z_2/a$ fails because hop(c, b) is not in the input. Other

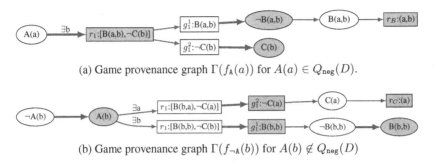

(a) Game provenance graph $\Gamma(f_A(a))$ for $A(a) \in Q_{\text{neg}}(D)$.

(b) Game provenance graph $\Gamma(f_{\neg A}(b))$ for $A(b) \notin Q_{\text{neg}}(D)$

Fig. 7. Provenance graphs for Q_{neg} with database $D = \{B(a,b), B(b,a), C(a)\}$. Both why and why-not graphs might contain leaf nodes representing existent and missing input facts.

instantiations, such as $X/c, Y/a, Z_1/c, Z_2/b$, fail because two facts are missing from the input, here $\text{hop}(c, b)$ and $\text{hop}(c, c)$.

It is no coincidence that all leaf nodes represent missing EDB facts for why-not provenance in positive non-recursive Datalog programs:

Proposition 3. *Let Q be a non-recursive Datalog program, D a database, $\Gamma(f_A(\bar{x}))$ the game provenance for facts $A(\bar{x}) \notin Q(D)$. All leaves of $\Gamma(f_A(\bar{x}))$ have type $f_R(\bar{y})$ and represent ground EDB atoms $R(\bar{y})$ that are missing from the input.* □

The above proposition illustrates that for positive queries, the ultimate reason for failure to derive outputs are missing inputs, represented by the leaves in provenance games.

As defined, game provenance is sensitive to the active domain of query and input database, which can lead to interesting effects. Consider the following query variant $Q'_{\text{neg}} := Q_{\text{neg}} \cup \{C(y) :- E(y, z)\}$ with input $D = \{B(a, a)\}$. Here, game provenance shows that $A(a)$ depends on the presence of $B(a, a)$ as well as on the absence of $E(a, a)$. The game provenance graph does not mention that the absence, e.g., of $E(a, b)$ is important as well—simply because b is not in the active domain.

3.4 Game Provenance for First-Order Queries

In this section, we demonstrate examples for provenance games in the presence of negation within the query. When constructing game graphs for Datalog$^{\neg}$ queries with negated goals, we obtain graphs in which there exists a path of length three between positive relation nodes. This switches roles between player I and II. In other words, to explain why a *negated* subgoal is satisfied, an argument like in the why-not case is used. In general, this leads to provenance graphs that contain leaf nodes of both kinds: $f_C(\bar{x})$ representing missing facts $R(\bar{x}) \notin D$ and $f_{r_R}(\bar{x})$ representing input facts $R(\bar{x}) \in D$.

In the following, we provide examples based on the Q_{neg} query (cf. Fig. 4) with input database $D = \{B(a, b), B(b, a), C(a)\}$.

Why Provenance. Figure 7a shows the provenance graph for the output fact $A(a)$. One can see that $A(a)$ could be derived via rule r_1 with the bindings $X/a, Y/b$. The positive goal succeeds due to the existence of the EDB fact $B(a, b)$. The negative goal g_1^2 succeeds due to the missing fact $C(b)$ from the input D.

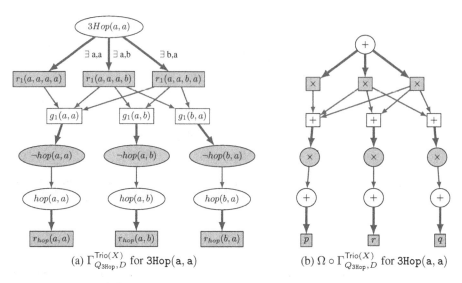

(a) $\Gamma_{Q_{3\text{Hop}},D}^{\text{Trio}(X)}$ for $\mathbf{3Hop(a, a)}$ (b) $\Omega \circ \Gamma_{Q_{3\text{Hop}},D}^{\text{Trio}(X)}$ for $\mathbf{3Hop(a, a)}$

Fig. 8. Creating $\text{Trio}(X)$ style provenance game variants for Q_{3Hop} by dropping positional identifiers in the Skolem function for goal nodes. The operator tree on the right reads $p + 2pqr$.

Why-Not Provenance. Figure 7b shows the provenance graph for $A(b)$ which is not part of $Q_{\text{neg}}(D)$. We can see that a player starting in $\neg A(b)$ will win the argument since $A(b)$ cannot be shown. Both attempts to derive $A(b)$ fail. With $X/b, Y/a$ the second goal $\neg C(a)$ is not satisfied since $C(a) \in D$. With $X/b, Y/b$ the first goal $B(b, b)$ fails since $B(b, b) \notin D$.

3.5   Evaluation Game Graph Variants

In the graph construction for provenance games, the definition of the Skolem functions is critical to capture provenance equivalent to $\mathbb{N}[X]$ povenance polynomials. Recall that the Skolem function for rule node identifiers, e.g., $f_{r_1}(X, Y)$, depend on the rule (here r_1) as well as the constants assigned to body variables. Skolem functions of goal node identifiers, e.g., $f_{g_1^2}(X, Y)$, depend on the rule they belong to (here 1), the exact position in the rule body at which that goal oocurs (here 2), and values of the bound variables.

By changing the definition of one or more Skolem functions, more compact but also less informative provenance can be encoded. We here only describe a simple variant that will create $\text{Trio}(X)$ [3] style provenance instead of $\mathbb{N}[X]$ provenance polynomials for $\mathcal{RA}^+$ queries. When changing the Skolem function of goal node identifiers by removing the positional argument for the goal, goals that appear at different positions in the body of a rule collapse into a single node. This construction yields a modified operator graph. In particular, using the same fact multiple times jointly in a rule will be recorded only as a single use—as it is the case in $\text{Trio}(X)$ provenance polynomials.

The game graph $\Gamma_{Q_{3\text{Hop}},D}^{\text{Trio}(X)} \left(f_{3\text{Hop}}(a, a) \right)$ and the corresponding operator graph are shown in Fig. 8. Reading out the polynomial results in the Trio-provenance-polynomial $p + 2pqr$ for the input fact annotations given in Fig. 5b.

4   Conclusions

In this paper we have defined the notion of *provenance games* to capture provenance of non-recursive Datalog¬. We have also shown how programs can be translated into a game form represented by a game graph. The game graph can be solved using the well-founded model of the well known win-move program. We have defined how the solved game for non-recursive Datalog¬ can provide valuable provenance information for the original program. In particular it can answer why and why-not provenance questions. We gave examples how to retrieve provenance information from a game graph.

Investigating approaches to mitigate the problem of domain dependency for why-not provenance is an interesting avenue for future work. Another possible extensions is the application of provenance games to full Datalog¬ programs, which requires the analysis of drawn positions.

Acknowledgements. Work supported by NSF awards IIS–1118088, DBI–1147273, and a gift from LogicBlox, Inc.

References

1. Amsterdamer, Y., Deutch, D., Tannen, V.: Provenance for aggregate queries. In: PODS, pp. 153–164. ACM (2011)
2. Amsterdamer, Y., Deutch, D., Tannen, V.: On the limitations of provenance for queries with difference. In: Workshop on Theory and Practice of Provenance (TaPP), Heraklion, Crete (2011)
3. Benjelloun, O., Sarma, A., Halevy, A., Widom, J.: Uldbs: Databases with uncertainty and lineage. In: VLDB, pp. 953–964 (2006)
4. Buneman, P., Khanna, S., Tan, W.-C.: Why and where: A characterization of data provenance. In: Van den Bussche, J., Vianu, V. (eds.) ICDT 2001. LNCS, vol. 1973, pp. 316–330. Springer, Heidelberg (2000)
5. Cheney, J., Chiticariu, L., Tan, W.: Provenance in databases: Why, how, and where. Foundations and Trends in Databases 1(4), 379–474 (2009)
6. Cui, Y., Widom, J., Wiener, J.: Tracing the lineage of view data in a warehousing environment. ACM Transactions on Database Systems (TODS) 25(2), 179–227 (2000)
7. Flum, J.: Games, kernels, and antitone operations. Order 17(1), 61–73 (2000)
8. Flum, J., Kubierschky, M., Ludäscher, B.: Total and partial well-founded datalog coincide. In: Afrati, F.N., Kolaitis, P.G. (eds.) ICDT 1997. LNCS, vol. 1186, pp. 113–124. Springer, Heidelberg (1997)
9. Flum, J., Kubierschky, M., Ludäscher, B.: Games and total datalog¬ queries. Theoretical Computer Science 239(2), 257–276 (2000)
10. Geerts, F., Poggi, A.: On database query languages for k-relations. Journal of Applied Logic 8(2), 173–185 (2010)
11. Green, T.: Containment of conjunctive queries on annotated relations. Theory of Computing Systems 49(2), 429–459 (2011)
12. Green, T., Ives, Z., Tannen, V.: Reconcilable differences. Theory of Computing Systems 49(2), 460–488 (2011)
13. Green, T., Karvounarakis, G., Ives, Z., Tannen, V.: Update exchange with mappings and provenance. In: VLDB, pp. 675–686 (2007)

14. Green, T., Karvounarakis, G., Tannen, V.: Provenance semirings. In: PODS, pp. 31–40 (2007)
15. Huang, S., Green, T., Loo, B.: Datalog and emerging applications: an interactive tutorial. In: SIGMOD, pp. 1213–1216 (2011)
16. Karvounarakis, G., Green, T.J.: Semiring-annotated data: queries and provenance. SIGMOD Record 41(3), 5–14 (2012)
17. von Neumann, J.: Zur Theorie der Gesellschaftsspiele. Mathematische Annalen 100, 295–320 (1928)
18. Schwalbe, U., Walker, P.: Zermelo and the early history of game theory. Games and Economic Behavior 34(1), 123–137 (2001)
19. Van Gelder, A.: The alternating fixpoint of logic programs with negation. Journal of Computer and System Sciences 47(1), 185–221 (1993)
20. Van Gelder, A., Ross, K., Schlipf, J.: The well-founded semantics for general logic programs. Journal of the ACM (JACM) 38(3), 619–649 (1991)
21. Zermelo, E.: Über eine Anwendung der Mengenlehre auf die Theorie des Schachspiels. In: Fifth Intl. Congress of Mathematicians, vol. 2, pp. 501–504. Cambridge University Press (1913)
22. Zinn, D., Green, T.J., Ludäscher, B.: Win-move is coordination-free (sometimes). In: Intl. Conf. on Database Theory (ICDT), pp. 99–113 (2012)

A   Proof of Theorem 3

PROOF. The evaluation of the transformed game graph $\Omega \circ \Gamma_{Q,D}(f_R(\bar{x}))$ is structurally equivalent to the evaluation of provenance semiring polynomials of the annotated $Q(D)$:

EDB Facts: Using provenance semirings, a fact $R(\bar{x})$ has the annotation $\mathcal{P}_{Q,D}^{\mathbb{N}[X]}(R(\bar{x}))$. The evaluation of provenance polynomials using provenance games starts at the positive relation node $f_R(\bar{x})$. Since $R(\bar{x}) \in Q(D)$ and by definition of the game graph this relation node has one reachable node $\mathsf{F}(f_R(\bar{x})) = \{f_{r_R}(\bar{x})\}$: $\Omega \circ \Gamma_{Q,D}(f_R(\bar{x})) = \Omega \circ \Gamma_{Q,D}(f_{r_R}(\bar{x}))$. The node $f_{r_R}(\bar{x})$ is a leaf node, so the evaluation Ω returns its label $L(f_{r_R}(\bar{x})) = \mathcal{P}_{Q,D}^{\mathbb{N}[X]}(R(\bar{x}))$ and we have:

$$\Omega \circ \Gamma_{Q,D}(f_R(\bar{x})) = L(f_{r_R}(\bar{x})) = \mathcal{P}_{\mathbb{N}[X]}(R(\bar{x})).$$

Union: Let $Q(D) := \{r_1 \colon U(\bar{x}) \leftarrow R_1(\bar{x}).\ r_2 \colon U(\bar{x}) \leftarrow R_2(\bar{x}).\}$ When evaluating $Q(D)$, the provenance semiring polynomial for fact $U(\bar{x}) \in Q(D)$ is: $\mathcal{P}_{\mathbb{N}[X]}(U(\bar{x})) = \mathcal{P}_{\mathbb{N}[X]}(R_1(\bar{x})) + \mathcal{P}_{\mathbb{N}[X]}(R_2(\bar{x}))$. The evaluation of provenance polynomials for $U(\bar{x}) \in Q(D)$ using provenance games starts at the positive relation node $f_U(\bar{x})$. By definition of the game graph for $Q(D)$, $\mathsf{F}(f_U(\bar{x})) = \{f_{r_1}(\bar{x}), f_{r_2}(\bar{x})\}$ and since $\gamma(f_U(\bar{x})) = \mathsf{W}$ we combine both terms with $L(f_U(\bar{x})) = "+"$:

$$\Omega \circ \Gamma_{Q,D}(f_U(\bar{x})) = \Omega \circ \Gamma_{Q,D}(f_{r_1}(\bar{x})) + \Omega \circ \Gamma_{Q,D}(f_{r_2}(\bar{x}))$$

Each rule node in $\Gamma_{Q,D}$ has exactly one outgoing edge to a goal node. Since the program is positive, each goal node has exactly one following negated relation node. Those negated relation nodes in turn have exactly one corresponding positive relation node. As shown above for EDB facts, for positive programs and a head node $U(\bar{x}) \in Q(D)$, positive relation nodes lead to the corresponding provenance annotations:

$$
\begin{aligned}
\Omega \circ \Gamma_{Q,D}(f_{\mathsf{U}}(\bar{x})) &= \Omega \circ \Gamma_{Q,D}(f_{\mathsf{g}_1^1}(\bar{x})) + \Omega \circ \Gamma_{Q,D}(f_{\mathsf{g}_2^1}(\bar{x})) \\
&= \Omega \circ \Gamma_{Q,D}(f_{\neg \mathsf{R}_1}(\bar{x})) + \Omega \circ \Gamma_{Q,D}(f_{\neg \mathsf{R}_2}(\bar{x})) \\
&= \Omega \circ \Gamma_{Q,D}(f_{\mathsf{R}_1}(\bar{x})) + \Omega \circ \Gamma_{Q,D}(f_{\mathsf{R}_2}(\bar{x})) \\
&= \mathcal{P}_{Q,D}^{\mathbb{N}[X]}(R_1(\bar{x})) + \mathcal{P}_{Q,D}^{\mathbb{N}[X]}(R_2(\bar{x}))
\end{aligned}
$$

Join: Let $Q(D) := \{r_1 \colon J(\bar{x}) \leftarrow R_1(\bar{x}), R_2(\bar{x}).\}$ When evaluating $Q(D)$ for a $J(\bar{x}) \in Q(D)$ using provenance semiring annotations we get: $\mathcal{P}_{Q,D}^{\mathbb{N}[X]}(J(\bar{x})) = \mathcal{P}_{Q,D}^{\mathbb{N}[X]}(R_1(\bar{x})) \times \mathcal{P}_{Q,D}^{\mathbb{N}[X]}(R_2(\bar{x}))$. The evaluation of provenance polynomials for $J(\bar{x}) \in Q(D)$ using provenance games starts at the positive relation node $f_J(\bar{x})$. By definition of the game graph for $Q(D)$, $f_J(\bar{x})$ connects to exactly one rule node: $\mathsf{F}(f_J(\bar{x})) = \{f_{r_1}(\bar{x})\}$. This rule node in turn leads to two goal nodes $\mathsf{F}(f_{r_1}(\bar{x})) = \{f_{\mathsf{g}_1^1}(\bar{x}), f_{\mathsf{g}_1^2}(\bar{x})\}$, which we combine with $L(f_{r_1}(\bar{x})) = \text{``} \times \text{''}$, since $\gamma(f_{r_1}(\bar{x})) = \mathsf{L}$:

$$
\begin{aligned}
\Omega \circ \Gamma_{Q,D}(f_J(\bar{x})) &= \Omega \circ \Gamma_{Q,D}(f_{r_1}(\bar{x})) \\
&= \Omega \circ \Gamma_{Q,D}(f_{\mathsf{g}_1^1}(\bar{x})) \times \Omega \circ \Gamma_{Q,D}(f_{\mathsf{g}_1^2}(\bar{x}))
\end{aligned}
$$

Since the program is positive, each goal node has exactly one following negated relation node. Those negated relation nodes in turn have exactly one corresponding positive relation node. As shown above for EDB facts and for positive programs with a head node $J(\bar{x}) \in Q(D)$, positive relation nodes lead to the corresponding provenance semiring annotations:

$$
\begin{aligned}
\Omega \circ \Gamma_{Q,D}(f_J(\bar{x})) &= \Omega \circ \Gamma_{Q,D}(f_{\neg \mathsf{R}_1}(\bar{x})) \times \Omega \circ \Gamma_{Q,D}(f_{\neg \mathsf{R}_2}(\bar{x})) \\
&= \Omega \circ \Gamma_{Q,D}(f_{\mathsf{R}_1}(\bar{x})) \times \Omega \circ \Gamma_{Q,D}(f_{\mathsf{R}_2}(\bar{x})) \\
&= \mathcal{P}_{Q,D}^{\mathbb{N}[X]}(R_1(\bar{x})) \times \mathcal{P}_{Q,D}^{\mathbb{N}[X]}(R_2(\bar{x}))
\end{aligned}
$$

Querying an Integrated Complex-Object Dataflow Database

Natalia Kwasnikowska and Jan Van den Bussche

Hasselt University and Transnational University of Limburg, Belgium

Abstract. We consider an integrated complex-object dataflow database in which multiple dataflow specifications can be stored, together with multiple executions of these dataflows, including the complex-object data that are involved, and annotations. We focus on dataflow applications frequently encountered in the scientific community, involving the manipulation of data with a complex-object structure combined with service calls, which can be either internal or external. Internal services are dataflows acting as a subprogram of an other dataflow, whereas external services are modeled as functions with a possibly non-deterministic behavior. Dataflow specifications are expressed in a high-level programming language based on the nested relational calculus, the operators of which provide the right "glue" needed to combine different service calls into a complex-object dataflow. All entities involved, whether complex-objects, dataflow executions or dataflow specifications, are first-class citizens of the integrated database: they are all data. We discuss how such dataflow repositories can be queried in a variety of ways, including provenance queries. We show that a modern SQL platform with support for (external) routines and SQL/XML suffices to support all types of dataflow repository queries.

Dedicated to Peter Buneman.

1 Introduction

A workflow is a high-level specification of a complex and possibly long-during task, consisting of different subtasks that must be performed in a certain order. This order does not need to be linear: some tasks can be performed concurrently, or alternatively. Workflow management has its origins in business process modeling [1], but in recent years workflows have gained importance in e-science, in parallel with the rise of Grid Computing [2]. Scientific workflows are distinguished from business workflows by their placing more importance on the data flow between the subtasks, than on the synchronization of subtasks [3]. (In e-science, the data flow frequently involves collections of complex data objects.) In accordance to this focus, in this paper, we use the terms "scientific workflow" and "dataflow" interchangeably.

With the rise of scientific workflows, the need for better database support became apparent. A nice overview of relevant topics in database support for

V. Tannen et al. (Eds.): Buneman Festschrift, LNCS 8000, pp. 400–417, 2013.

scientific workflow management has been given in a special issue of SIGMOD Record [4]. The needs in this area go well beyond what so-called workflow management systems (WFMS) provide, even if coupled to a DBMS such as Oracle Workflow or IBM WebSphere. Such WFMSs provide support for constructing workflow specifications and guiding and monitoring workflow executions.

In an e-science environment, however, one is confronted with multiple interrelated research projects, where in each project a multitude of different dataflows are in use, each of which has been executed many times, on different input data, using different versions of external services, by different users, and so on. Standard WFMSs, although they are implemented on top of a database, lack the support for ad-hoc querying of all this information in an integrated manner. Such database support is important to manage computational experiments, to allow reproducibility, and more generally, to "enforce the scientific method" [5].

In response to this problem, in an earlier paper [6], we gave the formal specification of an integrated dataflow repository. In the current paper, we show how an implementation of this system on top of a modern but standard SQL platform, enables the querying of dataflows and dataflow executions in an integrated manner. We intensively use such features as external routines, user-defined table functions, SQL/XML and XQuery capabilities.

Of course we are not the first to address the challenge of querying dataflow executions; in the scientific workflow community such queries are known as "provenance queries". The participants of the Provenance Challenges[1] have already intensively investigated this direction.

Our present approach focuses on the following aspects:

1. We explicitly represent the complex-data manipulations that are performed in a dataflow. We do this using the nested relational calculus (NRC [9]): an elementary functional programming language composed of all the natural manipulation operators on collection- and record-oriented data.
2. We investigate the feasibility of a 100% database solution. Using the full power of the modern SQL:2003 standard, we will see that all types of provenance queries can be solved directly in SQL. Many present solutions of the Provenance Challenge mentioned above involve coding of diverse programs outside of the database. In contrast, our approach focuses on a fixed set of user-defined functions that can then be used in SQL select statements.
3. We address querying not only of dataflow executions but also of the specifications of the dataflows. In the same vein, we address querying of executions of dataflows, the specification of which is not determined in advance. Previous approaches to dataflow provenance typically focus on querying executions of a fixed dataflow specification, given outside of the query.
4. Thanks to our explicit complex-object data model, we can support a new, finer-grained notion of provenance tracking, where we can derive connections directly among *subvalues* occurring in the result and the intermediate results of a dataflow execution.

---

[1] `http://twiki.ipaw.info/bin/view/Challenge/WebHome`

This paper is organized as follows. In Section 2 we describe related work. In Section 3 we briefly discuss the types of queries which illustrate the need for an integrated dataflow database. In Section 4 we use simple examples to discuss the database representation of complex data, NRC dataflows, and the integration of external services. In Section 4.4 we briefly describe the execution of dataflows, taking into account such issues as binding of input data, binding of external function calls, and binding of subdataflows. We conclude the section with the representation of past executions in the dataflow database. In Section 4.5 we briefly describe how the database can integrate annotations.

Finally, in Section 5, we show how the integrated complex-object dataflow database can be queried in a variety of ways.

2 Related Work

Support for the complex-object structure of data flowing in a scientific workflow is present in various systems, e.g., Taverna [10, 11], Kepler/CoMaD [12, 13], and Chimera [14, 15]. The operation of applying a function on all elements of a collection is typically provided. However, that operation is just one of the many possible kinds of "glue" needed to connect different subtasks in a complex data flow together. Indeed, the NRC which we use provides exactly the natural set of operations to deal with complex-object data. It has evolved from a long tradition of complex-object data modeling in the database research literature.

Also a database-oriented approach has been advocated by many others [16–20]. However, the querying of an unbounded number of dataflow executions, as given by the database instance and not fixed in advance, as well as the querying of dataflow specifications inside the database, has not been addressed before. Our approach is based on our earlier experience with database meta-querying [21, 22]. We should also mention the topic of process mining [23, 24], although the scope of process mining is quite different from that of repository querying.

We represent a dataflow execution in the database as a "log", i.e., a set of triples of the form (input, function, output). This representation is natural and common [25, 26, 19, 27, 28], and is often equivalently viewed as a causality graph. Specific to our approach is that we can define a finer-grained tracking of provenance not just from output to input, but also from a *subvalue* occurring in the output to a *subvalue* occurring in the input. Note that in our previous paper [29] we have given a conversion from our execution model to the proposed standard Open Provenance Model [30], which uses an explicit causality graph.

We should also mention some more distantly related work. Beeri, Milo et al. have an interesting project on querying the *potential* executions of a given workflow specification [31]. That approach is mainly verification-oriented rather than repository-oriented, although they did also consider monitoring [32]. The NRC was used in the Kleisli system [33, 34] not as a dataflow specification language, but as a bioinformatics data integration query language, where the entire structure of the biological data is modeled as a complex object. We use complex objects in a different way, to model the data flow in a scientific workflow.

The NRC is also used as a framework to formalize provenance and dependency analysis for queries over annotated databases [35, 36].

We conclude by pointing out that the need for a workflow repository is also acknowledged in other fields, as shown by Blockeel and Vanschoren's Experiment Databases for Machine Learning [37, 38].

3 Motivation

The participants of the Provenance Challenges[2] have already informally formulated various queries, involving both a dataflow specification and its past executions.

For example, for a specified part of a workflow output, say *out*, they have formulated queries that ask (i) which workflow inputs have contributed to the computation of *out* (Q1,Q5 from PC3); (ii) which part of the execution contributed to the computation of *out*, possibly further restricted by annotations, or only up to a specified task (Q1-Q3 from PC1, Q3 from PC3); (iii) to verify if certain tasks were involved in the computation of *out* (Q2 of PC3); (iv) to look for tasks that can be swapped during execution without affecting *out* (optional Q5 from PC3).

Queries that involve many executions of the same workflow ask (i) to find all invocations of a specified task, using a specified input, and having specified annotations (Q4); (ii) to retrieve (intermediate) results produced by a specified task and/or having specified annotations (Q8-Q9 from PC1), or even preceded by another specified task (Q6 from PC1); (iii) to find all workflow outputs produced from a specified input (Q5 from PC1); (iv) to find differences between specified past executions (Q7 from PC1). We concur that a dataflow repository should allow formulating such queries, and we illustrate in Section 5 how it can be done in our model.

In general, there are various types of queries that a dataflow repository should support, including:

- Queries involving *subvalues* of a (final) result. Indeed, in some dataflows, both intermediate values and the final result value may be huge data sets, and the user might be only interested in some part.
- Querying vast amounts of past executions, in order to identify dataflows and their executions involving a particular external service. Indeed, if that service produced erroneous results, or there is a better implementation available, such queries are necessary if we want to rerun the affected dataflows with another external service.
- Queries that allow modifying of dataflow specifications and immediate execution of the modified dataflows.

We show in Section 5 how such queries can be constructed for our integrated dataflow repository, after a description of a possible implementation in the following section.

---

[2] `http://twiki.ipaw.info/bin/view/Challenge/WebHome`, we refer to the first challenge as PC1, and to the third as PC3.

4 Complex-Object Dataflow Database

In an earlier paper [6], we gave the formal specification of a dataflow repository. In this section we show how we can represent all aspects of that formal model on top of a modern SQL platform.

4.1 Complex Data

Data objects flowing in a scientific workflow can either be atomic for the workflow, or can have a structure that is important for the workflow. The two basic data structures in databases are the set, e.g., $\{sequence_1, \ldots, sequence_{76}\}$, and the tuple, e.g., $\langle organism: mouse, \ldots, filename: \text{GPZ158} \rangle$. These structures can be arbitrarily nested: we use the complex-object data model [39]. For more details on the theory, including the type system, we refer to our previous paper [6], as here we are focusing more on the implementation and use of the system.

It is important to note that an "atomic" object can be quite complex, e.g., it can be a file, it can be an XML document. However, for a dataflow that has only actions that operate on the file as a whole, it is not relevant to model the file as a set of records. On the other hand, if the structure of the file as a collection is important, because we want to apply some operation to each of its elements, then we model the file as a complex object.

We represent atomic objects as strings. For small types of atomic objects, such as numbers, strings or dates, the string can hold the entire value of the object. For large atomic objects such as files, we could still represent them as a string by means of a path name of the file.

In many cases, however, it is more desirable to store the large atomic object in the database as a BLOB (which can contain a text file or an XML document as well as a binary file). In that case, the string representing the object is an identifier that can be used as a foreign key to the object in table `Pool(ID, object)`.

As to storing complex objects, we discuss two basic ways: *decomposition* and *XML* representation.

Decomposition of complex objects. A complex object, together with its nested subobjects, can be naturally viewed as a tree. We generate a string ID for each tuple and set node; the atomic objects, which occur as leaves in the tree, already have their string representation. We then store the tree in two tables: `Sets(ID, eID)` and `Tuples(ID, att, fID)`. Here, `eID` stands for element ID, `att` stands for attribute, and `fID` for field ID. Figure 1 shows an illustration for the following complex object:

$$\{\langle \text{exp}: \text{P2T42}, \text{targets}: \{\text{human}, \text{mouse}\}, \text{result}: \text{report123} \rangle,$$
$$\langle \text{exp}: \text{P42T3}, \text{targets}: \{\text{human}, \text{chimp}\}, \text{result}: \text{report456} \rangle \}$$

XML representation of complex objects. We can also take advantage of the XML data type supported by modern database systems, and store the complex-object

Fig. 1. Tree representation and decomposition of a complex object

tree directly as an XML value. This is illustrated in Figure 2. There is an additional choice when the complex object contains XML documents as large atomic objects at the leaves: we can just have the IDs of these objects at the leaves of the XML tree, or we can include their full XML content. For example, in Figure 2, the results are represented by IDs **report123** and **report456** referring to the **Pool** table, but alternatively we could have replaced these IDs inside the XML tree by the corresponding full XML reports.

The best choice among decomposition, intermediate XML, and full XML for complex objects depends on the application. We can provide library routines to move between the three representations; these routines can then be called in SQL statements.

4.2   NRC Dataflows

In its most simple form, a dataflow is a pipeline of function applications, as illustrated in Figure 4, or expressed in the dataflow language we use in Figure 5.

The function names **analyze**, **compare** and **annotate** represent the basic actions or tasks of which the dataflow is composed. In e-science and e-commerce settings, these tasks are often called *services*, so we refer to the function names in a dataflow as *abstract service names*. They are abstract in the sense that they serve only as placeholders for actions: only when the dataflow is actually executed, the abstract service names are bound to concrete actions.

Since the data objects flowing in the pipeline can have complex structure, a language with just variable definitions (the **let**-construct) and function application, as used in the above example, is not sufficient. For example, if x is a set, we want to apply **analyze** to every element of x and collect the results. We can accommodate this by adding a mapping construct $\{\texttt{analyze}(u) \mid u \in x\}$ to the language, in the form of **for** $u \in x$ **return** $\texttt{analyze}(u)$. In order to be able to organize the data flow, we also want the basic operations on tuples and sets: tuple formation, tuple projection, singleton set formation, set union, and big union, also known as "flatten".[3] Finally, we need an if-then-else construct. This rounds up the operations of a natural language for complex objects known as the *nested relational calculus* or NRC.

So, as already seen in Figure 5, a dataflow consists of a name, a specification of its input parameters, and a specification of its behavior in the form of an

---

[3] The flattening $\bigcup s$ of a set of sets $s = \{s_1, \ldots, s_n\}$ equals $s_1 \cup \cdots \cup s_n$.

```
<set>
<tuple>
  <att> exp </att>
  <atom> P2T42 </atom>
  <att> targets </att>
  <set>
    <atom> human </atom>
    <atom> mouse </atom>
  </set>
  <att> result </att>
  <atom> report123 </atom>
</tuple>
<tuple>
  <att> exp </att>
  <atom> P42T3 </atom>
  <att> targets </att>
  <set>
    <atom> human </atom>
    <atom> chimp </atom>
  </set>
  <att> result </att>
  <atom> report456 </atom>
</tuple>
</set>
```

```
<expr ID="0">
  <let ID="1">
    <var ID="2"> z </var>
    <for ID="3">
      <var ID="4"> u </var>
      <var ID="5"> x </var>
      <tuple  ID="6">
        <att> a </att>
        <project ID="7">
          <att> a </att>
          <var ID="8"> u </var>
        </project>
        <att> b </att>
        <call ID="9">
          <name> extract </name>
          <project ID="10">
            <att> c </att>
            <var ID="11"> u </var>
          </project>
        </call>
      </tuple>
    </for>
    <call ID="12">
      <name> validate </name>
      <call ID="13">
        <name> search1 </name>
        <var ID="14"> z </var>
        <var ID="15"> y </var>
      </call>
      <call ID="16">
        <name> search2 </name>
        <var ID="17"> z </var>
        <var ID="18"> y </var>
      </call>
    </call>
  </let>
</expr>
```

Fig. 2. XML representation of a complex object

Fig. 3. XML representation of the NRC expression of Figure 6

NRC expression. Another example is shown in Figure 6. Actually, our system is typed [6], so input and return types, as well as service signatures should also be specified. For simplicity of presentation, however, we omit the typing system.

Storing dataflow specifications in the repository. Dataflow specifications are stored in a table Dataflows with attributes ID and expr in which the name and the NRC expression are stored. (There are also attributes to store type information.) Here, attribute expr is of type XML: we store the expressions by their syntax tree in XML format, as illustrated in Figure 3.

Note that the element nodes in the XML syntax tree have unique ID attributes. This allows us to create an index on XML column expr based on the XPath pattern //*[@ID]. This is useful to support efficient querying of stored expressions using SQL/XML. Indeed, as we will see later, some other tables in the repository database contain references to these IDs, so many queries use conditions involving the above XPath pattern. We show examples in Section 5.

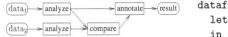

```
dataflow AFlow(x, y) returns
  let z := analyze(x)
  in annotate(compare(z, analyze(y)), z)
```

Fig. 4. A dataflow   **Fig. 5.** Specification of `AFlow`

```
<btree>
  <entry>
    <aname>extract</aname><ename>EXTR</ename>
  </entry>
  <entry>
    <aname>validate</aname><ename>VAL</ename>
  </entry>
  <entry>
    <aname>search1</aname><sub>CFlow</sub>
    <btree>
      <entry>
        <aname>dbsearch</aname><ename>SQST</ename>
      </entry>
    </btree>
  </entry>
  <entry>
    <aname>search2</aname><sub>CFlow</sub>
    <btree>
      <entry>
        <aname>dbsearch</aname><ename>MSCT</ename>
      </entry>
    </btree>
  </entry>
</btree>
```

```
dataflow BFlow(x, y) returns
let z := for u in x return
         <a: u.a, b: extract(u.c)>
in validate(search1(z,y),
            search2(z,y))
```

Fig. 6. Specification of `BFlow`   **Fig. 7.** Binding tree

4.3   External Services and Subdataflows

The functions we want to call in a dataflow execution are called *external services*, because they represent a computation that is external to the dataflow specification, i.e., not further modeled within the dataflow specification. In e-science, services can be local programs, remote programs, Grid service calls or Web service calls, and so on.

In order to integrate external services in the dataflow database, we assume Java wrappers for them, which are registered as external routines (user-defined Java functions). These functions take XML representations of complex objects as input and output. In this way, external services can be called directly in SQL statements, but also, dataflow executions can be initiated from inside the database server.

So, before we start the execution of a dataflow, we bind some of the abstract service names occurring in the body to names of external routines. Other abstract service names, however, may be bound to names of other dataflows in the repository. Indeed, in order to support modular programming of workflows, we want to be able to let one dataflow call another one as a subdataflow.

The specification of binding of abstract service names to external routines or subdataflows, together with the further binding of abstract service names occurring in those subdataflows, is called a *binding tree* and can be naturally represented in XML. Recall, for example, dataflow `BFlow` from Figure 6. To execute `BFlow` we might want to bind `extract` and `validate` to external routine names `EXTR` and `VAL`, and both `search₁` and `search₂` to another dataflow `CFlow`. Assume that `CFlow` calls just one abstract service name `dbsearch`. In the `CFlow` executions within `BFlow` that are called as `search₁`, we want to bind `dbsearch` to external routine `SQST`, but in the subdataflow executions called as `search₂`, we want to bind `dbsearch` to `MSCT`. The binding tree that specifies all this is shown in XML in Figure 7.

4.4   Executions

To execute a dataflow known to the repository, the system offers, as a library routine, the stored procedure *Execute(flowID, vassign, btree)*, where *flowID* designates a dataflow from the `Dataflows` table, *btree* is a binding tree for the dataflow, and *vassign* is an assignment of input values to the input parameters of the dataflow.

This value assignment is given in XML in the following format:

```
<vassign>
  <entry> <name> x </name> <val> v </val> </entry>
  ...
</vassign>
```

Here, x stands for an input parameter and v for the input value for x. When using the decomposed representation of complex objects, we can give v as an identifier to be found in the `Sets` and `Tuples` tables. When using XML representation, v is itself a further XML subtree. So, formally, we have different variants of *Execute*, but we omit this here from our notation.

The behavior of *Execute* is such that a log of the execution is stored in the repository. We call such a log a "run". Runs are stored in tables `Runs(ID, flowID, vassign, btree)` and `Triples(ID, caller, cassign, subexpr, vassign, value)`. Here, the ID of the run is newly generated. With this ID, a number of tuples, called "tagged triples", are inserted in the `Triples` table: one holding the final result value, and one for each service call that has been made. This is necessary because external services need to be considered as non-deterministic functions. For example, in Bioinformatics, public search services (for genes, proteins, etc) are heavily used and called through Web interfaces, but the underlying contents change daily. So, in order to allow for querying of past executions of dataflows in the repository, it is crucial that the results returned by the service calls are stored, because we cannot simply rerun the dataflow later on the same inputs and still be certain to get the same results.

The columns of the `Triples` table have the following meaning. Let us first consider the service calls made in the main dataflow execution, so not in subdataflows. Column `subexpr` holds the ID of the place of the call in the syntax tree of the dataflow expression. Column `vassign` holds the values of the dataflow parameters at the time of the call. Column `value` holds the return value of the call. For the tuple holding the final result value, subexpr is simply the identifier of the root element of the syntax tree, and vassign is the original input assignment.

```
dataflow mapF(input) returns          dataflow myFlow(input) returns
    for x in input return f(x)            <c: f(g(input.a)), d: f(g(input.b))>
```

Fig. 8. A simple flow   **Fig. 9.** Another simple flow

Let us illustrate the Triples table on the simple dataflow of Figure 8. Assume the node ID of the call f(x) in the syntax tree is 4, and that of the entire expression equals 1. Assume the input value equals the set $S = \{a, b, c\}$; then a possible run could generate the following triples: (we write the value assignments in an abbreviated form, and abbreviate input by i)

$$(1, [i = S], \{55, 66\});$$
$$(4, [i = S, x = a], 55); \quad (4, [i = S, x = b], 55); \quad (4, [i = S, x = c], 66).$$

So we see that $f(a)$ and $f(b)$ both returned 55, and $f(c)$ returned 66.

So far we have ignored the columns caller and cassign. In the triples corresponding to the execution of the main dataflow, these columns are NULL. In triples corresponding to subdataflow executions, these columns hold the ID of the call subexpression and the values of the dataflow parameters at the moment of the call.

Implementation. Execute can be implemented quite straightforwardly by compiling NRC into SQL/XML. Indeed, under the decomposed representation of complex objects, NRC operations can be quite simply programmed in SQL. We have already seen that external services can be called in SQL as external routines. Under the XML representation of complex objects, either decomposition can be applied first (this is the approach we take in our prototype), or a direct compilation of the NRC operations into XQuery may be performed.

4.5   Annotations

The basic set of tables Dataflows, Runs, and Triples that constitute the dataflow repository can, of course, be supplemented with extra tables in which extra information, known as *annotations* or *meta-data*, can be stored. These tables are application-dependent, and can refer to the IDs of the elements stored in the basic tables. Examples of meta-data can be authorship, dates and times, version information, categories of dataflows according to projects, and so on.

Annotation hooks. There is one kind of annotation that must be performed by the execution system. This is when we want to record the start or end date&time of runs, or properties of external service calls, such as date&time again, but also possible error codes and so on. In order to provide applications with a flexible annotation recording of runs, the procedure *Execute* can provide a hook that is called before and after each service call. The application developer can instantiate this hook with the code necessary to record the meta-data required by the application.

Note that for dataflows with known specification, no date&time information is necessary to determine the order of execution of (external) services. If the execution of a service depends on the result of another service, the order of execution of services can be determined from the subexpression identifiers stored in the `Triples` table and the dataflow specification in the `Dataflows` table.

5   Querying the Repository

In this section we show that our approach facilitates querying in various ways:

(i) Queries involving subvalues
   Apart from the obvious provenance queries, i.e., asking for the part of the run that has contributed to a certain subvalue, we can use information stored in the `Triples` table, e.g., to query the runs of relevant subdataflows if the subvalue is an element of a collection. Table `Triples` can also be used for querying multiple executions of different dataflows, even without knowing their specifications, to determine, e.g., executions that involved calls to a certain internal service. We note that with the addition of dataflow specifications stored as XML, more sophisticated queries can be formulated, to determine, e.g., executions involving certain subexpressions as well as the order in which the subexpressions were executed. For provenance queries involving dataflows which specifications are unknown, we provide function *Prov.*

(ii) Queries involving (external) services.
   Table `Triples` in combination with the binding trees stored as XML in table `Runs` can be used for querying multiple executions of dataflows, to determine, e.g., executions that involved calls to a certain external service, or which external services have produced a certain subvalue.

(iii) Queries executing modified dataflow specifications.
   We provide function *Eval* for the on-the-fly execution of dataflows with modified specification, with modifications in the subexpressions, as well as in binding to external services.

Queries involving subvalues. Some of the sample queries of the Provenance Challenge [7] are of the following kind. We are given a dataflow, for example, `myFlow` shown in Figure 9. Suppose we have run this flow, with run-ID `myRun`, and we observe the output value `<c: 55, d: 66>`. Consider now the query "What is the process that produced the value `55` in the output?" From the dataflow specification we see that `55` is the output of `f` applied to the output of `g` applied to `input.a`. We can thus retrieve the two relevant triples as follows:

```
select 'input.a', R.value
  from Triples R, Dataflows D
 where R.ID='myRun' and D.ID='myFlow'
   and xmlexists('$e//*[@ID=$s][name()="project"][att="a"]'
                 passing D.expr as "e", R.subexpr as "s")
 union
select 'g', R.value
  from Triples R, Dataflows D
 where R.ID='myRun' and D.ID='myFlow'
   and xmlexists('$e//*[@ID=$s][name()="call"][name="g"][project/att="a"]'
                 passing D.expr as "e", R.subexpr as "s")
```

Note the use of the SQL/XML predicate XMLEXISTS [40, 41] to retrieve the IDs of the nodes in the syntax tree of the dataflow's NRC expression.

Things get a bit more subtle when working with collections. Recall dataflow mapF from Figure 8.

Suppose the run of mapF with ID myRun2 yields a final result value {55,66}, and we again want to know the process that produced the subvalue 55. From the dataflow specification we see that 55 is the result of f applied to at least one element of the input collection. We thus want to retrieve all elements x in input for which f(x) resulted in 55:

```
select xmlquery('$a/var[name="x"]/val'
                passing R.vassign as "a")
  from Triples R, Dataflows D
 where R.ID='myRun2' and D.ID='mapF'
   and xmlexists('$e//*[@ID=$s][name()=call]'
                 passing D.expr as "e", R.subexpr as "s")
   and xmlexists('$v[.="55"]' passing R.value as "v")
```

Note the use of the SQL/XML function XMLQUERY to extract the value of variable x from the value assignment of the triple.

So far we have been querying one execution of a given dataflow. However, we can as well pose queries across all dataflows, and all their executions, in the database instance. For example, queries like "List all bioinformatics dataflows in which a function named f is called with parameter p equal to 5, and the value 'GPZ158' appears in the result of the call." can be expressed using similar techniques as above (assuming an annotation table that lists the IDs of bioinformatics dataflows).

The two earlier example queries over the executions myRun and myRun2 are simple but typical examples of provenance queries, where we ask for the process that lead to a given value occurring as a subvalue of the output. When the dataflow specification is known in advance (in the examples, myFlow and mapF), we have seen that provenance can be directly expressed in SQL. This is no longer straightforward, however, when the dataflow specification is unknown. Our solution is to provide a generic *provenance* computation as a library routine, which can be implemented in a programming language like Java, or even as an SQL/PSM routine. Concretely, we provide a user-defined table function *Prov* with the following signature:

```
function Prov(runID integer, subval integer)
  returns table (caller_expr XML, caller_vassign XML,
                 subexpr XML, vassign XML, subval2 integer)
```

Here, *subval* is the ID of an occurrence of a subvalue in the output of run *runID*. The returned set of tagged triples is much like the set of tagged triples representing a run, but there are three important differences:

1. In the set of triples representing a run, there is one triple for each service call. We have seen that this is sufficient to reconstruct all the intermediate results of NRC operators in between the calls, but that is true only if the dataflow specification is given. Since this is not the case here, the function *Prov* returns triples for NRC operators as well as for service calls.
2. Moreover, *Prov* returns triples only for those operators and service calls that played a role in the generation of *subval*.
3. Indeed, normal run-triples contain the result values of the intermediate steps of the run. However, here we are asking for the process that lead to a *subvalue* of the final output. Accordingly, the function *Prov* returns all *subvalues* (column `subval2`) of intermediate results of the dataflow execution that lead to *subval*.

For example, the earlier query about `myRun2` can now be expressed using *Prov* without any reference to `mapF`, so that it can be applied to, say, all dataflow executions done on a given date:

```
select P.subval2
  from Runs R, RunDates D,
       lateral (values xmlcast(xmlquery('$r//*[.="55"]/@ID'
                                         passing R.result as "r")
                         as integer)) as I(thesubvalue),
       table(Prov(R.ID, I.thesubvalue)) as P
 where D.runID=R.ID and D.when='2009-02-24'
```

For a formal specification of *Prov* we refer to our previous paper [6].

Queries involving (external) services. Consider an external service that is registered in the database as the external function `BLAST2008`. The database may contain many dataflow executions that have called this service. To retrieve them, it suffices to look in the binding tree of each execution, which is stored together with the run-ID in the `Runs` table. The following query also retrieves the abstract service name that is bound to `BLAST2008`.

```
create view B2008calls as
    select U.ID, Tree.aname
      from Runs U, xmltable('$tr/tree/entry'
                            passing U.btree as "tr"
                            columns aname varchar(30),
                                    ename varchar(30)) as Tree
     where Tree.ename='BLAST2008'
```

Now suppose we want to understand the effect of replacing the external function BLAST2008 by another one, say, BLAST2009. We are interested, across all executions in the database, which calls to BLAST2008 would give a different result when replaced by a call to BLAST2009. (We assume that the data used by all those dataflows remained unchanged.) We can find this out by the following query:

```
select O.ID, O.subexpr, O.argval, O.value, N.newvalue
 from
    (select U.ID, D.subexpr, R1.value, R2.value as argval
       from Runs U, B2008calls B, Dataflows D, Triples R1, Triples R2
      where U.ID=B.ID and U.flowID=D.ID
        and U.ID=R1.runID and U.ID=R2.runID and R1.vassign=R2.vassign
        and xmlexists(
               '$e//*[@ID=$s1][name()="call"][name=$b]/child::*[2][@ID=$s2]'
               passing D.expr as "e", R1.subexpr as "s1",
               B.aname as "b",  R2.subexpr as "s2")
    ) as O,
    lateral (values BLAST2009(O.argval)) as N(newvalue)
where is_different(O.value, N.newvalue)
```

Observe how the query directly calls BLAST2009 on the inputs of the recorded calls to BLAST2008. We also use a Boolean user-defined function is_different to compare the two resulting XML values, as a literal non-equality is not what we want.

Queries executing modified dataflow specifications. What if we want to find those dataflow executions whose *final result* would change if we replaced BLAST2008 by BLAST2009? Note that a difference in an individual call might not result in a difference in the final result. To answer this query, we can no longer directly call BLAST2009 as before, because we have to continue the process with the rest of the dataflow, which is unknown at query time. (Of course, if we are only interested in the executions of a dataflow whose specification is known in advance, we can simply rerun it, either through the repository or directly in a query, and compare the differences.)

The solution lies in the provision of dynamic dataflow execution through a library function. More specifically, we provide a user-defined table-valued function *Eval* with the following signature:

```
function Eval(expr XML, vassign XML, btree XML)
  returns table (caller XML, cassign XML, subexpr integer,
                 vassign XML, value XML)
```

This function returns the set of tagged triples representing the run of NRC expression expr on value assignment vassign and binding tree btree. So, *Eval* is like a lightweight version of procedure *Execute*, where the run is not stored in the repository but is merely made available for ad-hoc querying.

The astute reader will note that there is an issue with the subexpr column in the table returned by *Eval*. In a normal execution stored in the integrated repository, this column refers to the unique ID attribute of the nodes in the syntax tree of the dataflow expression. However, here, the input to an *Eval* call is an arbitrary expression `expr`, dynamically produced in XML format during the query, where we do not want to require that every node in *expr* has a unique ID attribute. This issue is solved by letting the `subexpr` column now refer to the numbers of the nodes, in document order. To retrieve nodes, instead of `$e//[@ID=$s]`, we can use `$e/descendant-or-self::*[$s]`.

We are now able to express our query asking for those dataflow executions whose final result would change if we replaced BLAST2008 by BLAST2009.

```
select O.ID, O.result, E.value
  from (select U.result, D.expr, U.vassign, U.btree
          from Runs U, Dataflows D
         where U.flowID=D.ID
           and xmlexists('$b//ename[.="BLAST2008"]
                         passing U.btree as "b") ) as O,
       lateral ( values
                   xmlquery('copy $newb := $b
                             modify for $n in $newb//entry
                                    where $n/ename="BLAST2008"
                                    return
                                       replace value of node $n/ename
                                       with "BLAST2009"
                             return $newb'
                             passing O.btree as "b" ) as N.newbtree,
       table ( Eval(O.expr, O.vassign, N.newbtree ) as E
 where E.subexpr=1 and is_different(O.result, E.value)
```

The condition `E.subexpr=1` on the last line selects the top-level node so as to retrieve the final result value of each rerun. Note also the use of XQuery Update facilities. These are already supported in some SQL/XML implementations, for example, DB2 v9.5.

In the above example, we only rewrite the binding trees, not the actual NRC expressions themselves. It should be clear by now that such rewritings are equally possible. For example, we might want to see the effect of shutting out certain parts of certain dataflows. We can express such queries using the same techniques.

6   Concluding Remarks

We have shown how an integrated complex-object dataflow database, implemented on top of a modern SQL platform, enables answering diverse provenance queries. (We are currently developing a prototype.)

Of course, querying such a complex database requires expression in advanced SQL and XQuery, a skill we can expect from programmers working in an e-science team. Nevertheless, it would be nice if a domain-specific query language could be designed, for example, in the field of bioinformatics dataflows. Such a language should be more intuitive, possibly graphical, and usable by the scientists themselves, who are not trained as programmers. This is an interesting direction for further research. The challenge will be to find the right balance between expressive power and ease of use.

References

1. van der Aalst, W., van Hee, K.: Workflow Management. MIT Press (2004)
2. Foster, I., Kesselman, C. (eds.): The Grid: Blueprint for a New Computing Infrastructure, 2nd edn. Elsevier (2004)
3. Shankar, S., et al.: Integrating databases and workflow systems. SIGMOD Record 34(3), 5–11 (2005)
4. Ludaescher, B., Goble, C. (eds.): Special Section on Scientific Workflows. SIGMOD Record, vol. 34(3). ACM (2005)
5. Brown Jr., A.L.: Enforcing the scientific method. In: Freire, J., Koop, D., Moreau, L. (eds.) IPAW 2008. LNCS, vol. 5272, p. 2. Springer, Heidelberg (2008)
6. Hidders, J., Kwasnikowska, N., Sroka, J., Tyszkiewicz, J., Van den Bussche, J.: A formal model of dataflow repositories. In: Cohen-Boulakia, S., Tannen, V. (eds.) DILS 2007. LNCS (LNBI), vol. 4544, pp. 105–121. Springer, Heidelberg (2007)
7. Provenance challenge Wiki, http://twiki.ipaw.info/bin/view/Challenge/
8. Moreau, L., Ludäscher, B., et al.: Special issue: The first provenance challenge. Concurrency and Computation: Practice and Experience 20(5), 409–597 (2008)
9. Buneman, P., Naqvi, S., Tannen, V., Wong, L.: Principles of programming with complex objects and collection types. Theoretical Computer Science 149(1), 3–48 (1995)
10. Turi, D., Missier, P., Goble, C., et al.: Taverna workflows: Syntax and semantics. In: 3rd e-Science, pp. 441–448. IEEE Computer Society (2007)
11. Missier, P., Belhajjame, K., Zhao, J., Roos, M., Goble, C.A.: Data lineage model for Taverna workflows with lightweight annotation requirements. In: Freire, J., Koop, D., Moreau, L. (eds.) IPAW 2008. LNCS, vol. 5272, pp. 17–30. Springer, Heidelberg (2008)
12. McPhillips, T., Bowers, S., Ludäscher, B.: Collection-oriented scientific workflows for integrating and analyzing biological data. In: Leser, U., Naumann, F., Eckman, B. (eds.) DILS 2006. LNCS (LNBI), vol. 4075, pp. 248–263. Springer, Heidelberg (2006)
13. Bowers, S., McPhillips, T., Ludäscher, B.: Provenance in collection-oriented scientific workflows. Concurrency and Computation: Practice and Experience 20(5), 519–529 (2008)
14. Foster, I., Völcker, J., Wilde, M., Zhao, Y.: Chimera: A virtual data system for representing, querying, and automating data derivation. In: 14th SSDBM, pp. 27–46. IEEE Computer Society (2002)
15. Clifford, B., Foster, I., et al.: Tracking provenance in a virtual data grid. Concurrency and Computation: Practice and Experience 20(5), 519–529 (2008)
16. Chen, I., Markowitz, V.: An overview of the object protocol model (OPM) and the OPM data management tools. Information Systems 20(5), 393–418 (1995)
17. Ailamaki, A., Ioannidis, Y., Livy, M.: Scientific workflow management by database management. In: 10th SSDBM, pp. 190–199. IEEE Computer Society (1998)
18. Biton, O., Cohen Boulakia, S., Davidson, S.: Querying and managing provenance through user views in scientific workflows. In: 24th ICDE, pp. 1072–1081. IEEE Computer Society (2008)

19. Cohen Boulakia, S., Biton, O., Cohen, S., Davidson, S.: Addressing the provenance challenge using ZOOM. Concurrency and Computation: Practice and Experience 20(5), 497–506 (2008)
20. Chebotko, A., Fei, X., Lin, C., Lu, S., Fotouhi, F.: Storing and querying scientific workflow provenance metadata using an RDBMS. In: 3rd e-Science, pp. 611–618. IEEE Computer Society (2007)
21. Van den Bussche, J., Vansummeren, S., Vossen, G.: Towards practical meta-querying. Information Systems 30(4), 317–332 (2005)
22. Van den Bussche, J., Vansummeren, S., Vossen, G.: Meta-SQL: Towards practical meta-querying. In: Bertino, E., Christodoulakis, S., Plexousakis, D., Christophides, V., Koubarakis, M., Böhm, K. (eds.) EDBT 2004. LNCS, vol. 2992, pp. 823–825. Springer, Heidelberg (2004)
23. van der Aalst, W., Reijers, H., Weijters, A., et al.: Business process mining: An industrial application. Information Systems 32(5), 713–732 (2007)
24. Santos, E., Lins, L., Ahrens, J.P., Freire, J., Silva, C.T.: A first study on clustering collections of workflow graphs. In: Freire, J., Koop, D., Moreau, L. (eds.) IPAW 2008. LNCS, vol. 5272, pp. 160–173. Springer, Heidelberg (2008)
25. Ludäscher, B., Podhorszki, N., et al.: From computation models to models of provenance: the RWS approach. Concurrency and Computation: Practice and Experience 20(5), 507–518 (2008)
26. Zao, J., et al.: Mining Taverna's semantic web of provenance. Concurrency and Computation: Practice and Experience 20(5), 463–472 (2008)
27. Barga, R., Digiampietri, L.: Automatic capture and efficient storage of e-science experiment provenance. Concurrency and Computation: Practice and Experience 20(5), 419–429 (2008)
28. Miles, S., et al.: Extracting causal graphs from an open provenance model. Concurrency and Computation: Practice and Experience 20(5), 577–586 (2008)
29. Kwasnikowska, N., Van den Bussche, J.: Mapping the NRC dataflow model to the open provenance model. In: Freire, J., Koop, D., Moreau, L. (eds.) IPAW 2008. LNCS, vol. 5272, pp. 3–16. Springer, Heidelberg (2008)
30. Moreau, L., et al.: The open provenance model. Technical Report 14979, University of Southampton, School of Electronics and Computer Science (2007)
31. Beeri, C., Eyal, A., Kamenkovich, S., Milo, T.: Querying business processes with BP-QL. Information Systems 33(6), 477–507 (2008)
32. Beeri, C., Eyal, A., Milo, T., Pilberg, A.: Monitoring business processes with queries. In: 33rd VLDB, pp. 603–614. ACM (2007)
33. Chen, J., Chung, S.Y., Wong, L.: The Kleisli query system as a backbone for bioinformatics data integration and analysis. In: Lacroix, Z., Critchlow, T. (eds.) Bioinformatics: Managing Scientific Data, pp. 147–187. Morgan Kaufmann (2003)
34. Davidson, S., Wong, L.: The Kleisli approach to data transformation and integration. In: Gray, P., Kerschberg, L., King, P., Poulovassilis, A. (eds.) The Functional Approach to Data Management, pp. 135–165. Springer (2004)
35. Buneman, P., Cheney, J., Vansummeren, S.: On the expressiveness of implicit provenance in query and update languages. In: Schwentick, T., Suciu, D. (eds.) ICDT 2007. LNCS, vol. 4353, pp. 209–223. Springer, Heidelberg (2006)
36. Cheney, J., Ahmed, A., Acar, U.: Provenance as dependency analysis. In: Arenas, M. (ed.) DBPL 2007. LNCS, vol. 4797, pp. 138–152. Springer, Heidelberg (2007)
37. Blockeel, H.: Experiment databases: A novel methodology for experimental research. In: Bonchi, F., Boulicaut, J.-F. (eds.) KDID 2005. LNCS, vol. 3933, pp. 72–85. Springer, Heidelberg (2006)

38. Blockeel, H., Vanschoren, J.: Experiment databases: Towards an improved experimental methodology in machine learning. In: Kok, J.N., Koronacki, J., Lopez de Mantaras, R., Matwin, S., Mladenič, D., Skowron, A. (eds.) PKDD 2007. LNCS (LNAI), vol. 4702, pp. 6–17. Springer, Heidelberg (2007)
39. Abiteboul, S., Hull, R., Vianu, V.: Foundations of Databases. Addison-Wesley (1995)
40. Eisenberg, A., Melton, J.: Advancements in SQL/XML. SIGMOD Record 33(3), 79–86 (2004)
41. Özcan, F., Chamberlin, D., Kulkarni, K., Michels, J.E.: Integration of SQL and XQuery in IBM DB2. IBM Systems Journal 45(2), 245–270 (2006)

Types, Functional Programming and Atomic Transactions in Hardware Design

Bluespec, Inc.
nikhil@bluespec.com

Abstract. Most hardware design languages have not benefited from modern ideas in programming languages. We describe aspects of BSV, a recent language for designing hardware systems that makes extensive use of Haskell types (Hindley-Milner types and type classes), functional programming (higher-order functions, monads) and atomic transactions in the form of concurrent rewrite rules.

Keywords: Haskell, Term Rewriting Systems, TRSs, Rewrite Rules, BSV, Bluespec SystemVerilog, Hardware Design Languages, Functional Programming.

1 Introduction

The hardware design languages most commonly used today, Verilog [8] and VHDL [6], are almost 30 years old but are being used for designs that, due to Moore's Law, are orders of magnitude larger and more complex. These languages are very low-level by the standards of modern software programming languages. Verilog (by far the more widely used) does not really have any data type other than bits and no serious abstraction mechanisms beyond a basic module structure. SystemVerilog [7] is a recent upgrade of Verilog, but other than slightly richer types, it does not offer much new expressive power for the designer (it does offer more expressive facilities for the verification engineer).

The situation has worsened in the last five years because the need for expressive hardware design languages has expanded beyond the traditional ASIC (Application Specific Integrated Circuits) designer. System architects need to experiment with complete system models (CPUs, caches, interconnects, memories, I/O devices) that run real software loads. Verification engineers need to test complex subsystems or complete systems. Software and firmware developers need to run on full system models well before ASIC silicon is available. Increasingly, these activities require emulation platforms based on FPGAs (Field Programmable Gate Arrays), because traditional software simulators are now many orders of magnitude too slow. FPGAs have the same fine-grained parallelism as ASICs, albeit somewhat slower clock speeds. But to run on FPGAs, system models and verification environments now need to be written in a hardware design language.

V. Tannen et al. (Eds.): Buneman Festschrift, LNCS 8000, pp. 418–431, 2013.

The high performance computing community (HPC) has also recently become interested in hardware design languages. Although they have long used vector supercomputers and clusters/farms with attached GPGPUs, HPC application developers are now looking at servers with attached FPGAs for compute kernels that have fine-grain, heterogeneous parallelism, which is not well served by existing HPC platforms.

BSV [13,14] is a recent hardware design language significantly raising the level of abstraction, compared to Verilog and VHDL, by incorporating ideas from Haskell [15] and Term Rewriting Systems [9]. It takes its type system from Haskell: the Hindley-Milner type system, and Haskell typeclasses. It is a Haskell-like language for circuit description, having the full power of functional programming including monadic evaluation. It takes its hardware execution semantics from Term Rewriting Systems—the execution behavior of the elaborated circuits is expressed as atomic, serializable rewrite rules.

In this paper, we describe how these ideas, familiar to those who know Haskell and Term Rewriting Systems, are applied profitably in the context of hardware design. This is more than a research exercise—BSV and its tools have been available commercially since 2005, and components designed with BSV are present in mobile and multimedia devices currently in the marketplace.

2   Using Haskell's Type System in BSV

BSV's types are essentially the same as Haskell's, except in a syntax that is based on SystemVerilog idioms: enums, structs, and tagged unions, which in Haskell are unified into the single notion of algebraic data types. Within *bsc*, the BSV compiler, they are in fact treated exactly like Haskell's algebraic data types. BSV's types can be polymorphic, just like Haskell's, and type-checking is essentially standard Hindley-Milner type-checking [12], except that the range of type inference is deliberately limited by requiring explicit type declarations in many places, in order to produce better error messages.

2.1   Strongly Typed Clocks and Static Checking of Clock Domains

In large hardware systems, different blocks and subsystems must often be driven with different clocks, based on considerations of performance, power consumption, conformance with protocol standards, and so on. Clocks are often *gated*, i.e., capable of being temporarily switched off, in order to reduce power consumption. Further, in high performance circuits, clocks must be treated very carefully in order to balance wire lengths to minimize skew (variance in the time at which a particular clock edge arrives at different places on the silicon die). In many organizations, clock circuits are designed only by experienced specialists.

Hardware is usually organized into *clock domains*, which is a partitioning of the system into disjoint regions, each of which has its own clock. "Clock domain discipline" is a design rule that requires that any signals that cross from one domain to another *must* go through a so-called "synchronizer" to avoid metastability (a pathological situation where a register's output voltage is not within the legal ranges that we designate as "0" or "1", and is stuck in the middle, for an unpredictable duration). Syncronization between two clock domains is typically not needed if both clocks are derived from a common original clock by gating or frequency division.

Despite all this, in Verilog there is in fact no distinction between clocks and ordinary signals. Clock domain discipline is merely a coding style (which can vary from one organization to the next), and a variety of brittle "linting" tools are available to check for conformance to these styles, but it is still easy to make mistakes.

BSV uses an abstract type Clock, and standard strong type-checking ensures that they can never be confused with any other signals. BSV has a precise and simple yet general notion of clock domains that is orthogonal to module structure—essentially, each *rule* (described later), along with its fragments (interface methods) that reach into other modules can be in its own clock domain. Static checking keeps track of clocks even across separately-compiled modules, so that the compiler knows which clocks are from the same "clock family", i.e., derived from the a common original clock. This, in turn, is used to verify that communication between clock domains with unrelated clocks always goes through a synchronizer. Thus many common clocking errors in Verilog are reported as compile-time errors in BSV.

2.2   Numeric Kinds and Typeclasses for Hardware Sizes and Size Constraints

Hardware resources (buses, registers, FIFOs, memories) typically have fixed sizes, and we would of course like to define modules that are polymorpic in the size of their resources. Further, different resources often have sizes that have a definite relationship. For example, a module that implements a FIFO of depth n is likely to contain a buffer of depth n, and registers containing "head" and "tail" buffer offsets which are likely to be $\log(n)$ bits wide. We would like to express such relationships and have them checked by the compiler.

BSV uses "numeric types" to represent sizes. In effect, the BSV type system has two Kinds: value types and numeric types. Relationships between numeric types are expressed either in functional form, using numeric type constructors such as TAdd#(n1,n2) and TLog#(n) or, equivalently, in relational form using numeric type classes such as Add#(n1,n2,n3) and Log#(n1,n2). These relational assertions are essentially Haskell typeclasses on types of numeric kind, and are solved by *bsc* during type-checking. Haskell's typeclass constraints appear in BSV syntax as "provisos". For example, here is a skeleton of a FIFO module constructor called mkMyFIFO.

```
module mkMyFIFO (MyFIFO #(n,t))
   provisos (Log #(n, ln),
             ... other provisos ... );
```

```
// Instantiate sub-modules (local state)
Vector #(n, Reg #(t))     buffer <- replicateM (mkRegU);
Reg #(Bits #(TLog #(n))) head   <- mkReg (0);
Reg #(Bits #(ln))         tail   <- mkReg (0);
...
endmodule
```

Here, `MyFIFO#(n,t)` is the interface type, polymorphic in `n`, the depth of the FIFO and `t`, the type of the data stored in the FIFO. The variable `buffer` is a vector of `n` registers, each containing a datum of type `t`. The `head` register and `tail` registers both hold bit vectors of width $\log(n)$. The former is declared with `TLog#(n)`, using the functional style. The latter is declared with `ln`, which is bound in the `provisos` clause by the relational typeclass `Log#(n,ln)`. The right-hand sides of the declarations are monadic instantiations of the state elements (we discuss this in more detail in a later section).

2.3 Typeclasses for Abstracting Bit Representation

Hardware designers are meticulous about bit representations (how an algebraic type or array is represented in bits), unlike software programmers who usually leave this decision to the compiler. In hardware, a representation that wastes storage bits or needs more logic in computational circuits has a direct economic impact because silicon area almost directly impacts chip cost. Redundant bits also consume power unnecessarily. Verilog's only data type is bits, so representation decisions are not even reflected in the language. SystemVerilog has language-specified representations for data types so that if you wish to change the representation you have to change the type declaration.

BSV uses Haskell's typeclasses to achieve representation independence. We define a `Bits#(t,n)` typeclass:

```
typeclass Bits #(t, n);
   function Bit #(n) pack    (t x);
   function t         unpack (Bit #(n) bs);
endtypeclass
```

The typeclass asserts that type `t` is represented in `n` bits, specifically the type `Bit#(n)`. The next two lines declare witness functions `pack` and `unpack` that convert back and forth between the type `t` and the type `Bit#(n)`.

As in Haskell, for each user-defined type, the user can create an "instance" of this typeclass, and define the specific `pack` and `unpack` functions for that type. Thus, the designer has precise control over bit representations.

Any primitive that needs the bit representation, such as a register module, a FIFO module, or a memory module, uses these overloaded `pack` and `unpack` to perform the conversion. Thus, the rest of the user code is written purely with the standard algebraic type notations (constructors, field selectors, pattern-matching, vector indexing, and so on), completely independent of the representation. The representation can be changed by simply changing the instance declaration; the rest of the code that uses the type is unaffected.

As in Haskell, for certain typeclasses in BSV the user can avoid the labor of writing explicit typeclass instances by attaching a "deriving" clause to a type declaration:

```
typedef ... some type declaration ... deriving (Bits);
```

BSV defines a fairly obvious "canonical" typeclass instance scheme for user-defined enums, structs, tagged unions and vectors. These are dense representations, using the minimum number of bits (within the canonical framework) and hence are satisfactory in almost all cases. In rare cases, a non-canonical representation exploiting some additional property of a type can use fewer bits (such as the knowledge that certain byte addresses are in fact word-aligned and therefore can omit or reuse the lower order bits). In these cases, the designer can create an explicit `Bits#(_,_)` instance declaration.

2.4   Other Uses of Typeclasses

Typeclasses are used extensively in BSV, both in the standard libraries and in user-written code. Some uses will be familiar to any Haskell programmer: the Eq typeclass for equality, the Ord typeclass for orderings, the Arith typeclass for arithmetic operations and functions, the FShow typeclass for pretty-printing, and so on. We list some other examples here to provide a flavor of their utility in expressing typically hardware concepts.

ToPut and ToGet

Two standard module interfaces in BSV are Put and Get. The former contains one method, put, and the latter one method get, using which one can send a value into a module or receive one from it, respectively (they essentially map to input and output buses, along with some handshaking signals).

Many other interfaces can be viewed as Put and Get interfaces. For example, enqueing a value into a FIFO is like a put; dequeing a value is like a get. Driving a read request on an ARM AXI bus is like a put, receiving a read response is like a get. BSV thus defines typeclasses ToPut and ToGet which contain functions toPut and toGet, respectively. Creating typeclass instances for FIFOs, AXI buses and other types allow them all to be used uniformly with the Put and Get communication interface, even though the particular signals and protocols they use vary widely.

Connectable

In hardware designs there are many pairs of compatible interfaces that can be connected together. These connections may involve not merely wires, but also combinational logic and state elements. In BSV, the idea of being able to connect two compatible interface types is expressed in the `Connectable` typeclass:

```
typeclass Connectable #(t1, t2);
   module mkConnection #(t1 ifc1, t2 ifc2) (Empty);
endtypeclass
```

Each instance of this typeclass provides a definition for a `mkConnection` module that takes two interfaces as arguments and instantiates whatever logic and state and protocols are necessary to connect those two interfaces. Thus, whether we are connecting a `Get` interface to a `Put` interface, or one FIFO to another, or an ARM AXI Master component to a Master socket on an ARM AXI bus, we uniformly use `mkConnection` to create the connection.

These facilities also enable flexible *composition* of interfaces. For example, even if two interfaces `ifcA` and `ifcX` are not directly connectable, it may be possible to connect them by converting them to `Get` and `Put` interfaces:

```
   mkConnection (toGet (ifcA), toPut (ifcX));
```

3   Functional Programming for Circuit Description

The full power of functional programming can be utilized in the *static elaboration* phase of a hardware design language. In software languages there are usually two distinct parts or phases in the semantics. The static semantics is defined on the source text: syntactic correctness, type-checking, scoping rules, and so on. The dynamic semantics describes the run time or execution behavior.

In hardware design languages there is another distinct phase called static elaboration. For example, in Verilog, this phase creates the hardware module hierarchy: the top-level module instantiates its sub-modules which recursively instantiate their sub-modules, and so on. A single module definition in the source text may be instantiated multiple times. Static elaboration results in a tree of module instances, connected by the language's communication channels (in Verilog, these are just wires). The language's dynamic execution semantics are defined on this module hierarchy and not on the source text.

Static elaboration can be viewed as a one-time execution of the original source text to describe an actual hardware circuit. In existing hardware design languages, static elaboration is mostly about straightforward module instantiation. However, there is no reason to limit the power of static elaboration in this way. In BSV, static elaboration is essentially Haskell execution: it is a full, pure, higher-order, lazy functional language, including monadic evaluation of modules. In the following sections we show examples of how this enables powerful abstraction in circuit description.

3.1   A Simple Example: A Routing Function Argument for a Polymorphic Switch

Here is the skeleton of the declaration of a module implementing a packet switch:

```
1  module mkSwitch
2     #(function Bit #(TLog #(n)) destination (t pkt))
3     (Switch_IFC #(m, n, t));
4     ...
5     body of module
6     ...
7  endmodule
```

Line 3 is the interface type of the switch, parametrized by m, the number of input ports, n the number of output ports, and t, the type of packets that flow through the switch. Line 2 is the module argument, and is a function from packets to output port numbers (note that the output port number must be $\log(n)$ bits wide, in order to name one of the n output ports). This function is used in the module body to route each incoming packet to its proper destination.

An example like this may at first seem surprising, raising questions like "what does it mean to pass a function argument in hardware". But this is not what is happening—we are merely passing a function argument during static elaboration. As long as the final result of static elaboration is something that can feasibly be implemented in hardware, the language of static elaboration need not be restricted in any way. In BSV, static elaboration essentially has the power of Haskell.

3.2   Higher-Order Functions to Capture Pipeline Structures

Higher-order functions are excellent for capturing common design patterns (maps and folds being two of the most famous). In hardware designs, pipelining is an area rich in design patterns, and we can use the full power of higher-order polymorphic functions to abstract common activities in building complex pipeline structures. We start by defining a standard interface for the output of a pipeline component:

```
interface PipeOut #(type t);
   method t       first ();      // view the next element from the pipe
   method Action deq ();         // pop the next element from the pipe
   method Bool   notEmpty ();    // test if the pipe has an element
endinterface
```

The compositional building blocks have the type Pipe#(ta,tb), representing a pipeline with an input stream of elements of type ta and an output stream of elements of type tb:

```
typedef
    (function Module #(PipeOut #(tb)) mkFoo (PipeOut #(ta) ifc))
    Pipe#(type ta, type tb);
```

or, to express it in more conventional notation, `Pipe(ta,tb)` is a synonym for:

```
PipeOut #(ta) → Module #(PipeOut #(tb))
```

In other words, a `Pipe#(ta,tb)` value is a function from the pipe output of the preceding (upstream) pipe to a new module whose interface is the new pipe output. For example, a constructor to serially compose two existing pipelines is declared like this:

```
module mkCompose_buffered  #(Bool param_with_buffer,
                             Pipe #(a, b) pab,
                             Pipe #(b, c) pbc,
                             PipeOut #(a) pa)
                            (PipeOut #(c));
```

Input data of type `a` are taken from `pa`, the output interface of the upstream pipe, and are fed into the first pipe `pab`. Its outputs, of type `b`, are fed into the second pipe `pbc`. Its outputs, of type `c`, are the outputs of the composite pipe. The additional boolean argument `param_with_buffer` optionally inserts a pipeline register between `pab` and `pbc`. BSV functions can be curried, so when partially applied to 3 arguments, `mkCompose_buffered(bool,pab,pbc)`, we get a value of type `Pipe#(a,c)`, i.e., a standard building block.

Here is a constructor to create an "if-then-else" pipeline structure:

```
module mkIfThenElse  #(Pipe #(a,b)  pipeT,
                       Pipe #(a,b)  pipeF,
                       PipeOut #(Tuple2 #(a, Bool)) poa)
                      (PipeOut #(b));
```

The upstream pipe `poa` delivers a stream of pairs of values of type `a` and `Bool`. Depending on the boolean, the corresponding value is either sent into `pipeT` or into `pipeF`. The outputs of these pipes, of type `b`, are delivered as the final output of the composite structure. When partially applied to two arguments, `mkIfThenElse(pt,pf)`, we once again get a standard building block with type `Pipe#(Tuple2#(a,Bool),b)`.

These are examples of functions from a BSV library called PAClib (Pipeline Architecture Constructor library) that contains many other functions for creating pipeline structures representing while loops, for loops, forks and joins, maps, folds, and more. They implement all the control circuits and pipeline buffering needed to build complex, flow-controlled pipelines, independent of the specific computational logic of particular applications.[1]

3.3 Monadic Static Elaboration

Static elaboration in BSV is a functional program evaluation in a "module monad". Conceptually, execution begins at a top-level module and sequentially processes the statements in the module, collecting semantic entities in the module such as sub-module instantiations, rules and interfaces. At each sub-module instantiation, we recursively process that sub-module.

For most users of BSV, this monadic evaluation is invisible, happening inside the *bsc* compiler. However, since the module monad is polymorphic, users can extend this monadic evaluation to solve certain common problems encountered in hardware design.

Control and Status Regsiters

In a hardware system, which is organized as a module hierarchy, various modules in the hierarchy may contain so-called Control and Status Registers (CSRs) for configuring the modules and reading back status while the hardware is running. All these registers, across the entire module hierarchy, are usually accessible over a separate CSR bus in a memory-mapped manner. Thus, in addition to its normal operational interface, every module has an extra set of highly stylized inputs and outputs for accessing its own CSRs and the CSRs in sub-modules. It is usually quite laborious to create the CSR bus interfaces to these registers and to create the "plumbing" of the CSR bus down the module hierarchy to all the places where it is needed. This extra code also compromises the simplicity and clarity of normal module code (consider a module that does not itself has any CSRs, but must pass the CSR bus through to sub-modules that do have CSRs). Maintenance of such code, when written in Verilog, is a nightmare, various ad hoc tools have been developed for "stitching" in CSR resources as a separate step.

Monadic evaluation provides a simple and elegant solution to this problem. CSRs become just another type of entity collected in the monad, and we can completely automate the creation of their bus interfaces and the plumbing of the CSR bus. Since all this information is carried in the "hidden" state of the monad, the source code is no longer cluttered with all this boilerplate CSR plumbing.

Probes and I/O

In a hardware design, we may wish to examine certain internal signals or perform some I/O of certain values, from arbitrary points in the module hierarchy. When running in simulation, these are typically just side-effects handled

---

[1] The general idea of using higher-order functions to describe circuit structures has also been explored earlier in Lava [2].

magically by the simulator. But when running on real hardware (such as on an FPGA), this requires actual hardware circuits to carry the data along the module hierarchy to and from the interface of the top-level (outermost) module. Monadic evaluation provides a way to automatically perform this plumbing of probe and I/O signals without cluttering the source code.

4 Rewrite Rules and Atomicity

Everything we have described so far is about circuit *structure*: types, and functional programming to describe circuits. The final output of static elaboration is a module hierarchy. What do these modules do (how do they execute?) and how do they communicate with each other? In other words, what is their dynamic semantics?

All behavior in BSV is expressed using *rules*. Here is the rest of the mkSwitch module whose skeleton we presented earlier:

```
1   module mkSwitch
2       #(function Bit #(TLog #(n)) destination (t pkt))
3       (Switch_IFC #(m, n, t));
4
5       // ----------------
6       // STATE: input and output queues
7       Vector #(m, FIFO #(t_pkt)) vf_ins  <- replicateM (mkFIFO);
8       Vector #(n, FIFO #(t_pkt)) vf_outs <- replicateM (mkFIFO);
9
10      // ----------------
11      // BEHAVIOR (atomic transactional rules)
12      for (Integer i = 0; i < valueOf (m); i = i + 1)
13         for (Integer j = 0; j < valueOf (n); j = j + 1)
14            rule transfer_packet (destination(vf_ins [i].first)
15                                  == fromInteger (j));
16               let pkt = vf_ins [i].first;
17               vf_ins [i].deq;
18               vf_outs [j].enq (pkt);
19            endrule
20
21      // ----------------
22      // INTERFACE (atomic transactional methods)
23      interface inputs  = map (toPut, vf_ins);
24      interface outputs = map (toGet, vf_outs);
25   endmodule
```

Lines 12 and 13 are statically elaborated for-loops that create $m \times n$ rules. The $(i, j)^{\text{th}}$ rule examines the packet at the head of the ith input FIFO, and tests if its destination is j. If so, it performs the action of dequeueing the packet and enqueueing it into the jth output FIFO.

Every rule has a CAN_FIRE condition and an action. In each rule above, its CAN_FIRE has several components. The boolean expression on lines 14-15 is an obvious component, but other components are booleans implicitly accompanying the methods first, deq and enq. These method conditions are specified inside the FIFO module by the implementer of that module. For example, the conditions of first and deq are true only when the FIFO is not empty, and the condition of the enq method is true only when the FIFO is not full.

Thus, an atomic unit of behavior is constructed from fragments that may span many module boundaries (a rule in one module invokes a method of another module, which may, in turn, invoke further methods of other modules and so on). A method is, in effect, a rule fragment. The CAN_FIRE condition of a rule involves the conditions of the rule itself and the conditions of all methods invoked, directly or transitively. Similarly, the overall action of a rule includes the actions of all methods invoked, directly or transitively. It is this cross-module composition of atomic units that gives rules tremendous expressive power.

To first approximation, BSV rule semantics are the same as for classical rewrite rules, which are explained very simply:

> while (True)
>   Choose any rule whose CAN_FIRE is true
>   Perform the rule's action

Thus, a BSV program's state evolves by repeated rule execution. Note that the semantics is non-deterministic in picking any enabled rule (since the conditions of many rules may be true), and describes a sequential trajectory through a space of possible states. Modulo syntactic differences and minor details, this is a classical Term Rewriting System (TRS) [9], and all the theoretical machinery of TRSs can be brought to bear on reasoning about the correctness of BSV programs. These semantics are also found in languages like Guarded Commands [4], UNITY [3], TLA+ [10], and Event B [11] for formal specification of concurrent state-based systems.

When the *bsc* compiler translates BSV into hardware, it creates circuits that, in effect, execute multiple rules "concurrently" in each clock cycle. In particular, it tries to execute as many rules as possible in each clock, in order to maximize performance. However, the hardware execution will always be consistent with the TRS semantics, i.e., there is always a logical sequential order to concurrent rule execution (which we call a rule *schedule*). Another way of saying this is that despite concurrent execution of rules within a clock, rules can be regarded as distributed (across modules), user-defined atomic transactions, so that one can continue to reason about invariants on a rule-by-rule basis, without worrying about interleavings of actions from different rules.

4.1   Structured Processes (FSMs) from Rules and Higher-Order Static Elaboration

A rule in BSV is a unit of behavior. There is no a priori sequencing of rules; they execute when their conditions are true, as described in the previous section. However, one often sets up rule conditions and actions in such a way that their collective behavior forms a structured process. Consider the following code fragment:

```
typedef enum  S0, S1, S2, ...   State deriving (Bits, Eq);

module mkFoo (...);
   Reg #(State) state <- mkReg (S0);

   rule r0 (state == S0);
      ... do state S0 actions ...
        state <= S1;                            // next state
   endrule

   rule r1 (state == S1);
      ... do state S1 actions ...
        state <= (cond ? S1 : S2);  // loop back to S1, or to S2
   endrule

   rule r2 (state == S2);
      ... do state S2 actions ...
      ... transition to next state ....
   endrule
endmodule
```

The `state` register is initialized to S0, so initially rule r0 can fire. It sets `state` to S1, enabling rule r1. This rule sets `state` either to S1 or to S2; in the former case, rule r1 is enabled again, and in the latter case rule r2 is enabled. This is essentially a structured sequential process (known as FSMs in hardware design), one that would be expressed in a more traditional imperative language like this:

```
   ... do state S0 actions ...
   repeat
      ... ... do state S1 actions ...
   until (! cond)
   ... ... do state S2 actions ...
```

During BSV static elaboration, rules and actions are first-class objects, with type `Rules` and `Action`, respectively. One can write functions to create rules and actions, collect them in data structures, and so on. Thus, it is possible write higher-order functions that are essentially constructors for various process structures: sequential and parallel composition, conditionals, while/for/until loops, and so on. In fact, such FSM structures are so common in hardware design that BSV contains an embedded FSM language, but users can, in addition, extend this with their own FSM constructors.

5 Conclusion

Perhaps because of the cultural separation of Electrical Engineering and Computer Science commonly seen in universities, many hardware designers have not been exposed to types and abstraction in modern programming languages, nor to functional programming, and have not seen the relevance of those topics to what they do. This is reflected in significant weaknesses in hardware design languages. Conversely, software engineers take their computing platforms as given and have not so far considered hardware design as relevant to what they do, and perhaps even view hardware design as a fundamentally "low-level" activity. This may change as FPGA acceleration becomes more common.

Such a separation is of course absurd. Ultimately, it's all just computation, and the choice of software or hardware execution is an implementation choice based on pragmatic considerations of speed of developement, speed of execution, power consumption, cost, convenience, and so on. The principles of types and abstraction are orthogonal to this choice, and are equally important whether designing software or hardware.

In this paper we have described BSV, a language that tries to bridge this gap by using ideas from Haskell (types and functional programming) and Term Rewriting Systems (atomic concurrent rewrite rules) to create a semantically clean and expressive language for hardware design that can appeal both to hardware and software designers.

Acknowledgements. In 1977, Peter Buneman introduced me, a fresh graduate student at the University of Pennsylvania, to the joys of Landin, ISWIM and Burge in one of his courses. Working with him, I was privileged to use my first higher-order functional programming language, POP-10, which Peter had brought from Edinburgh and had installed on the Wharton School DEC-10. This led to studying Backus' FP and FFP, Hope, SASL and KRC, Combinator Reduction and Graph Reduction, and to my thesis work on the Functional Query Language (FQL). I also had the pleasure of interacting with many exciting people who came to UPenn through Peter's influence, such as Malcolm Atkinson (PS-Algol), Dave MacQueen (ML) and Luca Cardelli (my UPenn PhD thesis was implemented using Luca's ML). You can see the connection from those wonderful influences at UPenn to the ideas discussed in this paper. I am still enthralled by the beauty of typeful and functional programming, to which I was first introduced by Peter.

The TRS aspects of BSV has its origins in research by Hoe and Arvind at MIT in the late 1990s [5]. The Haskell aspects of BSV were originally conceived by Lennart Augustsson [1].

References

1. Augustsson, L., Schwartz, J., Nikhil, R.S.: Bluespec Language Definition, The earliest version of BSV (2001)
2. Bjesse, P., Claessen, K., Sheeran, M., Singh, S.: Lava: Hardware Design in Haskell. In: Proc. ACM Intl. Conf. on Functional Programming, ICFP (1998)
3. Chandy, K., Misra, J.: Parallel Program Design: A Foundation. Addison Wesley (1988)
4. Dijkstra, E.W.: Guarded Commands, Nondeterminacy and Formal Derivation of Programs. Communications of the ACM 18(8), 453–457 (1975)
5. Hoe, J.C., Arvind: Synthesis of Operation-Centric Hardware Descriptions. In: IEEE/ACM Intl. Conf. on Computer Aided Design (ICCAD), pp. 511–518 (2000)
6. IEEE: IEEE Standard VHDL Language Reference Manual, IEEE Std 1076-1993 (2002)
7. IEEE: IEEE Standard for System Verilog—Unified Hardware Design, Specification and Verification Language, IEEE Std 1800-2005 (2005)
8. IEEE: IEEE Standard Verilog Hardware Description Language, iEEE Std 1364-2005 (2005)
9. Klop, J.: Term Rewriting Systems. In: Abramsky, S., Gabbay, D.M., Maibaum, T.S.E. (eds.) Handbook of Logic in Computer Science, vol. 2, pp. 1–116. Oxford University Press (1992)
10. Lamport, L.: Specifying Systems: The TLA+ Language and Tools for Hardware and Software Engineers. Addison-Wesley Professional (Pearson Education) (2002)
11. Metayer, C., Abrial, J.R., Voisin, L.: The Event-B Language (May 31, 2005), http://rodin.cs.ncl.ac.uk/deliverables.htm
12. Milner, R.: A Theory of Type Polymorphism in Programming. J. of Computer and System Sciences 17, 348–375 (1978)
13. Nikhil, R.S.: Abstraction in Hardware System Design. Communications of the ACM 54(10), 36–44 (2011)
14. Nikhil, R.S., Czeck, K.R.: BSV by Example. CreateSpace (December 2010) (book form: Amazon.com; PDF: bluespec.com)
15. Peyton Jones, S., (ed.): Haskell 98 Language and Libraries: The Revised Report. Cambridge University Press (2003), haskell.org

Record Polymorphism:
Its Development and Applications*

Atsushi Ohori

Research Institute of Electrical Communication
Tohoku University
ohori@riec.tohoku.ac.jp

Abstract. Record polymorphism plays an essential role in developing a static type system for labeled record structures such as relational databases. Moreover, compilation method for record polymorphism serves as the basis for efficiently compiling various advanced features in statically typed polymorphic programming languages. This article overviews the power and applicability of record polymorphism that have been implemented in SML♯, an extension of Standard ML been developed at RIEC, Tohoku University.

1 Introduction

Labeled records are ubiquitous data structures in programming languages and systems. They are basic data type constructors in programming languages. Classes and objects in object-oriented programming and tuples and tables in relational databases are also regarded as labeled record structures. They differ in details of their properties and associated operations, but all of them share the same underlying principles, namely *record polymorphism*. Record polymorphism concerns both static typing and compilation.

Static typing attempts to identify the set of well-behaved programs as the set of well-typed ones. It is relatively easy to exclude all the erroneous programs. The challenging part is to accept many useful programs including all the basic operations. For a language with functions and products, this is realized by polymorphic type discipline, which has been successfully used in the ML family of programming languages. In the polymorphic type system of the pure ML language, such as the one defined in [2], the polymorphic property of each of the primitive operations is represented by its most general polymorphic type. This property is the key to the flexibility and type-safety of ML programming. Labeled records should be given the same status. For a language with labeled records, a polymorphic type system must therefore be one that accepts all the basic record operations. The precise definition of the basic record operations may depend on the systems and languages, but there is the fundamental one, namely the operation to access a labeled field, which is the basis for any system

---

* This work was partially supported by Grant-in-aid for scientific research (C), grant no:22500023, and Grant-in-aid for scientific research (B), grant no:25280019.

V. Tannen et al. (Eds.): Buneman Festschrift, LNCS 8000, pp. 432–444, 2013.

manipulating labeled records. The polymorphic typing discipline [15,3] of the lambda calculus cannot represent the polymorphic nature of this operation. As a consequence, the conventional polymorphic type systems including that of ML cannot accept polymorphic record operations. Record polymorphism solves this problem.

Program execution is, in principle, independent of a static type system. However, a properly defined type system should reflect the essence of the computation. Through this property, a type system can lead to efficient compilation. This is indeed the case for record polymorphism, which yields type-directed compilation that compiles record operations to efficient codes. Moreover, the mechanism developed for polymorphic record compilation can be used to compile a number of advanced program constructs.

These two features of record polymorphism are the key aspects in the design and implementation of SML♯ [16], a new programming language in the ML family developed at RIEC, Tohoku University. The purpose of this paper is to present the essence of record polymorphism: its static polymorphic type system and its expressiveness, type-directed record compilation method and its applications through examples in the development of the SML♯ compiler. This would shed some light on the design and implementation of languages and systems involving record structures.

The rest of this paper is organized as follows. Section 2 overviews the development of the polymorphic type discipline for labeled records. Section 3 demonstrates the expressiveness of record polymorphism through examples and shows its application to SQL integration in SML♯. Section 4 outlines the central idea of polymorphic record compilation. Section 5 discusses applications of record compilation used in the SML♯ compiler. Section 6 concludes the paper.

2   Type System with Record Polymorphism

Investigation of type systems for record polymorphism started as an attempt to construct a complete type inference system for a language with labeled records. Except for an incomplete system [17], the first sound and complete type inference system for records was presented by Ohori and Buneman [10], as a type inference system for a functional language extended with a (nested) relational algebra. The basic idea underlying this type system is to include a constraint of the form $(l : \tau) \in \alpha$ on type variable α, indicating that any instance of α must be a record type containing a field $l : \tau$.

Soon after this proposal, Rémy [14] presented another polymorphic typing discipline for records. His system uses a constraint of the form $\alpha^{\{l\}}$ indicating that α ranges only over those record fields that do not contain the l field. Compared to the Ohori-Buneman system, a type system with this negative constraint is strictly stronger, and a variety of record operations are cleanly represented. However, perhaps due to this generality, Remy's type system does not yields efficient compilation method. One advantage of the Ohori-Buneman approach is that its constraint $l : \tau \in \alpha$ directly reflects the runtime computation performed by the record operation #l to access the l field of a record. This property yields a type-directed compilation of record polymorphism.

The Ohori-Buneman type system has been refined in [8,9] to a second-order kinded polymorphic type system, which leads to the development of SML♯, an extension of Standard ML supporting record polymorphism and other features. This language contains two basic record operations shown in the following interactive session in SML♯, where the user input is prompted by # and the system response is displayed with its type.

```
$ smlsharp
SML# version 1.2.0 (2013-06-26 15:21:29 JST) for x86-linux
# fun getX P = #X P;
val getX = _ : ['a#{X:'b},'b. 'a -> 'b]
# fun incX (P as {X,...})= P # {X = X + 1};
val incX = _ : ['a#{X:int}. 'a -> 'a]
```

Here, #X e extracts the X field from a record e, while e_1 # $\{X = e_2\}$ creates a new record by modifying the X field of a record e_1 with e_2. $\{X, \ldots\}$ is a flexible record pattern that matches any record having a label X. The notation 'a#$\{X:\tau\}$ is a type variable 'a with the constraint that its instance must be a record type containing the field X:τ. The type ['a#{X:'b},'b. 'a -> 'b] is a polymorpic type where the type variables 'a and 'b are universally bound; it corresponds to the logical notation $\forall(b, a :: \{X : b\}).a \to b$.

3   Representing Various Record Structures

Polymorphic record operations allow us to represent various record structures directly within the type system of Standard ML. This section demonstrates the expressiveness of record polymorphism through examples in SML♯.

3.1   Modular Programming through Record Polymorphism

With record polymorphism, one can write extensible generic codes by focusing only on the relevant properties of problems. This provides a powerful tool for modular construction of a large software.

To demonstrate this feature, let us consider a problem to simulate object movement in a Cartesian coordinate system. An object can be represented as a record containing X and Y fields of the current position, and Vx and Vy fields of the current velocity vector. We assume that the object is freely falling in a parabolic path, and develop a function **update** that computes the object states after one time unit. The X and Y positions can be computed independently as follows.

```
# fun moveX (p as {X,Vx,...}) = p # {X = X + Vx};
val moveX = fn
   : ['a#{Vx:'b,X:'b},'b::{int,word,word8,intInf,real,real32}.
```

```
      'a -> 'a]
# fun moveY (p as {Y,Vy,...}) = p # {Y = Y + Vy};
val moveY = fn
  : ['a#{Vy:'b,Y:'b},'b::{int,word,word8,intInf,real,real32}.
    'a -> 'a]
```

Here, `'b::{int,word,word8,intInf,real,real32}` is type variable `'b` whose possible instances are constrained to the specified set. This constraint comes from the overloaded primitive operation +. This feature is explain in Subsection 5.2. Acceleration functions can also be coded independently.

```
# fun accelerateX (p as {Vx,...}) = p # {Vx = Vx + 0.0};
val accelerateX = _ : ['a#{Vx:real}. 'a -> 'a]
# fun accelerateY (p as {Vy,...}) = p # {Vy = Vy - 9.8};
val accelerateY = _ : ['a#{Vy:real}. 'a -> 'a]
```

The function **update** is then defined by simply composing all of them as shown below.

```
# fun update p = (accelerateX o accelerateY o moveX o moveY) p;
val update = _ : ['a#{Vx:real,Vy:real,X:real,Y:real}. 'a -> 'a]
```

Here, o is the function composition operator in Standard ML. The resulting code is highly modular and type safe, and can be further combined with other behaviors of the objects quite easily. Our experience of developing a 2-D game program in SML♯ shows that this approach yields modular and declarative description of complex system behaviors.

3.2   Representing Relational Databases

Record polymorphism [10] was originally invented for representing relational databases in a polymorphic language. Based on this result and the observation that SQL statements are expressions that are polymorphic in their record structures, Machiavelli was designed [11,1]. In this language, one can write the following function on complex objects (nested relations).

```
fun Wealthy(S) = select x.Name
                 where x <- S
                 with x.Salary > 100000;
  : ['a#{Name:'b,Salary:int}, 'b. 'a -> 'b set]
```

where the type is presented in the notation used in the present paper.

As a database language, Machiavelli was only a conceptual one in the sense that it did not have practical implementation for database access, but it did demonstrate that if the type system of ML is extended with record polymorphism then it can cleanly represent SQL. This idea has been fully realized [12] in SML♯, which seamlessly integrate SQL expressions as first-class citizens in an extension of Standard ML. In SML♯, **Wealthy** above can be coded as the following function.

```
val Wealthy = _sql db => select #person.name as name
                        from #db.people as person
                        where SQL.>= (#person.salary,1000)
```

The `select` clause is SML♯ notation of an SQL expression that is evaluated by a remote database server. For this function, SML♯ infers the following typing.

```
val Wealthy = _
  : ['a#{people:'b},b#{name:'d,salary:int},'c,
     'd::{int,word,char,string,real,'e option},
     'e::{int,word,char,bool,string,real}.
       ('a, 'c) SQL.db -> {name:'d} SQL.query]
```

The type information is rather involved but it indeed represents the polymorphic properties of the SQL expression:

- It is a function that takes a database connection `db`.
- The connected database may be of any type `'a` as long as it contains a `people` table. This is represented by the type `('a, 'c) SQL.db` with the constraint `'a#{people:'b}`. The extra type parameter `'c` is here for enforcing the uniqueness of the database connection throughout the entire query expression. This is a subtle typing issue of integrating SQL in a higher-order language. The interested reader is referred to [12].
- The `people` table may be of any type `'b` as long as it contains a `name` column of any atomic type and a `salary` column of type `int`. This is represented by the constraint `'b#{name:'d,salary:int}`.
- The `name` column can be any atomic type including those of `NULL`. This property is represented by the constraint `'d::{int,word,char,string,real,'e option}` and `'e::{int,word,char,bool,string,real}`. The null value of type b is represented by `NONE` of the type b `option`.

The inferred type is indeed a principal type of this SQL expression. By this mechanism, SML♯ achieves seamless integration with SQL. SQL expressions can be freely combined with any other feature of the language.

3.3 Representing Objects

Although object-oriented programming involves a number of features beyond labeled record structures (see [4] for a survey on various typing issues in object-oriented programming), its polymorphic properties are based on the polymorphic operations on record structures. So one can enjoy some benefits of object-oriented programming in a functional language that supports record polymorphism.

An object can be represented in a variety of ways. In a simple view, an object is a reference to a record of attributes and a method is a function that takes such a state, accesses the necessary attributes and performs some computation. Under this simple view, methods for point objects may contain the following.

```
fun getX self = #X (!self)
fun setX self x = self := (!self # {X = x})
fun getY self = #Y (!self)
fun setY self x = self := (!self # {Y = x})
```

Here, ! is the pointer dereference operator and := is the pointer assignment operator in Standard ML. A class and an object can then be represented as follows.

```
val pointClass = {getX=getX, setX=setX, getY=getY, setY=setY}
val myPoint =
  let val state =  ref {X = 0.0, Y = 0.0}
  in fn selector => selector pointClass state
  end
val myColorPoint =
  let val state =  ref {X = 0.0, Y = 0.0, Color = "red"}
  in fn selector => selector pointClass state
  end
```

The defined object can be manipulated as follows.

```
# myPoint # setX 1.0;
val it = () : unit
# myPoint # getX;
val it = 1.0 : real
# myColorPoint # getX;
val it = 0.0 : real
# myPoint # getColor
(interactive):28.1-28.18 Error:
(type inference 007) operator and operand don't agree
    (further error information omitted.)
```

As shown in the last example, the system detects the type error statically.

3.4 Representing Polymorphic Variants

A commonly used feature of object-oriented programming is heterogeneous collections. One way to represent heterogeneous collections is using polymorphic variants. The polymorphic type system of [9] contains polymorphic variants, but this feature is not implemented in SML♯ considering the fact that Standard ML already contains variants tied with recursive type definition. However, as mentioned in [9], a variant type $\langle l_1 : \tau_1, \ldots, l_n : \tau_n \rangle$ can be encoded as $\forall t.\{l_1 : \tau_1 \to t, \ldots, l_n : \tau_n \to t\} \to t$. So programming with polymorphic variants can be done in a language with record polymorphism. Here we demonstrate this technique in SML♯.

As a simple example, consider a system where we have two representations for point objects, one in Cartesian coordinates and the other in polar coordinates. In this system, each representation is processed differently, so each point data has to be attached with a tag (label) indicating its representation. By regarding the label as a service selector from a given set of services, this system can be represented by polymorphic records. For example, the following codes show two representations of the same point.

```
# val myCPoint = fn M => #CPoint M {X=1.0, Y = 1.0};
val myCPoint = _
  : ['a#{CPoint: {X:real,Y:real} -> 'b}, 'b. 'a -> 'b]
# val myPPoint = fn M => #PPoint M {r=1.41421356, theta = 45.0 };
val myPPoint = _
  : ['a#{PPoint:{r:real,theta:real} -> 'b}, 'b. 'a -> 'b]
```

The idea is that a variant data with a tag T is considered as an object that receives a method suite, selects an appropriate method using T as the selector, and applies the selected method to itself. A method that works for all possible variants can be defined by writing the set of functions for all the variants, and creating a record consisting of these methods labeled with the corresponding variant tags. For example, a method to compute the distance from the origin can be coded as the following record.

```
val distance =
  {
    CPoint = fn {X,Y,...} => Real.Math.sqrt (X * X + Y * Y),
    PPoint = fn {r,...} => r
  };
```

This method suite is invoked on an object by applying the object function to the method suite as in the following.

```
# myCPoint distance ;
val it = 1.414213562373 : real
# myPPoint distance ;
val it = 1.41421356 : real
```

Record polymorphism allows us to create heterogeneous lists as in the following.

```
# val pointList = [myCPoint, myPPoint];
val pointList = _
  : ['a#{CPoint: {X:real,Y:real} -> 'b,
         PPoint: {r:real,theta:real} -> 'b},
     'b.
       ('a -> 'b) list]
# fun pointIter pointList method =
    map (fn x => x method) pointList;
val pointIter = _ : ['a, 'b. ('a -> 'b) list -> 'a -> 'b list]
# pointIter pointList distance;
val it = [1.414213562373, 1.41421356] : real list
```

In this way, various heterogeneous collections can be processed in a type safe way.

4 Type-Directed Compilation of Record Polymorphism

The other aspect of record polymorphism is type-directed compilation of polymorphic record operation. Without this, practical usefulness of record polymorphism is rather limited.

To see the problem, consider the expression `fn x => #Y x`. In a simple type system, the type of x is fixed to a concrete record type such as `{X:int, Y:int}`. The compiler then compiles a record of type `{X:int, Y:int}` to a vector of two consecutive `int` values, and compiles `#Y x` to an instruction to load the second element of the vector representation. This is a routine practice in a monomorphic language with records. However, in a language where field selection operation is polymorphic, compiling expression such as `fn x => #Y x` to efficient codes is a subtle problem. In a dynamically typed language, some form of dynamic look-up for the specified label is necessary. There have been some efforts to optimize the necessary dynamic look-up using a form of hashing [18], but certain amount of overhead in both space and time is inevitable even when the record structure is statically known.

The goal of type-directed record compilation is to compile polymorphic record operations into efficient codes. This is based on the following observation. The polymorphic typing of `#Y`

```
val f = fn x => #Y x : ['a#{Y:'b},'b. 'a -> 'b]
```

statically predicts its dynamic behavior that the Y field is selected from a record x of type `'a`. Furthermore, when this function is applied to some record such as `{X=1, Y=2}`, the type variable `'a` is instantiated to its type `{X:int, Y:int}`. At this time, the type system knows from the type instantiation for `'a#{Y:'b}` that the position of Y in `{X:int, Y:int}` is 2. The function can then be compiled to the following code.

```
val f = fn I => fn x => x[I]
    : ['a#{Y:'b},'b. index('a,Y) -> 'a -> 'b]
```

`x[I]` loads the I-th element from a vector representation of a record `x`. `index('a, Y)` is a type that denotes the singleton set of the index value corresponding to Y in a record `'a`. When this function is applied to `{X=1, Y=2}`, this type is instantiated to `index({X:int, Y:int}, Y)` which is equal to 2. From this information, the compiler generates the following code for application.

```
f 2 {X = 1, Y = 2}
```

By this way, polymorphic field operation can be implemented with small overhead of passing one extra integer value. Moreover, when the type of a record is statically known, this method does not introduce any overhead in both space and time. Based on these observations, a compilation method for polymorphic record operations has been developed in [8,9]. The SML♯ compiler is developed based on this method.

5   Applications of Type-Directed Compilation

As we have reviewed above, type-directed polymorphic record compilation is based on the combination of the following three ideas.

1. Introduce a special singleton type (e.g. a type of the form index('a,Y) in the above example) that denotes the singleton set of a runtime value needed for compilation.
2. When a kinded type variable (e.g. 'a#{Y:int}) is abstracted, insert a lambda abstraction over the corresponding singleton type (e.g. index('a,Y)).
3. When the abstracted kinded type variable is instantiated to a ground type (e.g. index({X:int, Y:int},Y)), generate the value denoted by the singleton type (e.g. 2) and insert a lambda application to pass this value.

The mechanism turns out to be a general compilation method having a number of applications in compiling various advance program constructs. Similar mechanisms have later been variously called in the literature as *evidences* [6] and *dictionary conversion* [13]. Although the literature did not seem to properly compare these mechanisms, the essence of these mechanisms appears to be the same as the one in [8], which first presented the ideas and developed them as a type-directed compilation method.

In the design and implementation of SML♯, this mechanism plays a central role in achieving its advanced features. In the rest of this section, we outline the applicability of using SML♯ implementation as examples.

5.1   Natural Data Representation

One major problem of functional languages is the lack of direct interoperability with the C language. The difficulty comes from the need of garbage collected memory management. Accurate garbage collection needs to identify all the pointer locations. For this purpose, conventional implementation of functional languages either represents all memory objects as pointers or introduces a tag bit within non-pointer objects such as integers. Due to these special runtime representations, conventional functional languages do not even have interoperability with C on atomic data such as integers and floating point numbers.

SML♯ solves this problem and achieves direct interface to C. Functions and libraries written in C can be directly called from SML♯ codes without writing data conversion function. Following codes is a fragment of an OpenGL demo program distributed with SML♯.

```
val glNormal3dv =
  dlsym (libgl, "glNormal3dv")
  : _import (real * real * real) -> unit
  ...
  map (fn (x,...) => (glNormal3dv x; ...)
  [((1.0,0.0,0.0),...),...]
```

This code dynamically links `glNormal3dv` function in the OpenGL library and calls it with a record created in SML♯. The key to the development is natural data representation [7] through type-directed compilation. In SML♯, a heap object has the following memory representation.

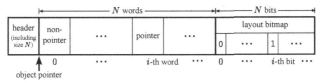

The actual object part (N-word part above) is the same as in C. For example, a heap-allocated object of type `real * real * real` is represented as 3 consecutive 64 bit floating point data, together with its layout bitmap indicating that all the words are non-pointers. The layout bitmap of an abject is used by the garbage collector to locate the set of pointer fields in the object.

In a monomorphic language, it is a simple matter to construct such an object representation. However, in a polymorphic language, constructing this natural representation is a hard problem. To see the problem, consider the following very simple code fragment, shown with its type, that creates a heap-allocated data.

```
fun f x = (x,x,x) : ['a. 'a -> 'a * 'a * 'a]
```

To compile this function, the compiler needs to generate codes that construct a heap-allocated object `(x,x,x)`. To allocate a heap block, the compiler needs to know the size and alignment constraint of `x`. To generate a layout bitmap for the garbage collector, the compiler needs to know whether `x` is a pointer or not. These properties are not available at the time when this function is compiled. Due to this problem, most conventional functional language compilers give up natural data representation.

This problem is essentially the same as that of polymorphic record field access we have analyzed. The occurrence of `'a` in a tuple type indicates that its size and the pointer property are required. We can then directly adopt the record compilation method and introduce the following types:

- `size(τ)` to denote the singleton set of the size of $τ$, and
- `tag(τ)` to denote one bit data indicating whether $τ$ is a pointer or not.

The compiler can then compile the above function to the following codes.

```
fun f (size, tag) x =
  let
    val bitmap = codes to compute a bitmap using size and tag
  in
    (x,x,x; bitmap)
  end
  : ['a. size('a) * tag('a) -> 'a -> 'a * 'a * 'a]
```

Since `size('a)` and `tag('a)` are constant for any concrete types of `'a`, the compiler can generate the following codes for application `f 1.0`

```
f (2,0) 1.0
```

where the extra parameter (2,0) is computed and inserted by the compiler using the instantiated type `size(real)` and `tag(real)`.

5.2   First-Class Overloaded Primitives

In Standard ML, commonly used built-in primitives are overloaded but they are statically resolved at the top-level. For example, if we write the following in Standard ML as a top-level program

fun plus x = x + x

then `Int.+` is selected for `+` and `plus` is bound to a function of type `int -> int`. This strategy works reasonably well, but this becomes a big obstacle in integrating SQL, where most of the primitives are overloaded. If we determine the types of all the primitives in a SQL query at the time of its definition, then we cannot make full use of ML polymorphism in dealing with databases.

One solution to this problem would be to introduce type classes of Haskell [5], which would complicate both the design and implementation of the language. With the record compilation mechanism, a limited form of overloading can be introduced without much additional machinery. SML♯ adopts this simpler solution. For example, SML♯ infers the following polymorphic type for `plus`.

```
fun plus x = x + x;
  : ['a::{int,IntInf.int,real,Real32.real,word,Word8.word}.
     'a -> 'a]
```

where the constraint `'a::{...}` on type variable `'a` indicates the set of allowable instance types. This function is compiled to the following function.

```
fun plus impl x = impl (x,x);
  : ['a::{int,IntInf.int,real,Real32.real,word,Word8.word}.
     plusImpl('a) -> 'a -> 'a]
```

where `plusImpl(b)` is a singleton type of the addition function on the base type b. When this function is applied, the compiler generates the appropriate plus function and passes it to the function `plus` as follows.

```
plus Real.+ 1.0
```

The rest of the development is essentially the same as that of record compilation.

6   Conclusions

We have reviewed the polymorphic typing and compilation method for polymorphic record operations developed in [10,8,9,1] and implemented in SML♯ language [16]. Its polymorphic type system allows modular software development, and is the basis for seamlessly integrating SQL. The type-directed polymorphic record compilation plays a central role in achieving natural data representation and first-class overloaded primitive operations. We hope that their expositions shed some light on the possibility of applying record polymorphism and its compilation method to various advanced features in programming languages and systems.

Acknowledgments. Katuhiro Ueno, a co-developper of the SML♯ compiler, has made numerous contributions to the development of type-directed compilation with record polymorphism and other features embodied in SML♯.

Detailed comments by the anonymous reviewer have been very helpful in improving the presentation of the paper.

References

1. Buneman, P., Ohori, A.: Polymorphism and type inference in database programming. ACM Transactions on Database Systems 21(1), 30–74 (1996)
2. Damas, L., Milner, R.: Principal type-schemes for functional programs. In: Proceedings of ACM Symposium on Principles of Programming Languages, pp. 207–212 (1982)
3. Girard, J.-Y.: Une extension de l'interpretation de gödel à l'analyse, et son application à l'élimination des coupures dans l'analyse et théorie des types. In: Second Scandinavian Logic Symposium. North-Holland (1971)
4. Gunter, C.A., Mitchell, J.C. (eds.): Theoretical Aspects of Object-Oriented Programming. MIT Press (1994)
5. Hudak, P., Peyton Jones, S., Wadler, P., Boutel, B., Fairbairn, J., Fasel, J., Guzman, M., Hammond, K., Hughes, J., Johnsson, T., Kieburtz, D., Nikhil, R., Partain, W., Perterson, J.: Report on programming language Haskell a non-strict, purely functional language version 1.2. SIGPLAN Notices, Haskell Special Issue 27(5) (1992)
6. Jones, M.: A theory of qualified types. In: Proc. European Symposium on Programming (1992)
7. Nguyen, H.-D., Ohori, A.: Compiling ML polymorphism with explicit layout bitmap. In: Proceedings of ACM Conference on Principles and Practice of Declarative Programming, pp. 237–248 (2006)
8. Ohori, A.: A compilation method for ML-style polymorphic record calculi. In: Proceedings of ACM Symposium on Principles of Programming Languages, pp. 154–165 (1992)
9. Ohori, A.: A polymorphic record calculus and its compilation. ACM Transactions on Programming Languages and Systems 17(6), 844–895 (1995), A preliminary summary appeared at ACM Symposium on Principles of Programming Languages, 1992 under the title "A compilation method for ML-style polymorphic record calculi"
10. Ohori, A., Buneman, P.: Type inference in a database programming language. In: Proc. ACM Conference on LISP and Functional Programming, Snowbird, Utah, pp. 174–183 (July 1988)
11. Ohori, A., Buneman, P., Breazu-Tannen, V.: Database programming in Machiavelli – a polymorphic language with static type inference. In: Proc. the ACM SIGMOD Conference, Portland, Oregon, pp. 46–57 (May-June 1989)

12. Ohori, A., Ueno, K.: Making Standard ML a practical database programming language. In: Proceedings of the ACM International Conference on Functional Programming, pp. 307–319 (2011)
13. Peterson, J., Jones, M.: Implementing type classes. In: Proc. ACM Conference on Programming Language Design and Implementation, pp. 227–236 (1993)
14. Remy, D.: Typechecking records and variants in a natural extension of ML. In: Proceedings of ACM Symposium on Principles of Programming Languages, pp. 242–249 (1989)
15. Reynolds, J.C.: Towards a theory of type structure. In: Paris Colloq. on Programming, pp. 408–425. Springer (1974)
16. SML♯ home page, http://www.pllab.riec.tohoku.ac.jp/smlsharp/
17. Wand, M.: Corrigendum: Complete type inference for simple object. In: Proceedings of the Third Symposium on Logic in Computer Science, p. 132 (1988), doi:10.1109/LICS.1988.5111
18. Wong, L.: An introduction to Remy's fast polymorphic record projection. ACM SIGMOD Record 24(3), 34–39 (1995)

A Calculus of Chemical Systems

Gordon D. Plotkin

LFCS, School of Informatics, University of Edinburgh

Abstract. We present the Calculus of Chemical Systems for the modular presentation of systems of chemical equations; it is intended to be a core calculus for rule-based modelling in systems biology. The calculus is loosely modelled after Milner's Calculus of Communicating Systems, but with communication replaced by chemical reactions. We give a variety of compositional semantics for qualitative and quantitative versions of our calculus, employing a commutative monoid semantical framework. These semantics include (qualitative and quantitative) Petri nets, transition relations, ordinary differential equations (ODEs), and stochastic matrices. Standard semantics of Petri nets, whether of transition relations, ODEs, or stochastic matrices, fit within the framework as commutative monoid homomorphisms. We give complete equational axiomatisations and normal forms for all the semantics, and full abstraction results for the ODE and stochastic semantics. Definability can be characterised in some cases, as was already known for ODEs; other cases, including the stochastic one, remain open.

1 Introduction

In recent years various calculi have been proposed for modelling biological systems, typically intracellular pathways. These calculi generally fall into one of two camps: ones based on process calculi, such as Milner's pi-calculus [25], and rule-based ones. Examples of the former include [32,33,31]; examples of the latter include BIOCHAM, κ, BioNetGen, and Dynamical Grammars [3,7,16,27]. One positive feature of the rule-based approach is that rules correspond naturally to biological events, with a main example being chemical reactions. However rule-based models usually consist of sets of rules, and these are completely unstructured. In sharp contrast, process calculi have natural means for specifying modularity such as a parallel combinator, to combine subsystems, and the ability to name and parameterise subsystems. They can thereby avoid much redundancy.

Here we aim at combining the naturalness of rules with the modularity of process calculi. We keep both sides of the endeavour simple. Our rules are simple reactions between species; our modularity provides parallelism and the ability to define modules (without parameters). We call the resulting formalism the *Calculus of Chemical Systems* and consciously model it on Milner's CCS [24], his *Calculus of Communicating Systems*. There are two versions of our calculus, a *qualitative* one and, more importantly, a *quantitative* one where the rules are

V. Tannen et al. (Eds.): Buneman Festschrift, LNCS 8000, pp. 445–465, 2013.

equipped with rates. In both cases modules are non-recursive; this is more suited to biological systems than the recursive modules of Milner's CCS.

There are strong arguments in favour of the existence of modules at the cellular level [14,1], although it is worth remarking that the extent to which biological systems are modular is controversial because of the high degree of interaction between supposed subsystems. Nonetheless, biologists do not describe entire cells but rather particular pathways and they further note recurring patterns; see, for example, [11] on the MAPK cascade. There is also speculation that modules have evolutionary significance and provide robustness to environmental perturbations [14,1]. In terms of Petri nets, where there has also been much research on modularity, e.g., [20,12,29,2], we combine nets sharing commonly named places (species) but not transitions (reactions). Whereas we provide means for describing modules one can also try to find modules within systems with given unstructured descriptions, often graphical; see [19] for a survey of work along these lines.

Following the CCS paradigm, we look at a number of equivalences, here naturally given via various compositional denotational semantics. In giving these semantics we take up a suggestion of Pedersen [30] to incorporate the various semantics within a general framework, here using commutative monoids. (This is strongly connected to the use of rings of operators by Mjolsness and Yosiphon [27].)

For the quantitative case, we consider two equivalencies, one based on ordinary differential equations (ODEs), and the other on stochastic matrices. For the qualitative case we consider a transition relation semantics and a Petri net one. As is well known, reactions can also be naturally represented by Petri nets, particularly P/T nets, and, indeed there is little difference between P/T nets and sets of reactions. See [5,15,26] for surveys of the now extensive applications of Petri nets to pathway simulation; see [36,17] for an early chemical reaction formalism using a bipartite graph structure equivalent to P/T nets; and see [9] for a survey of the application of graphical ideas to chemical reaction systems, including two bipartite graph formalisms [18,6].

We provide a complete axiomatisation of each semantics that we consider. We also consider definability, the main result here is a characterisation of the collection of definable sets of ODEs due to Hárs and Tóth [13,8]. Continuing to consider the analogy with Milner's CCS, one could also seek analogues of Hennesy-Milner logic, but we do not do so here.

Since our calculus and P/T nets are both ways of specifying sets of reactions, there is a tight relationship between them: the kind of P/T nets we consider form a complete model of the basic axiom system of the calculus, and all such nets are definable, up to isomorphism. This gives the calculus a reading as a modular way to describe Petri nets; conversely, the possibility arises of inputting programs via a graphical input system.

As is already well-known, one can give P/T nets themselves qualitative or quantitative semantics (for the quantitative semantics, see [15,37]: one has, of course, to equip the transitions with rates). We show that each such direct semantics agrees with the corresponding calculus semantics, by which we mean that the latter factors homomorphically through the former via the P/T net semantics of the calculus. As the various semantics of the P/T nets are standard, this acts as a verification of the corresponding semantics of the calculus. Another consequence is that properties of the semantics of P/T nets correspond with properties of the semantics of processes of the calculus; therefore any means of establishing that one holds provides a means of establishing that the other does.

The calculus of chemical systems is intended as a simulation language. So, in the cases of the quantitative semantics, one could argue that one is interested in the simulations that processes induce rather than the ODEs, or stochastic matrices, themselves. These simulations are the solutions to the ODEs, or (samples of) the Markov processes induced by the stochastic matrices, and are functionally dependent on given initial states. Unfortunately, such simulations do not have a prima facie compositional (here, commutative monoid) structure. Following a standard move in the programming language literature, see, e.g., [38,10], one could say that the correct equivalence should be an analogue of behavioural (a.k.a. observational, or, more neutrally, contextual) equivalence, that is, having the same behaviour, here simulations, in all contexts. Pleasingly, it turns out that we have full abstraction results in both cases, that is, the denotational and contextual equivalences agree.

Our calculus is intended as a simplest possible rule-based calculus. It should be possible to usefully add modularity to any rule-based calculus. Indeed the grammatical approach in [27] provides what amounts to a parameterised module mechanism. One can enrich our calculus with facilities for modifications and simple complexes along the general lines of BIOCHAM, and with a construction for (static) compartments: all of these are omnipresent in cellular networks. One then has a calculus briefly described in [30], and called there the *Calculus of Biochemical Systems*. That paper provided further linguistic facilities, for example parameterised modules, several kinds of declarations, and functional reaction rates; the aim was to provide a full-scale modular modelling language. In principle, such further developments can be carried out for any rule-based system.

After some technical preliminaries in Section 2, the calculus of chemical systems is presented in Section 3; we consider its syntax, an equational logic, and the general commutative monoid semantics. The following sections consider specific semantics. Section 4 gives "static" semantics for the qualitative and quantitative versions of the calculus in terms of, respectively, P/T nets and P/T nets equipped with reaction rates. The following three sections give "dynamic" semantics. Section 5 gives a transition relation semantics of the qualitative calculus. Sections 6 and 7 give ordinary differential equation (ODE) and stochastic semantics of the quantitative calculus.

Complete axiomatisations, and corresponding normal forms for the calculus, are given for all of these semantics (Theorems 1, 2, 4, and 6, and following discussions). In the two Petri net cases the equational logic is complete without adding further axioms. Characterisations of definability are given for the (immediately obvious) Petri net case and for the ODE case (Theorem 3); the other cases present interesting open problems. Finally, the full abstraction result for the ODE case is given by Theorem 5, and that for the stochastic case by Theorem 7.

2   Technical Preliminaries

For any set A we write $\mathcal{M}_f(A)$ for the collection of finite multisets on A. For any such multiset X, the multiplicity of $a \in A$ is written $X(a)$ and we write $\|X\|$ for its size, i.e., $\sum_{a \in A} X(a)$. The empty multiset is written as $\emptyset$; we may confuse an $a \in A$ with the multiset with unique element a occurring with multiplicity 1; and for any multisets X and Y we write mX and $X + Y$ for the multisets such that $(mX)(a) = mX(a)$ and $(X + Y)(a) = X(a) + Y(a)$, respectively. So, in particular, for natural numbers $m_1, \ldots, m_r$, and $a_1, \ldots, a_r \in A$ we have the multiset $m_1 a_1 + \ldots + m_r a_r$. Finally, for any function $f : A \to B$, and $a \in A$ and $b \in B$, $f[a \mapsto b]$ denotes the function everywhere equal to f except, possibly, at a where it has the value b.

3   The Calculus

We assume given a nonempty finite set Spec of *species*, ranged over by S, I, O. The set of species names is a parameter to our formalism and may be varied according to the area of application.

The set of *rules*, ranged over by R, is given by:

$$R ::= X \to Y$$

where X and Y are finite multisets of species.

We can use rules to describe chemical reactions, as in:

$$m_1 I_1 + \ldots + m_r I_r \longrightarrow n_1 O_1 + \ldots + n_p O_p$$

where the I_i are the reactants and the O_j are the products and the stoichiometry is given by the m_i and the n_j. Rules can also be used to describe complex formation, as in:

$$E + S \longrightarrow E\text{-}S$$

where $E\text{-}S$ is an assumed name for an E, S-complex, and to describe transport, as in:

$$S \to \text{nucleus}[S]$$

where $\text{nucleus}[S]$ is an assumed name for S inside the cell nucleus.

The set of *(qualitative) processes*, ranged over by P and Q, is then given by the following abstract syntax:

$$P ::= R \mid P|Q \mid \text{NIL} \mid A = P; Q \mid A$$

where A ranges over a countably infinite set ProcId of *process identifiers*. The first case is that of a rule, and the second case $P|Q$ is that of two systems P and Q acting in parallel: as a species name may occur in both they may interact. The third case is the empty system and the fourth case is a local definition: of A as P in Q. The last case is whatever system the identifier A denotes: as such it will normally be a fragment of a larger process in which it receives a definition.

Local definition is a binding construct with A having scope Q in $A = P; Q$. We have the usual notions of the free process identifiers $FP(P)$ occurring in a process P, of α-equivalence of processes, $P \equiv_\alpha Q$, and of the capture-avoiding substitution $P[Q/A]$ of a process Q for a process identifier A in a process P. We adopt a standard convention and regard α-equivalent processes as identical.

For the set of *quantitative* processes, rules instead have the form

$$X \xrightarrow{r} Y$$

where r is a positive real (i.e., $r > 0$), which gives the rate at which the rule occurs.

There are natural abbreviations. For reversible reactions, we could write

$$X \underset{s}{\overset{r}{\leftrightarrow}} Y$$

as an abbreviation for

$$X \xrightarrow{r} Y \mid Y \xrightarrow{s} X$$

in the quantitative language (and here, and below, we assume the evident corresponding abbreviations for the qualitative language).

For an enzymatic reaction in which an enzyme E converts a substrate S to a product P we could write

$$E : S \xrightarrow{r,s,t} P$$

as an abbreviation for

$$S + E \underset{s}{\overset{r}{\leftrightarrow}} E\text{-}S \mid E\text{-}S \xrightarrow{t} E + P$$

Finally for a reversible enzymatic reaction with different enzymes E and E' in the forwards and backwards directions we could write

$$E : S \underset{r',s',t'}{\overset{r,s,t}{\longleftrightarrow}} P : E'$$

for

$$E : S \xrightarrow{r,s,t} P \mid E' : P \xrightarrow{r',s',t'} S$$

There is an interesting empirical adequacy question here concerning the design of abbreviations: one needs to be able to use all the abbreviations commonly found in the literature. More ambitiously one may try to generate useful such abbreviations systematically. For example one may add those suggested in [39] in order to obtain natural, succinct descriptions of a variety of enzyme kinetics.

There is an evident, very simple, equational theory for processes (more precisely, one for each of the qualitative or quantitative cases). It has the standard rules of reflexivity, transitivity and symmetry and substitutivity for the parallel construct, together with the following congruence rule for local definitions:

$$\frac{P = P' \qquad Q = Q'}{(A = P; Q) = (A = P'; Q')}$$

The axioms are that the parallel construct and NIL form a commutative monoid:

$$(P_1 \mid P_2) \mid P_3 = P_1 \mid (P_2 \mid P_3) \qquad P_1 \mid P_2 = P_2 \mid P_1 \qquad P \mid \text{NIL} = P$$

together with:

$$(A = P; Q) = Q[P/A]$$

Every process can be put in the following *canonical form*:

$$A_1 \mid \ldots \mid A_m \mid R_1 \mid \ldots \mid R_n$$

associating parentheses to the left. We remark that the rule of substitutivity for local definitions is redundant as processes can be put in canonical form without using it.

It follows from Theorem 1, below (and from its analogue for the quantitative case) that two such canonical forms are provably equal if, and only if, the same process names and reactions occur in each, possibly in different orders; in other words if the two multisets of process names and reactions obtained from each canonical form are equal. With that we know that processes have *normal forms*, i.e., canonical forms unique up to reordering. The same situation obtains with respect to all the semantics considered below: there are evident canonical forms, and the relevant completeness theorems ensure that they are, in fact, normal forms, i.e., they are unique up to reordering.

We will give a variety of (denotational) semantics for both the qualitative and quantitative calculi. It proves convenient to organise all these under one scheme. Suppose that we have a structure

$$(M, \mid_M, \text{NIL}_M)$$

where $\mid_M$ is a binary operation on M and NIL_M is an element of M, and for every rule R we are given an element of M, its *semantics*, written $M[\![R]\!]$, slightly abusing notation. A *process environment* is a map

$$\rho : \text{ProcId} \to M$$

For every process P we give its semantics $M[\![P]\!](\rho)$ relative to a process environment ρ, by:

$$
\begin{aligned}
M[\![R]\!](\rho) &= M[\![R]\!] \\
M[\![P \mid Q]\!](\rho) &= M[\![P]\!](\rho) \mid_M M[\![Q]\!](\rho) \\
M[\![\text{NIL}]\!](\rho) &= \text{NIL}_M \\
M[\![A = P; Q]\!](\rho) &= M[\![Q]\!](\rho[A \mapsto M[\![P]\!](\rho)]) \\
M[\![A]\!](\rho) &= \rho(A)
\end{aligned}
$$

Note that $M[\![P]\!](\rho)$ depends only on the values that ρ assigns to the free process variables of M; we may therefore write $M[\![P]\!]$ instead of $M[\![P]\!](\rho)$ when M is closed; elements of M of the form $M[\![P]\!]$ are said to be *definable*. As is usual, denotational semantics commutes with substitution, by which is meant that:

$$M[\![P[Q/A]]\!](\rho) = M[\![P]\!](\rho[A \mapsto M[\![Q]\!](\rho)])$$

always holds.

If M is a commutative monoid then we obtain a model of the above equational theory, meaning that if $P = Q$ is provable then $M[\![P]\!](\rho) = M[\![Q]\!](\rho)$, for all ρ. Conversely, we say that such a model is *complete* if whenever $M[\![P]\!](\rho) = M[\![Q]\!](\rho)$ for all ρ then $P = Q$ is provable.

One may instead have a structure $(M, |_M, \mathrm{NIL}_M)$, which is not a commutative monoid, but can be equipped with a congruence $\sim$ such that $M/\sim$ is a commutative monoid: this occurs, for example, in the case of Petri nets. One then has a model in the weaker sense, that if $P = Q$ is provable then $M[\![P]\!](\rho) \sim M[\![Q]\!](\rho)$ for all ρ, and one defines completeness accordingly.

4   Petri Net Semantics

We begin our treatment of specific semantics with the main qualitative case, that of Petri nets. Following the above framework we first need to give a suitable set Net of Petri nets. We take these to be structures

$$(T, \mathrm{pre}, \mathrm{post})$$

where T, the set of transitions, is a finite subset of $\{0,1\}^*$ and $\mathrm{pre}, \mathrm{post} : T \to \mathcal{M}_f(\mathrm{Spec})$. We may write $\mathrm{pre}(t)$, $\mathrm{post}(t)$ as, respectively, $\dot{}t, t\dot{}$. We do not specify a set of places as we use the same set of places, Spec, for all our nets. Note too that places are identified with (basic) species, as is normally done when using Petri nets to describe biochemical processes, and which corresponds to the convention in pathway graphical formalisms of having each species occur just once in the graph. Further, transitions are kept anonymous: this could, of course be changed, but they are normally kept so, and we know no reason to depart from that practice. Our nets are P/T nets with the small differences that we have a fixed set of places and that we do not have an initial marking.

The semantics of rules is given by:

$$\mathrm{Net}[\![X \longrightarrow Y]\!] = (\{\varepsilon\}, \{\varepsilon \mapsto X\}, \{\varepsilon \mapsto Y\})$$

Next, the function $|_{\mathrm{Net}} : \mathrm{Net}^2 \to \mathrm{Net}$ is defined by:

$$(T, \mathrm{pre}, \mathrm{post}) \mid_{\mathrm{Net}} (T', \mathrm{pre}', \mathrm{post}') = (0T \cup 1T', \mathrm{pre}'', \mathrm{post}'')$$

where

$$\mathrm{pre}''(u) =_{\mathrm{def}} \begin{cases} \mathrm{pre}(w) & (\text{if } u = 0w) \\ \mathrm{pre}'(w) & (\text{if } u = 1w) \end{cases}$$

and

$$\text{post}''(u) =_{\text{def}} \begin{cases} \text{post}(w) & (\text{if } u = 0w) \\ \text{post}'(w) & (\text{if } u = 1w) \end{cases}$$

And we define:

$$\text{NIL}_{\text{Net}} = (\emptyset, \emptyset, \emptyset)$$

meaning the constantly $\emptyset$ function in the second and third components.

With these definitions (Net, $|_{\text{Net}}$, NIL_{Net}) is not a commutative monoid, because of slight differences of transitions. However we can define a congruence, putting

$$(T, \text{pre}, \text{post}) \sim (T', \text{pre}', \text{post}')$$

if, and only if, the two nets are isomorphic, meaning that there is a bijection $\theta : T \cong T'$ such that, for all $t \in T$ we have $\text{pre}(t) = \text{pre}'(\theta(t))$ and $\text{post}(t) = \text{post}'(\theta(t))$, and, dividing out by this congruence, we do obtain a commutative monoid, as required.

In a way, the calculus of chemical systems is little more than a way of writing down Petri nets, and this results in some natural formal relations between the two. Concerning definability, as is evident, every net in Net is definable by a program, up to isomorphism. This means that for every such net N there is a closed process P such that $[\![P]\!] \sim N$. This is the formal correlate of the pragmatic possibility of inputting processes by drawing nets, just as the semantics is the formal correlate of the pragmatic possibility of defining nets by processes.

We also have that the Petri net semantics is complete, and that the canonical forms are unique up to reordering (we then say that they are *normal* forms):

Theorem 1. *The following are equivalent for any two processes P and Q:*

1. *P and Q can be proven equal.*
2. *Any two canonical forms of P and Q are the same up to reordering.*
3. *$\text{Net}[\![P]\!](\rho) \sim \text{Net}[\![Q]\!](\rho)$ for all ρ.*

Proof. Clearly (2) $\Rightarrow$ (1) $\Rightarrow$ (3). So assume (3) and consider two processes P and Q with canonical forms $A_1 \mid \ldots \mid A_m \mid R_1 \mid \ldots \mid R_n$ and $A'_1 \mid \ldots \mid A'_{m'} \mid R'_1 \mid \ldots \mid R'_{n'}$. Recalling that Spec is nonempty, choose $S \in \text{Spec}$, and let $B_1, \ldots, B_n$ be a list of the process variables occurring freely in either one of P or Q, and let s be the maximum of the number of occurrences of S in an R_j or a $R'_{j'}$. Now choose ρ so that $\rho(B_k)$ is a net with one transition ε such that $\dot{\varepsilon}(S) = s + k$ and $\varepsilon\dot{}(S) = 0$. Then, as $\text{Net}[\![P]\!](\rho) \sim \text{Net}[\![Q]\!](\rho)$, one has that the two chosen canonical forms of P and Q are identical up to reordering (we omit further details). $\square$

There is a variant of the Petri net semantics worth remarking. One only allows nets not containing any transition w with $\dot{w} = w\dot{}$ and takes the semantics of $X \to X$ to be NIL_{Net}. Everything then goes through as before except that in the proof system one adds the axiom

$$X \to X = \text{NIL}$$

and in canonical forms one forbids rules of the form $X \to X$.

In the quantitative case rules have associated positive reals and we instead take our set of quantitative Petri nets, CNet to be structures

$$(T, \text{pre}, \text{post}, \text{rate})$$

where T, pre and post are as before and rate $: T \to \mathbb{R}^+$, where $\mathbb{R}^+$ is the set of positive reals. (Formally, these nets are stochastic nets but for the same small differences as before: there is a fixed set of places and there is no initial marking. However, our nets have no fixed intended interpretation, and, indeed, will receive both an ODE and a stochastic semantics.)

One then makes the evident changes to the semantics for the qualitative case: we do not spell them out here. The evident analogue of Theorem 1 holds, with the analogous proof. One also has the evident analogue of the above variant of the Petri net semantics, now with $X \xrightarrow{r} X = \text{NIL}$ as the additional axiom.

5   Qualitative Semantics: Transition Relations

Our other semantics of the qualitative calculus is of transition relations on *markings*, here finite multisets of species. The idea is that the marking gives the population of each species and the transitions correspond to the occurrence of a finite multiset of reactions, or other rules. So we set TRel to be the set of relations $\to$ on $\mathcal{M}_f(\text{Spec})$ satisfying the following closure conditions:

$$X \to X \qquad \frac{X \to Y \qquad X' \to Y'}{X + X' \to Y + Y'}$$

The first corresponds to the fact that the multiset of rules firing may be empty; the second corresponds to the fact that the firings of two multisets can be combined into their joint firing. Given any relation $\to$ on $\mathcal{M}_f(\text{Spec})$ there is a least such relation $\to^*$ containing it and closed under the rules; we have:

$$\to^* = \{(Z + \sum_{i=1,n} m_i X_i, \ Z + \sum_{i=1,n} m_i Y_i) \mid X_i \to Y_i, m_i \in \mathbb{N} \ (i = 1, n)\}$$

We say that $\to$ *generates* $\to^*$.

The semantics of rules is given by:

$$\text{TRel}[\![X \to Y]\!] = \{(Z + kX, Z + kY) \mid Z \in \mathcal{M}_f(\text{Spec}), k \in \mathbb{N}\} \ (= \{(X, Y)\}^*)$$

and we define a commutative monoid structure on TRel by:

$$\to |_{\text{TRel}} \to' = \{(kX + k'X', kY + k'Y') \mid k, k' \in \mathbb{N}, X \to Y, X' \to' Y'\} \ (= (\to \cup \to')^*)$$

and:

$$\text{NIL}_{\text{TRel}} = \{(X, X) \mid X \in \mathcal{M}_f(\text{Spec})\} \ (= \emptyset^*)$$

Note that $|_{\text{TRel}}$ is *absorptive*, i.e., that, for any transition relation $\to$, we have:

$$\to |_{\text{TRel}} \to \ = \ \to$$

We do not know any characterisation of the relations defined by closed processes, other than the obvious one that they are generated by a finite relation. An obvious necessary condition is that, for any X, the set $\{Y \mid X \to Y\}$ is finite. However there are closed non-finitely generated relations obeying this condition, e.g., $\{(mS, nS) \mid m \geq 1, m \leq n \leq m^2\}$ where the maximum gap size, $m^2 \quad m$, grows too quickly. This example also satisfies two other obvious conditions: that both the set $\{Y \mid X \to Y\}$ and its size are recursive in X.

As well as the axioms above, another three hold in TRel:

$$P \mid P = P$$

$$X \to X = \text{NIL}$$

$$X \to Y \mid X' \to Y' = X \to Y \mid X' \to Y' \mid X + X' \to Y + Y'$$

The first corresponds to the absorptiveness of $\mid_{\text{TRel}}$ and the others to the above closure conditions. Every process can be put in a canonical form. This is, as before, a composition of process names and rules but where, in addition, no process name or rule occurs twice, and where no rule is in the closure of the others (considered as forming a relation).

As we now see, with these additional axioms we obtain completeness for the transition relation semantics:

Theorem 2. *The following are equivalent for any two processes P and Q (assuming there is an element of Spec not occurring in P or Q):*

1. *P and Q can be proven equal using the above axioms for the qualitative semantics.*
2. *Any two canonical forms of P and Q are the same up to reordering.*
3. *$\text{TRel}[\![P]\!](\rho) = \text{TRel}[\![Q]\!](\rho)$ for all ρ.*

Proof. As in the case of Theorem 1 we need only assume (3) and prove (2). So let $A_1 \mid \ldots \mid A_m \mid R_1 \mid \ldots \mid R_n$ and $A'_1 \mid \ldots \mid A'_{m'} \mid R'_1 \mid \ldots \mid R'_{n'}$ be canonical forms of P and Q. For any A_i, first choose S not occurring in P or Q and then choose ρ such that $\rho(A_i) = \{(S, 0)\}^*$ and, otherwise, is NIL_{TRel}. Then $\text{TRel}[\![P]\!](\rho)$ is the least transition relation containing $(S, \emptyset)$ and the R_i (considered as ordered pairs of multisets). So, by assumption, $(S, \emptyset)$ also occurs in $\text{TRel}[\![Q]\!](\rho)$ and so, as S occurs in no $R'_{j'}$, A_i must be one of the $A'_{i'}$. With this, and the symmetric argument, we see that the A_i and the $A'_{i'}$ are the same.

Next, taking ρ constantly NIL_{TRel}, we see that the R_j and the $R'_{j'}$ generate the same transition relations using the above closure conditions as rules. Observe that if (X, Y) is generated from a set of pairs of multisets, then either $X = Y = \emptyset$ or (X, Y) is in the set or else it is generated from (X', Y') in the set with $\|X'\| + \|Y'\| < \|X\| + \|Y\|$. So as R_1 (say) is not $\emptyset \to \emptyset$ either it is some $R'_{j'}$ or else it is generated from $R'_{j'}$, which are smaller in this sense. But those $R'_{j'}$ are, in turn, generated from smaller R_i, and so, in this last alternative, R_1 is generated from strictly smaller R_i, which contradicts canonicity. Arguing symmetrically we see that the R_j and the $R'_{j'}$ coincide. $\square$

This theorem yields completeness for the set of transition relations formed from Spec expanded with an additional species name. As the additional species name is only used in the case that P and Q are open, the theorem holds generally for closed processes. The possibility of expanding Spec also ensures that that the equivalence of (1) and (2) holds without any assumption. It is worth noting that it follows from the proof that one can restrict the environments in (3) to be definable, by which we mean that all their values are definable.

One can, of course, directly define a transition relation in TRel on every net in Net. Specifically to every net $N = (T, \text{pre}, \text{post})$ one assigns the following transition relation:

$$\mathcal{R}(N) =_{\text{def}} \{(Y + \sum_{t \in T} X(t) \dot{}\, t,\ Y + \sum_{t \in T} X(t) t \dot{}\,) \mid X \in \mathcal{M}_f(T)\}\ (= \{(\dot{}\, t, t \dot{}\,)\}^*)$$

The function $\mathcal{R} : \text{Net} \to \text{TRel}$ preserves all the semantical structure:

Proposition 1. *For any rule R we have:*

$$\text{TRel}[\![R]\!] = \mathcal{R}(\text{Net}[\![R]\!])$$

and, further, $\mathcal{R}$ is a monoid homomorphism.

Consequentially, the Petri net and transition relation semantics are consistent with the usual multi-transition semantics of Petri nets in that, for any qualitative process P and any Net process environment ρ, we have:

$$\text{TRel}[\![P]\!](\mathcal{R} \circ \rho) = \mathcal{R}(\text{Net}[\![P]\!](\rho))$$

We can think of $\mathcal{R}$ as giving the semantics of Petri nets. As syntactic objects, Petri nets are generated from transitions by finite composition, and $\mathcal{R}$ preserves that structure. The qualitative calculus provides a syntax for nets with its rules and finite composition structure and the completeness of the axiom system identifies nets as equivalence classes of terms, and so as a kind of non-free syntax.

There are other possible transition relations one can associate to Petri nets, such as transitions occurring by virtue of a single transition firing, or by virtue of a set of transitions firing, or by virtue of a maximal set (or multiset) of transitions firing. Of these, the first two are *modular*, meaning that they can be equipped with a suitable monoidal structure, but the last two are not. We chose the multiset semantics as it seemed the most natural given that one is in any case working with markings as multisets. Another variant would have been to decorate the transition relation with the set or multiset of transitions involved, but we decided against that as we are keeping transitions anonymous.

Petri nets being at once graphs and supporting the fundamentals of chemistry themselves provide a fundamental graphical notation. Biologists make much use of informal graphical means of describing pathways; further, there has been work by Kohn, Kitano and others, see, e.g., [22,21,23], to produce more formal graphical notations adequate for flexible natural pathway description. By taking abbreviatory conventions seriously, meaning having them as additional language constructs, one can give a different graphical semantics than Petri nets, for example Petri nets extended with reversible transitions. In that way one's formalism would begin to make contact with the more informal graphical approaches, but still retain direct contact with the more basic Petri nets, and their various semantics.

6 Quantitative Semantics: Differential Equations

Our first semantics of the quantitative calculus is given in terms of systems of ordinary differential equations. We associate to a process a system of ODEs of the form:

$$\frac{\mathrm{d}[S_1]}{\mathrm{d}t} = p_1$$
$$\vdots$$
$$\frac{\mathrm{d}[S_m]}{\mathrm{d}t} = p_m$$

where, as usual, we write $[S]$ for the concentration of a species S, and $S_1, \ldots, S_m$ is an enumeration of the species in Spec, and $p_1, \ldots, p_m$ are real polynomials over the $[S_i]$. We need to make a commutative monoid Diff out of such sets of ODEs and to that end we identify them with maps from Spec to the commutative monoid of real polynomials over the $[S_i]$. They then have the standard pointwise monoid structure:

$$(\mathbf{p} \mid_{\text{Diff}} \mathbf{q})(S) = \mathbf{p}(S) + \mathbf{q}(S)$$

and:

$$\text{NIL}_{\text{Diff}}(S) = 0$$

It only remains to give the semantics of rules:

$$\text{Diff}[\![X \xrightarrow{r} Y]\!](S) = r(Y(S) - X(S)) \prod_{S \in \text{Spec}} [S]^{X(S)}$$

Not all sets of ODEs of the above form can arise as the semantics of (closed) processes or, equivalently, using Proposition 2 below, of quantitative Petri nets. However there is a simple condition, characterising those that are so definable. Expand each p_i as a linear sum of distinct monomials: $\sum_j a_{ij} q_{ij}$ $(a_i \neq 0)$. We then have the following theorem, due to Hárs and Tóth; we include a proof for the sake of completeness.

Theorem 3. *A set of ODEs of the above form is definable if, and only if, whenever any a_{ij} is negative then the power of $[S_i]$ in q_{ij} is non-zero.*

Proof. It is easy to see that this condition holds for all definable sets of equations. For the converse, it is enough to show that, for any i, j, we can define a rule R_{ij} such that $\text{Diff}[\![R_{ij}]\!](S) = 0$, if $S \neq S_i$, and $\text{Diff}[\![R_{ij}]\!](S) = a_{ij}q_{ij}$. With that, the parallel composition of the R_{ij} defines the given set of differential equations.

So, let q_{ij} have the form $\prod_{k=1,n}[S_k]^{m_k}$. There are two cases. Suppose first that a_{ij} is negative. Then $m_i \neq 0$ and we take the rule R_{ij} to be

$$m_1 S_1 + \cdots + m_n S_n \xrightarrow{a_{ij}/m_i} m_1 S_1 + \cdots + m_{i-1} S_{i-1} + m_{i+1} S_{i+1} + \cdots + m_n S_n$$

The other case is where a_{ij} is positive, when we take the rule R_{ij} to be

$$m_1 S_1 + \cdots + m_n S_n \xrightarrow{a_{ij}} S_i + (m_1 S_1 + \cdots + m_n S_n)$$

$\square$

There can be non-trivial examples of different quantitive (closed) processes (or, equivalently systems of reactions, or, as we see below, non-isomorphic quantitative Petri nets) having the same ODE semantics. The example

$$2A \xrightarrow{2r} B + A \; = \; 2A \xrightarrow{r} 2B$$

was (essentially) given in [4], and another example was given in [13]; see [34,35] for work on finding optimal reaction systems having given ODEs. We now axiomatise this equivalence. The following axioms hold:

$$X \xrightarrow{r} X = \text{NIL}$$
$$X \xrightarrow{r+s} Z = X \xrightarrow{r} Z \mid X \xrightarrow{s} Z$$
$$X + Y \xrightarrow{r} X + Z = X + Y \xrightarrow{r} X \mid X + Y \xrightarrow{r} X + Y + Z$$
$$X + Y + Z \xrightarrow{r} X = X + Y + Z \xrightarrow{r} X + Y \mid X + Y + Z \xrightarrow{r} X + Z$$
$$X \xrightarrow{r} X + Y + Z = X \xrightarrow{r} X + Y \mid X \xrightarrow{r} X + Z$$
$$X + Y \xrightarrow{r} X \mid X + Y \xrightarrow{s} (X+Y) + Y = \text{NIL} \qquad \qquad \text{(if } r = s)$$
$$X + Y \xrightarrow{r} X \mid X + Y \xrightarrow{s} (X+Y) + Y = X + Y \xrightarrow{r-s} X \qquad \text{(if } r > s)$$
$$X + Y \xrightarrow{r} X \mid X + Y \xrightarrow{s} (X+Y) + Y = X + Y \xrightarrow{s-r} (X+Y) + Y \qquad \text{(if } r < s)$$

The first two of these axioms are easy to understand. For the others, let us say that a rule of the form $X + Y \xrightarrow{r} X$ is of *consumption* type and that a rule of the form $X \xrightarrow{r} X + Y$ is of *production* type. Then the third axiom divides an arbitrary rule into one of each type; the fourth axiom divides a consumption rule into two other consumption rules that are simpler in the sense that less is consumed in each; the fifth axiom divides a rule of production type into two simpler such rules; and the last three concern the balance between production and consumption when a consumption rule is put in parallel with a production one.

The six consumption and production axioms may be easier to understand if we write $Y \xrightarrow[X]{r} Z$ for $X + Y \xrightarrow{r} X + Z$. Consumption and production axioms then take the respective forms $Y \xrightarrow[X]{r} \emptyset$ and $\emptyset \xrightarrow[X]{r} Y$, and the six axioms become:

$$Y \xrightarrow[X]{r} Z = Y \xrightarrow[X]{r} \emptyset \mid \emptyset \xrightarrow[X+Y]{r} Z$$

$$Y + Z \xrightarrow[X]{r} \emptyset = Z \xrightarrow[X+Y]{r} \emptyset \mid Y \xrightarrow[X+Z]{r} \emptyset$$

$$\emptyset \xrightarrow[X]{r} Y + Z = \emptyset \xrightarrow[X]{r} Y \mid \emptyset \xrightarrow[X]{r} Z$$

$$Y \xrightarrow[X]{r} \emptyset \mid \emptyset \xrightarrow[X+Y]{s} Y = \text{NIL} \qquad (\text{if } r = s)$$

$$Y \xrightarrow[X]{r} \emptyset \mid \emptyset \xrightarrow[X+Y]{s} Y = Y \xrightarrow[X]{r-s} \emptyset \qquad (\text{if } r > s)$$

$$Y \xrightarrow[X]{r} \emptyset \mid \emptyset \xrightarrow[X+Y]{s} Y = \emptyset \xrightarrow[X+Y]{s-r} Y \qquad (\text{if } r < s)$$

Note that in all the equations the left-hand-side of the rules do not change: in terms of the ODEs we are only reorganising the contributions to the coefficients of the monomials.

There is a canonical form. Say that a consumption, respectively production, rule is *unary* if it is of the form $S \xrightarrow[X]{r} \emptyset$, respectively $\emptyset \xrightarrow[X]{r} S$. Then a process is in canonical form if it is a composition of process names and such unary rules, with no species having both a consumption and a production rule. Every process can be put in canonical form: one eliminates trivial rules using the first axiom, reduces rules to compositions of unary ones using the next three axioms, and combines unary rules with identical left- and right-hand sides using the next, and finally uses the last two rules to ensure that no species has both a consumption and a production rule.

With the addition of the above axioms, the logic of the quantitative calculus is complete for the ODE semantics:

Theorem 4. *The following are equivalent for any two processes P and Q:*

1. *P and Q can be proven equal using the above axioms for the ODE semantics.*
2. *Any two canonical forms of P and Q are the same up to reordering.*
3. *$\text{Diff}[\![P]\!](\rho) = \text{Diff}[\![Q]\!](\rho)$ for all ρ.*

Proof. As always, we need only assume (3) and prove (2). So choose canonical forms $A_1 \mid \ldots \mid A_m \mid R_1 \mid \ldots \mid R_n$ and $A'_1 \mid \ldots \mid A'_{m'} \mid R'_1 \mid \ldots \mid R'_{n'}$ of P and Q. A consumption rule $X + S \xrightarrow{r} X$ has semantics with value 0 everywhere except at S where it has value

$$-r[S] \prod_i [S_i]^{X(S_i)}$$

A production rule $X \xrightarrow{r} X + S$ has semantics with value 0 everywhere except at S where it has value

$$r \prod_i [S_i]^{X(S_i)}$$

So, considering $\text{Diff}[\![P]\!](\rho)$ and $\text{Diff}[\![Q]\!](\rho)$, with ρ having value 0 everywhere, we see that the R_i and the $R'_{i'}$ must coincide.

To show that A_1, say, occurs with the same multiplicity in the two canonical forms one employs the environment ρ, which has value 0 everywhere except at A_1 where it has value $\text{Diff}[\![nS \xrightarrow{1} \emptyset]\!]$ where S is a chosen element of Spec and $n > 0$ is chosen greater than the multiplicity of S in the left-hand side of any R_i.   □

As before, it follows from the proof that one can restrict the environments in condition (3) to be definable.

One can directly assign ODE semantics to Petri nets in CNet, as was already done more generally in [15]. We set:

$$\mathcal{D}(T, \text{pre}, \text{post}, \text{rate})(S) = \sum_{t \in T} \text{rate}(t)(t^{\cdot}(S) - {}^{\cdot}t(S)) \prod_{S' \in \text{Spec}} [S']^{\cdot t(S')}$$

thereby defining the semantics $\mathcal{D} : \text{CNet} \to \text{Diff}$. As before this Petri net semantics preserves all the semantical structure:

Proposition 2. *For any rule R we have:*

$$\text{Diff}[\![R]\!] = \mathcal{D}(\text{CNet}[\![R]\!])$$

Further, $\mathcal{D} : (\text{CNet}, |_{\text{CNet}}, \text{NIL}_{\text{CNet}}) \to (\text{Diff}, |_{\text{Diff}}, \text{NIL}_{\text{Diff}})$ *is a monoid homomorphism.*

So the Petri net and ODE semantics are consistent in that, for any quantitative process P and any CNet process environment ρ, we have:

$$\text{Diff}[\![P]\!](\mathcal{D} \circ \rho) = \mathcal{D}(\text{CNet}[\![P]\!](\rho))$$

We now turn to our full abstraction results for the ODE semantics. We begin with a notion of "same simulation behaviour." For any $\mathbf{p}, \mathbf{q} \in \text{Diff}$, define $\mathbf{p} \sim \mathbf{q}$ to hold if, and only if, for all non-negative initial values (i.e., those in $\mathbf{x} \in \mathbb{R}_{\geq 0}^{|\text{Spec}|}$) there is a non-empty time interval $[0, t)$ on which the ODEs given by $\mathbf{p}$ and $\mathbf{q}$ have the same solutions with initial value $\mathbf{x}$. Thus $\mathbf{p} \sim \mathbf{q}$ if the ODEs given by $\mathbf{p}$ and $\mathbf{q}$ have the same solutions locally, for any given initial value. This relation is evidently an equivalence; it seems a reasonable definition as, in general, ODEs need not have global solutions.

One concern about the definition of same simulation behaviour is that solutions of the ODEs given by $\mathbf{p}$ may have negative components, even although the initial value is non-negative. However this does not happen for definable $\mathbf{p}$, as, in that case, solutions remain non-negative, as shown in [36,17]; one can prove this using an immediate consequence of the above definability condition, that if $[S_i] = 0$, then $\mathbf{p}_i \geq 0$.

Next we define the set of process contexts C, D by the following abstract syntax:

$$C ::= R \mid C|D \mid \text{NIL} \mid A = C; D \mid A \mid [\cdot]$$

which is the same as that for processes except that the possibility of a "hole" $[\cdot]$ has been added. Given any context C and process P one obtains a process $C[P]$ by replacing all the holes in C by P. We then define our notion of contextual equivalence by:

$$P \approx Q \text{ iff } \forall C. (C[P] \text{ and } C[Q] \text{ closed } \Rightarrow \text{Diff}[\![C[P]]\!] \sim \text{Diff}[\![C[Q]]\!])$$

We now show that our semantics is indeed fully abstract, in that contextual equivalence coincides with having the same ODE semantics. First we need a lemma.

Lemma 1. *For any* $\mathbf{p}, \mathbf{q} \in \text{Diff}$, $\mathbf{p} \sim \mathbf{q}$ *holds if, and only if,* $\mathbf{p} = \mathbf{q}$.

Proof. Assume $\mathbf{p} \sim \mathbf{q}$. Fix an initial value $\mathbf{x}$. By a standard existence theorem for ordinary differential equations (either that of Cauchy-Peano or that of Picard-Lindelöf), the ODEs given by $\mathbf{p}$ have a solution on some non-empty $[0, t)$ with the given initial value, and so, by the assumption, the ODEs given by $\mathbf{q}$ have the same solution. Such solutions determine the values of the $\frac{d[S_i]}{dt}$ at the given initial value, and so the polynomials $\mathbf{p}([S_i])$ and $\mathbf{q}([S_i])$ have the same values at the given initial value. As the initial value was chosen arbitrarily from $\mathbb{R}_{\geq 0}^{|\text{Spec}|}$, it follows that the two polynomials are identical. $\square$

Theorem 5. *For any processes P and Q we have:*

$$P \approx Q \quad \text{iff} \quad \forall \rho. \text{Diff}[\![P]\!](\rho) = \text{Diff}[\![Q]\!](\rho)$$

Proof. For the implication from right to left, assume that $\forall \rho. \text{Diff}[\![P]\!](\rho) = \text{Diff}[\![Q]\!](\rho)$. It is then easy to show for any context C that $\forall \rho. \text{Diff}[\![C[P]]\!](\rho) = \text{Diff}[\![C[Q]]\!](\rho)$; the proof is by induction on the structure of C.

Conversely, suppose that $P \approx Q$. Let ρ be a definable environment, and suppose that $\rho(A) = \text{Diff}[\![P_A]\!]$; and let $A_1, \dots, A_n$ be a list without repetition of all the free process variables of P or Q. Define C be the context

$$A_1 = P_{A_1};$$
$$\vdots$$
$$A_n = P_{A_n};$$
$$[\cdot]$$

Note that both $C[P]$ and $C[Q]$ are closed; this lets us apply the assumption:

$$\begin{aligned}
\text{Diff}[\![P]\!](\rho) &= \text{Diff}[\![P]\!](\rho[A_1 \mapsto \text{Diff}[\![P_{A_1}]\!]] \dots [A_n \mapsto \text{Diff}[\![P_{A_n}]\!]]) \\
&= \text{Diff}[\![P[P_{A_n}/A_n] \dots [P_{A_1}/A_1]]\!](\rho) \\
&\quad \text{(substitution and denotation commute)} \\
&= \text{Diff}[\![C[P]]\!](\rho) \quad \text{(using the proof rules)} \\
&= \text{Diff}[\![C[Q]]\!](\rho) \quad \text{(by assumption and Lemma 1)} \\
&= \text{Diff}[\![Q]\!](\rho)
\end{aligned}$$

The conclusion then follows by Theorem 4, and the remark after it on definable environments.

$\square$

7   Quantitative Semantics: Stochastic Matrices

Our other semantics of the quantitative calculus is given in terms of the set SMatrix of *stochastic transition matrices*. These are maps $Q : \mathcal{M}_f(\text{Spec})^2 \to \mathbb{R}$ such that

$$Q(X, Y) \geq 0 \quad (\text{if } Y \neq X)$$

and

$$Q(X, X) = -\sum_{Y \neq X} Q(X, Y)$$

They have the following pointwise commutative monoid structure:

$$(Q \mid_{\text{SMatrix}} Q')(X, Y) = Q(X, Y) + Q'(X, Y)$$

$$\text{NIL}_{\text{SMatrix}}(X, Y) = 0$$

For the semantics of rules, first define $(X, Y) \preceq (X', Y')$ to hold for multisets X, Y, X', Y' iff, for some (necessarily unique) Z we have $X' = Z + X$ and $Y' = Z + Y$. Then, in case $Y \neq X$ and $X' \geq X$, we put:

$$\text{SMatrix}[\![X \xrightarrow{r} Y]\!](X', Y') = \begin{cases} r\binom{X'}{X} & (\text{if } (X, Y) \preceq (X', Y')) \\ -r\binom{X'}{X} & (\text{if } Y' = X') \\ 0 & (\text{otherwise}) \end{cases}$$

where

$$\binom{X'}{X} =_{\text{def}} \prod_{S \in \text{Spec}} \binom{X'(S)}{X(S)}$$

In all other cases we put:

$$\text{SMatrix}[\![X \xrightarrow{r} Y]\!](X', Y') = 0$$

We do not know any characterisation of the stochastic transition matrices definable by nets. One necessary condition is that there is a k such that for all X we have $|\{Y \mid Q(X, Y) > 0\}| \leq k$. However a first problem seems to be, allowing nets with countably many transitions, to characterise the stochastic transition relations defined by such nets.

The following axioms hold:

$$X \xrightarrow{r} X = \text{NIL}$$

$$X \xrightarrow{r+s} Z = X \xrightarrow{r} Z \mid X \xrightarrow{s} Z$$

There is an evident canonical form: a composition of process names and rules in which no rule of the form $X \xrightarrow{r} X$ occurs and at most one rule with any given left- and right-hand side occurs. With the addition of the above two axioms, the logic of the quantitative calculus is complete for the stochastic semantics:

Theorem 6. *The following are equivalent for any two processes P and Q:*

1. P and Q can be proven equal using the above axioms for the stochastic semantics.
2. Any two canonical forms of P and Q are the same up to reordering.
3. $\mathrm{SMatrix}[\![P]\!](\rho) = \mathrm{SMatrix}[\![Q]\!](\rho)$ for all ρ.

Proof. As always, we need only assume (3) and prove (2). So choose canonical forms $A_1 \mid \ldots \mid A_m \mid R_1 \mid \ldots \mid R_n$ and $A'_1 \mid \ldots \mid A'_{m'} \mid R'_1 \mid \ldots \mid R'_{n'}$ of P and Q. Setting ρ to be constantly $\mathrm{NIL}_{\mathrm{SMatrix}}$ for any $X, Y \in \mathcal{M}_f(\mathrm{Spec})$ with $X \neq Y$, we have:

$$\mathrm{SMatrix}[\![P]\!](\rho)(X,Y) = \sum_{(X_j,Y_j)\preceq(X,Y)} r_j\left(\tbinom{X}{X_j}\right)$$

where $R_j = X_j \xrightarrow{r_j} Y_j$; a similar formula holds for Q, with $R'_k = X'_k \xrightarrow{r'_k} Y'_k$.

We prove that $X \xrightarrow{r} Y$ occurs in one canonical form iff it is in the other by induction on $\|X\|$. So consider an $R_j = X_j \xrightarrow{r_j} Y_j$, to show it is some R'_k. From the above formula for $\mathrm{SMatrix}[\![P]\!]$ we have:

$$\mathrm{SMatrix}[\![P]\!](\rho)(X_j,Y_j) = \sum_{\substack{(X_{j'},Y_{j'})\preceq(X,Y)\\ \|X_{j'}\|<\|X_j\|}} r_{j'}\left(\tbinom{X}{X_{j'}}\right) + r_j\left(\tbinom{X_j}{X_j}\right)$$

using the fact that if $(X',Y') \preceq (X,Y)$ and $\|X'\| = \|X\|$ then $X' = X$ and $Y' = Y$. Similarly, we have:

$$\mathrm{SMatrix}[\![Q]\!](\rho)(X_j,Y_j) = \sum_{\substack{(X'_k,Y'_k) \preceq (X_j,Y_j)\\ \|X'_k\| < \|X_j\|}} r'_k\left(\tbinom{X}{X_{j'}}\right) + \delta$$

where $\delta = 0$ unless there is a (necessarily unique) $R'_k = X'_k \xrightarrow{r'_k} Y'_k$ with $X'_k = X_j$ and $Y'_k = Y_j$, when $\delta = r'_k\left(\tbinom{X'_k}{X'_k}\right)(= r'_k\left(\tbinom{X_j}{X_j}\right))$.

We know that $\mathrm{SMatrix}[\![P]\!](\rho)(X_j,Y_j) = \mathrm{SMatrix}[\![Q]\!](\rho)(X_j,Y_j)$, so, applying the induction hypothesis, we see that $r_j\left(\tbinom{X_j}{X_j}\right) = \delta$. So, as $r_j \neq 0$, we have $r_j\left(\tbinom{X_j}{X_j}\right) = \delta = r'_k\left(\tbinom{X_j}{X_j}\right)$, and so $r'_k = r_j$. Therefore R_j occurs in the canonical form of Q, as required. The converse assertion, that rules appearing in the canonical form of Q also appear in the canonical form of P is proved similarly.

To see that the same process identifiers occur in both canonical forms, and with the same multiplicities, suppose that A has multiplicity m in P and multiplicity m' in Q. Define ρ to have value $\mathrm{NIL}_{\mathrm{SMatrix}}$ everywhere except at A where it has value $\mathrm{SMatrix}[\![nS \xrightarrow{1} \emptyset]\!]$, for chosen $S \in \mathrm{Spec}$, and $n > 0$ greater than the multiplicity of S in the left-hand side of any R_j or $R_{j'}$. Noting that $(X',Y') \preceq (X,\emptyset)$ iff $X' = X$ and $Y' = \emptyset$ we that $\mathrm{SMatrix}[\![R_1 \mid \ldots \mid R_n]\!](\rho)(nS,\emptyset) = 0$ and so $\mathrm{SMatrix}[\![P]\!](\rho)(nS,\emptyset) = mn!$. Arguing similarly, we see that $\mathrm{SMatrix}[\![Q]\!](\rho)(nS,\emptyset) = m'n!$ where m' is the multiplicity of A_1 in the canonical form of Q. It follows from the assumption that $m' = m$.

$\square$

As before, it follows from the proof that one can restrict the environments in condition (3) to be definable.

There is a standard Petri net stochastic semantics $\mathcal{S} : \mathrm{CNet} \to \mathrm{SMatrix}$, see, e.g., [37,15]. It is given for $Y \neq X$ by:

$$\mathcal{S}(T, \mathrm{pre}, \mathrm{post}, \mathrm{rate})(X, Y) = \sum_{t \in T} \{\mathrm{rate}(t)\tbinom{X}{{}^{\cdot}t} \mid ({}^{\cdot}t, t^{\cdot}) \preceq (X, Y)\}$$

and thereby determined on the diagonal.

Proposition 3. *For any rule R we have:*

$$\mathrm{SMatrix}[\![R]\!] = \mathcal{S}(\mathrm{CNet}[\![R]\!])$$

and $\mathcal{S}$ is a monoid homomorphism.

It follows that the Petri net and stochastic semantics are consistent in that, for any quantitative process P and any CNet process environment ρ, we have:

$$\mathrm{SMatrix}[\![P]\!](\mathcal{S} \circ \rho) = \mathcal{S}(\mathrm{CNet}[\![P]\!](\rho))$$

As in the case of the ODE semantics, we can consider notions of contextual equivalence for stochastic simulation. The analogue of a solution of the ODEs with a given initial value is the Markov process induced by a stochastic matrix $Q \in \mathrm{SMatrix}$, with a given initial point-mass probability distribution δ_X. (For an explanation of how Markov processes arise from stochastic matrices see, for example, Chapter 2 of [28].)

For any $Q, Q' \in \mathrm{SMatrix}$, define $Q \sim Q'$ to hold if, and only if, for any given initial point-mass probability distribution δ_X, Q and Q' induce the same Markov process. Contextual equivalence is then defined by:

$$P \approx Q \text{ iff } \forall C.\,(\mathrm{C}[P] \text{ and } \mathrm{C}[Q] \text{ closed } \Rightarrow \mathrm{SMatrix}[\![C[P]]\!] \sim \mathrm{SMatrix}[\![C[Q]]\!])$$

Lemma 2. *For any $Q, Q' \in \mathrm{SMatrix}$, $Q \sim Q'$ holds if, and only if, $Q = Q'$.*

Proof. The result is an immediate consequence of the fact that the X-th row of any $Q \in \mathrm{SMatrix}$ is determined by the induced Markov process starting at δ_X. To see this, first note that the first holding time of this process is exponentially distributed with parameter $Q_X =_{\mathrm{def}} -Q(X, X)$. If Q_X is 0 then so is the entire X-th row of Q. Otherwise, as the jump chain of the Markov process is the X-th row of the jump matrix Π of Q, and as $\Pi_{X,Y} = Q(X, Y)/Q_X$ off the diagonal when $Q_X \neq 0$, the X-th row of Q is again determined. $\square$

Using this lemma, we have that the stochastic matrix semantics is indeed fully abstract; the proof is entirely analogous to that of Theorem 5.

Theorem 7. *For any processes P and Q we have:*

$$P \approx Q \quad \textit{iff} \quad \forall \rho.\,\mathrm{SMatrix}[\![P]\!](\rho) = \mathrm{SMatrix}[\![Q]\!](\rho)$$

Acknowledgements. We would like to thank Michael Pedersen and János Tóth for helpful discussions.

References

1. Barabási, A.-L., Oltvai, Z.N.: Network biology: understanding the cell's functional organization. Nature Reviews Genetics 5(2), 101–113 (2004)
2. Bruni, R., Melgratti, H.C., Montanari, U.: A connector algebra for P/T nets interactions. In: Katoen, J.-P., König, B. (eds.) CONCUR 2011. LNCS, vol. 6901, pp. 312–326. Springer, Heidelberg (2011)
3. Calzone, L., Fages, F., Soliman, S.: BIOCHAM: an environment for modeling biological systems and formalizing experimental knowledge. Bioinformatics 22(14), 1805–1807 (2006)
4. Cardelli, L.: On process rate semantics. Theor. Comput. Sci. 391(3), 190–215 (2008)
5. Chaouiya, C.: Petri net modelling of biological networks. Briefings in Bioinformatics 8(4), 210–219 (2007)
6. Craciun, G., Feinberg, M.: Multiple equilibria in complex chemical reaction networks: II. The species-reaction graph. SIAM J. Appl. Math. 66(4), 1321–1338 (2006)
7. Danos, V., Laneve, C.: Formal molecular biology. Theor. Comput. Sci. 325(1), 69–110 (2004)
8. Érdi, P., Tóth, J.: Mathematical Models of Chemical Reactions: Theory and Applications of Deterministic and Stochastic Models. Princeton University Press (1989)
9. Domijan, M., Kirkilionis, M.: Graph theory and qualitative analysis of reaction networks. Networks and Heterogeneous Media 3(2), 295–322 (2008)
10. Fiore, M.P., Jung, A., Moggi, E., O'Hearn, P., Riecke, J., Rosolini, G., Stark, I.: Domains and denotational semantics: history, accomplishments and open problems. Bulletin of the European Association for Theoretical Computer Science 59, 227–256 (1996)
11. Garrington, T.P., Johnson, G.L.: Organization and regulation of mitogen-activated protein kinase signaling pathways. Current Opinion in Cell Biology 11, 211–218 (1999)
12. Groote, J.F., Voorhoeve, M.: Operational semantics for Petri net components. Theor. Comput. Sci. 379(1-2), 1–19 (2007)
13. Hárs, V., Tóth, J.: On the inverse problem of reaction kinetics. In: Farkas, M., Hatvani, L. (eds.) Qualitative Theory of Differential Equations. Coll. Math. Soc. J. Bolyai, vol. 30, pp. 363–379. North-Holland (1981)
14. Hartwell, L.H., Hopfield, J.J., Leibler, S., Murray, A.W.: From molecular to modular cell biology. Nature 402, C47–C52 (1999)
15. Heiner, M., Gilbert, D., Donaldson, R.: Petri nets for systems and synthetic biology. In: Bernardo, M., Degano, P., Zavattaro, G. (eds.) SFM 2008. LNCS, vol. 5016, pp. 215–264. Springer, Heidelberg (2008)
16. Hlavacek, W.S., Faeder, J.R., Blinov, M.L., Posner, R.G., Hucka, M., Fontana, W.: Rules for modeling signal-transduction systems. Sci. STKE 2006(344), re6 (2006)
17. Hudjaev, S.I., Vol'pert, A.I.: Analysis in classes of discontinuous functions and equations of mathematical physics. Mechanics: Analysis 8 (1985)
18. Ivanova, A.N.: Conditions for uniqueness of stationary state of kinetic systems related to structural scheme of reactions. Kinet. Katal. 20(4), 1019–1023 (1979)

19. Kaltenbach, H.-M., Stelling, J.: Modular analysis of biological networks. In: Advances in Systems Biology. Advances in Experimental Medicine and Biology, vol. 736, Part 1, pp. 3–17. Springer (2012)

20. Jensen, K.: Coloured Petri Nets: Basic Concepts, Analysis Methods and Practical Use. Monographs in Theoretical Computer Science, vol. 1. Springer (1992)

21. Kitano, H.: A graphical notation for biochemical networks. BIOSILICO 1(5), 169–176 (2003)

22. Kohn, K.W.: Molecular interaction map of the mammalian cell cycle control and DNA repair systems. Molecular Biology of the Cell 10, 2703–2734 (1999)

23. Kohn, K.W., Aladjem, M.I., Weinstein, J.N., Pommier, Y.: Molecular interaction maps of bioregulatory networks: A general rubric for systems biology. Mol. Biol. Cell 17, 1–13 (2006)

24. Milner, R.: Communication and Concurrency. Prentice-Hall (1989)

25. Milner, R.: Communicating and Mobile Systems - The Pi-Calculus. CUP (1999)

26. Matsuno, H., Li, C., Miyano, S.: Petri net based descriptions for systematic understanding of biological pathways. IEICE Trans. Fundam. Electron. Commun. Comput. Sci. 89-A(11), 3166–3174 (2006)

27. Mjolsness, E., Yosiphon, G.: Stochastic process semantics for dynamical grammars. Ann. Math. Artif. Intell. 47(3-4), 329–395 (2006)

28. Norris, J.R.: Markov Chains. Cambridge Series in Statistical and Probabilistic Mathematics, vol. 2. CUP (1998)

29. Pedersen, M.: Compositional definitions of minimal flows in Petri nets. In: Heiner, M., Uhrmacher, A.M. (eds.) CMSB 2008. LNCS (LNBI), vol. 5307, pp. 288–307. Springer, Heidelberg (2008)

30. Pedersen, M., Plotkin, G.D.: A language for biochemical systems: design and formal specification. T. Comp. Sys. Biology 12, 77–145 (2010)

31. Priami, C., Quaglia, P.: Beta binders for biological interactions. In: Danos, V., Schachter, V. (eds.) CMSB 2004. LNCS (LNBI), vol. 3082, pp. 20–33. Springer, Heidelberg (2005)

32. Priami, C., Regev, A., Shapiro, E.Y., Silverman, W.: Application of a stochastic name-passing calculus to representation and simulation of molecular processes. Inf. Process. Lett. 80(1), 25–31 (2001)

33. Regev, A., Panina, E.M., Silverman, W., Cardelli, L., Shapiro, E.Y.: BioAmbients: An abstraction for biological compartments. Theor. Comput. Sci. 325(1), 141–167 (2004)

34. Szederényi, G.: Computing sparse and dense realizations of reaction kinetic systems. Journal of Mathematical Chemistry 47, 551–568 (2009)

35. Szederkényi, G., Hangos, K.M., Péni, T.: Maximal and minimal realizations of reaction kinetic systems: Computation and properties. MATCH Communications in Mathematical and in Computer Chemistry 65(2) (2011), also available as arXiv:1005.2913v1 [q-bio.MN]

36. Vol'pert, A.I.: Differential equations on graphs. Mathematics of the USSR-Sbornik 17(4), 571–582 (1972)

37. Wilkinson, D.J.: Stochastic Modelling for System Biology. CRC Press, New York (2006)

38. Winskel, G.: The Formal Semantics of Programming Languages. MIT Press (1993)

39. Yang, C.-R., Shapiro, B.E., Mjolsness, E., Hatfield, G.W.: An enzyme mechanism language for the mathematical modeling of metabolic pathways. Bioinformatics 21(6), 774–780 (2005)

Schemaless Semistructured Data Revisited
—Reinventing Peter Buneman's Deterministic Semistructured Data Model—

Keishi Tajima

Kyoto University, Yoshida-Honmachi, Sakyo, Kyoto 603-8501 Japan
tajima@i.kyoto-u.ac.jp

Abstract. This paper reviews the design of data models for semistructured data, particularly focusing on their schemaless nature. Uniform treatment of schema information and data, in other words, uniform treatment of metadata and data, is important in the design of such data models. This paper discusses what data and metadata are, and argues that attribute names, which are usually regarded as metadata, and key values, which are usually regarded as data, play similar roles when we organize large data sets. The paper revises one of the standard semistructured data models in accordance with that argument, and eventually reinvents the deterministic semistructured data model proposed by Peter Buneman and his colleagues. The contribution of this paper is an additional rationale of the design of that data model, a rationale based on the similarity between attribute names and key values.

Keywords: semistructured, schemaless, self-describing, metadata, attribute name, key value, edge label, graph, table, multidimensional table.

1   Introduction

In the 1990s, data with nested irregular structure but without predefined schema became prevalent, and the management of such *semistructured* data became an important research topic in the database community [1,4]. Data models and query languages for semistructured data were first discussed [14,8,15,6], and they were soon followed by research on all other aspects of semistructured data management. After that, the focus of the research shifted to the management of XML data, which to some extent represents the convergence of semistructured data management and document management [2]. The XML data format, however, was not originally designed for semistructured data, and is not necessarily appropriate for such data. The design of data models for semistructured data, therefore, remains a technically interesting problem.

This paper reviews the data models for semistructured data that were proposed and studied in the 1990s. It particularly focuses on the *schemaless* nature of semistructured data. The term "schemaless" is related to a couple of aspects of semistructured data, but what is of interest here is the uniform treatment of schema information and data; in other words, the uniform treatment of *metadata*

V. Tannen et al. (Eds.): Buneman Festschrift, LNCS 8000, pp. 466–482, 2013.

and data. This paper therefore first discusses what data and metadata are, and argues that *attribute names*, which are usually regarded as metadata, and *key values*, which are usually regarded as data, play similar roles when we organize large data sets. Revising one of the standard semistructured data models proposed in the 1990s in accordance with the argument, we see that the result is the *deterministic semistructured data model* proposed by Peter Buneman and his colleagues in [9]. In other words, this paper reinvents that data model.

Much of the discussion in this paper has already been shown in the literature, such as [1,4,2] and, of course, [9]. This paper also includes many things that were not explicitly written in [9] but must have already been discussed by Peter Buneman and his colleagues. It may also even include something the author first heard from Peter Buneman or his colleagues but then forgot. The contribution of this paper is that it clarifies the similarity between attribute names and key values, thereby providing an additional rationale for the design of the deterministic semistructured data model in [9].

The remainder of this paper is organized as follows. The next section reviews key issues in the design of data models for schemaless semistructured data, and briefly explains one of the semistructured data models proposed in the 1990s. Section 3 discusses what data and metadata are, and shows that attribute names and key values play similar roles in indexing data items in large data sets. Section 4 extends the model previously explained in Section 2 in accordance with the discussion in Section 3, and "reinvents" the deterministic semistructured data model. Section 5 briefly discusses the relation between that data model and table-based data models, and Section 6 concludes the paper.

2   Semistructured Data Models

Two major data models for semistructured data were proposed in the 1990s, one by the Stanford University Database Group (which is now the Stanford University InfoLab) [3] and the other by Peter Buneman and his colleagues at the University of Pennsylvania [6].

One of the most important properties of these semistructured data models is that they are schemaless. That is, in these data models, data are not accompanied by a separate predefined schema that describes the structure of the data. In ordinary data models for database systems, e.g., in the relational data model, a schema mainly plays the following roles:

1. The most important role of a schema is to index and annotate each data item in the database. For example, attribute definitions in a relational schema are used by the system for parsing the tuples, and attribute names let users know the meaning of the attributes. Such data that describes the structure or meaning of another data is sometimes called *metadata*.

2. A schema also represents structural constraints on data. For example, attribute specifications in a relational schema work also as constraints on the structure and contents of tuples.

3. A schema as a whole also works as a data catalogue (i.e., a concise summary of the stored data) for users to browse or query the database.

In semistructured data models, however, the existence of a schema is not assumed [1,4,2] because

- data may have irregular structure, making it hard to define a compact schema,
- data may have a schema that changes frequently, and
- the information on the structure of data may not be available in advance when we start to store partial data.

When we do not assume a schema, we need some substitutes to play the roles explained above. For the roles of constraints and data catalogs (i.e., Items 2 and 3 above), graph schemas [5] and DataGuide [11] have been proposed. Graph schemas represent constraints on the structure of graph data in a looser way than ordinary rigid schemas (e.g., relational schemas in the relational data model). DataGuide is a summary of a database that is created a posteriori from the stored data. It can be used as a data catalog for users, and can also be used as data constraints in query optimization.

For indexing and annotation (i.e., Item 1 above), most existing semistructured data models take the same approach: they embed such metadata within the data itself. That is why semistructured data are sometimes called *self-describing*. This paper takes the same approach. When this approach is taken, how to embed metadata in data becomes the key issue in the design of data models.

The two data models proposed by the Stanford group and the UPenn group also embed metadata in data. Both data models are essentially labeled graphs. Graphs are used to represent nested irregular data structure, and both basic data values and metadata are represented by labels on nodes or edges. As a result of this, the distinction of data and metadata becomes unclear. In a semistructured data model, such a uniform representation of data and metadata has the following advantages [1,4,2]:

- Because the structure of semistructured data can be irregular and/or dynamic, we often want to query schema information as well as data. If both data and metadata are represented in a uniform way, we can use the same querying functions for both of them.
- In some applications, updates to schema information are also as frequent as updates to data. In such applications, if both data and metadata are represented in a uniform way, we can use the same updating functions for both of them.

In the data model proposed in [6], data and metadata are represented in an extremely uniform way: metadata are represented by edge labels, and atomic data are also represented by labels of terminating edges (i.e., edges to nodes without further outgoing edges).

Figure 1 shows an example graph in this data model, which represents a part of a movie database [6]. The root node at the top of the figure is the entry point of

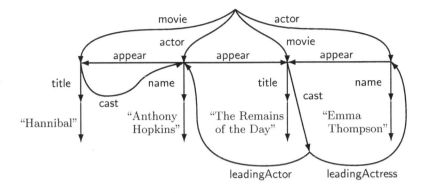

Fig. 1. An example data in the data model proposed in [6]

the database, and it has references to all entries of movies and actors/actresses. Movie entries have two attributes title and cast, and actor/actress entries have two attributes name and appear. Those attributes are represented by the edges outgoing from the node representing each entry. Because this is semistructured data, the structure inside attributes with the same attribute name can be heterogeneous. For example, the cast attribute of the movie "Hannibal" directly refers to an actor/actress entry, while the cast attribute of the movie "The Remains of the Day" leads to branching edges labeled leadingActress and leadingActor.

While attribute names, such as cast and title, are represented by edge labels, atomic values, such as the movie titles "The Remain of the Day" and "Hannibal," are also represented by edge labels. Because both attribute names and atomic values are represented by edge labels in this data model, there is no distinction between them in their query language.

Formally, the type τ of data in this data model is defined as follows [4]:

$$\tau = set(l \times \tau)$$
$$\text{where} \quad l = int \mid string \mid \ldots \mid symbol \ .$$

That is, a node in this data is a set of pairs of a label and another node. Each pair represents the label and the destination of each edge outgoing from the node. Labels can be either atomic values or symbols. Symbols are usually used as attribute names or other metadata. In this way, atomic data and metadata are modeled in a uniform way in this data model.

This model has already achieved the uniform treatment of data and metadata to some extent, but if we further pursue the interchangeability and intermingling of data and metadata, two questions arise:

– Although data and metadata are modeled in a uniform way in the data model, their usage in the example data is completely distinct. Symbols are used as metadata on internal edges, and the other atomic values are used as data on terminating edges. Are there any cases where symbols and other

atomic values should be used in a more intermingled way? One example explained in [4] is the encoding of arrays in this data model, where they use integers as labels on internal edges. Is there any more?
- In this data model, any atomic values can be used in place of metadata (i.e., as edge labels). Do we need to extend this "any atomic values" to "any data"?

To answer these questions, the next section examines what data and metadata are.

3   Data vs. Metadata

To examine what data and metadata are, this paper reviews the most classic and the most popular way to organize large amount of data: tables. In this paper, the term "tables" does not mean tables in relational databases, but it means tables used in print media or Web pages.

3.1   Simple Tables vs. Multidimensional Tables

We use a variety of types of tables, but the two most popular ones for organizing large data are *simple tables* representing some entities and *multidimensional tables*. Table 1 shows an example of a simple table representing some entities. It shows nutrition facts for menu items at some hamburger shop. On the other hand, Table 2 shows an example of a multidimensional table, which represents a mileage chart of a trail near Philadelphia.

Both Table 1 and Table 2 organize cells into two-dimensional structure in order to concisely represent two contexts of each cell by its horizontal and vertical positions, but their structure is slightly different. In the multidimensional table in Table 2, rows and columns are symmetric, but in the simple table in Table 1, rows and columns have asymmetric structure. In Table 1, cells in the same column store the same type of values. For example, the cells in the column **Item** store strings, those in the column **Cal** store integer values whose unit is "Cal.", and the last three columns store boolean values. On the other hand, cells in the same row store values related to the same menu item, but not necessarily of the same type.

In computer science, particularly in the relational data model, simple tables are usually interpreted as a special kind of n-ary relations that have column names (also called attribute names). If we interpret a table in that way, a table is a set of rows corresponding to entities, a row is a tuple consisting of n components representing n attributes of the entity, and the components are indexed by column names describing the meaning of the attributes. In that interpretation, column names are metadata, and values in other cells are data. In Table 1, the last three columns have hierarchical column names, but they can be expanded to simple column names, such as "Allergen.Milk".

On the other hand, in OLAP (OnLine Analytical Processing), multidimensional tables are interpreted as multidimensional arrays (or matrices when they

Table 1. An example of a simple table

Nutrition Facts

Item	Cal	Sugar	Fat	$\cdots$	Allergen		
					Milk	Wheat	Egg
Hamburger	250	5.5	9	$\cdots$	-	$\checkmark$	$\checkmark$
Cheeseburger	300	6.5	12	$\cdots$	$\checkmark$	$\checkmark$	$\checkmark$
Potato(S)	230	0.0	11	$\cdots$	-	$\checkmark$	-
Potato(M)	380	0.0	19	$\cdots$			
$\vdots$	$\vdots$	$\vdots$	$\vdots$	$\vdots$	$\vdots$	$\vdots$	$\vdots$
Gigaburger	540	8.8	29	$\cdots$	-	$\checkmark$	$\checkmark$

Table 2. An example of a multidimensional table

Schuylkill River Trail Mileage Chart

	Philadelphia	Manayunk	Conshohocken	$\cdots$	Tamaqua
Philadelphia	—	7	13	$\cdots$	114.5
Manayunk	7	—	6	$\cdots$	107.5
Conshohocken	13	6	—	$\cdots$	101.5
$\vdots$	$\vdots$	$\vdots$	$\vdots$	$\vdots$	$\vdots$
Tamaqua	114.5	107.5	101.5	$\cdots$	—

are two-dimensional). Arrays are usually indexed by integer values, but multi-dimensional tables in OLAP (also called DataCube [12]) are a special kind of arrays that are indexed by arbitrary values. For example, in Table 2, both rows and columns are indexed by place names. In this interpretation, the place names in the first row and the first column are regarded as column names and row names, which are metadata, while values in the other cells are data.

These examples show that simple tables and multidimensional tables have different structure for metadata. The distinction between them is, however, not always clear. In Table 2, rows and columns are completely symmetric, and it is quite unreasonable to interpret it as a simple table, but this is rather an extreme case. Table 3, which shows car sales data in each month and in each state in U.S., is a typical multidimensional table in OLAP (except that tables in OLAP usually have more dimensions), but this table can also be regarded as a simple table only if we add an attribute name "Month" to the first column, or if we add an attribute name "State" to the first row and transpose the table.

Similarly, Table 1 is usually interpreted as a simple table, but it can also be interpreted as a multidimensional table. In the previous interpretation, this table only has column names and does not have row names. The first column of this table, however, obviously plays a different role from those played by the other columns. The values in the first column are unique to each row, and they specify the meaning of each row, while no other column can play such a role. Therefore,

Table 3. An example of a multidimensional table in OLAP

Car Sales by Month and State

	NY	NJ	PA	⋯	CA
Jan 2012	233	149	183	⋯	258
Feb 2012	358	187	170	⋯	286
Mar 2012	285	174	191	⋯	225
⋮	⋮	⋮	⋮	⋮	⋮
Dec 2012	169	89	115	⋯	188

only if we regard the names of menu items in the first column, e.g., "Hamburger", as the row names, we can interpret this table as a multidimensional table.

In the relational data model, columns like the first column of this table are called "keys". Therefore, more generally speaking, we can interpret a simple table also as a multidimensional table only if we interpret its key values as its row names. Sometimes, we need more than one column to define keys. In such a case, we can produce composite row names from values of those columns, just as we did for hierarchical column names in Table 1.

Notice that we cannot clearly distinguish simple tables and multidimensional tables simply by whether all cells store the same type of values of which we can compute aggregation. Aggregation is required only for OLAP, and is not necessarily required for multidimensional tables in general. For example, it is unlikely that we want to compute any aggregation for Table 2, but this table is usually regarded as a multidimensional table. If aggregation is not required, the definition of "the same type of values" becomes ambiguous, because any value can be regarded as an instance of the type Object or the type Value.

As shown above, many tables can be interpreted either as a simple table or as a multidimensional table, and whether a given cell is data or metadata depends on how we interpret the table. If we interpret Table 1 as a simple table, the values in the first row are metadata, and the others are data. If we interpret it as a multidimensional table, the values in the first row and the first column are metadata, and the others are data. Similarly, if we interpret Table 3 as a multidimensional table, the values in the first row and the first column are metadata, while if we interpret it as a simple table, only the values in the first row or only the values in the first column are metadata.

In addition, when we have some data set, there are more than one way to organize it into a table. For example, the data in Table 3 can also be organized into a table shown in Table 4, as we actually do in ROLAP (Relational OLAP). In this representation, if we interpret this table as a simple table, "**Date**", "**State**", and "**Sales**" in the first row are metadata, and the other values are data.

The discussion above shows that we cannot uniquely determine which part of a given data set should be regarded as metadata. It depends on how we organize data. The examples above, however, demonstrate that two types of data are most likely to play a role of metadata: attribute names and key values. In addition,

Table 4. Relational encoding of a multidimensional table in ROLAP

Car Sales by Month and State

Date	State	Sales
Jan 2010	**NY**	233
Jan 2010	**NJ**	149
Jan 2010	**PA**	183
⋮	⋮	⋮
Jan 2010	**CA**	258
Feb 2010	**NY**	358
Feb 2010	**NJ**	187
Feb 2010	**PA**	170
⋮	⋮	⋮

there are advantages of organizing data as multidimensional tables, in other words, advantages of interpreting key values as metadata, as explained in the next subsection.

3.2   Advantages of Multidimensional Tables

We first compare the expressive power of simple tables and multidimensional tables. Both can represent information on some entities as shown in Table 1, which can be interpreted either as a simple table or as a multidimensional table.

Multidimensional data can also be represented either by a multidimensional table or by relational encoding as shown in Table 3 and Table 4. One difference between these two representations of multidimensional data is their space efficiency. For dense data, relational encoding is space-inefficient because the number of the repetition of the same values grows exponentially when the data has many dimensions. On the other hand, for sparse data, relational encoding can be more space-efficient if we omit rows corresponding to cases where we do not have data.

Exactly the same discussion also holds for information on many-to-many relationships. It can be represented either by multidimensional tables or by relational encoding, and their space efficiency depends on the data.

As shown above, the two types of tables have similar expressive power. Next, we compare their intuitiveness and easiness to understand. One advantage of relations is that they can always represent data in a flat two-dimensional structure. On the other hand, one advantage of multidimensional tables is that they are more intuitive when the data really have multidimensional nature. For example, Table 3 is easier to read for human readers than Table 4 is. More importantly, the interpretation of tables as multidimensional arrays is more intuitive than the interpretation as a relation even when tables represent information on some entities. For example, suppose we read out Table 1. If we interpret this table as a relation, we must read it out as:

"there is a row where the item is Hamburger, the calorie is 250,
the sugar is 5.5, ..., and the egg is true,

and,
there is a row where the item is Gigaburger, the calorie is 540,
the sugar is 8.8, ..., and the egg is true.

On the other hand, if we interpret this table as a matrix with column names and row names, we must read this table out as:

"the calorie of Hamburger is 250, the sugar of Hamburger is 5.5,
..., and the egg of Hamburger is true,

and,
the calorie of Gigaburger is 540, the sugar of Gigaburger is 8.8,
..., and the egg of Gigaburger is true.

For ordinary users who are not familiar with (and not biased toward) the relational data model, the latter description must be more natural.

Another advantage of multidimensional tables is their symmetricity. When we interpret Table 1 as a matrix indexed by column names (attribute names) and row names (key values), rows and columns have symmetric structure, and we do not need to distinguish attribute names and key values in the query languages. It means multidimensional tables treat data and metadata more interchangeably than relations. Such symmetricity of rows and columns is also useful when we interactively manipulate tables through some graphical user interface [16].

We should review why the relational data model adopted relations to represent data. In database systems, the set of attributes to be stored is usually static, while the set of entities in a database is usually changed frequently. Therefore, when we consider data models for ordinary database systems, it is reasonable to interpret tables as relations with static set of columns and dynamic set of rows. When we consider semistructured data, however, we do not assume that the set of attributes for entities is static, as explained before. Another asymmetricity of columns and rows in the relational data model is that cells in the same column store the same type of values, while cells in the same row may not. In semistructured data, however, we do not assume such regularity, either. Yet another, actually the most important, reason of the proposal of the relational data model is data independence [10]. This issue will be discussed later in the next section.

The discussion above is summarized as follows: where semistructured data is concerned, interpreting key values as metadata achieves more uniform treatment of data and metadata, and also achieves more intuitive representation of data. This conclusion leads to the design of the data model in the next section.

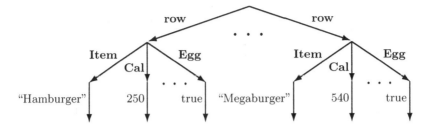

Fig. 2. Ordinary graph representation of a simple table

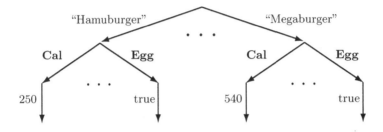

Fig. 3. Graph representation of a simple table using key values as labels

4 Deterministic Semistructured Data Model

This section gets back to the following two questions explained before:

- In edge-labeled graph models for semistructured data, are there cases where it is useful to use symbols and other atomic values in more intermingled way?
- Do we need to extend the edge-labeled graph models so that we allow any values including non-atomic values to be used as edge labels?

4.1 Symbols vs. Atomic Values

The answer to the first question is obvious from the discussion in the previous section. We should use key values as edge labels as well as attribute names. For example, the data in Table 1 is usually represented in a edge-labeled graph model as shown in Fig. 2. If we use key values as edge labels, however, this data can also be represented as shown in Fig. 3. Because we can use attribute names and key values interchangeably, this data can also be represented as shown in Fig. 4. As demonstrated in these examples, both key values and attribute names are useful to index data items in a data set, and therefore, we should use both of them for indexing, i.e., as edge labels, in semistructured data.

These examples raise another question: if we use key values and attribute names as edge labels, do we need to allow multiple edges with the same label outgoing from the same node? In semistructured data models, it is preferable

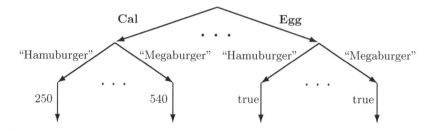

Fig. 4. Another graph representation of a simple table using key values as labels

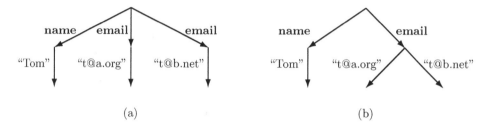

Fig. 5. Merging multiple edges representing a set value

not to distinguish set values and non-set values [1]. In that perspective, if we have a data shown in Fig. 5 (a), it is better represented by the graph shown in Fig. 5 (b). The advantage of the latter representation is that the value of some attribute can be extracted simply by extracting the subtree beneath the edge representing the attribute, no matter whether it is set-valued (e.g., **email** attribute in this example) or single-valued (e.g., **name** attribute in this example). In the existing data models that use the representation in Fig. 5 (a), similar uniformity is achieved by their carefully designed query languages [3,6].

Such merging of multiple edges, however, is not always possible. For example, suppose we have data shown in Fig. 6 (a). If we merge the car edges in this data and transform it into the graph shown in Fig. 6 (b), the correspondence between IDs and colors of the cars will be lost. However, if we use key values as labels, we can represent this data by the graph shown in Fig. 6 (c).

As demonstrated in these examples, if we use key values as edge labels, we do not need to allow multiple edges with the same label outgoing from the same node, as long as we have keys everywhere [9].

4.2   Atomic Values vs. Composite Values

Next, the second question is discussed: do we need to use not only atomic values but also composite values as edge labels? One possible answer is: *"Yes, because we often have composite keys"*. However, do we really need to use composite key values as edge labels?

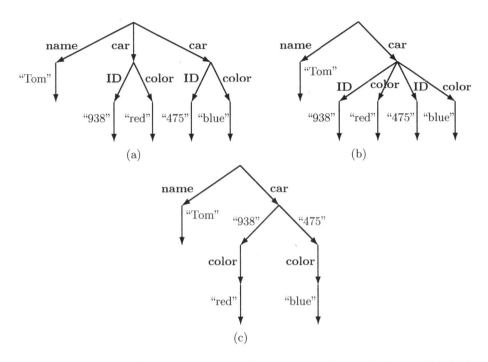

Fig. 6. Inappropriate (b) and appropriate (c) merging of edges with the same label (a)

For example, Table 5 shows information on a many-to-many relationship between students and courses, and it has a composite key consisting of **StudentID** and **CourseID**. Information in this table can be represented by a graph with hierarchical indexing structure, as shown in Fig. 7. Of course, we may also use the opposite order of **StudentID** and **CourseID**.

Such an interpretation of composite keys as hierarchical indices, however, is not always appropriate. For example, suppose there is a table that has a composite key consisting of **GivenName** and **Surname**. In this case, it does not make much sense to organize rows of this table hierarchically by first grouping them based on their **GivenName** and then grouping them based on their **Surname** (or in the opposite order), as shown in Fig. 8, because rows sharing the same **GivenName** (or the same **Surname**) are not necessarily related to each other, and a group of such rows has no useful meaning.

In addition, even in the former example of **StudentID** and **CourseID**, choosing and enforcing one specific order among these attributes causes the problem of *data independence*. That is, it enforces a specific access path on accessing programs, and if the order among the attributes is changed for some reason, we need to rewrite the programs.

The main motivation of the adoption of flat relations in the proposal of the relational data model was to achieve data independence [10]. Since one purpose of semistructured data model is to deal with data with irregular nested structure,

Table 5. Relation representing many-to-many relationship

Course Enrollment of Students

Student ID	Course ID	Grades
20091853	I295	80
20091853	E108	65
20091875	I117	75
20091875	E108	50
20101725	I295	70
⋮	⋮	⋮

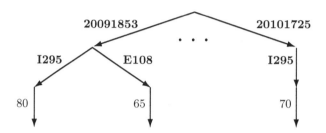

Fig. 7. Hierarchical representation of composite keys

it is difficult to fully eliminate hierarchical structure from the data model, but when hierarchical structure has no useful meaning, we should avoid it as much as possible.

There is yet another reason why we should use composite key values as edge labels: key values can be set values. When key values for some entities are set values, and each key value may have different number of elements, if we decompose these key values into hierarchical indexing structure with only atomic values on edges, each entity would have a different depth in the hierarchy, which introduces unnecessary irregularity. In addition, we need to define some canonical order among elements of a key value.

Table 6 is an example of a table whose key values are set values with different number of elements [13]. This table lists polygons, e.g., those in a CAD system, and here we assume that a polygon can be uniquely identified by specifying its set of vertices. If two polygons have the same set of vertices, they are regarded as the same polygon.

Because of these three reasons, the answer to the second question is: *"Yes, we should allow composite values as edge labels"*. Then, what kind of composite values should we allow? In the semistructured data model explained in Section 2, edge-labeled graph structure is the only data structure, and both records and sets are represented by this data structure. In addition, a key of some data may even include edge labels representing attribute names or class names, as shown in [7]. Therefore, we should allow any edge-labeled graph to be embedded as an edge label in another graph. For example, the data in Fig. 8 can be represented

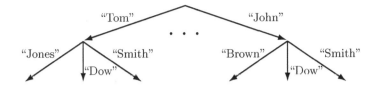

Fig. 8. Meaningless hierarchical representation of composite keys

Table 6. A table whose key values are set values

Polygons in CAD

vertices		color	owner
x	**y**		
3	5		
5	4	red	ken
4	2		
0	4		
1	6		
3	5	blue	joe
2	1		
⋮	⋮	⋮	⋮

as shown in Fig. 9. In the graph shown in Fig. 9, edges from the root node have labels representing composite values consisting of a given name and a surname.

4.3   Definition of the New Model

In this section, the model in Section 2 has been extended in the following two ways:

– Any edge-labeled graph can be used as an edge label in another graph.
– No node can have multiple outgoing edges with the same edge label.

Accordingly, the type τ of data in the data model is redefined as follows:

$$\tau = set(\tau \times \tau) \mid l$$
$$\text{where } l = int \mid string \mid \ldots \mid symbol .$$

That is, we now allow any value of type τ to be a label, and because we do not distinguish values and labels, any value of the type l is now regarded as a value of the type τ. Notice that l (i.e., atomic values) can also be used as the destination of an edge in this new definition.

If we emphasize the second extension, i.e., the uniqueness of labels of outgoing edges from a node, we can also define τ in the following way:

$$\tau = \tau \rightharpoonup_{fin} \tau \mid l$$
$$\text{where } l = int \mid string \mid \ldots \mid symbol$$

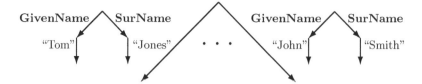

Fig. 9. Representation using composite keys as edge labels

where $\tau \rightharpoonup_{fin} \tau$ denotes a finite partial function from τ to τ.

Now, this is exactly the core part of the deterministic semistructured data model proposed by Peter Buneman and his colleagues in [9]. In this way, based on the discussion on the meanings of the term "schemaless" in the context of semistructured data model, and the discussion on what data and metadata are, this section revised the data model explained in Section 2, and reinvented the deterministic semistructured data model proposed in [9].

5   Graphs vs. Tables

The previous section reinvented the deterministic semistructured data model by starting from the graph-based data model explained in Section 2. Section 3, however, discussed data and metadata in the context of table representations of data. Then a question that may arise is: why do we use graphs rather than tables? To answer this question, this section briefly examines whether nested multidimensional tables are appropriate for representing semistructured data.

One advantage of the table-based representation of information over the graph-based representation is that it can naturally represent data indexed by combinations of two or more values. On the other hand, its disadvantage against the graph-based representation is that it is space-inefficient when the data is sparse. Because semistructured data has irregular structure, and its table representation can be sparse, we consider its relational encoding, which is more space-efficient for sparse data. In relational encoding of nested multidimensional tables, there is at most one row for each combination of indexing values. Therefore, the type τ' of such a data can be defined as a finite partial function below:

$$\tau' = (\tau' \times \cdots \times \tau') \rightharpoonup_{fin} \tau' \mid l$$
$$\text{where } l = int \mid string \mid \ldots \mid symbol \ .$$

In the definition above, the components of the tuple of indexing values are τ' because we should allow composite values and set values as indexing values, as shown in the previous examples. The codomain of the function is also τ' because the contents of a cell may be a nested table.

$(\tau' \times \cdots \times \tau')$ in this definition is a product of nested relations, but we can encode them in τ'. Therefore the type τ' above is a subset of the type τ defined in the previous section. That is, the deterministic semistructured data model can be used for concisely representing sparse nested multidimensional tables.

Then the next question is why we do not flatten nested tables into flat tables, as we do in the relational data model. The answer is simple. We can normalize nested tables into flat tables only if we can have key values that are not set-valued [10]. In semistructured data models, however, we want to allow keys that take set values, as explained before.

In general, an important difference between graph-based data models and table-based data models is how to represent references to other data. Most graph-based models use some kind of IDs, and most table-based models use foreign keys. In the model proposed in [9], two edges outgoing from the same node never have the same label, and therefore, any node can be identified by the sequence of edge labels on the path from the root to the node. Such a sequence of edge labels is used to represent a reference to a node in their model. That is, their model is value-based model just like the relational data model. Advantages and disadvantages of ID-based data models and value-based data models have been discussed extensively, and it is beyond the scope of this paper.

6   Conclusion

This paper reviewed what is schemaless semistructured data, and showed that one of the most important issues in the design of a data model for schemaless semistructured data, is the uniform treatment of data and metadata. Then this paper discussed what data and metadata are in the context of various table representations of data, and concluded that data which corresponds to attribute names or key values are most useful as metadata. In accordance with that discussion, this paper extended the standard edge-labeled graph model, which resulted in a reinvention of the deterministic semistructured data model proposed by Peter Buneman and his colleagues in [9]. Finally, this paper also showed that we can also reinvent the model by starting from nested multidimensional tables.

Acknowledgement. I would like to express the most sincere appreciation to Peter Buneman, who kindly allowed me to visit the database research group of the University of Pennsylvania from August 2000 to August 2001. This visit gave me a valuable opportunity to work with him and learn much from discussions with him. He also helped me and my wife enjoy life in Philadelphia during our stay there. Those thirteen months are a memorable period in both my research career and my personal life. He has also had a great influence on me through his research and his publications. I always enjoy reading his fascinating papers.

I also would like to thank Wenfei Fan, Leonid Libkin, Wang-Chiew Tan, Val Tannen, and Limsoon Wong, editors of the Festschrift in Honor of Peter Buneman, for providing me with the opportunity to contribute to it.

References

1. Abiteboul, S.: Querying semi-structured data. In: Afrati, F.N., Kolaitis, P.G. (eds.) ICDT 1997. LNCS, vol. 1186, pp. 1–18. Springer, Heidelberg (1996)

2. Abiteboul, S., Buneman, P., Suciu, D.: Data on the Web: From Relations to Semi-structured Data and XML. Morgan Kaufmann (1999)
3. Abiteboul, S., Quass, D., McHugh, J., Widom, J., Wiener, J.L.: The Lorel query language for semistructured data. International Journal of Digital Libraries 1(1), 68–88 (1997)
4. Buneman, P.: Semistructured data. In: Proc. of ACM PODS, pp. 117–121 (May 1997)
5. Buneman, P., Davidson, S., Fernández, M., Suciu, D.: Adding structure to unstructured data. In: Afrati, F.N., Kolaitis, P.G. (eds.) ICDT 1997. LNCS, vol. 1186, pp. 336–350. Springer, Heidelberg (1996)
6. Buneman, P., Davidson, S., Hillebrand, G., Suciu, D.: A query language and optimization techniques for unstructured data. In: Proc. of ACM SIGMOD, pp. 505–516 (June 1996)
7. Buneman, P., Davidson, S.B., Fan, W., Hara, C.S., Tan, W.C.: Keys for XML. In: Proc. of International WWW Conference, pp. 201–210 (January 2001)
8. Buneman, P., Davidson, S.B., Suciu, D.: Programming constructs for unstructured data. In: Proc. of International Workshop on DBPL, pp. 1–12 (September 1995)
9. Buneman, P., Deutsch, A., Tan, W.C.: A deterministic model for semistructured data. In: Proc. of the Workshop on Query Processing for Semistructured Data and Non-Standard Data Formats (in conjunction with ICDT), pp. 14–19 (January 1999)
10. Codd, E.F.: A relational model of data for large shared data banks. CACM 13(6), 377–387 (1970)
11. Goldman, R., Widom, J.: DataGuides: Enabling query formulation and optimization in semistructured databases. In: Proc. of VLDB, pp. 436–445 (August 1997)
12. Gray, J., Chaudhuri, S., Bosworth, A., Layman, A., Reichart, D., Venkatrao, M., Pellow, F., Pirahesh, H.: Data cube: A relational aggregation operator generalizing group-by, cross-tab, and sub totals. Data Mining and Knowledge Discovery 1(1), 29–53 (1997)
13. Makinouchi, A.: A consideration on normal form of not-necessarily-normalized relation in the relational data model. In: Proc. of VLDB, pp. 447–453 (1977)
14. Papakonstantinou, Y., Garcia-Molina, H., Widom, J.: Object exchange across heterogeneous information sources. In: Proc. of IEEE ICDE, pp. 251–260 (March 1995)
15. Quass, D., Rajaraman, A., Sagiv, Y., Ullman, J.D., Widom, J.: Querying semistructured heterogeneous information. In: Proc. of International Conference on Deductive and Object-Oriented Database Systems (DOOD), pp. 319–344 (December 1995)
16. Tajima, K., Ohnishi, K.: Browsing large HTML tables on small screens. In: Proc. of ACM Symposyum on User Interface Software and Technology (UIST), pp. 259–268 (October 2008)

Provenance Propagation in Complex Queries

Val Tannen

University of Pennsylvania,
Philadelphia, USA

PETRO BUNEMANNO CARISSIMO
ADMIRATIONE GRATIA VOTISQUE
AETERNAE AMICITIAE PIGNUS
DICTUM

Keywords. databases, query languages, provenance, complex values.

1 Introduction

Peter Buneman has exerted a major influence on my career. Among many other things, we worked together in early 1990s on the design of query languages for post-relational data models: nested relations, complex values, etc. Later on, his pioneering work on data provenance was the major influence on my own work on provenance. It therefore feels very appropriate to me to write for this Festschrift a piece in which languages for complex values and structures for provenance tracking come together.

In section 2 I tell the story of the intelectual filiation that led from Peter's work on why-provenace [4] to my own work on the semiring framework for annotations and provenance [13,10,1]. This is followed in section 3 by a synopsis of the algebraic foundations of the semiring framework. The synthesis mentioned above appears in section 4 where I review the constructs of the Nested Relational Calculus [5] with aggregations [16] while giving them a new semantics based on semiring-annotated sets and on semimodules. The last section comments briefly on the connections between all this and some concepts from category theory.

2 From Why-Provenance to the Semiring Framework

In 2001 Peter Buneman together with his Penn colleague Sanjeev Khanna and their student Wang-Chiew Tan published the seminal article: "Why and Where: A Characterization of Data Provenance" [4]. By then Peter had been interested in data provenance for several years. I recall listening to his views on the subject on many occasions. I recall him teaching me to think of provenance as an *annotation* on data and to focus on how such annotations are *transformed* when data is churned through query operations. His ideas, and the results of the Buneman, Khanna, and Tan paper, came back to me several years later when data provenance became a central concern of my collaboration [12,13] with Penn colleague

V. Tannen et al. (Eds.): Buneman Festschrift, LNCS 8000, pp. 483–493, 2013.
© Springer-Verlag Berlin Heidelberg 2013

Zack Ives and our students TJ Green and Grigoris Karvounarakis on the *semiring framework* for provenance. This section tries to explain the intuition behind this progression with the benefit of hindsight, of course.

While the input and the output of a query may be quite dissimilar in organization, every piece of information in the output is determined by the information in the input, since query languages are typically deterministic. In most cases a specific piece of the output is not determined by the whole input. One of the goals of provenance analysis is to figure out *which pieces of the input* contribute to the presence of a given piece in the output is. In the spirit of the title of [4] we will call this kind of analysis "which-provenance" [1] Let's look at the small example depicted in figure 1. Here the "pieces" of input or output are relational tuples. The input consists of two relations $R(A, B)$ and $S(B, C, D)$ and we show each tuple annotated with its unique *tuple id (tid)*, $r_1, \ldots, s_3$. The output of the relational algebra query $\pi_A(R \bowtie \pi_{BC} S)$ has a single tuple and we show as the first annotation its which-provenance, i.e., the set of input tids that contribute to the computation of this output tuple (only r_3 does not).

	R				S						$\pi_A(R \bowtie \pi_{BC} S)$	

A	B	tid
a	b	r_1
a	c	r_2
a	d	r_3

B	C	D	tid
b	d	e	s_1
b	d	f	s_2
c	g	h	s_3

A	which-provenance	why-provenance
a	$\{r_1, s_1, s_2, r_2, s_3\}$	$\{\{r_1, s_1\}, \{r_1, s_2\}, \{r_2, s_3\}\}$

Fig. 1. Which? Or why?

The output of a query contains many "atomic" pieces of data, for instance strings or numbers, and if the query does not compute these atomic output pieces itself, then each must have been copied from some atomic piece of the input. Figuring out which input piece it was copied from is "where-provenance", another goal of provenance analysis, pioneered in [4] and continued in, e.g., [19,3]. Although this is not a topic for this paper, let us observe that for the example in figure 1 the where-provenance of the a in the query output does not contain any reference to the a in r_3 and it contains references to either the a in r_1 or [2] the a in r_2.

It is however the "why-provenance" discussed in [4] that provided a fundamental new insight, making it significantly more valuable than which-provenance

---

[1] In fact, this kind of data provenance analysis for relational database operations in has been studied under the name *lineage* in [22,7,8] (even earlier work is referenced in [6]) but that term was later used for different kinds of provenance [2,18] possibly leading to confusion.

[2] Without a more detailed description of the implementation of the relational projection operator this is pretty much all we can say. A tree representation of relational data can, for example, provide such detail, see [10].

(lineage). Which-provenance, of course, answers the question "which pieces of the input are used by the query in computing a specific piece of the output?" This is too coarse-grain, because a query can compute (derive) a piece of output in more than one way. Why-provenance collects the annotations of the input pieces used in *each* of these ways and calls the result a *witness* for the output piece. The set of all the witnesses is then the why-provenance. The which-provenance can be recovered from the why-provenance by taking the union of all the witnesses. Looking again at figure 1 the why-provenance of the (just one) output tuple is its second annotation. It collects three witnesses: $\{r_1, s_1\}, \{r_1, s_2\}$, and $\{r_2, s_3\}$. Each of the witnesses is a *separate reason why* the output tuple is derived. Indeed take one of them, say $\{r_1, s_2\}$ and delete from R and S all tuples except r_1 and s_2. Recomputing the query we get the same output tuple again.

We claimed that which-provenance is too coarse-grain. In what applications is the finer-grain of why-provenance important? I will mention three such applications: trust, access control, and uncertainty.

In *trust* applications we have (a priori) different degrees of confidence in the various parts of a query input. This is very common in information integration, for instance. Now, given a query, we should ask what degree of confidence can be assigned to a piece of its output? Let's use again the example in figure 1 and a simple low/high confidence model. Assume that we have low confidence in r_1 and s_2 but high confidence in all the other tuples. Can we have high confidence in the output tuple? Which-provenance does not help since there are some contributing tuples of low confidence. Using which-provenance we would likely take a conservative view and assume that the output tuple has low confidence. However, why-provenance would save the reputation of the output tuple since it contains a witness, $\{r_2, s_3\}$, that has only tuples of high confidence!

In *access control* applications we need similar reasoning but we rely on clearance levels instead of degrees of confidence: if an output piece has both a witness of high clearance and a witness of low clearance then it can be given to a user of low clearance. Finally, in *uncertainty* applications that use probabilistic (or fuzzier) reasoning having multiple witnesses corresponds to unions of events while the pieces of input in the same witness correpond to intersections of events, a fundamental distinction that is not supported by which-provenance [3]

The interpretation we give to witnesses in the three applications above suggest that something very general is at work here. We can identify two fundamental ways in which a computation makes use of pieces of data: *joint use* as in using the input pieces in the same witness jointly, and *alternative use* as in using either of the data in two different witnesses. This insight has led us to an algebraic framework with two operations on annotations corresponding to the two kinds of uses we just listed. Further refinement led to a *semiring*-based framework that has unified and clarified much of the prior work on provenance propagation through database operations [13].

---

[3] Further evidence should have been obvious in Imielinski and Lipski's seminal work on querying incomplete databases [14].

Joint and alternative use of data can be very easily explained for the standard query operations on relational data. Again we refer to the example in figure 1. The tuple $\langle \text{B}:b, \text{C}:c \rangle \in \pi_{\text{BC}} S$ is obtained, alternatively, from s_1 or s_2. In the semiring framework we have a binary operation, $+$, that captures this and the provenance annotation of the tuple is $s_1 + s_2$. Alternative use also characterizes the relational union operation and $+$ on annotations is used there as well. The tuple $\langle \text{A}:a, \text{B}:b, \text{C}:c \rangle \in R \bowtie \pi_{\text{BC}} S$ is obtained by joining r_1 and $\langle \text{B}:b, \text{C}:c \rangle \in \pi_{\text{BC}} S$. In the semiring framework we have a different binary operation, $\cdot$, that captures this and the resulting provenance annotation is $r_1 \cdot (s_1 + s_2)$. Applying the same principles, the provenance of the output tuple $\langle \text{A}:a \rangle$ is $(r_1 \cdot (s_1 + s_2)) + (r_2 \cdot s_3)$. Using semiring algebraic laws [13] this can be rewritten as $r_1 \cdot s_1 + r_1 \cdot s_2 + r_2 \cdot s_3$. This gives exactly the why-provenance in figure 1 provided that (1) we interpret r_1 as $\{\{r_1\}\}$, and similarly for the other tids, (2) we interpret $+$ as union of sets (whose elements are sets of tids), and (3) we interpret $\cdot$ as $\uplus$ where

$$\mathcal{X} \uplus \mathcal{Y} = \{ X \cup Y \mid X \in \mathcal{X}, Y \in \mathcal{Y} \}$$

It also gives exactly the which-provenance, using a different interpretation in which $r_1 \mapsto \{r_1\}$ and $+$ and $\cdot$ are both interpreted *the same*, as union of sets of tids. The fact that alternative and joint use are not distinguished is at the root of the lack of wider usability for which-provenance.

The expressions we saw above are in fact more general than why-provenance since they can also *count* the number of times a tid is used in a witness as well as the number of different ways a tuple is derivable from the same witness. Using the algebraic laws of commutative semirings these expression can be rewritten as as multivariate *polynomials* whose indeterminates are the tids and whose coefficients are positive integers. These additional provenance tracking refinements become important when we use bag semantics or even when we just use aggregates, like summation, for which number of occurrences of the same value matters.

3   Semirings and K-Sets

A *commutative monoid* is an algebraic structures $(M, +_M, 0_M)$ where $+_M$ is an associative and commutative binary operation and 0_M is an identity for $+_M$. A **commutative semiring** is an algebraic structure $(K, +_K, \cdot_K, 0_K, 1_K)$ where $(K, +_K, 0_K)$ and $(K, \cdot_K, 1_K)$ are commutative monoids, $\cdot_K$ is distributive over $+_K$, and $a \cdot_K 0_K = 0_K \cdot_K a = 0_K$.

Basic examples of commutative semirings are $(\mathbb{N}, +, \cdot, 0, 1)$ and $(\mathbb{B}, \vee, \wedge, \mathsf{false}, \mathsf{true})$ where $\mathbb{B} = \{\mathsf{false}, \mathsf{true}\}$. General examples of commutative semirings are commutative rings (of course) but also distributive lattices (with top and bottom), hence boolean algebras. One distributive lattice of interest [10,1] is the *access control/"security"* semiring $(\mathbb{S}, \min, \max, 0_{\mathsf{s}}, 1_{\mathsf{s}})$ in which $\mathbb{S}$ is the ordered set $1_{\mathsf{s}} < \mathsf{C} < \mathsf{S} < \mathsf{T} < 0_{\mathsf{s}}$ where the intended meaning of the elements when used as annotations is: 1_{s} : public ("always available"), C : confidential, S : secret, T : top secret, and 0_{s} means "never available". Of course this is just an example of an access control classification; any finite distributive lattice (not necessarily totally ordered) could serve a similar purpose. Another commutative semiring of interest is (a version of) the so-called *tropical semiring*: $(\mathbb{R}_{\geq 0}^{\infty}, \min, +, \infty, 0)$ where we define $x + \infty = \infty$. Its elements can be interpreted as *costs*: for joint use we add up costs and for alternatives we assume that we pay the lower cost. This interpretation works particularly well if it is used for a *trust* model more refined than the low/high we discussed in section 1: the cost is read as an amount that we risk by trusting the data.

A fundamental example of distributive lattice is $(\mathsf{PosBool}(X), \vee, \wedge, \mathsf{false}, \mathsf{true})$. Its elements are equivalence classes of positive (no negation) boolean expressions constructed from variables in X together with false and true. Equivalence is defined in the usual way (same satisfying assignments) and it turns out to be exactly the same as equality modulo the laws of distributive lattices [4]. In fact, this semiring corresponds to the refinement of why-provenance to *minimal witnesses* only [4]. Its elements also give "enough provenance" for positive relational algebra queries (or non-recursive Datalog queries, or unions of conjunctive queries) over incomplete or probabilistic databases [14,18]. The role of the variables in X is to annotate input data and so we call them *provenance tokens*. They can be as fine-grain as tids or as coarse-grain as the same token for all the tuples from one data source. Given such a set X of provenance tokens we also consider the commutative semiring $(\mathbb{N}[X], +, \cdot, 0, 1)$ of *multivariate polynomials* with indeterminates from X and coefficients from $\mathbb{N}$. This semiring captures a very general kind of provenance, more general than which-, why- and PosBool-provenance and also capable of "counting" how many different ways there are to derive an output piece as well as how many times the same input piece is used (the latter is essential in cost/trust applications) [5].

Let D be a set. For any commutative semiring K, the set K^D of functions $D \to K$, with operations defined pointwise is a commutative monoid (in fact it is also a commutative semiring but the multiplicative structure is of less interest). For every $A \in K^D$ we define its *support* to be the following subset of D:

$$\mathsf{supp}(A) \;=\; \{x \in D \mid A(x) \neq 0_K\}$$

We now define a K-**set** with elements from D to be a function $D \to K$ that has *finite support*. The K-sets form a submonoid of K^D and we introduce the following notation for its operations:

$$A \uplus_K B \;=\; \lambda d.\ A(d) +_K B(d) \qquad\qquad \emptyset_K \;=\; \lambda d.\ 0_K$$

Now notice that $\mathbb{B}$-sets are ordinary sets with ordinary union while $\mathbb{N}$-sets are bags with bag union. For a finite arity r we can define [13] a K-*relation* to be a $\mathbb{D}^r$-set where $\mathbb{D}$ is a database domain.

---

[4] $\mathsf{PosBool}(X)$ is the distributive lattice freely generated by X.

[5] $\mathbb{N}[X]$ is the commutative semiring freely generated by X so it captures "enough" provenance to cover any other provenance approach that forms a commutative semiring, or any application that uses annotations from a commutative semiring [13,11].

In addition to forming a commutative monoid, the K-sets also can be "multiplied" by elements of K, an operation similar to multiplication by scalars in a vector space. For any $k \in K$ and any K-set A we define:

$$k *_{_K} A = \lambda d.\ k \cdot_{_K} A(d)$$

When there is no confusion we will omit the operation symbol and write kA instead of $k *_{_K} A$. This operation satisfies algebraic laws such as $k(A \uplus_{_K} B) = kA \uplus_{_K} kB$, $(k_1 +_{_K} k_2)A = k_1 A \uplus_{_K} k_2 A$, and $(k_1 \cdot_{_K} k_2)A = k_1(k_2 A)$ (for a complete list see below). It puts therefore a **semimodule** structure on K-sets. We will need semimodules for aggregation modeling so we give here the general definition.

Given a commutative semiring K, a structure $(W, +_w, 0_w, *_w)$ is a K-**semimodule** if $(W, +_w, 0_w)$ is a commutative monoid and $*_w$ is a binary operation $K \times W \to W$ such that (for all $k, k_1, k_2 \in K$ and $w, w_1, w_2 \in W$):

$$k *_w (w_1 +_w w_2) = k *_w w_1 +_w k *_w w_2 \qquad k *_w 0_w = 0_w$$

$$(k_1 +_{_K} k_2) *_w w = k_1 *_w w +_w k_2 *_w w \qquad 0_{_K} *_w w = 0_w$$

$$(k_1 \cdot_{_K} k_2) *_w w = k_1 *_w (k_2 *_w w) \qquad 1_{_K} *_w w = w$$

In the semimodule of K-sets the singletons form a *basis*. Indeed, for each $d \in D$ define

$$\mathsf{sng}\ d = \lambda d'.\ \textit{if}\ d' = d\ \textit{then}\ 1_{_K}\ \textit{else}\ 0_{_K}$$

Then, any K-set A such that $\mathsf{supp}(A) = \{d_1, \ldots, d_n\}$ can be written as a linear combination of singletons [6]:

$$A = A(d_1)\,\mathsf{sng}\ d_1 \uplus_{_K} \cdots \uplus_{_K} A(d_n)\,\mathsf{sng}\ d_n$$

In the next section we will see that the semimodule algebraic structure is precisely what allows us to define a semantics for the K-*nested relational calculus* as in [10], encompassing the standard particular cases for sets and bags [5]. We will also see that for any K-semimodule W we can define a semantics for the (K, W)-*nested relational calculus with aggregation* which captures additionally aggregations of K-sets of values from W, is part of the general approach in [16] and extends to complex values the work of [1].

4   A Calculus of K-Sets and Aggregation

Fix a commutative semiring K and let's define a calculus of K-sets. As with formalisms such a the lambda calculus, we need to describe *types, terms* and their semantics. In addition we also describe here an *equational theory* for the calculi.

---

[6] In fact, the K-sets form the K-semimodule freely generated by D.

We assume a base type ι whose meaning is $[\![\iota]\!] = \mathbb{D}$ (a domain of values of interest in some context). We also have a type constructor for K-sets: for a type τ whose meaning is some set $[\![\tau]\!] = D$, form the type $\mathsf{Set}_K\,\tau$ whose meaning is the set of K-sets of elements from D.

The terms of the calculus are built from constants c of base type and variables of all types. In the previous section we have identified an algebraic structure on K-sets and now we introduce syntax for terms in the calculus corresponding to this structure: if R, S are terms of type $\mathsf{Set}_K\,\tau$ and e is a term of type τ then $R \uplus_K S$, $\emptyset_K$ and $\mathsf{sng}\,e$ are terms of type $\mathsf{Set}_K\,\tau$. As you see, we use in the syntax the same symbols as in the semantics relying on the reader to disambiguate. Finally, we introduce the fundamental term construction of the calculus: if R is a term of type $\mathsf{Set}_K\,\sigma$ and S is a term of type $\mathsf{Set}_K\,\tau$ that may contain a variable x of type σ then

$$\biguplus_K (x \in R)\, S$$

is term of type $\mathsf{Set}_K\,\tau$. The variable x is bound and its scope is S but not R.

The semantics of $\biguplus_K (x \in R)\, S$ is indeed an indexed "big union" of K-sets. Suppose that the meaning of R is a K-set A whose support is $\{a_1, \dots, a_n\} \subseteq [\![\sigma]\!]$. Suppose also that the meaning of $\lambda x.S$ is the function F that associates to every $a \in [\![\sigma]\!]$ a K-set $F(a)$ of elements from $[\![\tau]\!]$. Then the meaning of $\biguplus_K (x \in R)\, S$ is defined to be the linear combination

$$A(a_1)\, F(a_1) \uplus_K \cdots \uplus_K A(a_n)\, F(a_n)$$

This semantics validates the following axioms for the equational theory of this calculus of K-sets:

$$\biguplus_K \left(x \in \biguplus_K (y \in R)\, S\right) T \;=\; \biguplus_K (y \in R) \biguplus_K (x \in S)\, T$$

$$\biguplus_K (x \in \mathsf{sng}\,e)\, S \;=\; S[e/x] \qquad\qquad \biguplus_K (x \in R)\, \mathsf{sng}\,x \;=\; R$$

$$\biguplus_K (x \in \emptyset_K)\, S \;=\; \emptyset_K \qquad\qquad \biguplus_K (x \in R)\, \emptyset_K \;=\; \emptyset_K$$

$$\biguplus_K (x \in R \uplus_K S)\, T \;=\; \biguplus_K (x \in R)\, T \;\uplus_K\; \biguplus_K (x \in S)\, T$$

$$\biguplus_K (x \in R)\, (S \uplus_K T) \;=\; \biguplus_K (x \in R)\, S \;\uplus_K\; \biguplus_K (x \in R)\, T$$

Next we extend this calculus of K-sets to express aggregations. In addition to the commutative semiring K let us also fix a K-semimodule W. We have one more base type α with $[\![\alpha]\!] = W$. To the terms of the calculus we add constants from W including 0_W and give them type α. Moreover if g, h are terms of type α then $g +_W h$ is also a term of type α. (Again we use the same notation for syntactic and semantic features.) The fundamental aggregation term construction is the following: if R is a term of type $\mathsf{Set}_K\,\sigma$ and g is a term of type α that may contain a variable x of type σ then

$$\sum_K (x \in R)\, g$$

is a term of type α. The variable x is bound and its scope is g but not R.

The semantics of $\sum_K (x \in R) S$ is an indexed "big sum" of elements in W. Suppose that the meaning of R is a K-set A whose support is $\{a_1, \ldots, a_n\} \subseteq [\![\sigma]\!]$ and let $k_i = A(a_i) \in K$ for $i = 1, \ldots, n$. Suppose also that the meaning of $\lambda x.g$ is the function f that associates to every $a \in [\![\sigma]\!]$ an element $f(a)$ of W. Then the meaning of $\sum_K (x \in R) g$ is defined to be the linear combination

$$k_1 *_w f(a_1) +_w \cdots +_w k_n *_w f(a_n)$$

One can see that this construct does for an arbitrary K-semimodule W what the $\uplus$ does for the K-semimodule of K-sets. Not surprisingly we get the analogous set of equational axioms:

$$\sum_K (x \in \uplus_K (y \in R) S) g \;=\; \sum_K (y \in R) \sum_K (x \in S) g$$

$$\sum_K (x \in \mathsf{sng}\ e) g \;=\; g[e/x]$$

$$\sum_K (x \in \emptyset_K) g \;=\; 0_W \qquad\qquad \sum_K (x \in R) 0_W \;=\; 0_W$$

$$\sum_K (x \in R \uplus_K S) g \;=\; \sum_K (x \in R) g \;+_w\; \sum_K (x \in S) g$$

$$\sum_K (x \in R) (g +_w h) \;=\; \sum_K (x \in R) g \;+_w\; \uplus_K (x \in R) h$$

The operations for which we introduced syntax so far do not include the "scalar multiplication" of the semimodule structures. Having such operations can be useful when we wish the queries of the calculus to perform (additional) annotations themselves. The idea was introduced in [10] and was exploited, for example, in *provisioning* [9].

For each $k \in K$ we add two unary constructs to the calculus. One of the constructs takes an expression R of type $\mathsf{Set}_K \tau$ and produces another expression $k R$ of the same type. If the meaning of R is the K-set A then the meaning of $k R$ is the K-set $k *_K A$. The other construct takes an expression g of type α and produces another expression $k g$ also of type α. If the meaning of g is $w \in W$ then the meaning of $k g$ is $k *_w w$. In addition to equalities directly derived from the semimodule axioms, these additional constructs satisfy the following:

$$\uplus_K (x \in k R) S \;=\; k \uplus_K (x \in R) S \;=\; \uplus_K (x \in R) k S$$

$$\sum_K (x \in k R) g \;=\; k \sum_K (x \in R) g \;=\; \sum_K (x \in R) k g$$

Together with the previous axioms about $\uplus_K$ and $+_w$ these are *linearity* properties. In fact, since the singletons form a basis for K-sets it follows that the semantics of $\sum_K (x \in R) g$ (and of $\uplus_K (x \in R) S$) is completely determined by linearity and by $\sum_K (x \in \mathsf{sng}\ e) g = g[e/x]$. We can show this within the equational theory of the calculus:

$$\sum_K (x \in k_1 \operatorname{sng} e_1 \uplus_K \cdots \uplus_K k_n \operatorname{sng} e_n) g \;=\;$$

$$\sum_K (x \in k_1 \operatorname{sng} e_1) g +_w \cdots +_w \sum_K (x \in k_n \operatorname{sng} e_n) g \;=\;$$

$$k_1 \sum_K (x \in \operatorname{sng} e_1) g +_w \cdots +_w k_n \sum_K (x \in \operatorname{sng} e_n) g \;=\;$$

$$k_1 \, g[e_1/x] +_w \cdots +_w k_n \, g[e_n/x]$$

Taking g to be just x and switching from syntax to semantics gives us the justification for the aggregations of annotated values in [1].

This calculation allows us also to see that the commutativity of $\uplus_K$ and $+_w$ validate the following *commutativity* axioms for $\uplus_K$ and $\sum_K K$:

$$\uplus_K (x \in R) \uplus_K (y \in S) \, T \;=\; \uplus_K (y \in S) \uplus_K (x \in R) \, T$$

$$\sum_K (x \in R) \sum_K (y \in S) \, g \;=\; \sum_K (y \in S) \sum_K (x \in R) \, g$$

Of course, the calculi described above cannot be legitimately called "query languages". However, as was shown in [5,16], only straightforward constructs for pairs (even better: for labeled records), conditionals and an equality test need to be added to get there. The equational theory we gave in this section justifies many of the query optimizations performed in database systems.

5   Connections with Concepts in Category Theory

In the 1970s and 80s, category theory, this desperately abstract branch of mathematics, has surprised programming language theorists by helping them organize their semantical landscape. When a couple of these PL theorists immigrated to databases, some category theory was smuggled in too, hidden among their supplies. So now that we have it we might as well make some use of it. Actually, we did. Pretty much all the constructs and equational laws in section 4 are taken directly from category theory, following [5,16]. For the reader interested in pursuing further connections I will summarize here how this worked out.

Fix a commutative semiring K and consider the category [7] K-SMod of K-semimodules. As usual for algebraic structures, the forgetful functor $U :$ K-SMod $\to$ SET has a left adjoint $F :$ SET $\to K$-SMod. Of interest to us, however, is that $F(D)$ can, in fact, be given as the semimodule of K-sets described in section 3.

Again as usual, the composition $T = U \circ F$ is a monad, in fact a strong monad with respect to the cartesian product of sets. Specializing to T the calculus associated with an arbitrary strong monad in [5] (following the work of Moggi, Wadler, and Trinder [17,21,20]) gives the calculus of K-sets described in section 4.

---

[7] See [15] for category, functor, left adjoint, monad, monad algebra, and monadic.

Moreover, since semimodules are (many-sorted) algebraic structures, Beck's theorem applies and the forgetful functor U is monadic (tripleable), i.e., the Eilenberg-Moore T-algebras are in canonical one-to-one correspondence with the K-semimodules. This allows us to specialize to T the calculus of algebraically "enriched" monad-based collections and their monad-algebra-based aggregates introduced in [16]. The result is the (K, W)-calculus described in section 4.

Other topics treated in [16] yield interesting concepts and results when specialized to K-semimodule monads. For example, the axiomatization of "collection conversions" (monad morphisms, here deriving from semiring homomorphisms) provides the core steps in proving a "commutation with homomorphisms" result for the query languages in section 4. This kind of result plays an essential role in making the provenance framework usable for, e.g., cost, trust, and access control/security applications [13,10,1].

Acknowledgements. I am also very grateful to all the people, aside from Peter, with whom I worked on the topics presented in this paper, and especially to Ramesh Subrahmanyam, Limsoon Wong, Kazem Lellahi, TJ Green, Grigoris Karvounarakis, Yael Amsterdamer, and Daniel Deutch.

References

1. Amsterdamer, Y., Deutch, D., Tannen, V.: Provenance for aggregate queries. In: PODS, pp. 153–164 (2011)
2. Benjelloun, O., Sarma, A.D., Halevy, A.Y., Widom, J.: ULDBs: Databases with uncertainty and lineage. In: VLDB, pp. 953–964 (2006)
3. Buneman, P., Cheney, J., Vansummeren, S.: On the expressiveness of implicit provenance in query and update languages. ACM Trans. Database Syst. 33(4) (2008)
4. Buneman, P., Khanna, S., Tan, W.-C.: Why and where: A characterization of data provenance. In: Van den Bussche, J., Vianu, V. (eds.) ICDT 2001. LNCS, vol. 1973, pp. 316–330. Springer, Heidelberg (2000)
5. Buneman, P., Naqvi, S.A., Tannen, V., Wong, L.: Principles of programming with complex objects and collection types. Theor. Comput. Sci. 149(1), 3–48 (1995)
6. Cheney, J., Chiticariu, L., Tan, W.C.: Provenance in databases: Why, how, and where. Foundations and Trends in Databases 1(4) (2009)
7. Cui, Y., Widom, J.: Practical lineage tracing in data warehouses. In: ICDE, pp. 367–378 (2000)
8. Cui, Y., Widom, J., Wiener, J.L.: Tracing the lineage of view data in a warehousing environment. ACM Trans. Database Syst. 25(2), 179–227 (2000)
9. Deutch, D., Ives, Z.G., Milo, T., Tannen, V.: Caravan: Provisioning for what-if analysis. In: CIDR (2013)
10. Foster, J.N., Green, T.J., Tannen, V.: Annotated XML: queries and provenance. In: PODS, pp. 271–280 (2008)
11. Green, T.J.: Containment of conjunctive queries on annotated relations. Theory Comput. Syst. 49(2), 429–459 (2011)
12. Green, T.J., Karvounarakis, G., Ives, Z.G., Tannen, V.: Update exchange with mappings and provenance. In: VLDB, pp. 675–686 (2007)

13. Green, T.J., Karvounarakis, G., Tannen, V.: Provenance semirings. In: PODS, pp. 31–40 (2007)
14. Imielinski, T., Lipski Jr., W.: Incomplete information in relational databases. J. ACM 31(4), 761–791 (1984)
15. Lane, S.: Categories for the Working Mathematician. Graduate Texts in Mathematics. Springer (1998)
16. Lellahi, S.K., Tannen, V.: A calculus for collections and aggregates. In: Moggi, E., Rosolini, G. (eds.) CTCS 1997. LNCS, vol. 1290, pp. 261–280. Springer, Heidelberg (1997)
17. Moggi, E.: Notions of computation and monads. Inf. Comput. 93(1), 55–92 (1991)
18. Suciu, D., Olteanu, D., Ré, C., Koch, C.: Probabilistic Databases. Synthesis Lectures on Data Management. Morgan & Claypool Publishers (2011)
19. Tan, W.-C.: Containment of relational queries with annotation propagation. In: Lausen, G., Suciu, D. (eds.) DBPL 2003. LNCS, vol. 2921, pp. 37–53. Springer, Heidelberg (2004)
20. Trinder, P.W.: Comprehensions, a query notation for dbpls. In: DBPL, pp. 55–68 (1991)
21. Wadler, P.: Comprehending monads. Mathematical Structures in Computer Science 2(4), 461–493 (1992)
22. Woodruff, A., Stonebraker, M.: Supporting fine-grained data lineage in a database visualization environment. In: ICDE, pp. 91–102 (1997)

Well-Defined NRC Queries Can Be Typed
(Extended Abstract)

Jan Van den Bussche[1] and Stijn Vansummeren[2]

[1] Hasselt University and Transnational University of Limburg, Belgium
[2] Université Libre de Bruxelles, Belgium

Abstract. We study the expressive power of the static type system of the Nested Relational Calculus $\mathcal{NRC}$ and show that on so-called *homogeneous* input and output types, the $\mathcal{NRC}$ type system is *expressively complete*: every untyped but homogeneously well-defined $\mathcal{NRC}$ expression can be equivalently expressed by a well-typed expression. The $\mathcal{NRC}$ static type system hence does not limit the expressive power of the query writer.

Dedicated to Peter Buneman.

1 Introduction

Peter Buneman has been a longtime advocate of database query languages in the style of functional programming [3,4,9]. He has also repeatedly pointed out the relevance of union or variant types in the context of database applications [2,5,8]. Hence it seems fitting to contribute a paper on the expressive power of a typed first-order functional database query language, where we make a heavy use of union and variant types in our technical development.

Conventional wisdom states that programming errors should be caught as soon as possible, preferably at program development time. To this end, most programming languages come equipped with a static type system that accepts only "well-defined" programs that do not "crash" or "go wrong". Unfortunately, however, although decidable static type systems can prove the absence of crashes, they cannot prove their presence. For example, a program like

$$\text{if <complex test> then <crash>}$$

will be rejected as ill-typed even if <complex test> never terminates and the <crash> expression is never executed, as termination of programs is undecidable and hence cannot be statically checked.

For this reason, practical type systems only need to be sound (i.e., accept only well-defined programs), but not complete (i.e., accept exactly all well-defined programs). Note, however, that devising a type system that only needs to be sound is trivial. It suffices to let every expression be ill-typed, as soundness vacuously holds in the absence of well-typed programs. Of course, such a type

V. Tannen et al. (Eds.): Buneman Festschrift, LNCS 8000, pp. 494–506, 2013.

system is useless as it precludes the definition of *all* programs that can be expressed in a well-defined (but untyped) manner. Although real type systems are far from trivial, the question of their expressive power with regard to the class of well-defined programs remains interesting: are there well-defined programs that cannot be expressed by a well-typed program? If so, then the type system limits the expressiveness of the programmer, and more expressive type systems should be considered instead. If not, then we say that the type system is *expressively complete*.

In this paper, we study the expressive power of the static type system of the Nested Relational Calculus $\mathcal{NRC}$ [4]. The $\mathcal{NRC}$ is a database query language that provides a generalization and elegant abstraction of the familiar select-from-where SQL, OQL, and $C^\sharp$ queries. In earlier work [12], we have studied the decision problem of well-definedness for $\mathcal{NRC}$, obtaining that the problem is undecidable for $\mathcal{NRC}$ in general, but decidable for certain restricted fragments. These results motivate the need for an (incomplete) static type system for $\mathcal{NRC}$, such as the one proposed by Buneman et al. [4] during $\mathcal{NRC}$'s inception. Here we show that, on so-called *homogeneous* input and output types, the $\mathcal{NRC}$ type system is *expressively* complete. This hence confirms in the positive a conjecture made by the authors in [11].

Most type systems for imperative Turing complete programming languages are easily shown expressively complete: it suffices to show that one can simulate all Turing machine operations (including encoding and decoding of the programming language objects on Turing machine tapes) in a well-typed manner. Proving expressive completeness for the $\mathcal{NRC}$ type system, in contrast, is more difficult exactly because $\mathcal{NRC}$ is not Turing complete.

Interestingly enough, there are type systems for functional turing complete programming languages that are *not* expressively complete. For example, the untyped lambda calculus can define all computable functions, while in the simply typed lambda calculus only a restricted class of functions, the so-called *extended polynomials*, are definable [1,10]. Moreover, as shown by Kahrs, the type system of the Programmable language for Computable Functions PCF is expressively complete [7], while the type system of ML 1990 is not [6].

This paper is further organized as follows. In Section 2 we formally introduce the $\mathcal{NRC}$ and its static type system. We obtain our main result in Section 3. In this extended abstract, we will omit the detailed proof but we indicate the main steps toward the proof. It is anticipated that the full paper will appear in a scientific journal.

2   Preliminaries

From the outset we assume a non-empty set of atomic data constants (which in practice will include integers, strings, and so on). The $\mathcal{NRC}$ operates on *complex objects* o, which are nested combinations of atomic data constants c; records; and sets:

$$o ::= c \mid () \mid (o,o') \mid \{o,\dots,o'\}.$$

Here, () is the empty record, and (o, o') is the pair of objects formed by o and o'. Note that larger-arity records like, e.g., (o_1, o_2, o_3) can be simulated by nesting pairs as, e.g., $(o_1, (o_2, o_3))$.

The $\mathcal{NRC}$ expressions e themselves are given by the syntax

$$e ::= x \mid c \mid () \mid (e, e') \mid \pi_1(e) \mid \pi_2(e)$$
$$\mid \ \{\} \mid \{e\} \mid e_1 \cup e_2 \mid \{e_2 \mid x \in e_1\} \mid \bigcup e$$
$$\mid \ \text{if } e_1 = e_2 \text{ then } e_3 \text{ else } e_4.$$

(Parentheses may be used to avoid ambiguity.) Here, x ranges over *variables* that can be bound to input objects; c is data constant formation; () is empty record formation; (e, e') is pair formation; $\pi_1(e)$ and $\pi_2(e)$ is left and right projection on pairs, repsectively; $\{\}$ and $\{e\}$ are empty and singleton set construction, respectively; $e_1 \cup e_2$ is set union; and $\{e_2 \mid x \in e_1\}$ is set comprehension. The set comprehension evaluates e_2 for every x in the set returned by e_1. For example, $\{\pi_1(x) \mid x \in R\}$ returns the projection on the first component of the set of pairs R. The expression $\bigcup e$ flattens the set of sets e. Finally, if $e_1 = e_2$ then e_3 else is a conditional expression that evaluates e_3 if e_1 and e_2 evaluate to the same object, and evaluates e_4 otherwise.

It should be emphasized that the $x \in e_1$ part in the $\{e_2 \mid x \in e_1\}$ construct is *not* a membership test. It is an abstraction which introduces and binds the variable x, whose scope is the expression e_2. In light of this view, the *free variables* $FV(e)$ of an expression e are hence inductively defined as follows: $FV(x) = \{x\}$, $FV(o) = \{\}$, $FV(\{e_2 \mid x \in e_1\}) = FV(e_1) \cup (FV(e_2) - \{x\})$, and $FV(e)$ is the union of the free variables of e's immediate subexpressions otherwise. We write $e(x, \ldots, y)$ to indicate that e is an expression with $FV(e) \subseteq \{x, \ldots, y\}$. An expression without free variables is *closed*.

Some expressions, like $\pi_1(\{4\})$ and $5 \cup \{6\}$, clearly apply primitive operators to inappropriate objects and will therefore crash during evaluation. This intuition is formalized as follows. First, define an *environment* to be a mapping α that maps each variable x to an object $\alpha(x)$. We use the notation $x/o, \alpha$ to stand for the environment that equals α on all variables except x, which it maps to o. Let $e[\alpha]$ denote the expression obtained from e by replacing all free occurrences of x by $\alpha(x)$, for every $x \in FV(e)$. Clearly, $e[\alpha]$ is fully determined by the free variables of e: if α and α' agree on $FV(e)$ then $e[\alpha] = e[\alpha']$. We may therefore write $e[x/o, \ldots, y/o']$ as a shorthand of the more verbose $e[x/o, \ldots, y/o', \alpha]$ when $FV(e) = \{x, \ldots, y\}$. Evaluation of $e(x, \ldots, y)$ on $o, \ldots, o'$ can then be seen as running the operational semantics of Figure 1 on $e[x/o, \ldots, y/o']$. There, we use the notation $e \to o$ to indicate that *closed* expression e evaluates to object o. Evaluation *crashes* when there is no o such that $e \to o$.

Example 1. Evaluation of the expression $\bigcup\{\{(\pi_1(y), z) \mid z \in x_2\} \mid y \in x_1\}$ with x_1 bound to $o_1 = \{(1, 2)\}$ and x_2 bound to $o_2 = \{3\}$ is successful:

$$\bigcup\{\{(\pi_1(y), z) \mid z \in \{3\}\} \mid y \in \{(1, 2)\}\} \to \{(1, 3)\}.$$

$$\frac{}{c \to c} \qquad \frac{}{() \to ()} \qquad \frac{e_1 \to o_1 \quad e_2 \to o_2}{(e_1, e_2) \to (o_1, o_2')} \qquad \frac{e \to (o_1, o_2)}{\pi_1(e) \to o_1} \qquad \frac{e \to (o_1, o_2)}{\pi_2(e) \to o_2}$$

$$\frac{}{\{\} \to \{\}} \qquad \frac{e \to o}{\{e\} \to \{o\}} \qquad \frac{e_1 \to \{o_1, \ldots, o_m\} \quad e_2 \to \{o_1', \ldots, o_n'\}}{e_1 \cup e_2 \to \{o_1, \ldots, o_m, o_1', \ldots, o_n'\}}$$

$$\frac{e_1 \to \{o_1', \ldots, o_m'\} \quad e[x/o_i'] \to o_i \text{ for } 1 \le i \le m}{\{e \mid x_1 \in e_1\} \to \{o_1, \ldots, o_m\}}$$

$$\frac{e \to \{o_1, \ldots, o_m\} \text{ where each } o_i \text{ is a set}}{\bigcup e \to o_1 \cup \cdots \cup o_m}$$

$$\frac{e_1 \to o_1 \quad e_2 \to o_2 \quad o_1 = o_2 \quad e_3 \to o}{\text{if } e_1 = e_2 \text{ then } e_3 \text{ else } e_4 \to o} \qquad \frac{e_1 \to o_1 \quad e_2 \to o_2 \quad o_1 \ne o_2 \quad e_4 \to o}{\text{if } e_1 = e_2 \text{ then } e_3 \text{ else } e_4 \to o}$$

Fig. 1. The operational semantics of $\mathcal{NRC}$

Evaluation of this expression with x_1 bound to $o_1' = (1,2)$ instead of o_1 crashes, however, as no inference rule applies to $\{\{(\pi_1(y), z) \mid z \in \{3\}\} \mid y \in (1,2)\}$.

Note that crashes only occur when (1) we apply projection to non-pairs, and (2) when we apply set union, comprehension, or flattening to non-sets.

We are interested in the crashing behavior of expressions when the inputs are taken from certain prescribed classes of objects. To this end, let the $\mathcal{NRC}$ *types* be given by the syntax

$$s, t ::= \mathsf{atom} \mid \mathsf{unit} \mid s \times t \mid \{s\} \mid s \vee t.$$

The semantics of a type is just a set of objects: atom is the set of all atomic data constants; unit is the type of the empty record (); $s \times t$ is the set of all pairs (o, o') with o of type s and o' of type t; $\{s\}$ is the set of all finite sets of objects of type s; and $s \vee t$ it is the set of all objects of type s or of type t. We write $o \colon s$ to indicate that o is an object of type s. Note that every object belongs to a type (in fact infinitely many). For example, $\{5, (1,2)\}$ has type $\{\mathsf{atom} \vee (\mathsf{atom} \times \mathsf{atom})\}$ but also $\{\mathsf{atom} \vee (\mathsf{atom} \times \mathsf{atom}) \vee s\}$ for every s.

Types of the form $s \vee t$ are called *union types*. A type in which no union type occurs is called a *homogeneous type*. So, $\{\mathsf{atom}\}$ is a homogeneous type, but $\{\mathsf{atom} \vee (\mathsf{atom} \times \mathsf{atom})\}$ is not. An object is *homogeneous* if it has a homogeneous type. It is *heterogenous* otherwise. So, $\{5, 1, 2\}$ is a homogeneous set object (of homogeneous type $\{\mathsf{atom}\}$), but $\{5, (1,2)\}$ is heterogenous.

Definition 1. *A type assignment is a mapping* T *that assigns a type* $\mathrm{T}(x)$ *to each variable* x. *An environment* α *is compatible with a type assignment* T, *written* $\alpha \colon \mathrm{T}$ *if* $\alpha(x) \colon \mathrm{T}(x)$, *for every* x. *An* $\mathcal{NRC}$ *expression* e *is said to be well-defined under* T *if for every* $\alpha \colon \mathrm{T}$ *there exists* o *with* $e[\alpha] \to o$. *We write* $\mathrm{T} \models e \colon t$ *to indicate that* e *is well-defined under* T *and, moreover, every output* o *of* e *under all* $\alpha \colon \mathrm{T}$ *is of type* t.

$$\overline{T \vdash x \colon T(x)} \qquad \overline{T \vdash c \colon \text{atom}} \qquad \overline{T \vdash () \colon \text{unit}}$$

$$\frac{T \vdash e_1 \colon s_1 \quad T \vdash e_2 \colon s_2}{T \vdash (e_1, e_2) \colon s_1 \times s_2} \qquad \frac{T \vdash e \colon s_1 \times s_2 \quad i = 1,2}{T \vdash \pi_i(e) \colon s_i}$$

$$\overline{T \vdash \{\} \colon \{s\}} \qquad \frac{T \vdash e \colon s}{T \vdash \{e\} \colon \{s\}} \qquad \frac{T \vdash e_1 \colon \{s\} \quad T \vdash e_2 \colon \{s\}}{T \vdash e_1 \cup e_2 \colon \{s\}}$$

$$\frac{T \vdash e_1 \colon \{s\} \quad x \colon s, T \vdash e_2 \colon t}{T \vdash \{e_2 \mid x \in e_1\} \colon \{t\}} \qquad \frac{T \vdash e \colon \{\{s\}\}}{T \vdash \bigcup e \colon \{s\}}$$

$$\frac{T \vdash e_1 \colon s \quad T \vdash e_2 \colon s \quad T \vdash e_3 \colon t \quad T \vdash e_4 \colon t}{T \vdash \text{if } e_1 = e_2 \text{ then } e_3 \text{ else } e_4 \colon t}$$

Fig. 2. Static type system of $\mathcal{NRC}$

Traditionally, the $\mathcal{NRC}$ is defined to operate only on homogeneous objects, and its type system (which we will define shortly) hence considers only homogeneous types. For the discussion that follows, however, it will be convenient to be able to assign a type also to heterogenous objects. Whence our inclusion of the union types.

The static type system for $\mathcal{NRC}$ is given in Fig. 2. There, the notation $x \colon s, T$ stands for the type assignment that equals T on all variables except x, which it maps to s. As usual, the notation $T \vdash e \colon s$ indicating that e *has type s under* T should be read as "assuming that the free variables x of e are bound to objects of type $T(x)$, e outputs objects of type s". Observe that this relation only depends on the free variables of an expression: if T and T' agree on $FV(e)$ and $T \vdash e \colon s$, then also $T' \vdash e \colon s$. We may therefore write $x \colon r, \ldots, y \colon s \vdash e \colon t$ as a shorthand of the more verbose $x \colon r, \ldots, y \colon s, T \vdash e \colon t$ when $FV(e) = \{x, \ldots, y\}$.

The obvious property one expects from a type system is *soundness*:

Theorem 1. *The static type system of Fig. 2 is sound. That is, if $T \vdash e \colon t$ then $T \models e \colon t$.*

Well-typedness hence implies well-definedness. The converse implication does not hold however, as the static type system rejects certain well-defined expressions. For example, $\{\pi_1(\{\}) \mid x \in \{\}\}$ is well-defined, but is not *well-typed* (i.e., there is no s such that $\vdash e \colon s$). In the following Section we will show, however, that e can equivalently be expressed by a well-typed $\mathcal{NRC}$ expression.

A Note on the $\mathcal{NRC}$ Static Type System. As mentioned earlier, traditionally the type system of $\mathcal{NRC}$ does not include union types. Formally, this means that, traditionally, in Fig. 2 the meta-variables s and t are restricted to range over homogeneous types, and T is restricted to *homogeneous type assignments* (i.e., a mapping from variables to homogeneous types). We do not require this restriction, and are hence able to derive, for example $x\colon \{r_1 \vee r_2\}, y\colon \{r_1 \vee r_2\} \vdash x \cup y\colon \{r_1 \vee r_2\}$.

Still, our setting treats union types in a conservative way, in the following sense.

Proposition 1. *Let* T *be a homogeneous type assignment (i.e., a mapping from variables to homogeneous types) and let* e *be an* $\mathcal{NRC}$ *expression. If* T $\vdash e\colon t$ *then* t *is also a homogeneous type.*

This implies that on homogeneous type assignments, the type system of Fig. 2 hence coincides with the traditional one.

3 Completeness

Our goal in this section is to obtain the following result. Let $e \equiv^{\mathrm{T}} f$ denote that e and f are *equivalent* on inputs of type T. That is, for every $\alpha\colon$ T, either $e[\alpha]$ and $f[\alpha]$ both crash or they evaluate to the same object o.

Theorem 2. *Homogeneous well-defined* $\mathcal{NRC}$ *expressions can be expressed in a well-typed way, in the following sense. For every* $\mathcal{NRC}$ *expression* e, *every homogeneous type assignment* T *and every homogeneous type* t *such that* T $\models e\colon t$ *there exists an* $\mathcal{NRC}$ *expression* h *such that (1)* T $\vdash h\colon t$ *and (2)* $e \equiv^{\mathrm{T}} h$.

The proof is effective and allows us to transform e into h, given T and t. Intuitively, there are two problems to overcome. The first problem is that well-defined expressions may contain ill-defined subexpressions. For example, $e = \{\pi_1(\{\}) \mid x \in \{\}\}$ is well-defined, but its subexpression $e' = \pi_1(\{\})$ is not. Of course, e' is "dead code" (it is never executed) and we can therefore alternatively express e by $\{\bot_t \mid x \in \{\}\}$ where $\bot_t$ is an arbitrary constant object of type t, the desired output type. Our transformation of e into f will therefore need to detect dead subexpressions, and replace them by harmless constants. The second problem is that even when evaluated on homogeneous inputs, well-defined expressions may manipulate heterogeneous objects while well-typed expressions cannot. For example, $e = \{\pi_1(z) \mid z \in (x \cup y)\}$, is well-defined under $x\colon \{s \times s\}, y\colon \{s \times t\}$ with s and t are two different types. It is not well-typed under this type assignment, however, as the type rule for $x \cup y$ requires x and y to have the same set type. Nevertheless, the same query is expressed by $e' = \{\pi_1(z) \mid z \in x\} \cup \{\pi_1(x) \mid z \in y\}$, which is well-typed. In general, we will deal with this problem by simulating heterogeneous objects by homogeneous ones.

The proof of Theorem 2 is divided into three steps as follows, where step 1 and 2 deal with the first problem, and step 2 and 3 deal with the second problem.

1. First, we show that homogeneous well-defined $\mathcal{NRC}$ expressions can be defined in a well-typed way in $\mathcal{NRC}(\mathit{cast})$, an extension of $\mathcal{NRC}$ with a typecast operator.

2. Next, we show that well-typed $\mathcal{NRC}(cast)$ can be simulated in well-typed $\mathcal{NRC}^+$, a variant of the $\mathcal{NRC}$ in which we disallow union types but add *sum types* (also known as *variant types*) instead. In particular, since $\mathcal{NRC}^+$ does not have a typecasting operator, we show that casts can be simulated on sum types.

3. We are thus left with well-typed $\mathcal{NRC}^+$ expressions with homogeneous input and output types, which are already known to be expressible in a well-typed manner in $\mathcal{NRC}$ itself [13].

We now develop each of these steps in turn.

3.1   Adding Casts

Let $\mathcal{NRC}(cast)$ be the extension of $\mathcal{NRC}$ with expressions of the form $\langle s \rangle\, e$, for every type s:
$$e ::= \cdots \mid \langle s \rangle\, e.$$
Semantically, $\langle s \rangle\, e$ returns the same object as e if that object is of type s, otherwise it returns an arbitrary (but fixed) object $\perp_s$ of type s.

$$\frac{e \to o \quad o : s}{\langle s \rangle\, e \to o} \qquad \frac{e \to o \quad \neg(o : s)}{\langle s \rangle\, e \to \perp_s}$$

Note that the output of $\langle s \rangle\, e$ is always of type s. We therefore add the following type rule to the typesystem of $\mathcal{NRC}$:

$$\frac{\mathrm{T} \vdash e : t}{\mathrm{T} \vdash \langle s \rangle\, e : s}$$

It is easy to see that with this addition the typesystem of $\mathcal{NRC}(cast)$ is sound.

The following proposition shows that the typecast operator allows us to extend *any* expression into a well-typed (and therefore, well-defined) expression. Intuitively, this is because we can always typecast subexpressions that do not meet the type rule constraints of Fig. 2 into a type that does meet these constraints. Consider, for example, that we are type-checking $\pi_1(e)$ and suppose that we have already derived $\mathrm{T} \vdash e : t$ with $t = \{\mathsf{unit}\} \vee (s_1 \times s_2)$. Then clearly, $\pi_1(e)$ cannot be well-typed under T since the type rule for π_1 requires e to have a pair type. Suppose, however, that we know that $\pi_1(e)$ is well-defined under T. Then clearly, although the type system derives $\{\mathsf{unit}\} \vee (s_1 \times s_2)$ as the output type of e, we know that e can never output an object of type $\{\mathsf{unit}\}$, otherwise $\pi_1(e)$ would crash. Hence, $\pi_1(e)$ can equivalently be expressed on T by $\pi_1(\langle s_1 \times s_2 \rangle\, e)$, which is well-typed under T.

Similarly, suppose that we have derived $\mathrm{T} \vdash e : t$ with $t = (s_1 \times s_2) \vee (s_1' \times s_2')$. Again, $\pi_1(e)$ is not well-typed under T since the type rule for π_1 requires e to have a pair type $t_1 \times t_2$ instead of a union type. In this case, however, it suffices to recognize that all objects of type $(s_1 \times s_2) \vee (s_1' \times s_2')$ also have type $t' := (s_1 \vee s_1') \times (s_2 \vee s_2')$. Hence, $\pi_1(e)$ can equivalently be expressed on T by $\pi_1(\langle t' \rangle\, e)$, which is well-typed under T.

These two simple ideas form the basis of the following proposition.

Proposition 2. *For every $\mathcal{NRC}$ expression e and every type assignment T there exists an expression $f^{e,T} \in \mathcal{NRC}(cast)$ and type $t^{e,T}$ such that*

(a) $T \vdash f^{e,T} \colon t^{e,T}$; and
(b) for every $\alpha \colon T$, if $e[\alpha] \to o$ then $f^{e,T}[\alpha] \to o$.

Corollary 1. *For every $\mathcal{NRC}$ expression e, every type assignment T, and every type t with $T \models e \colon t$ there exists a well-typed $\mathcal{NRC}(cast)$ expression $T \vdash f \colon t$ such that then $e \equiv^T f$.*

3.2   Simulating Union Types and Casts

In this subsection we explain how the union types and casts of $\mathcal{NRC}(cast)$ can be simulated in $\mathcal{NRC}^+$, a variant of $\mathcal{NRC}$ in which we disallow union types but add *sum types* (also known as *variant types*) instead. Note that $\mathcal{NRC}^+$ does not have a typecasting operator.

$\mathcal{NRC}^+$ extends $\mathcal{NRC}$ on three levels: on the level of objects themselves, on the level of types, and on the level of expressions. On the level of objects, $\mathcal{NRC}^+$ adjoins the atomic, records, and set objects of $\mathcal{NRC}$ with *tagged* objects of the form *left o* and *right o*:

$$o ::= c \mid () \mid (o, o') \mid \{o, \dots, o'\} \mid \textit{left } o \mid \textit{right } o.$$

One can see tagged objects as objects paired with either the label *left* or the label *right*.

On the level of types, $\mathcal{NRC}^+$ adjoins the atomic, record, and set types of $\mathcal{NRC}$ with sum types, as given by the syntax:

$$\sigma, \tau ::= \mathsf{atom} \mid \mathsf{unit} \mid \sigma \times \tau \mid \{\sigma\} \mid \sigma{+}\tau.$$

Note that every homogeneous type s as defined in Section 2 is syntactically also an $\mathcal{NRC}^+$ type. Like $\mathcal{NRC}$ types, the semantics of a $\mathcal{NRC}^+$ type is just a set of objects: atom is the set of all atomic data constants; unit is the type of the empty record (); $\sigma \times \tau$ is the set of all pairs (o, o') with o of type σ and o' of type τ; $\{\sigma\}$ is the set of all finite sets of objects of type σ; and $\sigma{+}\tau$ is the set of all objects *left o* and *right o* with o of type σ and τ, respectively.

On the level of expressions $\mathcal{NRC}^+$ extends $\mathcal{NRC}$ with two tagged object assembly operations, and one dissembly operation:

$$e ::= \dots \mid \mathtt{left}^{\sigma,\tau}\, e \mid \mathtt{right}^{\sigma,\tau}\, e \mid \mathsf{when}\ e_1\ \mathsf{is}\ \mathsf{left}\, x\ \mathsf{do}\ e_2\ \mathsf{or}\ \mathsf{right}\, y\ \mathsf{do}\ e_3$$

where σ and τ range over $\mathcal{NRC}^+$ types. Intuitively, applying assembly operation $\mathtt{left}^{\sigma,\tau}$ to object o adds the *left* label to o, returning *left o*. $\mathtt{right}^{\sigma,\tau}$ works similarly. The dissembly operation $\mathsf{when}\ e_1\ \mathsf{is}\ \mathsf{left}\, x\ \mathsf{do}\ e_2\ \mathsf{or}\ \mathsf{right}\, y\ \mathsf{do}\ e_3$ first inspects the result of e_1. If this is a tagged object *left o* then it evaluates e_2 with x bound to o. If this is a tagged object *right o* then it evaluates e_3 with y bound to o. The free variables of $\mathtt{left}^{\sigma,\tau}\, e$ and $\mathtt{right}^{\sigma,\tau}\, e$ are hence simply the free variables of e. In contrast, the free variables of $\mathsf{when}\ e_1\ \mathsf{is}\ \mathsf{left}\, x\ \mathsf{do}\ e_2\ \mathsf{or}\ \mathsf{right}\, y\ \mathsf{do}\ e_3$ is $FV(e_1) \cup (FV(e_2) - \{x\}) \cup (FV(e_3) - \{y\})$.

$\mathcal{NRC}^+$ OPERATIONAL SEMANTICS.

$$\frac{e \to o}{\texttt{left}^{\sigma,\tau} e \to \textit{left } o} \qquad \frac{e \to o}{\texttt{right}^{\sigma,\tau} e \to \textit{right } o}$$

$$\frac{e_1 \to \textit{left } o_1 \quad e_2[x/o_1] \to o}{\text{when } e_1 \text{ is left } x \text{ do } e_2 \text{ or right } y \text{ do } e_3 \to o}$$

$$\frac{e_1 \to \textit{right } o_1 \quad e_3[y/o_1] \to o}{\text{when } e_1 \text{ is left } x \text{ do } e_2 \text{ or right } y \text{ do } e_3 \to o}$$

$\mathcal{NRC}^+$ STATIC TYPE SYSTEM.

$$\overline{\text{T} \vdash^+ x : \text{T}(x)} \qquad \overline{\text{T} \vdash^+ c : \text{atom}} \qquad \overline{\text{T} \vdash^+ () : \text{unit}}$$

$$\frac{\text{T} \vdash^+ e_1 : \sigma_1 \quad \text{T} \vdash^+ e_2 : \sigma_2}{\text{T} \vdash^+ (e_1, e_2) : \sigma_1 \times \sigma_2} \qquad \frac{\text{T} \vdash^+ e : \sigma_1 \times \sigma_2 \quad i = 1,2}{\text{T} \vdash^+ \pi_i(e) : \sigma_i}$$

$$\overline{\text{T} \vdash^+ \{\} : \{\sigma\}} \qquad \frac{\text{T} \vdash^+ e : s}{\text{T} \vdash^+ \{e\} : \{\sigma\}} \qquad \frac{\text{T} \vdash^+ e_1 : \{\sigma\} \quad \text{T} \vdash^+ e_2 : \{s\}}{\text{T} \vdash^+ e_1 \cup e_2 : \{\sigma\}}$$

$$\frac{\text{T} \vdash^+ e_1 : \{\sigma\} \quad x : \sigma, \text{T} \vdash^+ e_2 : \tau}{\text{T} \vdash^+ \{e_2 \mid x \in e_1\} : \{\tau\}} \qquad \frac{\text{T} \vdash^+ e : \{\{\sigma\}\}}{\text{T} \vdash^+ \bigcup e : \{\sigma\}}$$

$$\frac{\text{T} \vdash^+ e_1 : \sigma \quad \text{T} \vdash^+ e_2 : \sigma \quad \text{T} \vdash^+ e_3 : \tau \quad \text{T} \vdash^+ e_4 : \tau}{\text{T} \vdash^+ \text{if } e_1 = e_2 \text{ then } e_3 \text{ else } e_4 : \tau}$$

$$\frac{\text{T} \vdash^+ e : \sigma}{\text{T} \vdash^+ \texttt{left}^{\sigma,\tau} e : \sigma + \tau} \qquad \frac{\text{T} \vdash^+ e : \tau}{\text{T} \vdash^+ \texttt{right}^{\sigma,\tau} e : \sigma + \tau}$$

$$\frac{\text{T} \vdash^+ e_1 : \sigma_1 + \sigma_2 \quad x : \sigma_1, \text{T} \vdash^+ e_1 : \tau \quad y : \sigma_2, \text{T} \vdash^+ e_2 : \tau}{\text{T} \vdash^+ \text{when } e_1 \text{ is left } x \text{ do } e_2 \text{ or right } y \text{ do } e_3 : \tau}$$

Fig. 3. The operational semantics and type system of $\mathcal{NRC}^+$

In the type system, $\texttt{left}^{\sigma,\tau} e$ will have type $\sigma + \tau$, provided that e has type σ. Similarly, $\texttt{right}^{\sigma,\tau} e$ has type $\sigma + \tau$ provided that e has type τ. Finally, when e_1 is left x do e_2 or right y do e_3 has type τ provided that e_1 has type $\sigma_1 + \sigma_2$, and e_2 and e_3 both have type τ under the assumption that $x : \sigma_1$ and $y : \sigma_2$, respectively.

The formal evaluation rules, as well as the rules of the $\mathcal{NRC}^+$ static type system are given in Fig. 3. There, we use the notation $\text{T} \vdash^+ e : \tau$ that $\mathcal{NRC}^+$ expression e has $\mathcal{NRC}^+$ type τ under $\mathcal{NRC}^+$ type assignment T. It is straightforward to show that this type system is sound.

Example 2. The expression

$$e = \text{when } z \text{ is left } x \text{ do } \pi_1(x) \text{ or right } y \text{ do } \bigcup y$$

is well-typed under the type assignment $z\colon (\{\text{atom}\} \times \text{atom}) + \{\{\text{atom}\}\}$. Intuitively, this type assignment indicates that z can take values that are either of type $\{\text{atom}\} \times \text{atom}$ or of type $\{\{\text{atom}\}\}$. The expression evaluates π_1 on its input object z if that object is of pair type $\{\text{atom}\} \times \text{atom}$. (To be precise, it evaluates π_1 on o when z is of the form *left o*). It evaluates $\bigcup$ on its input object if it is of type $\{\{\text{atom}\}\}$ (i.e., z is of the form *right o*).

As this example illustrates, one can see sum types as a (better-behaved) variant of union types. The crucial difference between union types and sum types lies in the fact that, by means of the *left* and *right* labels, objects of a sum type carry runtime type information, whereas objects of a union type (not having labels) do not. Indeed, an expression similar to e in the example above can intuitively not be defined in a well-defined manner in $\mathcal{NRC}(\textit{cast})$ under the type assignment $z\colon (\{\text{atom}\} \times \text{atom}) \vee \{\{\text{atom}\}\}$ since we have no means in $\mathcal{NRC}(\textit{cast})$ to inspect whether z is of type $\{\text{atom}\} \times \text{atom}$ or $\{\{\text{atom}\}\}$. We will exploit the fact that $\mathcal{NRC}^+$ has this form of runtime type information to show that well-typed $\mathcal{NRC}(\textit{cast})$ can be simulated in well-typed $\mathcal{NRC}^+$. The simulation is based on the following encoding.

The Encoding. We will use $\mathcal{NRC}^+$'s sum types to simulate $\mathcal{NRC}$'s union types by means of the following one-to-one correspondence between the syntax of sum types and union types. Let s^+ be the $\mathcal{NRC}^+$ type obtained by recursively replacing every union type $t_1 \vee t_2$ in $\mathcal{NRC}$ type s by $t_1^+ + t_2^+$.

$$\text{atom}^+ = \text{atom} \qquad \text{unit}^+ = \text{unit} \qquad (s \times t)^+ = s^+ \times t^+$$
$$\{s\}^+ = \{s^+\} \qquad (s \vee t)^+ = s^+ + t^+$$

Similarly, let $\overline{\sigma}$ be the $\mathcal{NRC}$ type obtained by recursively replacing every sum type $\tau_1 + \tau_2$ occurring in $\mathcal{NRC}^+$ type σ by the union type $\overline{\tau_1} \vee \overline{\tau_2}$.

$$\text{atom}^+ = \text{atom} \qquad \text{unit}^+ = \text{unit} \qquad (s \times t)^+ = s^+ \times t^+$$
$$\{s\}^+ = \{s^+\} \qquad (s \vee t)^+ = s^+ + t^+$$

Clearly, $\overline{s^+} = s$ and $\overline{\sigma}^+ = \sigma$. Moreover, if s is a homogeneous type, then $s^+ = \overline{s} = s$. We extend these operations pointwise to type assignments and write, for example, T^+ for $\mathcal{NRC}^+$ type assignment that maps $x \mapsto \text{T}(x)^+$, for every x. The type assignment $\overline{\text{T}}$ is defined similarly.

Finally, let the erasure $\overline{o}$ of $\mathcal{NRC}^+$ object o be the object obtained by recursively replacing all subobjects of the form *left o'* and *right o'* in o by $\overline{o'}$.

$$\overline{c} := c \qquad\qquad \overline{()} = () \qquad\qquad \overline{(o_1, o_2)} = (\overline{o_1}, \overline{o_2})$$
$$\overline{\{o, \ldots, o'\}} := \{\overline{o}, \ldots, \overline{o'}\} \qquad \overline{\textit{left } o} := \overline{o} \qquad \overline{\textit{right } o} := \overline{o}$$

Note that if o is a homogeneous object, then $\overline{o} = o$. We extend erasure pointwise to $\mathcal{NRC}^+$ environments, and write $\overline{\alpha}$ for the environment with domain $dom(\alpha)$ that maps $x \mapsto \overline{\alpha(x)}$, for every $x \in dom(\alpha)$.

Definition 2. *Let s be an $\mathcal{NRC}$ type. We say that $u \colon s^+$ is an* encoding *of $o \colon s$ with respect to s if $\overline{u} = o$.*

It is easy to see that for every $\mathcal{NRC}$ type s and every $o \colon s$ there is at least one encoding. Hence, for every $\alpha \colon \mathrm{T}$ there always an environment $\alpha' \colon \mathrm{T}^+$ encoding α (i.e., $\overline{\alpha'} = \alpha$).

Lemma 1. *Type casts can be simulated in $\mathcal{NRC}^+$. That is, for all $\mathcal{NRC}$ types s and t there exists an $\mathcal{NRC}^+$ expression $cast^{s,t}(x)$ such that:*

(a) $x \colon s^+ \vdash^+ cast^{s,t}(x) \colon t^+$; and
(b) $cast^{s,t}[x/o] \to o'$ implies $\langle t \rangle\, \overline{o} \to \overline{o'}$, for every $o \colon s^+$.

Let us illustrate the proof idea by means of the following example.

Example 3. Let $atom^n$ with $n \geq 1$ stand for the type of n-ary tuples of atomic data constants: $atom^1 = atom$; $atom^2 = atom \times atom$; $atom^3 = atom \times atom^2$; and so on. Let $s = atom^2 \vee atom^3$ and $t = atom^3 \vee atom^4$. Suppose that $\bot_t = (c, (c, (c, c)))$. Then $cast^{s,t}(x)$ is given by

when x is left y do $\mathrm{right}^{atom^3, atom^4}(c, (c, (c, c)))$ or right z do $\mathrm{left}^{atom^3, atom^4}(z)$.

Lemma 2. *For all $\mathcal{NRC}$ types s and t there exists an expression $eq^{s,t}(x, y)$ in $\mathcal{NRC}^+$ that checks equality modulo encodings:*

(a) $x \colon s^+, y \colon t^+ \vdash^+ eq^{s,t}(x, y) \colon \{unit\}$; and
(b) $eq^{s,t}[x/o_x, y/o_y] \to \{()\}$ iff $\overline{o_x} = \overline{o_y}$, for every $o_x \colon s^+, o_y \colon t^+$.

Let us illustrate the proof idea by means of the following example.

Example 4. Using the notation of Example 3, let $s = atom^2 \vee atom^3$ and $t = atom^3 \vee atom^4$. Then $eq^{s,t}(x, y)$ is given by

> when x is left u do $\{\}$
> or right u do
>   when y is left v do (if $u = v$ then $\{()\}$ else $\{\}$)
>   or right v do $\{\}$

Proposition 3. *For every $\mathcal{NRC}(cast)$ expression e, type assignment T and type t with $\mathrm{T} \vdash e \colon t$ there exists $\mathcal{NRC}^+$ expression e^+ such that:*

(a) $\mathrm{T}^+ \vdash^+ e^+ \colon t^+$; and
(b) $e^+[\alpha] \to o$ iff $e[\overline{\alpha}] \to \overline{o}$, for every $\alpha \colon \mathrm{T}^+$.

Corollary 2. *For every $\mathcal{NRC}(cast)$ expression e, every homogeneous type assignment T, and every homogeneous type t with $\mathrm{T} \vdash e \colon t$ there exists a well-typed $\mathcal{NRC}^+$ expression $\mathrm{T} \vdash^+ e^+ \colon t$ such that $e^+ \equiv^{\mathrm{T}} e$.*

3.3   Removing Sum Types

To finalize the proof, we recall the following result by Wong [13, Corollary 2.3.5].

Proposition 4 (Wong [13]). *For every $\mathcal{NRC}^+$ expression e, every homogeneous type assignment* T *and every homogeneous type t with* T $\vdash^+$ $e\colon t$ *there exists a well typed $\mathcal{NRC}$ expression* T $\vdash f\colon t$ *such that $e \equiv^{\mathrm{T}} f$.*

We hence obtain the following proof of Theorem 2.

Proof (of Theorem 2). Let e be an $\mathcal{NRC}$ expression; let T be a homogeneous type assignment; and let t be a homogeneous type such that T $\models e\colon t$. By Corollary 1 there exists $\mathcal{NRC}(\mathit{cast})$ expression $f \equiv^{\mathrm{T}} e$ with T $\vdash f\colon t$. By Corollary 2 there exists $\mathcal{NRC}^+$ expression $g \equiv^{\mathrm{T}} f$ with T $\vdash g\colon t$. Then, by Proposition 4 there exists $\mathcal{NRC}$ expression $h \equiv^{\mathrm{T}} f$ such that T $\vdash f\colon t$, as desired.   □

4   Discussion

One may wonder whether Theorem 2 can be strengthened to the case where e is well-typed under a *heterogeneous* type assignment T with output in a *heterogeneous* type t. It turns out that the static type system of Fig. 2 is too weak for this purpose since it never introduces or manipulates union types; it merely propagates them from the input type assignment to output type. Indeed, the following proposition is straightforward to obtain by induction on e.

Proposition 5. *Let* T $\vdash e\colon t$. *Then every union type $t_1 \vee t_2$ that occurs in t also occurs in* T(x) *for some $x \in FV(e)$.*

Hence, we cannot find a well-typed equivalent of the well-defined $x\colon \{s\}, y\colon \{t\} \models x \cup y\colon \{s \vee t\}$ when s and t are distinct types.

Alternatively, can Theorem 2 be strengthened to the case where e is well-typed under a *heterogeneous* type assignment T with output in a *homogeneous* type t? Proposition 5 does not exclude this possibility. We conjecture, however, that it is also not possible to strengthen Theorem 2 in this sense.

Conjecture 1. There exists a heterogeneous type assignment T, $\mathcal{NRC}$ expression e and homogeneous type t with T $\models e\colon t$ that cannot be equivalently expressed by a well-typed $\mathcal{NRC}$ expression.

References

[1] Barendregt, H.: The Lambda Calculus: its Syntax and Semantics. North-Holland (1984)
[2] Buneman, P., Davidson, S., Watters, A.: A semantics for complex objects and approximate answers. J. Comput. Syst. Sci. 43(1), 170–218 (1991)
[3] Buneman, P., Frankel, R., Nikhil, R.: An implementation technique for database query languages. ACM Trans. Database Syst. 7(2), 164–186 (1982)

[4] Buneman, P., Naqvi, S.A., Tannen, V., Wong, L.: Principles of programming with complex objects and collection types. Theor. Comput. Sci. 149(1), 3–48 (1995)

[5] Buneman, P., Pierce, B.: Union types for semistructured data. In: Connor, R., Mendelzon, A. (eds.) DBPL 1999. LNCS, vol. 1949, pp. 184–207. Springer, Heidelberg (2000)

[6] Kahrs, S.: Limits of ML-definability. In: Kuchen, H., Swierstra, S.D. (eds.) PLILP 1996. LNCS, vol. 1140, pp. 17–31. Springer, Heidelberg (1996)

[7] Kahrs, S.: Well-going programs can be typed. In: Hofmann, M.O. (ed.) TLCA 2003. LNCS, vol. 2701, pp. 167–179. Springer, Heidelberg (2003)

[8] Ohori, A., Buneman, P.: Polymorphism and type inference in database programming. ACM Trans. Database Syst. 21(1), 30–76 (1996)

[9] Ohori, A., Buneman, P., Breazu-Tannen, V.: Database programming in Machiavelli—a polymorphic language with static type inference. In: Clifford, J., Lindsay, B., Maier, D. (eds.) Proceedings of the 1989 ACM SIGMOD International Conference on the Management of Data. SIGMOD Record, vol. 18(2), pp. 46–57. ACM Press (1989)

[10] Schwichtenberg, H.: Definierbare funktionen in λ-kalkül mit typen. Archiv für Mathematische Logik und Grundlagenforschung 174, 113–114 (1976)

[11] Van den Bussche, J., Van Gucht, D., Vansummeren, S.: A crash course on database queries. In: Proceedings of the Twenty-Sixth ACM SIGACT-SIGMOD-SIGART Symposium on Principles of Database Systems (PODS), pp. 143–154. ACM (2007)

[12] Van den Bussche, J., Van Gucht, D., Vansummeren, S.: Well-definedness and semantic type-checking for the nested relational calculus. Theor. Comput. Sci. 371(3), 183–199 (2007)

[13] Wong, L.: Querying Nested Collections. PhD thesis, University of Pennsylvania (1994)

Nine Years with Peter Buneman

Stratis D. Viglas

School of Informatics
University of Edinburgh
sviglas@inf.ed.ac.uk

The first time I met Peter was a typical rainy Edinburgh morning. I was already aware of his tremendous reputation, achievements, and contributions to database systems, but I had not officially met him until that day. It was Thursday, the first day of May, back in 2003; the time was about 8:30am. It is not so much that I have a good memory, as much as it that it was a special day for me. At the time, I was a graduating PhD student at the University of Wisconsin-Madison and I was in Edinburgh for my interview.

During my interview season back in 2003 I was ambivalent on whether I should stay in the US after graduation, or move back to Europe. Edinburgh was certainly not the database powerhouse that it is today. Peter had only recently joined Edinburgh after his long stint at UPenn. I originally sent him an email asking whether there would be any open positions in Edinburgh to which he replied saying there would be, but I needed to be a bit patient as he worked through the bureaucracy to make the official announcement. We exchanged a few emails until the interview and, when the day came and I was in Edinburgh, he made sure to communicate his vision about building something great. The interview went well, even though I never felt being interviewed at all; it felt more like a visit to a former colleague. By the end of the day, I was certain that if Edinburgh would make me an offer I would prefer it over any other offer I had at the time. Peter's presence in Edinburgh was largely the reason for my decision. His email offering me a Lecturer's position at Edinburgh came a few weeks later, and I immediately accepted the offer.

I cannot count the number of times that Peter has impressed me over the last nine years that we have co-existed in Edinburgh. I will likely digress in this essay as I will not focus as much on his research output. I am sure other colleagues who have had a more extensive collaboration with him can write entire books on his research and scientific merits. Personally, I have always thought of Peter equally as a colleague and as a mentor and I will aim to do both sides justice. So what I will do is provide a few anecdotes indicative of our time together in Edinburgh and of the rare opportunity I was given to collaborate and interact with him on a daily basis. At the same time, I will try to showcase why these moments left a great impression on me.

V. Tannen et al. (Eds.): Buneman Festschrift, LNCS 8000, pp. 507–515, 2013.

1   The Collaborator

I joined Edinburgh in September 2003 and, around that time, semi-structured data and XML were still hot research topics. To say that Peter has had a long-lasting impact on the field would be an understatement. I was involved in XML data management as part of my PhD and internship work and it seemed natural that we would at least discuss certain ideas on fast XML query processing after I arrived in Edinburgh.

Peter was the Principal Investigator of an EPSRC grant on what he had termed *XML Vectorisation*: essentially an application of vertical partitioning to the XML data model by supplementing his prior work on structural compression with an efficient storage scheme for data values. This was generalising some of his prior work on XML skeletons with Martin Grohe and Christoph Koch [2] and also the XML compression work of Hartmut Liefke and Dan Suciu [3]. What he was hoping to do at that point was to combine efficient schema and raw-data management techniques through a fast query processor. We started working on the topic on and off for a few months, but at a very superficial level: Peter was heavily involved in getting the Digital Curation Centre[1] off the ground, while I was still becoming accustomed to a new life in Edinburgh. So our collaboration mainly consisted of bouncing ideas off one another every now and then, and helping Peter's PhD students at the time with certain implementation issues.

After the Christmas break, and in January 2004, Wenfei Fan also officially joined Edinburgh. At that point, and after a few discussions and some steps forward in the implementation, we decided to aim to submit a paper to VLDB 2004; that initial work became our ICDE 2005 paper [1]. The division of work was that Wenfei would work on raising the theoretical technical content of the paper, I would work on designing the query processing algorithms and help the students with translating this design into a system, while Peter would oversee the entire process and provide the missing glue to turn all this work into a coherent paper.

The first anecdote is an example of Peter's acute skills in comprehending other people's ideas and turning them into coherent, sensible and easily understandable statements. One of the main issues with our work was that we had to combine frameworks and pieces of code from various ideas and glue them together through an execution engine. Two such frameworks were Christoph's skeleton processing code, and a path-based vertical partitioning implementation the PhD students were working on. The problem was that skeleton processing disregarded the data values; while the data values stored in vectors disregarded the notion of a skeleton as a traversal mechanism. This was not too much of a conceptual problem, but mainly an implementation problem: some type of mapping was necessary to keep the two in sync. At some point in the process, I was looking over one student's idea for tackling the problem. As it typically the case with overworked graduate students, what I had to look at were two hand-written pages with an example and a few bullet points. I had managed to decipher enough to get going but was

---

[1] http://www.dcc.ac.uk

stuck on some part of the example where what looked like a linear arrangement of nodes all of a sudden exploded into a multi-node graph. I was pacing around the hallway when I came across Peter. It was late in the evening and he asked me what I was working on. After I told him, his eyes lit up just as a child's eyes light up when given a new toy. We immediately went back into his office and he started recreating the example on his whiteboard until at some point he sat in his chair and started simply looking at the whiteboard looking as puzzled as I had looked a few minutes before. We decided it was too late in the evening to solve this, so we should head back home and he offered to give me a ride. I went back to my office to pack, and after returning to his office a couple of minutes later he was still sitting in his chair looking at the whiteboard but now with a smile on his face: "It's a line, but not the skeleton," he told me. "It's not the actual XML graph, but it's the operations on the graph. He's just saying that if you have an entire skeleton that has been reduced to a single line and you need to decompress it to process, then different operations need different types of decompression." The example immediately made sense. Depending on the operation and the type of compression, you needed to select how to decompress the skeleton. This was then generalised to the graph reduction technique we used in the actual paper. It was already too close to the deadline at that point and even though we managed to submit the paper after and an all-night editing session with Wenfei, it did not make it through. It received good reviews though, and with a few more experimental tests and mainly cosmetic changes we sent it to ICDE 2005 where it got accepted.

The final editing of the ICDE 2005 submission took place over a weekend in Peter's house in Arnisdale, in the Scottish Highlands. Peter had invited Wenfei and myself over for a long weekend. I still remember the time when while both Wenfei and I were getting a bit stressed about the upcoming deadline and were more-or-less frantically editing the paper Peter was urging us to finish up not so we could submit it, but so we could help him mow the lawn and get his boat in the water and go for a sail around the loch.

What impressed me most throughput this whole process were two things. The first was Peter's need to be challenged. He really likes to solve practical problems that real systems face as opposed to inventing problems for the sake of having something to work on, even though the practical applications may be limited. Overall, he views such problems as puzzles. He simply thinks it is a fascinating new puzzle that someone has put in front of him and he wants to solve it in the most elegant way possible. This has been indeed true throughout our overlap here in Edinburgh. I am one of these dry people that does not like this "invention of problems for having something to work on" referred to above (what qualifies as such a problem is a different discussion). However, the first person to ask the question of the practical aspects of a piece of work is not me, but it usually is Peter. Research should be used to identify our limitations and solve practical problems. This has been constant throughout his career: his prior work on data models and his latest work on provenance, for instance, are prime examples of practically-driven work that touches both theory and practice.

The second attitude to note is how laid-back he is towards research and our work in general. He does not work for the paper or towards a specific deadline. He views research as part of his work and will not push for it at any cost. I think this is intertwined with his viewing of a problem as a puzzle. The only person you challenge in such a situation is yourself and as such you are the one to set the pace. And there is equal enjoyment in sailing in Arnisdale and getting an ICDE submission out of the way: the difference is that most people enjoy finishing the latter so they might be able to enjoy the former. Peter simply wants to enjoy both equally and he views them as steps towards the same goal: solve another puzzle.

2   The Mentor

The transition from graduate student to faculty member is abrupt and its difficulty is underestimated. I cannot believe anyone can be well-prepared for it. As a graduate student, you are somewhat shielded from all that comes with a job in academia. You work on your problem and on that problem alone. Funding is likely taken care of one way or another and you are likely one of the chosen few that work on something they feel passionate about. This all changes when you become a faculty member. You need to arrange for your own and your research group's funding; to publish at a greater rate as when a graduate student and in more diverse topics; to undertake administrative posts and carry out various such tasks in your department (posts and tasks you could not imagine existed let alone associate them with a faculty position); and, amidst all this, be prepared to teach to audiences ranging from first year undergraduate students to mature graduate students. And the above are all in the first few months of starting.

The best analogy I can think of is that as a graduate student you get an entry-level job at a theatre that routinely hosts your favourite acts. Even better, you are chosen to work back-stage for the next big show. Then, the day of the performance, as you are taking care of the last few finishing touches a few minutes before the start of the main act, you graduate. And all of a sudden, you are centre-stage, the curtain is lifted immediately, big lights blind you and every single member of the audience in a packed theatre throws you a juggling club and demands you start juggling with no prior training. Yes, this is an exaggeration, but not too far from the truth of the first few days when you are exposed to the entire machinery of academia.

Barring the above, perhaps one of the most accurate descriptions of academia I have come across is that it is perfect since you get to choose *which* twelve (or more) hours of the day you get to work; but you do have to work as much. This was certainly true in my case at least, and also for some of my contemporaries.

Peter has come to my rescue more than a few times when such frustrations were getting the better of me. A couple of more incidents I recall had to do with such rescues. The first one was after the results of my first EPSRC funding proposal. The process in the UK is that you first receive the reviews of the proposal to which you can reply if necessary (which means if you think it has a chance of going through) before the proposal is put forward in front of a panel in order to be ranked among all similar proposals. The highest ranked proposals will be funded. The proposal was on a new dataflow for query processing and the reviewers all thought it was an ambitious piece of work that should be funded, though they had a few reservations regarding whether query processing was indeed all that important, and not a "solved problem." To say that I was irritated by the latter statement would be an understatement. I asked Peter about how I should prepare the response and, likely using a few expletives in the process. He argued that my response should be factual: "just count the papers on query processing in the last five SIGMOD and VLDB conferences." This is what we did. We sat down and went through the proceedings and counted the number of query processing papers; in the end it was some percentage in the region of 70% —not small by any means. We sent this as our response, but the proposal did not get funded in the end. Upon receiving the news I was dejected and could not really figure out what to do next. At that time I feared that I had made the wrong choice by joining Edinburgh: clearly, the School was a lot more theoretical than I would like it to be, which meant that the pool of PhD applicants I could select from was very limited; while the funding agencies were not too keen to fund systems research. I discussed all these with Peter and he, again, made a simple suggestion that would prove to be a good step towards ironing all these issues out. "Do it anyway," he said. "If they are not willing to fund what they should be funding, maybe they will be willing to fund what they should have funded." And it was really that simple. I started working on implementing certain ideas myself, even though that meant even longer working hours and having to juggle even more things. In the process, that taught me to be efficient in allocating time to the various issues that I had to deal with over the day. I knew that I could not spend as much time as I would like to on some particular topic. Instead, I had to be diligent and finish things as quickly as possible and with minimal backtracking. In the process, I managed to see Edinburgh as a challenge and not as a potentially bad choice. I managed to find funding from elsewhere, publish some work on my own, attract good PhD students, and build by own research group in Edinburgh. All these would make life a lot better over the next few years. Peter's lesson was a valuable one: some times, if you know an idea is good, you should not wait for approval in the shape of funding. You can follow it yourself through limited means. If it is good it will certainly find its way. The four PhD students I have graduated so far, along with all our published work from that day forward were directly related to Peter's "do it anyway" advice.

A little further down the line, I was again getting frustrated by not having found something "big" to work on, so I had this discussion with Peter on what we thought would be good problems to work on. At some point, the discussion revolved around our previous work on XML and how it all started from dropping the schema assumption of the relational model and coming up with semi-structured data in the process. I think I said something along the lines of trying something similar again and Peter's response was that "the last thing the world needs is another data model." This was definitely a surprising statement coming from the one who established both the functional data model and semi-structured data as the research areas that they are today. But, at the same time, it was refreshing and enabling. It is true that we get sometimes too involved in our own work and expertise: when you have a hammer, everything looks like a giant nail. So we try to apply this expertise to everything that we see around us—much like we would use our giant hammer to hammer in every single pro-truding nail, regardless of its small size. In these cases, we need to take a step back and look at other problems that are masquerading as uninteresting ones. In my case, these problems had to do with hardware-conscious query processing, and led to our work on data management over flash memory and code genera-tion for SQL. Having a background in distributed processing and data streams, I was too eager to showhorn other areas into my own, missing interesting ideas in the process. But this is not what research is about. It should be the other way: my expertise should be an enabler to see other areas in new light, and not simply view them through a well-known lens. I believe this is what Peter has done throughout his career and what he meant during that conversation. You need to reinvent your work, not reapply it. He invented a new data model only when one was necessary — not simply when he needed something new to work on. And looking at existing and practical problems from other areas enabled him to identify the need and produce sea-changing research in the process.

3   The Spirit

Peter has certainly taught me that not only you should pick your battles, but also that you should not leave a battle if you find yourself in it through no fault of your own. In academia, this happens more often than usual. My view as to why is that academia is generally full of smart people who feel passionate about their work. It is as if there is a hidden imperative that springs into action with an academic job: focussing on an area and becoming an authority. Otherwise you will not get tenured or promoted, or receive funding, or be able to build your own group, or be invited to collaborations—I could go on, but these are relatively well-known facts. This entire mentality, coupled with a passion for research means that we can become too self-involved and, even worse, self-important. I have seen this happen countless times, and I am certainly as guilty of this as the next person. This means that, at times, we think we know more than we do and get arrogant in the process, or try to discount every new idea as a "yet-another" one that we have seen so many times before.

I have had the opportunity to witness Peter defuse such situations with per-fectly combined amounts of grace and force, depending on the situation. He would brush off negative comments with a joke or a carefully selected pointed remark that nobody could return from. But he would also go head on to battle if necessary. He would do that in the most elegant way possible. Not by shouting over the other person or by pointing them to prior work or by simply disagreeing and thinking he knows best. But by constructing counter-examples and proving to them they were wrong. Or by better understanding their point of view and reaching a common understanding. It has been the case countless times that he would disagree with something during one of our seminars and would say "well, let's not move on, can't we just solve this now?" We would stick there for as long as necessary and only move on when the problem was solved. And in the end we would all know something more.

A different aspect that I have found deeply inspirational is his way of engaging with everything. He views whatever he is doing, however big or small, as a blessing disguised as a chore and strives to turn it into a way to enjoy himself. I recall that we were discussing our MSc programme here in Edinburgh and decided that with the up and coming fire-power that we would have, it was about time that we got a database-specific strand, a specialism in Edinburgh terminology, in the MSc programme in place. This was no simple task, as we had to propose and argue for, roughly, two courses per faculty member. With only three known established courses at the time and projecting to four faculty members (Wenfei and Leonid had not officially joined us at the time), we had to invent five new courses. This had to be dealt with by the next day to meet certain University deadlines, so we had no choice as to the time. Peter suggested that we do this in his flat, since we would not want to be stuck in the office late at night. This being Edinburgh where the weather does tend to be a bit unwelcoming, the suggestion seemed a sensible idea. So, armed with two laptops and two bottles of wine, we started working on the case for support. We ploughed through the creation and description of four new courses and an entire study programme for twenty or so students (that was our estimation for the maximum capacity of the programme at the time) in a few hours. Most of our exchanges were along the lines of "Well, why not? Let's try this." We finished late at night and brought this to the relevant committee over the next few days and even though there was some resistance (which Peter defused by being adamant that our programme as it stands is necessary if we want to attract good students—conceding only to one criticism: "I profusely apologise for misplacing a comma.") it was accepted and put in effect for the next academic year. This was back in late 2004. Since then, the database specialism is one of the flagship specialisms of our MSc programme and accounts for almost fifty students per year—more than twice the number of students we were hoping for, and about 20% of our MSc student intake. I have been involved in designing and delivering various courses and programmes since, but no preparation was as efficient or as enjoyable as that first one.

Similarly, what would also always pleasantly surprise me was the kind of "geek" he is. He would never mind getting his hands dirty with intricate technical details. We would have these long discussions and arguments about which Linux distribution we should use and what sort of packaging mechanism each uses; or whether

Equally, whenever he wanted to get something done quickly he would simply sit down with his laptop and fire up Emacs to write a Python script that would get the job done. I remember how he went through this exercise so he could sanitise text dumps of various protein databases he was experimenting with, or the CIA World Factbook—his favourite example for his work on provenance and the database wiki. Or how when we needed to have some internal voting at the School he whipped up the Python-script equivalent of Scotland's single transferable vote system. Seeing as a lot of colleagues mainly dealing with research management, idea debugging and paper editing, and not so much actively involved in development and all the nitty-gritty aspects of research, it was most refreshing to see someone like Peter as eager to try things himself instead of only providing direction.

His deep need for understanding things is evident in anything he gets his hands on. I believe that Peter is one of the most genuinely curious spirits I know. He is simply eager to learn and try new things. And in doing that, one cannot become self-involved. People like Peter want to know how things work and try new ideas for the sake of the journey not the destination. Whether it is picking up woodwork in his workshop in the Highlands; or sailing his boat; or building a wireless network from scratch so he can read his email at Arnisdale; or inventing and establishing entire new research areas.

It might have been a side-effect of collaborating with Peter later in his career and after he was well established. This meant that he never exhibited this self-involved attitude that I referred to earlier. But I somehow doubt that he ever had this attitude to begin with. The reason is that someone who has been around for as long as he has, is acquainted with pretty much everyone in our area. Granted, my sample may be small, but I have never come across anyone who does not think highly of Peter not only as an academic, but also as a person. And who did not have an interesting story to share, or did not ask me to give him his best when I next saw him in Edinburgh. Of all the things I have heard about him or have witnessed over the years, there are two things that are prevalent. His curiosity and his drive to see things through. These two qualities epitomise him as a researcher and, primarily, as a person.

4   In Closing

Reading over the last few pages I cannot help but fear that the tone is wrong. I think I focussed more on my interpretation of Peter, as opposed to a subjective assessment and celebration of his contributions, which may be more of what one would expect in such an essay. As scientists, we have been trained to look for these subjective truths and base any assessment we make on facts. But, in Peter's case, I think that his work speaks for itself. Furthermore, it has been documented in every aspect possible: his publications, his students, the research groups he has built and the values he has instituted in them are his greatest legacy and they will have a lasting impact. It would be trite and commonplace to talk about it in any detail.

The other aspect I do not like about this essay and the Festschirft in general is that even though it is supposed to be a celebration it can easily be misinterpreted as if there is a sadness lurking, in the sense that we talk about Peter's contributions as if he will not be contributing anything more. This is simply not true. Peter's legacy is vast and will be the source of inspiration for many generations of database researchers to come. Moreover, it is not only his legacy that is an inspiration. It is the man himself who is around doing what he does best: solving puzzles in the most elegant ways possible and enjoying every single step of the process, eager to learn and eager to teach.

Isaac Newton, in a letter to none other than Richard Hooke, famously reiterated Bernard of Chartes' syllogism [4]: "If I have seen a little further, it is by standing on the shoulders of Giants." Time has already proved that Peter is such a Giant on whose shoulders we stand. Personally, I have been lucky enough to witness his greatness and interact with him. I can only hope that a small portion of his quality has rubbed off on me though this interaction. It would make me immensely proud.

References

[1] Buneman, P., Choi, B., Fan, W., Hutchison, R., Mann, R., Viglas, S.D.: Vectorizing and querying large xml repositories. In: ICDE Conference (2005)
[2] Buneman, P., Grohe, M., Koch, C.: Path queries on compressed xml. In: VLDB Conference (2003)
[3] Liefke, H., Suciu, D.: Xmill: An efficient compressor for xml data. In: SIGMOD Conference (2000)
[4] John of Salisbury: The Metalogicon of John of Salisbury: A Twelfth-century Defense of the Verbal and Logical Arts of the Trivium. University of California Press (1955); Translated by Daniel McGarry

Modal Logic for Preference Based on Reasons

Daniel Osherson[1] and Scott Weinstein[2]

[1] Princeton University, Princeton NJ 08544, USA
osherson@princeton.edu
[2] University of Pennsylvania, Philadelphia PA 19104, USA
weinstein@cis.upenn.edu

Abstract. We discuss the logic of preferences, introducing modal connectives that reflect reasons to prefer that one formula rather than another be true. An axiomatic analysis of two such logics is presented.

1 Introduction

The second author is grateful for the opportunity to contribute to this volume in honor of Peter Buneman, whose colleagueship he enjoyed for many years at Penn. Peter's passionate and powerful intellect, his generosity, and his kindness have enriched the lives of all who worked with him. We dedicate this chapter to him. Our hope is that he, or one among his legion of distinguished students, find something here which they can elaborate in ways beyond our capacity to imagine.

The present paper focusses on the modal logic of preference, following up earlier work (Osherson and Weinstein, 2012) on the interaction between preference and *reasons*. An example may help to communicate the kind of situation under investigation. You are deciding whether to adopt a certain dog, Fido; alternatively, you might choose the cat Thomasina. To make up your mind, you first imagine how life would be with Fido, taking into account the companionship and safety he would provide but also the expense and bother. Then you do the same for Thomasina. You observe that, compared to Thomasina, life with Fido would have greater value along the first two dimensions (companionship and safety) but entail less with respect to the second pair (expense and bother). Somehow, you aggregate these four considerations, and plump for Fido.

Our formal reconstruction of this episode is as follows. The world you live in is one of many possibilities including some in which "I adopt Fido" is true and others in which "I adopt Thomasina" is true. In choosing between the two plans, you imagine a world rather similar to yours except that the Fido sentence is true, and another world for the Thomasina sentence. These two worlds are compared for the amount of companionship they provide as well as for safety, expense and bother. A scheme for combining these comparisons is applied, which yields your decision.

The Fido world was delivered by a *selection function* applied to your current world under the thought of adopting Fido, and similarly for the Thomasina world. In other words, selection makes a choice among possible worlds that

V. Tannen et al. (Eds.): Buneman Festschrift, LNCS 8000, pp. 516–541, 2013.

satisfy whatever proposition is being entertained. In the most basic logic, no conditions regulate how the function operates. But stronger theories impose requirements that fill out the idea that selection seeks a world "close" to its starting point among the worlds that satisfy the target proposition. The most elementary constraint is *reflexivity*, which requires that if the starting world satisfies a proposition A, then that world be selected when seeking an A-world. A more consequential constraint is that selection be interpreted metrically, in the sense that the chosen world be uniquely nearest to the starting point among A-worlds, for some underlying metric that situates all the worlds in play. Several constraints are investigated in Osherson and Weinstein (2012).

The basic logic will be presented shortly, followed by an alternative version that dispenses with selection. It will be seen that the two systems validate the same formulas, a fact not available in Osherson and Weinstein (2012). We then proceed to extend the basic logic in another direction, by introducing quantifiers. Before getting started, let us acknowledge some of the prior literature on the logic of preference.

Contemporary work includes several systems that elucidate the interaction between choice and epistemic possibility (see Lang et al., 2003; van Benthem et al., 2009 for an overview). Liu (2008, Ch. 3) is particularly pertinent since it introduces "priorities," which function somewhat like reasons in our theory. Liu's approach is nonetheless different from the one described below inasmuch as selection is absent. A different perspective on the integration of preferences is embodied in the graph-theoretic approach offered in Andréka et al. (2002); different graphs represent different orderings of the alternatives in play, and can be conceived as separate reasons for choice among them. Within another tradition, multi-attribute utility theory (Keeney and Raiffa, 1993) analyses the aggregation of reasons by combining utilities based on separate dimensions. The theory reveals the conditions under which aggregation can proceed additively but stops short of exploring the logical structure of reasons and preference, as we shall do here. Finally (in this abbreviated review), Dietrich and List (2009) provide a representation theorem relating choice to the respective bundles of reasons that apply to the available choices; the simple axioms invoked for their theorem clarify several issues relating to combining reasons.

We shall not attempt to further summarize the extensive literature on the logic of preference. An excellent review up to 1989 is offered by Hansson (1989). Surveys of later work are available in Liu (2008) and Dietrich and List (2009). It is, however, worth emphasizing that the formalisms presented below share many features with earlier work. For example, Hansson (1989) introduces a *selection function* for choosing worlds relevant to an affirmation of preference; a somewhat different kind of selection function (based on the analysis of counterfactuals in Stalnaker, 1968) is central to our own theory. Similarly, the idea of attaching values to possible worlds in order to analyze preference among statements appears in several works (e.g., Rescher, 1967), and is pivotal here as well. Our approach thus builds on many earlier discussions; but (so far as we can see) it puts familiar pieces together in a novel way.

2 The Basic Theory

Turning to our own proposal, we first introduce the family of languages that are used to express preferences, then provide their semantics.

2.1 Syntax

Signatures. A given language is determined by its *signature*, which consists of

(a) a non-empty set $\mathbb{P}$ of propositional variables, and
(b) a nonempty collection $\mathbb{S}$ of nonempty subsets of $\mathbb{N}$ (the set $\{0, 1, \dots\}$ of natural numbers). The elements of $\mathbb{S}$ serve as indexes for utility functions.

The numbers appearing in $X \in \mathbb{S}$ represent specific reasons for preference such as the desire for companionship in our introductory example. A set X of reasons influences preference through aggregation of its members. If $\bigcup \mathbb{S} \in \mathbb{S}$ then preference according to $\bigcup \mathbb{S}$ amounts to preference *tout court*; for, such preference takes into account all reasons in play.

Formulas. The language determined by signature $(\mathbb{P}, \mathbb{S})$ is denoted $\mathcal{L}(\mathbb{P}, \mathbb{S})$, and is built from the following symbols.

(a) the set $\mathbb{P}$ of propositional variables
(b) the unary connective $\neg$
(c) the binary connective $\wedge$
(d) for every set $X \in \mathbb{S}$, the binary connective $\succeq_X$
(e) the two parentheses

Formulas are defined inductively via:

$$p \in \mathbb{P} \mid \neg \varphi \mid (\varphi \wedge \psi) \mid (\varphi \succeq_X \psi) \text{ for } X \in \mathbb{S}.$$

We rely on obvious abbreviations for the boolean connectives including the constants $\top$, $\bot$. We also write: $(\varphi \succ_X \psi)$ for $(\varphi \succeq_X \psi) \wedge \neg(\psi \succeq_X \varphi)$, $(\varphi \approx_X \psi)$ for $(\varphi \succeq_X \psi) \wedge (\psi \succeq_X \varphi)$, $(\varphi \preceq_X \psi)$ for $(\psi \succeq_X \varphi)$, and $(\varphi \prec_X \psi)$ for $(\psi \succ_X \varphi)$.

To illustrate a formula with modal embedding, suppose that utility indexes refer to commercial agents like businesses. Then in a domain that represents economic conditions (availability of raw materials, tax laws, etc.), $\varphi \succ_i \psi$ might mean that φ is more conducive to the profitability of business i than is ψ. Due to competition (e.g., for scarce resources or market share), i might be better off if j does not benefit from the same economic situations as i, yielding, for example:

$$(\varphi \succ_i \psi) \rightarrow ((\varphi \succ_j \psi) \prec_i (\psi \succ_j \varphi)).$$

A similar interpretation concerns the fitness of species i, j in a given ecological environment.

2.2   Semantics

According to the semantics provided below, $\varphi \succ_1 \psi$ can be understood as follows. As a function of the world you actually inhabit, a world w satisfying φ, and a world v satisfying ψ are selected. The formula is true just in case $u_1(w) > u_1(v)$, where u_1 is a utility function from worlds to numbers, with index 1. Let φ, ψ express the adoption of Fido and Thomasina, respectively. If the indexes $1 \ldots 4$ measure companionship, safety, expense, and bother then $X = \{1 \ldots 4\}$ is the aggregate index for all four together. So, if w is the world in which Fido is adopted, and v is the world for Thomasina then Fido is your choice if $u_X(w) > u_X(v)$, in which case $\varphi \succ_X \psi$ is true at the world you inhabit.

Models.   A *model* for signature $(\mathbb{P}, \mathbb{S})$ is based on a nonempty set of points called "worlds." Subsets of worlds are termed *propositions*. As discussed above, given a nonempty proposition A and world w, we pick an alternative to w among the worlds in A. (If $w \in A$ then the "alternative" might be w itself.) Such choices are formalized as follows.

(1) DEFINITION: A *selection function s* over a set $\mathbb{W}$ of worlds is a mapping from $\mathbb{W} \times \{A \subseteq \mathbb{W} \mid A \neq \emptyset\}$ to $\mathbb{W}$ such that for all $w \in \mathbb{W}$ and $\emptyset \neq A \subseteq \mathbb{W}$, $s(w, A) \in A$.

Intuitively, s chooses a member of A that is similar to w.

Next, recall that each world can be evaluated according to different utility scales, indexed by members of $\mathbb{S}$.

(2) DEFINITION: A *utility function u over* $\mathbb{W}$ *and* $\mathbb{S}$ is a mapping from $\mathbb{W} \times \mathbb{S}$ to $\Re$ (the reals).

For $w \in \mathbb{W}$ and $\{i\}, X \in \mathbb{S}$, we write $u(w, \{i\})$ as $u_i(w)$, and $u(w, X)$ as $u_X(w)$.

In a given signature $(\mathbb{P}, \mathbb{S})$, $\mathbb{P}$ is a nonempty set of propositional variables. The last component of a model is the assignment of a proposition to each variable in $\mathbb{P}$.

(3) DEFINITION: A *truth-assignment (over* $\mathbb{W}$ *and* $\mathbb{P}$*)* is a mapping from $\mathbb{P}$ to the power set of $\mathbb{W}$.

For a truth-assignment t, the idea is that $p \in \mathbb{P}$ is true in $w \in \mathbb{W}$ just in case $w \in t(p)$.

(4) DEFINITION: A *(basic) model* for a signature $(\mathbb{P}, \mathbb{S})$ is a quadruple $(\mathbb{W}, s, u, t)$ where
   (a) $\mathbb{W}$ is a nonempty set of worlds;
   (b) s is a selection function over $\mathbb{W}$;
   (c) u is a utility function over $\mathbb{W}$ and $\mathbb{S}$;
   (d) t is a truth-assignment over $\mathbb{W}$ and $\mathbb{P}$.

Propositions. We may now specify the proposition (set of worlds) expressed by a given formula φ in a model $\mathcal{M}$. This proposition is denoted $\varphi[\mathcal{M}]$, and defined as follows.

(5) DEFINITION: Let signature $(\mathbb{P}, \mathbb{S})$, $\varphi \in \mathcal{L}(\mathbb{P}, \mathbb{S})$, and model $\mathcal{M} = (\mathbb{W}, s, u, t)$ for $(\mathbb{P}, \mathbb{S})$ be given.
   (a) If $\varphi \in \mathbb{P}$ then $\varphi[\mathcal{M}] = t(\varphi)$.
   (b) If φ is the negation $\neg\theta$ then $\varphi[\mathcal{M}] = \mathbb{W} \setminus \theta[\mathcal{M}]$.
   (c) If φ is the conjunction $(\theta \wedge \psi)$ then $\varphi[\mathcal{M}] = \theta[\mathcal{M}] \cap \psi[\mathcal{M}]$.
   (d) If φ has the form $(\theta \succeq_X \psi)$ for $X \in \mathbb{S}$, then $\varphi[\mathcal{M}] = \emptyset$ if either $\theta[\mathcal{M}] = \emptyset$ or $\psi[\mathcal{M}] = \emptyset$. Otherwise:
   $$\varphi[\mathcal{M}] = \{w \in \mathbb{W} \mid u_X(s(w, \theta[\mathcal{M}])) \geq u_X(s(w, \psi[\mathcal{M}]))\}.$$

Note that $(\theta \succeq_X \psi)[\mathcal{M}]$ is defined to be empty if there is no world that satisfies θ or none that satisfies ψ. Thus, we read $(\theta \succeq_X \psi)$ with existential import ("the θ-world is weakly X-better than the ψ-world," where the definite description is Russellian). In the nontrivial case, let $A \neq \emptyset$ be the proposition expressed by θ in $\mathcal{M}$, and $B \neq \emptyset$ the one expressed by ψ. Then world w satisfies $(\theta \succeq_X \psi)$ in $\mathcal{M}$ iff the world selected from A has X-utility no less than that of the world selected from B.

In the sequel, we rely on standard model theoretic locutions, notably: model $\mathcal{M}$ *satisfies* φ just in case $\varphi[\mathcal{M}] \neq \emptyset$, φ is *valid* in $\mathcal{M}$ just in case $\varphi[\mathcal{M}] = \mathbb{W}$, and φ is *valid* just in case φ is valid in every model. The *basic theory* is the set of φ that are valid in every basic model.

Global Modality. Finally, observe that the "global modality" (Blackburn et al., 2001, §2.1) can be expressed in the following manner. Choose any $X \in \mathbb{S}$, and for $\varphi \in \mathcal{L}(\mathbb{P}, \mathbb{S})$ let:

(6) $\square\varphi \overset{\text{def}}{=} \neg(\neg\varphi \succeq_X \neg\varphi)$ and $\Diamond\varphi \overset{\text{def}}{=} (\varphi \succeq_X \varphi)$.

Then applying (5)d yields:

(7) PROPOSITION: For all $\varphi \in \mathcal{L}(\mathbb{P}, \mathbb{S})$ and models $\mathcal{M} = (\mathbb{W}, s, u, t)$:
   (a) $\square\varphi[\mathcal{M}] \neq \emptyset$ iff $\square\varphi[\mathcal{M}] = \mathbb{W}$ iff $\varphi[\mathcal{M}] = \mathbb{W}$.
   (b) $\Diamond\varphi[\mathcal{M}] \neq \emptyset$ iff $\Diamond\varphi[\mathcal{M}] = \mathbb{W}$ iff $\varphi[\mathcal{M}] \neq \emptyset$.

Proposition (7) implies that the axioms of S5 are valid for $\square$ and $\Diamond$. Other validities are shown in (8), below.

3   Axioms for the Basic Theory

The axioms for the basic theory, which we call O, include all $\mathcal{L}(\mathbb{P}, \mathbb{S})$-instances of any standard schematic axiomatization of S5 [using the modality defined in (6)], together with all $\mathcal{L}(\mathbb{P}, \mathbb{S})$-instances of the following additional axiom schemata. $X \in \mathbb{S}$, and $\varphi, \psi, \theta \in \mathcal{L}(\mathbb{P}, \mathbb{S})$:

(8) (a) $((\varphi \succeq_X \psi) \wedge (\psi \succeq_X \theta)) \to (\varphi \succeq_X \theta)$

   (b) $(\Diamond\varphi \wedge \Diamond\psi) \leftrightarrow ((\varphi \succeq_X \psi) \vee (\psi \succeq_X \varphi))$

   (c) $\Box(\varphi \leftrightarrow \psi) \to (((\varphi \succeq_X \theta) \leftrightarrow (\psi \succeq_X \theta)) \wedge ((\theta \succeq_X \varphi) \leftrightarrow (\theta \succeq_X \psi)))$

The theorems of O consist of the closure of these axioms under the rules of *modus ponens* and necessitation. The adequacy of O follows from Theorem (10) below.

4   Generalized Models

In the basic theory, $\varphi \succeq_X \psi$ asserts that u_X attributes at least as much value to the proposition expressed by φ as to the proposition expressed by ψ. The latter two propositions are represented by elements of each, selected on the basis of the world at which the formula is evaluated. In the present section, we generalize this idea by comparing the value of propositions directly, without recourse to selected worlds as representatives. To begin, let $(\mathbb{P}, \mathbb{S})$ be our background signature, and recall that a *total preorder* is transitive and connected over its domain.

   (9) DEFINITION: Let a set $\mathbb{W}$ of worlds be given.

      (a) By a *value-ordering for $\mathbb{W}$ and $\mathbb{S}$* is meant a function v from $\mathbb{W} \times \mathbb{S}$ to the set of total preorders over the class of nonempty subsets of $\mathbb{W}$.

      (b) Let a truth-assignment t and a value-ordering v for $\mathbb{W}$ and $\mathbb{S}$ be given. Then $(\mathbb{W}, t, v)$ is a *generalized model*.

Thus, a value-ordering arranges propositions by utility, relative to index $X \in \mathbb{S}$ and vantage point $w \in \mathbb{W}$. The semantics of generalized models is given by Definition (5) with the following substitution for clause (5)d. Let $\varphi \in \mathcal{L}(\mathbb{P}, \mathbb{S})$ and generalized model $\mathcal{M} = (\mathbb{W}, t, v)$ for $(\mathbb{P}, \mathbb{S})$ be given.

(5)d′ If φ has the form $(\theta \succeq_X \psi)$ for $X \in \mathbb{S}$, then $\varphi[\mathcal{M}] = \emptyset$ if either $\theta[\mathcal{M}] = \emptyset$ or $\psi[\mathcal{M}] = \emptyset$. Otherwise:

$$\varphi[\mathcal{M}] = \{w \in \mathbb{W} \mid \theta[\mathcal{M}] \text{ comes no earlier than } \psi[\mathcal{M}] \text{ in } v(w, X)\}.$$

We call $\varphi \in \mathcal{L}(\mathbb{P}, \mathbb{S})$ a *generalized validity* just in case φ is valid in all generalized models (that is, just in case for all generalized models $\mathcal{M} = (\mathbb{W}, t, v)$, $\varphi[\mathcal{M}] = \mathbb{W}$).

   Here is the sense in which Definition (9) generalizes the basic theory presented in Section 2. Let (basic) model $\mathcal{M} = (\mathbb{W}, s, u, t)$ be given. Then a value-ordering v is induced by the following condition. For $w \in \mathbb{W}$, $X \in \mathbb{S}$, and nonempty $A, B \subseteq \mathbb{W}$, A is (weakly) ordered after B iff $u_X(w_A) \geq u_X(w_B)$ where $w_A = s(w, A)$ and $w_B = s(w, B)$. (The truth-assignment t plays no role.) In Osherson and Weinstein (2012) we exhibit classes of generalized models whose value orderings cannot be induced in this way. The excess of generalized models, however, does not affect the class of generalized validities. For, the latter class is axiomatized by the same system presented in Section 3 for the basic theory.

   (10) THEOREM: For all $\varphi \in \mathcal{L}(\mathbb{P}, \mathbb{S})$ the following are equivalent.

(a) φ is a theorem of O.
(b) φ is a generalized validity.
(c) φ is a basic validity.

The proof is provided in Appendix 1. The small model property for basic and generalized satisfiability is a corollary to the proof, from which decidability follows immediately.

The axioms O are striking for their simplicity, expressing little more than the preordering of $\succeq_X$, an obvious substitution property, and the apparatus of S5 (along with familiar rules of inference). Apparently, both basic and generalized models represent a wide range of reason-based preferences. As noted in Section 4, there are natural classes of generalized models that are not induced by any basic model. So the fact that the two kinds of models define the same set of validities is perhaps the most noteworthy aspect of Theorem (10).

The generality of the basic theory provides reason to study subclasses of models, such as the metrical models (mentioned in the Introduction). Each such subclass can be evaluated as a theory of rational preference, as well as inviting additions to O.

5   Quantified Preference Logic

The basic system described above can be seen as a propositional calculus extended with modal binary connectives. Our present purpose is to show how the propositional part can be replaced with predicate calculus. We start with syntax.

5.1   Syntax for Quantified Preference Logic

Signatures.   A quantified language is built from its "signature."

(11) DEFINITION: By a *signature (for quantified preference logic* is meant a pair $(\mathbb{L}, \mathbb{S})$ where
(a) $\mathbb{L}$ is a collection of predicates and function symbols of various arities.
(b) $\mathbb{S}$ is a nonempty collection of nonempty subsets of natural numbers $(0, 1 \ldots)$.

As before, members of $\mathbb{S}$ stand for sets of reasons thought of as dimensions for evaluating possible worlds.

Formulas.   We may now specify the language $\mathcal{L}(\mathbb{L}, \mathbb{S})$ parameterized by the signature $(\mathbb{L}, \mathbb{S})$. Formulas are built from the following symbols.

(a) the members of $\mathbb{L}$ along with the identity sign $=$
(b) for each $X \in \mathbb{S}$, the binary connective $\succeq_X$
(c) the binary connective $\wedge$ and the unary connective $\neg$
(d) the quantifier $\exists$
(e) the two parentheses, (,)
(f) a denumerable collection $v_0, v_1 \ldots$ of individual variables (denoted below by x, y, z).

The set of *terms* is constructed from functions and variables as usual. The set $\mathcal{L}(\mathbb{L}, \mathbb{S})$ of *formulas* is likewise built in the usual way except that we add the clause:

Given $\varphi, \psi \in \mathcal{L}(\mathbb{L}, \mathbb{S})$ and $X \in \mathbb{S}$, $\varphi \succeq_X \psi$ also belongs to $\mathcal{L}(\mathbb{L}, \mathbb{S})$.

In addition to our earlier abbreviations, we write $\forall x \varphi$ for $\neg \exists x \neg \varphi$. Also, the global modalities $\Box \varphi$ and $\Diamond \varphi$ are defined as before [via $\neg(\neg \varphi \succeq_X \neg \varphi)$ and $\varphi \succeq_X \varphi$, respectively].

Examples of Formulas.   The following formulas serve as illustration.

(12) (a) $\exists x (Px \succ_X \forall y Py)$
     (b) $\exists x Px \succ_X \forall y Py$

In the domain of people, (12)a affirms that there is someone for whom satisfying P is preferable to everyone satisfying it. This might well be true. For example, from my perspective, it's better that I discover a metric ton of gold than that everyone does (where the reasons encoded in X are basely materialistic). In contrast, (12)b entails that someone getting the gold is better than everyone getting it, which might be false if it doesn't strike me as plausible that I'm the lucky person. We return to (12) later on.

The next example is more complicated inasmuch as it exhibits modal embedding. Let the domain of discourse consist of citizens in a modern state. Suppose that the predicate P picks out the charismatic, socialist politicians (if any) in a given possible world. Suppose Q picks out the fabulously wealthy citizens in a given world. We'll also rely on two utility scales. Let u_c measure the level of consumer confidence in a given world (greater consumer confidence yielding greater u_c utility); let u_j measure the level of social and economic justice in a given world (more justice means greater u_j utility). Now consider:

$$\forall x(\, (\, \exists y Qy \, \succ_c \, Px \,) \, \succ_j \, Px)$$

According to the semantics provided below, this formula is true in a given world w_0 just in case the following circumstances obtain. For all citizens (say, Tom), there is greater social justice in the nearest world w_1 to w_0 in which

(13) the existence of charismatic socialist leaders provokes more consumer confidence than does Tom's being fabulously wealthy

compared to the nearest world w_2 to w_0 in which Tom is fabulously wealthy. That is, $u_j(w_1) > u_j(w_2)$. Of course, we must also interpret (13) according to our semantics. It means that the nearest world w_3 to w_1 with charismatic socialist leaders has greater consumer confidence than the nearest world w_4 to w_1 in which Tom is fabulously wealthy. That is, $u_c(w_3) > u_c(w_4)$. Of course, the nearest world that satisfies a certain formula might be your own.

5.2   Semantics in Quantified Preference Logic

Models in Quantified Preference Logic.   Recall that a signature $(\mathbb{L}, \mathbb{S})$ consists of vocabulary $(\mathbb{L})$ and sets of utility indices $(\mathbb{S})$.

(14)   DEFINITION: Let a signature $(\mathbb{L}, \mathbb{S})$ be given. By a *model* for the signature is meant a quintuple $\mathcal{M} = \langle D, \mathbb{W}, t, u, s \rangle$ where:
   (a) D is a nonempty set, the *domain* of $\mathcal{M}$.
   (b) $\mathbb{W}$ is a nonempty set of points, the *worlds* of $\mathcal{M}$.
   (c) t maps $\mathbb{W} \times \mathbb{L}$ to the appropriate set-theoretic objects over D. (For example, if $Q \in \mathbb{L}$ is a binary relation symbol then $t(w, Q)$ is a subset of $D \times D$.) Identity is assigned to $=$.
   (d) u is a function from $\mathbb{S} \times \mathbb{W}$ to the real numbers. For $X, \{i\} \in \mathbb{S}$ we write $u_X(w)$ in place of $u(X, w)$ and $u_i(w)$ in place of $u(\{i\}, w)$.
   (e) s is a function from $\mathbb{W} \times \{A \subseteq \mathbb{W} \mid \emptyset \neq A\}$ such that for all $w \in \mathbb{W}$ and $\emptyset \neq A \subseteq \mathbb{W}$, $s(w, A) \in A$.

Thus, $\mathbb{W}$ corresponds to a set of potential situations; via t, each gives extensions in D to the vocabulary in $\mathbb{L}$. The function u_X measures the utility of worlds according to the considerations encoded in $X \in \mathbb{S}$. Finally, given a world w_0 and a set A of worlds, s selects a "cognitively salient" member of A, where salience may depend on the vantage point w_0.

Propositions in Quantified Preference Logic.   Subsets of worlds are called *propositions*. In the context of a given model, our semantic definition assigns a proposition (subset of $\mathbb{W}$) to each closed formula. To explain, fix a signature $(\mathbb{L}, \mathbb{S})$, and let a model $\mathcal{M} = \langle D, \mathbb{W}, t, u, s \rangle$ be given. By an *assignment (for $\mathcal{M}$)* is meant a map of the individual variables of $\mathcal{L}(\mathbb{L}, \mathbb{S})$ into D. Given a variable x and assignment d, an x *variant* of d is any assignment that differs from d at most in the member of D assigned to x. Assignments are extended to terms of $\mathcal{L}(\mathbb{L}, \mathbb{S})$ in the usual way.

(15)   DEFINITION: Let a model $\mathcal{M} = \langle D, \mathbb{W}, t, u, s \rangle$ and assignment d be given. For $\varphi \in \mathcal{L}(\mathbb{L}, \mathbb{S})$, the proposition $\varphi[\mathcal{M}, d]$ is defined as follows.
   (a) If φ is $Pt_1 \ldots t_n$ for $P \in \mathbb{L}$ and terms $t_1 \ldots t_n$ then:
   $$\varphi[\mathcal{M}, d] = \{w \in \mathbb{W} \mid \langle d(t_1) \ldots d(t_n) \rangle \in t(w, P)\}.$$
   (b) If φ is the negation $\neg\theta$ then $\varphi[\mathcal{M}, d] = \mathbb{W} \setminus \theta[\mathcal{M}, d]$.
   (c) If φ is the conjunction $(\theta \wedge \psi)$ then $\varphi[\mathcal{M}, d] = \theta[\mathcal{M}, d] \cap \psi[\mathcal{M}, d]$.
   (d) If φ is the existential $\exists x \psi$ then $\varphi[\mathcal{M}, d]$ is the set of $w \in \mathbb{W}$ such that $w \in \psi[\mathcal{M}, d']$ for some x variant d' of d.
   (e) If φ has the form $(\theta \succeq_X \psi)$ for $X \in \mathbb{S}$, then $\varphi[\mathcal{M}, d] = \emptyset$ if either $\theta[\mathcal{M}, d] = \emptyset$ or $\psi[\mathcal{M}, d] = \emptyset$. Otherwise:
   $$\varphi[\mathcal{M}, d] = \{w \in \mathbb{W} \mid u_X(s(w, \theta[\mathcal{M}, d])) \geq u_X(s(w, \psi[\mathcal{M}, d]))\}.$$

Thus, relative to $\mathcal{M}$ and d, the formula $(\theta \succeq_X \psi)$ expresses the null proposition if evaluating it requires that s choose a world from $\emptyset$. (Preference makes a covert existential claim in the present theory, namely, that there is something to choose between.) Otherwise $w \in \mathbb{W}$ belongs to the proposition expressed by $(\theta \succeq_X \psi)$ just in case the world chosen by s to represent $\theta[\mathcal{M}, d]$ has greater X-utility than the world chosen by s to represent $\psi[\mathcal{M}, d]$ — where s's choices depend on the current situation w. Informally, we think of s as choosing the most similar world to w among those available in the proposition at issue.

We extract the assignment-invariant core of a formula's proposition in the standard way.

(16) DEFINITION: Let $\varphi \in \mathcal{L}(\mathbb{L}, \mathbb{S})$ and model $\mathcal{M} = \langle D, \mathbb{W}, t, u, s \rangle$ be given. We write $\varphi[\mathcal{M}]$ for the intersection of $\varphi[\mathcal{M}, d]$ over all assignments d.

It follows that for closed $\varphi \in \mathcal{L}(\mathbb{L}, \mathbb{S})$ (no free variables), $\varphi[\mathcal{M}] = \varphi[\mathcal{M}, d]$ for any assignment d. As usual, we call closed $\varphi \in \mathcal{L}(\mathbb{L}, \mathbb{S})$ *satisfiable* just in case $\varphi[\mathcal{M}] \neq \emptyset$ for some model $\mathcal{M}$; and φ is valid iff $\neg\varphi$ is not satisfiable.

Analysis of the Formulas in Example (12). The formula (12)a is true at w_0 in model $\langle D, \mathbb{W}, t, u, s \rangle$ just in case there is $a \in D$ such that

the nearest world w_1 (according to s) in which $a \in t(w_1, P)$

has higher u_X value than

the nearest world w_2 (according to s) in which $t(w_2, P) = D$.

On the other hand, (12)b is true at w_0 in $\langle D, \mathbb{W}, t, u, s \rangle$ just in case

the nearest world w_1 (according to s) in which $t(w_1, P) \neq \emptyset$

has higher u_X value than

the nearest world w_2 (according to s) in which $t(w_2, P) = D$.

6   Basic Properties of Quantified Preference Logic

6.1   Expressive Power of Modal Formulas

It is worth verifying that our modal vocabulary allows additional propositions to be expressed.

(17) DEFINITION:
  (a) The *modal depth* of formulas is defined inductively. First-order (non-modal) formulas have modal depth zero. If $\varphi, \psi \in \mathbb{L}$ have respective modal depths m, n then $\varphi \succeq_X \psi$ has modal depth $1 + \max\{m, n\}$.
  (b) We say that a model $\mathcal{M}$ *has a modal hierarchy* just in case there are closed formulas $\varphi_0, \varphi_1 \ldots$ such that for all $n \geq 0$:
    i. φ_n has modal depth n;
    ii. for all closed $\psi \in \mathcal{L}$ of modal depth n or less, $\varphi_{n+1}[\mathcal{M}] \neq \psi[\mathcal{M}]$.

(18) DEFINITION: Let $\mathcal{N} = \langle D, \mathbb{W}, t \rangle$ be the first three components of a model, missing just the utility and selection functions, u, s. Notice that $\langle D, \mathbb{W}, t \rangle$ assigns a proposition $\psi[\mathcal{N}] \subseteq \mathbb{W}$ to each non-modal $\psi \in \mathcal{L}$. We call $\mathcal{N}$ a *normal core* just in case D is countable, $\mathbb{W}$ is countably infinite, and there is non-modal, closed $\psi \in \mathcal{L}$ with $\emptyset \neq \psi[\mathcal{N}] \neq \mathbb{W}$.

Now fix a countable signature $(\mathbb{L}, \mathbb{S})$. The following proposition reveals the near ubiquity of modal hierarchies.

(19) PROPOSITION: Let $\mathcal{N} = \langle D, \mathbb{W}, t \rangle$ be a normal core. Then there is a utility function $u : \mathbb{S} \times \mathbb{W} \to \Re$ and a selection function $s : \mathbb{W} \times \{A \subseteq \mathbb{W} \mid A \neq \emptyset\} \to \mathbb{W}$ such that the model $\mathcal{M} = \langle D, \mathbb{W}, t, u, s \rangle$ has a modal hierarchy.

PROOF: Choose utility index $X \in \mathbb{S}$, let $\mathcal{N} = \langle D, \mathbb{W}, t \rangle$ be a normal core, and fix closed, non-modal $\psi \in \mathcal{L}$ with $\emptyset \neq \psi[\mathcal{N}] \neq \mathbb{W}$. By replacing ψ with its negation if necessary, we can ensure that $\psi[\mathcal{N}]$ has at least two elements. Let φ_0 be ψ and let φ_{n+1} be $(\top \prec_X \varphi_n)$. Observe that for all $n \in \mathbb{N}$, φ_n has modal depth n. We will define s and u in such a way that $\varphi_0, \varphi_1 \ldots$ is a modal hierarchy for $\mathcal{M} = \langle D, \mathbb{W}, t, u, s \rangle$.

Let $\{w_0, w_1, \ldots\}$ enumerate $\mathbb{W}$. Since $\psi[\mathcal{N}] = \varphi_0[\mathcal{N}]$ has at least two elements, we may assume without loss of generality that $\{w_0, w_1\} \subseteq \varphi_0[\mathcal{N}]$. Let u be any utility function that meets the conditions:

(20) $u_X(w_0) = 0$ and for all $i > 0$, $u_X(w_i) = 1$.

It remains to specify the selection function s, and to show that it generates a modal hierarchy. This is achieved by inductively defining a sequence of "partial selection" functions s_n, $n \in \mathbb{N}$. At stage n, the partial selector s_n defines a partial model $\mathcal{M}_n = \langle D, \mathbb{W}, t, u, s_n \rangle$ which yields a proposition $\chi[\mathcal{M}_n, d]$ for each assignment d, and each $\chi \in \mathcal{L}$ of modal depth n or below. It will be easy to see that for each such χ and d, $\chi[\mathcal{M}_n, d] = \chi[\mathcal{M}, d]$ where $\mathcal{M} = \langle D, \mathbb{W}, t, u, s \rangle$ with $\bigcup_n s_n \subset s$. Let $\mathfrak{P}_n$ denote the family of nonempty propositions expressed by formulas of modal depth n or below with arbitrary assignments of members of D to their free variables. It is easy to verify that $\mathfrak{P}_n$ is countable. At stage $n = 0$, we let $s_0 = \emptyset$.

For stage $n + 1$, we will define s_{n+1} so that:

(a) s_{n+1} is defined for every pair (w, X) where $w \in \mathbb{W}$ and $X \in \mathfrak{P}_n$; hence, for every assignment d and $\chi \in \mathcal{L}$ of modal depth n or below, $\chi[\mathcal{M}_n, d]$ is well defined.

(b) $\varphi_{n+1}[\mathcal{M}_{n+1}] \notin \mathfrak{P}_n$ hence $\varphi_{n+1}[\mathcal{M}] \notin \mathfrak{P}_n$;

Moreover, at every stage n, it will be the case that $\{w_0, w_1\} \subseteq \varphi_n[\mathcal{M}_n]$. In particular, $\{w_0, w_1\} \subseteq \varphi_0[\mathcal{M}_0] = \psi[\mathcal{N}]$ follows from our choice of ψ.

Now we complete stage $n + 1$. For all $w \in \mathbb{W}$, set $s_{n+1}(w, \mathbb{W}) = w_0$ (hence we always draw w_0 from the proposition expressed by $\top$). For all $w \in \mathbb{W}$ and all $C \in \mathfrak{P}_n - \{\varphi_n[\mathcal{M}_n], \mathbb{W}\}$, choose $s_{n+1}(w, C)$ to be an arbitrary member of C. For the remainder of s_{n+1}, choose $A \subseteq \mathbb{W} - \{w_0, w_1\}$ such that $A \notin \{B - \{w_0, w_1\} \mid B \in \mathfrak{P}_n\}$. Such an A exists because $\mathfrak{P}_n$ is countable. For all $w \in \mathbb{W}$, we define:

$$s_{n+1}(w, \varphi_n[\mathcal{M}_n]) = \begin{cases} w_1 & \text{if } w \in A \cup \{w_0, w_1\} \\ w_0 & \text{otherwise.} \end{cases}$$

It follows immediately from (20) that $\varphi_{n+1}[\mathcal{M}_{n+1}] = A \cup \{w_0, w_1\} \notin \mathfrak{P}_n$.   □

A natural question about Proposition (19) is whether modal hierarchies still appear when models satisfy various *frame properties*. To illustrate, model $\mathcal{M} = \langle D, \mathbb{W}, t, u, s \rangle$ is called "reflexive" just in case for all $w \in \mathbb{W}$ and $A \subseteq \mathbb{W}$, if $w \in A$ then $s(w, A) = w$. Reflexivity embodies the idea that the actual world is closer to home than any other world. Several frame properties are examined in Osherson and Weinstein (2012), and also below. In the case of reflexivity, the foregoing proof can be adjusted to show that any normal core can be extended to a reflexive model with modal hierarchy. We leave unexplored the larger project of characterizing the frame properties that allow modal hierarchies, or identifying natural properties that do not.

6.2   Undecidability of Satisfaction

Suppose that the signature $(\mathbb{L}, \mathbb{S})$ contains two unary predicates $P, Q \in \mathbb{L}$. Then it follows from the argument in Kripke (1962) that:

(21)   PROPOSITION: The satisfiable subset of $\mathcal{L}(\mathbb{L}, \mathbb{S})$ is not decidable.

Kripke's argument hinges on a mapping from first-order sentences with just the binary relation symbol R to modal sentences that replace Rxy with $\Diamond(Px \wedge Qy)$. On the other hand, the validities are axiomatizable:

(22)   PROPOSITION: If the signature is effectively enumerable then so is the set of valid formulas in quantified preference logic.

This fact follows from Proposition (27), below.

6.3   Size of Models

Suppose that the signature contains a binary predicate G. Then the upward Löwenheim-Skolem property fails to apply to quantified preference logic. Indeed:

(23)   PROPOSITION: There is $\varphi \in \mathcal{L}(\mathbb{L}, \mathbb{S})$ such that:
(a) Some model $\langle D, \mathbb{W}, t, u, s \rangle$ with D countable satisfies φ.
(b) No model $\langle D, \mathbb{W}, t, u, s \rangle$ with D uncountable satisfies φ.

PROOF: Basically, φ says that $\prec$ is a lexicographical order on $D \times D$; such an order cannot be embedded in $\langle \Re, < \rangle$ if D is uncountable. For typographical simplicity, we choose $X \in \mathbb{S}$, and write $\prec$ in place of $\prec_X$.

Specifically, we take φ to be the conjunction of the following formulas.

(24) (a) $\forall x \forall y (x \neq y \rightarrow ((Gxx \prec Gyy) \vee (Gyy \prec Gxx))$
   (b) $\forall x_1 y_1 x_2 y_2 ((Gx_1 y_1 \prec Gx_2 y_2) \leftrightarrow ((Gx_1 x_1 \prec Gx_2 x_2) \vee ((x_1 = x_2) \wedge (Gy_1 y_1 \prec Gy_2 y_2))))$

Let a model $\mathcal{M} = \langle D, \mathbb{W}, t, u, s \rangle$ and $w_0 \in \mathbb{W}$ be given with $w_0 \in \varphi[\mathcal{M}]$. We define:

$$X = \{ u(s(w_0, Gxx[\mathcal{M}, d(a/x)])) \mid a \in D \}.$$

Then (24)a implies that X (a set of reals) has the same cardinality as D. Define:

$$Y = \{ u(s(w_0, Gxy[\mathcal{M}, d(a/x, b/y)])) \mid a, b \in D \}.$$

Then (24)b implies that $\langle Y, < \rangle$ is isomorphic to the lexicographic ordering of $X \times X$.

We leave to the reader the verification that φ is satisfiable in a model with countable domain. On the other hand, suppose that the domain is uncountable, whence X is uncountable. Then the existence of an isomorphism between $\langle Y, < \rangle$ and the lexicographic ordering of $X \times X$ contradicts the separability of the real line.   □

6.4   Preorder Models

We can recover the upward Löwenheim-Skolem property by introducing a more general way to compare the value of worlds. Recall that a (*total*) *preorder* is transitive, connected, and reflexive over its domain. Given a signature $(\mathbb{L}, \mathbb{S})$, we achieve more generality by replacing u in a model $\langle D, \mathbb{W}, t, u, s \rangle$ with a map $\unrhd$ from $\mathbb{S}$ to the set of preorders over $\mathbb{W}$. [We write $\unrhd_X$ for $\unrhd(X)$, $X \in \mathbb{S}$.] In such a model $\langle D, \mathbb{W}, t, \unrhd, s \rangle$, we evaluate $(\theta \succeq_X \psi)$ according to the following rule, in place of (15)e.

(15)e′ If φ has the form $(\theta \succeq_X \psi)$ for $X \in \mathbb{S}$, then $\varphi[\mathcal{M}, d] = \emptyset$ if either $\theta[\mathcal{M}, d] = \emptyset$ or $\psi[\mathcal{M}, d] = \emptyset$. Otherwise:

$$\varphi[\mathcal{M}, d] = \{ w \in \mathbb{W} \mid s(w, \theta[\mathcal{M}, d]) \unrhd_X s(w, \psi[\mathcal{M}, d]) \}.$$

In what follows, we'll call the semantics based on (15)e′ *preorder logic*. The original semantics, based on (15)e, will be called *utility logic*. It is easy to see that utility logic is a special case of preorder logic (since assigning utilities to worlds preorders them). Also, it is straightforward to show that the formula φ in the proof of Proposition (23) is satisfied in a preorder model with uncountable domain D. Indeed, the following Löwenheim-Skolem Theorem holds for preorder models.

(25) PROPOSITION: Let $\langle D, \mathbb{W}, t, \unrhd, s \rangle$ be a preorder model for a countable signature.
   (a) If $\mathbb{W}$ is infinite, then for every infinite cardinal κ there is a preorder model $\mathcal{M}' = \langle D', \mathbb{W}', t', \unrhd', s' \rangle$ such that $\mathrm{card}(\mathbb{W}') = \kappa$ and for every sentence φ,
   $$\mathcal{M} \models \varphi \text{ if and only if } \mathcal{M}' \models \varphi.$$

(b) If D is infinite, then for every infinite cardinal κ there is a preorder model $\mathcal{M}' = \langle D', \mathbb{W}', t', \unrhd', s' \rangle$ such that $\mathsf{card}(D') = \kappa$ and for every sentence φ,
$$\mathcal{M} \models \varphi \text{ if and only if } \mathcal{M}' \models \varphi.$$

Despite the greater generality of preorder logic, and the contrast between Propositions (25) and (23), the distinction between utility and preorder models is not discernible by formulas. Indeed:

(26) PROPOSITION: A formula θ is valid in the class of utility models if and only if it is valid in the class of preorder models.

Finally, the next proposition shows that the set of formulas which are valid in preorder models (and hence utility models, by the preceding proposition) is axiomatizable. We assume that the signature is effectively enumerable.

(27) PROPOSITION: The set of formulas which are valid in preorder models is effectively enumerable.

Proofs of Propositions (25), (26), and (27) are given in the Appendix 2. We have not investigated the quantified version of "generalized logic," introduced in Section 4 above.

7   Subclasses of Utility Models

For the remainder of the discussion, only utility models (introduced in Section 5.2) are at issue. (We leave preorder models to one side.)

7.1   Metricity

Many interesting properties of a model $\langle D, \mathbb{W}, t, u, s \rangle$ can formulated just in terms of $\mathbb{W}$ and s (the model's "frame"). For example, Osherson and Weinstein (2012) consider the following way to express the idea that s chooses "the nearest world."

(28) DEFINITION: A model $\langle D, \mathbb{W}, t, u, s \rangle$ is *metric* just in case there is a metric $d \colon \mathbb{W} \times \mathbb{W} \to \Re$ such that for all $w \in \mathbb{W}$ and $\emptyset \neq A \subseteq \mathbb{W}$, $s(w, A)$ is the unique d-closest member of A to w.

Note that a model is metric only if d-closest worlds exist (there are no chains of worlds ever d-closer to a given world). It is easy to see that in a metric model the set of worlds is countable. There are several properties of models that are implied by metricity, including the following two, articulated by Stalnaker (1968).

(29) DEFINITION: Let model $\mathcal{M} = \langle D, \mathbb{W}, t, u, s \rangle$ be given.
   (a) $\mathcal{M}$ is *reflexive* just in case for all $A \subseteq \mathbb{W}$ and $w \in A$, $s(w, A) = w$.
   (b) $\mathcal{M}$ is *regular* just in case for all $A \subseteq B \subseteq \mathbb{W}$ and $w \in \mathbb{W}$, $s(w, B) \in A$ implies $s(w, A) = s(w, B)$.

These properties are explored in Osherson and Weinstein (2012). Here we focus on:

(30) DEFINITION: A model $\langle D, \mathbb{W}, t, u, s \rangle$ is *transitive* just in case for all $A, B, C \subseteq \mathbb{W}$ with $A, B \neq \emptyset$, and $w_0 \in \mathbb{W}$, if $s(w_0, A \cup B) \in A$ and $s(w_0, B \cup C) \in B$ then $s(w_0, A \cup C) = s(w_0, A \cup B)$.

Exploiting our quantificational apparatus, we can write a formula that is true in all transitive models but not valid. We assume that the signature includes the predicate P. For notational ease, we suppress the X on $\approx_X$.

(31) PROPOSITION: Let φ be the conjunction of the following formulas.
   (a) $\forall xy (x \neq y \to (Px \not\approx Py))$
   (b) $\forall xyz ((x \neq y \wedge y \neq z \wedge x \neq z) \to ((((Px \vee Py) \approx Px) \wedge ((Py \vee Pz) \approx Py)) \to (Px \vee Pz) \approx Px))$
   Then φ is invalid but valid in the class of transitive models.

The proposition can be viewed as expressing the transitivity of revealed preference, e.g., $(Px \vee Py) \approx Px$ says that Px is chosen from the mutually exclusive options Px, Py.

PROOF: Let model $\mathcal{M} = \langle D, \mathbb{W}, t, u, s \rangle$, $w_0 \in \mathbb{W}$ and assignment d be given. Let $Px[\mathcal{M}, d] = A$, $Py[\mathcal{M}, d] = B$ and $Pz[\mathcal{M}, d] = C$. If any of $d(x), d(y), d(z)$ are identical or either A or B are empty then we are done. Otherwise, in the presence of (31)a, $(Px \vee Py) \approx Px$ and $(Py \vee Pz) \approx Py$ imply respectively that $s(w_0, A \cup B) \in A$ and $s(w_0, B \cup C) \in B$. So transitivity implies $s(w_0, A \cup C) = s(w_0, A \cup B)$ which entails $w_0 \in (Px \vee Pz) \approx (Px \vee Py)[\mathcal{M}, d]$. So the proposition follows by the transitivity of $\approx$ from $w_0 \in (Px \vee Py) \approx Px[\mathcal{M}, d]$. $\square$

7.2   Beyond the Frame

Rational agents might not be able to discriminate between isomorphic worlds. To formulate this idea, fix a signature $(\mathbb{L}, \mathbb{S})$, and let model $\mathcal{M} = \langle D, \mathbb{W}, t, u, s \rangle$ be given. We say that $v, w \in \mathbb{W}$ are *isomorphic* ($v \simeq w$) just in case there is a permutation h of D such that for all $Q \in \mathbb{L}$, h (applied component-wise) maps $t(v, Q)$ onto $t(w, Q)$.

(32) DEFINITION: Model $\langle D, \mathbb{W}, t, u, s \rangle$ is *utility-invariant* just in case for all isomorphic $v, w \in \mathbb{W}$, $u_X(v) = u_X(w)$ for all $X \in \mathbb{S}$.

This is not a frame property because all components of the model are involved in its formulation. Validity in the utility-invariant models doesn't imply validity in the strict sense. Indeed, we have:

(33) PROPOSITION: Let signature $(\mathbb{L}, \mathbb{S})$ be given with $\mathbb{L}$ finite, and distinct $X, Y \in \mathbb{S}$. Then there is invalid $\varphi \in \mathcal{L}(\mathbb{L}, \mathbb{S})$ that is valid in the class of utility-invariant models.

PROOF: There is $\chi \in \mathcal{L}(\mathbb{L}, \mathbb{S})$ such that for all models $\mathcal{M} = \langle D, \mathbb{W}, t, u, s \rangle$, $\chi[\mathcal{M}] = \mathbb{W}$ iff $| D | = 2$. Hence, by the finitude of $\mathbb{L}$ and the presence of identity, there is closed, satisfiable $\psi \in \mathcal{L}(\mathbb{L}, \mathbb{S})$ such that for all models $\mathcal{M}$, if $w_1, w_2 \in \psi[\mathcal{M}]$ then $w_1 \simeq w_2$. Let the promised φ be:

$$(\psi \wedge (\psi \succ_X \top) \wedge (\psi \succ_Y \top)) \to ((\psi \wedge (\psi \succ_X \top)) \approx_X (\psi \wedge (\psi \succ_Y \top))).$$

We indicate why φ is invalid. The antecedent of φ is easily seen to be satisfiable, and a ψ-world satisfying $\psi \wedge (\psi \succ_X \top)$ need not be the same world that satisfies $\psi \wedge (\psi \succ_Y \top)$; and u_X may be chosen to be injective.

On the other hand, suppose that model $\mathcal{M} = \langle D, \mathbb{W}, t, u, s \rangle$ is utility-invariant and let $w_0 \in \mathbb{W}$. Suppose that the antecedent of φ is satisfiable in $\mathcal{M}$ (otherwise, we are done). Then $(\psi \wedge (\psi \succ_X \top))[\mathcal{M}] \neq \emptyset$ and $(\psi \wedge (\psi \succ_Y \top))[\mathcal{M}] \neq \emptyset$. So, let $w_1 = s(w_0, (\psi \wedge (\psi \succ_X \top))[\mathcal{M}])$ and $w_2 = s(w_0, \psi \wedge (\psi \succ_Y \top)))[\mathcal{M}])$. Then each of w_1, w_2 satisfies ψ so $w_1 \simeq w_2$. Hence $u_X(w_1) = u_X(w_2)$ by utility-invariance. $\qquad \square$

8   Anonymity

Our next topic concerns the manner in which utilities are associated with formulas. First, a condition is exhibited that makes the utility of a conjunction depend on just the utilities of each conjunct separately. According to this condition the vocabulary appearing in a conjunct is not permitted to influence the utility of the conjunction; rather, the conjunct contributes its utility "anonymously." A second condition is then introduced that entails a similar kind of anonymity for the contribution of utility indexes 1 and 2 to the aggregated utility $\{1, 2\}$. The material in this section is inspired by the discussion in Krantz et al. (1971, §7.2).

8.1   Decomposing the Utility of Conjunctions

Let a signature $(\mathbb{L}, \mathbb{S})$ be given with predicate $P \in \mathbb{L}$. Conjunctive anonymity with respect to P is expressed by the following formula. (To lighten notation, we suppress $X \in \mathbb{S}$ in subscripts.)

$$(34) \quad \varphi \overset{\text{def}}{=} \forall xy((Px \approx Py) \to \forall z((Px \wedge Pz) \approx (Py \wedge Pz)))$$

The next proposition gives the sense in which φ causes the utility of $Px \wedge Py$ to be a function (F) of the utilities of Px and Py.

(35) PROPOSITION: Let model $\mathcal{M} = \langle D, \mathbb{W}, t, u, s \rangle$ be given with $w_0 \in \varphi[\mathcal{M}]$. Then there is a function $F : \Re^2 \to \Re$ such that for all assignments d with $Px \wedge Py[\mathcal{M}, d] \neq \emptyset$,

$$u(s(w_0, Px \wedge Py[\mathcal{M}, d])) = F(u(s(w_0, Px[\mathcal{M}, d])),$$
$$u(s(w_0, Py[\mathcal{M}, d]))).$$

PROOF: For numbers of the form $u(s(w_0, Px[\mathcal{M}, d]))$ and $u(s(w_0, Py[\mathcal{M}, d]))$ define:

(36) $F(u(s(w_0, Px[\mathcal{M}, d])), u(s(w_0, Py[\mathcal{M}, d]))) \overset{\text{def}}{=} u(s(w_0, Px \wedge Py[\mathcal{M}, d])).$

For all other numbers r_1, r_2, $F(r_1, r_2)$ is defined arbitrarily. We must show that F is a function. For this purpose, let variable q be given, and suppose that

(37) $u(s(w_0, Px[\mathcal{M}, d])) = u(s(w_0, Pq[\mathcal{M}, d])).$

To finish the proof it suffices to show that

(38) $u(s(w_0, Px \wedge Py[\mathcal{M}, d])) = u(s(w_0, Pq \wedge Py[\mathcal{M}, d])),$

the second argument of F being treated in the same way. It follows immediately from (37) that $w_0 \in (Px \approx Pq)[\mathcal{M}, d]$, hence by (34)

$w_0 \in ((Px \wedge Py) \approx (Pq \wedge Py))[\mathcal{M}, d],$

which implies (38).   □

Observe that φ and Proposition (35) can be formulated with disjunction in place of conjunction — or with many other formulas. The proof proceeds in the same way.

8.2 Decomposing a Complex Utility Index

Suppose for this section that the signature $(\mathbb{L}, \mathbb{S})$ contains unary $P \in \mathbb{L}$ along with $\{1\}, \{2\}, \{1, 2\} \in \mathbb{S}$. Define:

(39) $\varphi \overset{\text{def}}{=} \forall xy(((Px \approx_1 Py) \wedge (Px \approx_2 Py)) \to (Px \approx_{1,2} Py)).$

Then φ implies that the contributions of 1 and 2 to the complex utility index $\{1, 2\}$ can be separated then brought back together via a binary mapping on $\mathfrak{R}$. Specifically:

(40) PROPOSITION: Let model $\mathcal{M} = \langle D, \mathbb{W}, t, u, s \rangle$ be given with $w_0 \in \varphi[\mathcal{M}]$. Then there is a function $F : \mathfrak{R}^2 \to \mathfrak{R}$ such that for all assignments d:

$u_{1,2}(s(w_0, Px[\mathcal{M}, d])) = F(u_1(s(w_0, Px[\mathcal{M}, d])), u_2(s(w_0, Px[\mathcal{M}, d]))).$

PROOF: Call a pair $(p, q) \in \mathfrak{R}^2$ *critical* just in case there is an assignment d such that

(41) (a) $p = u_1(s(w_0, Px[\mathcal{M}, d]))$
      (b) $q = u_2(s(w_0, Px[\mathcal{M}, d])).$

Let $F : \mathfrak{R}^2 \to \mathfrak{R}$ be such that for any critical pair (p, q) as in (41), $F(p, q) = u_{1,2}(s(w_0, Px[\mathcal{M}, d]))$. The behavior of F on noncritical pairs is arbitrary. Suppose that for some assignment d':

(42) (a) $p = u_1(s(w_0, Px[\mathcal{M}, d']))$
    (b) $q = u_2(s(w_0, Px[\mathcal{M}, d']))$.

To verify that F is a function, thereby completing the proof, we must show that

$$(43)\quad u_{1,2}(s(w_0, Px[\mathcal{M}, d])) = u_{1,2}(s(w_0, Px[\mathcal{M}, d'])).$$

Let y be a variable distinct from x, and let $d'' = d(d'(x)/y)$. From (41) and (42) we infer: $w_0 \in Px \approx_1 Py[\mathcal{M}, d'']$ and $w_0 \in Px \approx_2 Py[\mathcal{M}, d'']$. From (39) we then obtain $w_0 \in Px \approx_{1,2} Py[\mathcal{M}, d'']$ from which (43) is an immediate consequence.   □

9 Arrow's Theorem in the Context of Quantified Preference Logic

Finally, we illustrate how results in the theory of Social Welfare can be cast as constraints on the relation between the separate utility indexes $\{1\} \ldots \{k\}$ and their aggregate $\{1 \ldots k\}$. For this purpose, we focus on Kenneth Arrow's classic theorem beginning with a review of its usual formulation (following Reny, 2001).

9.1 Review

Let A be a set of cardinality at least three. Let slo denote the set of strict linear orders (or *rankings*) on A, and let wlo be their weak counterparts. Fix a positive integer k. Members of slo are thought of as potential citizens in a community of size k. Each citizen expresses (rank order) preferences about the set A of agenda items (or "alternatives"). Any function from $\text{slo}^k \to \text{wlo}$ is called a *social welfare function*. For $C \in \text{slo}^k$, the members of C are denoted by C_i. (C is a community of k citizens.)

Let f be a social welfare function, and consider four potential properties of f.

(44) DEFINITION:

    (a) (Universality): f is total.

    (b) (Pareto efficiency): Let $a, b \in A$ and $C \in \text{slo}^k$ be given. Suppose that for all $i \le k$, a is ranked above b in C_i. Then a is ranked above b in $f(C)$.

    (c) (Independence of irrelevant alternatives): Let $a, b \in A$ and $C, C' \in \text{slo}^k$ be given. Suppose that for all $i \le k$, a is ranked below b in C_i if and only if a is ranked below b in C'_i. Then a is ranked below b in $f(C)$ if and only if a is ranked below b in $f(C')$

    (d) (Dictatorship): There is $i \le k$ such that for all $C \in \text{slo}^k$, $f(C) = C_i$.

(45) THEOREM: Every social welfare function that satisfies Universality, Pareto efficiency, and Independence of irrelevant alternatives is dictatorial.

9.2   Reconstruction within Preference Logic

Let our signature include a monadic predicate P and utility indices $\{1\}\ldots\{k\}$, $\{1\ldots k\}$. As usual, we abbreviate the index $\{i\}$ to just i. The language $\mathcal{L}(\mathbb{L},\mathbb{S})$ is assumed to include distinct variables x, y, z possibly with subscripts, superscripts and primes. The formulas defined below are meant to recapitulate the four properties in Definition (44). We consider $m \geq 3$ agenda items.

Universality.   Fix m variables $x^1 \ldots x^m$ where $m \geq 3$. For variables $x_1 \ldots x_m$, let $\chi(x_1 \ldots x_m)$ be the formula that says that each of $x_1 \ldots x_m$ is equal to exactly one of $x^1 \ldots x^m$.

(46) DEFINITION: (Universality): Let ψ be the conjunction of

$$\chi(x_1 \ldots x_m) \wedge (Px_1 \succ_1 Px_2) \wedge (Px_2 \succ_1 Px_3) \wedge \cdots \wedge (Px_{m-1} \succ_1 Px_m)$$
$$\vdots$$
$$\chi(x_1 \ldots x_m) \wedge (Px_1 \succ_k Px_2) \wedge (Px_2 \succ_k Px_3) \wedge \cdots \wedge (Px_{m-1} \succ_k Px_m)$$

Let φ_{univ} be the universal closure of $\Diamond\psi$.

That is, each conjunct of ψ imposes a complete $\succ_i$-ordering on the Px_j where $1 \leq i \leq k$ and $1 \leq j \leq m$. So φ_{univ} is true in a model $\langle D, \mathbb{W}, t, u, s \rangle$ just in case every community is realized in some $w \in W$.

Pareto Efficiency

(47) DEFINITION: Let φ_{pareto} be the universal closure of $\Box((Px \succ_1 Py \wedge \cdots \wedge Px \succ_k Py) \to Px \succ_{\{1\ldots k\}} Py)$.

Independence of Irrelevant Alternatives.   Fix two variables x, y. For variables x', y', let $\psi(x', y')$ be the formula that says that each of x', y' is equal to exactly one of x, y.

(48) DEFINITION: Let φ_{iia} be the universal closure of the formula

$$(\psi(x_1, y_1) \wedge \cdots \wedge \psi(x_k, y_k)) \to$$
$$(\Diamond((Px_1 \succ_1 Py_1) \wedge \cdots \wedge (Px_k \succ_k Py_k) \wedge (Px \succ_{\{1\ldots k\}} Py)) \to$$
$$\Box(((Px_1 \succ_1 Py_1) \wedge \cdots \wedge (Px_k \succ_k Py_k)) \to Px \succ_{\{1\ldots k\}} Py)).$$

Then φ_{iia} is expresses that $\succ_{\{1\ldots k\}}$ has the property of independence of irrelevant alterantives (with respect to formulas of the form Pv).

Dictatorship

(49) DEFINITION: Let φ_{dict} be the disjunction of the following formulas.

$$\forall x_1 \dots x_m \Box(((Px_1 \succ_1 Px_2) \wedge (Px_2 \succ_1 Px_3) \dots (Px_{m-1} \succ_1 Px_m)) \leftrightarrow$$
$$((Px_1 \succ_{\{1\dots k\}} Px_2) \wedge (Px_2 \succ_{\{1\dots k\}} Px_3) \dots (Px_{m-1} \succ_{\{1\dots k\}} Px_m)))$$

$$\vdots$$

$$\forall x_1 \dots x_m \Box(((Px_1 \succ_k Px_2) \wedge (Px_2 \succ_k Px_3) \dots (Px_{m-1} \succ_k Px_m)) \leftrightarrow$$
$$((Px_1 \succ_{\{1\dots k\}} Px_2) \wedge (Px_2 \succ_{\{1\dots k\}} Px_3) \dots (Px_{m-1} \succ_{\{1\dots k\}} Px_m)))$$

Then φ_{dict} asserts that one of the individual indexes reveals the collective preference. Notice that dictatorship extends beyond the particular m-tuple that we might wish to fix at the start of the discussion. The (unique) dictator described in (49) determines all preferences.

9.3 Arrow's Theorem Revisited

The next theorem follows easily from the definitions above along with any proof of Arrow's Theorem.

(50) THEOREM: In quantified preference logic:

$$\{\varphi_{univ}, \varphi_{pareto}, \varphi_{iia}\} \models \varphi_{dict}.$$

Appendix 1: Proof of Theorem (10)

It is easy to see that (10)a implies (10)b and that (10)b implies (10)c. We proceed to establish that (10)c implies (10)a. For this purpose, we first establish that (10)b implies (10)a. For the latter, we prove the dual, namely,

(51) For all $\varphi \in \mathcal{L}(\mathbb{L}, \mathbb{S})$, if φ is consistent, then φ is satisfiable in a generalized model.

The proof of (51) will be based on a canonical model construction. In order to explain the construction we require the notion of *modal depth*.

(52) DEFINITION: We define $\mu(\varphi)$, the modal depth of φ, by recursion on $\varphi \in \mathcal{L}(\mathbb{L}, \mathbb{S})$ as follows.

$$\mu(\varphi) = \begin{cases} 0 & \text{if } \varphi \in \mathbb{P} \\ \mu(\psi) & \text{if } \varphi = \neg\psi \\ \max\{\mu(\psi), \mu(\theta)\} & \text{if } \varphi = (\psi \wedge \theta) \\ \max\{\mu(\psi), \mu(\theta)\} + 1 & \text{if } \varphi = (\psi \preceq_X \theta) \end{cases}$$

Since the satisfiability of single formulas is at issue, we may assume that our signature $(\mathbb{P}, \mathbb{S})$ is finite. For any such signature, it is easy to verify that if $(\mathbb{P}, \mathbb{S})$ is finite, then for any $n \in \mathbb{N}$, there are only finitely many $\varphi \in \mathcal{L}(\mathbb{L}, \mathbb{S})$ with $\mu(\varphi) \leq n$ up to equivalence in sentential logic. In light of this, we may enforce the convention that any set of formulas of bounded modal depth that we mention is finite. To reduce notational clutter, we fix throughout a finite signature $(\mathbb{P}, \mathbb{S})$ and omit further reference to it. Moreover, we suppose that $\mathbb{S}$ is a singleton and suppress the subscripts on occurrences of $\preceq$. Likewise, they are suppressed on utility functions u. It will be seen that these simplifications affect nothing of substance in our construction.

If Σ is a set of formulas, we let $\nu(\Sigma) = \{\Box\varphi \mid \Box\varphi \in \Sigma\}$. If Σ and Σ' are sets of formulas, we say Σ is *compatible* with Σ' just in case $\nu(\Sigma) = \nu(\Sigma')$.

A set of formulas Σ is *consistent* just in case $\bot$ is not O-derivable from Σ; a set of formulas Σ is *maximally consistent* just in case it is consistent and no proper extension of it is consistent. We say a set of formulas Γ is *n-maximally consistent* if and only if there is a maximally consistent set Σ such that $\Gamma = \{\varphi \in \Sigma \mid \mu(\varphi) \leq n\}$. We abbreviate "$n$-maximally consistent set of formulas" to "n-mcs." Note that by our aforementioned convention, every n-mcs is finite. We repeatedly use the following fundamental property of maximally consistent sets of formulas.

(53) For every maximally consistent set of formulas Γ and formula φ, if φ is O-derivable from Γ, then $\varphi \in \Gamma$. Moreover, for every $n \in \mathbb{N}$, n-mcs Σ, and φ of modal depth $\leq n$, if φ is O-derivable from Σ, then $\varphi \in \Sigma$.

For each $n, m \geq 0$ and n-mcs Σ, we define the *canonical generalized model*, $\mathcal{M}^{n,m}(\Sigma) = (\mathbb{W}^{m,n}, v^{n,m}, t^{n,m})$ of depth n and width m generated by Σ. Given n-mcs Σ, let $\Xi^n(\Sigma)$ be the family of n-mcs's which are compatible with Σ. The collection of worlds $\mathbb{W}^{n,m}$ of $\mathcal{M}^{n,m}(\Sigma)$ is $\Xi^n(\Sigma) \times \{0, \ldots, m\}$. In order to specify the remaining components of $\mathcal{M}^{n,m}(\Sigma)$, we fix an n-mcs Σ_0. We also fix $m \in \mathbb{N}$ to be "large enough" (a lower bound for m appears at the end of the proof). For brevity, we write $\mathcal{M}^n$ for our canonical generalized model $\mathcal{M}^{n,m}(\Sigma_0)$ and we write $\mathbb{W}^n$, v^n, and t^n for $\mathbb{W}^{n,m}$, $v^{n,m}$, and $t^{n,m}$, respectively. Moreover, if $w \in \mathbb{W}^n$, we call w an n-mcs (ignoring its second coordinate) and likewise we write $\varphi \in w$ just in case φ is a member of the first coordinate of w. For each $p \in \mathbb{P}$, $t^n(p) = \{w \in \mathbb{W}^n \mid p \in w\}$. Toward defining the value ordering v^n, we begin by defining a sequence of partial value orderings v_j^n and partial models $\mathcal{M}_j^n$ simultaneously by induction on j, for $0 \leq j \leq n$. Let $v_0^n = \emptyset$ (the empty partial function) and $\mathcal{M}_0^n = (\mathbb{W}^n, v_0^n, t^n)$. Note that for every φ of modal depth 0, $\varphi[\mathcal{M}_0^n]$ is well-defined since the evaluation of such formulas does not make use of the value ordering. Moreover, for all $w \in \mathbb{W}^n$ and for all φ of modal depth 0, $w \in \varphi[\mathcal{M}_0^n]$ if and only if $\varphi \in w$. This follows immediately from (53), the definition of t^n, and the fact that each $w \in \mathbb{W}^n$ is an n-mcs, since every formula of modal depth 0 is a boolean combination of sentence letters.

Suppose that our construction has proceeded to some stage j, with $0 \leq j < n$ resulting in a partial model $\mathcal{M}_j^n = (\mathbb{W}^n, v_j^n, t^n)$. Moreover, suppose, as induction hypothesis, that for every formula of modal depth $\leq j$,

(54) $w \in \varphi[\mathcal{M}_j^n]$ if and only if $\varphi \in w$.

Let $\Omega_j^n = \{\varphi[\mathcal{M}_j^n] \mid \mu(\varphi) \leq j\} - \{\emptyset\}$.

We proceed to specify v_{j+1}^n. For each $w \in \mathbb{W}^n$, $v_{j+1}^n(w)$ is the relation on Ω_j^n defined as follows.

(55) For all φ and ψ with $\mu(\varphi), \mu(\psi) \leq j$ and $\varphi[\mathcal{M}_j^n]$, $\psi[\mathcal{M}_j^n]$ non-empty,

$$\langle \varphi[\mathcal{M}_j^n], \psi[\mathcal{M}_j^n] \rangle \in v_{j+1}^n(w) \text{ if and only if } (\varphi \preceq \psi) \in w.$$

To complete the construction, we must verify that

(56) for all $w \in \mathbb{W}^n$ and all formulas φ of modal depth $\leq j+1$,
  (a) $v_{j+1}^n(w)$ is a pre-order of Ω_j^n, and
  (b) $w \in \varphi[\mathcal{M}_{j+1}^n]$ if and only if $\varphi \in w$.

In order to establish (56)a, we argue as follows. Fix $w \in \mathbb{W}^n$. We first show that $v_{j+1}^n(w)$ is well-defined, that is, if φ, ψ, and θ are formulas of modal depth $\leq j$ and $\varphi[\mathcal{M}_j^n] = \psi[\mathcal{M}_j^n]$, then

(57) $\langle \varphi[\mathcal{M}_j^n], \theta[\mathcal{M}_j^n] \rangle \in v_{j+1}^n(w)$ if and only if $\langle \psi[\mathcal{M}_j^n], \theta[\mathcal{M}_j^n] \rangle \in v_{j+1}^n(w)$,

and similarly with φ and θ and ψ and θ reversed. So suppose that

(58) φ and ψ are formulas of modal depth $\leq j$ and $\varphi[\mathcal{M}_j^n] = \psi[\mathcal{M}_j^n]$.

It follows at once from (58), (54), and (53), recalling the fact that every $w' \in \mathbb{W}^n$ is an n-mcs, that

(59) for all $w' \in \mathbb{W}^n$, $(\varphi \leftrightarrow \psi) \in w'$.

Let χ be the conjunction of the formulas in $\nu(w)$. It follows from (59) and the definition of $\mathbb{W}^n$ that

(60) $\chi \to (\varphi \leftrightarrow \psi)$ is a theorem of O,

for otherwise, there would be an n-mcs $w' \in \mathbb{W}^n$ with $\neg(\varphi \leftrightarrow \psi) \in w'$ contradicting (59). Since the theorems of O are closed under necessitation, (60) implies that

(61) $\Box(\chi \to (\varphi \leftrightarrow \psi))$ is a theorem of O.

Moreover, since each $w' \in \mathbb{W}^n$ is an n-mcs, $\Box\theta \to \Box\Box\theta$ is a theorem of S5, and each of the conjuncts of χ is a "boxed" formula, it follows from (53) that

(62) for all $w' \in \mathbb{W}^n$, and all maximally consistent sets of formulas $\Gamma \supset w'$, $\Box\chi \in \Gamma$.

It follows from (61), (62), and (53), and the S5 modal principle

$$(\Box\chi \wedge \Box(\chi \to (\varphi \leftrightarrow \psi))) \to \Box(\varphi \leftrightarrow \psi),$$

that

(63) $\Box(\varphi \leftrightarrow \psi) \in w$.

But then, by (53), (63), Axiom (8)c and the fact that w is an n-mcs,

(64) $(\varphi \preceq \theta) \in w$ if and only if $(\psi \preceq \theta) \in w$.

Therefore v_{j+1}^n is well-defined, since (57) follows directly from (64) and (55). In order to see that $v_{j+1}^n(w)$ is a pre-order of Ω_j^n, it suffices to show that

(65) (a) $\emptyset$ is not in the field of $v_{j+1}^n(w)$,

(b) $v_{j+1}^n(w)$ is transitive on Ω_j^n, and

(c) $v_{j+1}^n(w)$ is connected on Ω_j^n.

Toward establishing condition (65)a, we show that if A is in the field of $v_{j+1}^n(w)$, then $A \neq \emptyset$. So suppose that

(66) $\langle \varphi[\mathcal{M}_j^n], \psi[\mathcal{M}_j^n] \rangle \in v_{j+1}^n(w)$,

with $\mu(\varphi), \mu(\psi) \leq j$. We show that $\varphi[\mathcal{M}_j^n] \neq \emptyset$. (The argument for $\psi[\mathcal{M}_j^n] \neq \emptyset$ is virtually identical.) To show this, it suffices, by (54), to show that for some $w' \in \mathbb{W}^n$, $\varphi \in w'$. Suppose, for *reductio*, that for all $w' \in \mathbb{W}^n$, $\varphi \notin w'$. Since all $w' \in \mathbb{W}^n$ are n-mcs's, it follows at once that for all $w' \in \mathbb{W}^n$, $\neg \varphi \in w'$. As before, let χ be the conjunction of the formulas in $\nu(w)$. Arguing as we did for (63), we may conclude that $(\chi \to \neg \varphi)$ is a theorem of O, and thence that $\Box \neg \varphi \in w'$ for all $w' \in \mathbb{W}^n$. It follows immediately by (53) that

(67) $\neg \Diamond \varphi \in w'$, for all $w' \in \mathbb{W}^n$.

On the other hand, it is a direct consequence of (55) and (66) that

(68) $\varphi \preceq \psi \in w$.

It follows from (53), (68), and the right-to-left direction of Axiom (8)b that

(69) $\Diamond \varphi \in w$.

But (69) contradicts (67), thereby establishing that $\varphi[\mathcal{M}_{j+1}^n] \neq \emptyset$.

In order to establish (65)b, suppose that φ, ψ, and θ are formulas of modal depth $\leq j$, $w \in \mathbb{W}^n$ and that

(70) $\langle \varphi[\mathcal{M}_j^n], \psi[\mathcal{M}_j^n] \rangle \in v_{j+1}^n(w)$ and $\langle \psi[\mathcal{M}_j^n], \theta[\mathcal{M}_j^n] \rangle \in v_{j+1}^n(w)$.

It follows immediately from (70) and (55) that

(71) $\varphi \preceq \psi \in w$ and $\psi \preceq \theta \in w$.

Therefore, by Axiom (8)a and (53),

(72) $\varphi \preceq \theta \in w$.

Hence, by (72) and (55)

(73) $\langle \varphi[\mathcal{M}_j^n], \theta[\mathcal{M}_j^n] \rangle \in v_{j+1}^n(w)$.

We leave the argument for (65)c to the reader – it is virtually the same as the argument for (65)b, using the left-to-right direction of Axiom (8)b in place of Axiom (8)a.

We now verify (56)b. Note that by (56)a, for every φ with $\mu(\varphi) \leq j+1$, $\varphi[\mathcal{M}_{j+1}^n]$ is a well-defined. It is clear from (55) and the choice of v_0^n as the empty partial function that for all $0 \leq i \leq j$ and all $w \in \mathbb{W}^n$, $v_i^n(w) \subseteq v_{i+1}^n(w)$. It follows at once that

(74) for all φ of modal depth $\leq j$, $\varphi[\mathcal{M}_j^n] = \varphi[\mathcal{M}_{j+1}^n]$.

Hence, by (54) and (74), it follows at once that in order to prove (56)b, we need only show that for every $w \in \mathbb{W}^n$ and every formula φ, if $\mu(\varphi) = j + 1$, then

(75) $w \in \varphi[\mathcal{M}^n_{j+1}]$ if and only if $\varphi \in w$.

Every formula of modal depth $j + 1$ is a boolean combination of formulas of the form $\psi \preceq \theta$, with $\mu(\psi), \mu(\theta) \leq j$. Thus, by (53) and the fact that all $w \in \mathbb{W}^n$ are n-mcs's, in order to establish (75), it suffices to show that for all ψ and θ with $\mu(\psi), \mu(\theta) \leq j$,

(76) $w \in (\psi \preceq \theta)[\mathcal{M}^n_{j+1}]$ if and only if $(\psi \preceq \theta) \in w$.

But (76) is an immediate consequence of (55). This concludes the construction of the partial generalized model $\mathcal{M}^n$. By (56)b, it has the "canonical model property"

(77) for all φ of modal depth $\leq n$, $w \in \varphi[\mathcal{M}^n]$ if and only if $\varphi \in w$.

Let v^n be a value ordering such that for every $w \in \mathbb{W}^n$, $v^n(w)$ extends $v^n_n(w)$ and let $\mathcal{M}^n = (\mathbb{W}^n, v^n, t^n)$. It follows immediately from (77) that $\mathcal{M}^n$ satisfies Σ_0. Since every formula φ is contained in an n-mcs for some n, this concludes the proof of (51).

We proceed to establish that (10)c implies (10)a. In order to do so, we will make use of the neglected parameter m in our definition of the model $\mathcal{M}^n (= \mathcal{M}^{n,m})$. In particular, recall that the collection of worlds $\mathbb{W}^{n,m}$ of $\mathcal{M}^{n,m}$ is $\Xi^n(\Sigma_0) \times \{0, \ldots, m\}$. By our proof above that (10)b implies (10)a, it will suffice to show that for a sufficiently large choice of m, there is a basic partial model $\mathcal{M} = \langle \mathbb{W}^n, s, u, t^n \rangle$ such that v^n_n is the value ordering of Ω^n_{n-1} induced by $\mathcal{M}$, for this will establish that every consistent φ is satisfied by some basic model. It is easy to see that no matter how m is chosen,

(78) for every proposition $A \in \Omega^n_{n-1}$, $\mathsf{card}(A) \geq m$.

Let Π be the set of pre-orderings of Ω^n_{n-1}, and choose $m \geq \mathsf{card}(\Pi) \cdot \mathsf{card}(\Omega^n_{n-1})$. It then follows from (78) that there is a function $f : \Pi \times \Omega^n_{n-1} \mapsto \mathbb{W}^n$ such that

(79) (a) for all $\pi \in \Pi$ and $A \in \Omega^n_{n-1}$, $f(\pi, A) \in A$, and
　　(b) for all distinct $\pi, \pi' \in \Pi$ and all distinct $A, B \in \Omega^n_{n-1}$, $f(\pi, A) \neq f(\pi', B)$.

It follows at once from (79) that we may define u in such a way that

(80) for all $\pi \in \Pi$ and all $A, B \in \Omega^n_{n-1}$,

$$u(f(\pi, A)) \leq u(f(\pi, B)) \text{ if and only if } \langle A, B \rangle \in \pi.$$

Finally, define the selector s as follows.

(81) For all $w \in \mathbb{W}^n$ and $A \in \Omega^n_{n-1}$, $s(w, A) = f(v^n_n(w), A)$.

It follows at once from (80) and (81) that if we let $\mathcal{M}$ be the partial basic model $\langle \mathbb{W}^n, s, u, t^n \rangle$, then v^n_n is the value ordering of Ω^n_{n-1} induced by $\mathcal{M}$. $\qquad\square$

Appendix 2: Proofs of Propositions (25), (26), and (27)

All three proofs elaborate a construction that appears in the demonstration of Theorem (55) in Osherson and Weinstein (2012). Specifically, the earlier construction can be adapted to show that there is an effective translation from sentences $\varphi \in \mathcal{L}(\mathbb{L}, \mathbb{S})$ to formulas $\varphi^\dagger(x)$ of first-order logic, and a map from preorder models $\mathcal{M} = \langle D, \mathbb{W}, t, \trianglerighteq, s \rangle$ to relational structures $\mathcal{F}_\mathcal{M}$ such that

(82) $w \in \varphi[\mathcal{M}]$ iff $\mathcal{F}_\mathcal{M} \models \varphi^\dagger[w]$.

Moreover, assuming that $(\mathbb{L}, \mathbb{S})$ is recursive, there is a recursively axiomatizable first-order theory T in the signature of $\mathcal{F}_\mathcal{M}$ such that

(83) for every preorder model $\mathcal{M}$, $\mathcal{F}_\mathcal{M} \models T$

and

(84) for every first-order structure A, if $A \models T$, then for some preorder model $\mathcal{M}$, $A = \mathcal{F}_\mathcal{M}$.

Proposition (27) now follows from the completeness theorem for first-order logic, since (82), (83), and (84) imply that $\varphi \in \mathcal{L}(\mathbb{L}, \mathbb{S})$ is valid in preorder logic if and only if $\forall x \varphi^\dagger(x)$ is a consequence of T. In like fashion, Proposition (25) follows from the Löwenheim-Skolem Theorem for first-order logic. Proposition (26) now follows immediately, since every countable preorder model is induced by a corresponding utility model, a consequence of the fact that the rational numbers are universal among countable linear orders. □

References

Andréka, H., Ryan, M., Schobbens, P.-Y.: Operators and laws for combining preferential relations. Journal of Logic and Computation 12, 12–53 (2002)

Blackburn, P., de Rijke, M., Venema, Y.: Modal Logic. Cambridge University Press (2001)

Dietrich, F., List, C.: A reason-based theory of rational choice. Technical Report, London School of Economics (2009)

Hansson, S.O.: A new semantical approach to the logic of preference. Erkenntnis 31(1), 1–42 (1989)

Keeney, R.L., Raiffa, H.: Decisions with Multiple Objectives: Preferences and Value Trade-Offs. Cambridge University Press, Cambridge (1993)

Krantz, D.H., Luce, R.D., Suppes, P., Tversky, A.: Foundations of Measurement, vol. I. Academic Press, New York (1971)

Kripke, S.: The undecidability of monadic modal quantification theory. Zeitschr. f. math. Logik und Grundlagen d. Math. 8, 113–116 (1962)

Lang, J., van der Torre, L., Weydert, E.: Hidden uncertainty in the logical representation of desires. In: Proceedings of Eighteenth International Joint Conference on Artificial Intelligence, IJCAI 2003 (2003)

Liu, F.: Changing for the Better: Preference Dynamics and Agent Diversity. PhD thesis, ILLC, University of Amsterdam (2008)

Osherson, D., Weinstein, S.: Preference based on reasons. The Review of Symbolic Logic 5(1), 122–147 (2012)

Reny, P.J.: Arrow's Theorem and the Gibbard-Satterthwaite Theorem: A Unified Approach. Economics Letters 70, 99–105 (2001)

Rescher, N.: Semantic foundations for a the logic of preference. In: The Logic of Decision and Action, University of Pittsburgh Press (1967)

Stalnaker, R.: A theory of conditionals. In: Rescher, N. (ed.) Studies in Logical Theory. Blackwell, Oxford (1968)

van Benthem, J., Girard, P.K., Roy, O.: Everything else being equal: A modal logic for *Ceteris Paribus* preferences. Journal of Philosophical Logic 38, 83–125 (2009)

The Dichotomous Intensional Expressive Power of the Nested Relational Calculus with Powerset*

Limsoon Wong

National University of Singapore
wongls@comp.nus.edu.sg

Abstract. Most existing studies on the expressive power of query languages have focused on what queries can be expressed and what queries cannot be expressed in a query language. They do not tell us much about whether a query can be implemented efficiently in a query language. Yet, paradoxically, efficiency is a key concern in computer science. In this paper, the efficiency of queries in $\mathcal{NRC}(powerset)$, a nested relational calculus with a powerset operation, is discussed. A dichotomy in the efficiency of these queries on a large general class of structures—which include long chains, deep trees, etc.—is proved. In particular, it is shown that these queries are either already expressible in the usual nested relational calculus or require at least exponential space. This Dichotomy Theorem, when coupled with the bounded degree and locality properties of the usual nested relational calculus becomes a powerful general tool in studying the intensional expressive power of query languages. The bounded degree and locality properties make it easy to prove that a query is inexpressible in the usual nested relational calculus. Then, if the query is expressible in $\mathcal{NRC}(powerset)$, subject to the conditions of the Dichotomy Theorem, the query must take at least exponential space.

1 Introduction

Existing research on the power of query languages has focused almost exclusively on the expressive power of query languages. So we have many results of the following kinds:

- Is a specific function expressible in a given query language? For example, Libkin & Wong showed that all usual nested relational calculi and algebras cannot express the transitive closure function in general [12].
- What complexity class do functions expressible in a given query language belong to? For example, Buneman et al. showed that functions expressible in all the usual nested relational calculi and algebras have polynomial complexity [4].
- What general properties do functions expressible in a given query language have? For example, Dong et al. [7] showed that all functions on unordered

---

* Supported in part by a Singapore Ministry of Education grant MOE-T1-251RES1206.

V. Tannen et al. (Eds.): Buneman Festschrift, LNCS 8000, pp. 542–556, 2013.

graphs expressible in a nested relational calculus with aggregate functions have the bounded degree property and, thus, cannot transform a simple graph (which has an arbitrarily large but fixed degree) into a complex graph (which has an arbitrary number of distinct degrees).

These results are purely extensional. They basically state that a large class of queries is expressible or representable in a query language. However, they say nothing about the efficiency of such a representation, even though the efficiency aspect is of primary concern for computer science.

A function f that is expressible in a query language can be implemented in many different ways, each corresponding to a different algorithm. These different algorithms—which implement that same function f, as far as input/output is concerned—may have rather different complexity. Moreover, some algorithms for f may not even be expressible in the given query language, though some other algorithm for f is expressible in the given query language. Seldom do we see results that study the power of query languages from this "intensional" perspective.

This lack of results may be due to the tradition of logical vs physical separation in the database community. This separation is beneficial as it allows a database system to use radically different execution plans for the same query depending on a variety of optimization factors, such as what relevant indices are available. Nevertheless, the syntax of a query suggests an natural implementation, even if an unoptimized one. So, as argued by Suciu, Paredeans, and Wong [14,15], there is a natural operational semantics for a query language and intensional expressive power can be studied with respect to it.

Some of the exceptional papers that are in the spirit of intensional expressive power include:

- The work of Colson [5] which showed that the function which computes the minimum of two integers in unary representation cannot be programmed using primitive recursion in $O(min(m, n))$ complexity.
- The work of Abiteboul and Vianu [2] which proved that the parity query cannot be expressed in PTIME by a generic machine.
- The work of Suciu and Wong [15] which proved that any uniform translation of sequential iteration queries (sri queries) into data-parallel iteration queries (sru queries) over a nested relational algebra must map some PTIME queries into exponential space ones.
- The work of Suciu and Paredaens [14] which proved that any implementation of the transitive closure query in Abiteboul and Beeri's complex object algebra must use an exponential amount of space.

However, these intensional results tend to be very query specific. Furthermore, the proofs tend to be complex and are not easily portable to other queries. So they do not shed sufficient light on the structure of the query languages concerned or the structure of inefficient queries in these query languages that render the cause of the inefficiency clear.

In contrast, the intensional expressive power of $\mathcal{NRC}(powerset)$, a nested relational calculus endowed with a powerset operation, is studied here in a more general non-query-specific setting—I think this is probably the first time that intensional expression power is studied in such a general setting. This calculus, to be presented in Section 2, is equivalent to the complex object algebra of Abiteboul and Beeri [1] which, as mentioned earlier, was shown by Suciu and Paredaens [14] to use exponential space to implement the transitive closure query.

Here, all flat relational queries on a general class of structures that exhibit a "severely dichotomous" property are considered. Intuitively, a severely dichotomous structure has two groups of "motifs" that characterize all the elements in the structure. One group of motifs have small radius and are populated by a small predictable number of elements in the structure, while the other group of motifs are populated by an arbitrarily large number of elements in the structure. Graphs with a few long chains or a few deep trees are severely dichotomous structures. Specifically, the points near the ends of the few long chains satisfy the first group of motifs, while the rest of the chains—being long and thus arbitrarily many—satisfy the second group of motifs. Similarly, the points near the roots of the few deep trees satisfy the first group of motifs, while the rest of the trees—being deep and thus arbitrarily many—satisfy the second group of motifs.

Intuitively, it is the presence of the second group of motifs that make the class of severely dichotomous structures those that really require an arbitrarily deep level of recursion or the full power of the powerset operation (if recursion is unavailable) to manipulate. Indeed, this paper proves—in Section 4—that all flat relational queries in $\mathcal{NRC}(powerset)$ on severely dichotomous structures either (i) are already expressible without the powerset operation and, hence, has a PTIME implementation in $\mathcal{NRC}(powerset)$; or (ii) are inexpressible without using the powerset operation on a non-trivial amount of data and, hence, can only be implemented in $\mathcal{NRC}(powerset)$ using an exponential amount of space.

The proof of this Dichotomy Theorem reveals the exact cause of the blow-up and, briefly, it proceeds as follows. $\mathcal{NRC}(powerset)$ is known to have the conservative extension property [17,10], which is described later in Section 3.1. Moreover, the normal form induced by this property does not increase the complexity of the query. Inspecting this normal form, the subexpression containing the first instance of the powerset operation—say $powerset\ e$—to be executed is analyzed. By the conservative extension property, e is known to be equivalent to a first-order formula $\varphi(\boldsymbol{x}, \boldsymbol{y})$, where $\boldsymbol{x}$ are free variables corresponding to input that is bound before e is excuted, and $\boldsymbol{y}$ are free variables corresponding to output produced after e finishes execution. There are only three situations that need to be considered:

1. y_j in $\boldsymbol{y}$ is connected to some x_i in $\boldsymbol{x}$; that is, the point that y_j is instantiated with is close to some point that is used to instantiate an input x_i. If the query is restricted to input structures with a known maximum fan-out, then the number of possible values that y_j can take with respect to each instantiation of x_i can be calculated in advance.

2. y_j has to be instantiated to a point characterized by the first type of motifs in a seriously dichotomous structure, and it is not close to any x_i. The first type of motifs are populated by a small predictable number of elements. So the number of possible values that y_j can take can be calculated in advance.

3. y_j has to be instantiated to a point that is not close to any point x_i and is characterized by the second kind of motifs in a seriously dichotomous structure. As mentioned, this kind of motifs are populated by an arbitraily large number of elements in the structure. By the locality property of first-order formula [8,7,12,9], which is described later in Section 3.2, y_j must take on an arbitrarily large number of values. Unfortunately, this number cannot be calculated in advance independent of the size of the input relations.

If each y_j in $\boldsymbol{y}$ takes only a predictable number of possible values that can be calculated in advance and independent of the size of the input relations, then the number of tuples—say, $H*$—in the result of evaluating e can be estimated in advance and independent of the input relations. Then this *powerset e* can be replaced by *powerset*$_{H*}$ e, where *powerset*$_{H*}$ is an operation that computes subsets of size up to $H*$. Clearly, *powerset*$_{H*}$ can be implemented in $\mathcal{NRC}(powerset)$ without using the powerset operation. If all the powerset operations can be eliminated in this manner, we get a PTIME implementation of the query in $\mathcal{NRC}(powerset)$. On the other hand, if the third situation is encountered, then that *powerset e* cannot be eliminated. It is easy to see that, in a seriously dichotomous input structure $\mathcal{A} = \langle A, O \rangle$, the expression e in *powerset e* is guaranteed to produce $\Omega(|A|)$ number of elements. Consequently, *powerset e* is forced to produce $\Omega(2^{|A|})$ number of elements, causing the exponential blow up.

2   Nested Relational Calculus with Powerset

Let me first recall the nested relational calculus $\mathcal{NRC}$ from Buneman et al. [4]. The types and expressions in $\mathcal{NRC}$ are given in Figure 1. The type superscripts in the figure are usually omitted because they can be inferred.

The semantics of a type is just a set of complex objects. There are some unspecified base types b and the usual Boolean base type *bool*. An object of type $s_1 \times \cdots \times s_n$ is a tuple whose ith component is an object of type s_i, for $1 \le i \le n$. An object of type $\{s\}$ is a finite set whose elements are objects of type s; an object of type $\{s\}$ is called a "relation". Moreover, if $s = b \times \cdots \times b$, then an object of type $\{s\}$ (or s) is called a "flat relation". On the other hand, if s contains some set brackets, then an object of type $\{s\}$ is called a "nested relation". More generally, a type s containing n levels of nested set brackets is said to be of height n; e.g., $b \times b$ has height 0, $\{b \times b\}$ has height 1, and $\{b \times \{b\}\}$ has height 2.

The semantics of the expression constructs are described below. The expression c denotes some constants of base type b. The expressions *true*, *false*, and *if e_1 then e_2 else e_3* have their usual semantics. The expression $(e_1, \ldots, e_n)$ denotes the tuple whose ith component is the object denoted by e_i, for $1 \le i \le n$. The expression π_i e denotes the ith component of the tuple denoted by e.

$$\boxed{\begin{array}{c}
\text{Types in } \mathcal{NRC} \\[2mm]
s ::= b \mid bool \mid s_1 \times \cdots \times s_n \mid \{s\} \\[3mm]
\text{Expressions in } \mathcal{NRC}
\end{array}}$$

$$\frac{}{c : b} \qquad \frac{}{x^s : s} \qquad \frac{e_1 : s_1 \quad \dots \quad e_n : s_n}{(e_1, \dots, e_n) : s_1 \times \cdots \times s_n} \qquad \frac{e : s_1 \times \cdots \times s_n}{\pi_i \, e : s_i} 1 \leq i \leq n$$

$$\frac{}{\{\}^s : \{s\}} \qquad \frac{e : s}{\{e\} : \{s\}} \qquad \frac{e_1 : \{s\} \quad e_2 : \{s\}}{e_1 \cup e_2 : \{s\}} \qquad \frac{e_1 : \{s\} \quad e_2 : \{t\}}{\bigcup\{e_1 \mid x^t \in e_2\} : \{s\}}$$

$$\frac{}{true : bool} \qquad \frac{}{false : bool} \qquad \frac{e_1 : bool \quad e_2 : s \quad e_3 : s}{if \; e_1 \; then \; e_2 \; else \; e_3 : s}$$

$$\frac{e_1 : b \quad e_2 : b}{e_1 = e_2 : bool} \qquad \frac{e : \{b \times \cdots \times b\}}{isempty \; e : bool}$$

$$\begin{array}{c}
\text{Powerset Operator in } \mathcal{NRC}(powerset) \\[3mm]
\dfrac{e : \{b \times \cdots \times b\}}{powerset \; e : \{\{b \times \cdots \times b\}\}}
\end{array}$$

Fig. 1. $\mathcal{NRC}$ and its extension $\mathcal{NRC}(powerset)$

The expression $\{\}$ denotes the empty set. The expression $\{e\}$ denotes the singleton set containing the object denoted by e. The expression $e_1 \cup e_2$ denotes the union of the sets e_1 and e_2. The expression $\bigcup\{e_1 \mid x \in e_2\}$ denotes the set obtained by first applying the function $f(x) = e_1$ to each object in the set e_2 and then taking their union; that is, $\bigcup\{e_1 \mid x \in e_2\} = f(C_1) \cup \ldots \cup f(C_n)$, where $f(x) = e_1$ and $\{C_1, \dots, C_n\}$ is the set denoted by e_2.

Note that the $x \in e_2$ part in the $\bigcup\{e_1 \mid x \in e_2\}$ construct is not a membership test. It is an abstraction that introduces the variable x whose scope is the expression e_1. This construct is the sole means in $\mathcal{NRC}$ for iterating over a set. For example, the cartesian product of two sets X and Y can be defined as $cartprod(X, Y) =_{df} \bigcup\{\bigcup\{\{(x,y)\} \mid x \in X\} \mid y \in Y\}$. As a second example, the flattening of a nested set X can be defined as $flatten(X) =_{df} \bigcup\{x \mid x \in X\}$. As a last example, the projection of the first column of a relation X can be defined as $\Pi_1(X) =_{df} \bigcup\{\{\pi_1 \, x\} \mid x \in X\}$.

The notation $e[\boldsymbol{R}]$ stands for the an expression e with free variables $\boldsymbol{R}$; however, when it is not important to explicitly list the free variables, it is written simply as e. For a list of objects $\boldsymbol{O}$ that conform to the types of $\boldsymbol{R}$, the notation $e[\boldsymbol{O}/\boldsymbol{R}]$ stands for the expression obtained by substituting $\boldsymbol{O}$ for $\boldsymbol{R}$ in the standard way. The expression $e[\boldsymbol{R}]$ can be thought of as a "query" where

R are its input; equivalently, it can be thought of as a function $f(R) = e[R]$. The expression $e[R]$ is said to be a "flat relational query" if each R in R is a flat relation and $e[R] : \{b \times \cdots \times b\}$. Recall that a flat relation can have type $\{b \times \cdots \times b\}$ or type $b \times \cdots \times b$. So, the notation $e[R, x]$ is used here when it is important to explicitly separate the two kinds of variables in a flat relational query. The result below on the expressive power of $\mathcal{NRC}$ is well known.

Proposition 1 (Wong [17]).

1. $\mathcal{NRC}$ is in PTIME.
2. $\mathcal{NRC}$ is equivalent to the classical nested relational algebra.
3. $\mathcal{NRC}$, when restricted to flat relational queries, is equivalent to the classical relational algebra.

As $\mathcal{NRC}$ is not more powerful than the classical relational algebra, recursive queries such as the transitive closure query are inexpressible in $\mathcal{NRC}$. In fact, as shown by Libkin and Wong [12], these queries remain inexpressible even when $\mathcal{NRC}$ is augmented with arithmetics and aggregate functions. One proposal to enable a nested relational calculus or algebra to express complex queries, without resorting to explicit recursion, is to endow the calculus or algebra with a powerset operation. Indeed, this option was proposed by Abiteboul and Beeri [1] and by Suciu and Paredaens [14].

Following in their foot steps, a more powerful nested relational calculus $\mathcal{NRC}(powerset)$ is defined here by augmenting $\mathcal{NRC}$ with a powerset operation on flat relations, as shown in Figure 1. Here, *powerset e* produces a set containing all the subsets of the set denoted by e, provided e is a flat relation. By factoring through the equivalence [4] between $\mathcal{NRC}$ and a corresponding nested relational algebra, the result below on the expressive power of $\mathcal{NRC}(powerset)$ is readily obtained.

Proposition 2 (Buneman et al. [4]). $\mathcal{NRC}(powerset)$ *is equivalent to the complex object algebras of Abiteboul and Beeri and of Suciu and Paredaens.*

Following Suciu and Paredaens [14], a call-by-value operational semantics is defined for $\mathcal{NRC}(powerset)$, as shown in Figure 2. In this operational semantics, $e \Downarrow C$ means the closed expression e is evaluated to the object C. The notation $C_1 \cup \cdots \cup C_n$ denotes the set of objects obtained by the union of the sets C_1, ..., C_n. This evaluation is sound in the sense that, when $e : s$ and $e \Downarrow C$, then C is an object of type s and $e = C$. Thus, each $e : s$ evaluates to a unique C. The notation $e \Downarrow$ is used here to refer to the unique evaluation tree of e.

The complexity $sizeof(e \Downarrow)$ of an evaluation is normally defined in terms of the size of the evaluation tree. However, for the purpose of this paper, and analogous to Suciu and Paredaens [14], it is sufficient to define it in terms of the size of the largest object in the evaluation tree. That is, $sizeof(e \Downarrow) = \max\{sizeof(C) \mid$ the object C occurs in the evaluation tree $e \Downarrow\}$. The size of an object is defined in some standard way, e.g., the number of atomic objects (i.e., objects of base type b) in it.

$$\frac{}{c \Downarrow c} \qquad \frac{e_1 \Downarrow C_1 \quad \cdots \quad e_n \Downarrow C_n}{(e_1, \ldots, e_n) \Downarrow (C_1, \ldots, C_n)} \qquad \frac{e \Downarrow (C_1, \ldots, C_n)}{\pi_i \, e \Downarrow C_i} 1 \le i \le n$$

$$\frac{}{\{\} \Downarrow \{\}} \qquad \frac{e \Downarrow C}{\{e\} \Downarrow \{C\}} \qquad \frac{e_1 \Downarrow C_1 \quad e_2 \Downarrow C_2}{e_1 \cup e_2 \Downarrow C_1 \cup C_2}$$

$$\frac{e_2 \Downarrow \{C_1, \ldots, C_n\} \quad e_1[C_1/x] \Downarrow C_1' \quad \cdots \quad e_1[C_n/x] \Downarrow C_n'}{\bigcup \{e_1 \mid x \in e_2\} \Downarrow C_1' \cup \cdots \cup C_n'}$$

$$\frac{}{true \Downarrow true} \qquad \frac{}{false \Downarrow false}$$

$$\frac{e_1 \Downarrow true \quad e_2 \Downarrow C}{if \ e_1 \ then \ e_2 \ else \ e_3 \Downarrow C} \qquad \frac{e_1 \Downarrow false \quad e_3 \Downarrow C}{if \ e_1 \ then \ e_2 \ else \ e_3 \Downarrow C}$$

$$\frac{e_1 \Downarrow C_1 \quad e_2 \Downarrow C_2}{e_1 = e_2 \Downarrow true} C_1 = C_2 \qquad \frac{e_1 \Downarrow C_1 \quad e_2 \Downarrow C_2}{e_1 = e_2 \Downarrow false} C_1 \ne C_2$$

$$\frac{e \Downarrow C}{isempty \ e \Downarrow true} C = \{\} \qquad \frac{e \Downarrow C}{isempty \ e \Downarrow false} C \ne \{\}$$

$$\frac{e \Downarrow \{C_1, \ldots, C_n\}}{powerset \ e \Downarrow \{C_1', \ldots, C_{2^n}'\}}$$
$$\text{where } C_1', \ldots, C_{2^n}' \text{ are the subsets of } \{C_1, \ldots, C_n\}$$

Fig. 2. A call-by-value operational semantics of $\mathcal{NRC}(powerset)$

Suciu and Paredaens [14] showed a deep result that can be restated in $\mathcal{NRC}(powerset)$ as follows:

Proposition 3. *[Suciu and Paredaens [14]] Let $e[R]$ be a query that implements the transitive closure of an input flat relation $R : \{b \times b\}$ in $\mathcal{NRC}(powerset)$. Let O be a sufficiently long chain of type $\{b \times b\}$. Then $sizeof(e[O/R] \Downarrow)$ is $\Omega(2^{|O|})$. That is, every implementation of transitive closure in $\mathcal{NRC}(powerset)$ requires exponential space.*

In this paper, an alternative proof of this result is presented. Moreover, it is generalized here to a dichotomy result on practically all flat relational queries expressible in $\mathcal{NRC}(powerset)$. In particular, practically all flat relational queries expressible in $\mathcal{NRC}(powerset)$ are shown here to be dichotomous in the sense that either they are already expressible in $\mathcal{NRC}$ or they require at least exponential space. Hence, the extra expressive power that the powerset operation buys for $\mathcal{NRC}(powerset)$ comes strictly with an exponential cost.

3   Conservative Extension and Locality Properties

Two sets of techniques are needed to prove the Dichotomy Theorem. The first is the conservative extension property of $\mathcal{NRC}$ and the system of rewrite rules used for proving this property. The second is the locality property of first-order queries.

3.1   Conservative Extension

The conservative extension property and the associated system of rewrite rules were initially described by Wong [17] and, later, generalized by Libkin and Wong [10,12]. This system of rewrite rules is given in Figure 3.

$$\bigcup\{e \mid x \in \{\}\} \mapsto \{\}$$
$$\bigcup\{e_1 \mid x \in \{e_2\}\} \mapsto e_1[e_2/x]$$
$$\bigcup\{e \mid x \in (e_1 \cup e_2)\} \mapsto \bigcup\{e \mid x \in e_1\} \cup \bigcup\{e \mid x \in e_2\}$$
$$\bigcup\{e_1 \mid x \in \bigcup\{e_2 \mid y \in e_3\}\} \mapsto \bigcup\{\bigcup\{e_1 \mid x \in e_2\} \mid y \in e_3\}$$
$$\bigcup\{e \mid x \in (if\ e_1\ then\ e_2\ else\ e_3)\} \mapsto if\ e_1\ then\ \bigcup\{e \mid x \in e_2\}\ else\ \bigcup\{e \mid x \in e_3\}$$
$$\pi_i(e_1, \ldots, e_2) \mapsto e_i$$
$$\pi_i\ (if\ e_1\ then\ e_2\ else\ e_3) \mapsto if\ e_1\ then\ \pi_i\ e_2\ else\ \pi_i\ e_3$$
$$if\ true\ then\ e_2\ else\ e_3 \mapsto e_2$$
$$if\ false\ then\ e_2\ else\ e_3 \mapsto e_3$$

Fig. 3. A system of rewrite rules for $\mathcal{NRC}(powerset)$

The following properties of this system of rewrite rules are well known.

Proposition 4 (Conservative Extension [17,10]).

1. *This system of rewrite rules is sound.*
2. *This system of rewrite rules is strongly normalizing.*
3. *Let e be an expression in $\mathcal{NRC}(powerset)$ that is in normal form with respect to this system of rewrite rules. That is, no rule can be applied to further rewrite e. Let $e'[\boldsymbol{R}] : s$ be a subexpression in e. Suppose $\boldsymbol{R}$ have types whose height is at most h, and the type s has height h'. Then all the types appearing in the type derivation of $e'[\boldsymbol{R}] : s$ have height at most $\max(h, h')$, if the powerset operation does not appear in $e'[\boldsymbol{R}]$; or, they have height at most $\max(h, h', 2)$, if the powerset operation appears in $e'[\boldsymbol{R}]$.*

It is straightforward to show that this system of rewrite rules does not increase the complexity of evaluation.

Proposition 5. *Let $e[\boldsymbol{R}] \mapsto e'[\boldsymbol{R}]$. Let $\boldsymbol{O}$ be a list of objects conforming to the types of $\boldsymbol{R}$. Then $sizeof(e[\boldsymbol{O}/\boldsymbol{R}] \Downarrow) \geq sizeof(e'[\boldsymbol{O}/\boldsymbol{R}] \Downarrow)$.*

3.2   Locality

The second main machinery needed to prove the dichotomy result is the locality property. Let me first introduce the notions of "τ structure", "Gaifman graph", "r-sphere", and "r-neighbourhood", before explaining what the locality property is.

A signature τ is a list of symbols $\mathbf{R}$, where $\mathbf{R}$ is to be regarded as input for a query. The signature τ_m is obtained by extending the signature τ with m new constant symbols. For the purpose of this paper, each R_i in $\mathbf{R}$ has type of the form $\{b \times \cdots \times b\}$. A τ structure $\mathcal{A} = \langle A, \mathbf{O} \rangle$ has a universe A (which is a finite nonempty set of objects of type b) and a list of objects $\mathbf{O}$ (where each object O_i in $\mathbf{O}$ is the interpretation of the corresponding R_i and, thus, having the type of R_i). Also, all elements of $\mathbf{O}$ are in the universe A. The class of τ structures is denoted by STRUCT$[\tau]$. The symbol $\simeq$ is used to denote isomorphism of τ structures.

Given a τ structure $\mathcal{A} = \langle A, \mathbf{O} \rangle$, its Gaifman graph $\mathcal{G}(\mathcal{A})$ is defined as a graph such that its vertices are the universe of $\mathcal{A}$ and its edges are precisely those pairs (a, b) where there is a tuple $t_i \in O_i$, for some O_i in $\mathbf{O}$, such that both a and b are in t_i. The distance $d^{\mathcal{A}}(a, b)$ is defined as the length of the shortest path from a to b in $\mathcal{G}(\mathcal{A})$. Given a tuple $\mathbf{a} = (a_1, \ldots, a_m)$ of objects in A, and some $r \geq 0$, the r-sphere of $\mathbf{a}$ is defined as $S_r^{\mathcal{A}}(\mathbf{a}) = \bigcup_{1 \leq i \leq m} S_r^{\mathcal{A}}(a_i)$, where $S_r^{\mathcal{A}}(a_i) = \{b \in A \mid d^{\mathcal{A}}(a_i, b) \leq r\}$. Also, the r-neighbourhood of $\mathbf{a}$ is defined as the τ_m structure $N_r^{\mathcal{A}}(\mathbf{a}) = \langle S_r^{\mathcal{A}}(\mathbf{a}), \mathbf{O}|_{S_r^{\mathcal{A}}(\mathbf{a})}, a_1, \ldots, a_m \rangle$. That is, $N_r^{\mathcal{A}}(\mathbf{a})$ is obtained by restricting $\mathcal{A}$ to the universe $S_r^{\mathcal{A}}(\mathbf{a})$ and adding some extra constants that are the elements of $\mathbf{a}$.

Gaifman [8] showed that first-order queries exhibit a kind of locality property in the sense that the result of these queries can be determined by considering "small neighbourhoods" of its input. It follows easily from the work of Gaifman and Part 3 of Proposition 1 that flat relational queries in $\mathcal{NRC}$ has this kind of locality property.

Proposition 6 (Locality [8,7,9]). *Every flat relational query $e[\mathbf{R}]$ in $\mathcal{NRC}$ has the locality property. That is, there is a finite natural number r such that, for every $\mathcal{A} = \langle A, \mathbf{O} \rangle \in STRUCT[\mathbf{R}]$, for every two m-ary vectors $\mathbf{a}$ and $\mathbf{b}$ of elements of A, it is the case that $N_r^{\mathcal{A}}(\mathbf{a}) \simeq N_r^{\mathcal{A}}(\mathbf{b})$ implies $\mathbf{a} \in e[\mathbf{O}/\mathbf{R}]$ if and only if $\mathbf{b} \in e[\mathbf{O}/\mathbf{R}]$.*

In short, for every flat relational query expressible in $\mathcal{NRC}$ there is some number r such that, for every pair $(\mathbf{a}, \mathbf{b})$, so long as a and b have neighbourhoods that are isomorphic up to radius r, they must either be both in the result of the query or both not in the result of the query. The smallest such number r is called the "locality index" of the query.

An equivalence relation $\mathbf{a} \approx_r^{\mathcal{A}} \mathbf{b}$ is induced by $N_r^{\mathcal{A}}(\mathbf{a}) \simeq N_r^{\mathcal{A}}(\mathbf{b})$. The resulting isomorphism types are called r-neighbourhood types here. If a restriction is imposed so that $\mathcal{G}(\mathcal{A})$ has degree at most k, then the number of r-neighbourhood types realised for each $r > 0$ is finite. Thus, under this restriction, for any flat relational query $e[\boldsymbol{R}]$ in $\mathcal{NRC}$, its result is completely characterized by a finite number of r-neighbourhood types. Each r-neighbourhood type induced by $N_r^{\mathcal{A}}(\boldsymbol{a})$ can be thought of as a "diagram" showing how objects in this neighbourhood type are "connected" to each other and to the fixed reference objects (i.e., $\boldsymbol{a}$). Each neighbourhood type is definable by a first-order formula $\xi(\boldsymbol{u})$ such that $\boldsymbol{a} \approx_r^{\mathcal{A}} \boldsymbol{b}$ if and only if $\mathcal{A} \models \xi(\boldsymbol{a})$.

The following proposition on objects that are connected in a neighbourhood type is easily proved.

Proposition 7. *Given a neighbourhood type $\xi(u_1, \ldots, u_m)$ induced by some r-neighbourhood. Suppose u_i and u_j are connected to each other in $\xi(u_1, \ldots, u_m)$. Then for any τ_m structure $A = \langle A, \boldsymbol{O}, o_1, \ldots, o_m \rangle$ realizing $\xi(u_1, \ldots, u_m)$, it is the case that $d^A(o_i, o_j) \leq mr + 1$.*

4 Complexity of Queries on Dichotomous Structures

Given a signature τ. A "motif" of radius r is a first-order formula $\rho(u)$ with a single free variable u such that $\rho(u)$ has locality index r on all τ structures. A τ structure $\mathcal{A}$ is said to be "bounded" by a motif $\rho(u)$ at a threshold g if $|\{a \in A \mid \mathcal{A} \models \psi(a)\}| \leq rg$, where r is the radius of $\rho(u)$. That is, there are at most rg elements in the universe of $\mathcal{A}$ that make $\rho(u)$ true. A class $\mathcal{C}$ of τ structures is said to be "bounded" by a motif $\rho(u)$ at a threshold g if that motif $\rho(u)$ bounds all structures in $\mathcal{C}$ at the threshold g. On the other hand, $\mathcal{C}$ is said to be "unbounded" by $\rho(u)$ if for every $g > 0$, there is some $\mathcal{A} \in \mathcal{C}$ that is not bounded by $\rho(u)$ at threshold g.

Definition 1. *A class $\mathcal{C}$ of τ structures is said to be "dichotomous" at threshold g if and only if (i) $\mathcal{C}$ is unbounded by some motifs, and (ii) $\mathcal{C}$ is bounded by all other motifs at threshold g. A dichotomous class is said to be "deep" if, at every r, it is unbounded by some motifs of radius r. A dichotomous class $\mathcal{C}$ is said to have "severity" l if for every motif $\rho(u)$ that unbounds $\mathcal{C}$, there is a series of structures $\mathcal{A}_1, \mathcal{A}_2, \ldots,$ in $\mathcal{C}$ having universe of increasing size, and the ratio $|\{a \in A_i \mid A_i \models \rho(a)\}|/|A_i|$ tends to 1 as i tends to infinity. A "severely dichotomous" class is one that has severity 1.*

I am now ready to sketch a proof of the Dichotomy Theorem for such general classes of structures. Given a flat relational structure $\mathcal{A} = \langle A, \boldsymbol{O} \rangle$, the size of the structure is defined as the size of its universe: $|\mathcal{A}| = |A|$.

Theorem 1 (Dichotomy). *Let $e[\boldsymbol{R}] : \{b \times \cdots \times b\}$ be a flat relational query in $\mathcal{NRC}(powerset)$, such that the input $\boldsymbol{R}$ comes from a class $\mathcal{C}$ of seriously dichotomous structures whose Gaifman graph has degree at most k. Then either $e[\boldsymbol{R}]$ is expressible in $\mathcal{NRC}$; or, there is a structure $\mathcal{A} = \langle A, \boldsymbol{O} \rangle \in \mathcal{C}$ such that $sizeof(e[\boldsymbol{O}/\boldsymbol{R}] \Downarrow)$ is $\Omega(2^{|A|})$.*

Proof. Let $\mathcal{C}$ be severely dichotomous at threshold g, and the Gaifman graphs of structures in it have degree at most k. Let $\mathcal{A} = \langle A, \boldsymbol{O} \rangle \in \mathcal{C}$ be the input to the query $e[\boldsymbol{R}]$.

By Proposition 5, the system of rewrite rules in Figure 3 does not increase complexity. By Proposition 4, it preserves semantics and is strongly normalizing. Thus it can be assumed without loss of generality that $e[\boldsymbol{R}]$ is an expression in normal form with respect to this system of rewrite rules.

If the powerset operation does not appear in $e[\boldsymbol{R}]$, then the theorem trivially holds. So, let it contain some occurrences of the powerset operation. Let *powerset* $e'[\boldsymbol{R}, \boldsymbol{x}]$ be the occurrence of the powerset operation that corresponds to the earliest instance of the powerset operation to be evaluated when $e[\boldsymbol{R}]$ is evaluated according to the operational semantics given in Figure 2.

Since the $\bigcup\{e_1 \mid x \in e_2\}$ construct is the only way to introduce a new variable in $\mathcal{NRC}(powerset)$, each new free variable x_i in $\boldsymbol{x}$ must have been introduced in an enclosing expression of the form $\bigcup\{\cdots powerset\ e'[\boldsymbol{R}, \boldsymbol{x}] \cdots \mid x_i \in E\}$. As the entire expression $e[\boldsymbol{R}]$ is in normal form, and $e'[\boldsymbol{R}, \boldsymbol{x}]$ is the earliest instance of the powerset operation to be evaluated, E must be one of the R_i in $\boldsymbol{R}$, which is a flat relation. Consequently, x_i has height 0 and a type of the form $b \times \cdots \times b$. Furthermore, as $e'[\boldsymbol{R}, \boldsymbol{x}]$ is an input to a powerset operation, its type must have the form $\{b \times \cdots \times b\}$. Thus $e'[\boldsymbol{R}, \boldsymbol{x}]$ is a flat relational query in $\mathcal{NRC}$.

In fact, by the conservative extension property (Proposition 4), all the types that appear in the typing derivation of $e'[\boldsymbol{R}, \boldsymbol{x}]$ have height at most 1 (i.e., must be flat). By Proposition 1, $e'[\boldsymbol{R}, \boldsymbol{x}]$ is equivalent to a first-order formula $\varphi(\boldsymbol{x}, \boldsymbol{y})$ such that, for every τ_m structure $\mathcal{A} = \langle A, \boldsymbol{O}, \boldsymbol{o} \rangle$ and objects $\boldsymbol{o'}$ of the appropriate types, it is the case that $\boldsymbol{o'} \in e'[\boldsymbol{O}/\boldsymbol{R}, \boldsymbol{o}/\boldsymbol{x}]$ if and only if $\mathcal{A} \models \varphi(\boldsymbol{o}, \boldsymbol{o'})$.

I am now almost ready to use the locality property, except for the variables $\boldsymbol{x}$. To deal with this inconvenience, we inspect the original expression $e[\boldsymbol{R}]$, in an outside-in manner until we reach the expression $e'[\boldsymbol{R}, \boldsymbol{x}]$, to extract all the conditions that must hold on $\boldsymbol{x}$ before $e'[\boldsymbol{R}, \boldsymbol{x}]$ gets evaluated. We define the extraction function $\overrightarrow{e[\boldsymbol{R}]}$ by induction on the structure of e using rules like those given below, where the symbol $\odot$ represents a subexpression that contains the occurrence of the expression $e'[\boldsymbol{R}, \boldsymbol{x}]$ and we write φ_E for the first-order formula that the expression E in $\mathcal{NRC}$ translates to. The existence of φ_E is guaranteed by Proposition 1.

- $\overrightarrow{\bigcup\{if\ E\ then\ \odot\ else\ F \mid x \in R\}} = (x, \boldsymbol{x'} : R, \boldsymbol{R'} : \varphi_E \wedge \psi)$, where $\overrightarrow{\odot} = (\boldsymbol{x'} : \boldsymbol{R'} : \psi)$.
- $\overrightarrow{\bigcup\{if\ E\ then\ F\ else\ \odot \mid x \in R\}} = (x, \boldsymbol{x'} : R, \boldsymbol{R'} : \neg\varphi_E \wedge \psi)$, where $\overrightarrow{\odot} = (\boldsymbol{x'} : \boldsymbol{R'} : \psi)$.
- $\overrightarrow{\bigcup\{if\ \odot\ then\ E\ else\ F \mid x \in R\}} = (x, \boldsymbol{x'} : R, \boldsymbol{R'} : \psi)$, where $\overrightarrow{\odot} = (\boldsymbol{x'} : \boldsymbol{R'} : \psi)$.
- $\overrightarrow{\odot \cup E} = \overrightarrow{\odot}$,
- $\overrightarrow{E \cup \odot} = \overrightarrow{\odot}$,
- the remaining rules are omitted.

So, the original expression $e[\boldsymbol{R}]$ is inspected, using the extraction function above, to obtain all the conditions that must hold on $\boldsymbol{x}$ before $e'[\boldsymbol{R}, \boldsymbol{x}]$ gets evaluated. This gives us a first-order formula $\psi(\boldsymbol{x})$. Let $\phi(\boldsymbol{x}, \boldsymbol{y}) =_{df} \boldsymbol{R}(\boldsymbol{x}) \wedge \psi(\boldsymbol{x}) \wedge \varphi(\boldsymbol{x}, \boldsymbol{y})$.

It follows by Proposition 6 that $\phi(\boldsymbol{x}, \boldsymbol{y})$ enjoys the locality property. Let r be its locality index. Since I am only considering structures $\mathcal{A} = \langle A, \boldsymbol{O} \rangle$ whose Gaifman graph has degree at most k, there is a finite number of neighbourhood types $\xi_h(\boldsymbol{x}, \boldsymbol{y})$ such that $\neg(\xi_h(\boldsymbol{x}, \boldsymbol{y}) \Rightarrow \neg\phi(\boldsymbol{x}, \boldsymbol{y}))$ holds. I refer to these as the "qualifying neighbourhood types".

For each qualifying neighbourhood type $\xi_h(\boldsymbol{x}, \boldsymbol{y})$ and each y_i in $\boldsymbol{y}$, we try to determine a number $H_{h,i}$ that is an upperbound on the number of distinct objects in the universe of the input structure $\mathcal{A}$ that y_i can be instantiated to. Then the number of tuples that can result from evaluating $e'[\boldsymbol{R}, \boldsymbol{x}]$ is bounded by $H* = \sum_h \prod_i H_{h,i}$. Then the number of tuples that can result from evaluating *powerset* $e'[\boldsymbol{R}, \boldsymbol{x}]$ is bounded by 2^{H*}. If $H*$ (i.e., each $H_{h,i}$) can be determined independently of the input structure, then we can replace *powerset* $e'[\boldsymbol{R}, \boldsymbol{x}]$ by *powerset*$_{H*} e'[\boldsymbol{R}, \boldsymbol{x}]$, where *powerset*$_{H*}$ is an expression in $\mathcal{NRC}$ to produce all subsets of a set up to $H*$ elements.

There are only three scenarios that need to be considered in determining $H_{h,i}$. The first scenario is when y_i is connected to some x_j in the neighbourhood formula $\xi_h(\boldsymbol{x}, \boldsymbol{y})$. By Proposition 7, the distance between x_j and y_i is at most $mr + 1$, where m is the length of the tuples of variables denoted by $\boldsymbol{x}, \boldsymbol{y}$. Since the Gaifman graph of the input sturcture $\mathcal{A}$ has degree at most k, given any instantiation for x_j, there are at most k^{mr+1} possible instantiations for y_i. So, in this scenario, $H_{h,i}$ can be simply set as k^{mr+1}.

However, when y_i is not connected to any x_j in $\xi_h(\boldsymbol{x}, \boldsymbol{y})$, we cannot constrain the number of instantiations for y_i this way. Let $\xi'_h(y_i) =_{df} \exists \boldsymbol{x}, \boldsymbol{y}' : \xi_h(\boldsymbol{x}, y)$, where $\boldsymbol{y}'$ are all the variables in $\boldsymbol{y}$, except y_i. Since y_i is not connected to any x_j in $\xi_h(\boldsymbol{x}, \boldsymbol{y})$, the instantiations for y_i that make $\xi_h(\boldsymbol{x}, \boldsymbol{y})$ true must be the same ones that make $\xi'_h(y_i)$ true. By the locality property, let the locality index of $\xi'_h(y_i)$ be r'. Again, due to the constraint that the Gaifman graph of the input structure has degree at most k, the number of qualifying r'-neighbourhood types $\rho_{h,d}(y_i)$ such that $\neg(\rho_{h,d}(y_i) \Rightarrow \neg\xi'_h(y_i))$ is finite. Let $H'_{h,i,d}$ be an upperbound— to be determined shortly—on the size of the neighbourhood $\xi'_h(y_i)$. Obviously, $H_{h,i}$ is bounded by the total size $\sum_d H'_{h,i,d}$ of these qualifying neighbourhoods.

It remains to determine $H'_{h,i,d}$. Since $\mathcal{C}$ is severely dichotomous at threshold g, each $\rho_{h,d}(y_i)$ is a motif that either bounds $\mathcal{C}$ at threshold g or unbounds $\mathcal{C}$. This leads to the second and third scenarios of the proof.

The second scenario is when $\rho_{h,d}(y_i)$ is a motif that bounds $\mathcal{C}$ at threshold g. By definition of bounding motifs, there are at most $r'g$ number of instantiations that makes $\rho_{h,d}(y_i)$ true, where r' is the radius of $\rho_{h,d}(y_i)$, which obviously has the same radius as $\xi'_h(y_i)$. So, in this scenario, $H_{h,i,d}$ can be set to $r'g$.

The third and last scenario is when $\rho_{h,d}(y_i)$ is a motif that unbounds $\mathcal{C}$. Since $\mathcal{C}$ is severely dichotomous, by definition, it has a series of structures $\mathcal{A}_1 = \langle A_1, \boldsymbol{O}_1 \rangle$, $\mathcal{A}_2 = \langle A_2, \boldsymbol{O}_2 \rangle$, ..., with universe of increasing size such that the ratio $|\{a \in A_i \mid \mathcal{A}_i \models \rho_{h,d}(y_i)\}|/|A_i|$ tends to 1, as $\rho_{h,d}(y_i)$ is a motif that unbounds it. Since $\rho_{h,d}(y_i)$ is a neighbourhood type, by the locality property, all of the objects a in $\{a \in A_i \mid \mathcal{A}_i \models \rho_{h,d}(y_i)\}$ must be used to instantiate y_i. Thus, the number of instantiations for y_i is essentially $|A_i|$. In this case, we cannot set $H_{h,i,d}$ to a finite value independently of the input structure. Therefore, the powerset operation in *powerset* $e'[\boldsymbol{R}, \boldsymbol{x}]$ cannot be eliminated in this scenario. On the other hand, the number of instantions for $\boldsymbol{y}$ is $\Omega(|A_i|)$ since one of its component, y_i, has $|A_i|$ instantiations. Thus $e'[\boldsymbol{R}, \boldsymbol{x}]$ has $\Omega(|A_i|)$ elements, and *powerset* $e'[\boldsymbol{R}, \boldsymbol{x}]$ has $\Omega(2^{|A_i|})$ elements. Then $sizeof(e[\boldsymbol{O}_i/\boldsymbol{R}] \Downarrow)$ is $\Omega(2^{|A_i|})$ as required, proving the theorem. □

The following corollary is immediate.

Corollary 1. *For any flat relational query on severely dichotomous structures whose Gaifman graphs have degree at most k, if it is inexpressible in $\mathcal{NRC}$ but is expressible in $\mathcal{NRC}(powerset)$, then all of its implementations in $\mathcal{NRC}(powerset)$ need an exponential amount of space.*

5   Discussion

It follows from the Dichotomy Theorem that, for any query in $\mathcal{NRC}(powerset)$ on seriously dichotomous structures, either it is already expressible in $\mathcal{NRC}$ (and hence in PTIME) or all of its implementations in $\mathcal{NRC}(powerset)$ need exponential space. Since the class of structures containing a single long chain is seriously dichotomous, and the transitive closure of single long chain is inexpressible in $\mathcal{NRC}$ [7], it follows immediately as a corollary of the Dichotomy Theorem above that all implementations of transitive closure in $\mathcal{NRC}(powerset)$ must use at least exponent space, as proven earlier by Suciu and Paredaens [14] in a brute-force manner.

Our the Dichotomy Theorem is more general in three important ways. Firstly, it is not limited to any single specific query like the transitive closure. Secondly, it is not limited to a simple input structure like a single chain. Thirdly, the proof is made more general by factoring through the conservative extension and locality properties of a query language. These advantages open the route to proving the dichotomous behaviour of a wider range of queries in a wider range of query languages.

Some further insights can be gained from the proof. It is the third scenario in the proof that cause the blow-up in complexity. Analyzing the unbounding motifs further, we can divide them into two classes: those in the deep dichotomous classes and those in the non-deep dichotomous classes given in Definition 1. The deep dichotomous classes contain structures like a small set of long chains. The non-deep classes contain structures like a set of arbitrarily many short chains. I believe the queries on the former truly need recursion, but queries on the latter probably do not. However, in the latter, the removal of the powerset operation as presented in the Dichotomy Theorem is not clever enough to remove all powerset operations if a programmer happens to unnecessarily use some powerset operations to implement these queries—after all, the Dichotomy Theorem is not a clever query optimizer.

6   Remarks

It was with Peter Buneman and Val Tannen that I first defined $\mathcal{NRC}$ in 1992 [3], two decades ago! It was also Peter and Val who first posed me the conservative extension property of $\mathcal{NRC}$ as an open question, which I solved in 1993 [16] by the analysing the normal forms of the system of rewrite rules presented earlier in this paper.

I first saw in 1994 Dan Suciu and Jan Paredaens' proof [13] that all implementations of the transitive closure query in $\mathcal{NRC}(powerset)$ are necessarily inefficient. This was my first encounter with the intensional aspect of expressive power. It intrigued me greatly and I soon co-authored, in 1995, a paper [15] with Dan comparing the efficiency of the algorithms that can be implemented by different forms of structural recursion.

I first learned in 1994 [11] the locality property of first-order query languages from Leonid Libkin. It took me three further years to fully appreciate this powerful property and to exploit it to prove, in 1997 [6], with Leonid and Guozhu Dong, the bounded degree property of query languages with aggregate function.

Leonid, Dan, and I were students in the same group led by Peter, Val, and Susan Davidson. While they have continued working in the database theory area, I have more or less left the field to explore challenges in computational biology since the late 1990s. After this ten-year break, I am delighted to briefly re-visit the field and contribute to this Festschrift to Peter. I am pleasantly surprised that I am able to chain together the series of our major past results ($\mathcal{NRC}$, normal forms of my favourite rewrite system, the conservative extension property, and the locality property) that Peter had a big role in nurturing, to solve a problem that Peter also had a big role in keeping my continued fascination with it. I hope you have enjoyed reading the paper as much as I have enjoyed working on it.

References

1. Abiteboul, S., Beeri, C.: The power of languages for the manipulation of complex values. The VLDB Journal 4(4), 727–794 (1995)
2. Abiteboul, S., Vianu, V.: Generic computation and its complexity. In: Proceedings of 23rd ACM Symposium on the Theory of Computing, pp. 209–219 (1991)
3. Breazu-Tannen, V., Buneman, P., Wong, L.: Naturally embedded query languages. In: Proceedings of 4th International Conference on Database Theory, Berlin, Germany, October 1992, pp. 140–154 (1992)
4. Buneman, P., Naqvi, S., Tannen, V., Wong, L.: Principles of programming with complex objects and collection types. Theoretical Computer Science 149(1), 3–48 (1995)
5. Colson, L.: About primitive recursive algorithms. Theoretical Computer Science 83, 57–69 (1991)
6. Dong, G., Libkin, L., Wong, L.: Local properties of query languages. In: Proceedings of 6th International Conference on Database Theory, pp. 140–154 (1997)
7. Dong, G., Libkin, L., Wong, L.: Local properties of query languages. Theoretical Computer Science 239, 277–308 (2000)

8. Gaifman, H.: On local and non-local properties. In: Proceedings of the Herbrand Symposium, Logic Colloquium '81, pp. 105–135 (1982)
9. Hella, L., Libkin, L., Nurmonen, J., Wong, L.: Logics with aggregate operators. Journal of the ACM 48(4), 880–907 (2001)
10. Libkin, L., Wong, L.: Conservativity of nested relational calculi with internal generic functions. Information Processing Letters 49(6), 273–280 (1994)
11. Libkin, L., Wong, L.: New techniques for studying set languages, bag languages, and aggregate functions. In: Proceedings of 13th ACM Symposium on Principles of Database Systems, pp. 155–166 (1994)
12. Libkin, L., Wong, L.: Query languages for bags and aggregate functions. Journal of Computer and System Sciences 55(2), 241–272 (1997)
13. Suciu, D., Paredaens, J.: Any algorithm in the complex object algebra needs exponential space to compute transitive closure. In: Proceedings of 13th ACM Symposium on Principles of Database Systems, pp. 201–209 (1994)
14. Suciu, D., Paredaens, J.: The complexity of the evaluation of complex algebra expressions. Journal of Computer and Systems Sciences 55(2), 322–343 (1997)
15. Suciu, D., Wong, L.: On two forms of structural recursion. In: Proceedings of 5th International Conference on Database Theory, pp. 111–124 (1995)
16. Wong, L.: Normal forms and conservative properties for query languages over collection types. In: Proceedings of 12th ACM Symposium on Principles of Database Systems, pp. 26–36 (1993)
17. Wong, L.: Normal forms and conservative extension properties for query languages over collection types. Journal of Computer and System Sciences 52(3), 495–505 (1996)

Provenance in a Modifiable Data Set

Jing Zhang and H.V. Jagadish

University of Michigan
{jingzh,jag}@umich.edu

Abstract. Provenance of data is now widely recognized as being of great importance, thanks in large part to pioneering work [4, 6] by Peter Buneman and his collaborators in a stream that continues to produce influential papers today [1–3, 7]. When we consume data from a database, we often care about where these data come from, how they were derived, and so forth. We may desire answers to such questions to establish trust in the data, to investigate suspicious values, to debug code in the system, or for a host of other reasons. Considerable recent work has addressed many issues related to provenance. However, the standard assumption is that data sources, from which result data have been derived, are static. In reality, we know that most data are modified over time, including data sources used for deriving results of interest. When we consider provenance in the context of such modifications, many new problems arise. This chapter addresses two key problems in this context:

1. Result data may no longer be valid after a source update. How can we efficiently determine whether a given result tuple is valid? When a result tuple is invalidated, can we explain what caused this invalidation?
2. We may have lost access to (some) source data. In such a situation, can we determine what is the missing source data on which some result tuple depends?

1 Validating an Answer

In a modern scientific project, there frequently is a huge body of raw data collected from experiments. Usually, this body of data is stored in a database, and processed by SQL queries to make it ready for further analysis. These derived data are vital for the final scientific conclusions the scientists draw from the experiments. When the raw data change, e.g., due to a re-collection or a curation of the raw data, in the form of database inserts, deletes and updates, it is important to know whether previously derived data and results are still valid or derivable.

Previously derived data can be validated by incrementally maintaining [11] the derived data set with regard to the updated database. However, scientists are often interested in only some particular portion of the derived data set, possibly even a single tuple. For example, this may be a specific result quoted in some publication or used in follow-on work. In such cases, one desires a more efficient way to validate the part in question without refreshing the whole derived data set, especially when the derived data set is large.

We propose an approach to validating the selected answer tuples derived from a nested query in case of modifications to the source database, and provide an explanation

V. Tannen et al. (Eds.): Buneman Festschrift, LNCS 8000, pp. 557–567, 2013.

of the invalidation of any of these tuples that is invalidated. For the former part, we base our approach on the incremental evaluation of materialized views enhanced with pruning predicates derived from the selected tuples and tailored for both positive and negative tuples[1] in delta tables; for the latter part, we treat the invalidated tuples as negative tuples in the delta result table and retrieve their provenance as a set of both positive and negative tuples within original and/or delta source tables.

Consider the following illustrative scenario, which we have designed using customers and orders, as is so common in the database literature. We use this as our running example, to make it accessible to the reader without requiring domain knowledge in any scientific discipline.

Example 1. Assume we have two simple tables *Orders* and *Customers* as shown in Figure 1. Every order in *Orders* consists of a unique order ID, a customer ID and the cost of the order. Every customer in *Customers* consists of a unique customer ID and a nation ID. There are four simple ASPJ queries Q_{cMax}, Q_{oCnt}, Q_{dist} and $Q_{cMaxNation}$ as shown in Figure 2. Q_{cMax} computes the the maximum cost of a single order for each customer; Q_{oCnt} computes the order count for each customer; $Q_{oCnt} \circ Q_{dist}$ computes the distribution of customers for each count of orders; $Q_{cMax} \circ Q_{cMaxNation}$ computes the maximum cost of a single order for each nation. The derived tables are *CostMax*, *OrderCount*, *CustomerDistribution* and *CostMaxNation* are also shown in Figure 1.

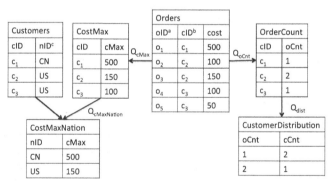

a: *oID* is a unique ID for each order.
b: *cID* is a unique ID for each customer.
c: *nID* is a unique ID for each nation.

Fig. 1. Source Table And Derived Tables

Suppose we have updates to *Orders* table as *ΔOrders*, shown in Figure 3. The *CNT* attribute in *ΔOrders* is the number of derivations of each tuple. Tuples with positive *CNT* are to-be-inserted tuples and tuples with negative *CNT* are to-be-removed tuples. *ΔOrders* leads to the update *ΔCostMax* to the result table *CostMax*. For example,

---

[1] Tuples in delta tables can have positive counts or negative counts [11]. We call tuples with positive counts positive tuples, and tuples with negative counts negative tuples.

Q_{oCnt}:
SELECT cID, $count(oID)$ as $oCnt$
FROM $Orders$ WHERE $cost >= 100$
GROUP BY cID

r_{oCnt}:
$OrderCount(cID, count(\langle oID \rangle)\ AS\ oCnt) :- Orders(oID, cID, cost)$
$? - OrderCount(cID, oCnt)$

Q_{dist}:
SELECT $oCnt$, $count(cID)$ as $cCnt$
FROM $OrderCount$ GROUP BY $oCnt$

r_{dist}:
$CustomerDistribution(oCnt, count(\langle cID \rangle)\ AS\ cCnt) :- OrderCount(cID, oCnt)$
$? - CustomerDistribution(oCnt, cCnt)$

Q_{cMax}:
SELECT cID, $max(cost)$ as $cMax$
FROM $Orders$
GROUP BY cID

r_{cMax}:
$CostMax(cID, max(\langle cost \rangle)\ AS\ cMax) :- Orders(oID, cID, cost)$
$? - CostMax(cID, cMax)$

$Q_{cMaxNation}$:
SELECT nID, $max(cMax)$ as $cMaxNation$
FROM $CostMax$, $Customers$
WHERE $CostMax.cID = Customers.cID$
GROUP BY nID

$r_{cMaxNation}$:
$CostMaxNation(nID, max(\langle cMax \rangle)\ AS\ cMaxNation) :-$
$CostMax(cID, cMax), Customers(cID, nID)$
$? - CostMaxNation(nID, cMaxNation)$

Fig. 2. Example Queries

$(o_6, c_3, 150) \in \Delta Orders$ is inserted into the source table $Orders$, and then $(c_3, 100) \in$ $CostMax$ is replaced with $(c_3, 150)$. We say that $(o_6, c_3, 150)$ contradicts the previous answer $(c_3, 100)$, and $(o_6, c_3, 150)$ serves as an explanation of the invalidation of $(c_3, 100)$ from $CostMax$.

Note that upon the insertion of $(o_6, c_3, 150)$, the derivation that produced $(c_3, 100)$ is still in $Orders$. However, $(c_3, 100)$ is no longer an answer in $CostMax$. Thus, the existence of contributory derivations is not sufficient to form an answer. Moreover, it is obvious that there is more than one way to contradict an answer. For example, $(o_7, c_3, 200)$ can contradict $(c_3, 100)$ as well. On the other hand, the removal of contributory source tuples, e.g., $(o_4, c_3, 100)$ can invalidate $(c_3, 100)$ too.

In general, an answer's validity can be changed by the insertion of contradictory source tuples or by the removal of contributory source tuples. The contributory provenance and the contradictory provenance have an interesting duality and correspondence. When an answer is invalidated, a negative version of it shows up in the delta answer set, e.g., $(c_1, 500, -1)$ in $\Delta CostMax$ indicates the invalidation of $(c_1, 500)$ in the original answer set $CostMax$. Therefore, the contributory provenance of the negative version of an answer in the delta answer set is in fact the contradictory provenance of the answer.

Orders

oID^a	cID^b	cost	CNT
o_1	c_1	500	1
o_2	c_2	100	1
o_3	c_2	150	1
o_4	c_3	100	1

ΔOrders

oID^a	cID^b	cost	CNT
o_6	c_3	150	1
o_1	c_1	500	-1

ΔOrderCount

cID	oCnt	CNT
c_1	1	-1
c_3	1	-1
c_3	2	1

ΔCustomerDistribution

oCnt	cCnt	CNT
2	1	-1
1	2	-1
2	2	1

ΔCostMax

cID	cMax	CNT
c_1	500	-1
c_3	100	-1
c_3	150	1

Fig. 3. (Delta) Tables Extended With *CNT*

The contributory provenance of the negative version consists of tuples from delta source tables and/or original source tables, and consists of both positive tuples and negative tuples. The queries that produce the negative version are delta query rules [11], which are derived from the original query. Then, the contributory provenance of the negative version of an answer can be retrieved by tracing queries based on the delta query rules that produced the negative version.

In general, we can validate selected answers in the following two steps.

Step 1. compute the delta result table by incrementally evaluating the (nested) query with pruning predicates;

Step 2. check the delta result table against the original result table to see if the given answers are invalidated, and explain the invalidation with the positive and/or negative tuples in the delta source tables (and possibly tuples in the original source tuples)

In Step 1, the key point is the construction of pruning predicates. The goal is to prune irrelevant source tuples in the (delta) source tables. The source tuples that can not possibly affect the selected answer(s) are considered irrelevant. Note that the view update results computed from the incremental evaluation with and without pruning predicates are possibly different, since the former does not care for updating answers other than the selected ones.

Since the pruning predicates are constructed for the delta rules and the delta rules evaluate over delta tables, the pruning predicates have to deal with both the positive tuples (i.e., to-be-inserted tuples) and the negative tuples (i.e., to-be-deleted tuples) in the delta tables. The positive tuples and negative tuples in the delta source tables affect the given answer in different ways. For example, if the given answer is the current maximum, then the positive tuples with a greater value have the potential to invalidate the current maximum while the negative tuples with the same value as the current maximum have the potential to invalidate the current maximum. Therefore, a pruning predicate is a disjunction of two predicates, one for the positive tuples and one for the negative tuples.

If the answer is derived through a single query rule, the pruning predicates are constructed directly based on the given answer. If the answer is derived through a stratified Datalog program consisting of multiple rules, and the single rule with the highest stratum produces the final answer. Then the pruning predicates for the rule with highest stratum is constructed directly based on the given answer; and the pruning predicates for any other rule are inferred from the pruning predicates for rules with higher strata.

In Step 2, if we find a negative version of the selected answer in the delta result table, we know that the given answer is invalidated. Since this negative version is produced by the delta rules from the delta source tables and possibly original source tables, we can find the contributory provenance of this negative version in the delta source tables (and original source tables) using classical tracing queries derived from the delta rules. This contributory provenance of the negative version, also being the contradictory provenance of the given answer, explains the invalidation of the given answer.

A related problem has also been studied in [10]. The update techniques given there for the count of the derivations of each view tuple can easily be generalized to update the complete provenance of the view tuple instead. However, the update technique in [10] only applies to SPJU queries without aggregations. Furthermore, this technique also updates the entire derived dataset instead of just the subset of interest to the user.

1.1 Explanation of the Absence of Expected Answer

We considered above the question of identifying updates to source data that caused a result tuple to be invalidated. We have previously studied a closely related question of explaining why some expected result tuple is missing from the answer set [8]. In this previous work, we are not specifically looking at source updates.

When some answer tuples that are expected to be in the result set are missing, we seek to identify particular source tuples or particular manipulations in the derivation responsible for their absence. Such input data are defined to be *unpicked* and such manipulations are defined to be *picky* manipulations for these unpicked data. We proposed both top-down and bottom-up approaches to search over the derivation process to find the picky manipulations.

In other related work, [13] showed that proper changes can be made to some attribute values in the source data that have previously failed to produce the expected result tuples, such that these modified source data can now go through the query evaluation and produce the expected result tuples. [14] introduced the concept of functional causes, which explains the presence and absence of answers. Similar to [13], [12] also provides instance-based explanations for missing answers, but is more general since its technique can apply to a set of SPJUA queries instead of SPJ queries.

2   Lost Source Provenance

Modifications to a source data set may delete (or update/overwrite) some or all of the source data from which a result of interest was derived. Even in the absence of modifications, it is possible that a data source becomes unavailable, for instance because it is remote and goes off-line or because it is owned by an entity that decides to take it private.

In consequence, the provenance of an answer can be (partially) removed from the source data set. In order to retrieve this (partially) lost provenance when requested, we have two possible strategies with different trade offs between the provenance we can provide and the storage/time overhead we are willing to pay.

One way to avoid this problem is to store a version of the source at the time the result was derived. We can thereby guarantee no provenance will be lost, but there is storage cost for keeping a duplicate of the source, and this cost could be substantial. Moreover, if we operate in an environment in which result tuples are lazily updated from the source, we may have to keep multiple versions of the source to meet the provenance needs of all result tuples.

In this section, we develop a second strategy. We show how we can add three (small) extra data structures to the database, and use these to recover the lost provenance.

First, we define the provenance of a given derived tuple as follows. It is a modified version of the definition introduced in [9].

Definition 1. *Given a database D of tables $T_1, ..., T_n$, a query Q and a derived tuple t, there exists a set of tables $T'_1, ..., T'_n$ such that*

- $T'_i \subseteq T_i$, where $i = 1, ..., n$
- $\{t\} = Q(T'_1, ..., T'_n)$
- $\forall T'_k : \forall t' \in T'_k : Q(T'_1, ..., T'_{k-1}, \{t'\}, T'_{k+1}, ..., T'_n) \neq \emptyset$

Notice that if a single table has more than one instance in the query, each instance is considered a separate table.

Second, we describe the three extra data structures we need to retrieve the possibly overwritten provenance. With these three data structures, we can have standard tracing queries modified to make use of them and retrieve the lost provenance. We refer to these queries as *extended tracing queries*.

1. We need a log, denoted as *provenance log*, recording the operations that have taken place over a time period till the current time point, beginning from some defined origin. Every entry records one operation and each entry has a unique log ID, which can be used to identify the operation in this entry.
2. We associate with each tuple in the current database an extra attribute, denoted as *since*, storing a log ID, which indicates the operation that introduced this tuple into the database.
3. We also associate with each table in the current database a so-called *shadow table* that keeps the tuples that were once in the database table but have been removed at some time point. In particular, the shadow table has the same schema as the database table except for two extra attributes storing log IDs, denoted as *begin* and *end*, with *begin* indicating the operation that introduced the tuple into the database and *end* indicating the operation that removed the tuple from the database.

The provenance log, denoted as *Plog*, consists of a sequence of log entries. Each entry corresponds to an operation executed in the database system. Each entry has the structure *(ID, timestamp, user, sqlStatement)*. *ID* is an unique ID assigned to every entry in the log, and an operation that is committed later has a greater ID for its corresponding log entry. That is to say, the ID indicates the order of the commission of all the operations. *sqlStatement* stores the SQL statement of the committed operation.

timestamp is the time when the operation is committed. *user* specifies the user who commits the operation.

The shadow tables are for the historical tuples. For each regular table in the database, we define a corresponding shadow table. For example, if a regular table is of schema $T : \langle a_1, a_2 \rangle$, then the shadow table of T is $T_{sh} : \langle a_1, a_2, begin, end \rangle$. The attributes *begin* and *end* are foreign keys referring to the attribute *ID* in the provenance log. The attribute *begin* stores an ID whose corresponding entry in the provenance log records the operation that generates this tuple. The attribute *end* stores an ID whose corresponding entry in the provenance log records the operation that removes this tuple.

The attributes *begin* and *end* are to specify the time period when the historical tuple was current. We choose to use the IDs of log entries instead of the actual times to avoid ambiguity: two committed operations can have the same time of commit but can not have a same log entry ID.

Current tuples are stored in regular tables. An extra annotation attribute called *since* is added to each regular table, which is a foreign key referring to the attribute *ID* in the provenance log. The attribute *since* stores an ID whose correspondent entry in the provenance log stores the operation that generates this tuple.

This extra annotation attribute is not visible to the users of the database, and thus it can not be manipulated by the users. Provenance capture and retrieval are the only procedures that can set its value or query it.

All the auxiliary data structures are populated whenever a database operation takes place.

1. When a database operation takes place, a new entry is created in the provenance log and a unique ID is assigned to this new entry.
2. When a tuple is inserted into a table due to this database operation, the value of its *since* attribute is set with the ID of the newly created entry in the provenance log.
3. When a tuple is removed from a table due to this database operation, either by a delete or by an update, the removed tuple is inserted into the corresponding shadow table. For this new tuple in the shadow table, the value of the *begin* attribute is set with the value of the *since* attribute in the removed tuple; the value of the *end* attribute is set with the value of the ID of the newly created entry in the provenance log.

This populating of auxiliary data structures is in fact our provenance capture procedure. All the provenance information we need is recorded in these auxiliary structures.

Given a derived tuple *t*, if its provenance is not current in the database, we can retrieve its provenance with our extended tracing queries. Compared to the standard tracing query, the extended tracing query need an extra piece of information, i.e., the ID of the provenance log entry that records the original query. The IDs of provenance log entries can be used as timestamps to indicate time points or periods of time, e.g., storing these IDs in the attributes *begin*, *end* and *since*. These IDs are even better than real timestamps since they incur no ambiguity.

Similarly, the ID of the provenance log entry that records the original query represents the derivation time, i.e., the time when the original query was executed. Therefore, with this ID, our extended tracing query is able to decide which historical data to retrieve provenance from, i.e., the data values that were current in the database at the derivation time. In particular, if a source tuple's life span (identified by *begin* and *end*) covers the derivation time, this source tuple is eligible to be in the provenance. The extended tracing query only uses those eligible source tuples and retrieves the (lost) provenance from them.

In general, the construction of an extended tracing query needs three pieces of information:

1. the derived tuple
2. the original query
3. the ID of the provenance log entry recording the original query

Given a tuple t, suppose it is derived from the original query Q shown in Equation 1, and further suppose Q is logged in a provenance log entry with ID being id, then the extended tracing query to retrieve provenance in the table T_k is as shown in Equation 2.

$$\left\{ \, t : \langle A_1, ..., A_n, G \; AS \; agg(A_{n+1}) \rangle \; | \atop \exists s_1, ..., s_m \atop (T_1(s_1) \wedge ... \wedge T_m(s_m) \wedge f(s_1, ..., s_m, t)) \, \right\} \tag{1}$$

$$\left\{ \, s_k : \langle B_1, ..., B_l \rangle \; | \atop \exists t, s_1, ..., s_{k-1}, s_{k+1}, ..., s_m \atop (T_1^H(s_1) \wedge ... \wedge T_m^H(s_m) \wedge f(s_1, ..., s_m, t) \atop \wedge t.A_1 = a_1 \wedge ... \wedge t.A_n = a_n) \, \right\} \tag{2}$$

where T_k^H, assuming the shadow table of T_k is T_{k_sh}, is

$$\left\{ \, s_k : \langle B_1, ..., B_l \rangle \; | \atop (T_k(s_k) \wedge s_k.since < id) \vee \atop \exists s_k'(T_{k\_sh}(s_k') \wedge s_k'.begin < id \wedge s_k'.end >= id \atop \wedge s_k'.B_1 = s_k.B_1 \wedge ... \wedge s_k'.B_l = s_k.B_l) \, \right\} \tag{3}$$

Notice that, although the original query is a conjunctive query, with aggregation in this case, the extended tracing query is not a conjunctive query, because of the union connective used in Equation 3.

These three data structures incur some space overhead. We discuss next how to minimize this overhead.

First of all, the provenance log does not need to take extra space in practice, since all database management systems keep some kind of log and the provenance log can be implemented as a view over the system maintained logs. This is almost always possible since the really vital attributes in the provenance log are the log ID and the operation, which are very basic information a typical system log will keep.

As for the space overhead due to the attribute *since*, the number of cells of this attribute is equal to the number of tuples in the database. Since the database tuples usually have multiple attributes and some of them are of more space-costly data types than integer type, the total cost of this extra attribute in integer type is only a fraction of the total size of the database.

The shadow tables are the costliest of the three auxiliary data structures in terms of space. The size of shadow tables grows with the number of tuples that have been updated or removed. In a database with a moderate amount of change to data, the space cost due to shadow tables may be acceptable. Intuitively, this cost is unavoidable: if there is change to data and we need past values, we have to store them somewhere. The cost of shadow tables is much less than the cost of storing a version of the source database for each derived value.

In general, the archiving of historical data can be done at different granularities. For example, if one attribute in one tuple in a table in a database is updated, to store the historical data, before the update, we can back up (i) the whole database, (ii) the updated table, (iii) the updated tuple, or (iv) just the updated attribute in the tuple.

The size of the storage of historical data obviously depends on the granularity used in archiving [5, 15]. In the above example, each way of archiving can enable the recovering of the database before update, however, the last one incurs the minimum amount of storage.

In our approach, we archive the historical data at the granularity level of tuples, i.e., we archive a tuple in a proper shadow table when one or multiple attributes in this tuple are updated. Assume the average size of a tuple is $size_t$, and the number of tuples affected by an operation is n. Thus, after this operation, the size of the shadow tables is increased by $(size_t + C) \times n$, where C is a constant being the size of the two attributes *begin* and *end*.

Notice that decreasing the space cost also means increasing the time cost of reconstructing previous versions using historical data. For example, if the whole database is archived, the reconstruction of any table in the database at a previous time involves no complex queries but almost merely selecting. Comparatively, since we only archive the updated tuple when one or more attributes in it are changed, the reconstruction of the involved table needs to run a query as shown in Equation 3.

The book-keeping of these three data structures also incurs some time overhead during the execution of an operation.

There are two types of time cost: the time cost of provenance capture and the time cost of provenance retrieval. The time cost of provenance capture is relatively smaller and more straightforward than that of provenance retrieval.

Provenance capture for every database operation is a two-step procedure: computing one new provenance log entry and/or new shadow table tuples; and inserting them into the provenance log and/or shadow tables.

The computation time is negligible, since the computation of both the log entry and the shadow table tuples is fairly simple. The insertion time of the log entry is constant, since there is always one log entry with a fixed size. The insertion time of shadow table tuples depends on the number of shadow table tuples generated by this operation. Assume n tuples are updated during an operation, and
$insert\_time_t$ is the average time of inserting one shadow table tuple. Then the time of inserting into shadow tables for this operation will be $insert\_time_t \times n$.

The time cost of our provenance retrieval primarily consists of constructing an extended tracing query and executing it. The construction of an extended tracing query takes roughly a constant amount of time. On the other hand, the time to execute it varies with the reconstructed historical versions.

The historical version of a table consists of tuples from the current table and from the shadow table. The execution time of the extended tracing query is affected by both the number of tuples in the historical version and the location of these tuples. The former is easier to understand, since retrieving from a table/view with more tuples takes more time than retrieving from a table/view with less tuples. However, the second relationship is not so obvious. If most of the tuples in the output of concatenation are from the same table, (the sort at the heart of) the union may be faster than in the case where tuples come evenly from the two tables.

3   Conclusions

We live in a dynamic world and the digital artifacts we rely on must change to keep pace with the world we live in. Provenance is more difficult to specify and to work with when we cannot rely on immutable objects and data sources. However, it is possible to do and, in any case, we have no choice in the matter given that we live in a dynamic world. This chapter considered some of the challenges that arise due to change, and suggested solutions to these challenges.

References

1. Buneman, P., Chapman, A., Cheney, J.: Provenance management in curated databases. In: Proceedings of the 2006 ACM SIGMOD International Conference on Management of Data, pp. 539–550 (2006)
2. Buneman, P., Cheney, J., Lindley, S., Müller, H.: Dbwiki: A structured wiki for curated data and collaborative data management. In: Proceedings of the 2011 ACM SIGMOD International Conference on Management of Data, pp. 1335–1338 (2011)
3. Buneman, P., Cheney, J., Tan, W.-C., Vansummeren, S.: Curated databases. In: Proceedings of the 27th ACM SIGMOD-SIGACT-SIGART Symposium on Principles of Database Systems, pp. 1–12 (2008)
4. Buneman, P., Khanna, S., Tan, W.C.: Data provenance: Some basic issues. In: Foundations of Software Technology and Theoretical Computer Science, pp. 87–93 (2000)
5. Buneman, P., Khanna, S., Tajima, K., Tan, W.C.: Archiving scientific data. ACM Trans. Database Syst. 29, 2–42 (2004)
6. Buneman, P., Khanna, S., Tan, W.-C.: Why and where: A characterization of data provenance. In: Van den Bussche, J., Vianu, V. (eds.) ICDT 2001. LNCS, vol. 1973, pp. 316–330. Springer, Heidelberg (2000)
7. Buneman, P., Tan, W.-C.: Provenance in databases. In: Proceedings of the 2007 ACM SIGMOD International Conference on Management of Data, pp. 1171–1173 (2007)
8. Chapman, A., Jagadish, H.V.: Why not? In: Proceedings of the 35th SIGMOD International Conference on Management of Data, pp. 523–534 (2009)
9. Cui, Y., Widom, J.: Practical lineage tracing in data warehouses. In: Proceedings of the 15th International Conference on Data Engineering, pp. 367–378 (1999)
10. Green, T.J., Karvounarakis, G., Ives, Z.G., Tannen, V.: Update exchange with mappings and provenance. In: Proceedings of the 33rd International Conference on Very Large Data Bases, pp. 675–686 (2007)

11. Gupta, A., Mumick, I.S., Subrahmanian, V.S.: Maintaining views incrementally. In: Proceedings of the 1993 ACM SIGMOD International Conference on Management of Data, pp. 157–166 (1993)
12. Herschel, M., Hernández, M.A.: Explaining missing answers to spjua queries. Proc. VLDB Endow. 3, 185–196 (2010)
13. Huang, J., Chen, T., Doan, A., Naughton, J.F.: On the provenance of non-answers to queries over extracted data. Proc. VLDB Endow. 1(1), 736–747 (2008)
14. Meliou, A., Gatterbauer, W., Moore, K.F., Suciu, D.: Why so? or why no? functional causality for explaining query answers. In: CoRR (2009)
15. Müller, H., Buneman, P., Koltsidas, I.: Xarch: Archiving scientific and reference data. In: Proceedings of the 2008 ACM SIGMOD International Conference on Management of Data, pp. 1295–1298 (2008)

Author Index